DEMO

WRITTEN BY
Brian Wood

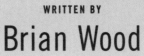

ILLUSTRATED BY
Becky Cloonan

Karen Berger Senior VP-Executive Editor
Will Dennis Editor-collected edition
Robbin Brosterman Senior Art Director
Paul Levitz President & Publisher
Georg Brewer VP-Design & DC Direct Creative
Richard Bruning Senior VP-Creative Director
Patrick Caldon Executive VP-Finance & Operations
Chris Caramalis VP-Finance
John Cunningham VP-Marketing
Terri Cunningham VP-Managing Editor
Alison Gill VP-Manufacturing
David Hyde VP-Publicity
Hank Kanalz VP-General Manager, WildStorm
Jim Lee Editorial Director-WildStorm
Paula Lowitt Senior VP-Business & Legal Affairs
MaryEllen McLaughlin VP-Advertising & Custom Publishing
John Nee Senior VP-Business Development
Gregory Noveck Senior VP-Creative Affairs
Sue Pohja VP-Book Trade Sales
Steve Rotterdam Senior VP-Sales & Marketing
Cheryl Rubin Senior VP-Brand Management
Jeff Trojan VP-Business Development, DC Direct
Bob Wayne VP-Sales

SPECIAL THANKS TO RYAN YOUNT

Cover design by Brian Wood
All artwork by Becky Cloonan
Publication design by Amelia Grohman

DEMO

DC Comics
1700 Broadway, New York, NY 10019
A Warner Bros. Entertainment Company.
Printed in Canada. First Printing.
ISBN 13: 978-1-4012-1621-4

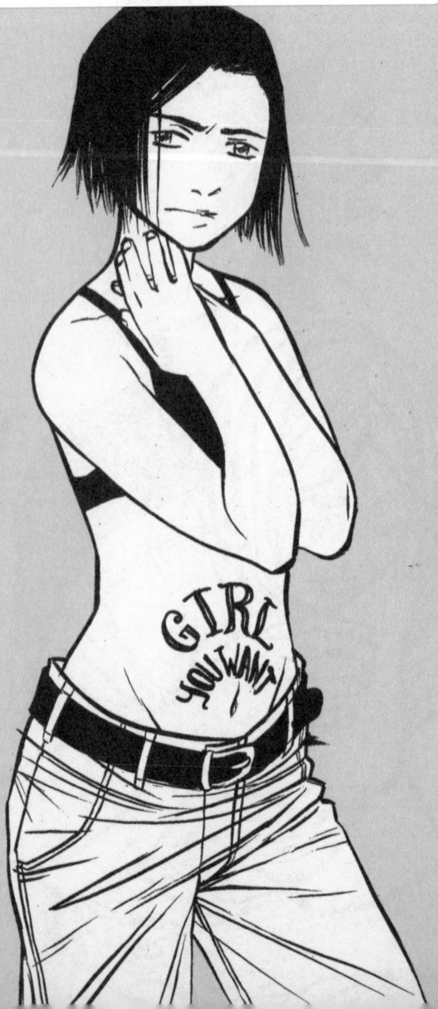
GIRL
YOU WANT

Contents

1

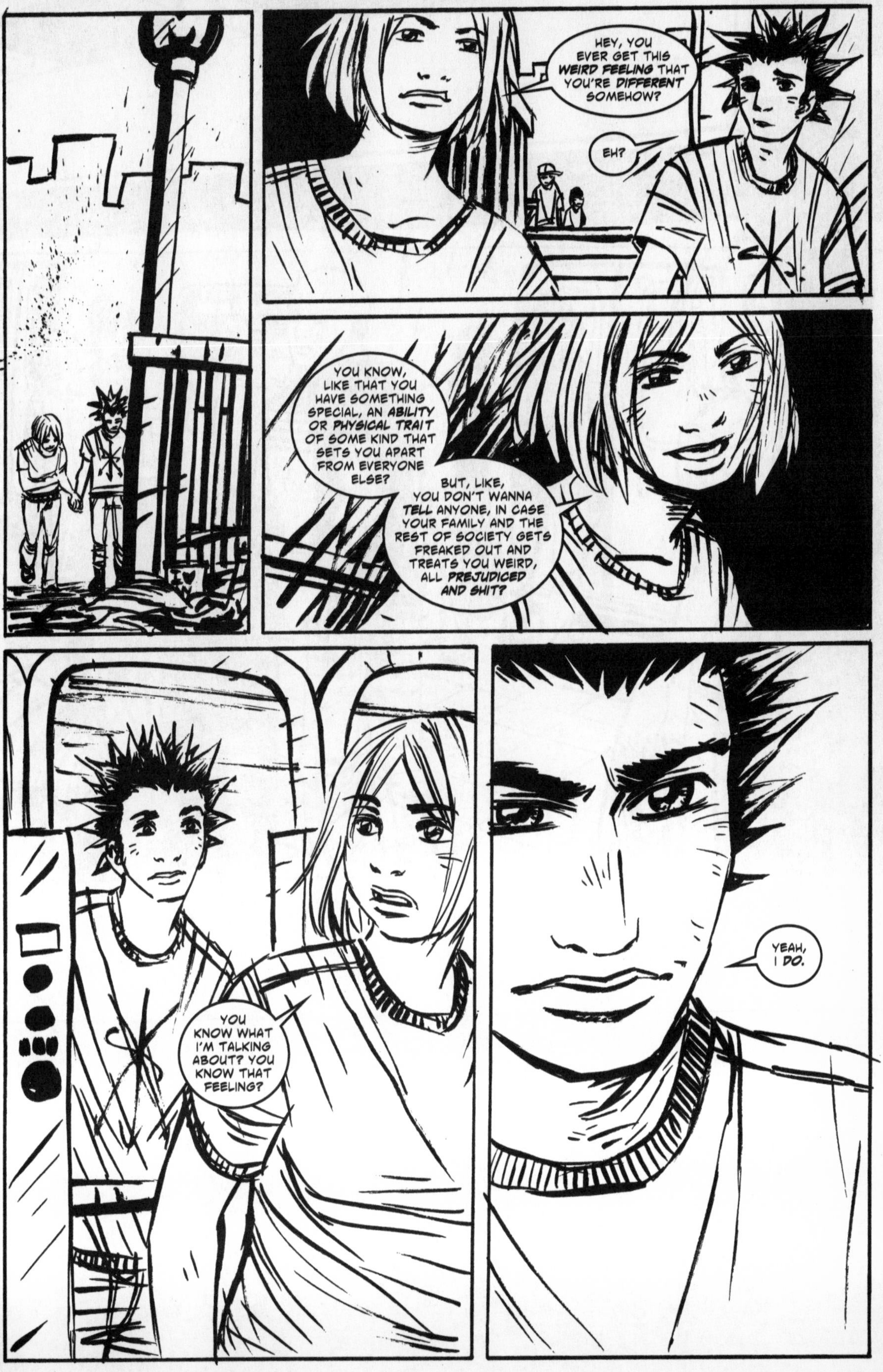
HEY, YOU EVER GET THIS WEIRD FEELING THAT YOU'RE DIFFERENT SOMEHOW?
EH?
YOU KNOW, LIKE THAT YOU HAVE SOMETHING SPECIAL, AN ABILITY OR PHYSICAL TRAIT OF SOME KIND THAT SETS YOU APART FROM EVERYONE ELSE?
BUT, LIKE, YOU DON'T WANNA TELL ANYONE, IN CASE YOUR FAMILY AND THE REST OF SOCIETY GETS FREAKED OUT AND TREATS YOU WEIRD, ALL PREJUDICED AND SHIT?
YOU KNOW WHAT I'M TALKING ABOUT? YOU KNOW THAT FEELING?
YEAH, I DO.

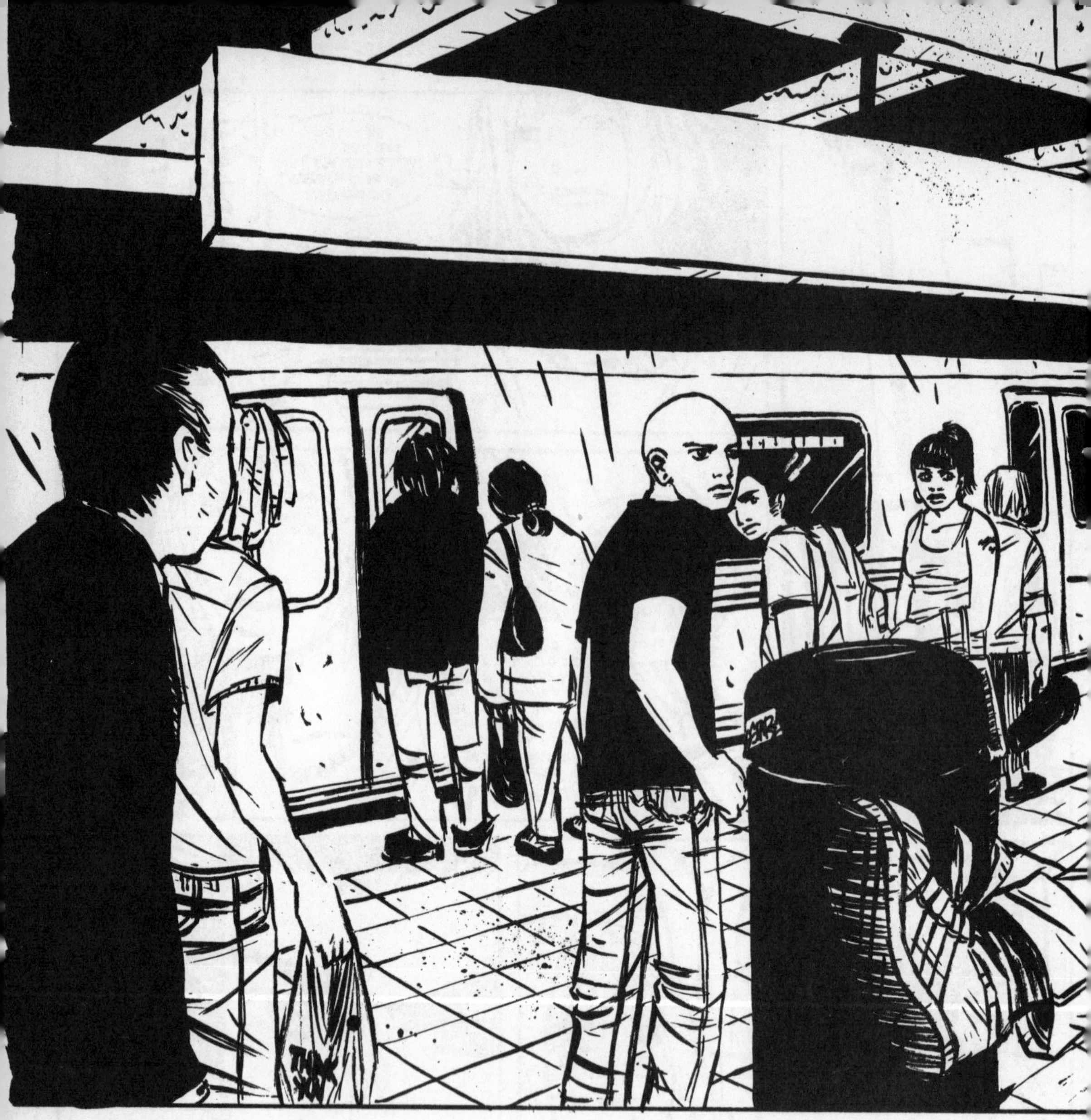

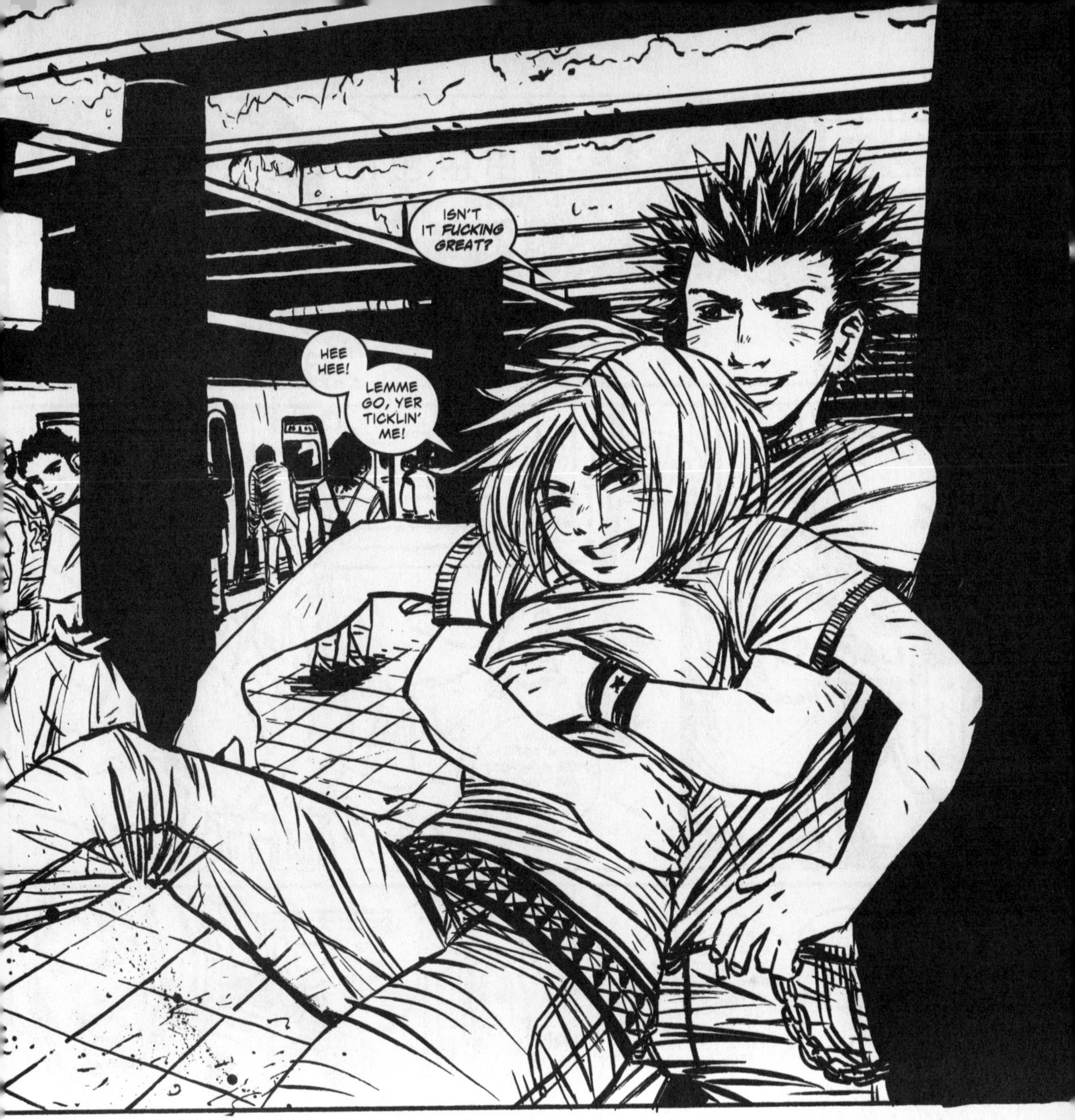
ISN'T IT FUCKING GREAT?
HEE HEE!
LEMME GO, YER TICKLIN' ME!

"NYC"

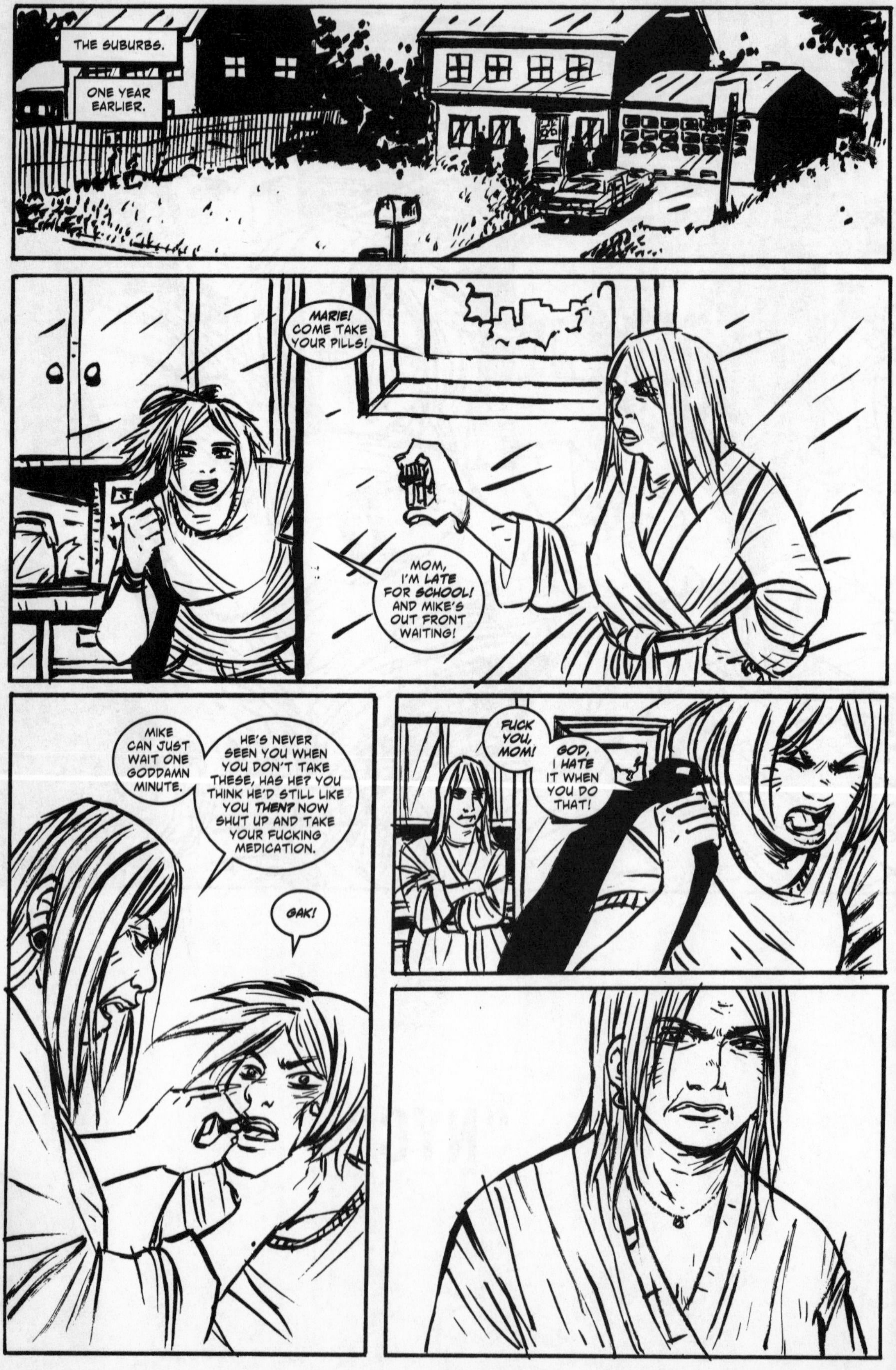
THE SUBURBS.
ONE YEAR EARLIER.
MARIE! COME TAKE YOUR PILLS!
MOM, I'M LATE FOR SCHOOL! AND MIKE'S OUT FRONT WAITING!
MIKE CAN JUST WAIT ONE GODDAMN MINUTE.
HE'S NEVER SEEN YOU WHEN YOU DON'T TAKE THESE, HAS HE? YOU THINK HE'D STILL LIKE YOU THEN? NOW SHUT UP AND TAKE YOUR FUCKING MEDICATION.
GAK!
FUCK YOU, MOM!
GOD, I HATE IT WHEN YOU DO THAT!

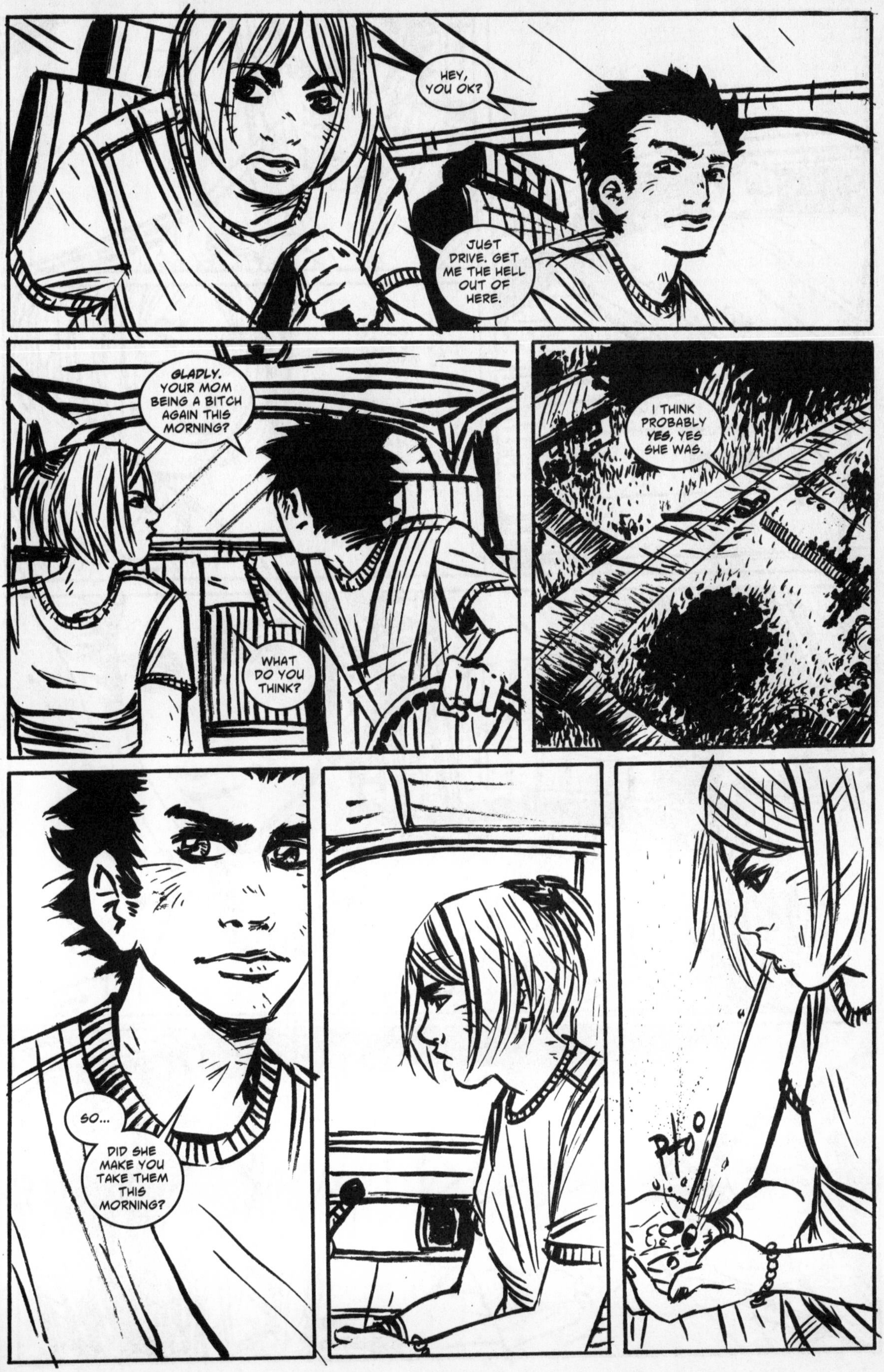
HEY, YOU OK?
JUST DRIVE. GET ME THE HELL OUT OF HERE.
GLADLY. YOUR MOM BEING A BITCH AGAIN THIS MORNING?
WHAT DO YOU THINK?
I THINK PROBABLY YES, YES SHE WAS.
SO...
DID SHE MAKE YOU TAKE THEM THIS MORNING?

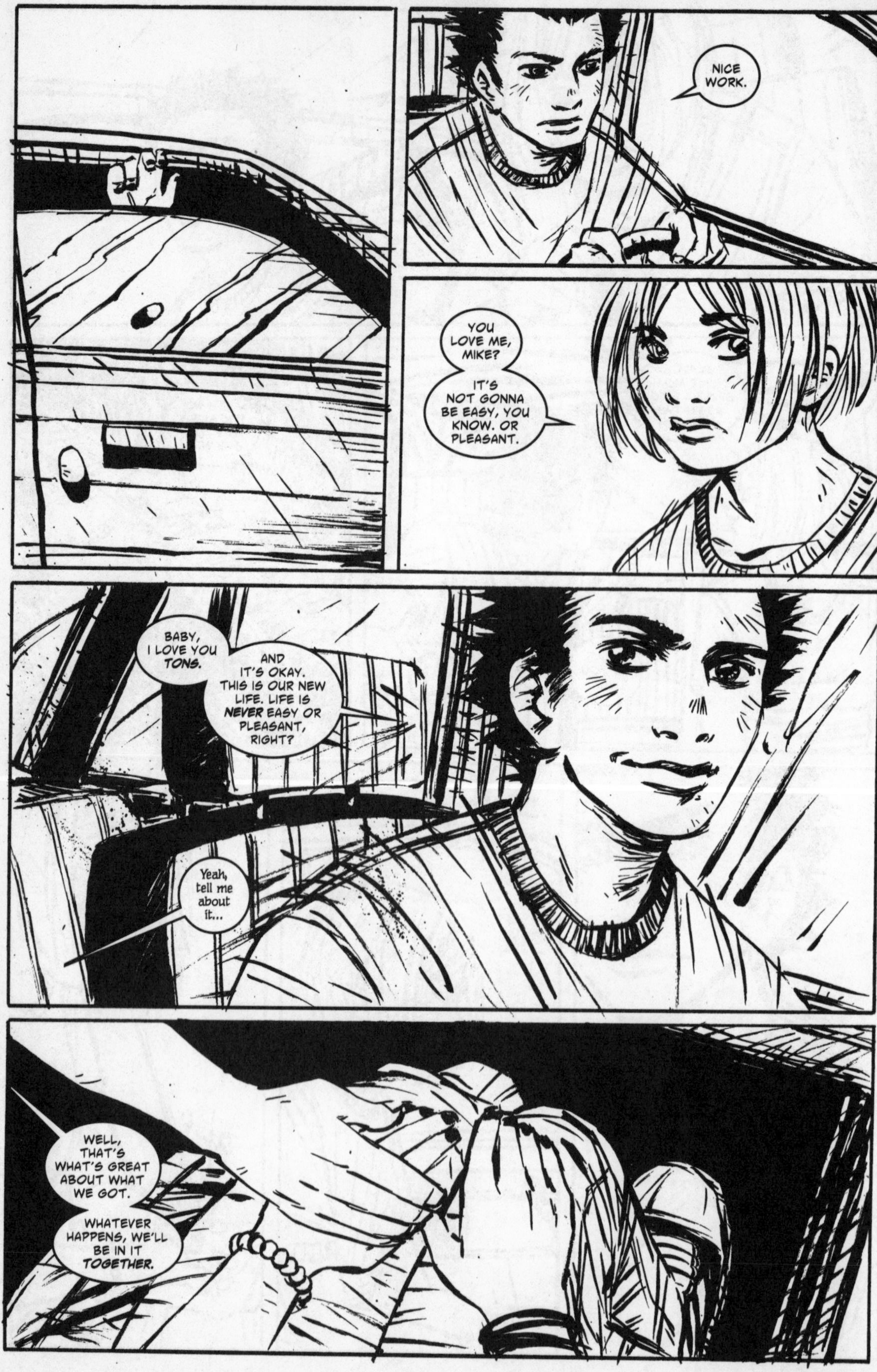
NICE WORK.
YOU LOVE ME, MIKE?
IT'S NOT GONNA BE EASY, YOU KNOW. OR PLEASANT.
BABY, I LOVE YOU TONS.
AND IT'S OKAY. THIS IS OUR NEW LIFE. LIFE IS NEVER EASY OR PLEASANT, RIGHT?
Yeah, tell me about it...
WELL, THAT'S WHAT'S GREAT ABOUT WHAT WE GOT.
WHATEVER HAPPENS, WE'LL BE IN IT TOGETHER.

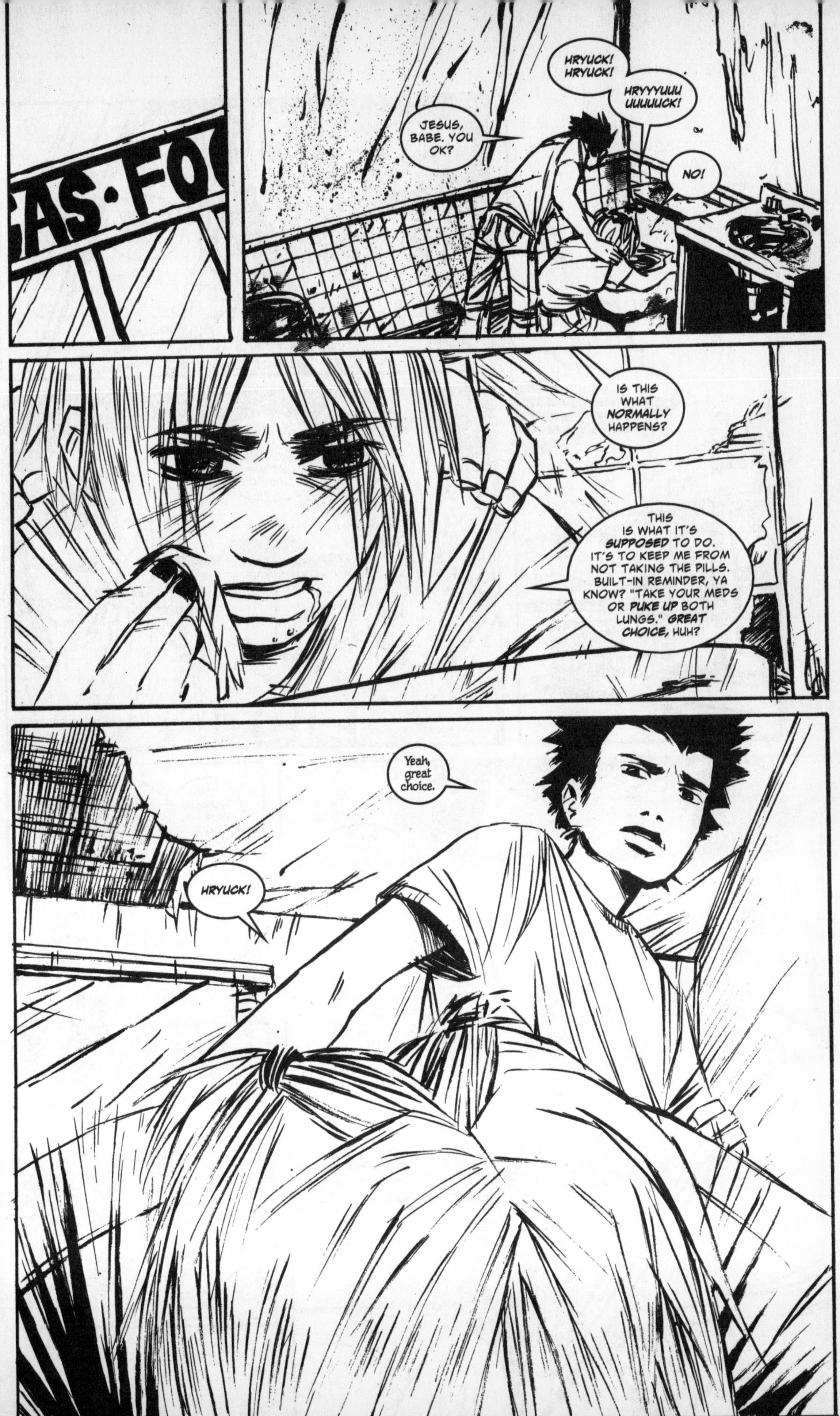
GAS·FO
HRYUCK! HRYUCK!
HRYYYUUU UUUUUCK!
JESUS, BABE. YOU OK?
NO!
IS THIS WHAT NORMALLY HAPPENS?
THIS IS WHAT IT'S SUPPOSED TO DO. IT'S TO KEEP ME FROM NOT TAKING THE PILLS. BUILT-IN REMINDER, YA KNOW? "TAKE YOUR MEDS OR PUKE UP BOTH LUNGS." GREAT CHOICE, HUH?
Yeah, great choice.
HRYUCK!

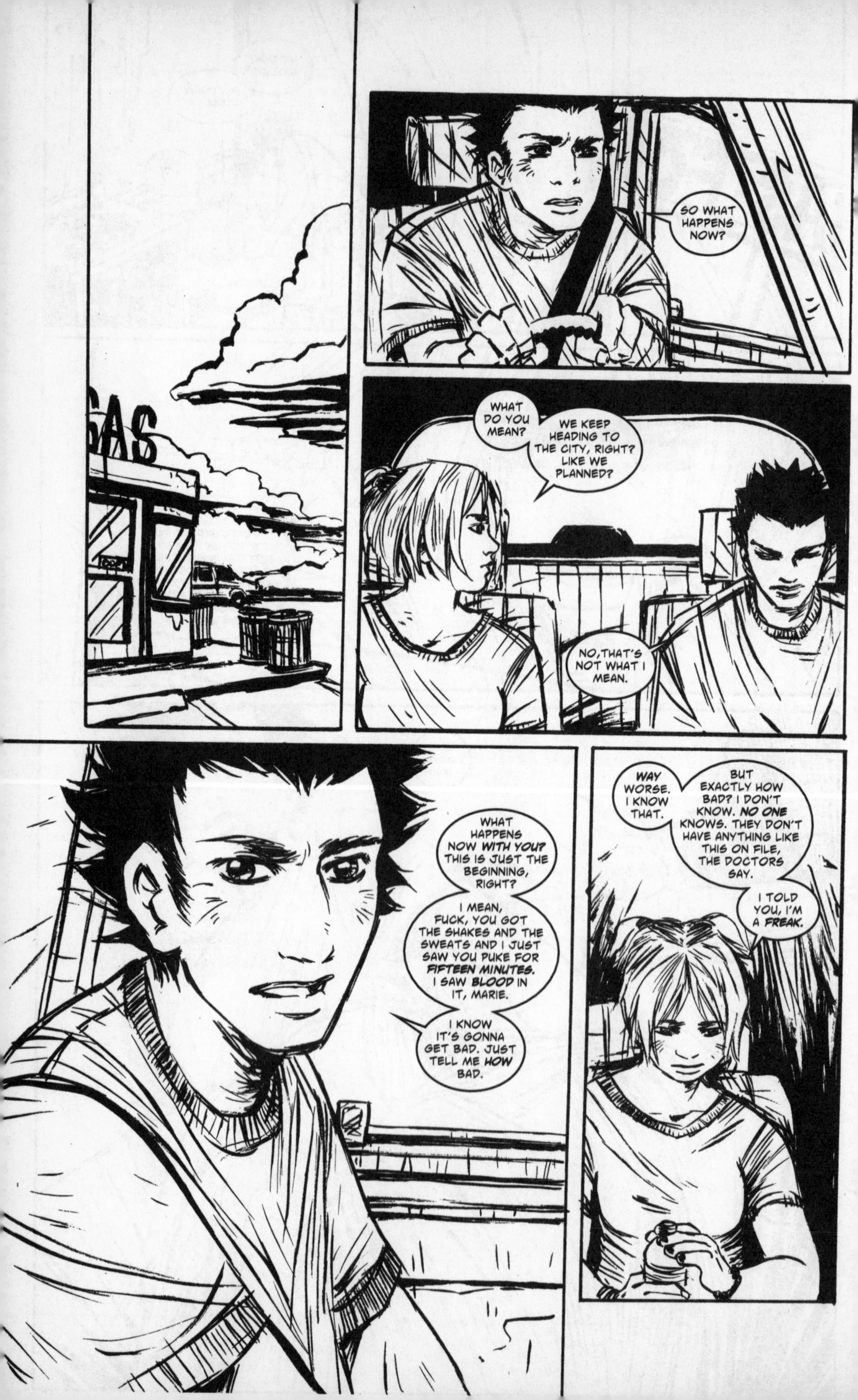
GAS
SO WHAT HAPPENS NOW?
WHAT DO YOU MEAN?
WE KEEP HEADING TO THE CITY, RIGHT? LIKE WE PLANNED?
NO, THAT'S NOT WHAT I MEAN.
WHAT HAPPENS NOW *WITH YOU?* THIS IS JUST THE BEGINNING, RIGHT?
I MEAN, FUCK, YOU GOT THE SHAKES AND THE SWEATS AND I JUST SAW YOU PUKE FOR *FIFTEEN MINUTES.* I SAW *BLOOD* IN IT, MARIE.
I KNOW IT'S GONNA GET BAD. JUST TELL ME *HOW* BAD.
WAY WORSE. I KNOW THAT.
BUT EXACTLY HOW BAD? I DON'T KNOW. *NO ONE* KNOWS. THEY DON'T HAVE ANYTHING LIKE THIS ON FILE, THE DOCTORS SAY.
I TOLD YOU, I'M A *FREAK.*

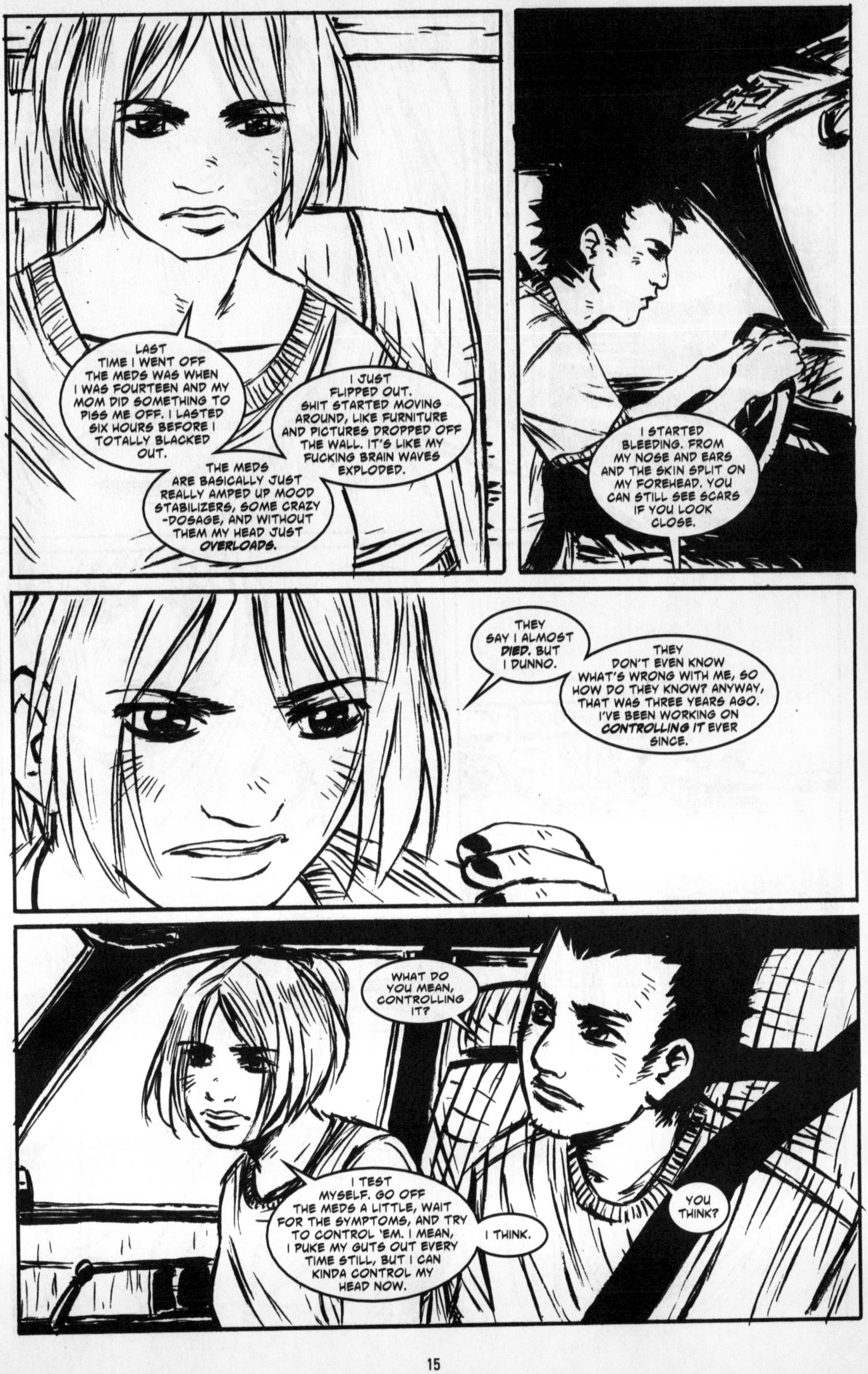
LAST TIME I WENT OFF THE MEDS WAS WHEN I WAS FOURTEEN AND MY MOM DID SOMETHING TO PISS ME OFF. I LASTED SIX HOURS BEFORE I TOTALLY BLACKED OUT.
THE MEDS ARE BASICALLY JUST REALLY AMPED UP MOOD STABILIZERS, SOME CRAZY -DOSAGE, AND WITHOUT THEM MY HEAD JUST OVERLOADS.
I JUST FLIPPED OUT. SHIT STARTED MOVING AROUND, LIKE FURNITURE AND PICTURES DROPPED OFF THE WALL. IT'S LIKE MY FUCKING BRAIN WAVES EXPLODED.
I STARTED BLEEDING. FROM MY NOSE AND EARS AND THE SKIN SPLIT ON MY FOREHEAD. YOU CAN STILL SEE SCARS IF YOU LOOK CLOSE.
THEY SAY I ALMOST DIED. BUT I DUNNO.
THEY DON'T EVEN KNOW WHAT'S WRONG WITH ME, SO HOW DO THEY KNOW? ANYWAY, THAT WAS THREE YEARS AGO. I'VE BEEN WORKING ON CONTROLLING IT EVER SINCE.
WHAT DO YOU MEAN, CONTROLLING IT?
I TEST MYSELF. GO OFF THE MEDS A LITTLE, WAIT FOR THE SYMPTOMS, AND TRY TO CONTROL 'EM. I MEAN, I PUKE MY GUTS OUT EVERY TIME STILL, BUT I CAN KINDA CONTROL MY HEAD NOW.
I THINK.
YOU THINK?

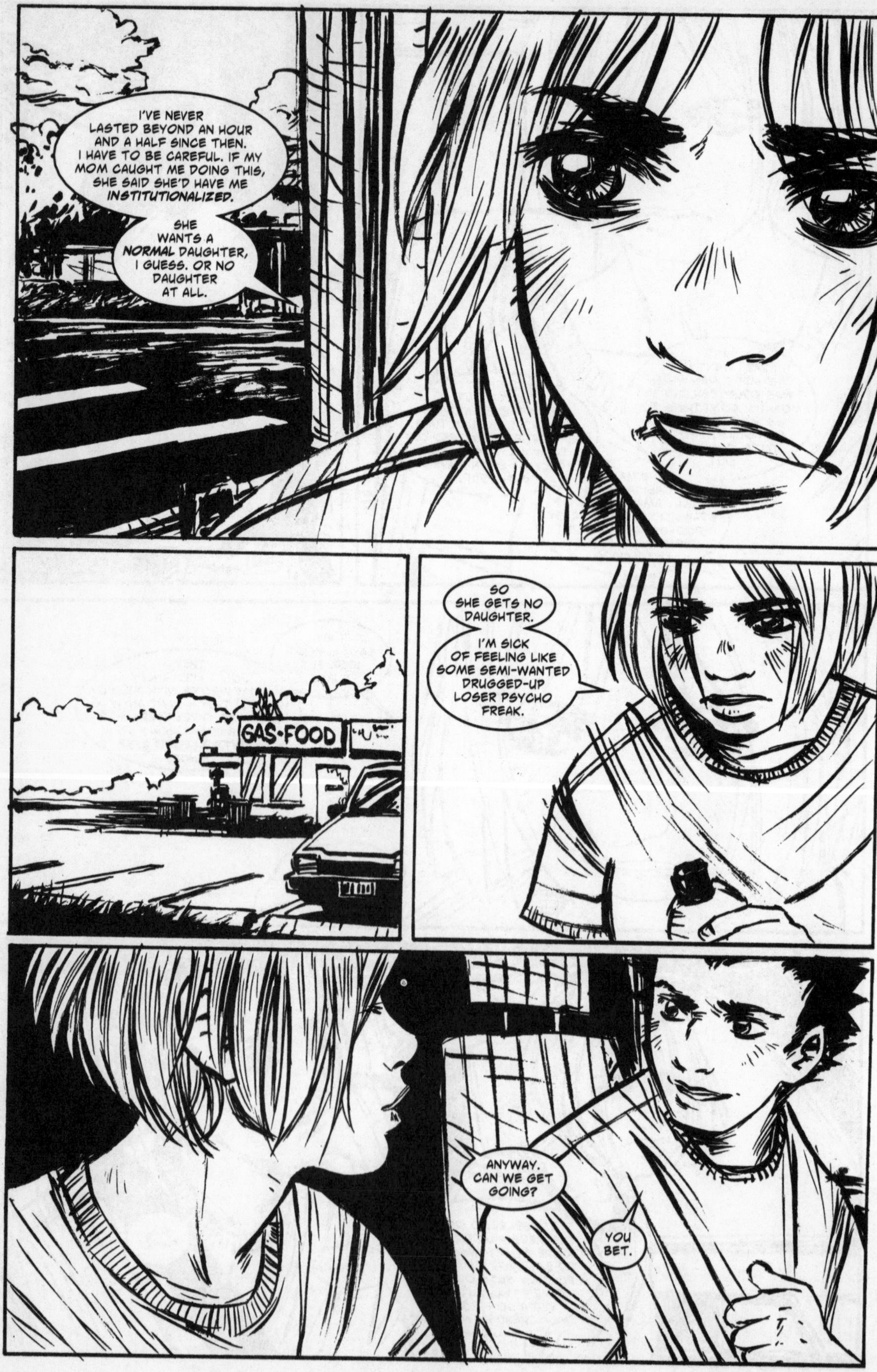
I'VE NEVER LASTED BEYOND AN HOUR AND A HALF SINCE THEN. I HAVE TO BE CAREFUL. IF MY MOM CAUGHT ME DOING THIS, SHE SAID SHE'D HAVE ME INSTITUTIONALIZED.
SHE WANTS A NORMAL DAUGHTER, I GUESS. OR NO DAUGHTER AT ALL.
GAS·FOOD
SO SHE GETS NO DAUGHTER.
I'M SICK OF FEELING LIKE SOME SEMI-WANTED DRUGGED-UP LOSER PSYCHO FREAK.
ANYWAY. CAN WE GET GOING?
YOU BET.

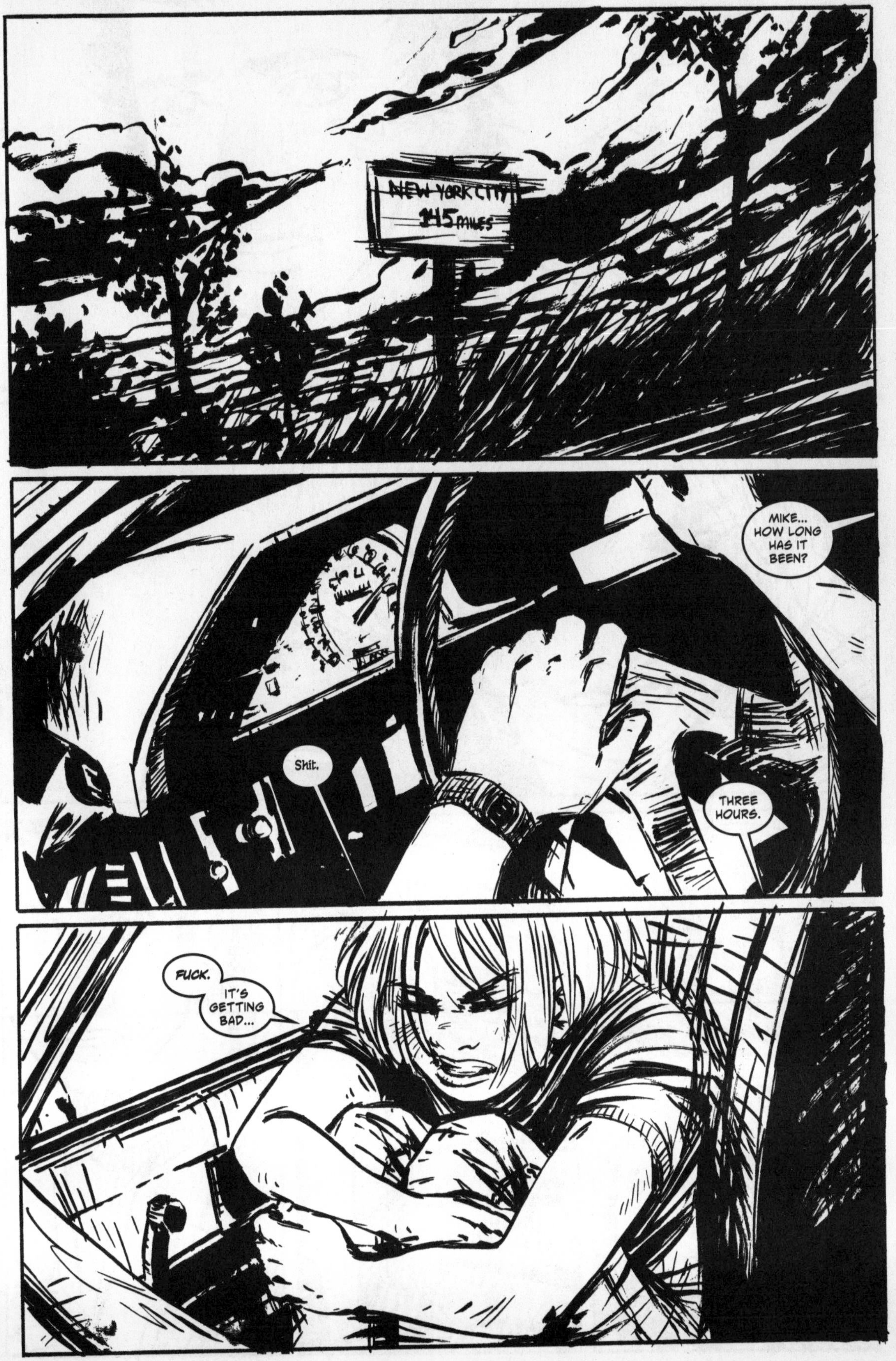

NEW YORK CITY
145 MILES
MIKE... HOW LONG HAS IT BEEN?
Shit.
THREE HOURS.
FUCK.
IT'S GETTING BAD...

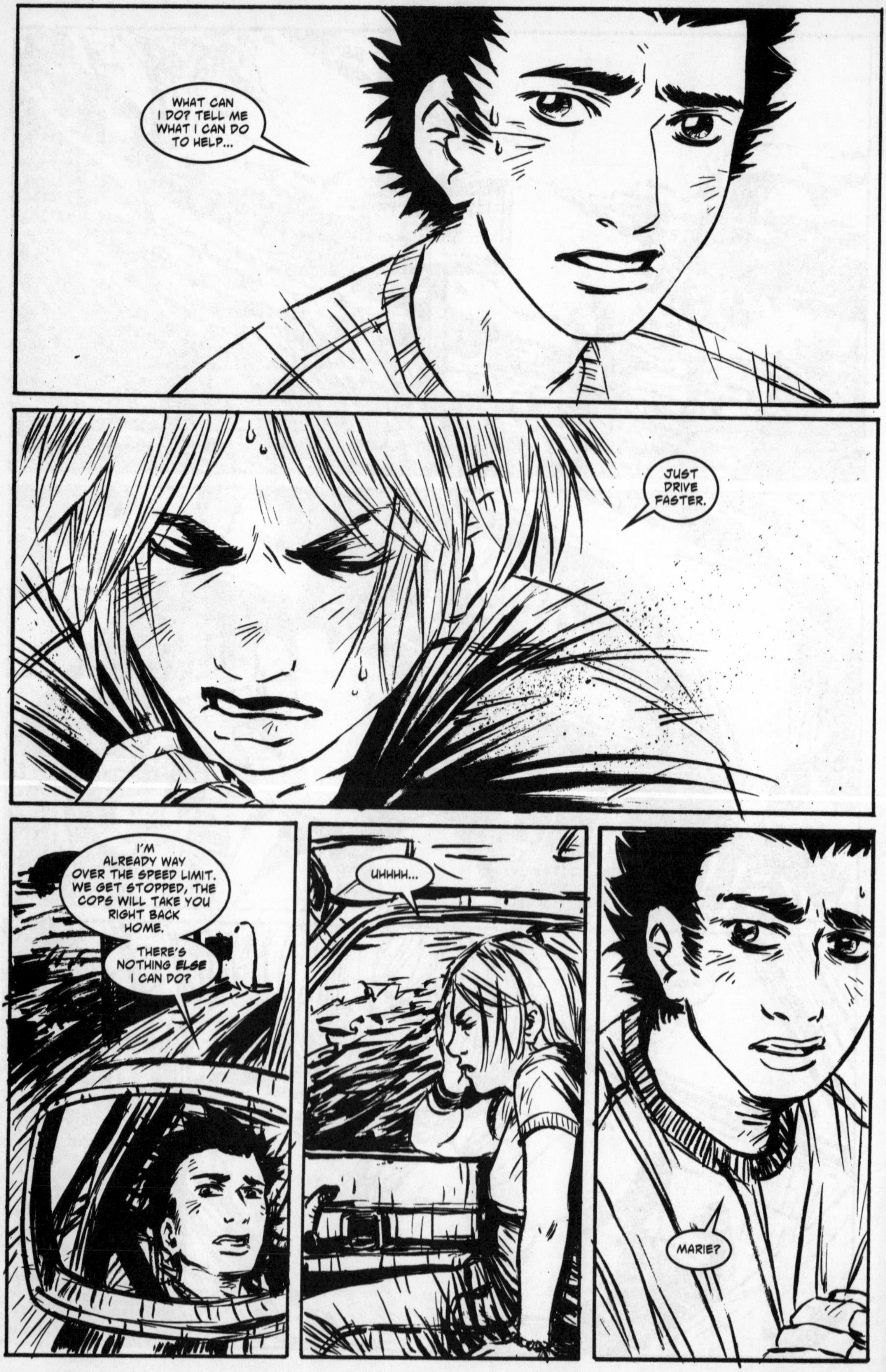
WHAT CAN I DO? TELL ME WHAT I CAN DO TO HELP...
JUST DRIVE FASTER.
I'M ALREADY WAY OVER THE SPEED LIMIT. WE GET STOPPED, THE COPS WILL TAKE YOU RIGHT BACK HOME.
THERE'S NOTHING ELSE I CAN DO?
UHHHH...
MARIE?

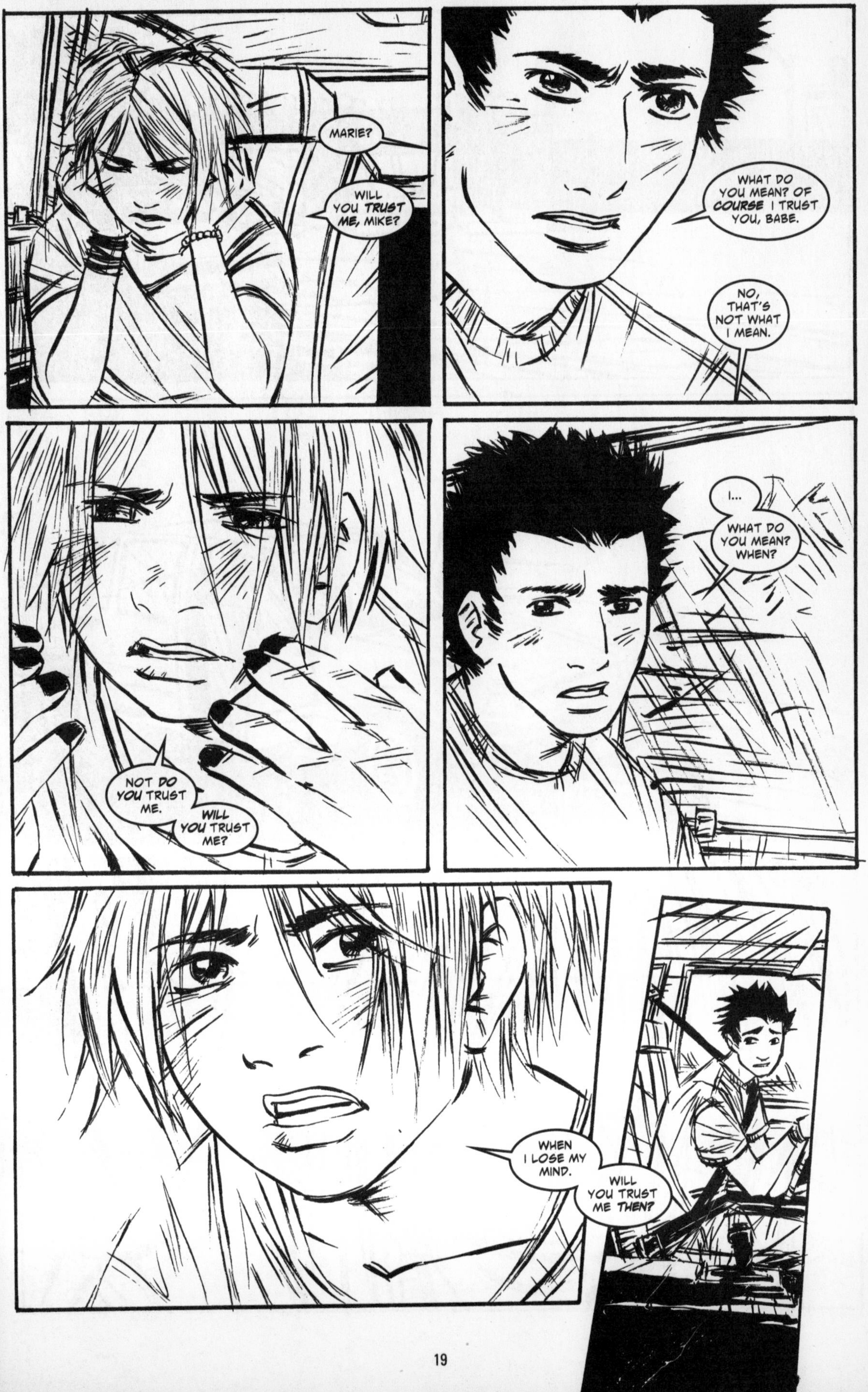
MARIE?
WILL YOU TRUST ME, MIKE?
WHAT DO YOU MEAN? OF COURSE I TRUST YOU, BABE.
NO, THAT'S NOT WHAT I MEAN.
NOT DO YOU TRUST ME.
WILL YOU TRUST ME?
I...
WHAT DO YOU MEAN? WHEN?
WHEN I LOSE MY MIND.
WILL YOU TRUST ME THEN?

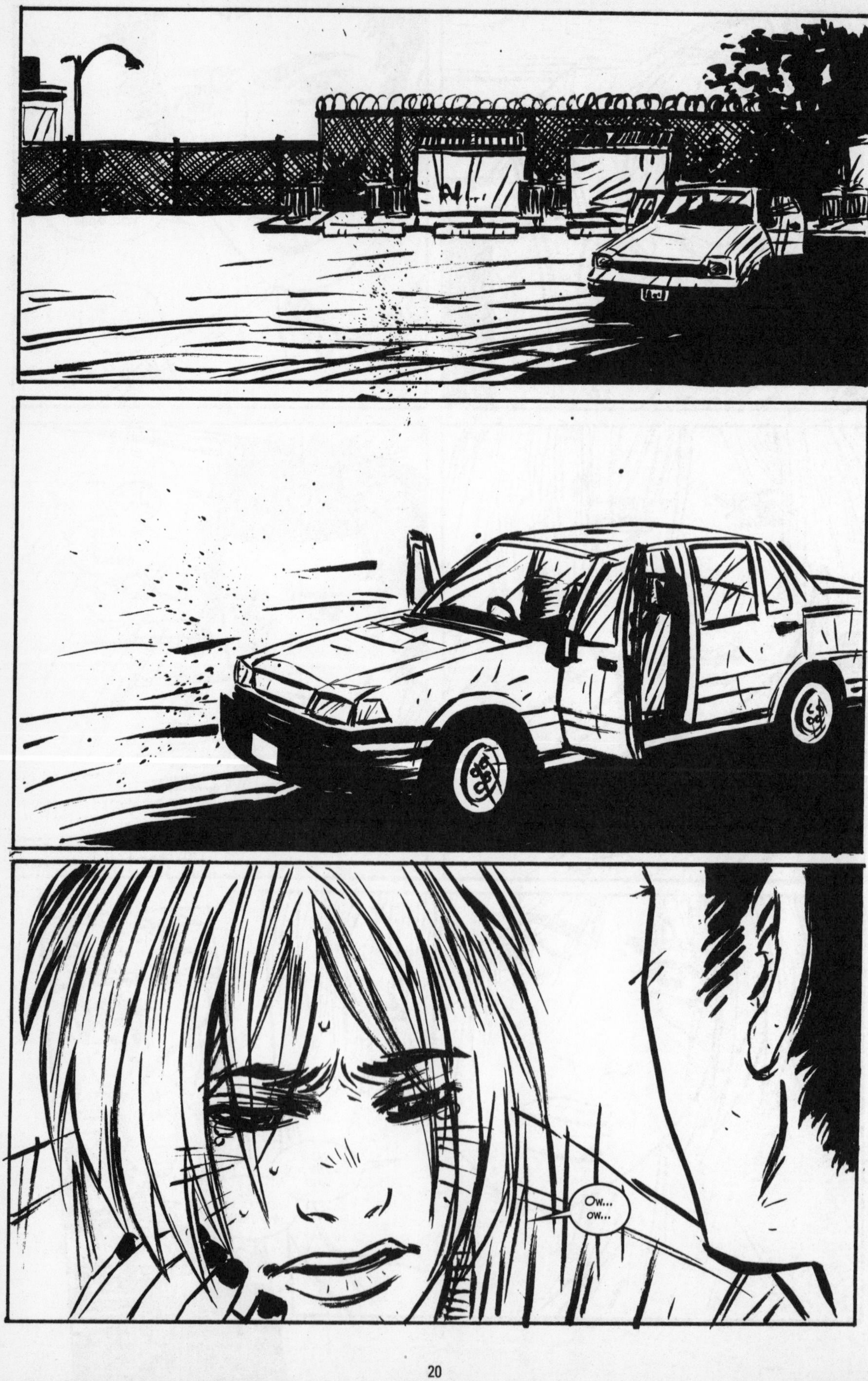
Ow... ow...

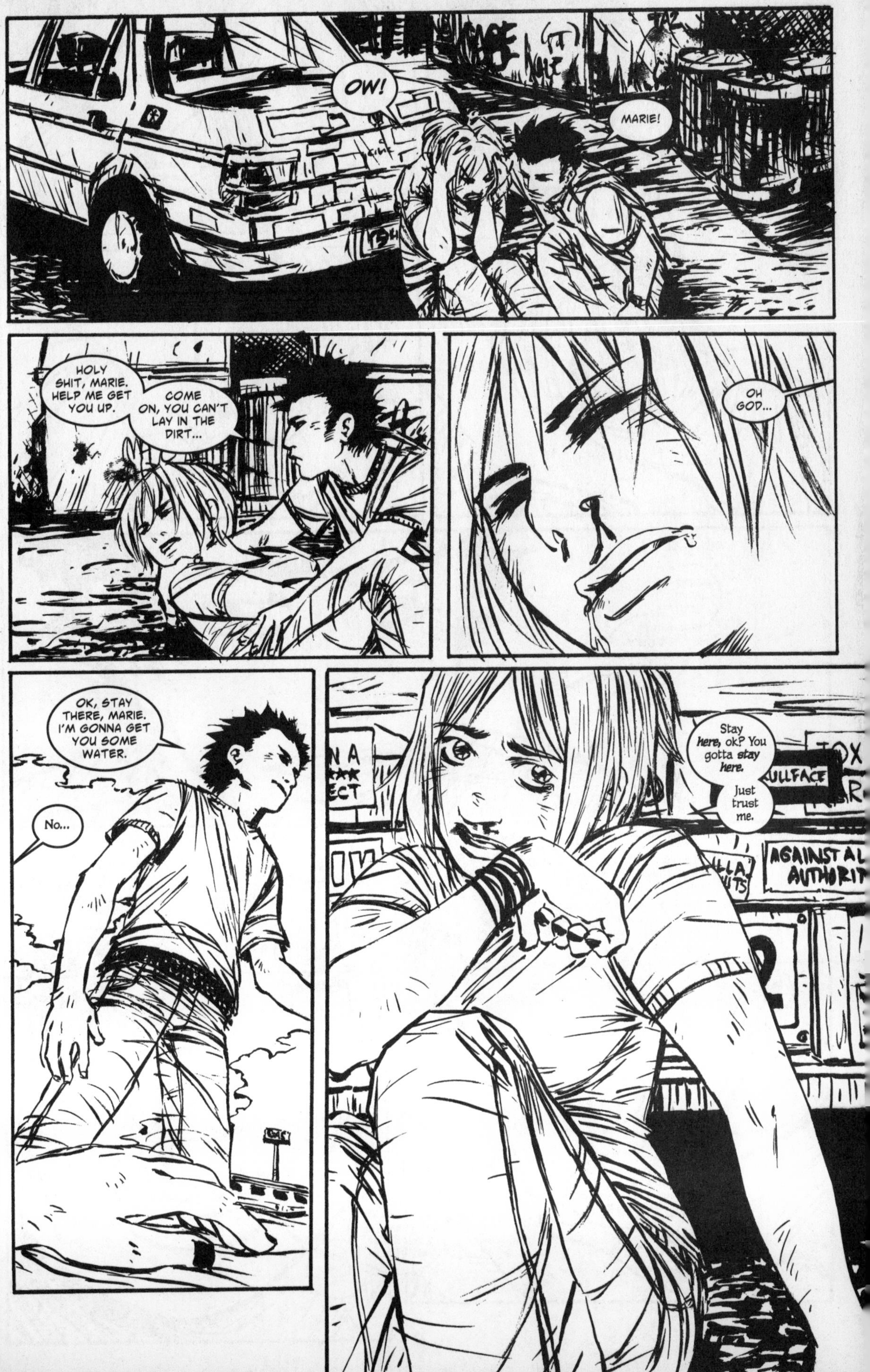
OW!
MARIE!
HOLY SHIT, MARIE. HELP ME GET YOU UP.
COME ON, YOU CAN'T LAY IN THE DIRT...
OH GOD...
OK, STAY THERE, MARIE. I'M GONNA GET YOU SOME WATER.
No...
Stay *here*, ok? You gotta *stay here*.
Just trust me.
AGAINST ALL AUTHORITY

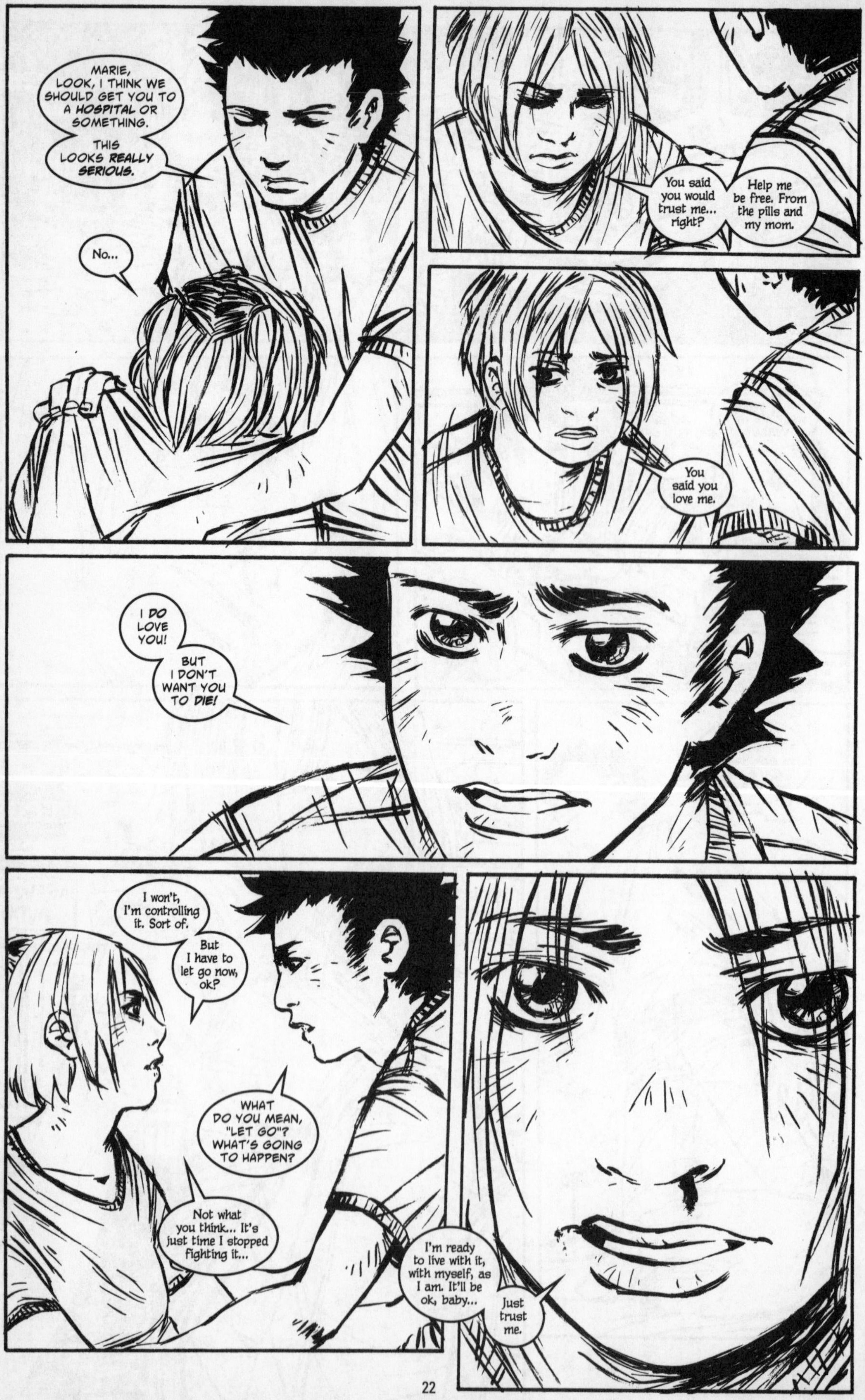
MARIE, LOOK, I THINK WE SHOULD GET YOU TO A HOSPITAL OR SOMETHING.
THIS LOOKS REALLY SERIOUS.
No...
You said you would trust me... right?
Help me be free. From the pills and my mom.
You said you love me.
I DO LOVE YOU!
BUT I DON'T WANT YOU TO DIE!
I won't, I'm controlling it. Sort of.
But I have to let go now, ok?
WHAT DO YOU MEAN, "LET GO"? WHAT'S GOING TO HAPPEN?
Not what you think... It's just time I stopped fighting it...
I'm ready to live with it, with myself, as I am. It'll be ok, baby...
Just trust me.

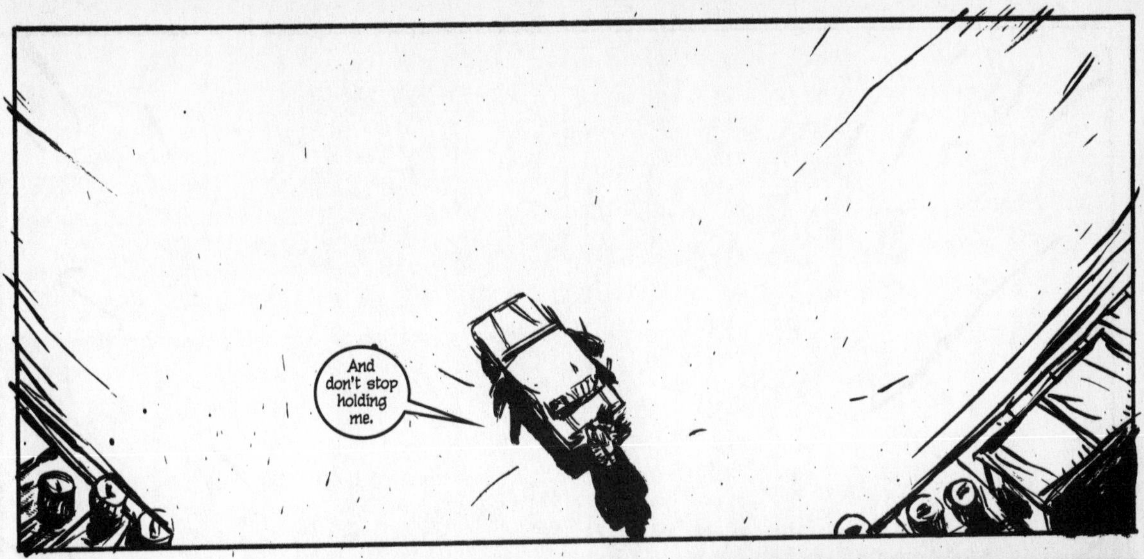
And don't stop holding me.

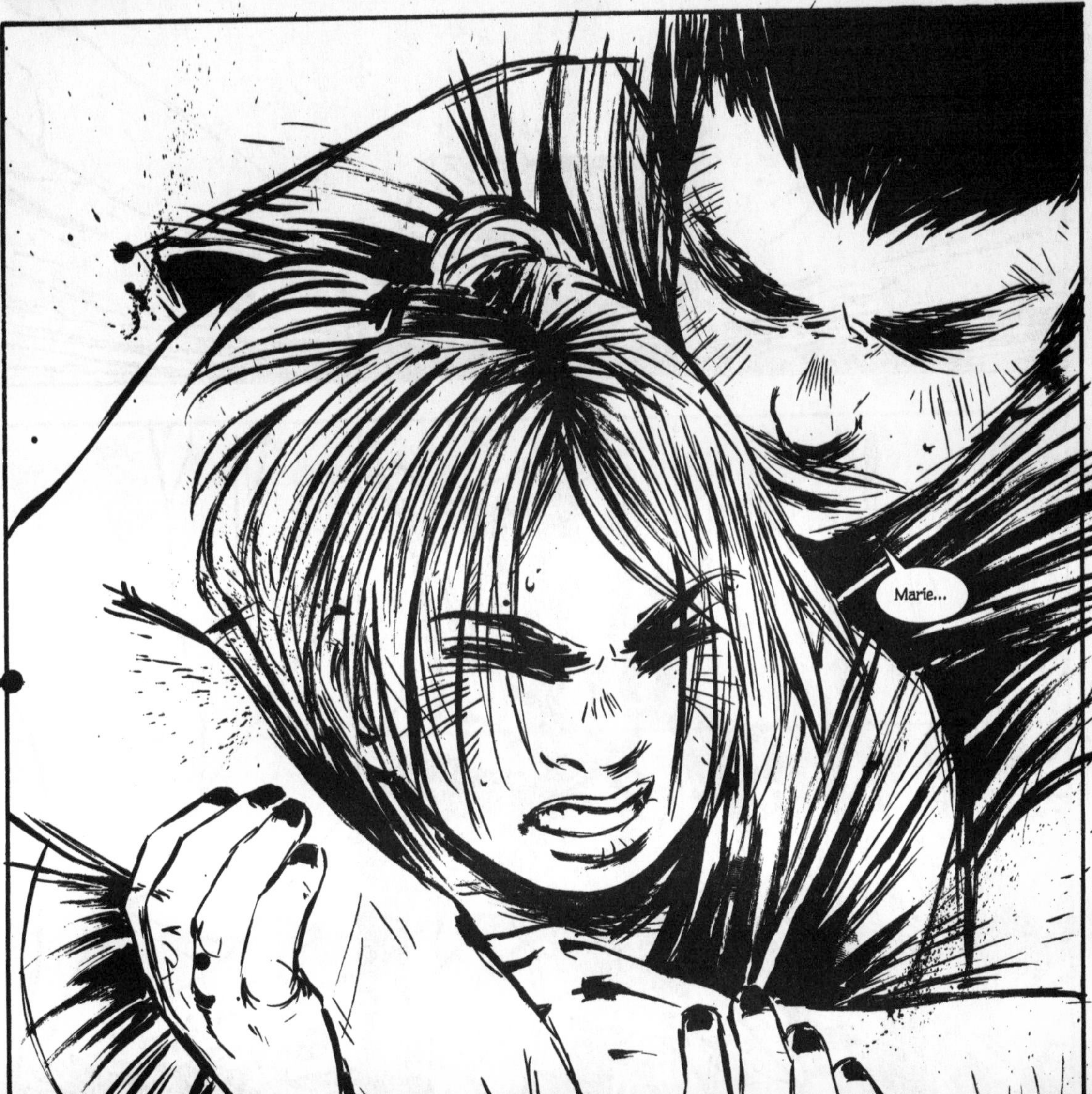
Marie...

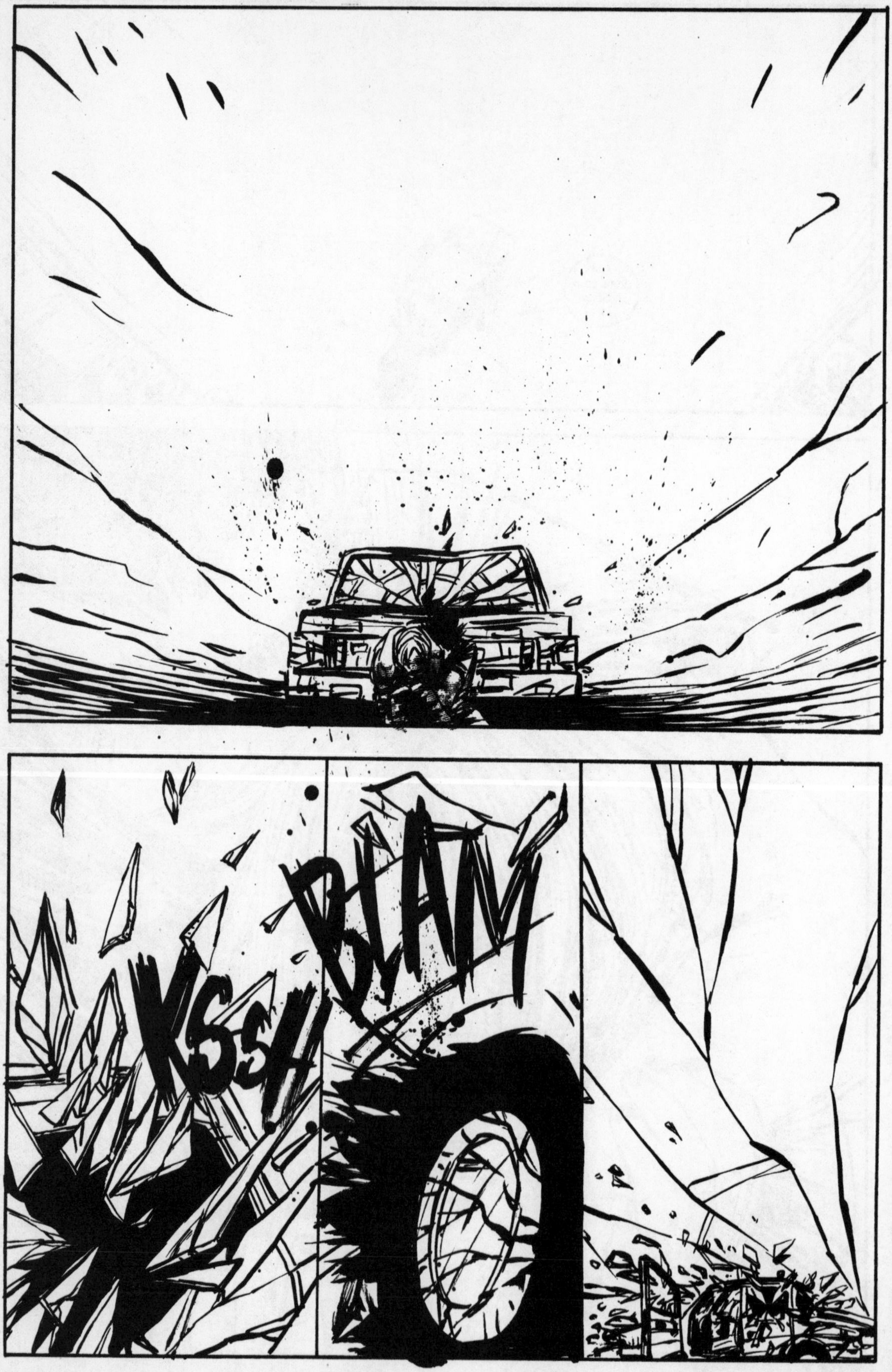
KSSH
BLAM

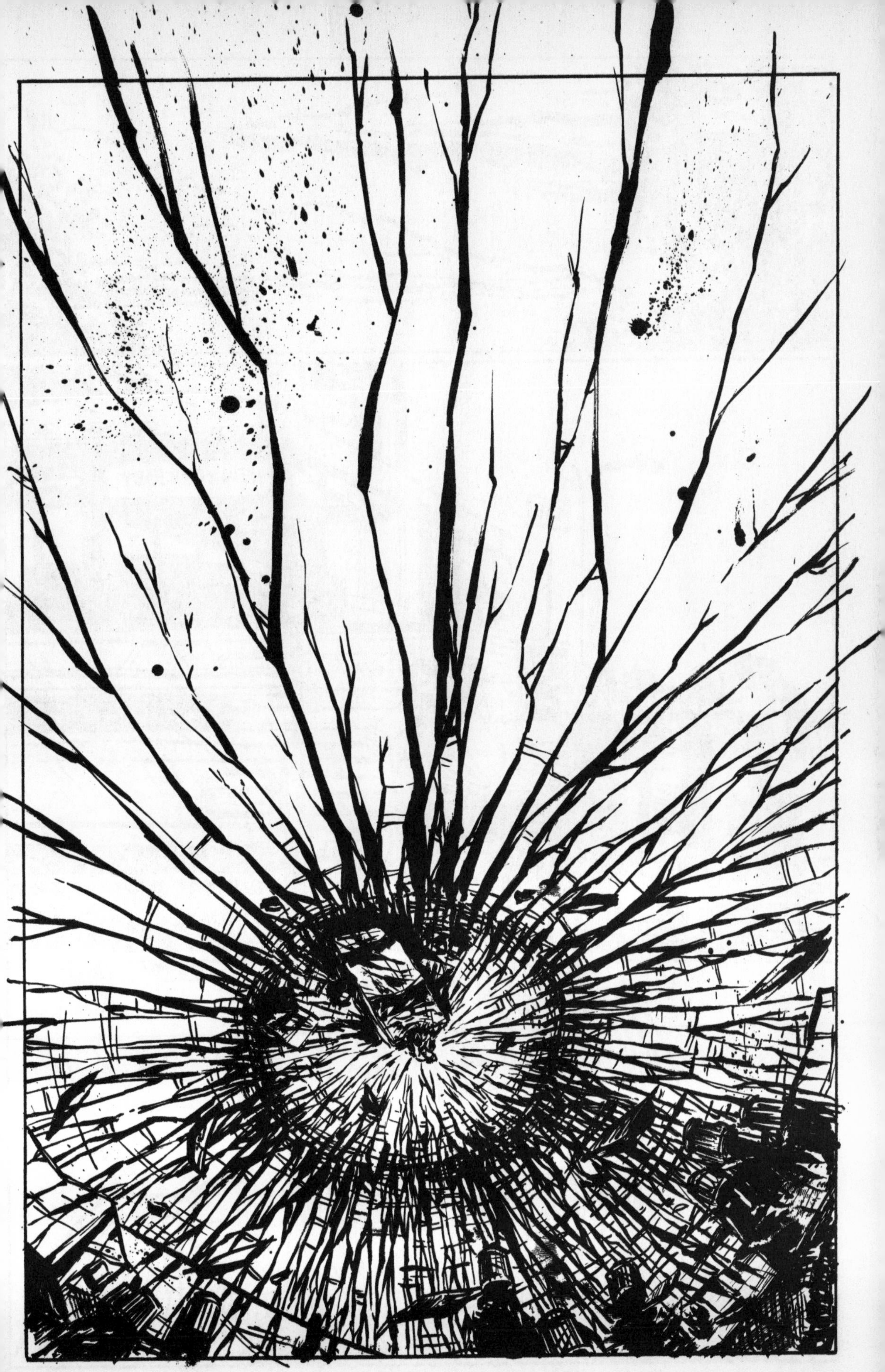

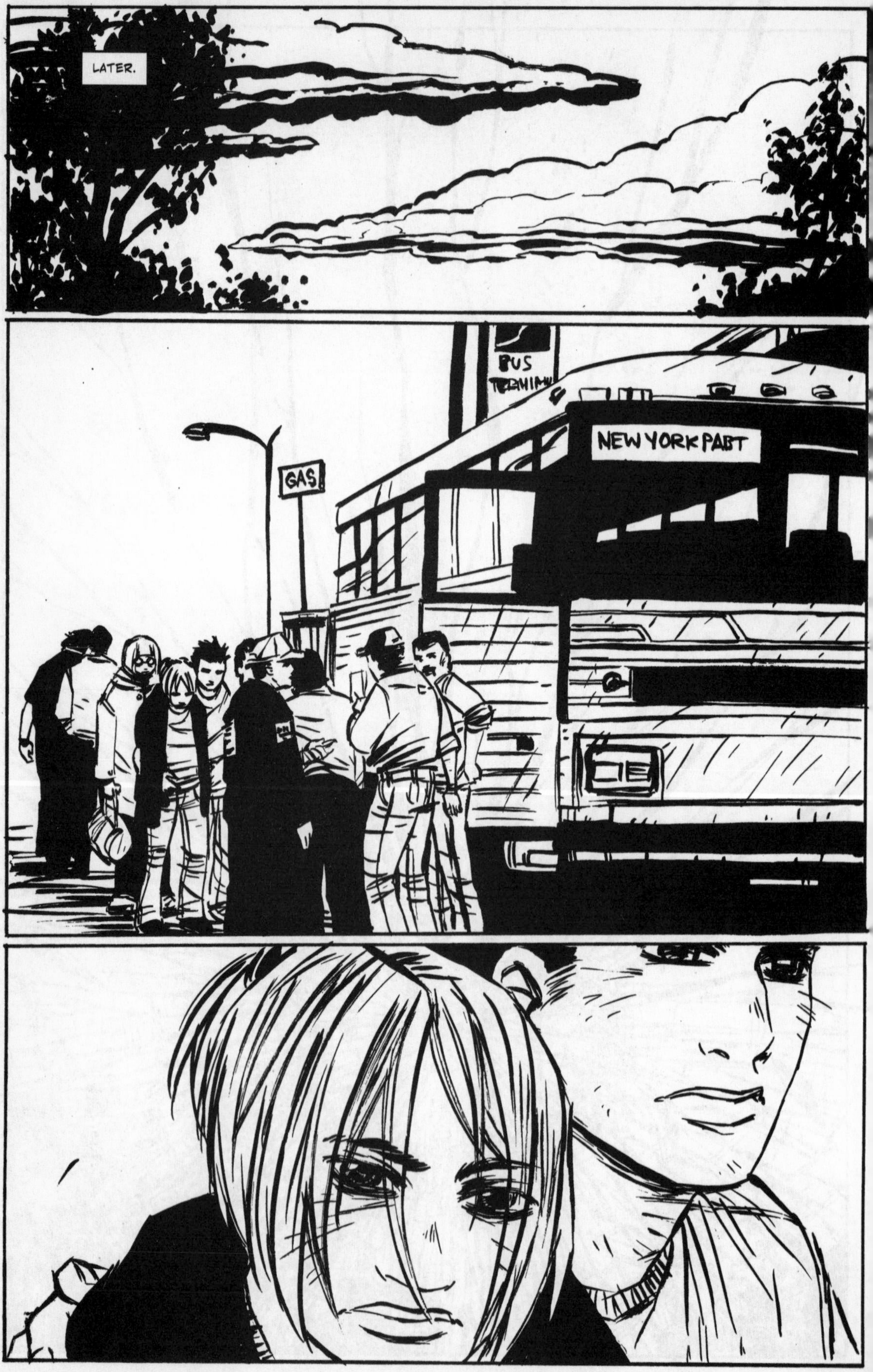
LATER.
BUS
NEW YORK PABT
GAS

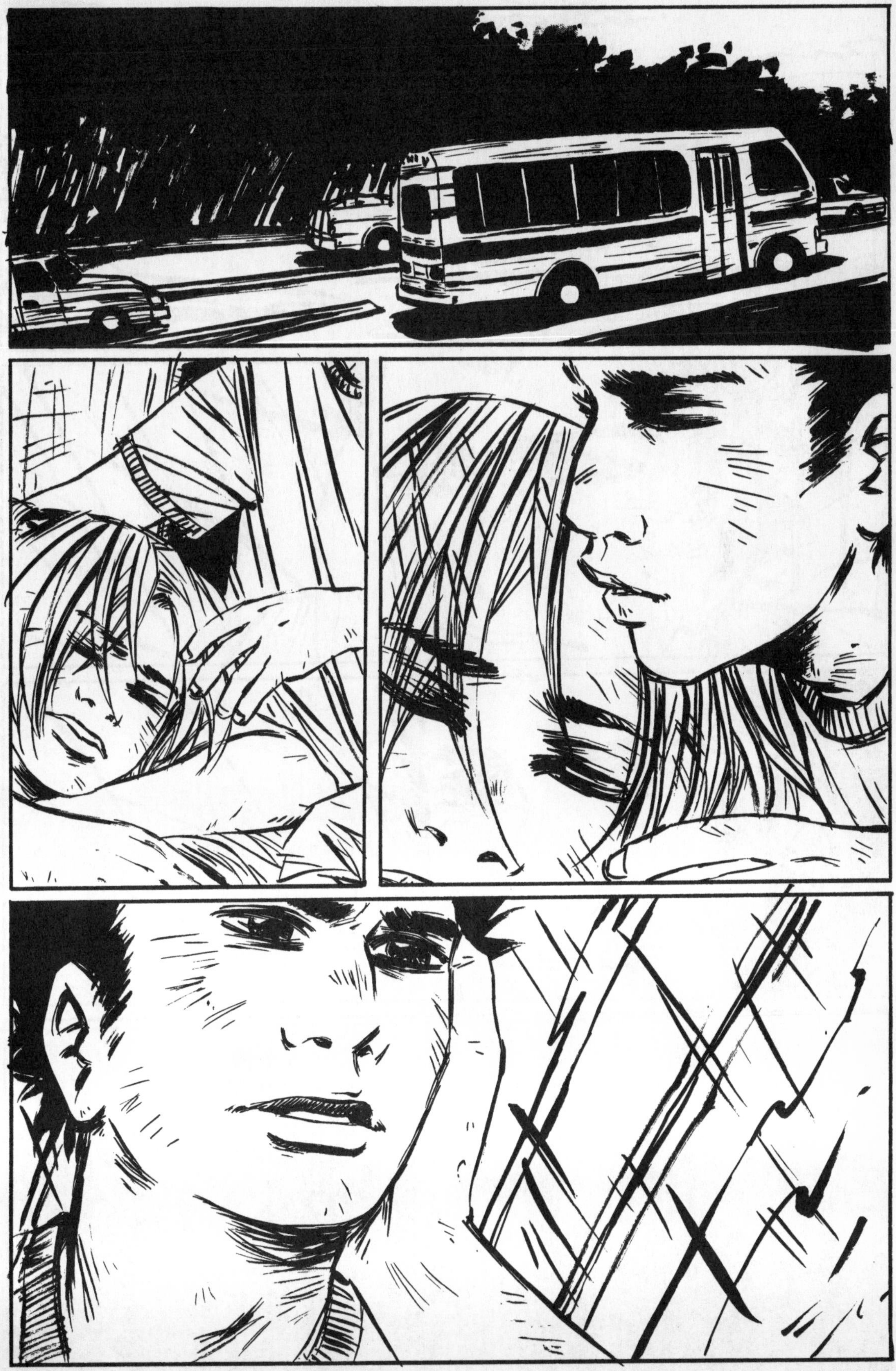

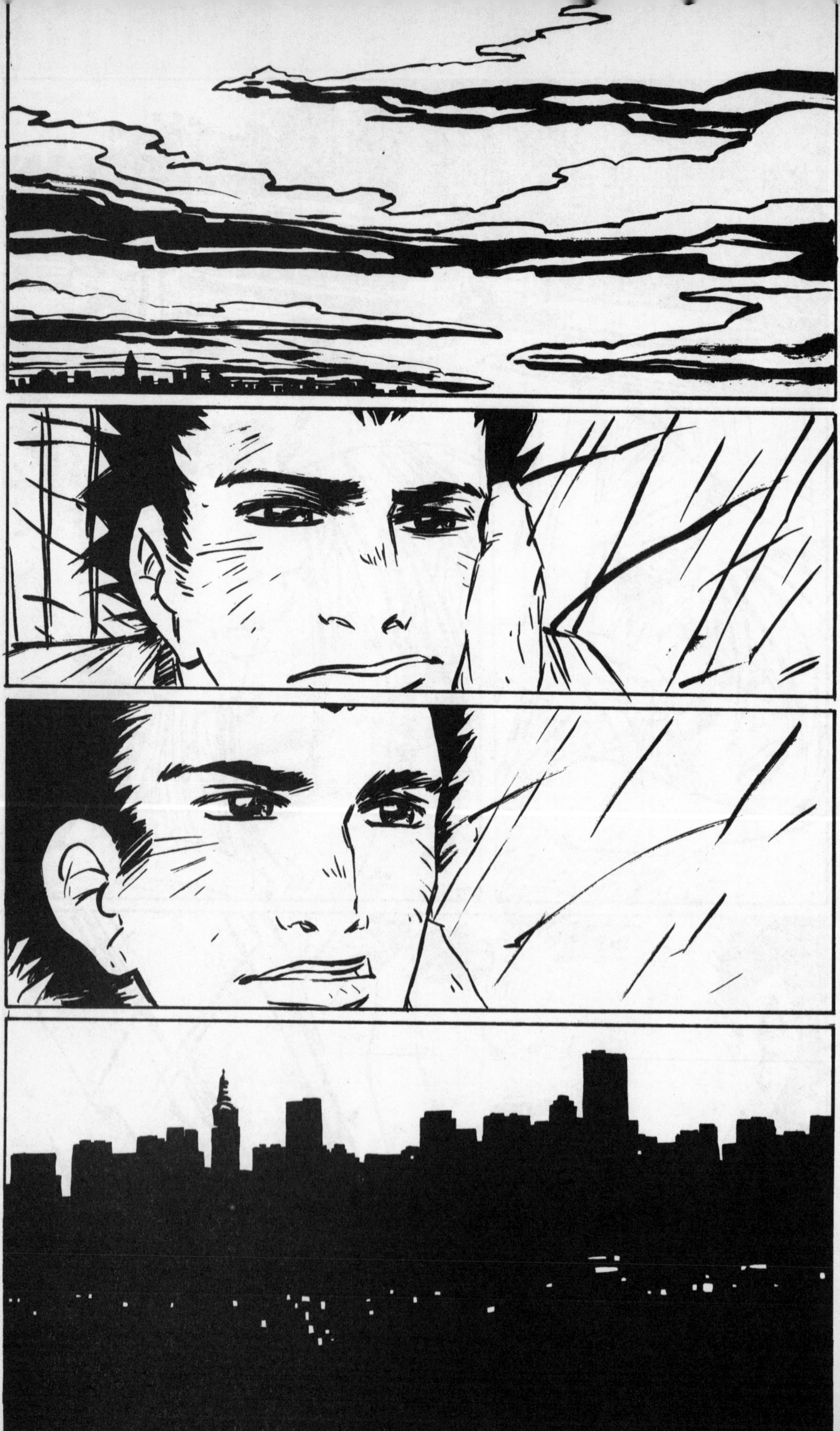

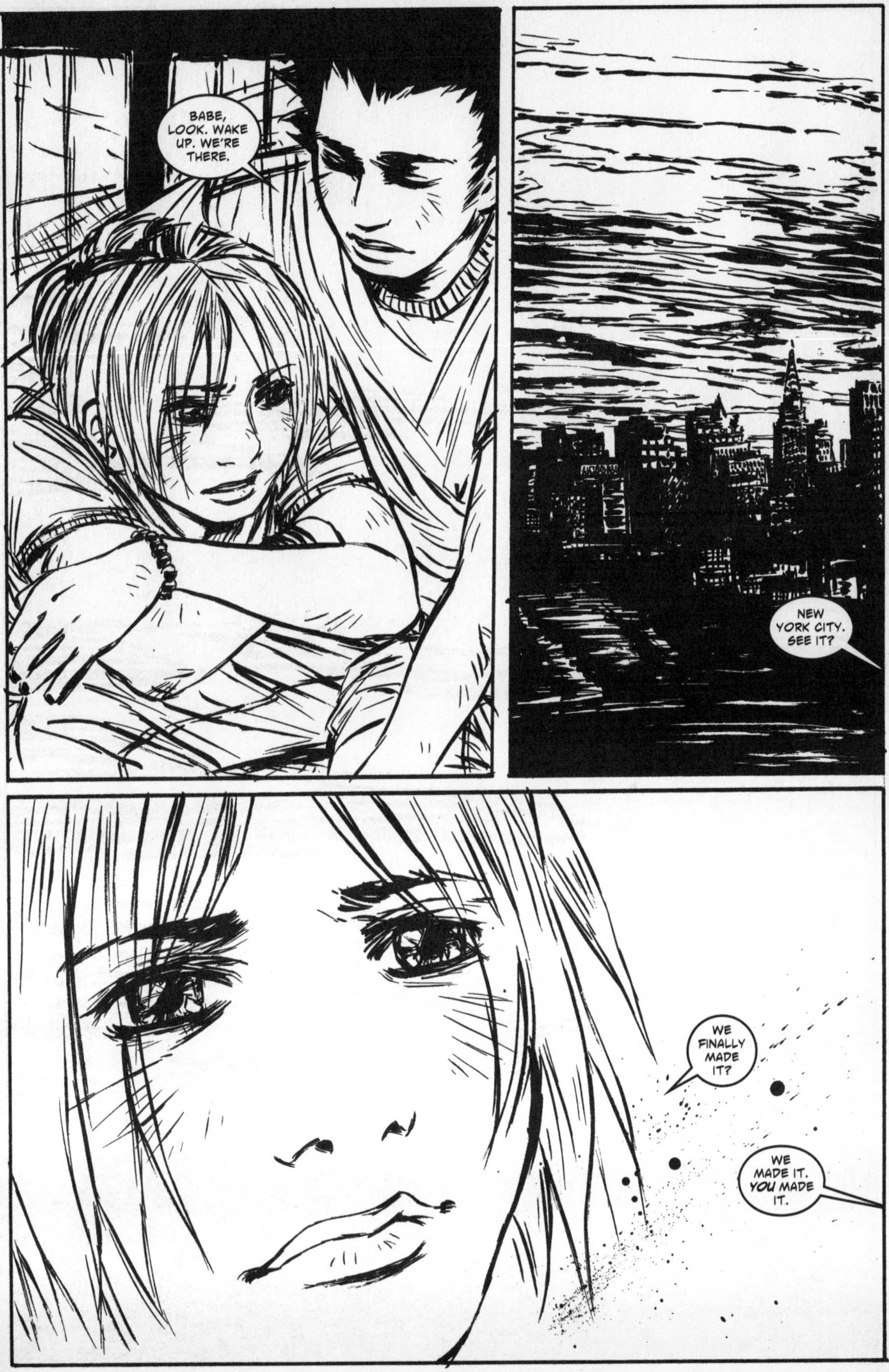
BABE, LOOK. WAKE UP. WE'RE THERE.
NEW YORK CITY. SEE IT?
WE FINALLY MADE IT?
WE MADE IT. *YOU* MADE IT.

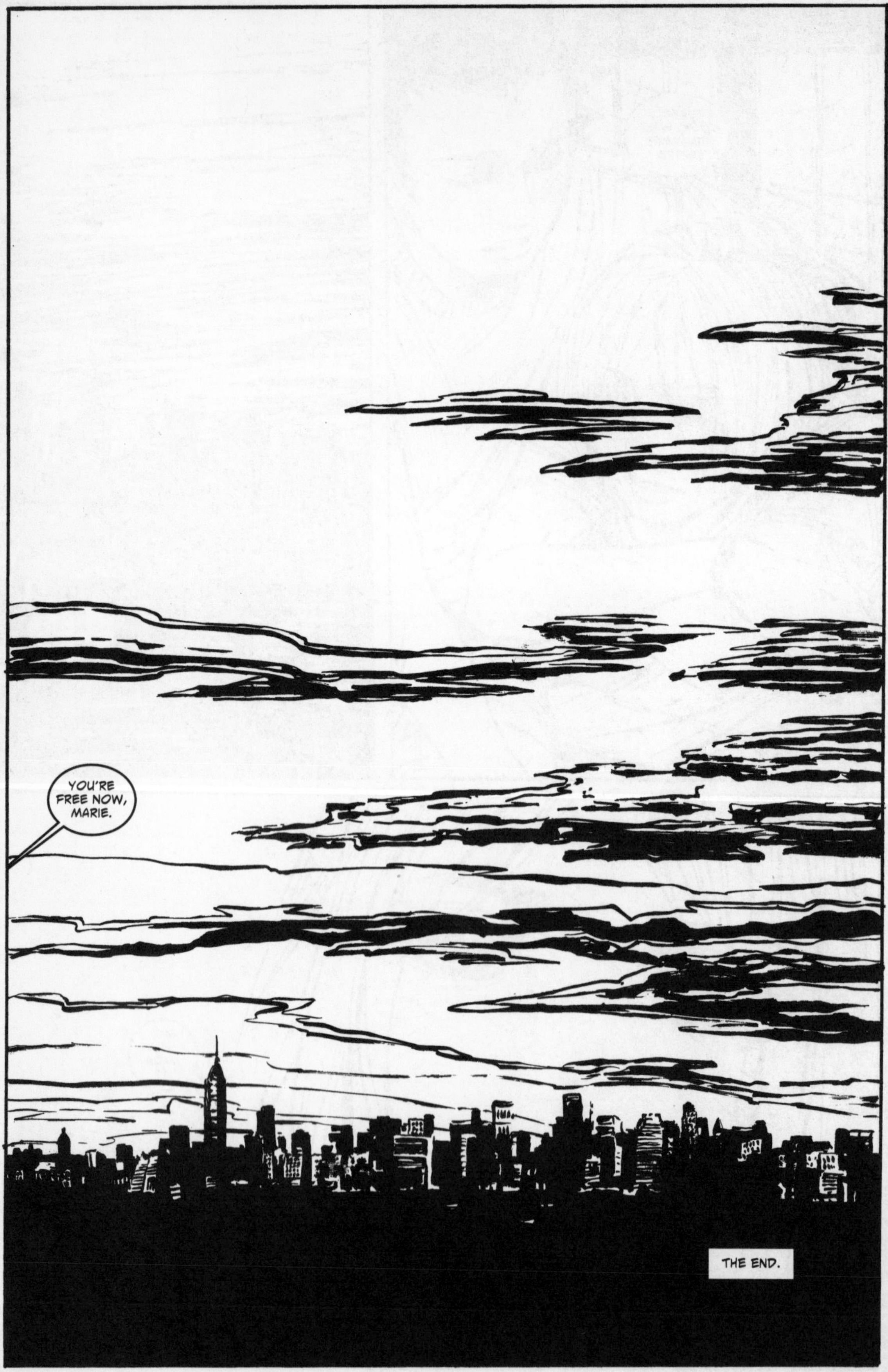
YOU'RE FREE NOW, MARIE.
THE END.

2

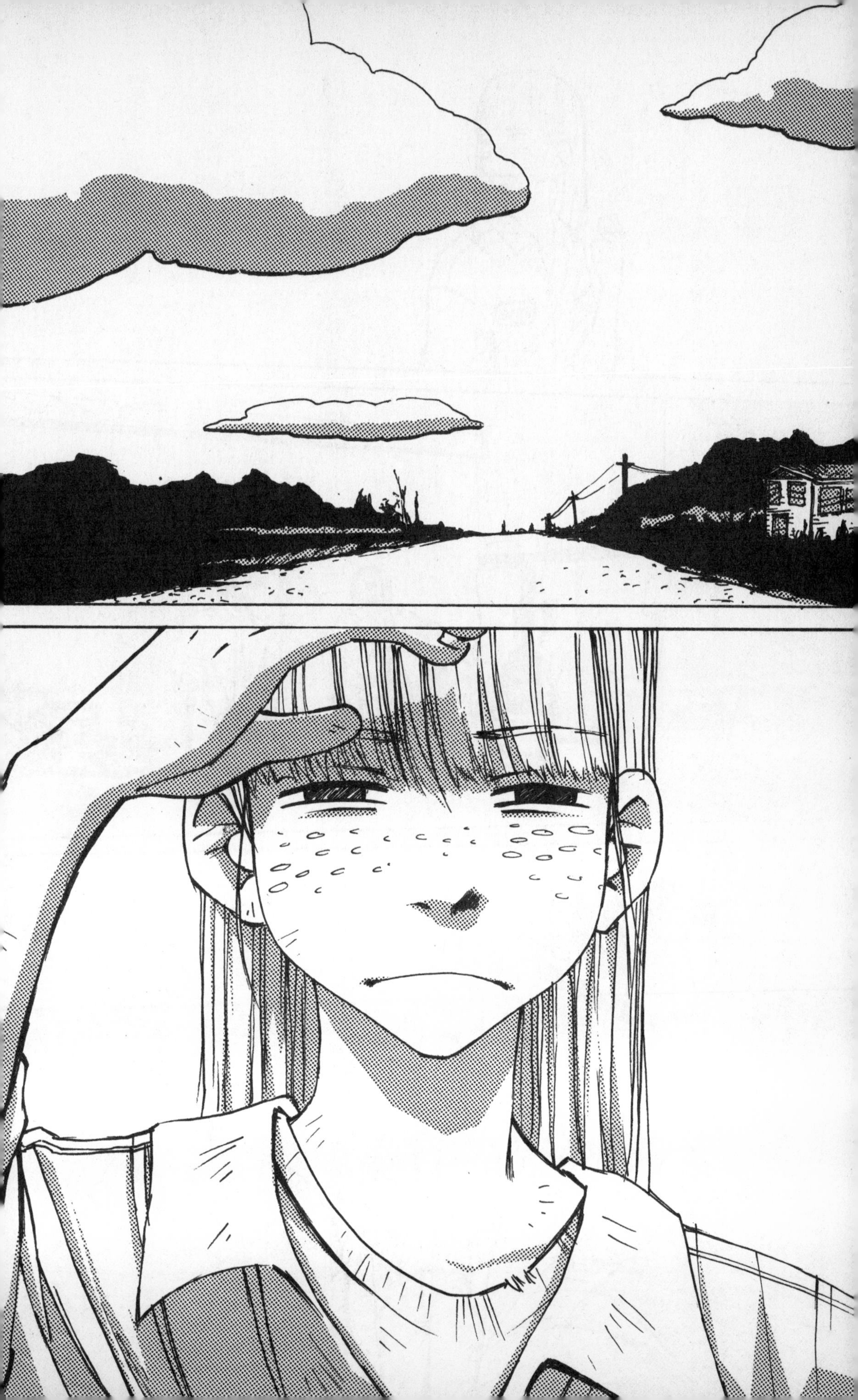

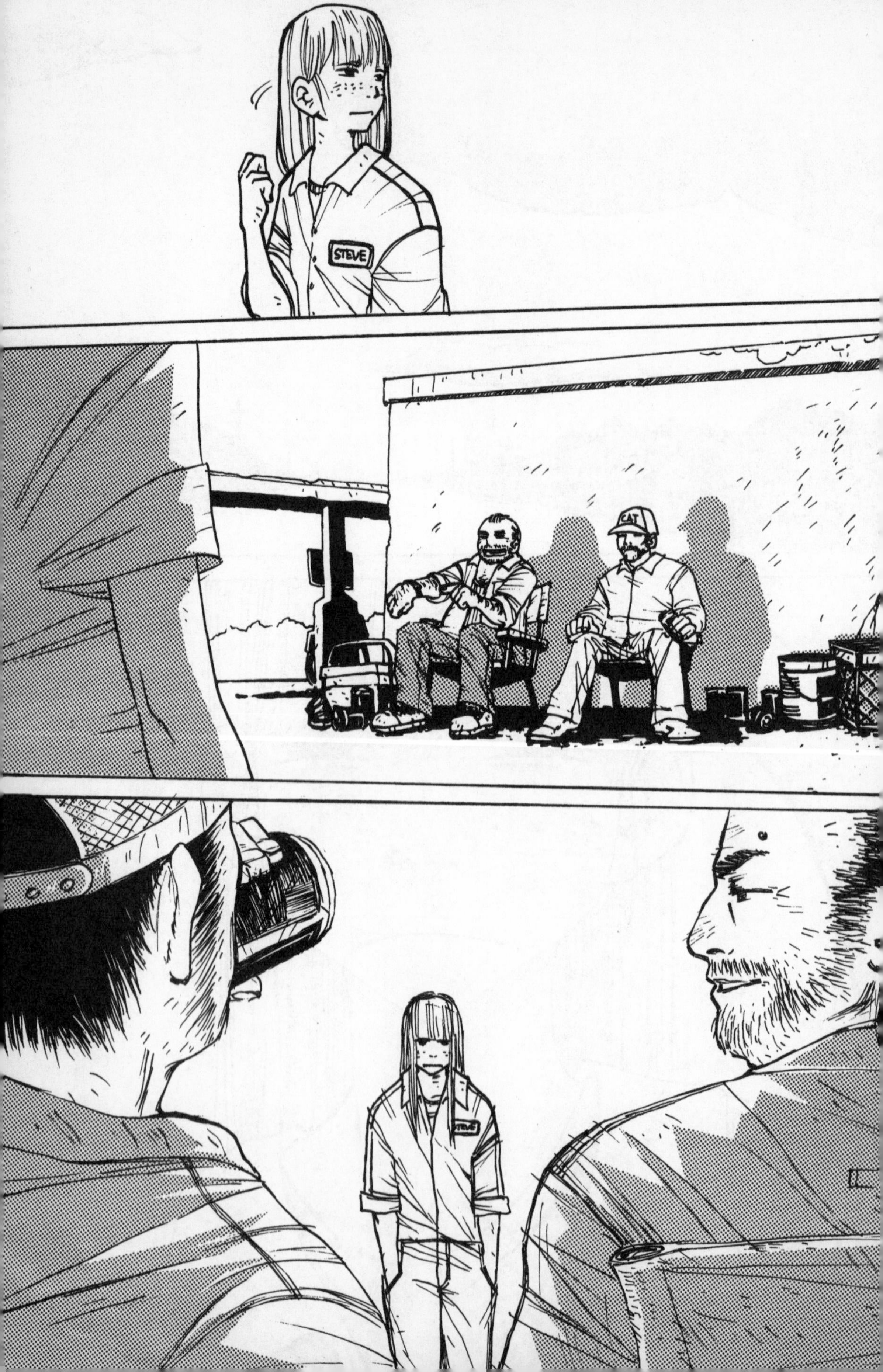
STEVE
CAT

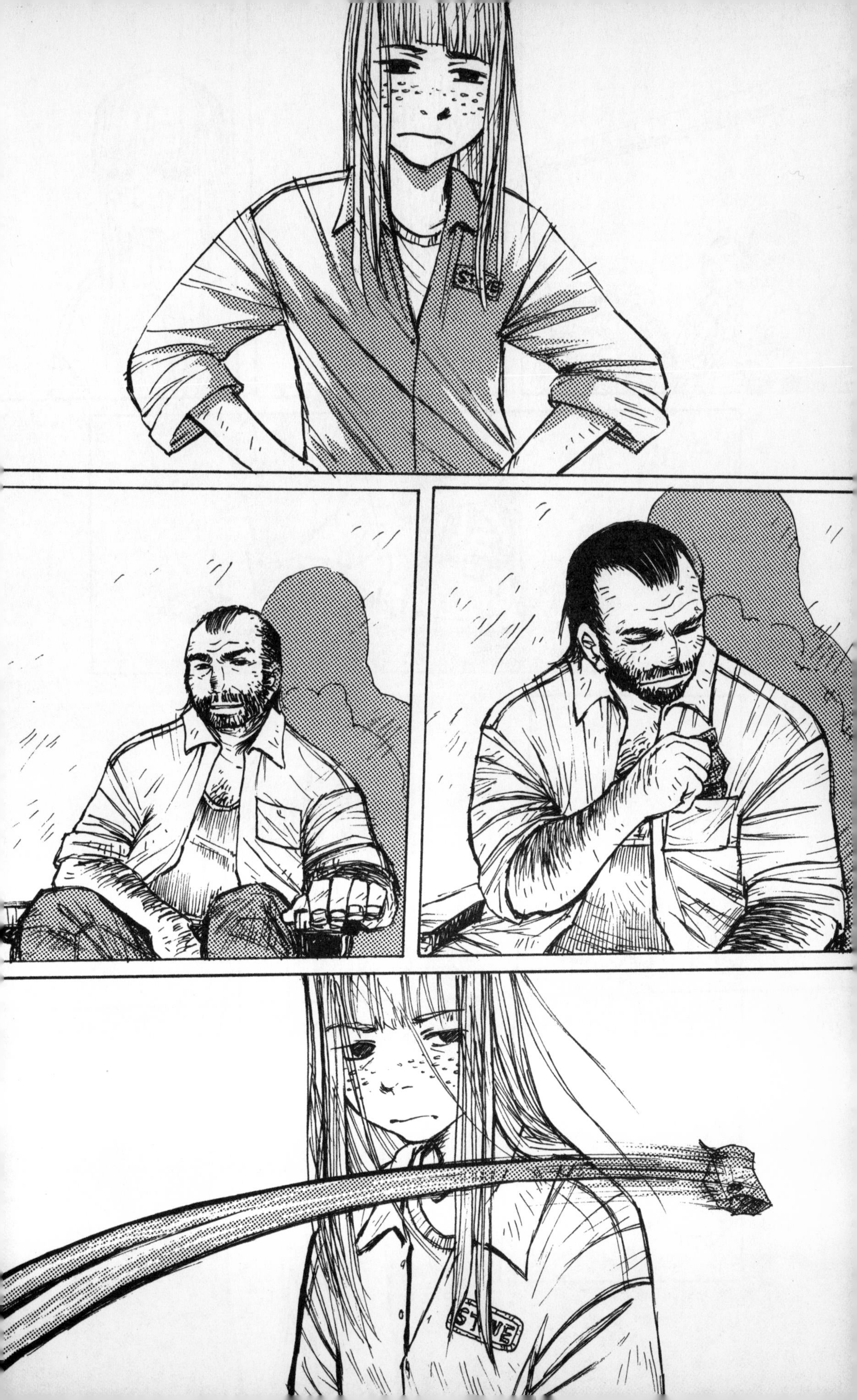
STEVE
STEVE

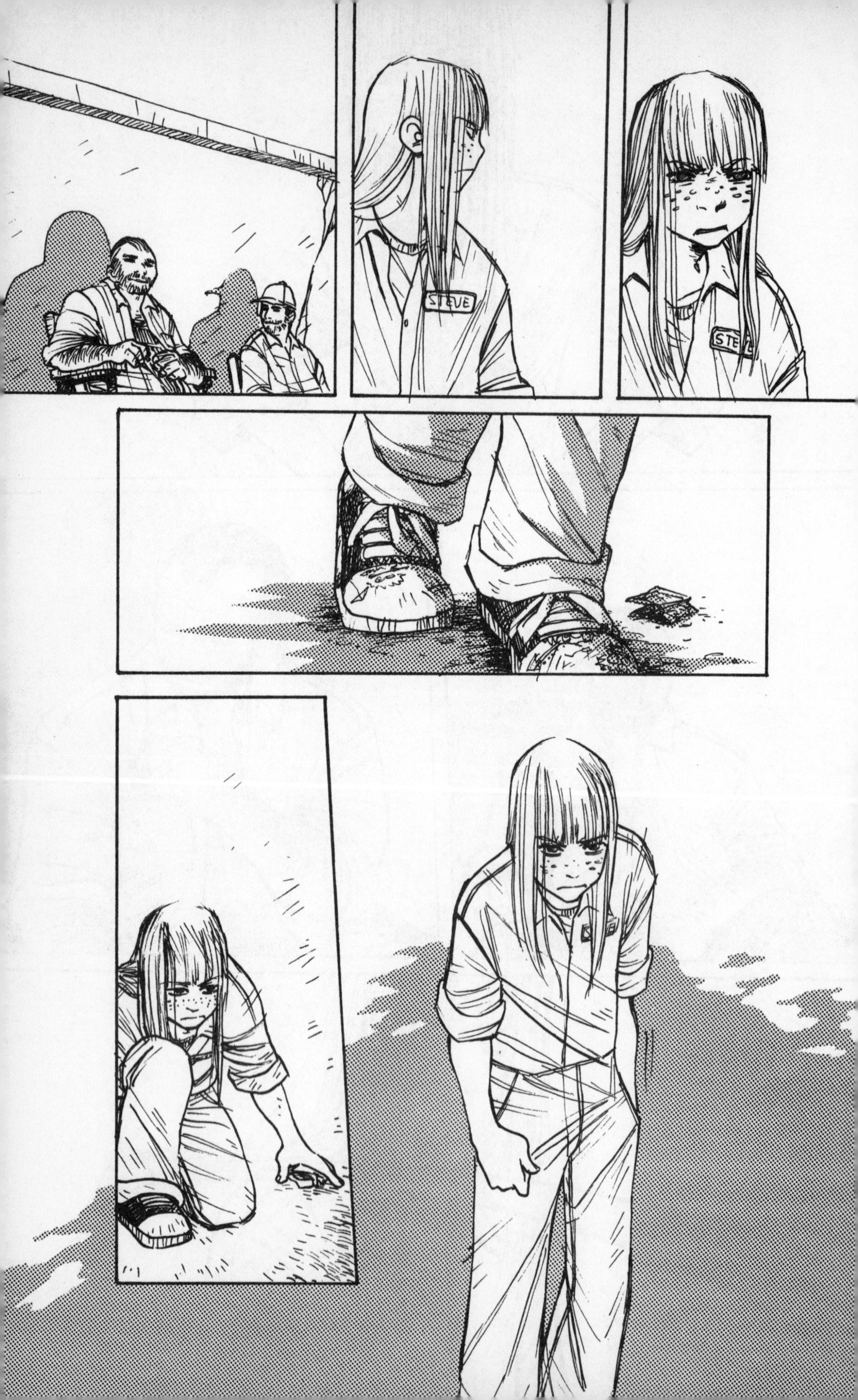
STEVE

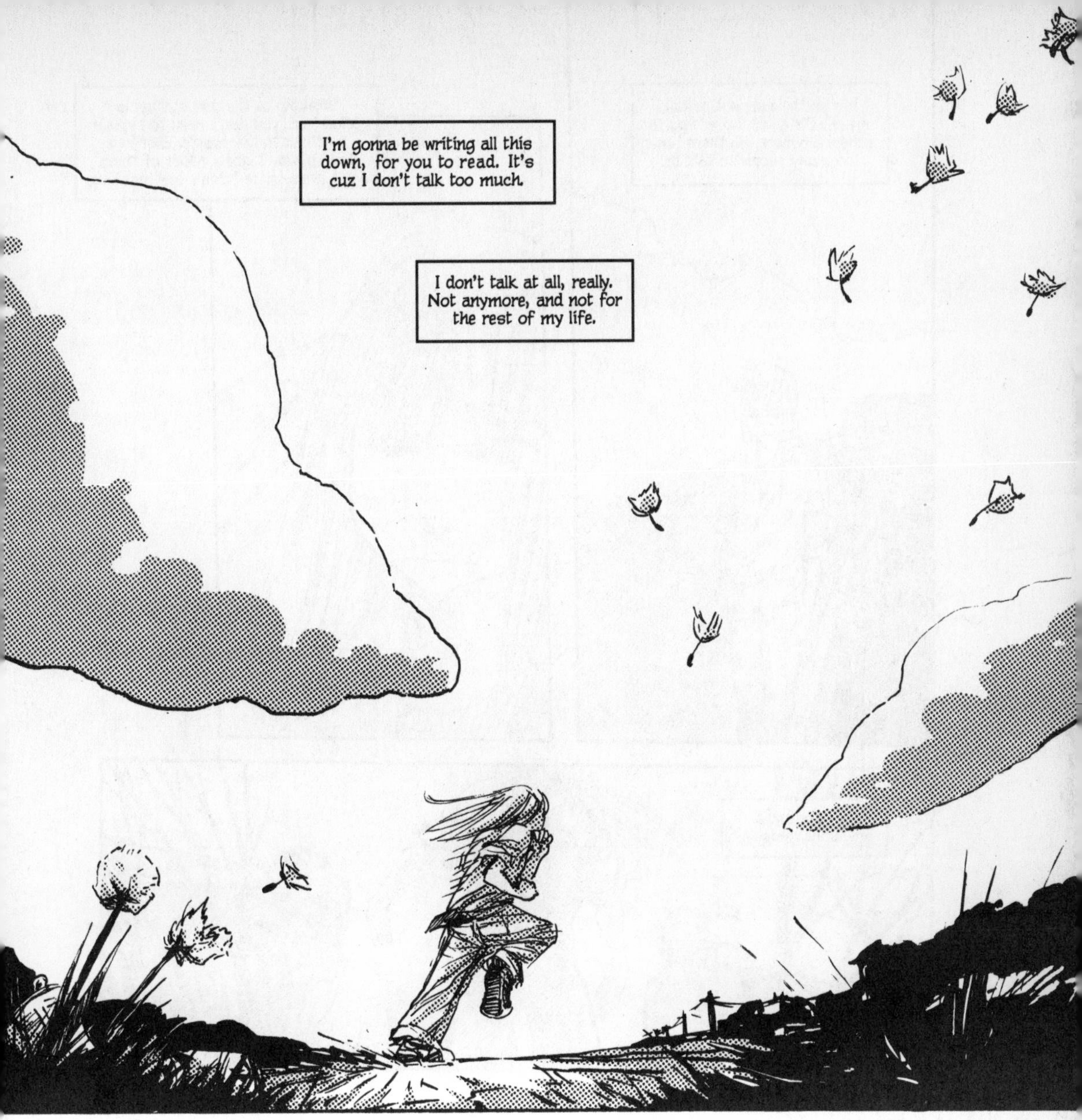
I'm gonna be writing all this down, for you to read. It's cuz I don't talk too much.
I don't talk at all, really. Not anymore, and not for the rest of my life.

"Emmy"

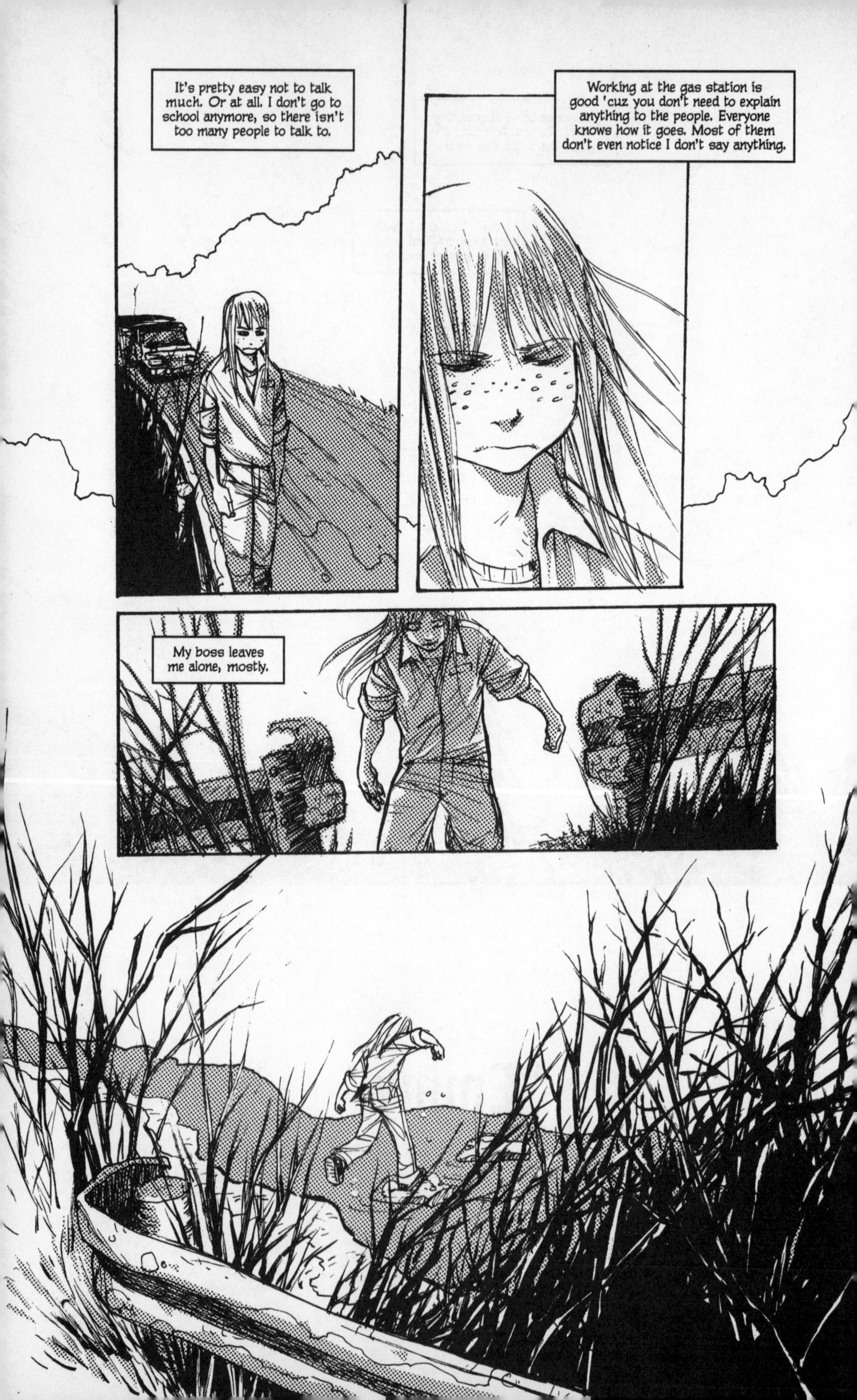
It's pretty easy not to talk much. Or at all. I don't go to school anymore, so there isn't too many people to talk to.
Working at the gas station is good 'cuz you don't need to explain anything to the people. Everyone knows how it goes. Most of them don't even notice I don't say anything.
My boss leaves me alone, mostly.

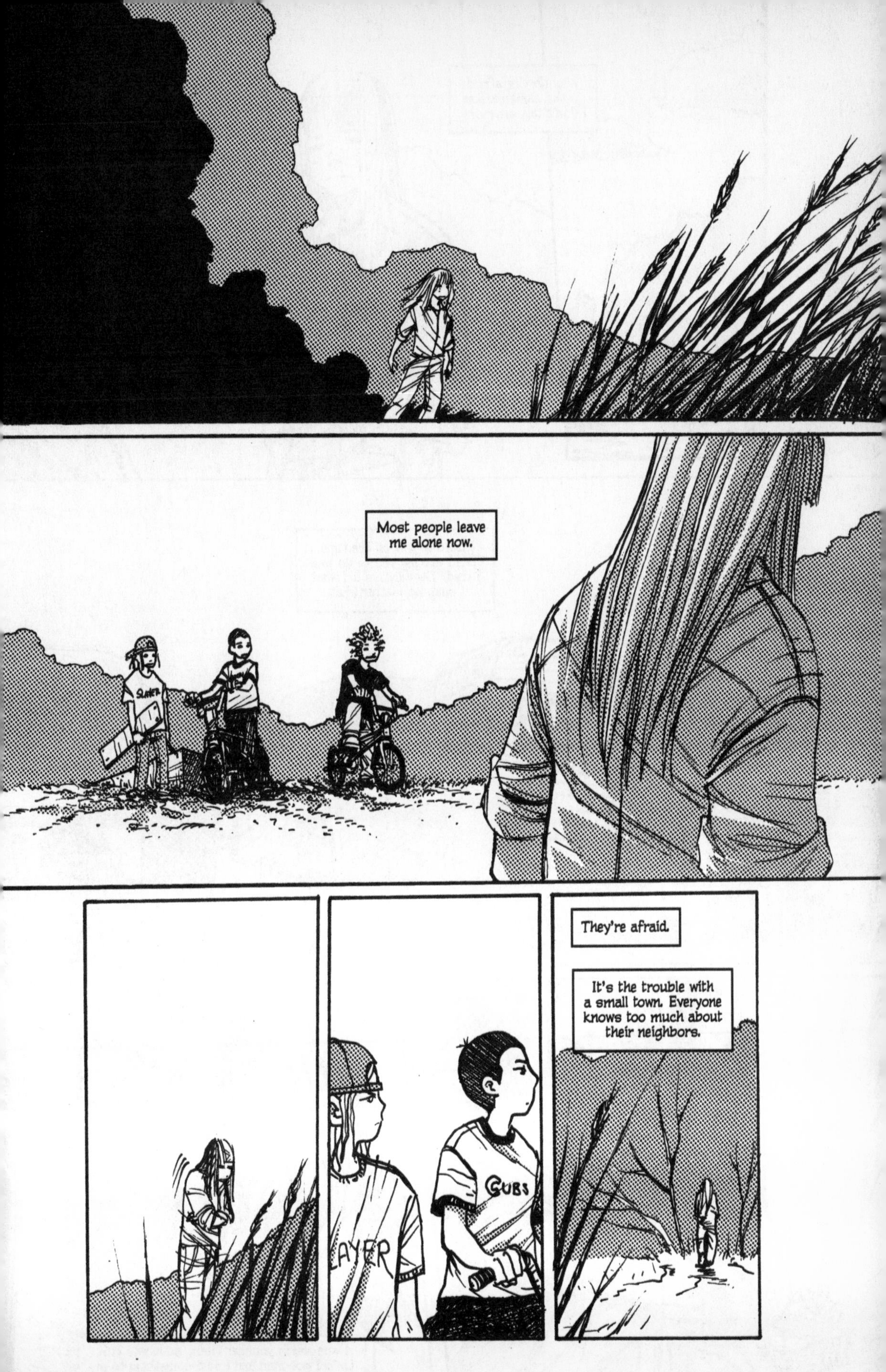
Most people leave me alone now.
They're afraid.
It's the trouble with a small town. Everyone knows too much about their neighbors.
CUBS

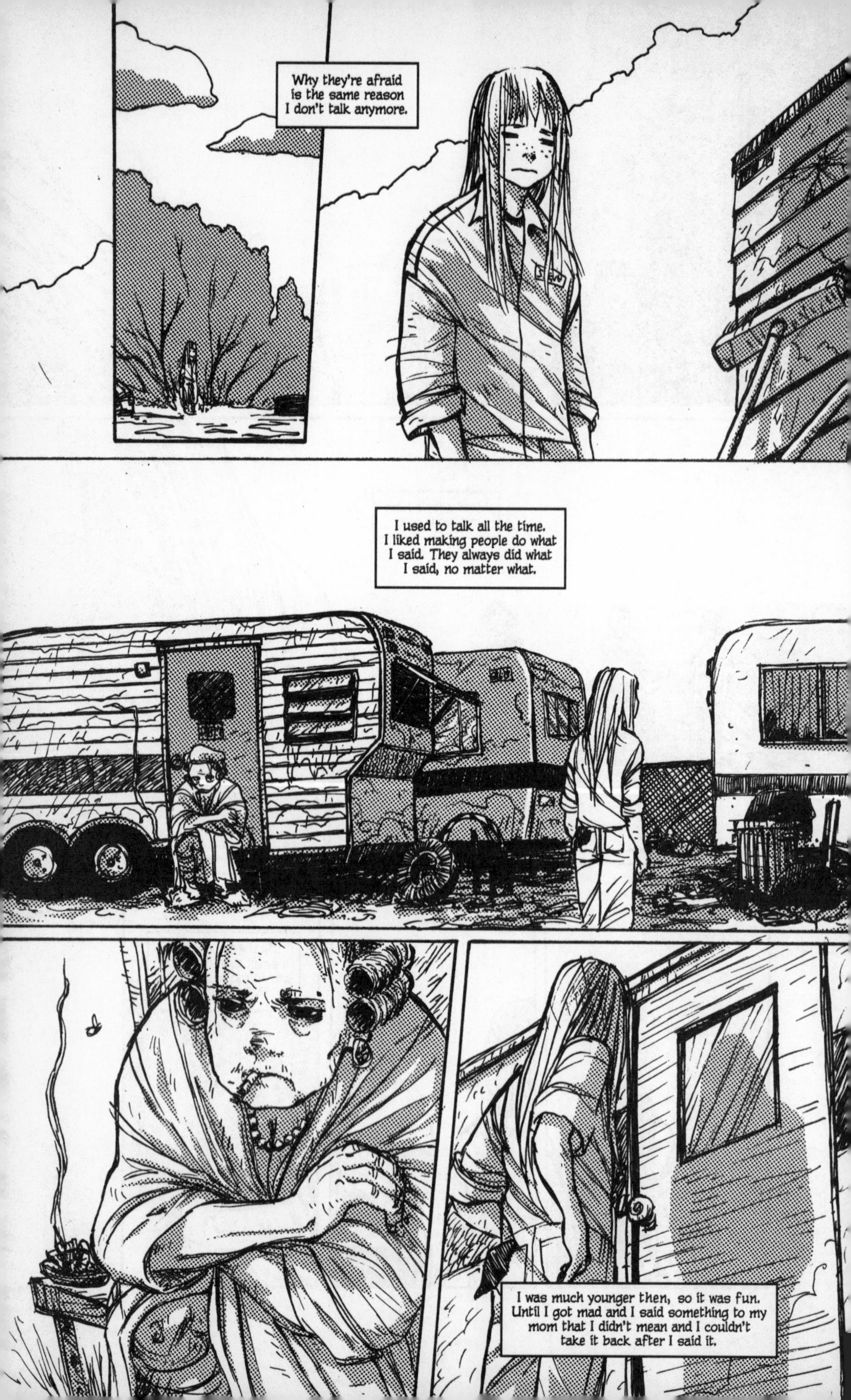
Why they're afraid
is the same reason
I don't talk anymore.
I used to talk all the time.
I liked making people do what
I said. They always did what
I said, no matter what.
I was much younger then, so it was fun.
Until I got mad and I said something to my
mom that I didn't mean and I couldn't
take it back after I said it.

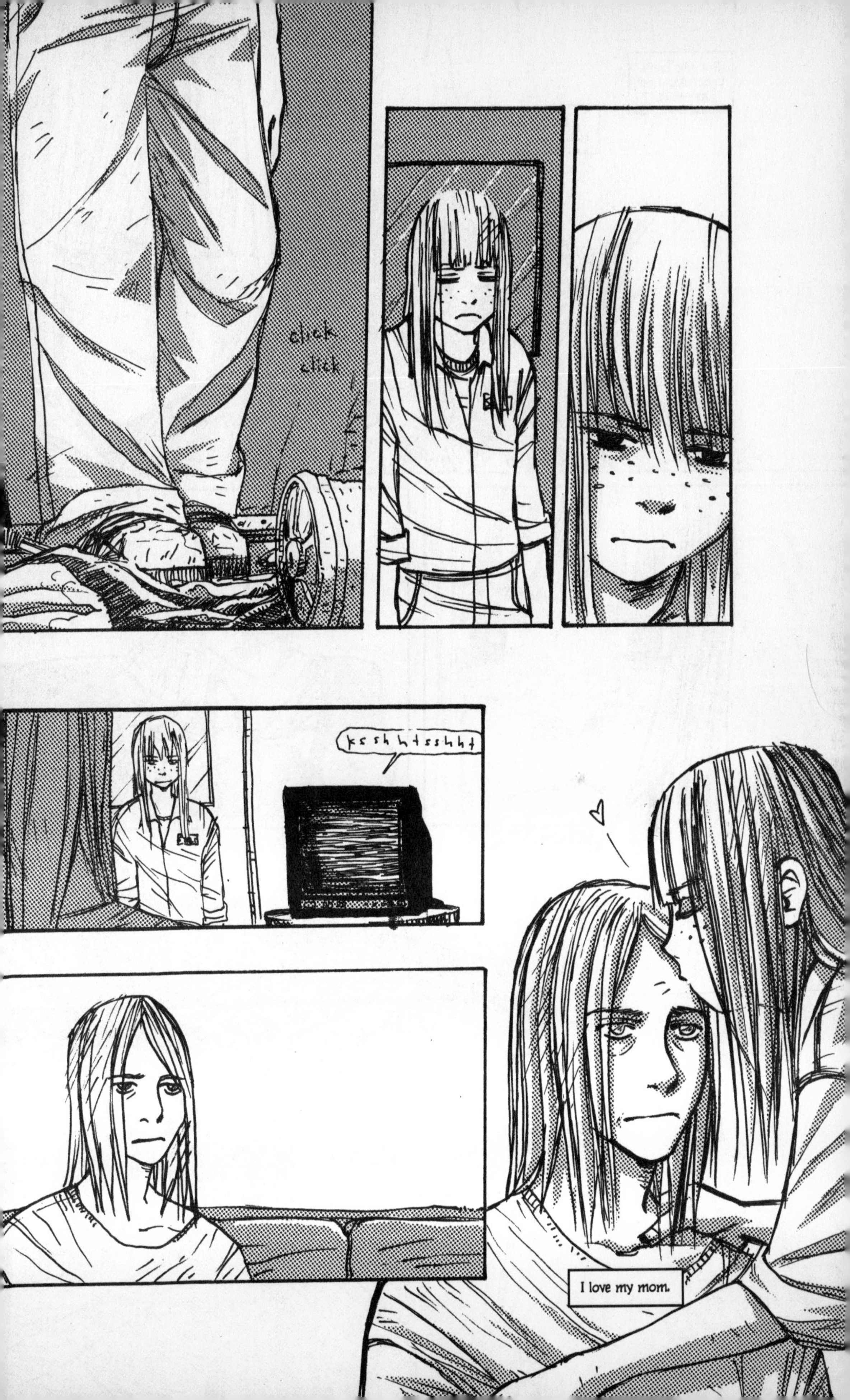
click
click
kssh htsshht
I love my mom.

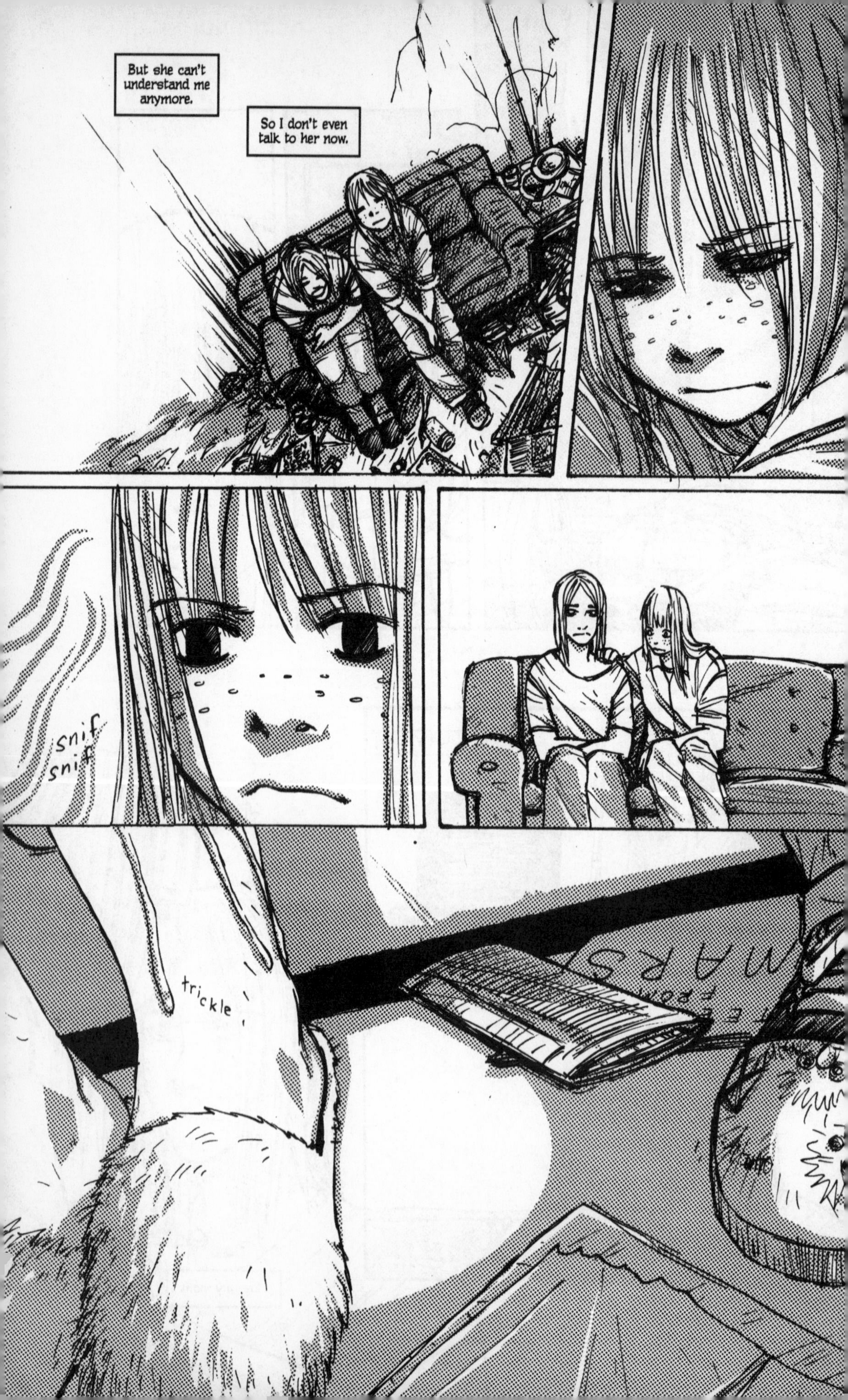
But she can't understand me anymore.
So I don't even talk to her now.
snif snif
trickle

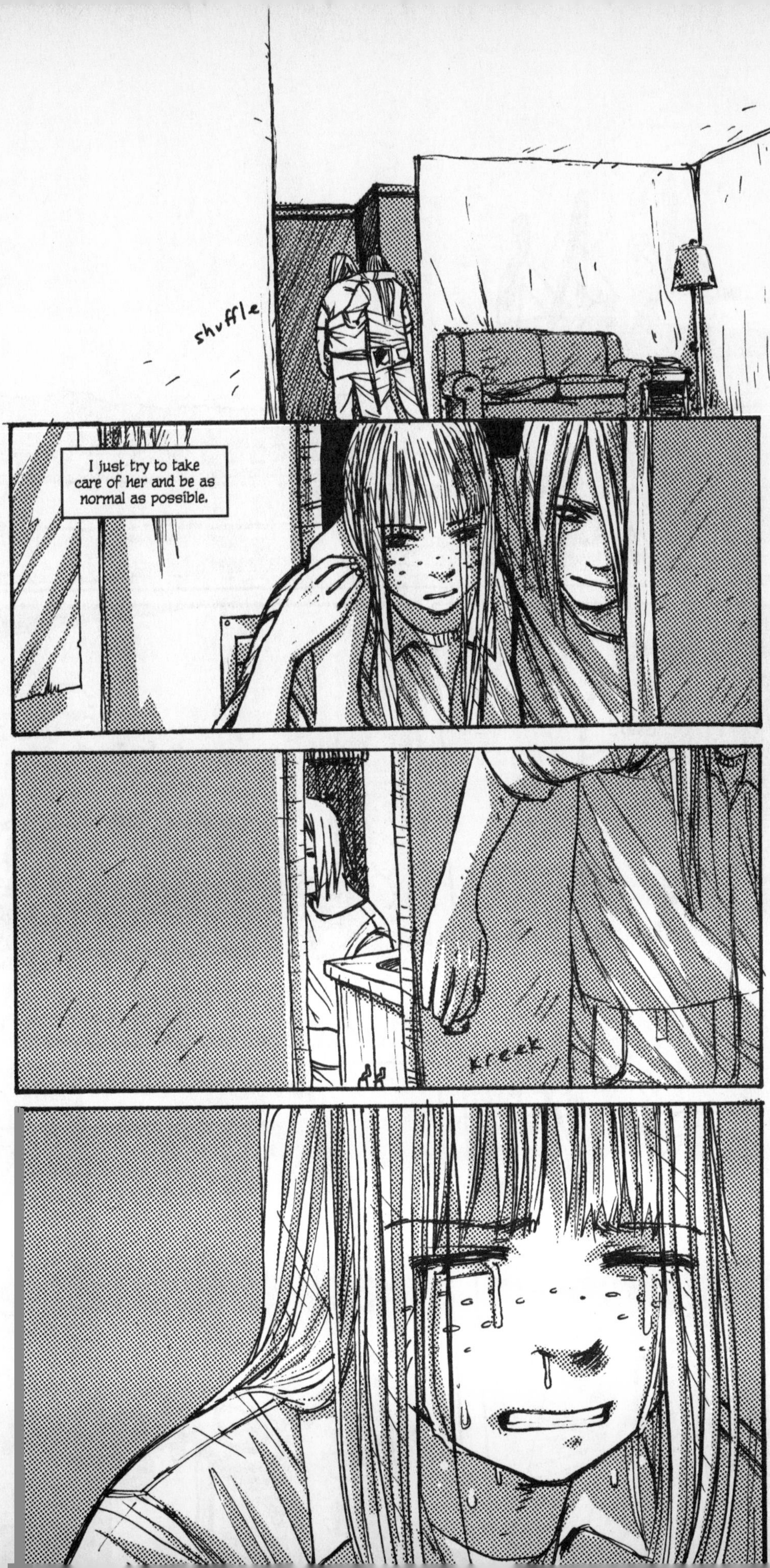
shuffle
I just try to take care of her and be as normal as possible.
kreek

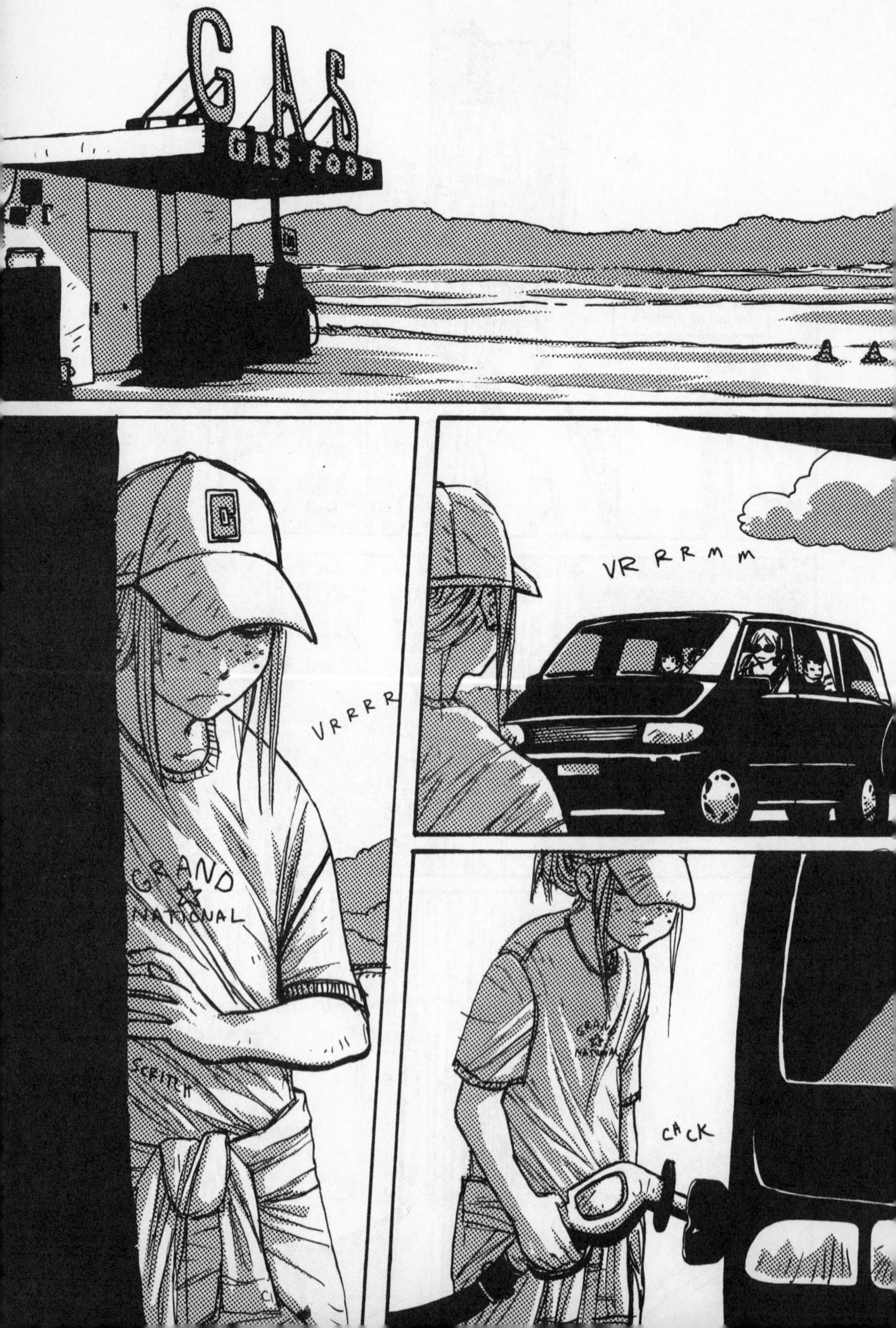
GAS
GAS·FOOD
VRRRR
GRAND
NATIONAL
SCRITCH
VR RRMM
CACK

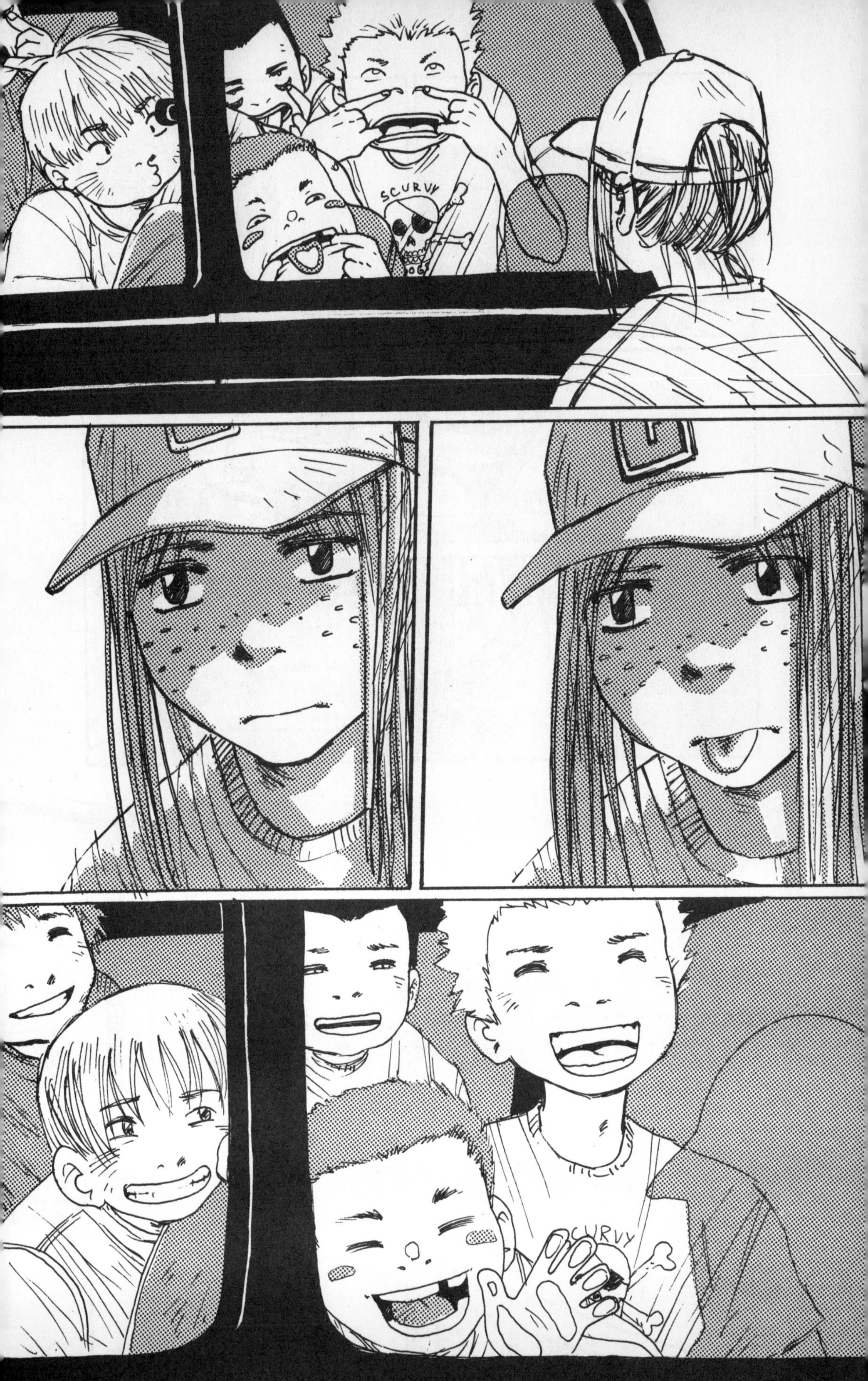
SCURVY
SCURVY

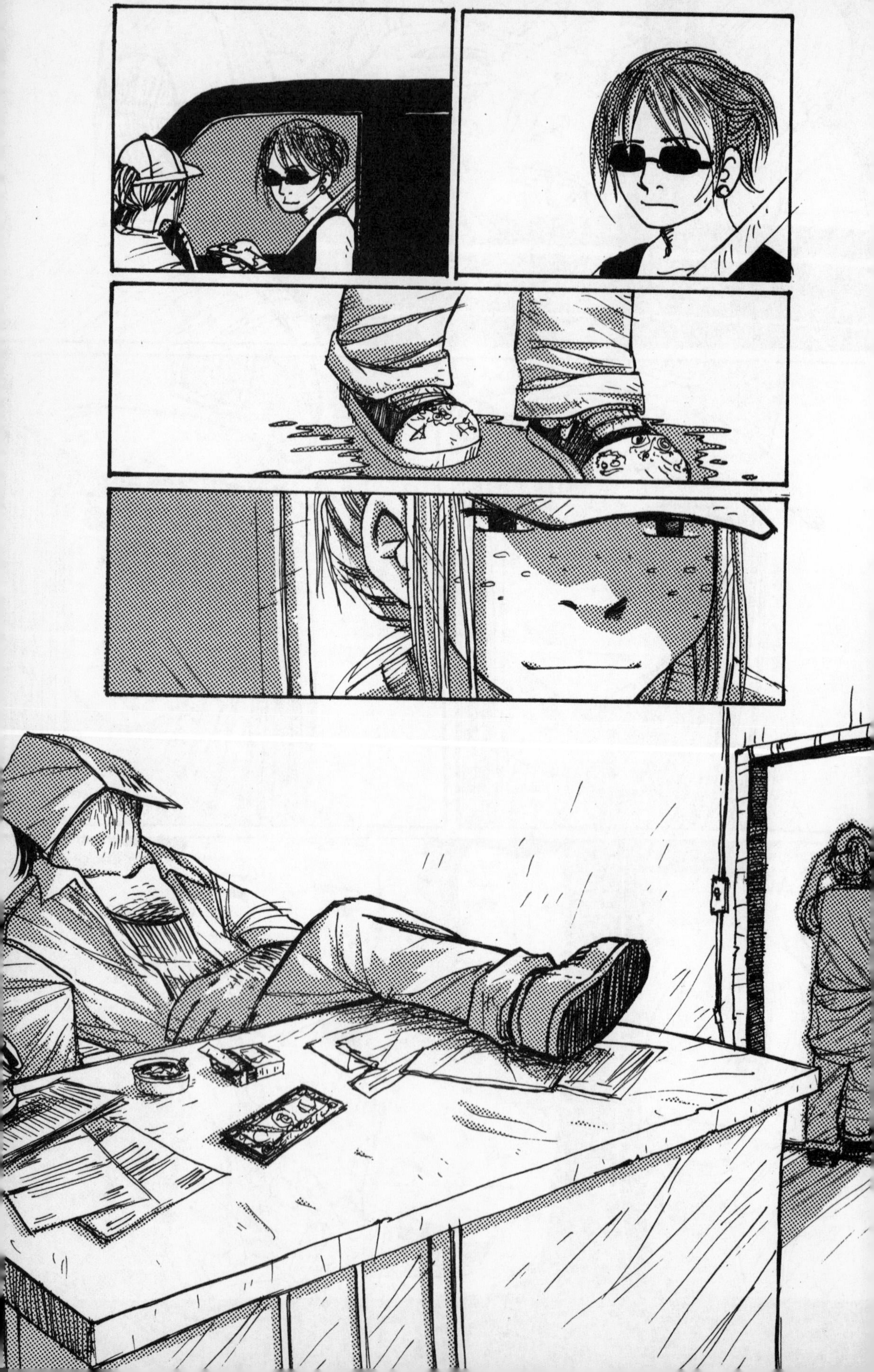

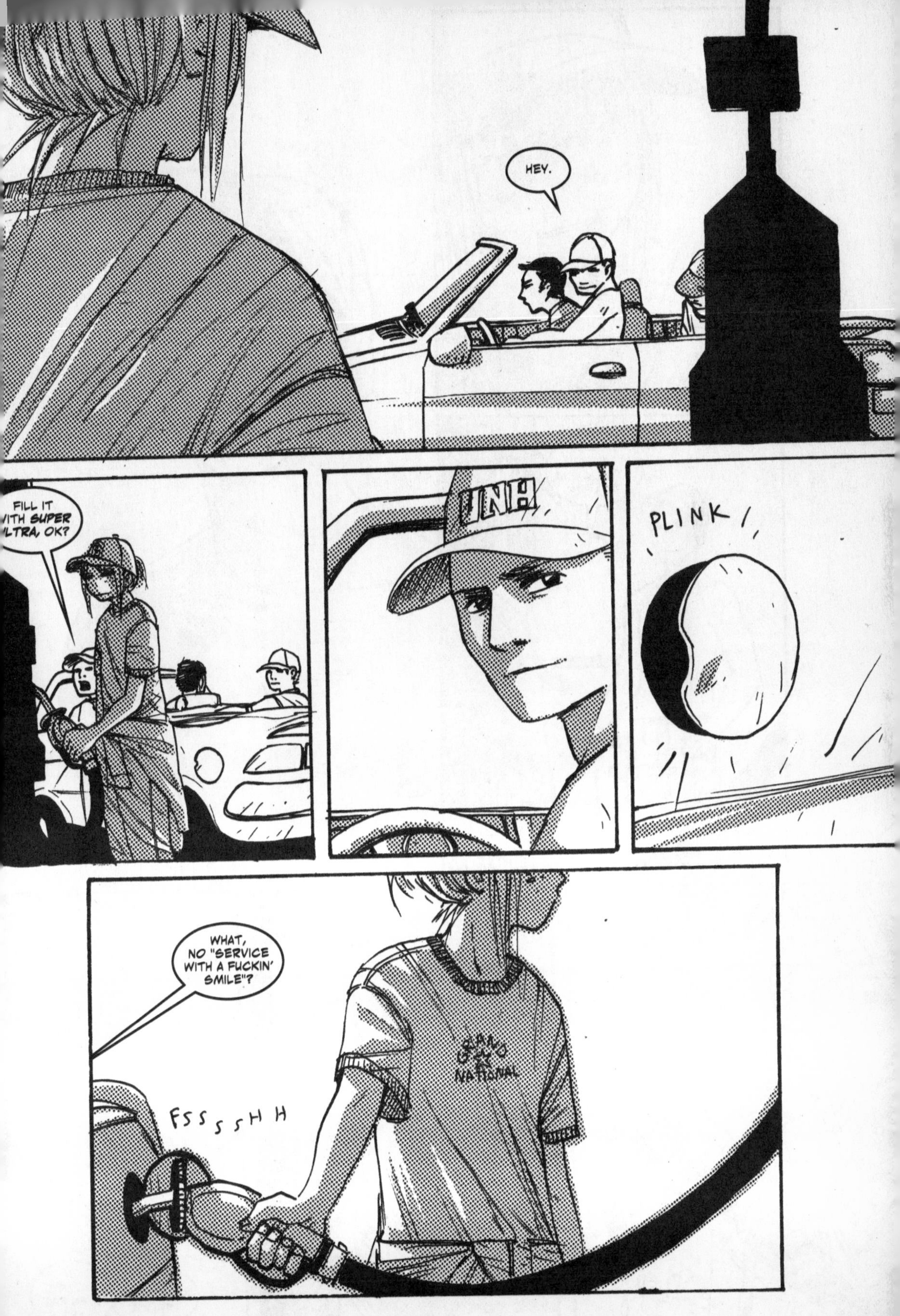
HEY.
FILL IT WITH SUPER ULTRA, OK?
UNH
PLINK
WHAT, NO "SERVICE WITH A FUCKIN' SMILE"?
NATIONAL
FSSSSHH

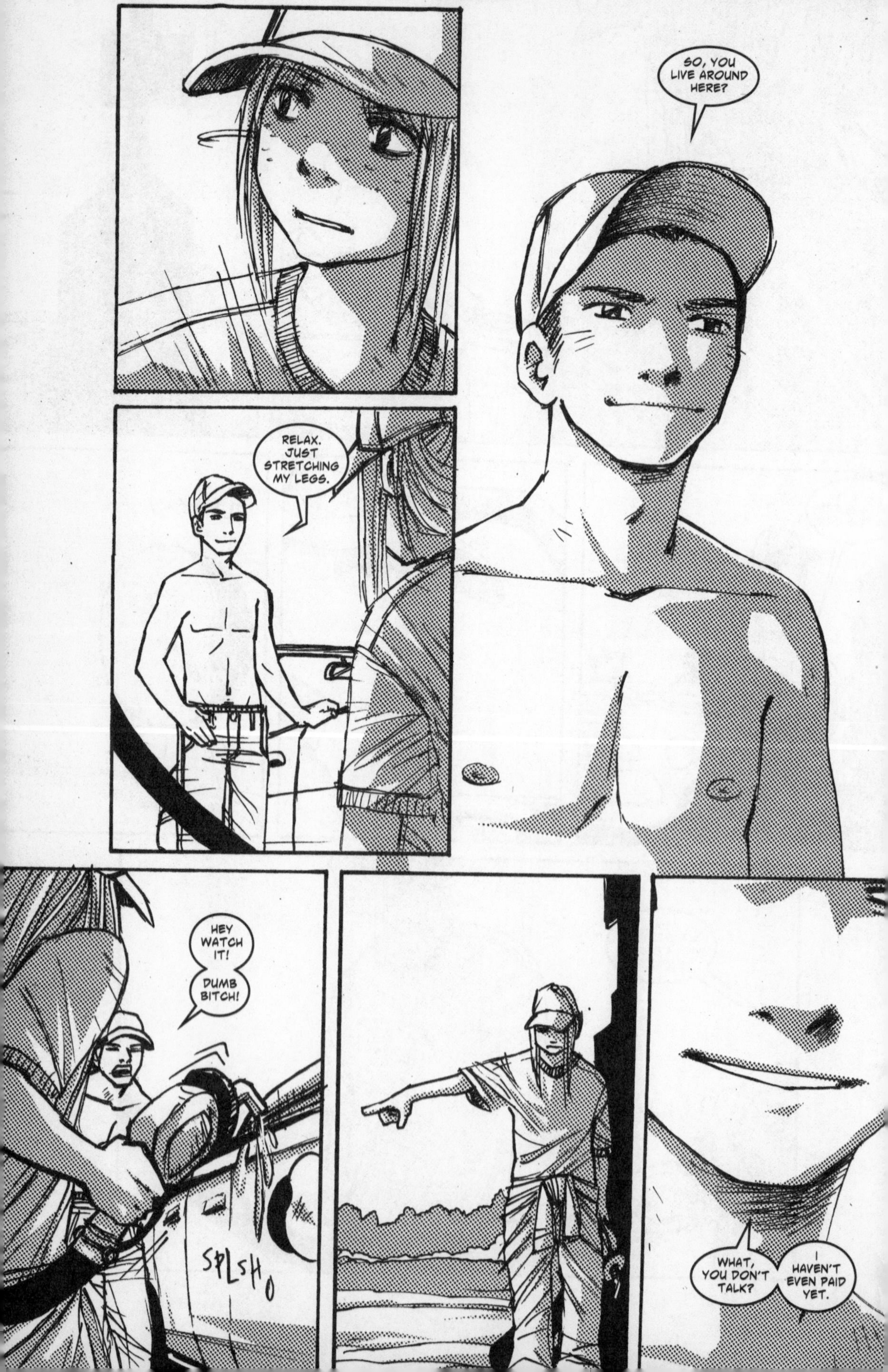
SO, YOU LIVE AROUND HERE?
RELAX. JUST STRETCHING MY LEGS.
HEY WATCH IT!
DUMB BITCH!
SPLSH
WHAT, YOU DON'T TALK?
I HAVEN'T EVEN PAID YET.

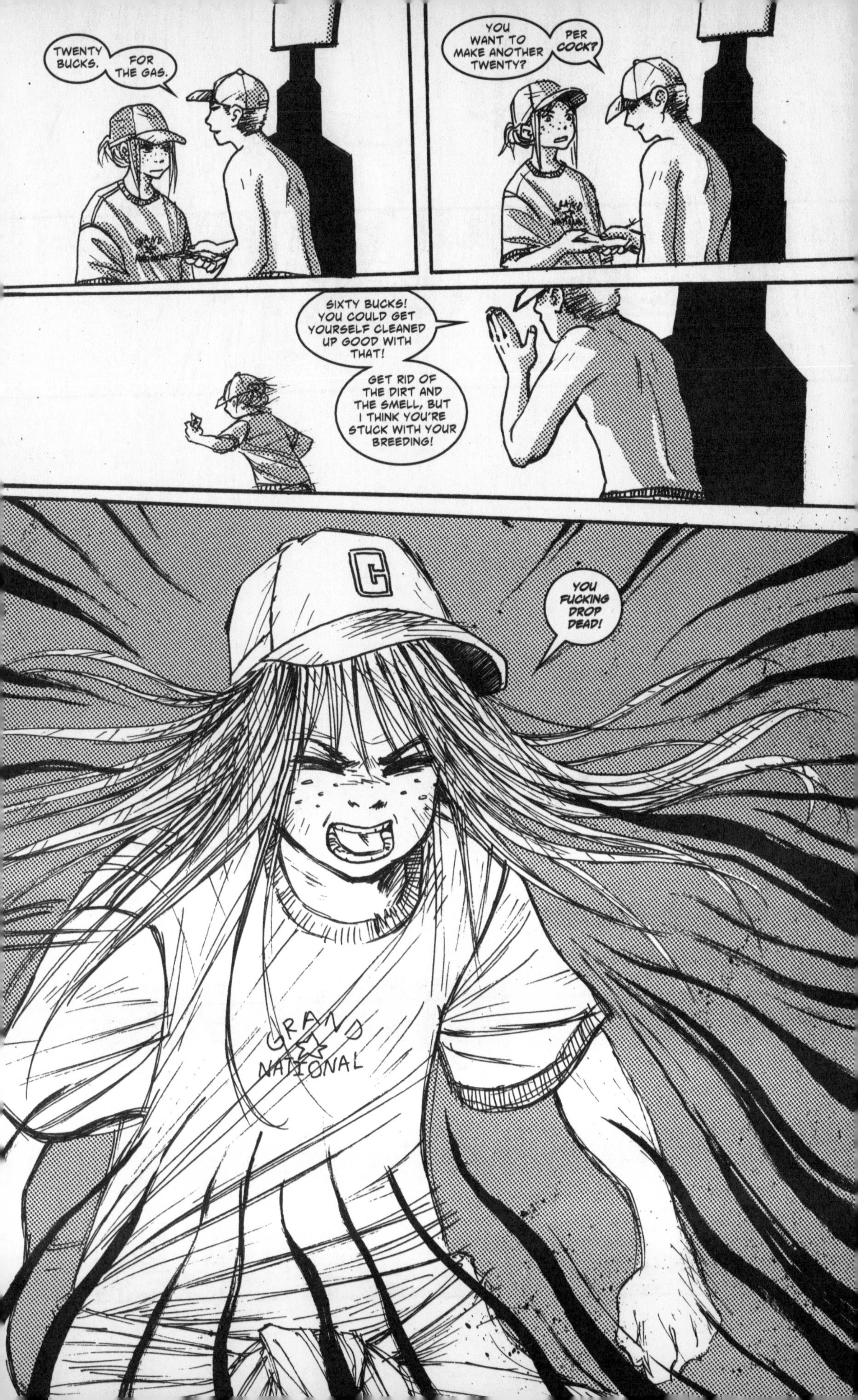

TWENTY BUCKS.
FOR THE GAS.
YOU WANT TO MAKE ANOTHER TWENTY?
PER COCK?
SIXTY BUCKS! YOU COULD GET YOURSELF CLEANED UP GOOD WITH THAT!
GET RID OF THE DIRT AND THE SMELL, BUT I THINK YOU'RE STUCK WITH YOUR BREEDING!
YOU FUCKING DROP DEAD!
GRAND NATIONAL

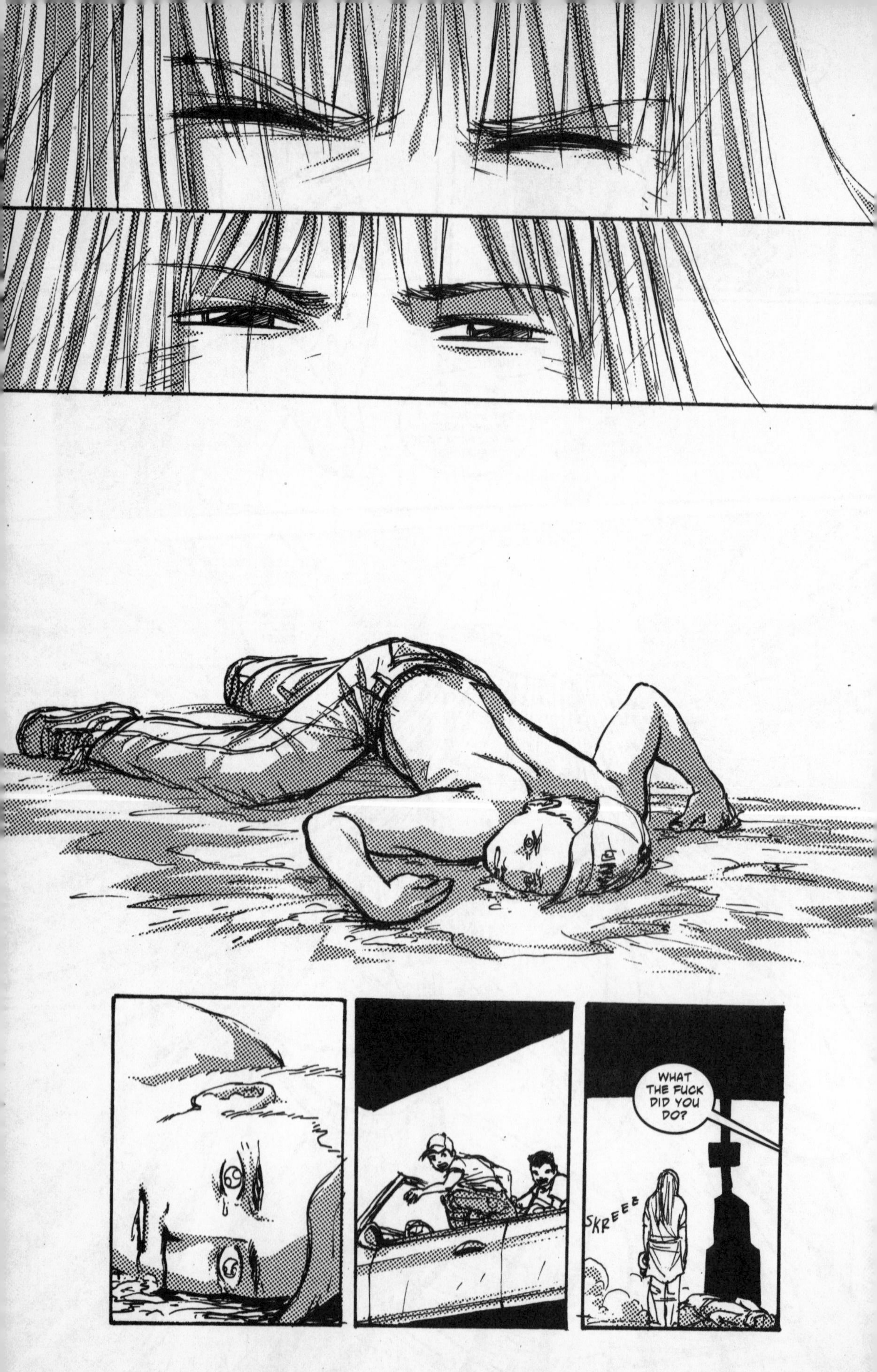
SKREEE
WHAT THE FUCK DID YOU DO?

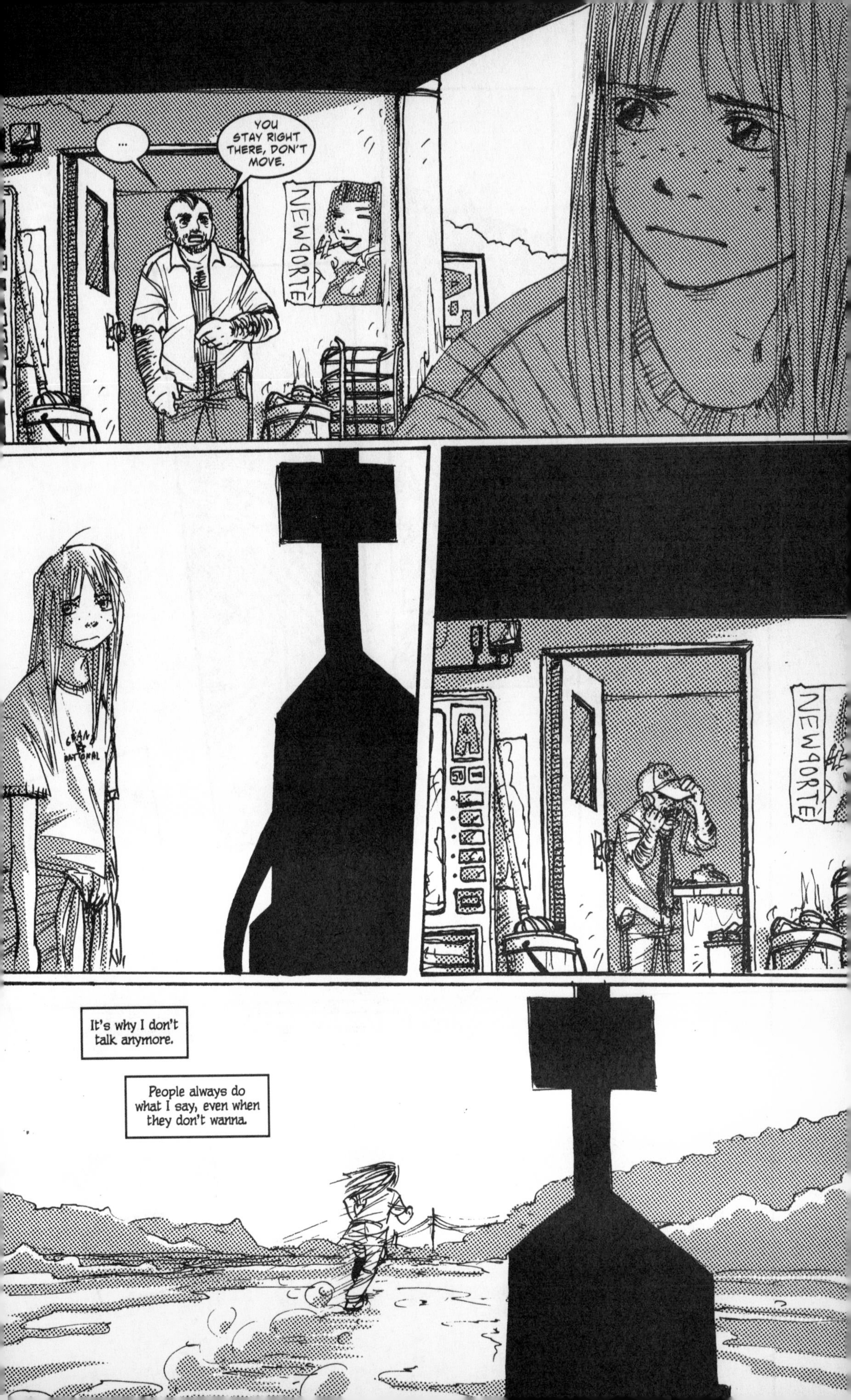
...
YOU STAY RIGHT THERE, DON'T MOVE.
NEWPORTE
NEWPORTE
It's why I don't talk anymore.
People always do what I say, even when they don't wanna.

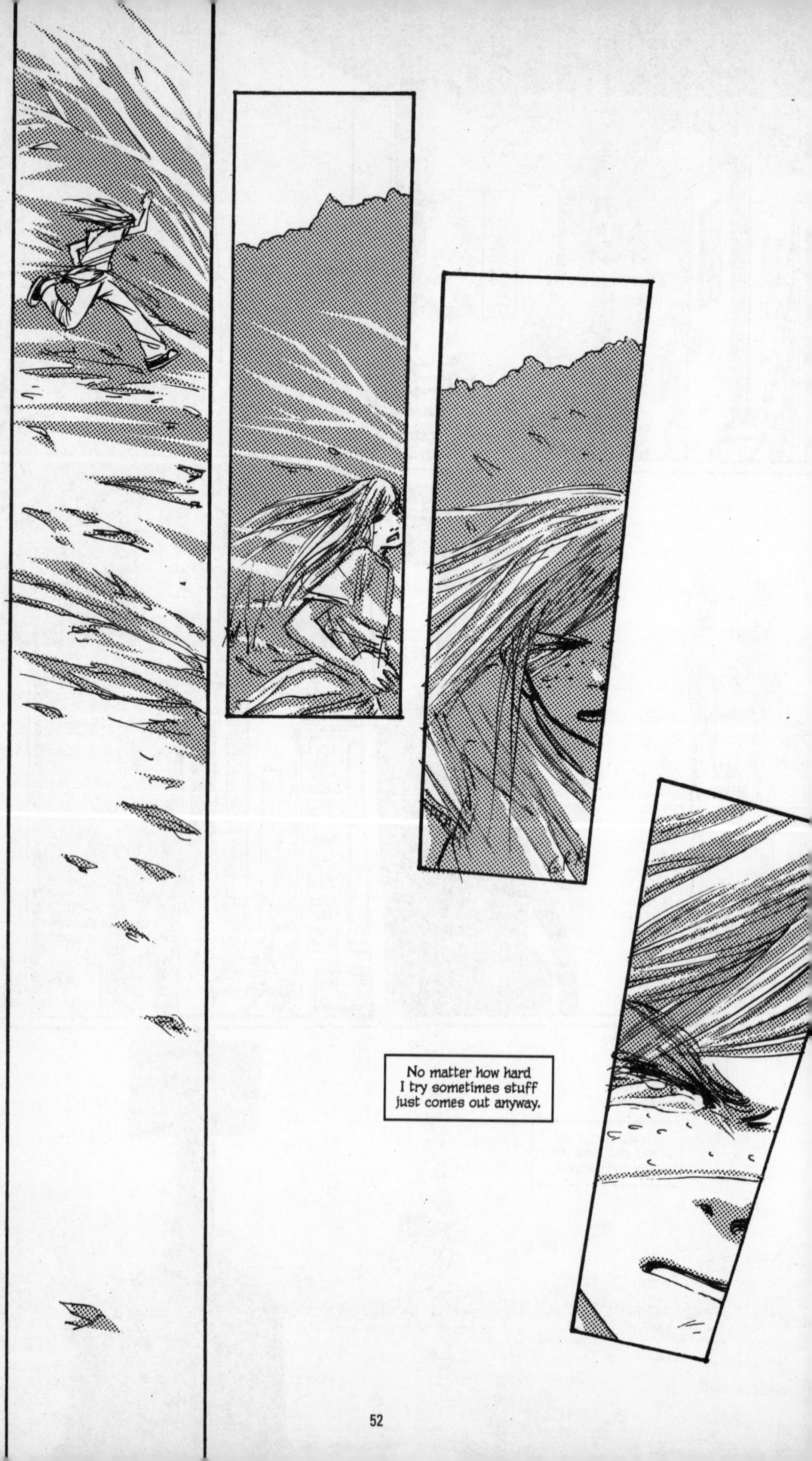
No matter how hard I try sometimes stuff just comes out anyway.

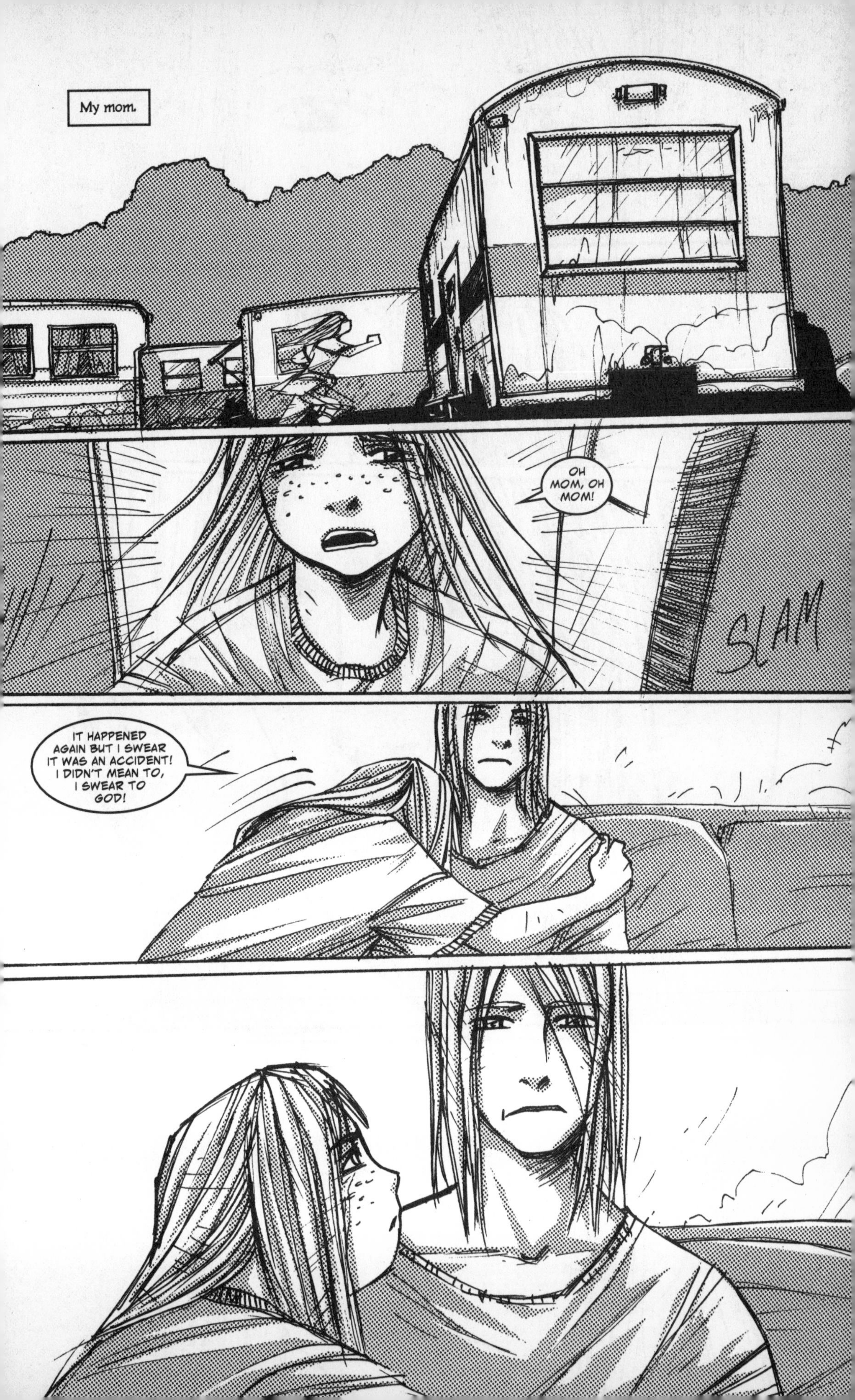
My mom.
OH MOM, OH MOM!
SLAM
IT HAPPENED AGAIN BUT I SWEAR IT WAS AN ACCIDENT! I DIDN'T MEAN TO, I SWEAR TO GOD!

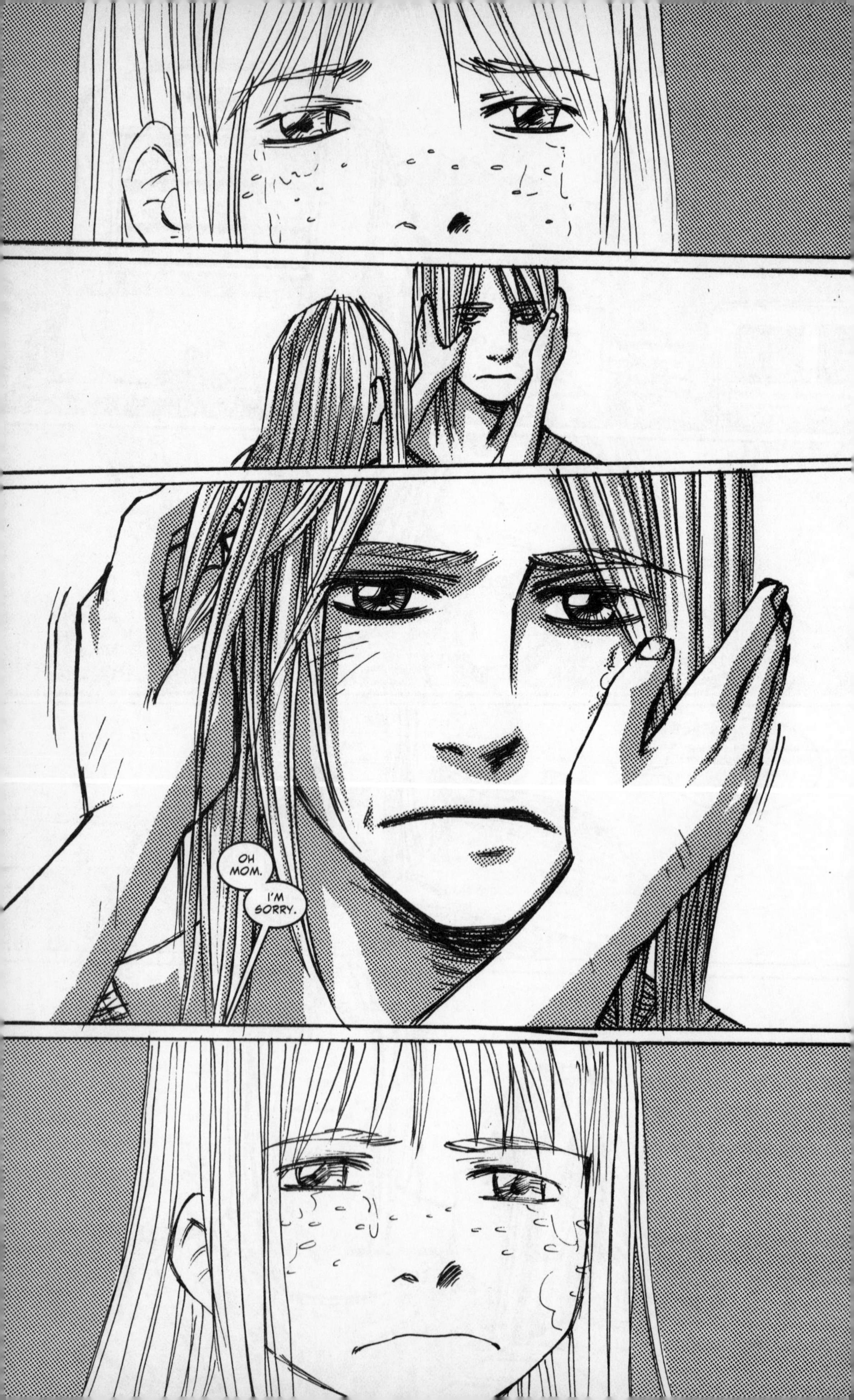
OH MOM.
I'M SORRY.

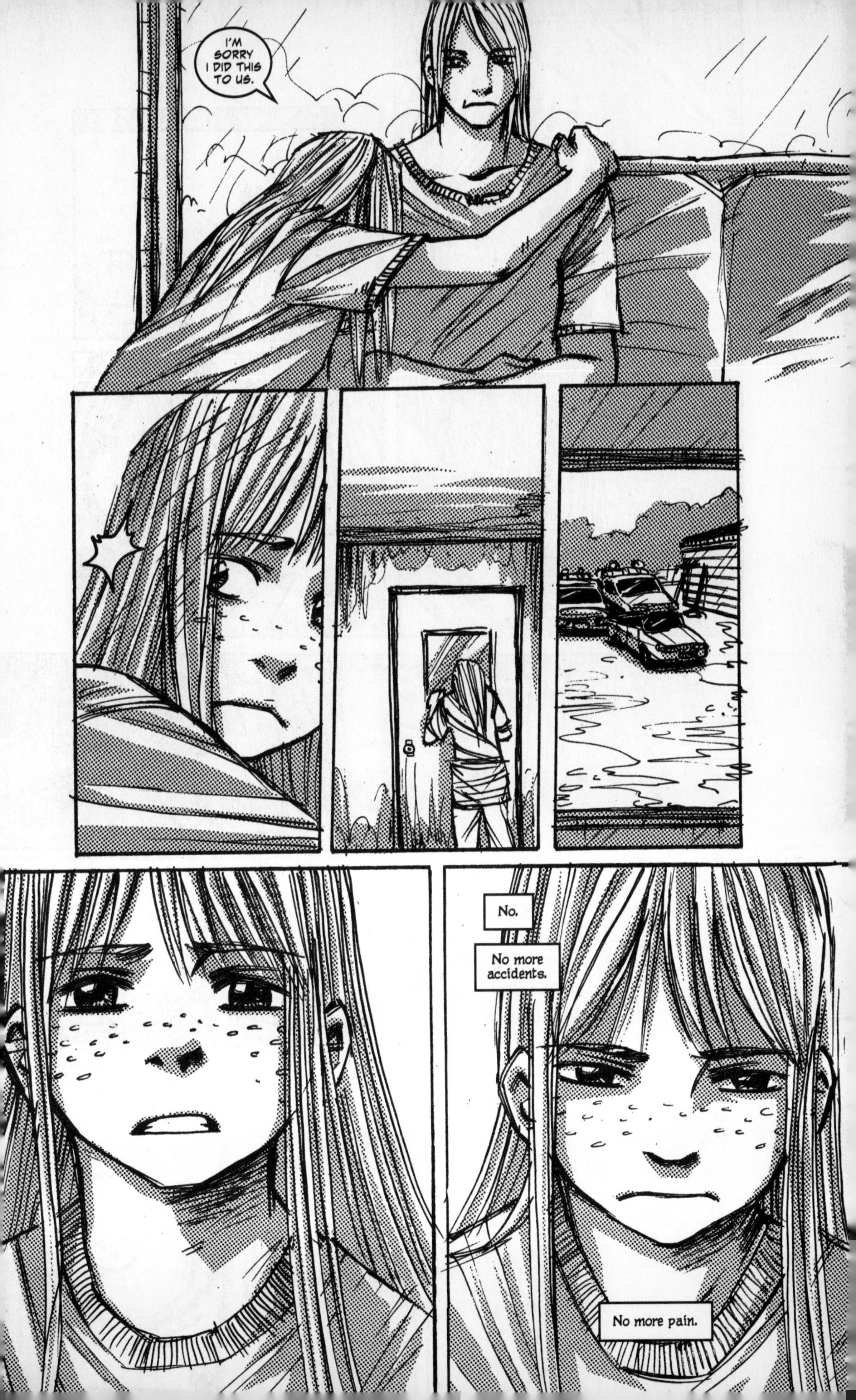
I'M SORRY I DID THIS TO US.
No.
No more accidents.
No more pain.

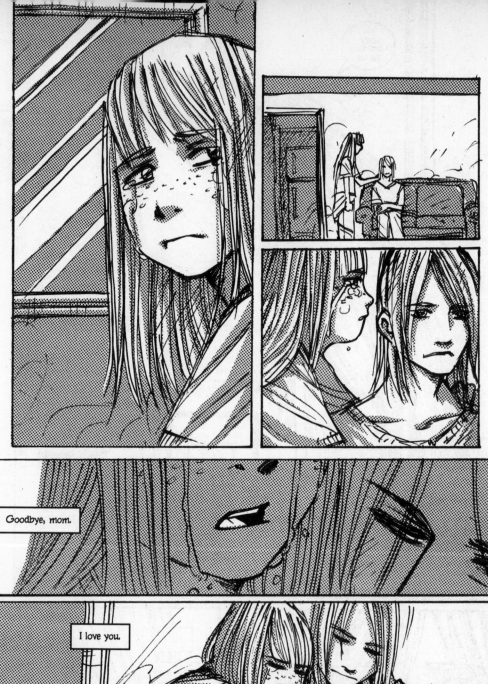

Goodbye, mom.

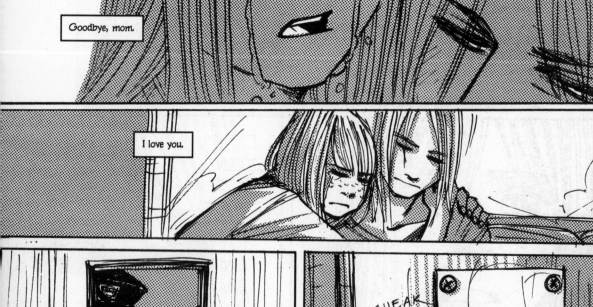

I love you.

knock knock

SQUEAK

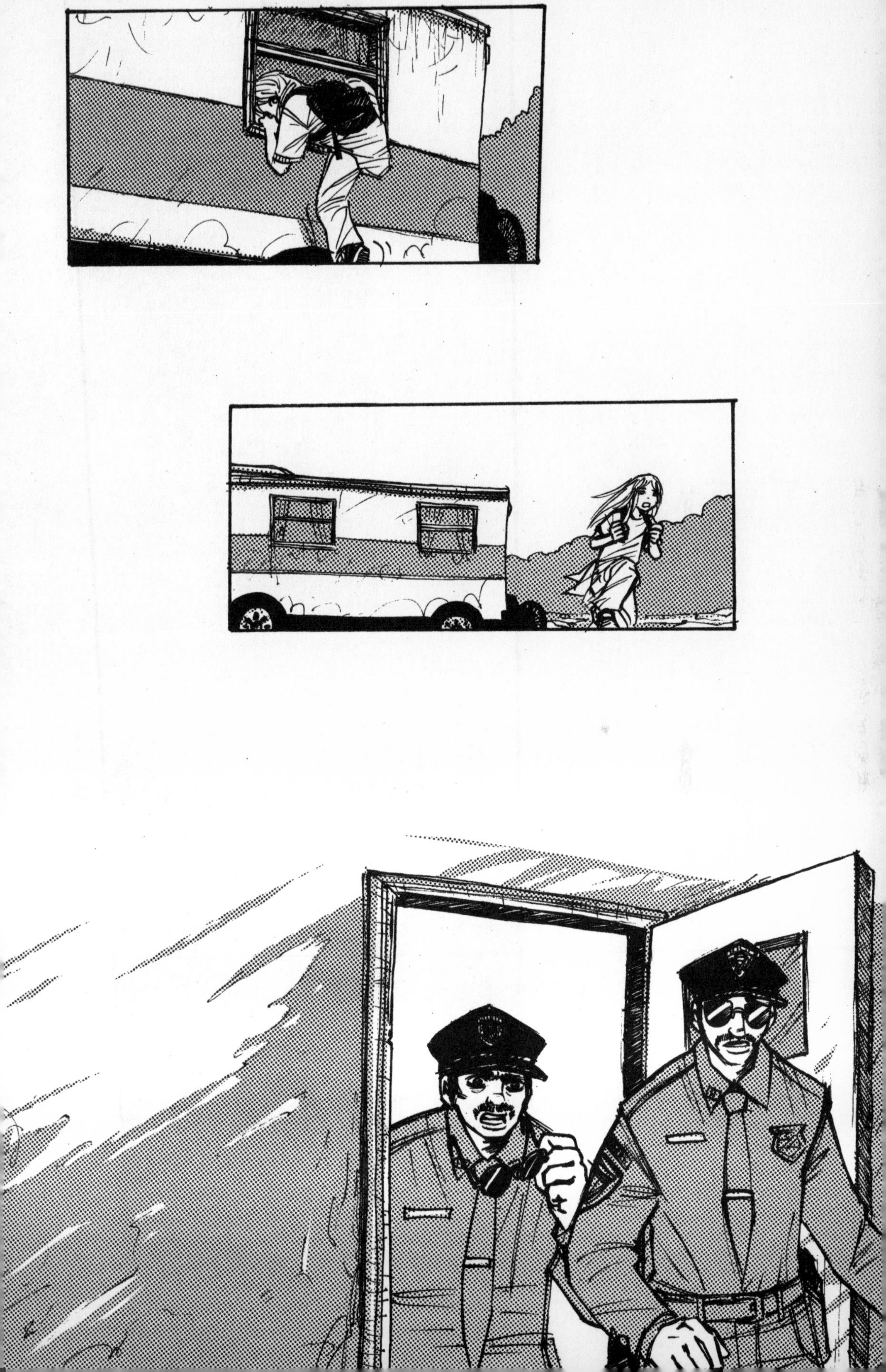

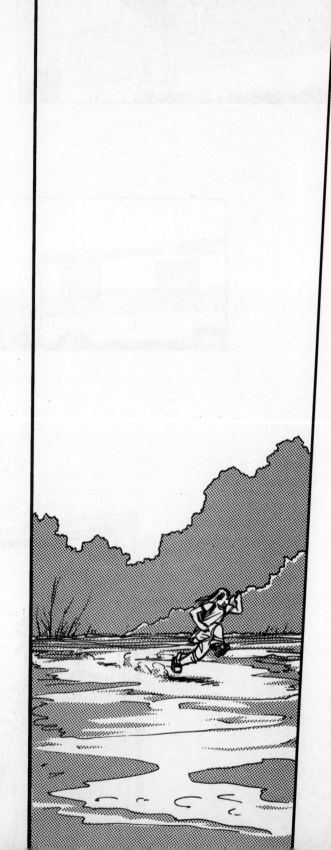

THE END

3

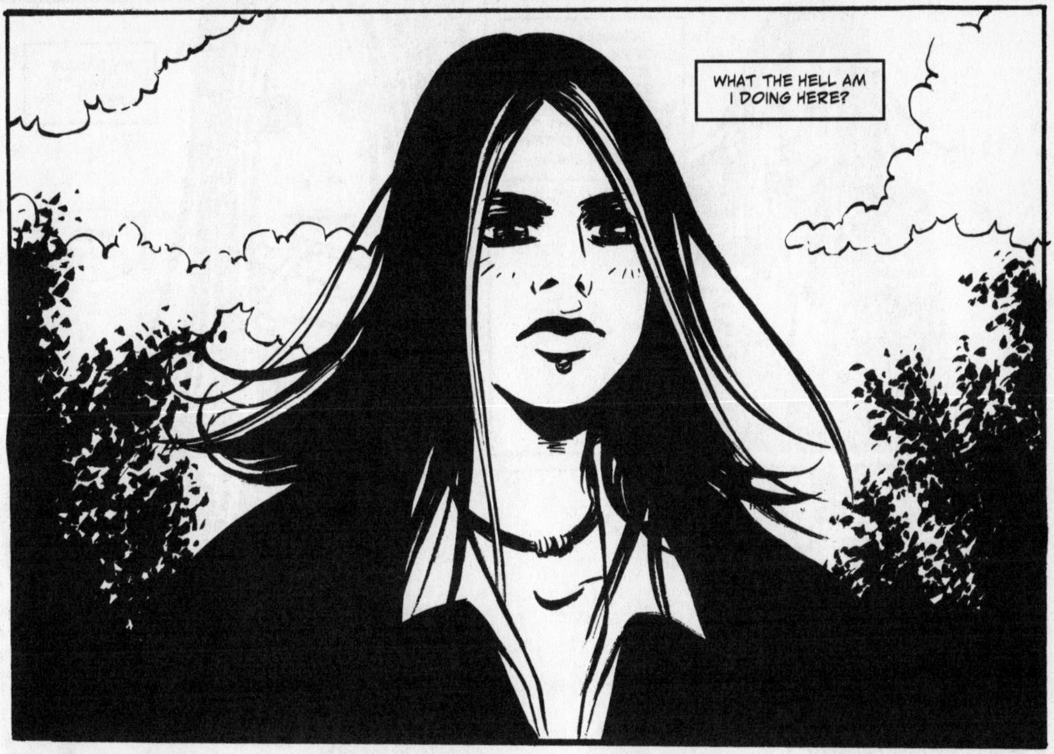
WHAT THE HELL AM I DOING HERE?

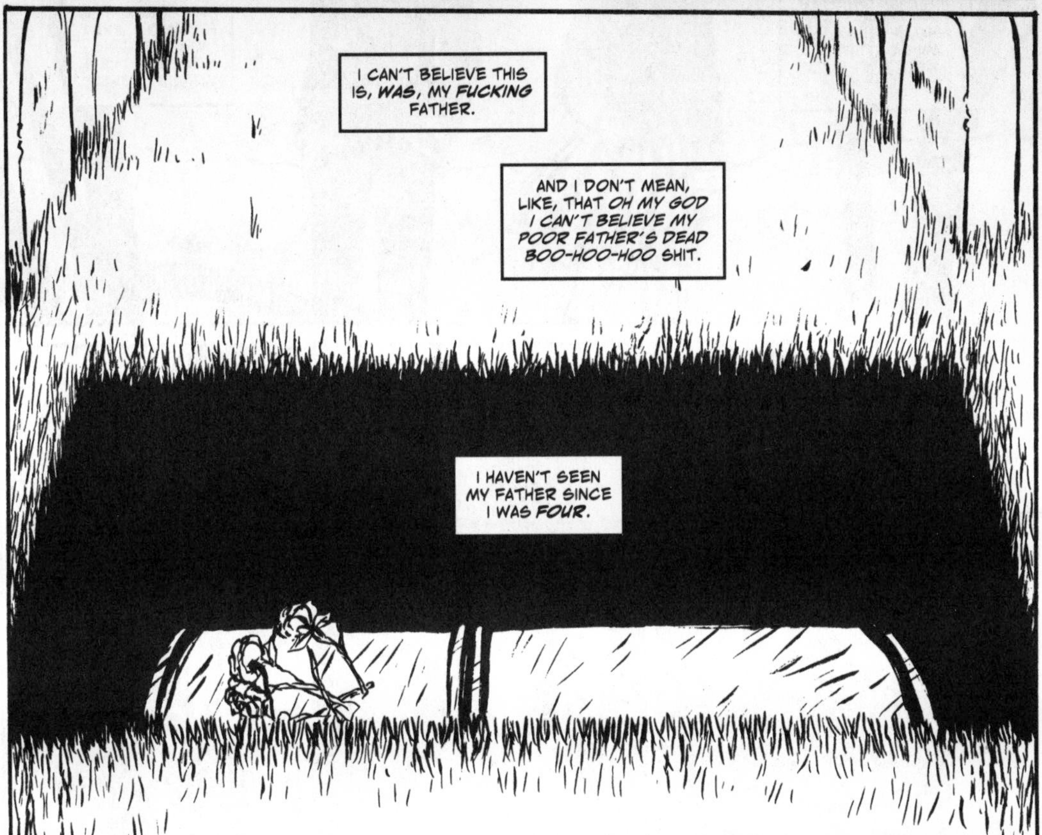
I CAN'T BELIEVE THIS IS, *WAS*, MY *FUCKING* FATHER.
AND I DON'T MEAN, LIKE, THAT *OH MY GOD I CAN'T BELIEVE MY POOR FATHER'S DEAD BOO-HOO-HOO* SHIT.
I HAVEN'T SEEN MY FATHER SINCE I WAS *FOUR*.

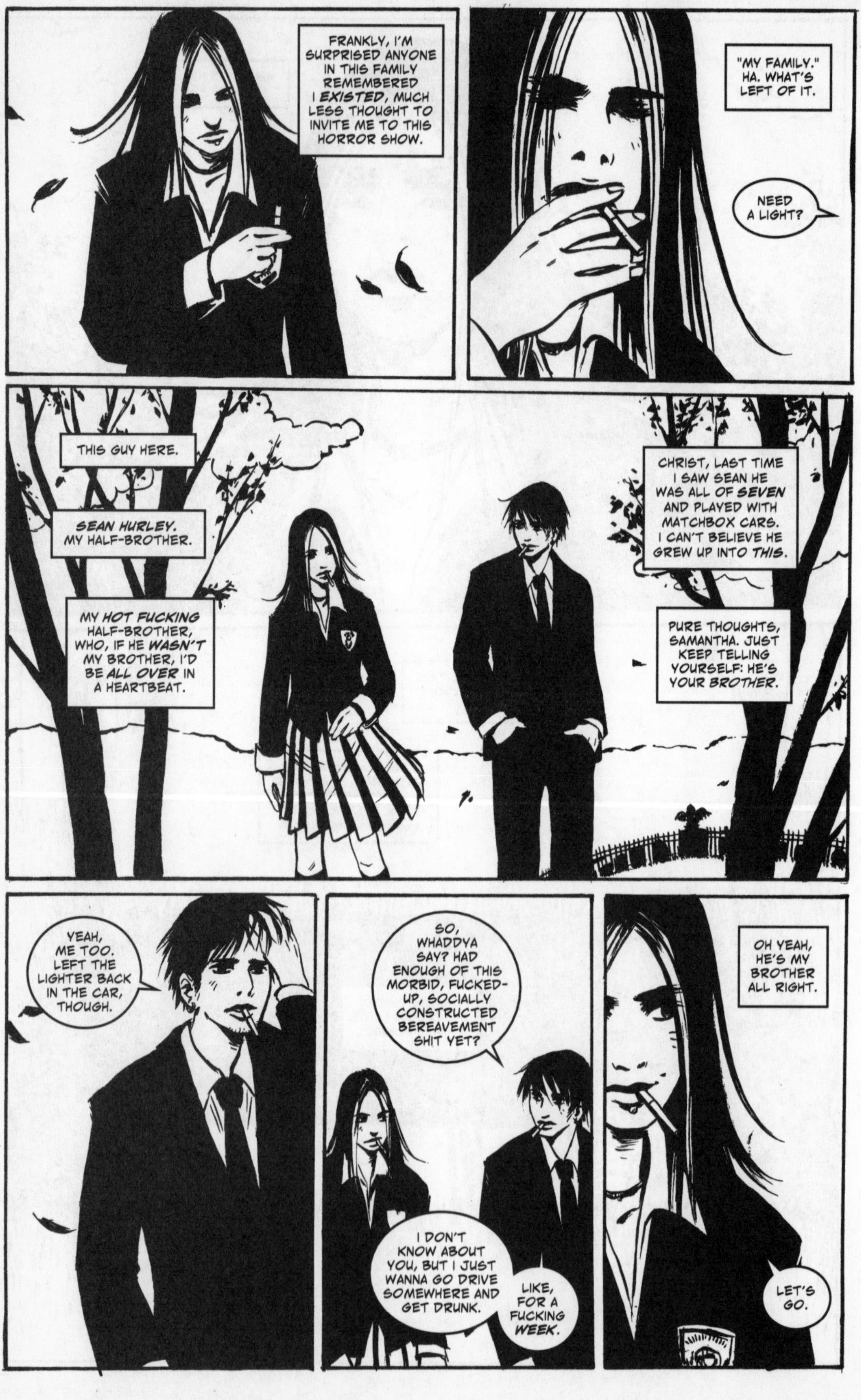
FRANKLY, I'M SURPRISED ANYONE IN THIS FAMILY REMEMBERED I EXISTED, MUCH LESS THOUGHT TO INVITE ME TO THIS HORROR SHOW.
"MY FAMILY." HA. WHAT'S LEFT OF IT.
NEED A LIGHT?
THIS GUY HERE.
SEAN HURLEY. MY HALF-BROTHER.
MY HOT FUCKING HALF-BROTHER, WHO, IF HE WASN'T MY BROTHER, I'D BE ALL OVER IN A HEARTBEAT.
CHRIST, LAST TIME I SAW SEAN HE WAS ALL OF SEVEN AND PLAYED WITH MATCHBOX CARS. I CAN'T BELIEVE HE GREW UP INTO THIS.
PURE THOUGHTS, SAMANTHA. JUST KEEP TELLING YOURSELF: HE'S YOUR BROTHER.
YEAH, ME TOO. LEFT THE LIGHTER BACK IN THE CAR, THOUGH.
SO, WHADDYA SAY? HAD ENOUGH OF THIS MORBID, FUCKED-UP, SOCIALLY CONSTRUCTED BEREAVEMENT SHIT YET?
I DON'T KNOW ABOUT YOU, BUT I JUST WANNA GO DRIVE SOMEWHERE AND GET DRUNK.
LIKE, FOR A FUCKING WEEK.
OH YEAH, HE'S MY BROTHER ALL RIGHT.
LET'S GO.

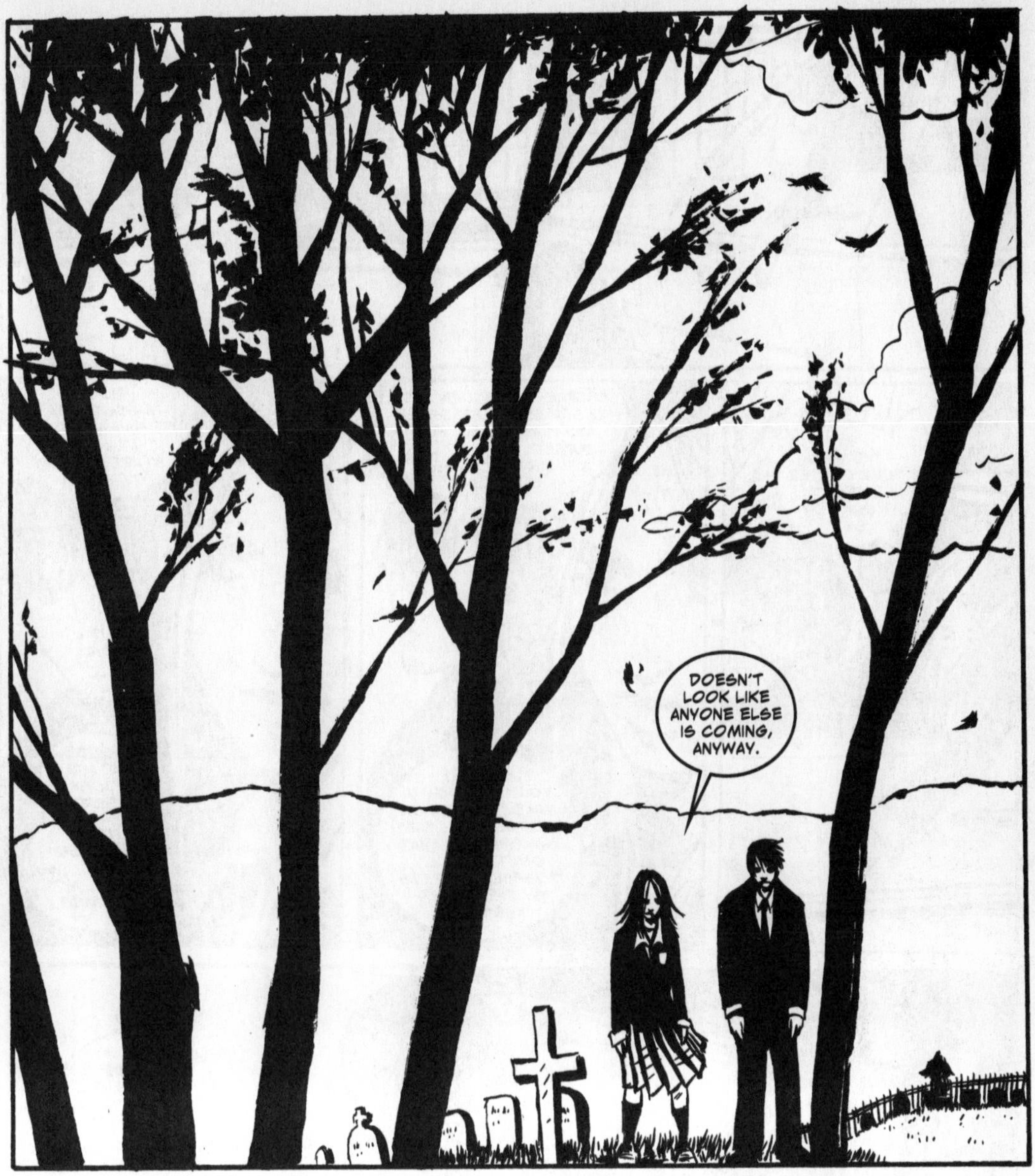
DOESN'T LOOK LIKE ANYONE ELSE IS COMING, ANYWAY.

"BAD BLOOD"

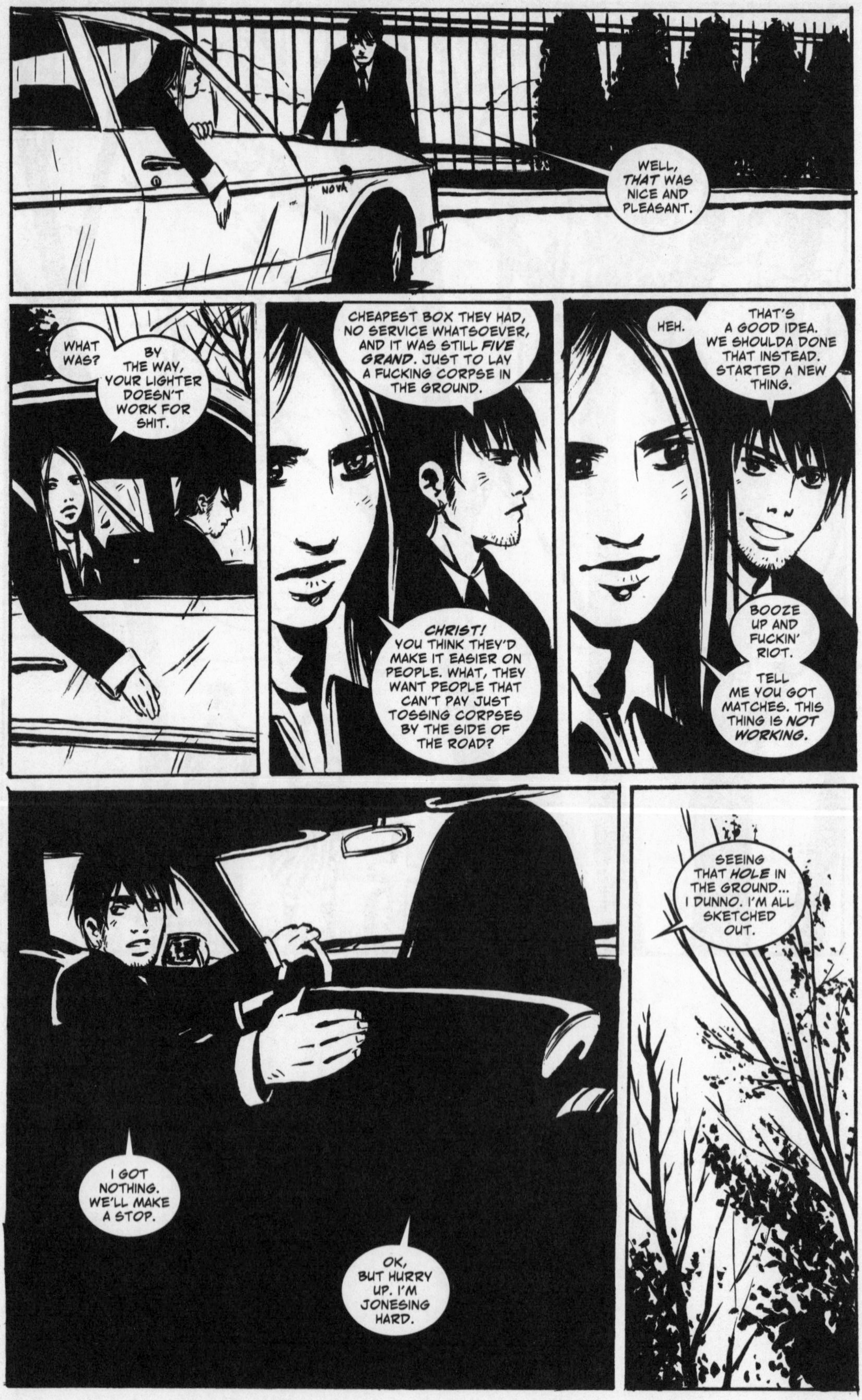

NOVA
WELL, THAT WAS NICE AND PLEASANT.
WHAT WAS?
BY THE WAY, YOUR LIGHTER DOESN'T WORK FOR SHIT.
CHEAPEST BOX THEY HAD, NO SERVICE WHATSOEVER, AND IT WAS STILL FIVE GRAND. JUST TO LAY A FUCKING CORPSE IN THE GROUND.
CHRIST! YOU THINK THEY'D MAKE IT EASIER ON PEOPLE. WHAT, THEY WANT PEOPLE THAT CAN'T PAY JUST TOSSING CORPSES BY THE SIDE OF THE ROAD?
HEH.
THAT'S A GOOD IDEA. WE SHOULDA DONE THAT INSTEAD. STARTED A NEW THING.
BOOZE UP AND FUCKIN' RIOT.
TELL ME YOU GOT MATCHES. THIS THING IS NOT WORKING.
I GOT NOTHING. WE'LL MAKE A STOP.
OK, BUT HURRY UP. I'M JONESING HARD.
SEEING THAT HOLE IN THE GROUND... I DUNNO. I'M ALL SKETCHED OUT.

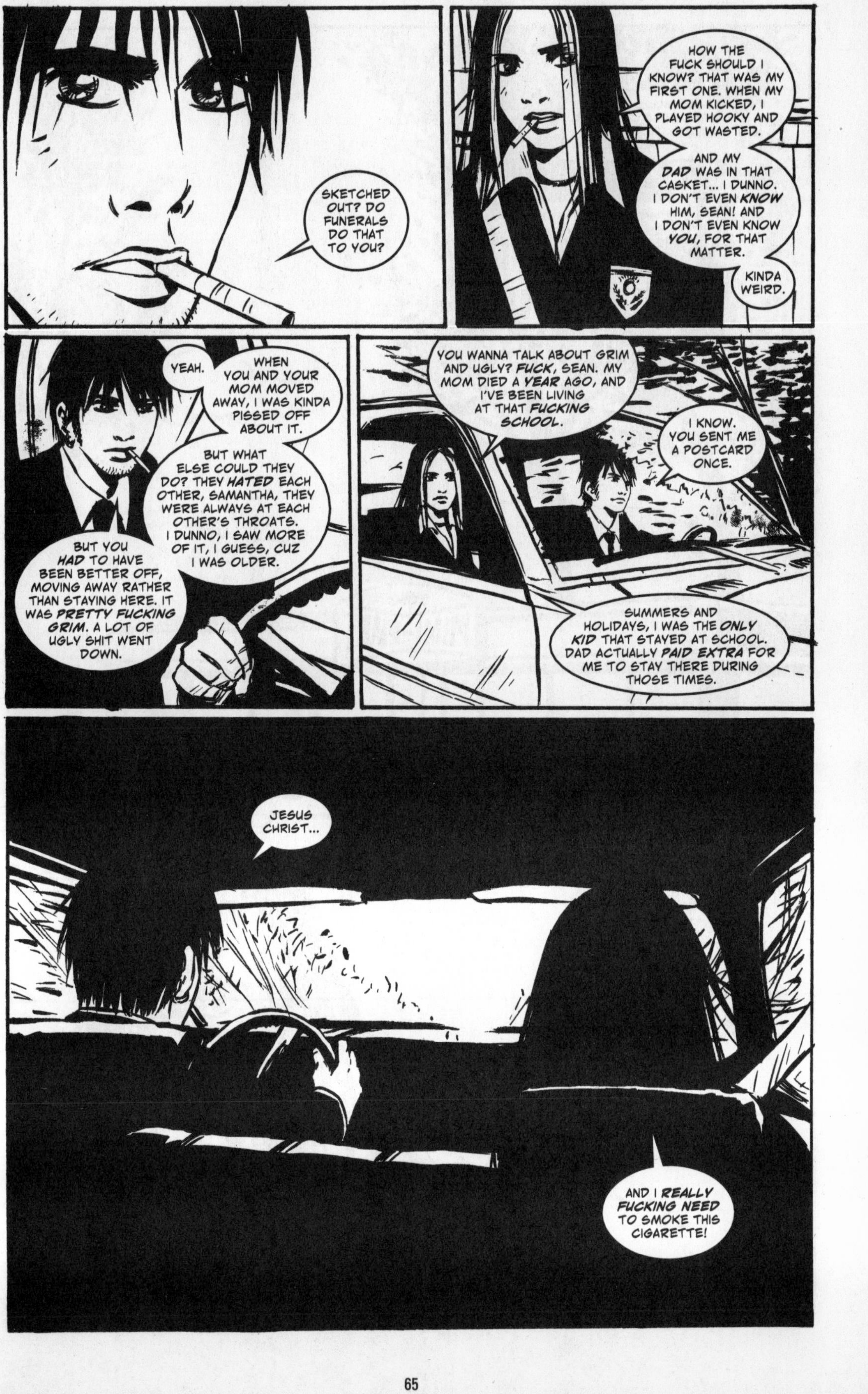
SKETCHED OUT? DO FUNERALS DO THAT TO YOU?
HOW THE FUCK SHOULD I KNOW? THAT WAS MY FIRST ONE. WHEN MY MOM KICKED, I PLAYED HOOKY AND GOT WASTED.
AND MY DAD WAS IN THAT CASKET... I DUNNO. I DON'T EVEN KNOW HIM, SEAN! AND I DON'T EVEN KNOW YOU, FOR THAT MATTER.
KINDA WEIRD.
YEAH.
WHEN YOU AND YOUR MOM MOVED AWAY, I WAS KINDA PISSED OFF ABOUT IT.
BUT WHAT ELSE COULD THEY DO? THEY HATED EACH OTHER, SAMANTHA, THEY WERE ALWAYS AT EACH OTHER'S THROATS. I DUNNO, I SAW MORE OF IT, I GUESS, CUZ I WAS OLDER.
BUT YOU HAD TO HAVE BEEN BETTER OFF, MOVING AWAY RATHER THAN STAYING HERE. IT WAS PRETTY FUCKING GRIM. A LOT OF UGLY SHIT WENT DOWN.
YOU WANNA TALK ABOUT GRIM AND UGLY? FUCK, SEAN. MY MOM DIED A YEAR AGO, AND I'VE BEEN LIVING AT THAT FUCKING SCHOOL.
I KNOW. YOU SENT ME A POSTCARD ONCE.
SUMMERS AND HOLIDAYS, I WAS THE ONLY KID THAT STAYED AT SCHOOL. DAD ACTUALLY PAID EXTRA FOR ME TO STAY THERE DURING THOSE TIMES.
JESUS CHRIST...
AND I REALLY FUCKING NEED TO SMOKE THIS CIGARETTE!

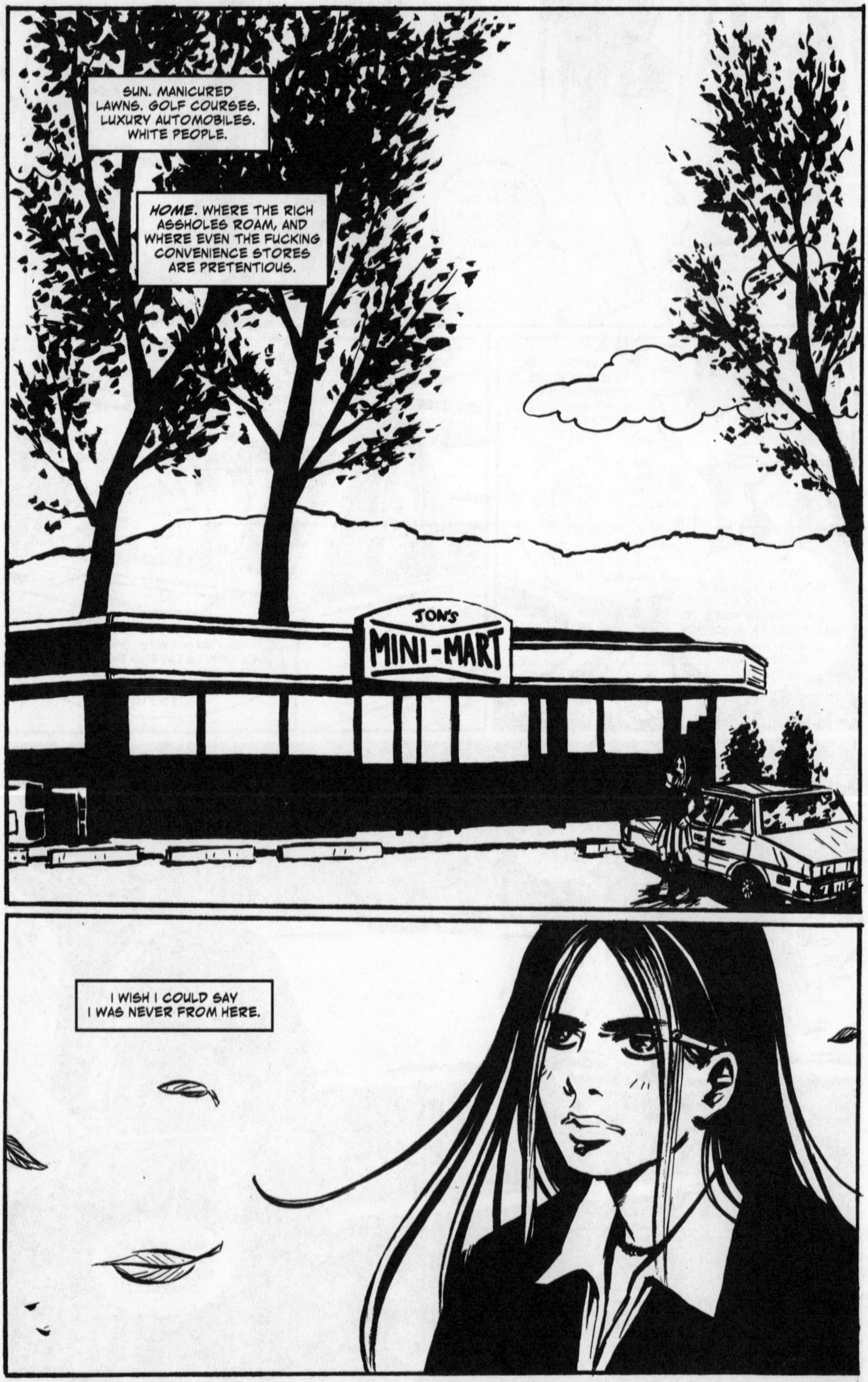
SUN. MANICURED LAWNS. GOLF COURSES. LUXURY AUTOMOBILES. WHITE PEOPLE.
HOME. WHERE THE RICH ASSHOLES ROAM, AND WHERE EVEN THE FUCKING CONVENIENCE STORES ARE PRETENTIOUS.
JON'S MINI-MART
I WISH I COULD SAY I WAS NEVER FROM HERE.

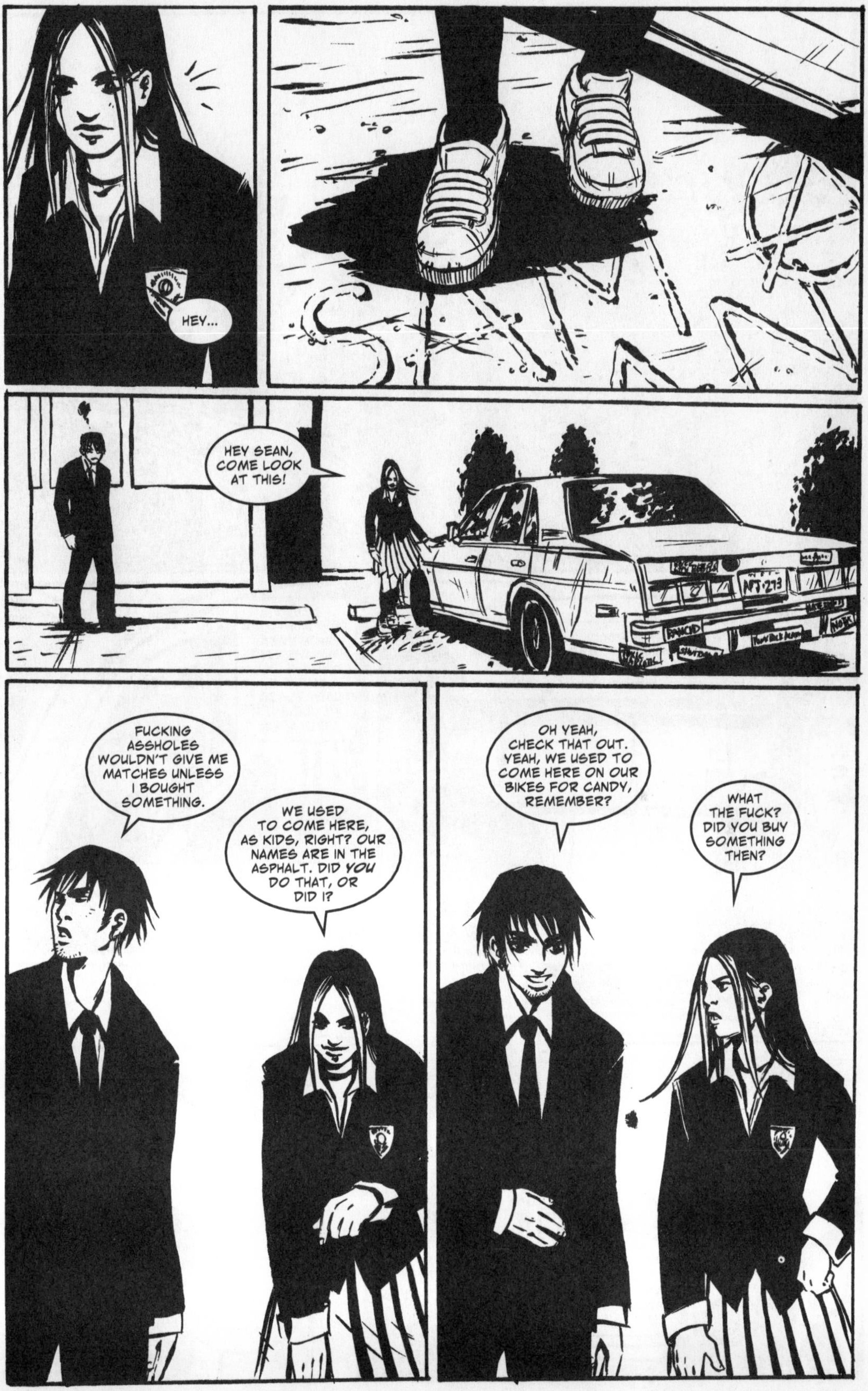
HEY...
HEY SEAN, COME LOOK AT THIS!
FUCKING ASSHOLES WOULDN'T GIVE ME MATCHES UNLESS I BOUGHT SOMETHING.
WE USED TO COME HERE, AS KIDS, RIGHT? OUR NAMES ARE IN THE ASPHALT. DID *YOU* DO THAT, OR DID I?
OH YEAH, CHECK THAT OUT. YEAH, WE USED TO COME HERE ON OUR BIKES FOR CANDY, REMEMBER?
WHAT THE FUCK? DID YOU BUY SOMETHING THEN?

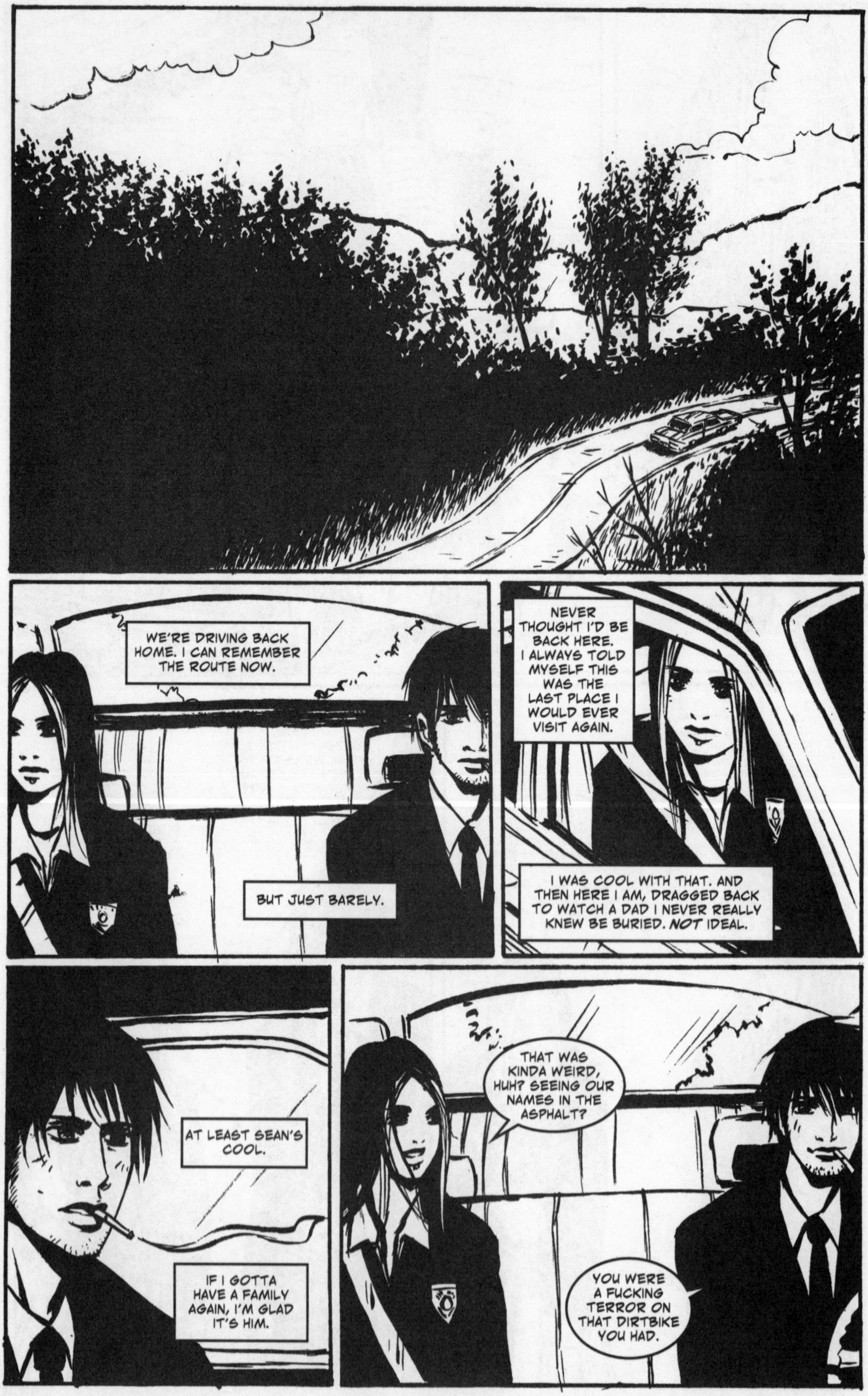
WE'RE DRIVING BACK HOME. I CAN REMEMBER THE ROUTE NOW.
BUT JUST BARELY.
NEVER THOUGHT I'D BE BACK HERE. I ALWAYS TOLD MYSELF THIS WAS THE LAST PLACE I WOULD EVER VISIT AGAIN.
I WAS COOL WITH THAT. AND THEN HERE I AM, DRAGGED BACK TO WATCH A DAD I NEVER REALLY KNEW BE BURIED. NOT IDEAL.
AT LEAST SEAN'S COOL.
IF I GOTTA HAVE A FAMILY AGAIN, I'M GLAD IT'S HIM.
THAT WAS KINDA WEIRD, HUH? SEEING OUR NAMES IN THE ASPHALT?
YOU WERE A FUCKING TERROR ON THAT DIRTBIKE YOU HAD.

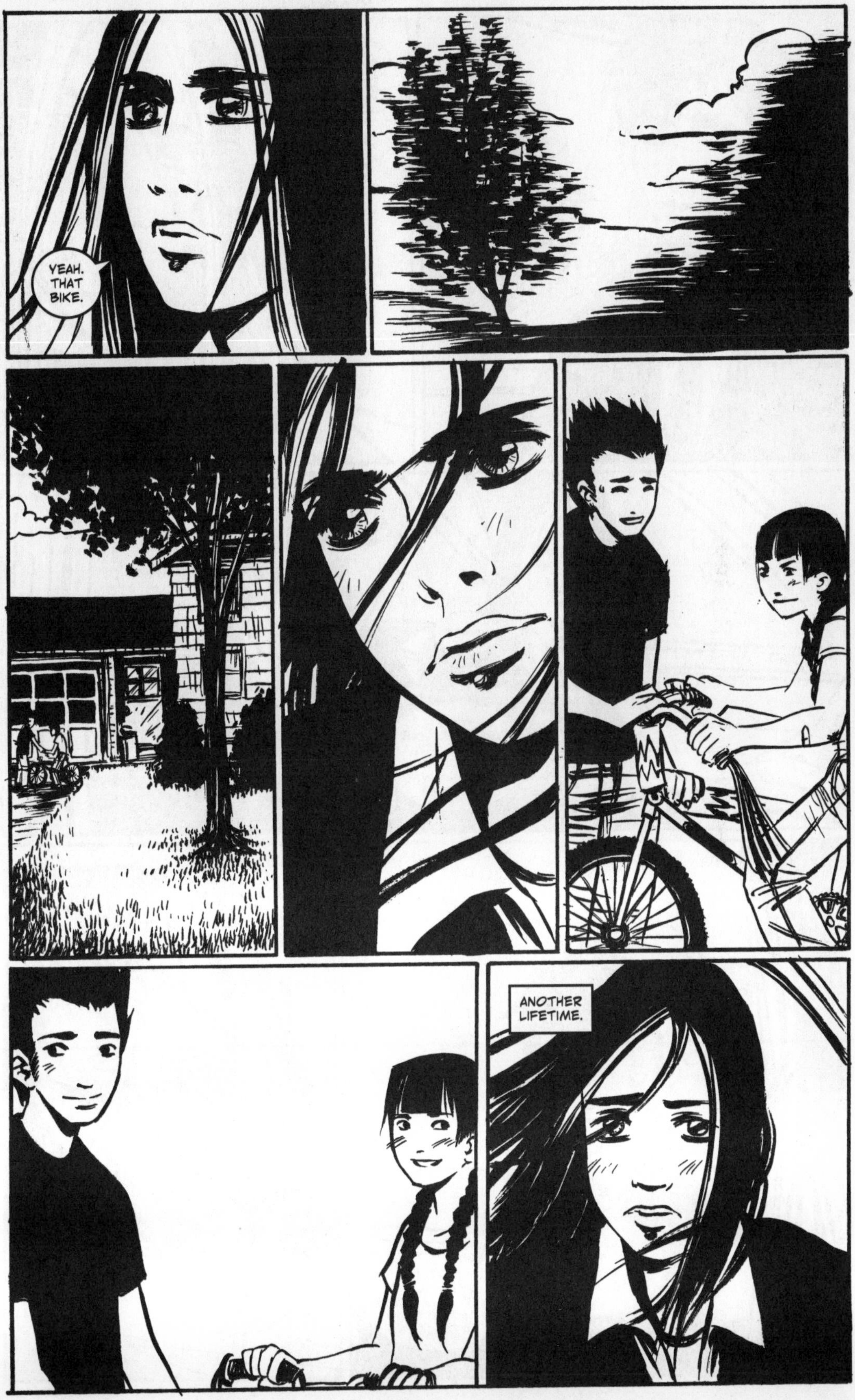
YEAH. THAT BIKE.
ANOTHER LIFETIME.

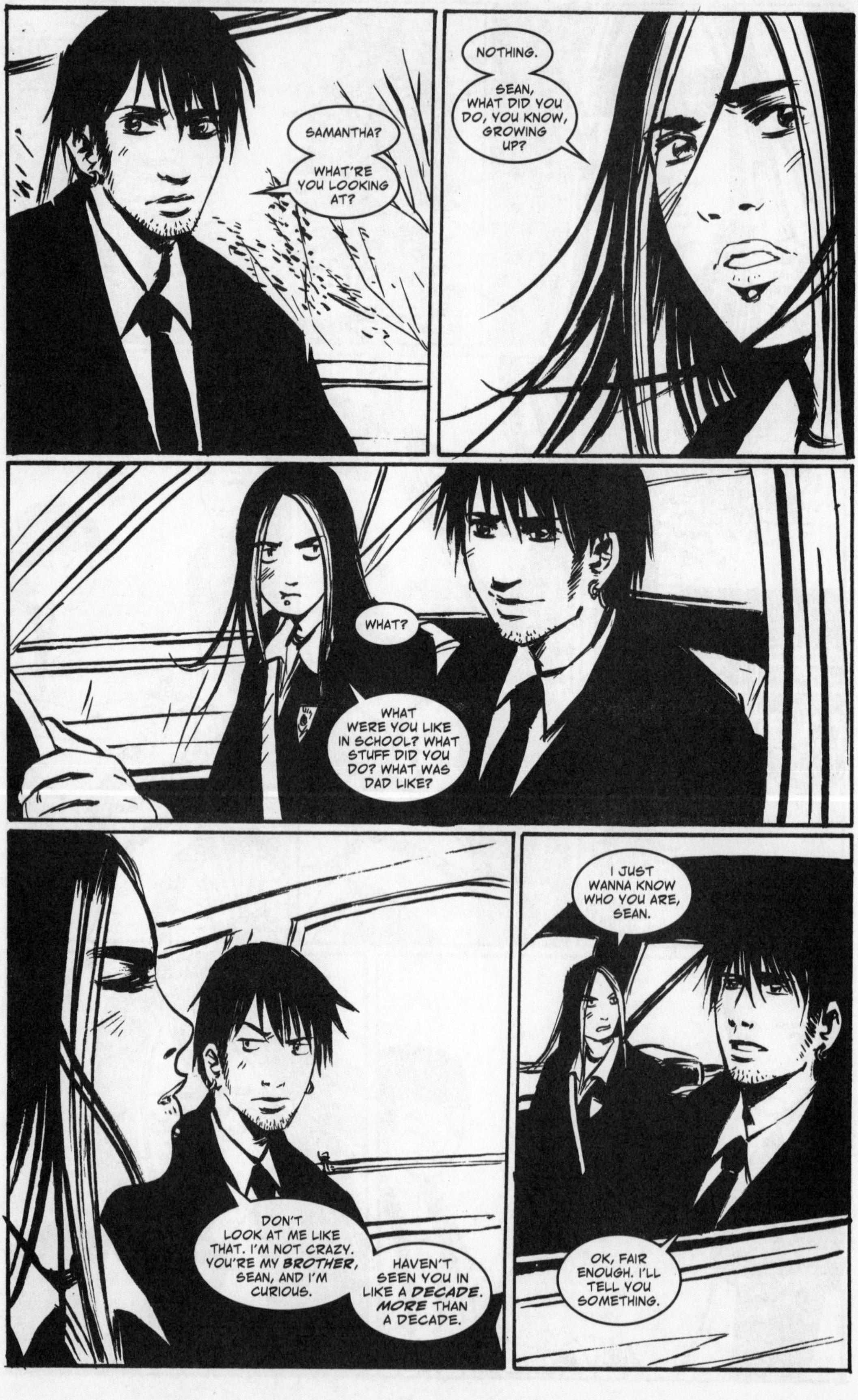
SAMANTHA?
WHAT'RE YOU LOOKING AT?
NOTHING.
SEAN, WHAT DID YOU DO, YOU KNOW, GROWING UP?
WHAT?
WHAT WERE YOU LIKE IN SCHOOL? WHAT STUFF DID YOU DO? WHAT WAS DAD LIKE?
DON'T LOOK AT ME LIKE THAT. I'M NOT CRAZY. YOU'RE MY BROTHER, SEAN, AND I'M CURIOUS.
HAVEN'T SEEN YOU IN LIKE A DECADE. MORE THAN A DECADE.
I JUST WANNA KNOW WHO YOU ARE, SEAN.
OK, FAIR ENOUGH. I'LL TELL YOU SOMETHING.

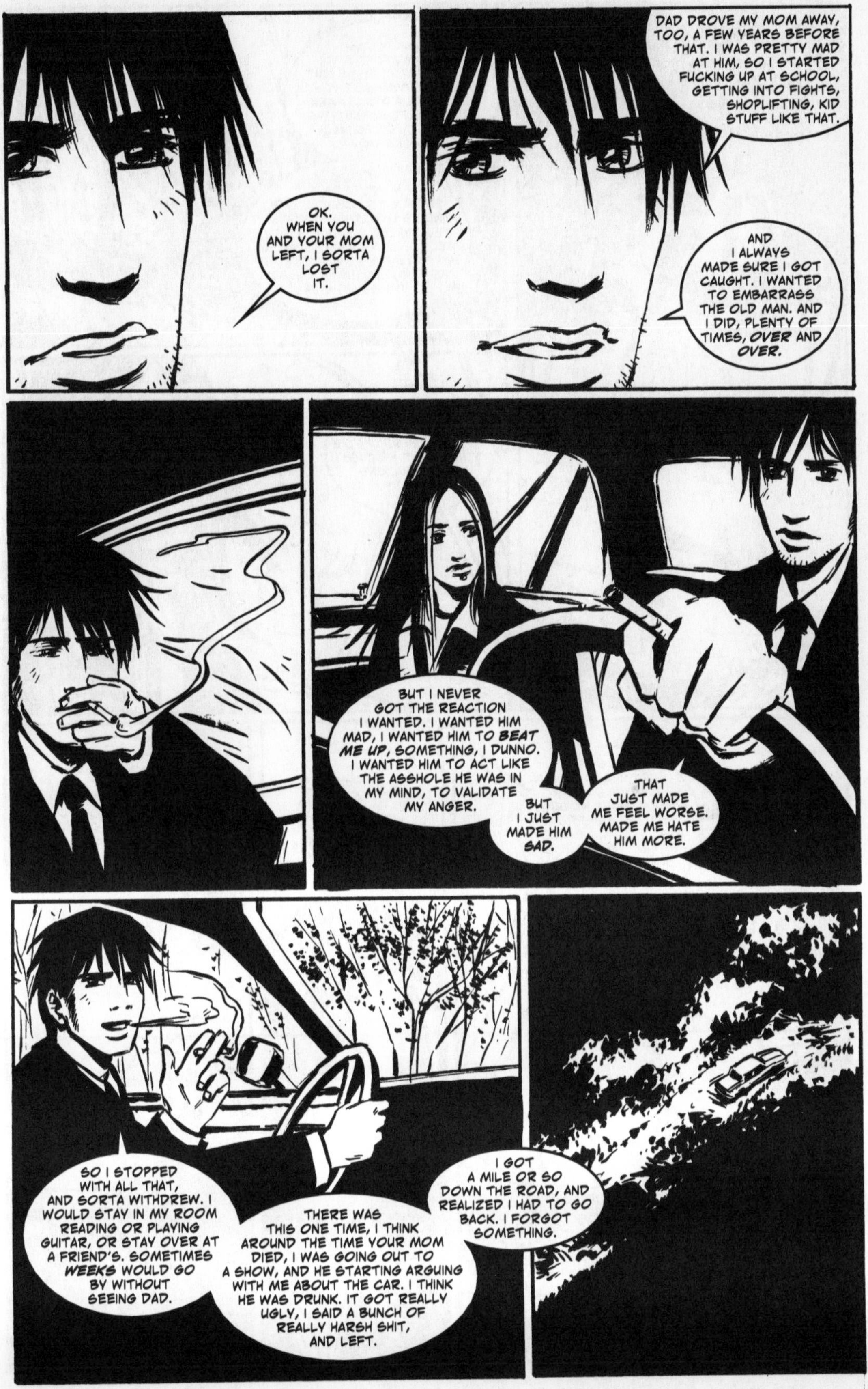
OK. WHEN YOU AND YOUR MOM LEFT, I SORTA LOST IT.
DAD DROVE MY MOM AWAY, TOO, A FEW YEARS BEFORE THAT. I WAS PRETTY MAD AT HIM, SO I STARTED FUCKING UP AT SCHOOL, GETTING INTO FIGHTS, SHOPLIFTING, KID STUFF LIKE THAT.
AND I ALWAYS MADE SURE I GOT CAUGHT. I WANTED TO EMBARRASS THE OLD MAN. AND I DID, PLENTY OF TIMES, OVER AND OVER.
BUT I NEVER GOT THE REACTION I WANTED. I WANTED HIM MAD, I WANTED HIM TO BEAT ME UP, SOMETHING, I DUNNO. I WANTED HIM TO ACT LIKE THE ASSHOLE HE WAS IN MY MIND, TO VALIDATE MY ANGER.
BUT I JUST MADE HIM SAD.
THAT JUST MADE ME FEEL WORSE. MADE ME HATE HIM MORE.
SO I STOPPED WITH ALL THAT, AND SORTA WITHDREW. I WOULD STAY IN MY ROOM READING OR PLAYING GUITAR, OR STAY OVER AT A FRIEND'S. SOMETIMES WEEKS WOULD GO BY WITHOUT SEEING DAD.
THERE WAS THIS ONE TIME, I THINK AROUND THE TIME YOUR MOM DIED, I WAS GOING OUT TO A SHOW, AND HE STARTING ARGUING WITH ME ABOUT THE CAR. I THINK HE WAS DRUNK. IT GOT REALLY UGLY, I SAID A BUNCH OF REALLY HARSH SHIT, AND LEFT.
I GOT A MILE OR SO DOWN THE ROAD, AND REALIZED I HAD TO GO BACK. I FORGOT SOMETHING.

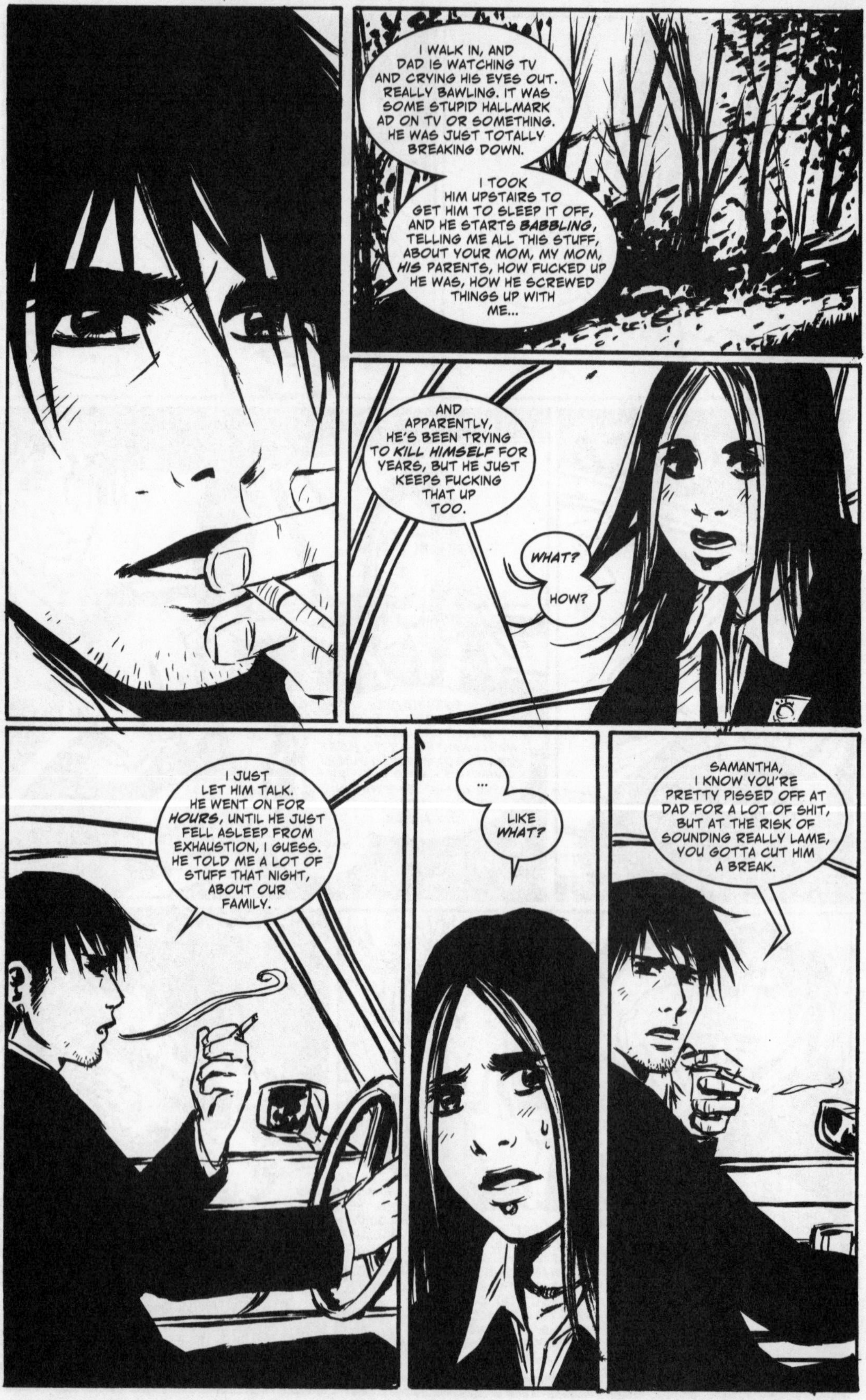
I WALK IN, AND DAD IS WATCHING TV AND CRYING HIS EYES OUT. REALLY BAWLING. IT WAS SOME STUPID HALLMARK AD ON TV OR SOMETHING. HE WAS JUST TOTALLY BREAKING DOWN.
I TOOK HIM UPSTAIRS TO GET HIM TO SLEEP IT OFF, AND HE STARTS *BABBLING*, TELLING ME ALL THIS STUFF, ABOUT YOUR MOM, MY MOM, *HIS* PARENTS, HOW FUCKED UP HE WAS, HOW HE SCREWED THINGS UP WITH ME...
AND APPARENTLY, HE'S BEEN TRYING TO *KILL HIMSELF* FOR YEARS, BUT HE JUST KEEPS FUCKING THAT UP TOO.
WHAT?
HOW?
I JUST LET HIM TALK. HE WENT ON FOR *HOURS*, UNTIL HE JUST FELL ASLEEP FROM EXHAUSTION, I GUESS. HE TOLD ME A LOT OF STUFF THAT NIGHT, ABOUT OUR FAMILY.
...
LIKE *WHAT?*
SAMANTHA, I KNOW YOU'RE PRETTY PISSED OFF AT DAD FOR A LOT OF SHIT, BUT AT THE RISK OF SOUNDING REALLY LAME, YOU GOTTA CUT HIM A BREAK.

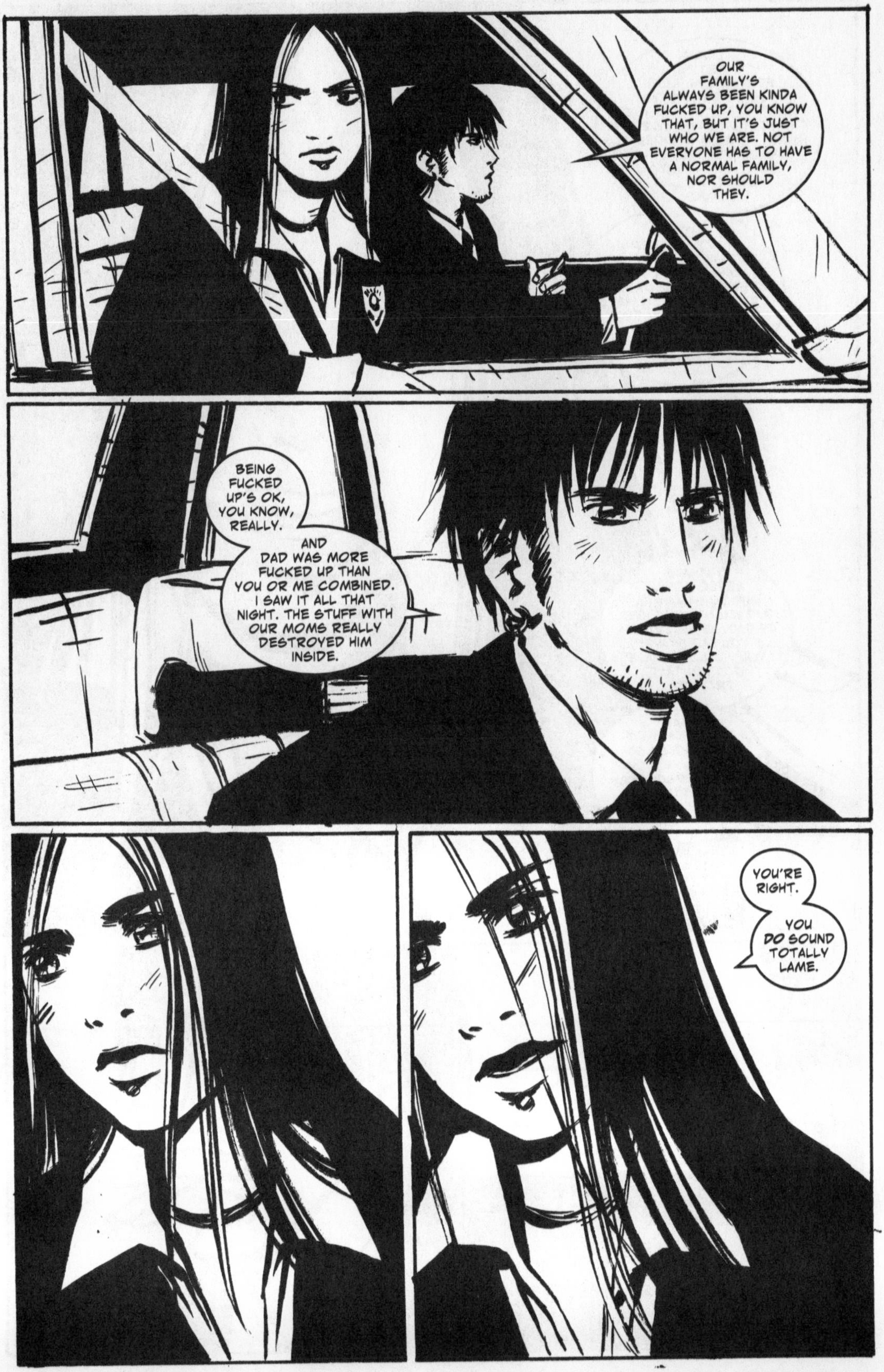
OUR FAMILY'S ALWAYS BEEN KINDA FUCKED UP, YOU KNOW THAT, BUT IT'S JUST WHO WE ARE. NOT EVERYONE HAS TO HAVE A NORMAL FAMILY, NOR SHOULD THEY.
BEING FUCKED UP'S OK, YOU KNOW, REALLY.
AND DAD WAS MORE FUCKED UP THAN YOU OR ME COMBINED. I SAW IT ALL THAT NIGHT. THE STUFF WITH OUR MOMS REALLY DESTROYED HIM INSIDE.
YOU'RE RIGHT.
YOU DO SOUND TOTALLY LAME.

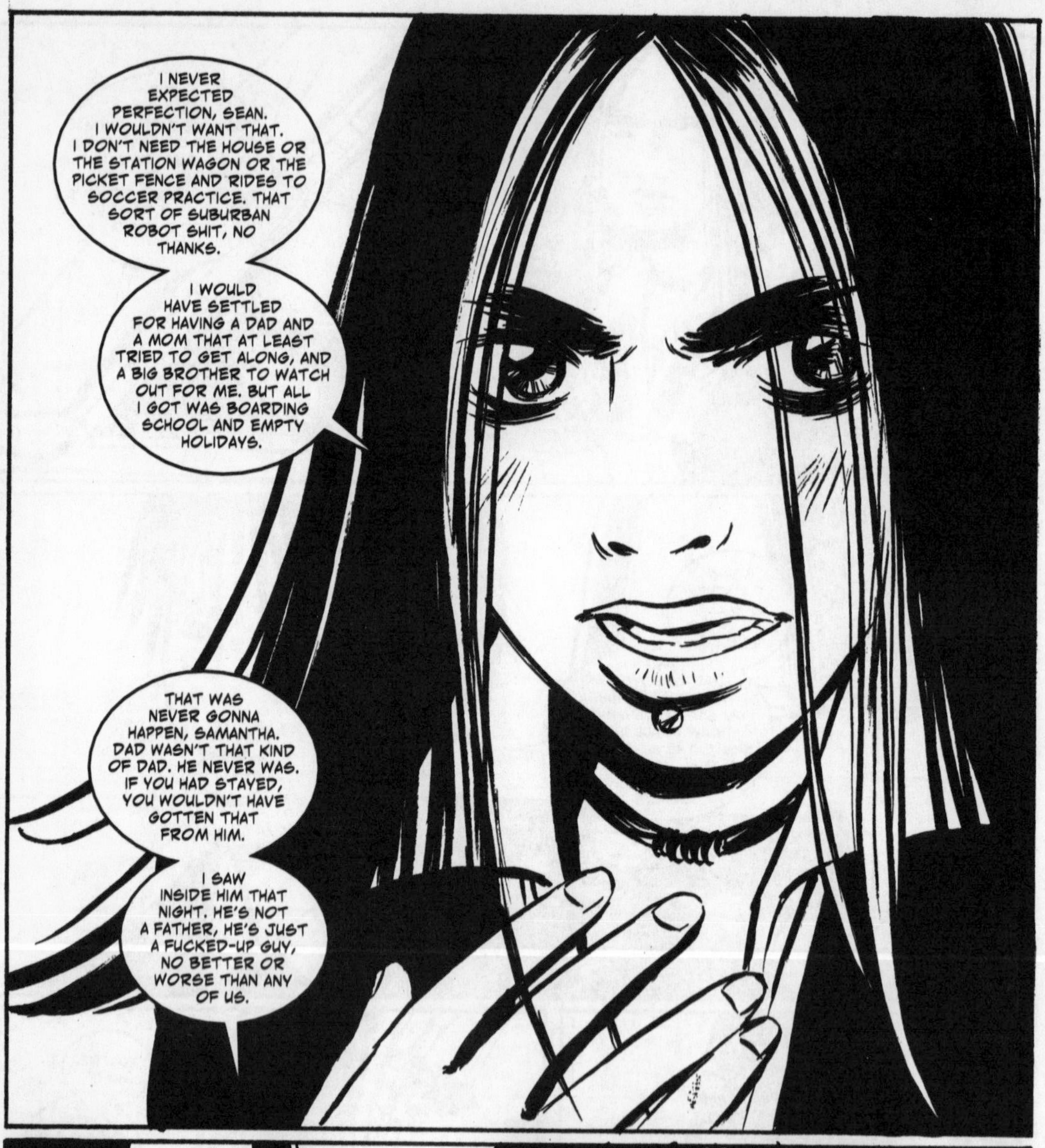
I NEVER EXPECTED PERFECTION, SEAN. I WOULDN'T WANT THAT. I DON'T NEED THE HOUSE OR THE STATION WAGON OR THE PICKET FENCE AND RIDES TO SOCCER PRACTICE. THAT SORT OF SUBURBAN ROBOT SHIT, NO THANKS.
I WOULD HAVE SETTLED FOR HAVING A DAD AND A MOM THAT AT LEAST TRIED TO GET ALONG, AND A BIG BROTHER TO WATCH OUT FOR ME. BUT ALL I GOT WAS BOARDING SCHOOL AND EMPTY HOLIDAYS.
THAT WAS NEVER GONNA HAPPEN, SAMANTHA. DAD WASN'T THAT KIND OF DAD. HE NEVER WAS. IF YOU HAD STAYED, YOU WOULDN'T HAVE GOTTEN THAT FROM HIM.
I SAW INSIDE HIM THAT NIGHT. HE'S NOT A FATHER, HE'S JUST A FUCKED-UP GUY, NO BETTER OR WORSE THAN ANY OF US.

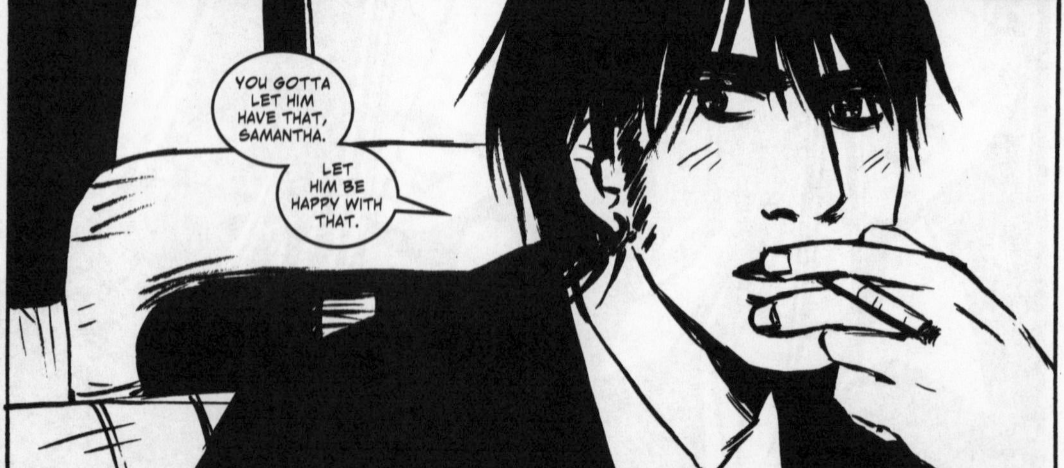
YOU GOTTA LET HIM HAVE THAT, SAMANTHA.
LET HIM BE HAPPY WITH THAT.

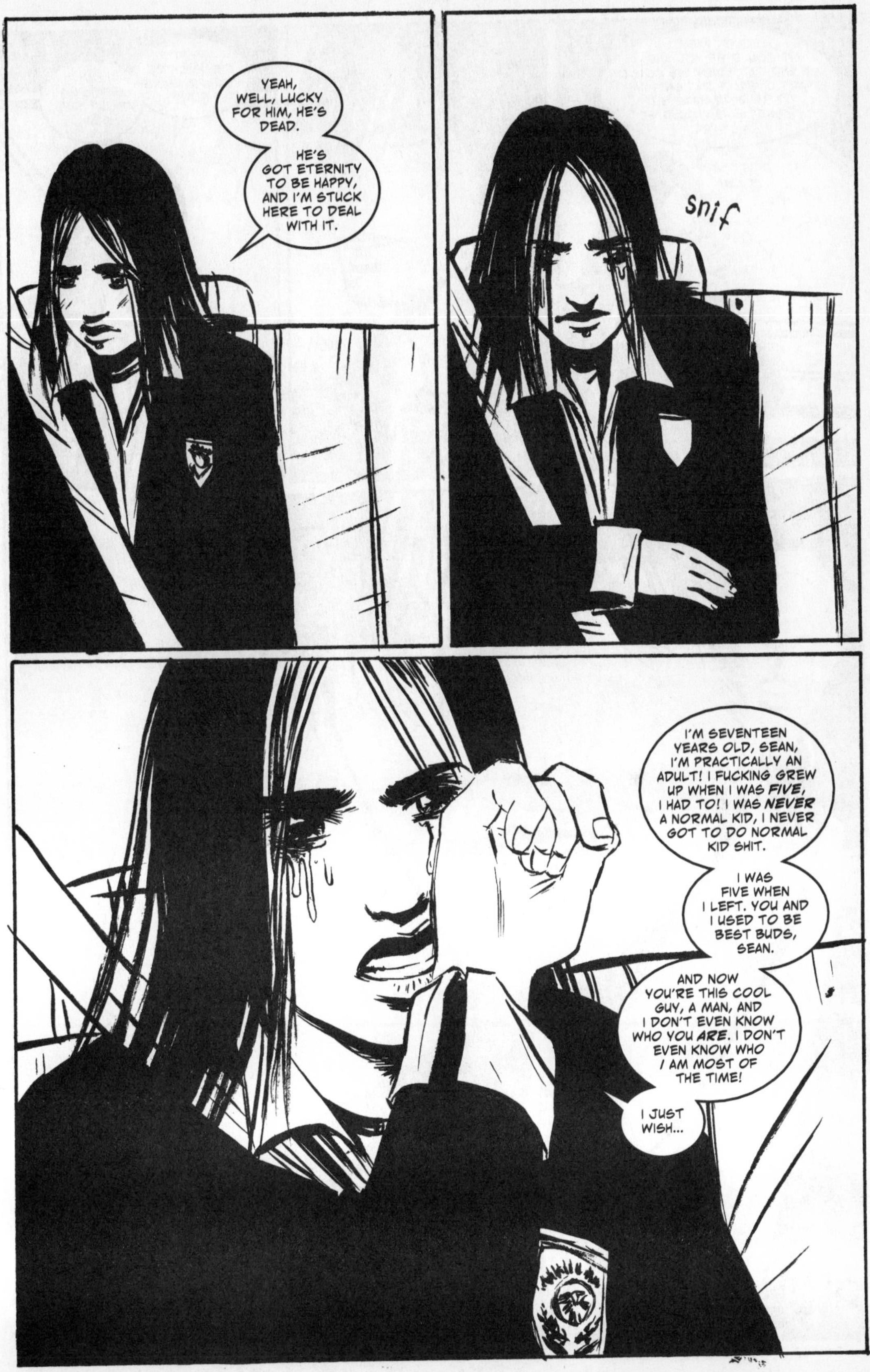
YEAH, WELL, LUCKY FOR HIM, HE'S DEAD.
HE'S GOT ETERNITY TO BE HAPPY, AND I'M STUCK HERE TO DEAL WITH IT.
snif
I'M SEVENTEEN YEARS OLD, SEAN, I'M PRACTICALLY AN ADULT! I FUCKING GREW UP WHEN I WAS *FIVE*, I HAD TO! I WAS *NEVER* A NORMAL KID, I NEVER GOT TO DO NORMAL KID SHIT.
I WAS FIVE WHEN I LEFT. YOU AND I USED TO BE BEST BUDS, SEAN.
AND NOW YOU'RE THIS COOL GUY, A MAN, AND I DON'T EVEN KNOW WHO YOU *ARE*. I DON'T EVEN KNOW WHO *I* AM MOST OF THE TIME!
I JUST WISH...

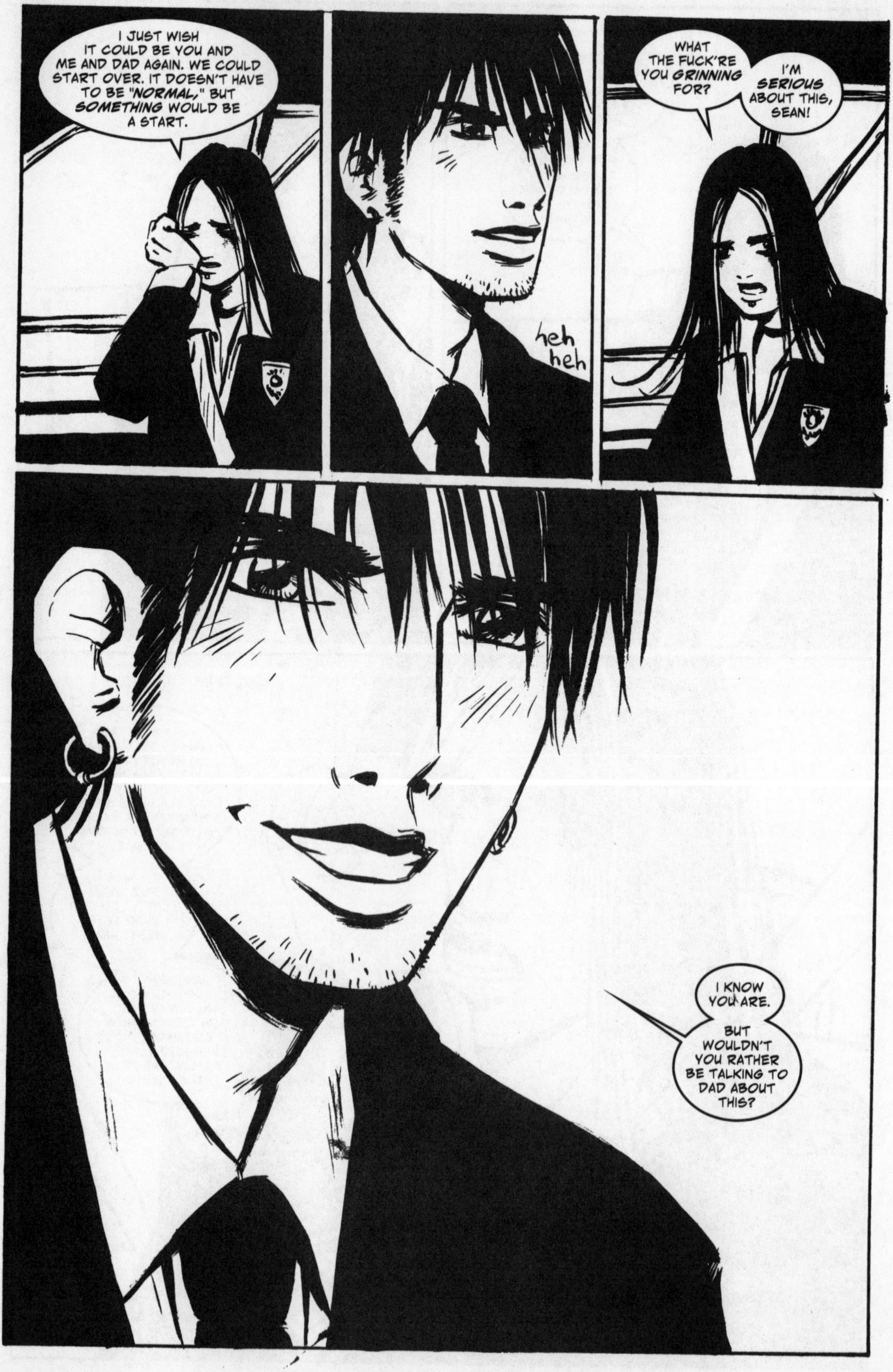
I JUST WISH IT COULD BE YOU AND ME AND DAD AGAIN. WE COULD START OVER. IT DOESN'T HAVE TO BE "NORMAL," BUT SOMETHING WOULD BE A START.
heh heh
WHAT THE FUCK'RE YOU GRINNING FOR?
I'M SERIOUS ABOUT THIS, SEAN!
I KNOW YOU ARE.
BUT WOULDN'T YOU RATHER BE TALKING TO DAD ABOUT THIS?

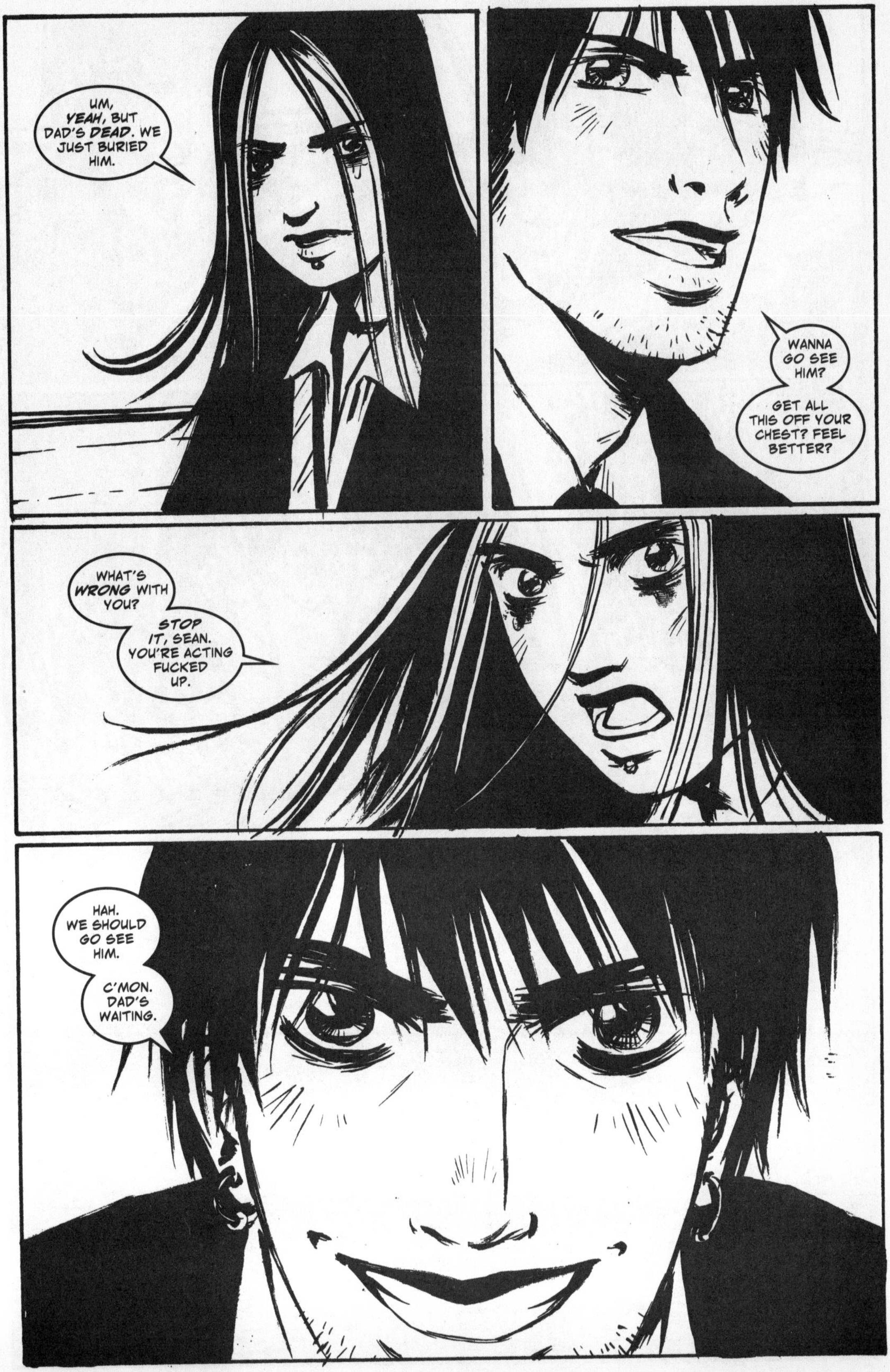
UM, YEAH, BUT DAD'S DEAD. WE JUST BURIED HIM.
WANNA GO SEE HIM?
GET ALL THIS OFF YOUR CHEST? FEEL BETTER?
WHAT'S WRONG WITH YOU?
STOP IT, SEAN. YOU'RE ACTING FUCKED UP.
HAH. WE SHOULD GO SEE HIM.
C'MON. DAD'S WAITING.

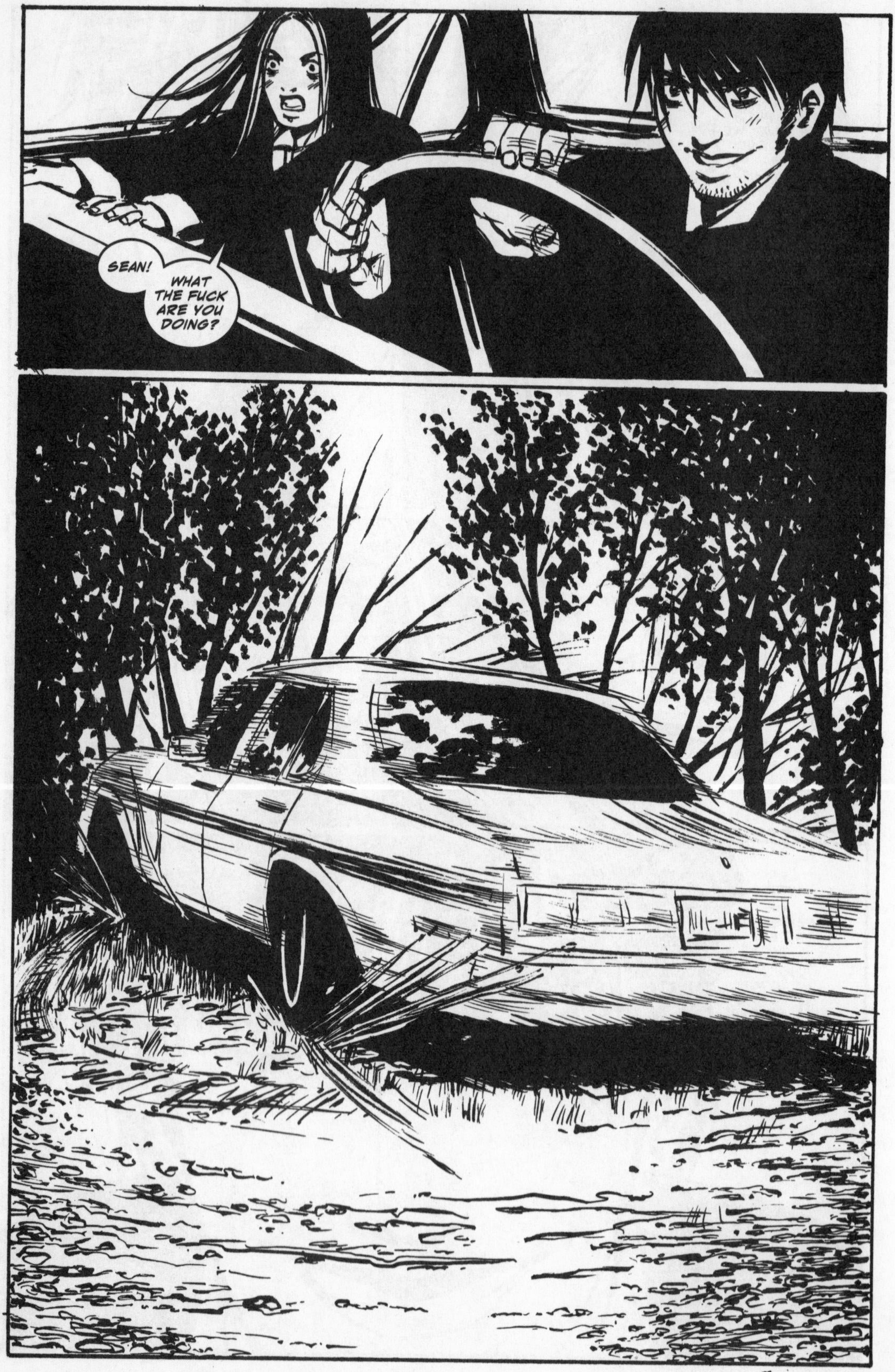
SEAN!
WHAT THE FUCK ARE YOU DOING?

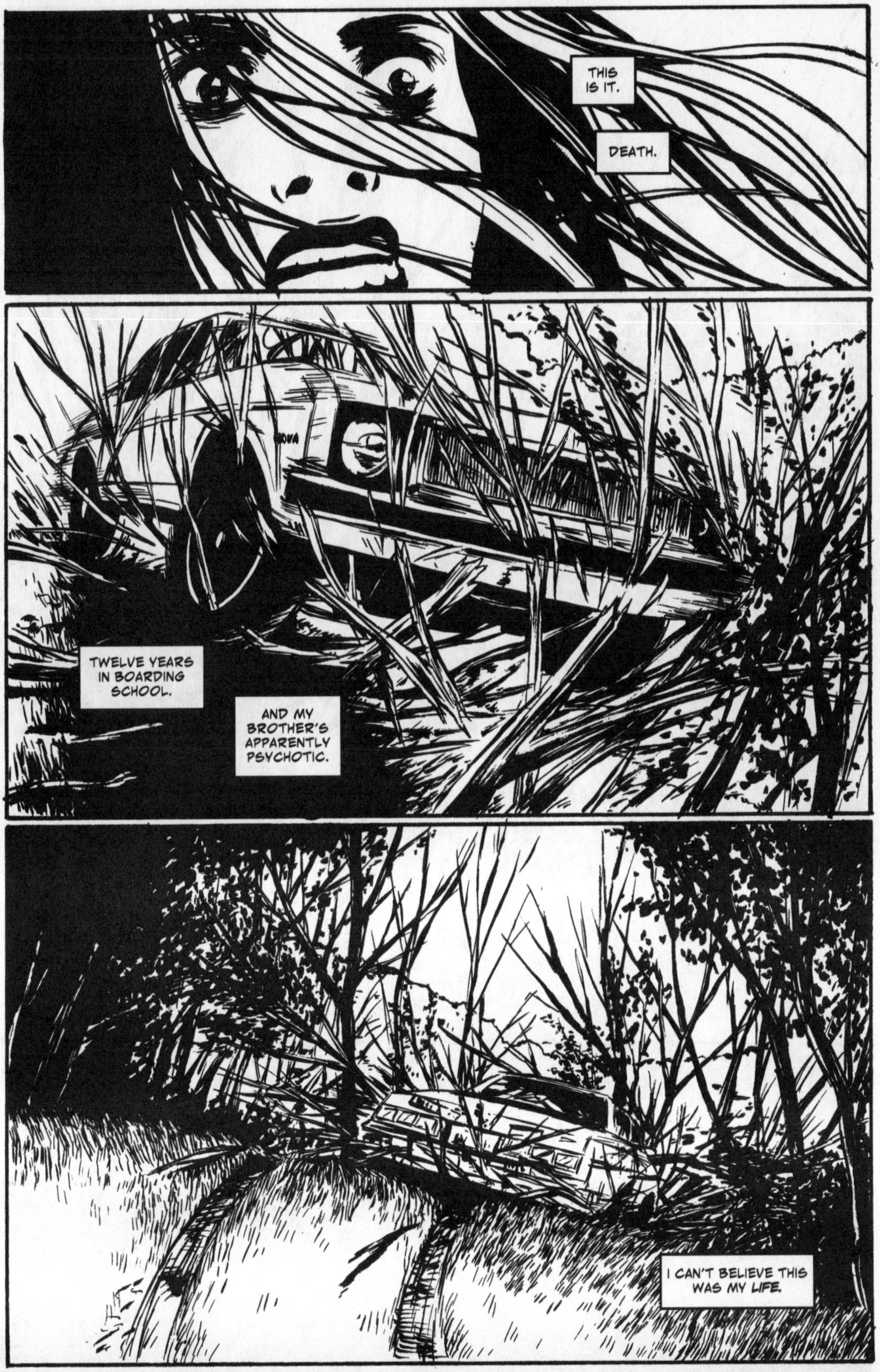

THIS IS IT.
DEATH.
TWELVE YEARS IN BOARDING SCHOOL.
AND MY BROTHER'S APPARENTLY PSYCHOTIC.
I CAN'T BELIEVE THIS WAS MY LIFE.

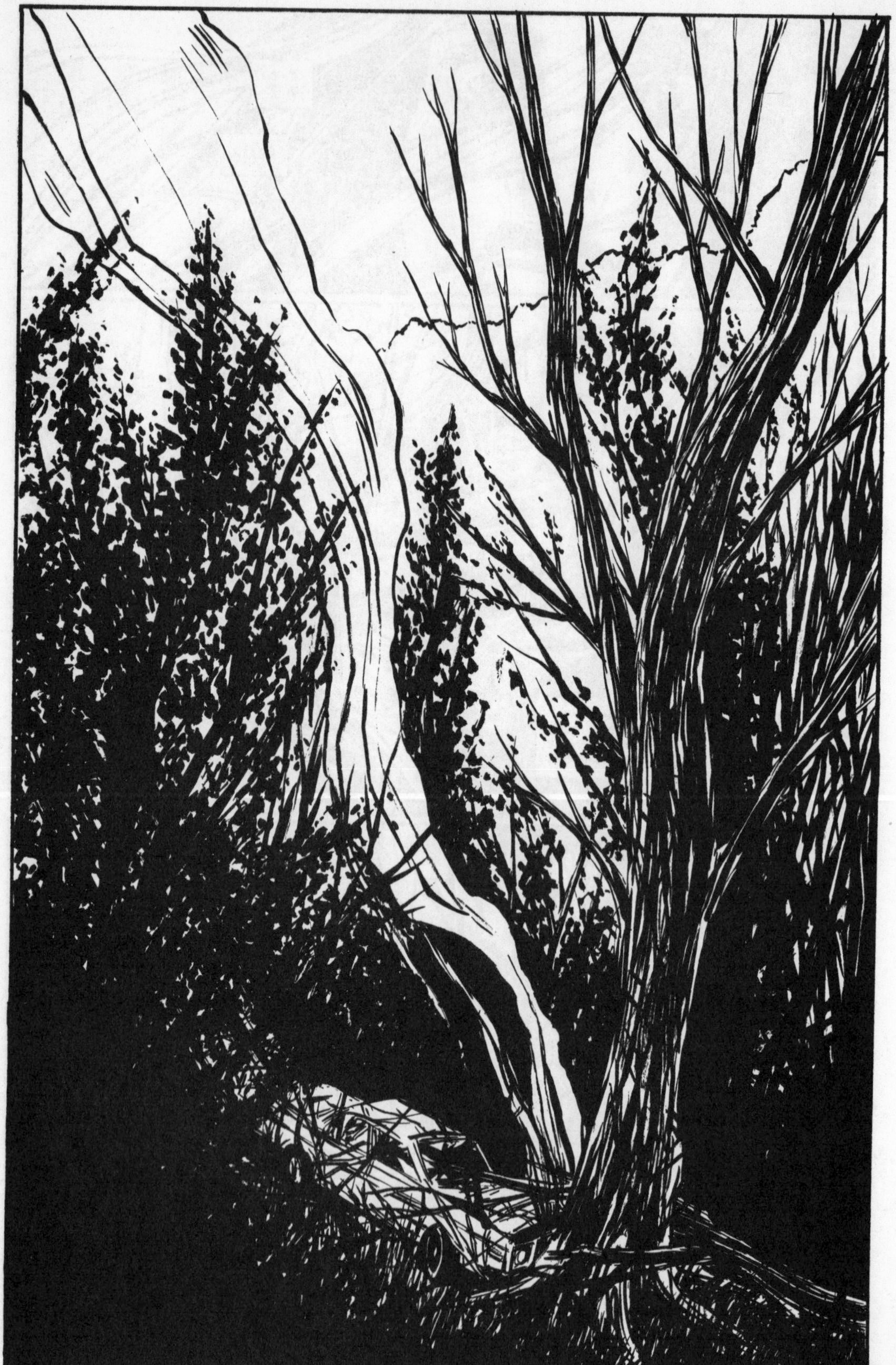

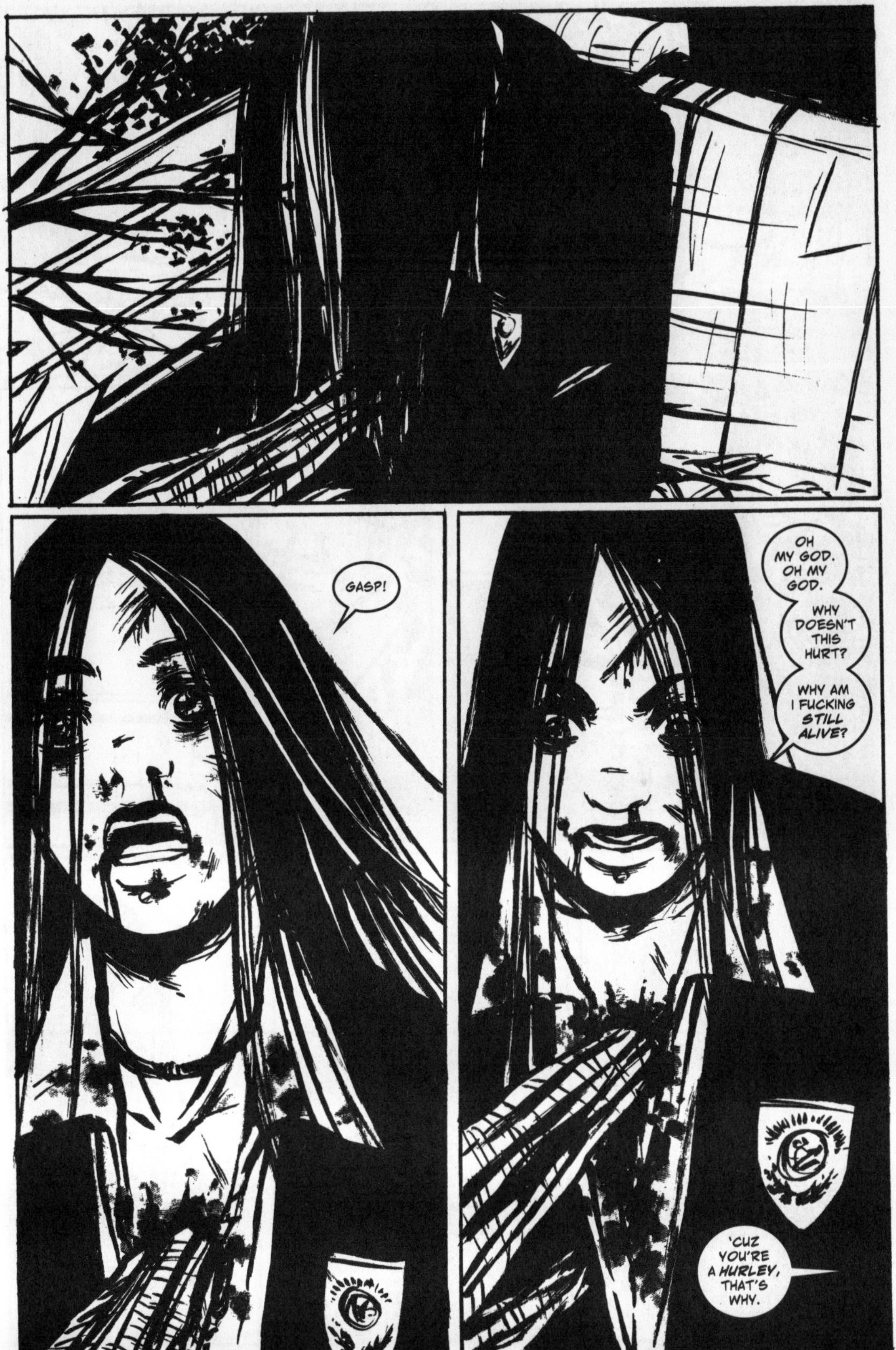
GASP!
OH MY GOD. OH MY GOD.
WHY DOESN'T THIS HURT?
WHY AM I FUCKING STILL ALIVE?
'CUZ YOU'RE A HURLEY, THAT'S WHY.

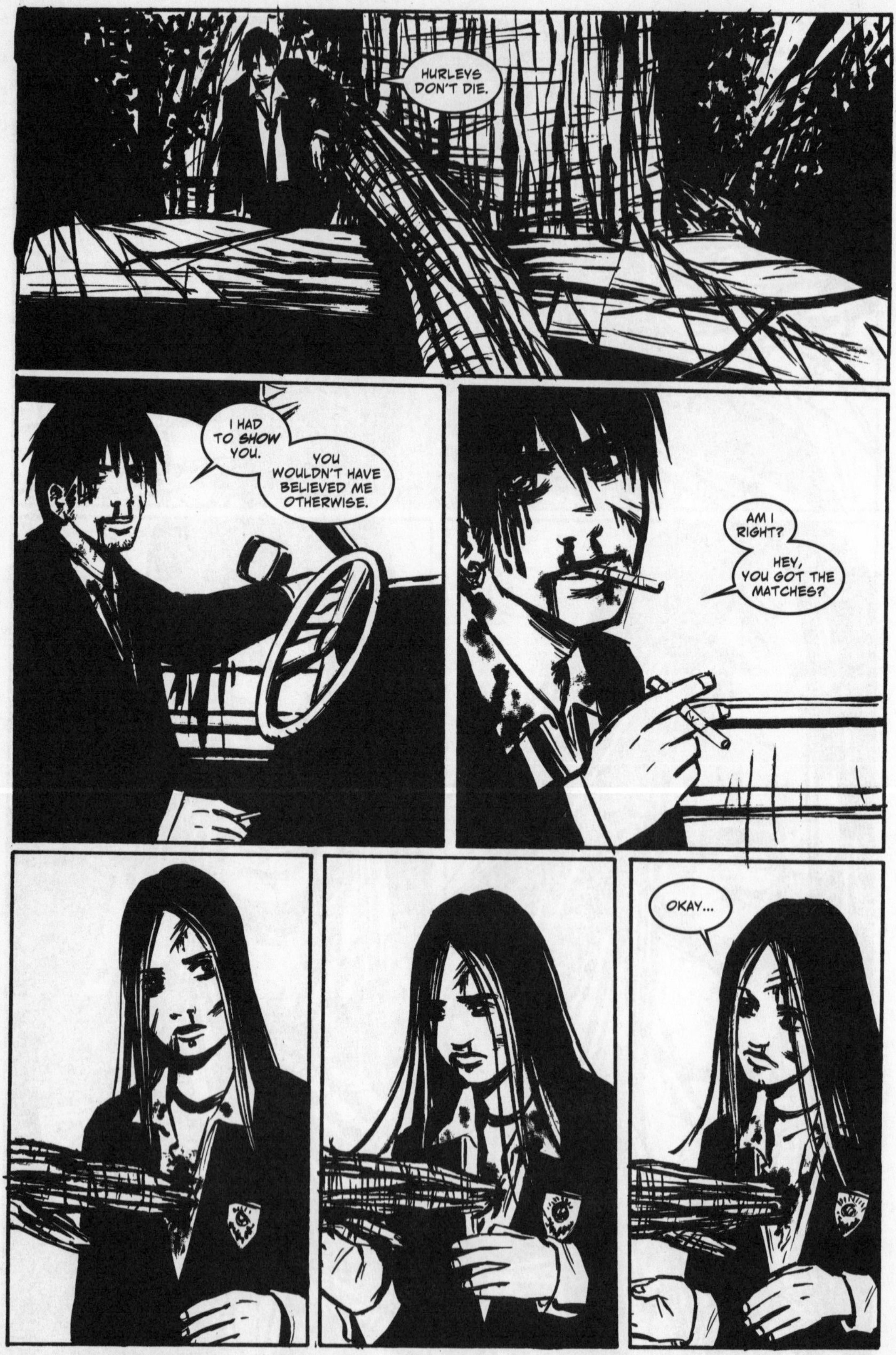
HURLEYS DON'T DIE.
I HAD TO SHOW YOU.
YOU WOULDN'T HAVE BELIEVED ME OTHERWISE.
AM I RIGHT?
HEY, YOU GOT THE MATCHES?
OKAY...

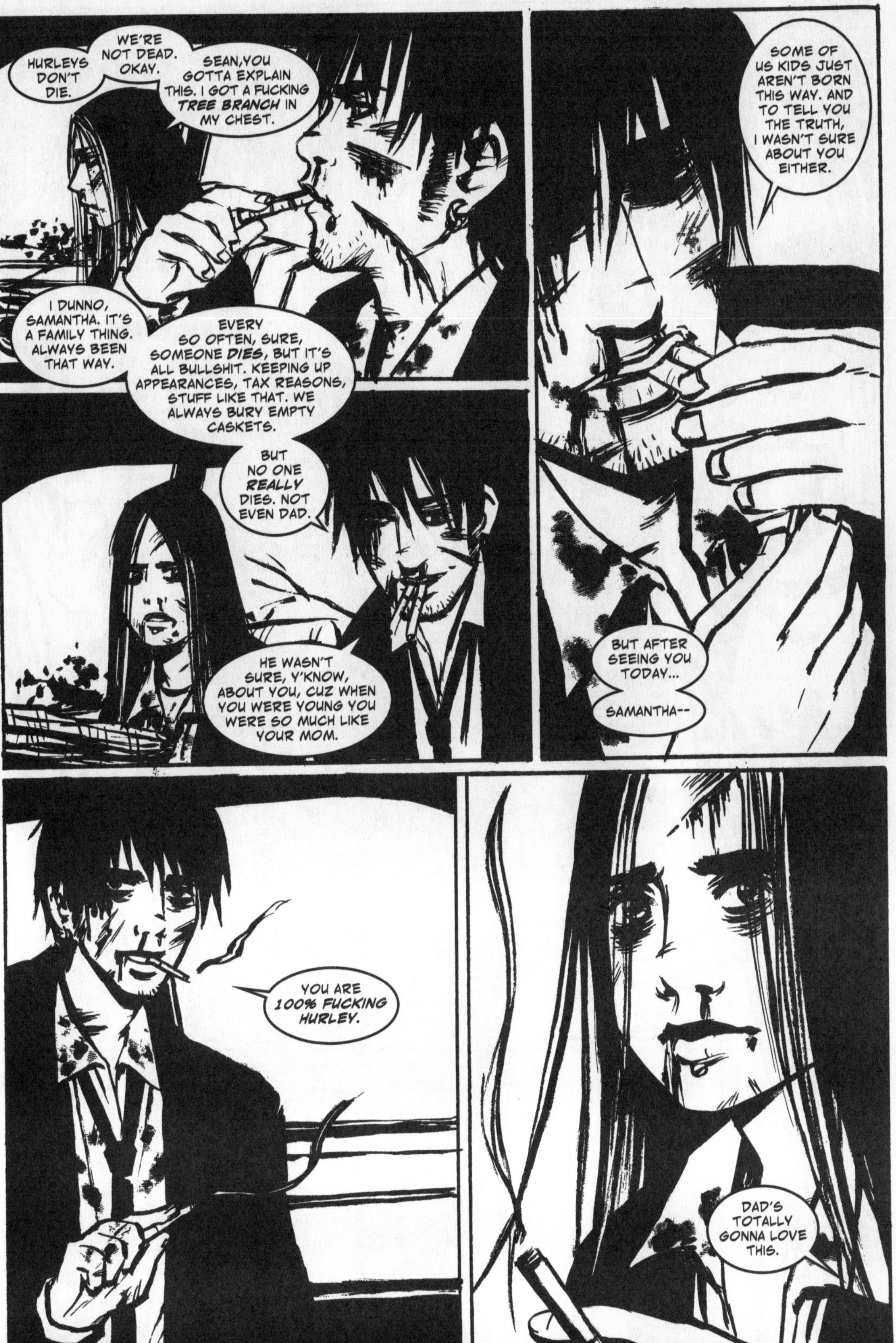
HURLEYS DON'T DIE.
WE'RE NOT DEAD. OKAY.
SEAN,YOU GOTTA EXPLAIN THIS. I GOT A FUCKING TREE BRANCH IN MY CHEST.
SOME OF US KIDS JUST AREN'T BORN THIS WAY. AND TO TELL YOU THE TRUTH, I WASN'T SURE ABOUT YOU EITHER.
I DUNNO, SAMANTHA. IT'S A FAMILY THING. ALWAYS BEEN THAT WAY.
EVERY SO OFTEN, SURE, SOMEONE DIES, BUT IT'S ALL BULLSHIT. KEEPING UP APPEARANCES, TAX REASONS, STUFF LIKE THAT. WE ALWAYS BURY EMPTY CASKETS.
BUT NO ONE REALLY DIES. NOT EVEN DAD.
HE WASN'T SURE, Y'KNOW, ABOUT YOU, CUZ WHEN YOU WERE YOUNG YOU WERE SO MUCH LIKE YOUR MOM.
BUT AFTER SEEING YOU TODAY...
SAMANTHA--
YOU ARE 100% FUCKING HURLEY.
DAD'S TOTALLY GONNA LOVE THIS.

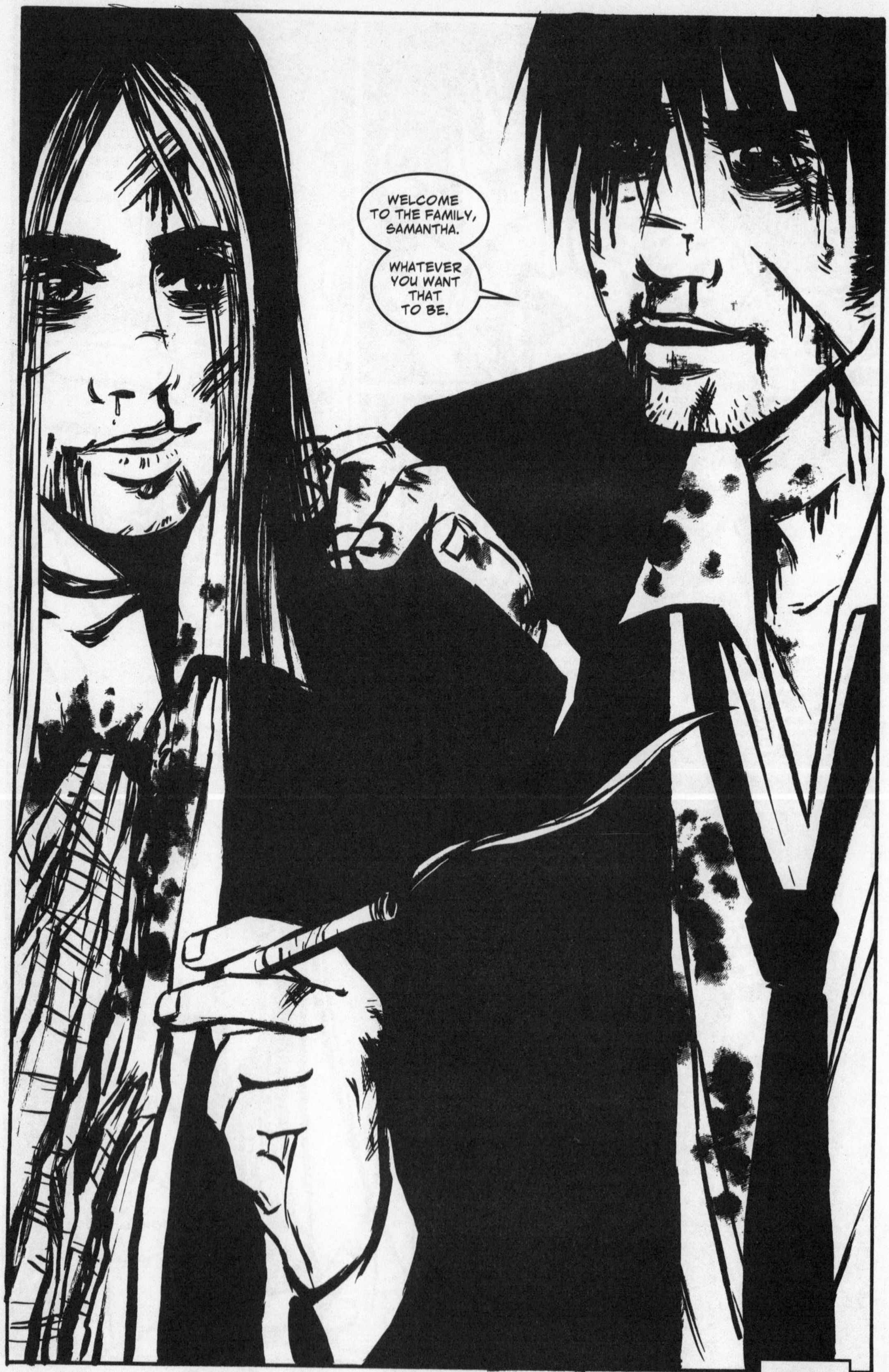
WELCOME TO THE FAMILY, SAMANTHA.
WHATEVER YOU WANT THAT TO BE.
THE END

4

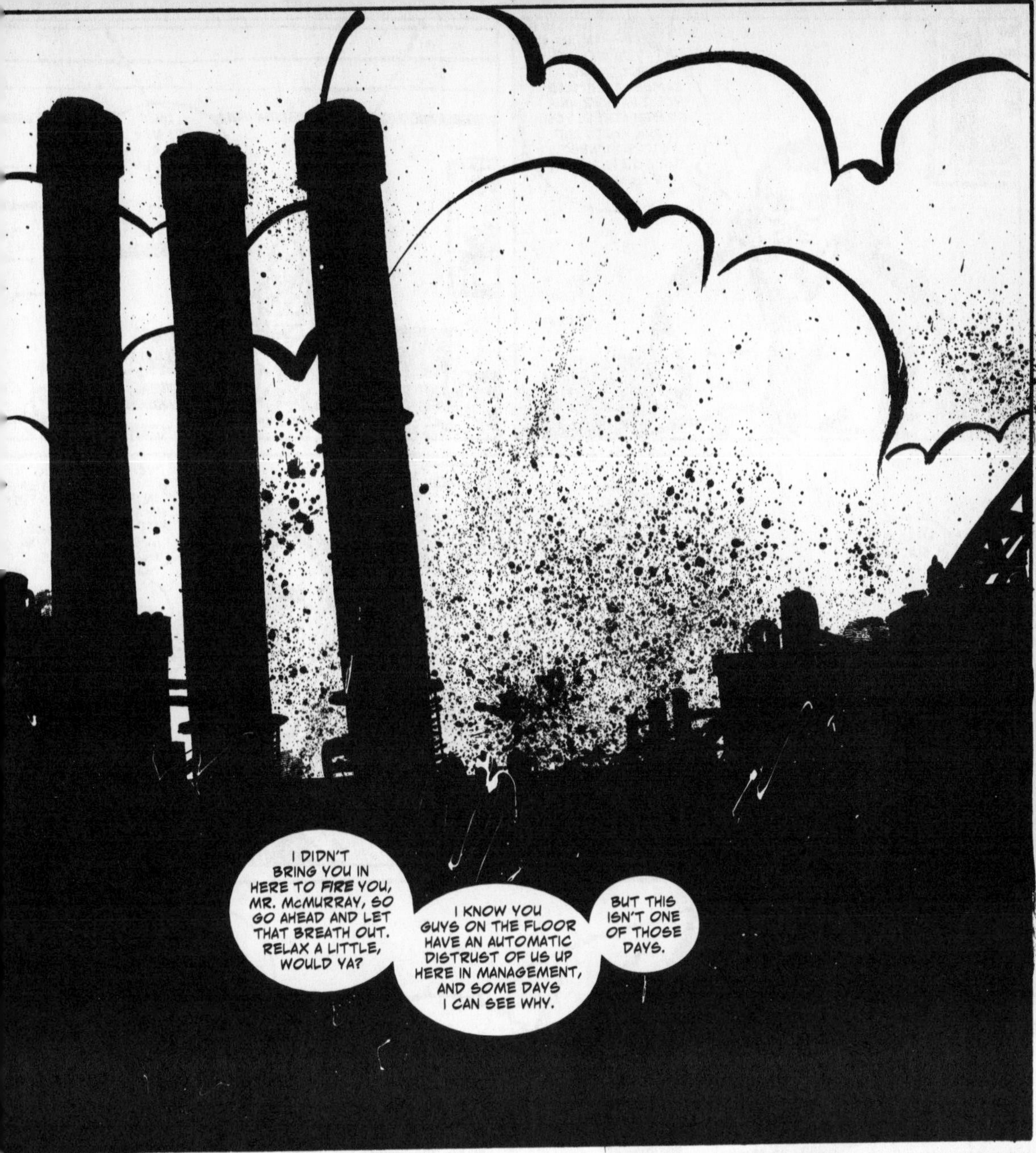
I DIDN'T BRING YOU IN HERE TO FIRE YOU, MR. McMURRAY, SO GO AHEAD AND LET THAT BREATH OUT. RELAX A LITTLE, WOULD YA?
I KNOW YOU GUYS ON THE FLOOR HAVE AN AUTOMATIC DISTRUST OF US UP HERE IN MANAGEMENT, AND SOME DAYS I CAN SEE WHY.
BUT THIS ISN'T ONE OF THOSE DAYS.

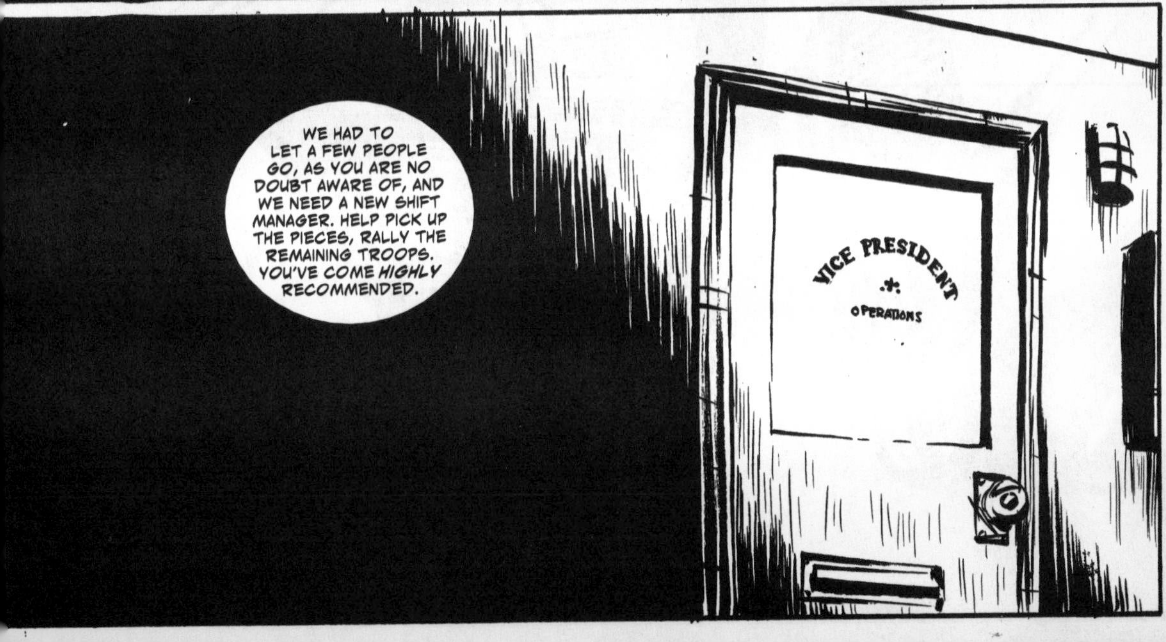
WE HAD TO LET A FEW PEOPLE GO, AS YOU ARE NO DOUBT AWARE OF, AND WE NEED A NEW SHIFT MANAGER. HELP PICK UP THE PIECES, RALLY THE REMAINING TROOPS. YOU'VE COME HIGHLY RECOMMENDED.
VICE PRESIDENT
OPERATIONS

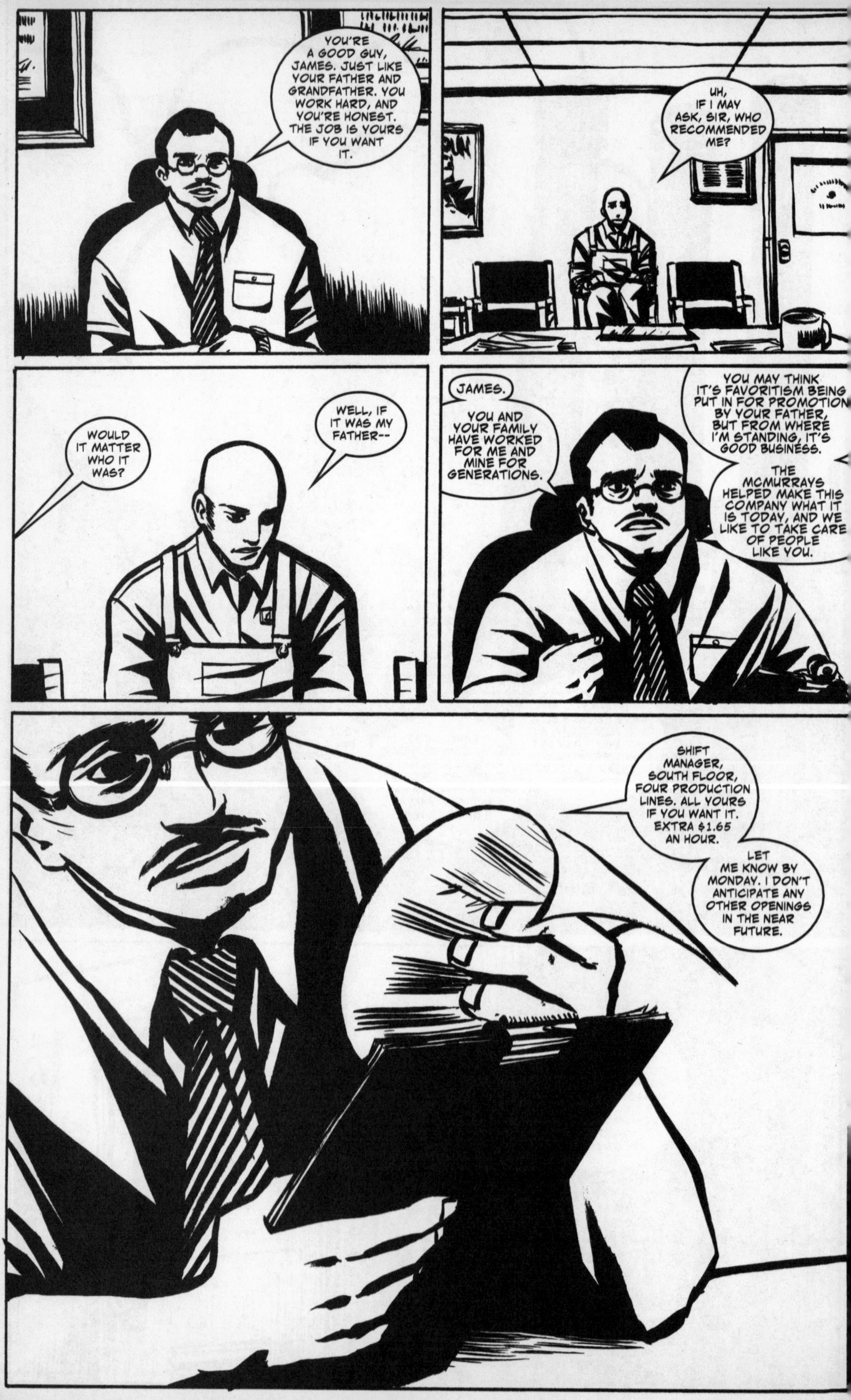

YOU'RE A GOOD GUY, JAMES. JUST LIKE YOUR FATHER AND GRANDFATHER. YOU WORK HARD, AND YOU'RE HONEST. THE JOB IS YOURS IF YOU WANT IT.
UH, IF I MAY ASK, SIR, WHO RECOMMENDED ME?
WOULD IT MATTER WHO IT WAS?
WELL, IF IT WAS MY FATHER--
JAMES.
YOU AND YOUR FAMILY HAVE WORKED FOR ME AND MINE FOR GENERATIONS.
YOU MAY THINK IT'S FAVORITISM BEING PUT IN FOR PROMOTION BY YOUR FATHER, BUT FROM WHERE I'M STANDING, IT'S GOOD BUSINESS.
THE MCMURRAYS HELPED MAKE THIS COMPANY WHAT IT IS TODAY, AND WE LIKE TO TAKE CARE OF PEOPLE LIKE YOU.
SHIFT MANAGER, SOUTH FLOOR, FOUR PRODUCTION LINES. ALL YOURS IF YOU WANT IT. EXTRA $1.65 AN HOUR.
LET ME KNOW BY MONDAY. I DON'T ANTICIPATE ANY OTHER OPENINGS IN THE NEAR FUTURE.

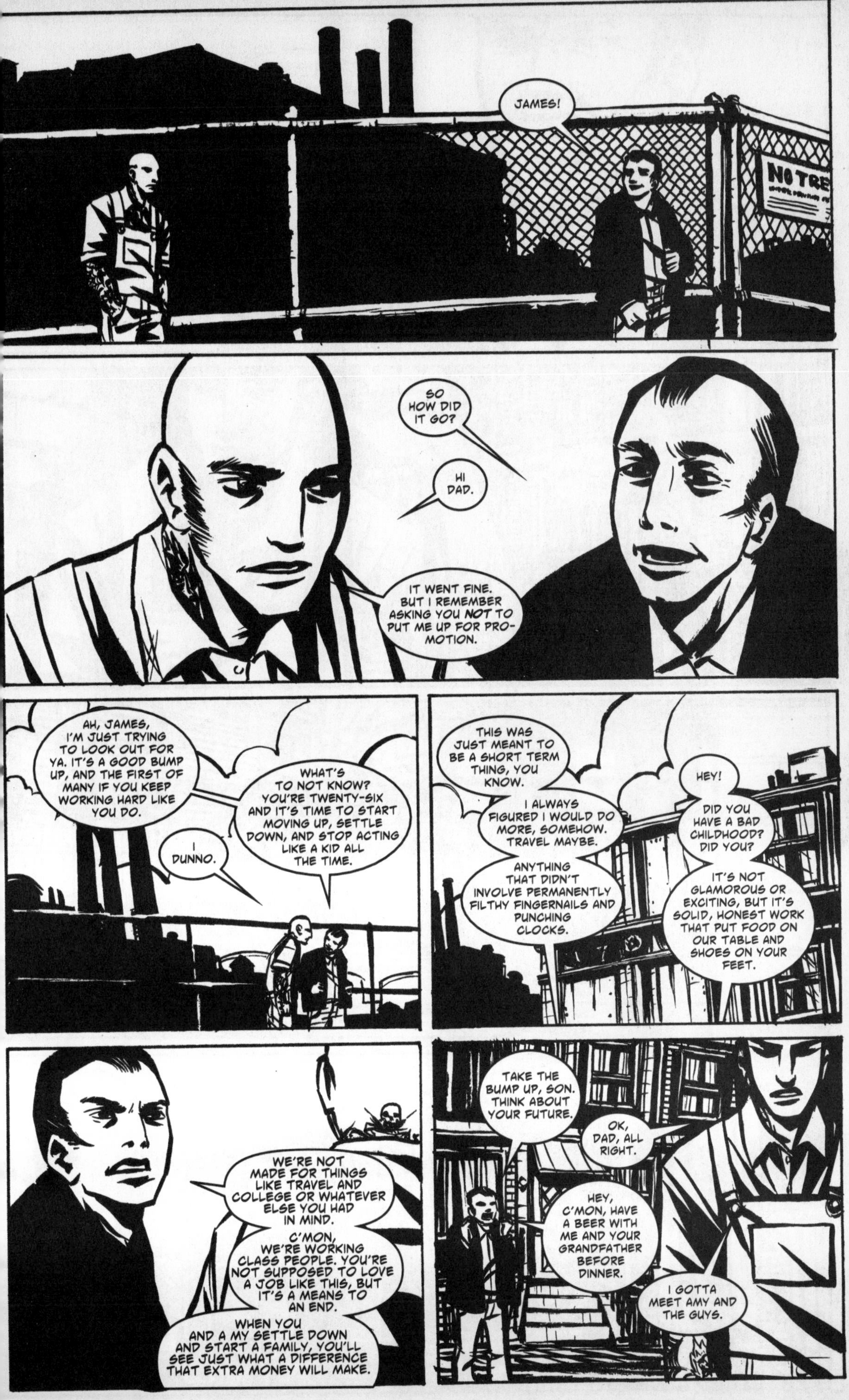
JAMES!
NO TRE
SO HOW DID IT GO?
HI DAD.
IT WENT FINE. BUT I REMEMBER ASKING YOU **NOT** TO PUT ME UP FOR PRO-MOTION.
AH, JAMES, I'M JUST TRYING TO LOOK OUT FOR YA. IT'S A GOOD BUMP UP, AND THE FIRST OF MANY IF YOU KEEP WORKING HARD LIKE YOU DO.
I DUNNO.
WHAT'S TO NOT KNOW? YOU'RE TWENTY-SIX AND IT'S TIME TO START MOVING UP, SETTLE DOWN, AND STOP ACTING LIKE A KID ALL THE TIME.
THIS WAS JUST MEANT TO BE A SHORT TERM THING, YOU KNOW.
I ALWAYS FIGURED I WOULD DO MORE, SOMEHOW. TRAVEL MAYBE.
ANYTHING THAT DIDN'T INVOLVE PERMANENTLY FILTHY FINGERNAILS AND PUNCHING CLOCKS.
HEY!
DID YOU HAVE A BAD CHILDHOOD? DID YOU?
IT'S NOT GLAMOROUS OR EXCITING, BUT IT'S SOLID, HONEST WORK THAT PUT FOOD ON OUR TABLE AND SHOES ON YOUR FEET.
WE'RE NOT MADE FOR THINGS LIKE TRAVEL AND COLLEGE OR WHATEVER ELSE YOU HAD IN MIND.
C'MON, WE'RE WORKING CLASS PEOPLE. YOU'RE NOT SUPPOSED TO LOVE A JOB LIKE THIS, BUT IT'S A MEANS TO AN END.
WHEN YOU AND A MY SETTLE DOWN AND START A FAMILY, YOU'LL SEE JUST WHAT A DIFFERENCE THAT EXTRA MONEY WILL MAKE.
TAKE THE BUMP UP, SON. THINK ABOUT YOUR FUTURE.
OK, DAD, ALL RIGHT.
HEY, C'MON, HAVE A BEER WITH ME AND YOUR GRANDFATHER BEFORE DINNER.
I GOTTA MEET AMY AND THE GUYS.

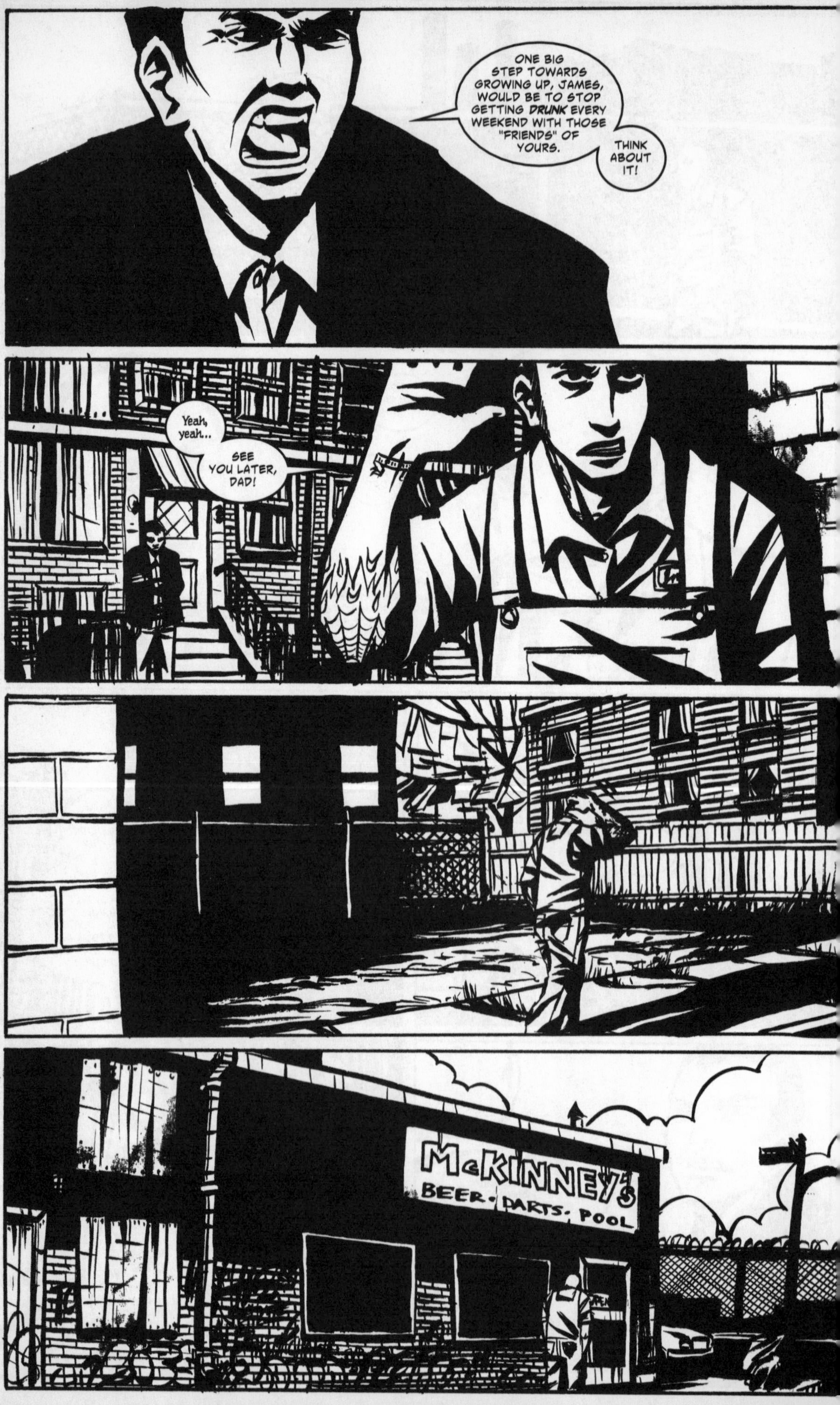
ONE BIG STEP TOWARDS GROWING UP, JAMES, WOULD BE TO STOP GETTING DRUNK EVERY WEEKEND WITH THOSE "FRIENDS" OF YOURS.
THINK ABOUT IT!
Yeah, yeah...
SEE YOU LATER, DAD!
McKINNEY'S
BEER - DARTS - POOL

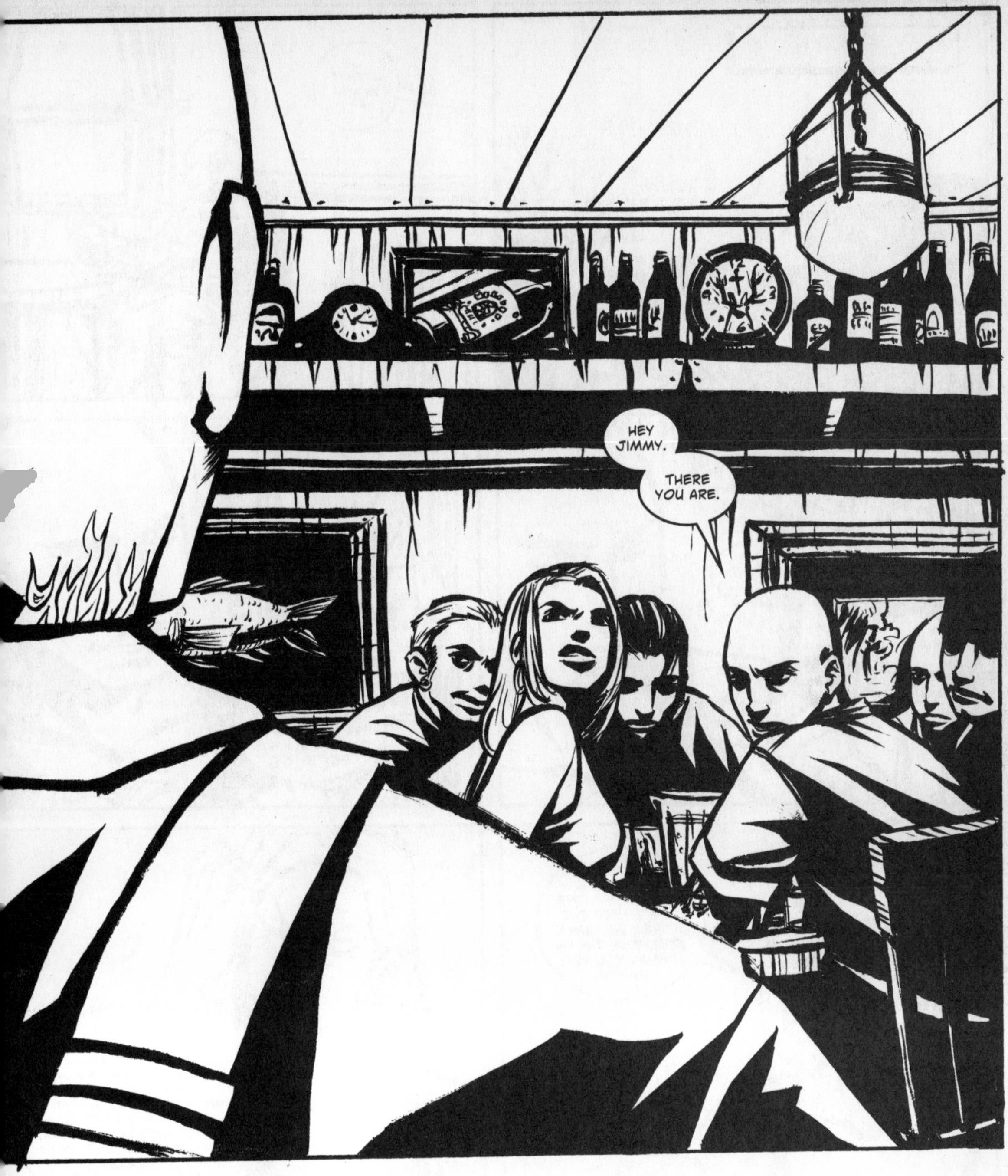
HEY JIMMY.
THERE YOU ARE.

“Stand Strong”

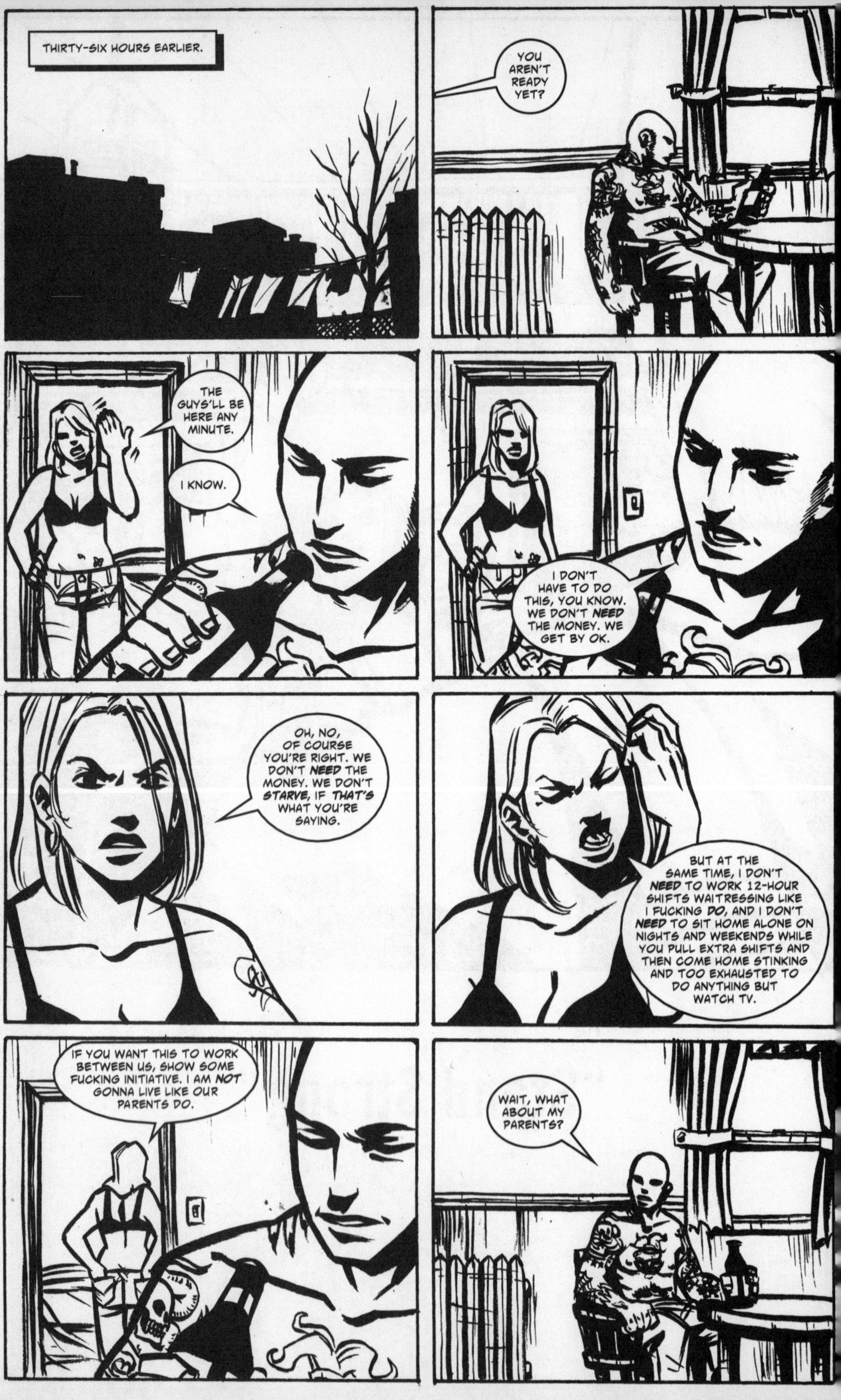
THIRTY-SIX HOURS EARLIER.
YOU AREN'T READY YET?
THE GUYS'LL BE HERE ANY MINUTE.
I KNOW.
I DON'T HAVE TO DO THIS, YOU KNOW. WE DON'T NEED THE MONEY. WE GET BY OK.
OH, NO, OF COURSE YOU'RE RIGHT. WE DON'T NEED THE MONEY. WE DON'T STARVE, IF THAT'S WHAT YOU'RE SAYING.
BUT AT THE SAME TIME, I DON'T NEED TO WORK 12-HOUR SHIFTS WAITRESSING LIKE I FUCKING DO, AND I DON'T NEED TO SIT HOME ALONE ON NIGHTS AND WEEKENDS WHILE YOU PULL EXTRA SHIFTS AND THEN COME HOME STINKING AND TOO EXHAUSTED TO DO ANYTHING BUT WATCH TV.
IF YOU WANT THIS TO WORK BETWEEN US, SHOW SOME FUCKING INITIATIVE. I AM NOT GONNA LIVE LIKE OUR PARENTS DO.
WAIT, WHAT ABOUT MY PARENTS?

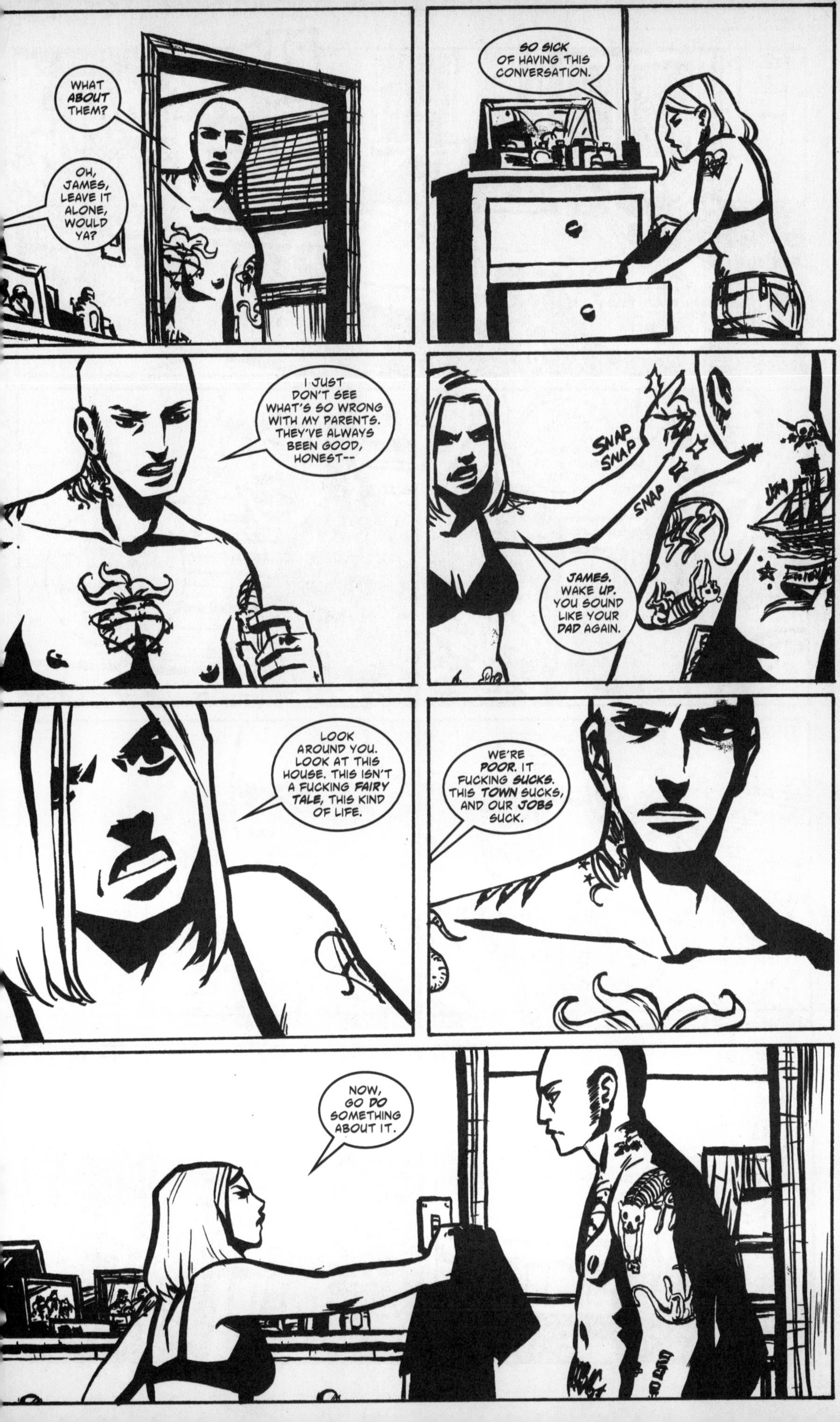
WHAT ABOUT THEM?
OH, JAMES, LEAVE IT ALONE, WOULD YA?
SO SICK OF HAVING THIS CONVERSATION.
I JUST DON'T SEE WHAT'S SO WRONG WITH MY PARENTS. THEY'VE ALWAYS BEEN GOOD, HONEST--
SNAP SNAP
SNAP
JAMES. WAKE UP. YOU SOUND LIKE YOUR DAD AGAIN.
LOOK AROUND YOU. LOOK AT THIS HOUSE. THIS ISN'T A FUCKING FAIRY TALE, THIS KIND OF LIFE.
WE'RE POOR. IT FUCKING SUCKS. THIS TOWN SUCKS, AND OUR JOBS SUCK.
NOW, GO DO SOMETHING ABOUT IT.

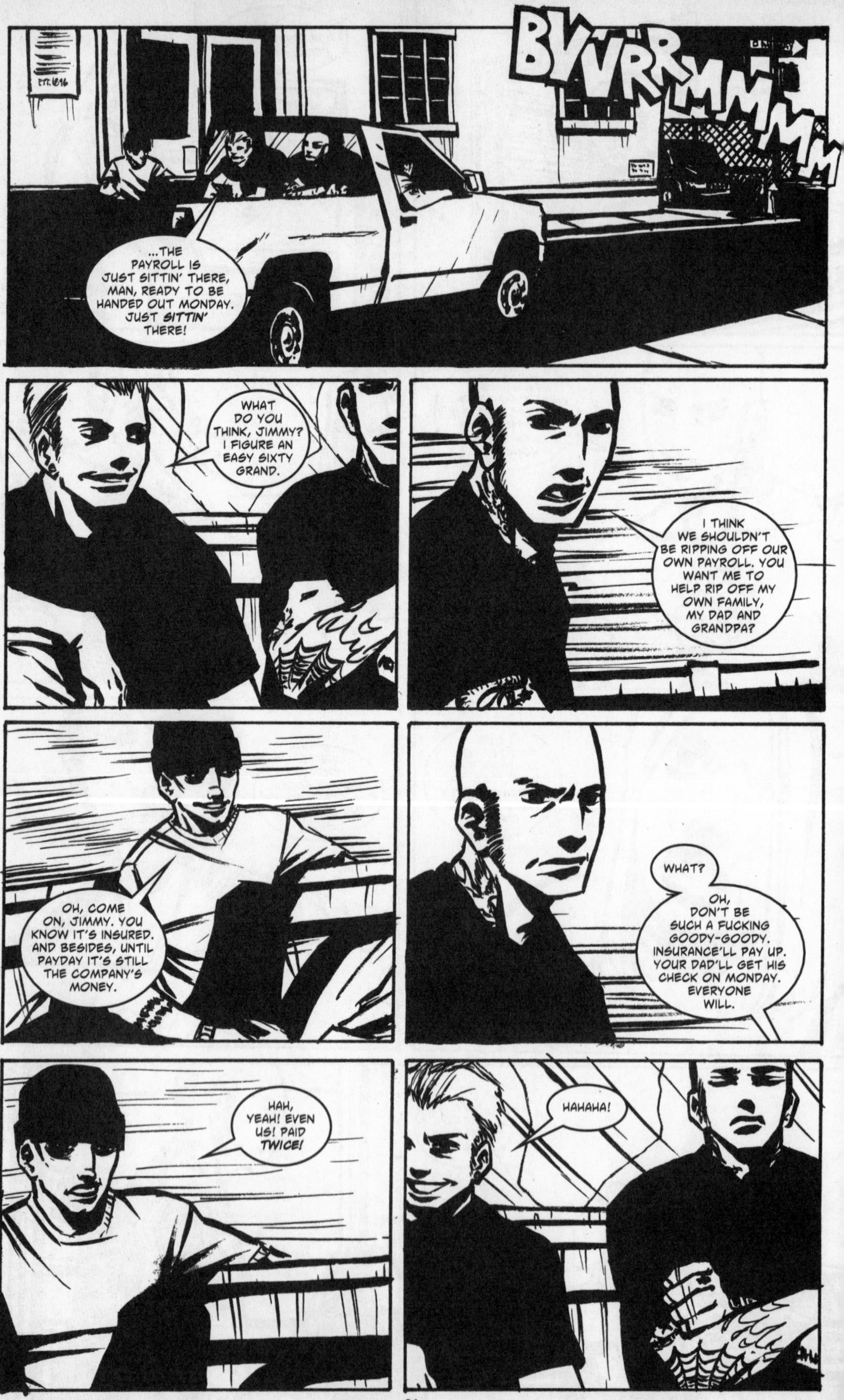
BVVRRMMMMMM
...THE PAYROLL IS JUST SITTIN' THERE, MAN, READY TO BE HANDED OUT MONDAY. JUST SITTIN' THERE!
WHAT DO YOU THINK, JIMMY? I FIGURE AN EASY SIXTY GRAND.
I THINK WE SHOULDN'T BE RIPPING OFF OUR OWN PAYROLL. YOU WANT ME TO HELP RIP OFF MY OWN FAMILY, MY DAD AND GRANDPA?
OH, COME ON, JIMMY. YOU KNOW IT'S INSURED. AND BESIDES, UNTIL PAYDAY IT'S STILL THE COMPANY'S MONEY.
WHAT?
OH, DON'T BE SUCH A FUCKING GOODY-GOODY. INSURANCE'LL PAY UP. YOUR DAD'LL GET HIS CHECK ON MONDAY. EVERYONE WILL.
HAH, YEAH! EVEN US! PAID TWICE!
HAHAHA!

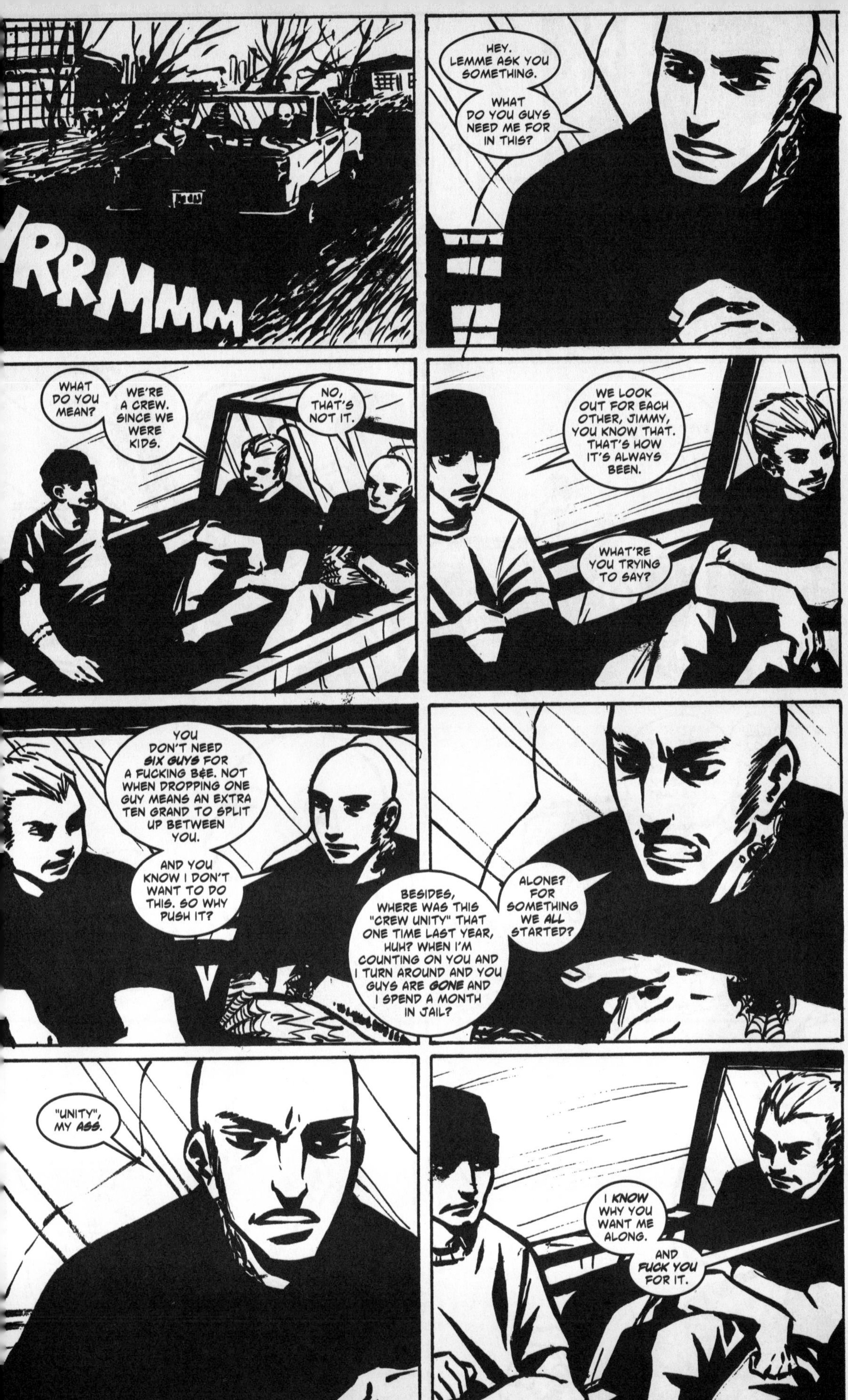
RRRMMM
HEY. LEMME ASK YOU SOMETHING.
WHAT DO YOU GUYS NEED ME FOR IN THIS?
WHAT DO YOU MEAN?
WE'RE A CREW. SINCE WE WERE KIDS.
NO, THAT'S NOT IT.
WE LOOK OUT FOR EACH OTHER, JIMMY, YOU KNOW THAT. THAT'S HOW IT'S ALWAYS BEEN.
WHAT'RE YOU TRYING TO SAY?
YOU DON'T NEED SIX GUYS FOR A FUCKING B&E. NOT WHEN DROPPING ONE GUY MEANS AN EXTRA TEN GRAND TO SPLIT UP BETWEEN YOU.
AND YOU KNOW I DON'T WANT TO DO THIS. SO WHY PUSH IT?
ALONE? FOR SOMETHING WE ALL STARTED?
BESIDES, WHERE WAS THIS "CREW UNITY" THAT ONE TIME LAST YEAR, HUH? WHEN I'M COUNTING ON YOU AND I TURN AROUND AND YOU GUYS ARE GONE AND I SPEND A MONTH IN JAIL?
"UNITY", MY ASS.
I KNOW WHY YOU WANT ME ALONG.
AND FUCK YOU FOR IT.

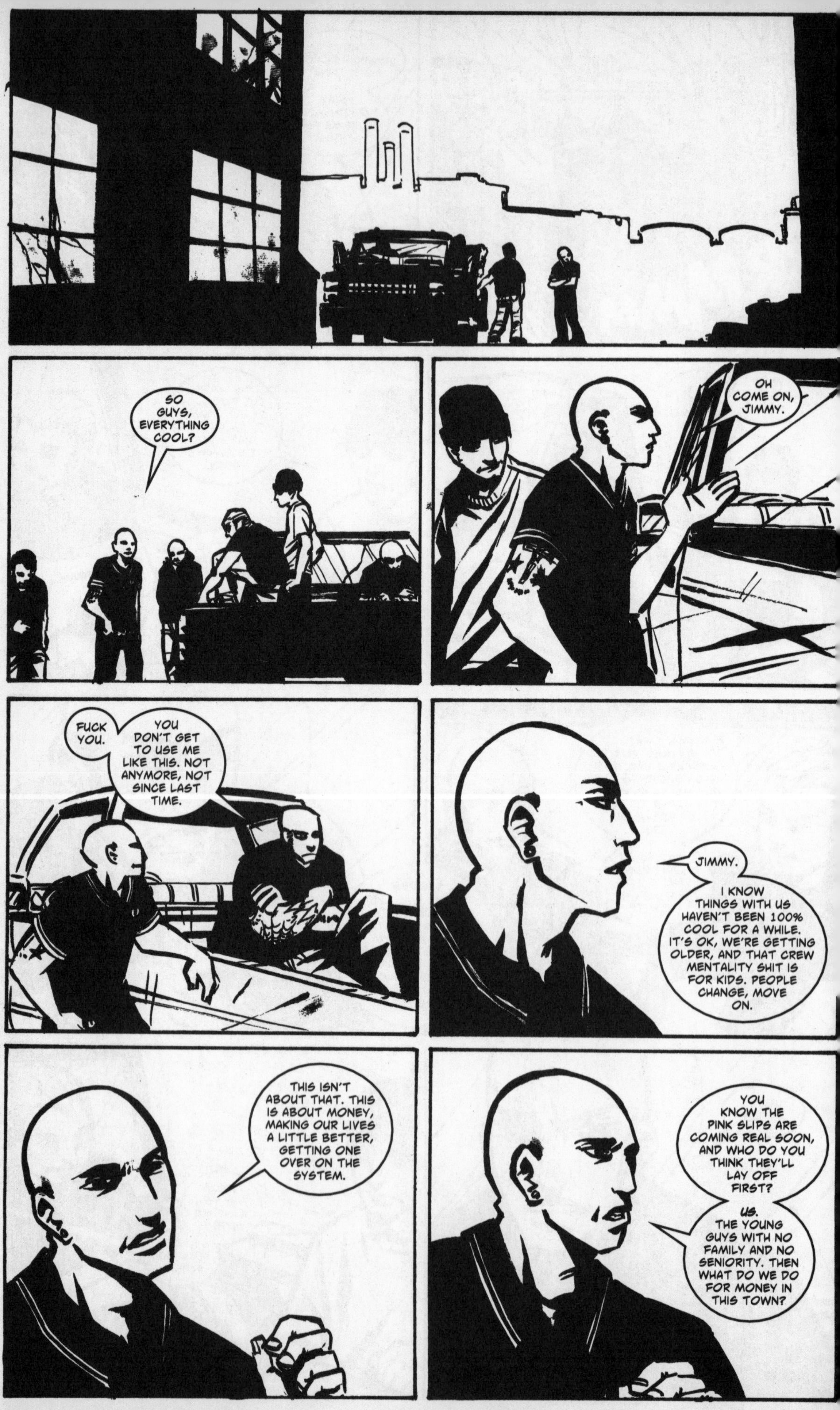
SO GUYS, EVERYTHING COOL?
OH COME ON, JIMMY.
FUCK YOU.
YOU DON'T GET TO USE ME LIKE THIS. NOT ANYMORE, NOT SINCE LAST TIME.
JIMMY.
I KNOW THINGS WITH US HAVEN'T BEEN 100% COOL FOR A WHILE. IT'S OK, WE'RE GETTING OLDER, AND THAT CREW MENTALITY SHIT IS FOR KIDS. PEOPLE CHANGE, MOVE ON.
THIS ISN'T ABOUT THAT. THIS IS ABOUT MONEY, MAKING OUR LIVES A LITTLE BETTER, GETTING ONE OVER ON THE SYSTEM.
YOU KNOW THE PINK SLIPS ARE COMING REAL SOON, AND WHO DO YOU THINK THEY'LL LAY OFF FIRST?
US. THE YOUNG GUYS WITH NO FAMILY AND NO SENIORITY. THEN WHAT DO WE DO FOR MONEY IN THIS TOWN?

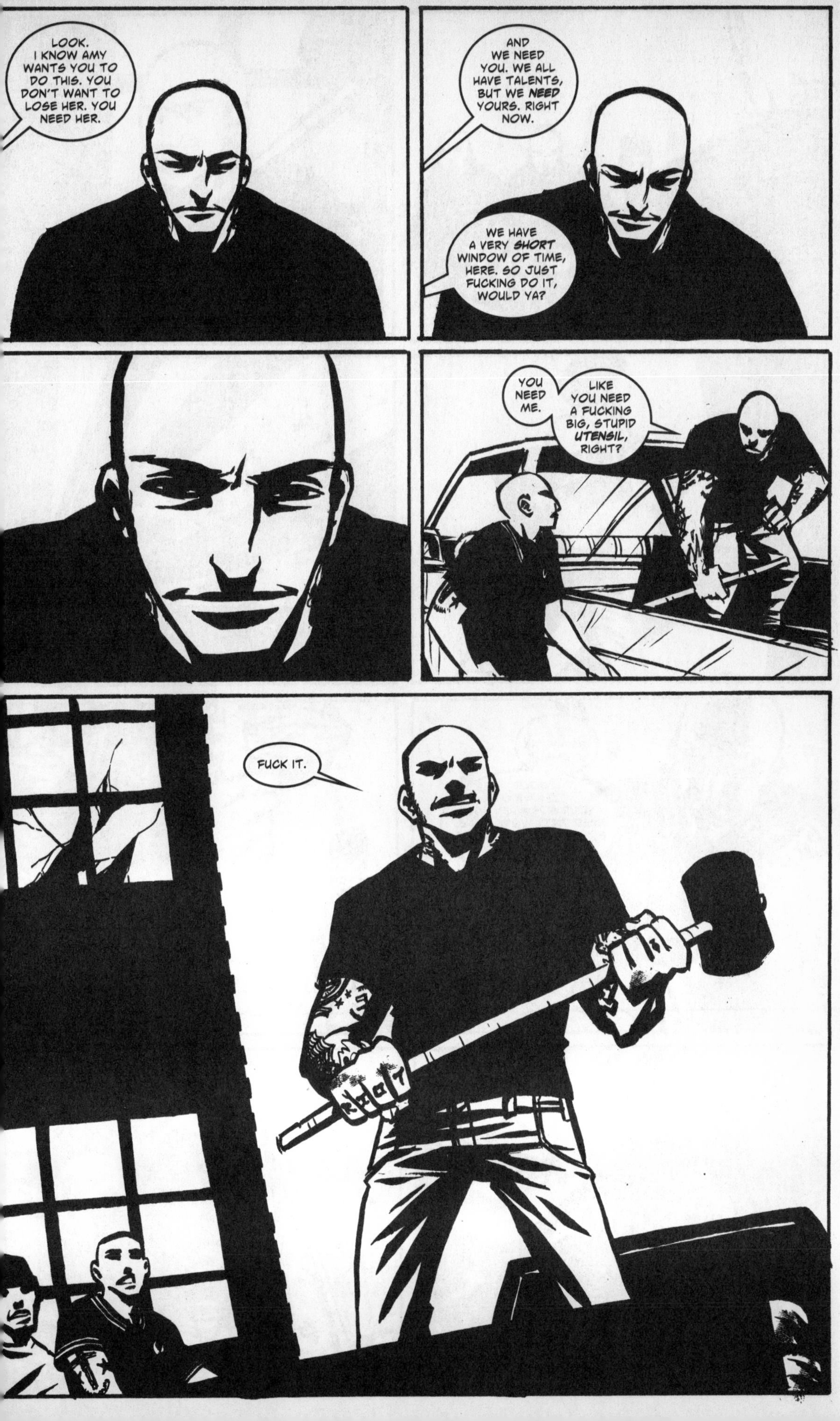
LOOK. I KNOW AMY WANTS YOU TO DO THIS. YOU DON'T WANT TO LOSE HER. YOU NEED HER.
AND WE NEED YOU. WE ALL HAVE TALENTS, BUT WE NEED YOURS. RIGHT NOW.
WE HAVE A VERY SHORT WINDOW OF TIME, HERE. SO JUST FUCKING DO IT, WOULD YA?
YOU NEED ME.
LIKE YOU NEED A FUCKING BIG, STUPID UTENSIL, RIGHT?
FUCK IT.
RIOT

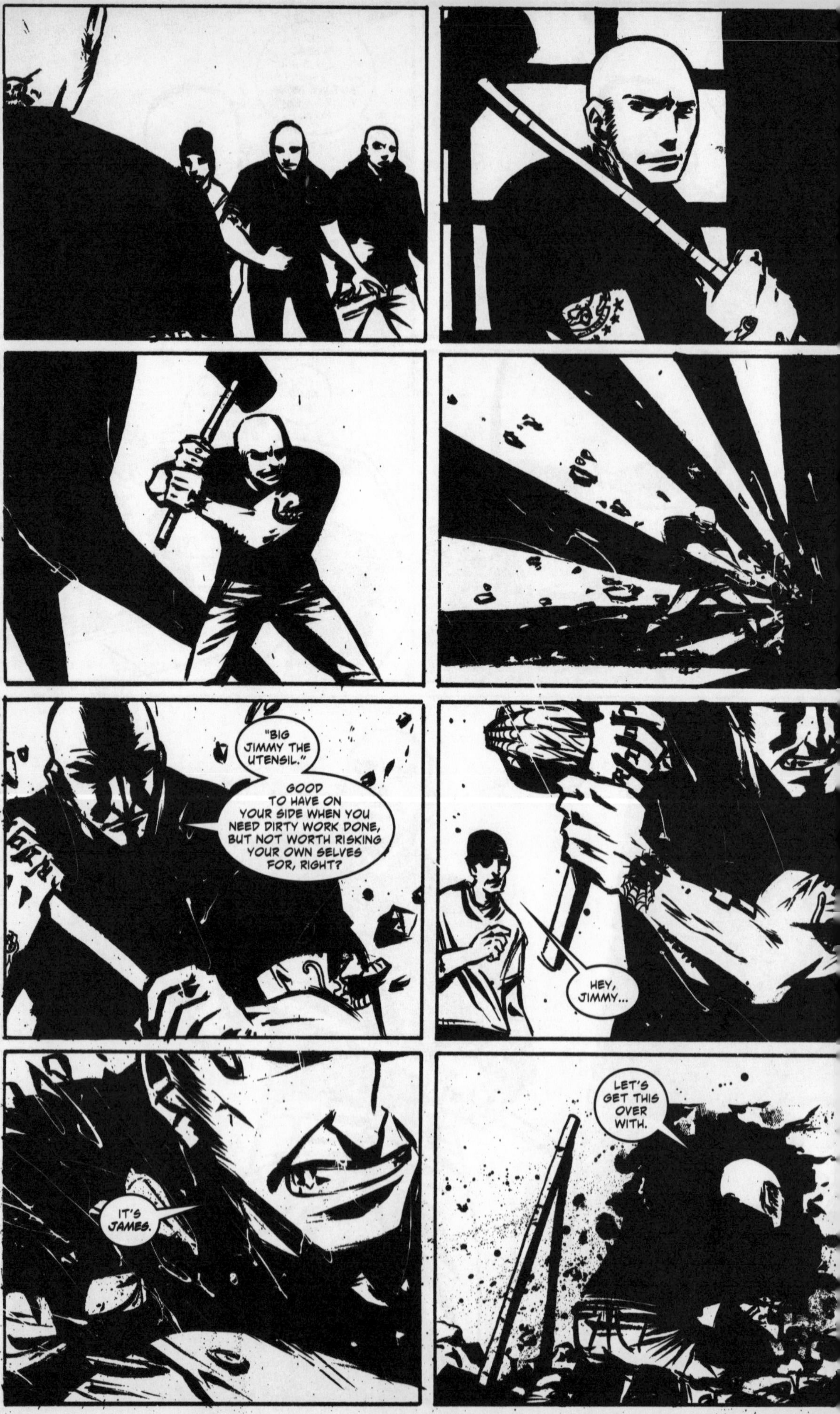
"BIG JIMMY THE UTENSIL."
GOOD TO HAVE ON YOUR SIDE WHEN YOU NEED DIRTY WORK DONE, BUT NOT WORTH RISKING YOUR OWN SELVES FOR, RIGHT?
HEY, JIMMY...
IT'S JAMES.
LET'S GET THIS OVER WITH.

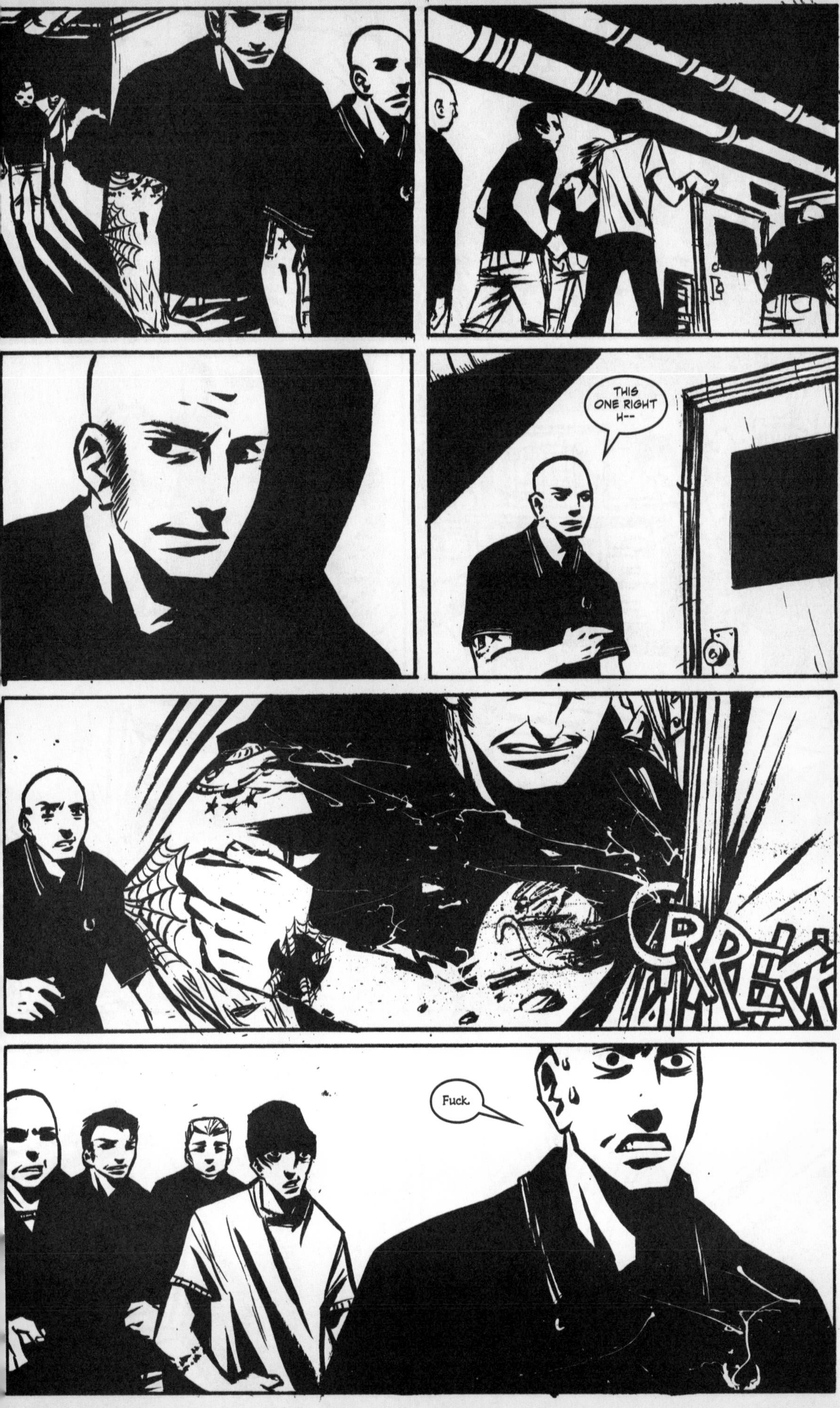
THIS ONE RIGHT H--
CRRK
Fuck.

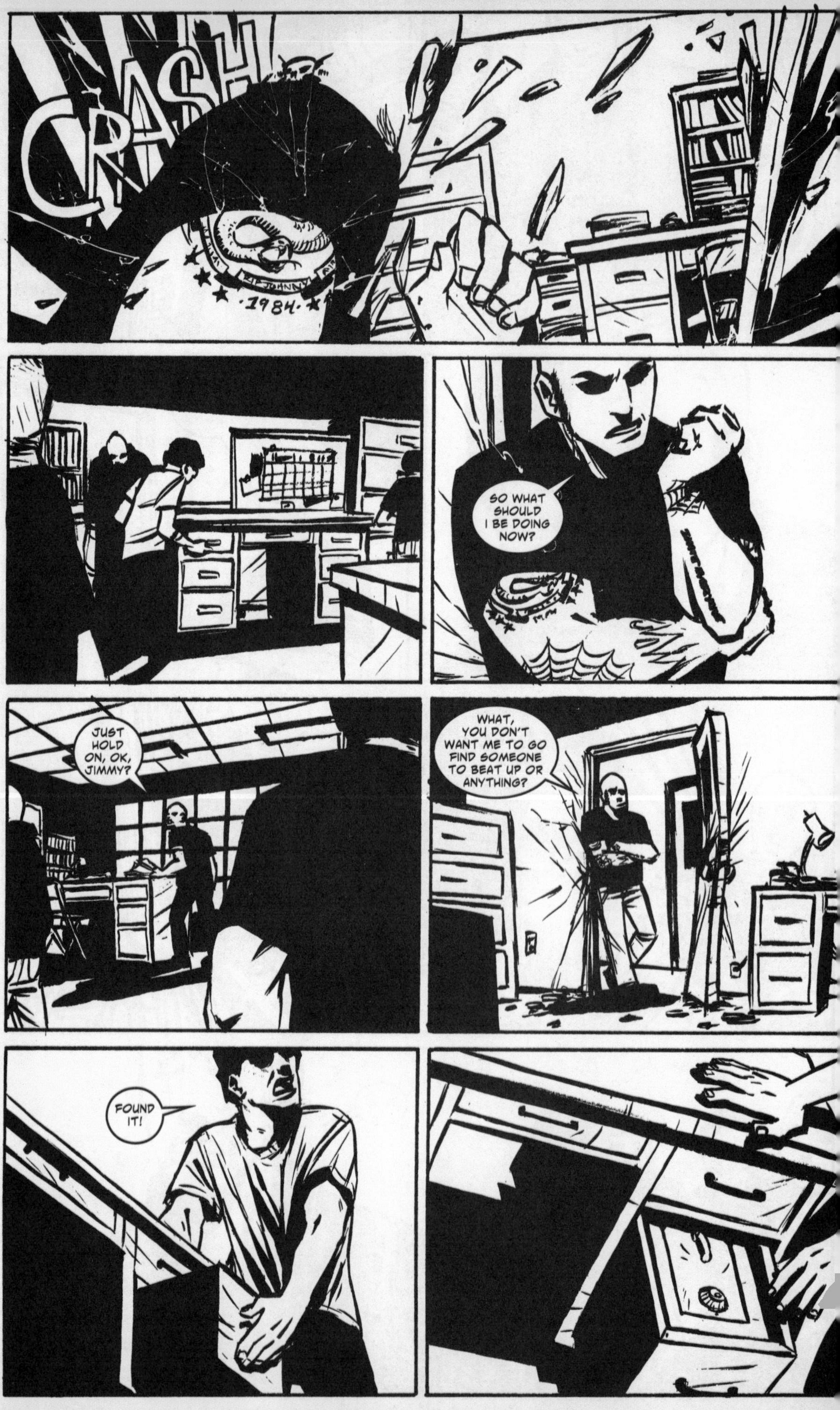
CRASH
RIP JOHNNY
1984
SO WHAT SHOULD I BE DOING NOW?
JUST HOLD ON, OK, JIMMY?
WHAT, YOU DON'T WANT ME TO GO FIND SOMEONE TO BEAT UP OR ANYTHING?
FOUND IT!

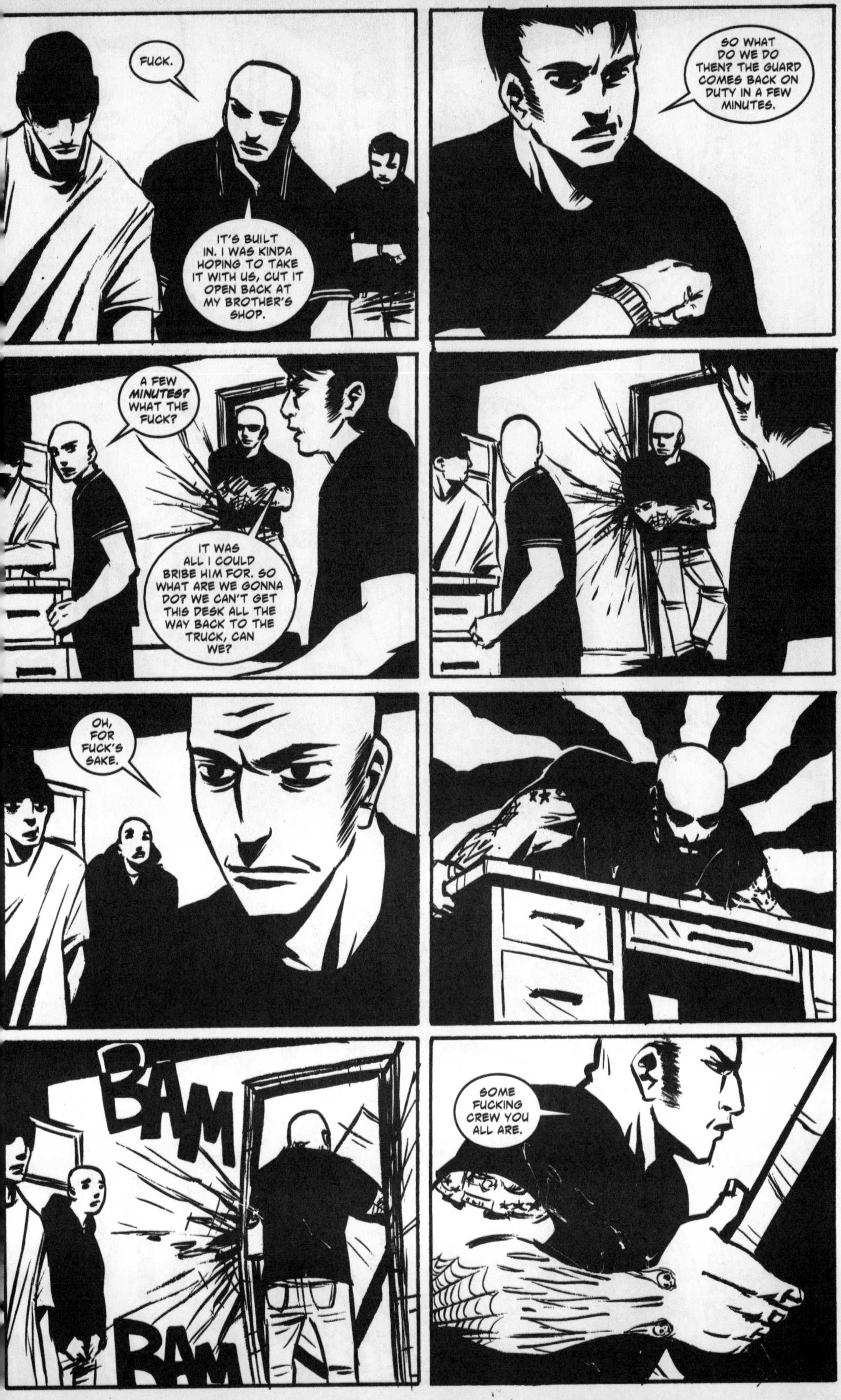
FUCK.
IT'S BUILT IN. I WAS KINDA HOPING TO TAKE IT WITH US, CUT IT OPEN BACK AT MY BROTHER'S SHOP.
SO WHAT DO WE DO THEN? THE GUARD COMES BACK ON DUTY IN A FEW MINUTES.
A FEW *MINUTES?* WHAT THE FUCK?
IT WAS ALL I COULD BRIBE HIM FOR. SO WHAT ARE WE GONNA DO? WE CAN'T GET THIS DESK ALL THE WAY BACK TO THE TRUCK, CAN WE?
OH, FOR FUCK'S SAKE.
BAM
BAM
SOME FUCKING CREW YOU ALL ARE.

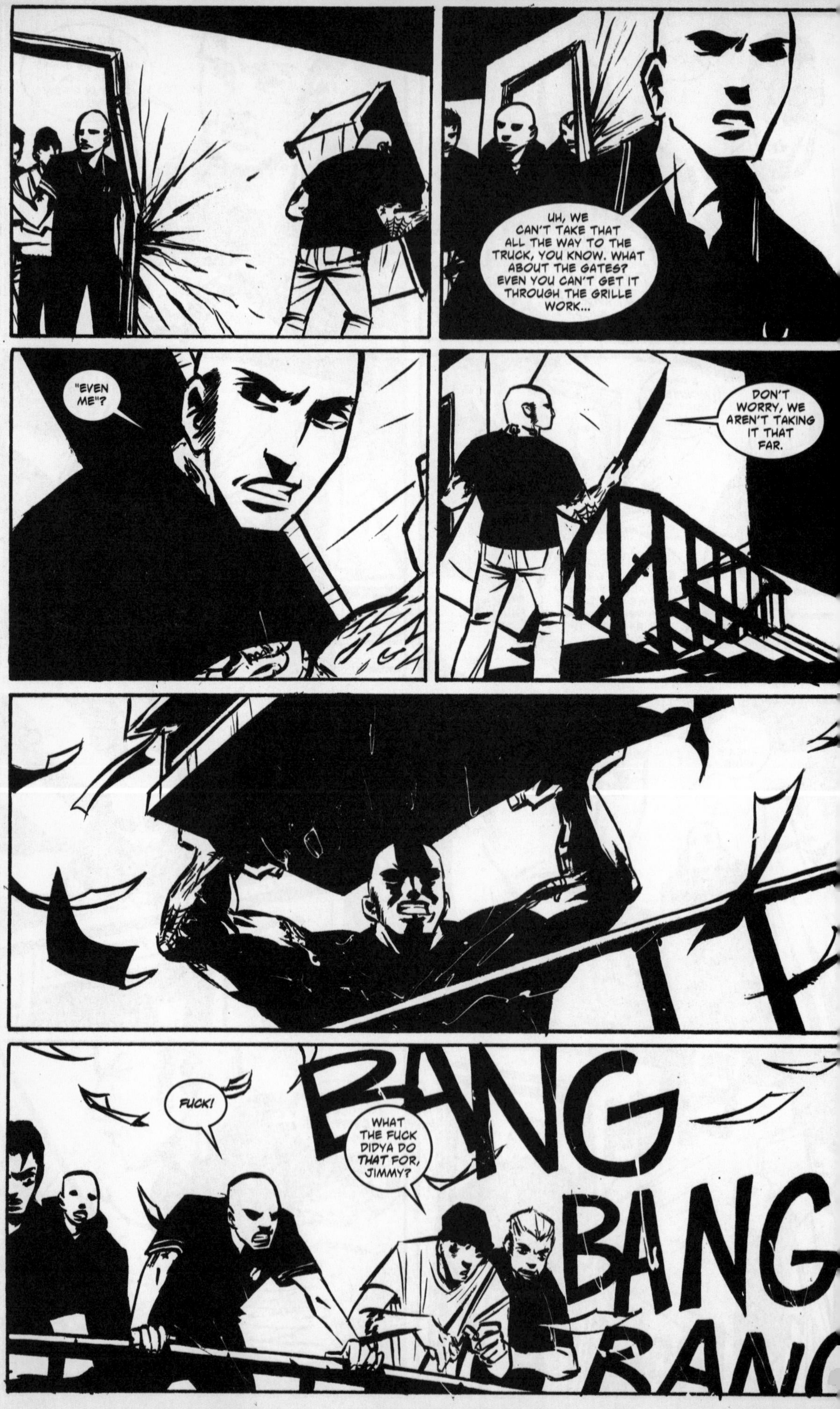
UH, WE CAN'T TAKE THAT ALL THE WAY TO THE TRUCK, YOU KNOW. WHAT ABOUT THE GATES? EVEN YOU CAN'T GET IT THROUGH THE GRILLE WORK...
"EVEN ME"?
DON'T WORRY, WE AREN'T TAKING IT THAT FAR.
BANG
BANG
FUCK!
WHAT THE FUCK DIDYA DO THAT FOR, JIMMY?

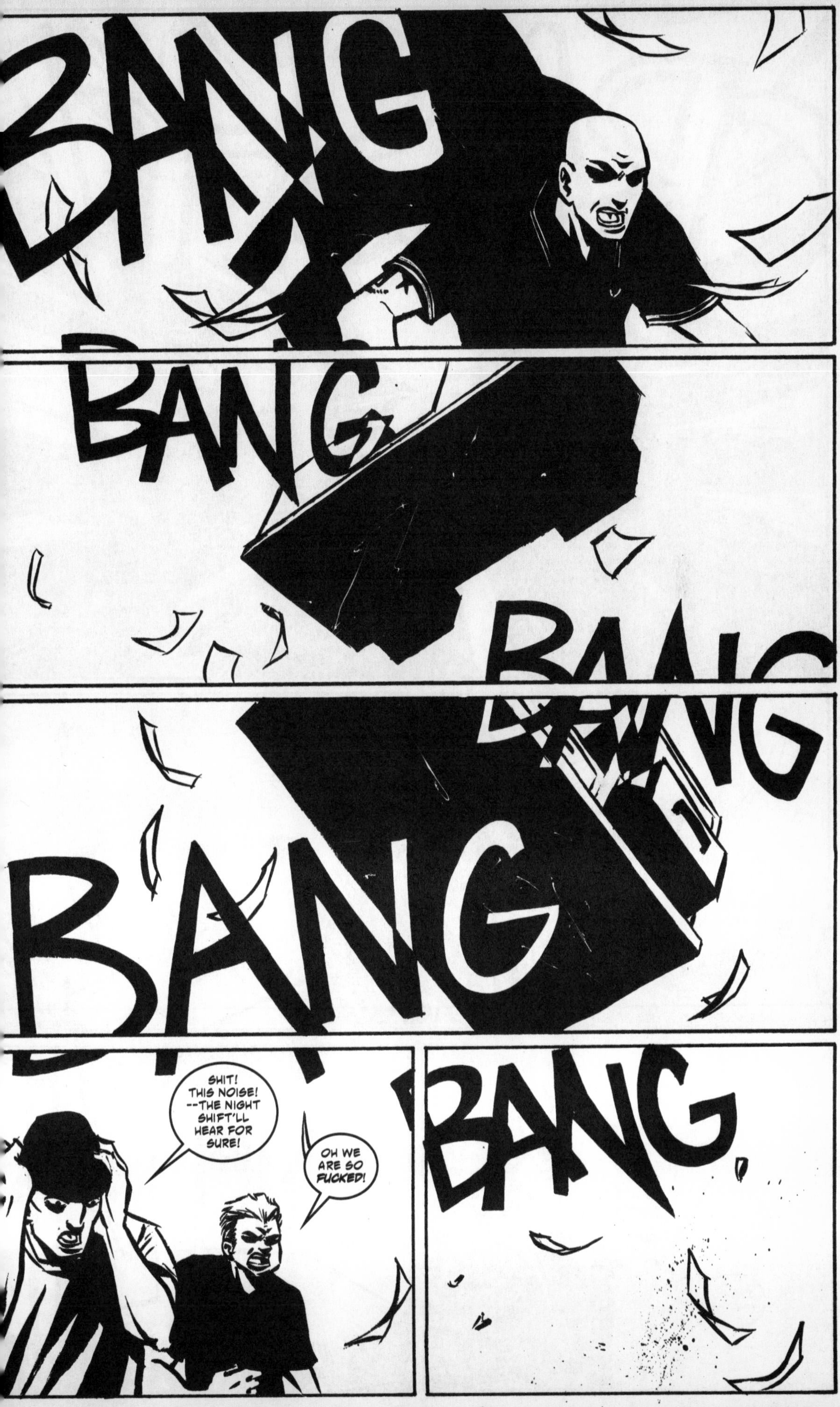
BANG
BANG
BANG
BANG
BANG
SHIT! THIS NOISE! --THE NIGHT SHIFT'LL HEAR FOR SURE!
OH WE ARE SO FUCKED!
BANG

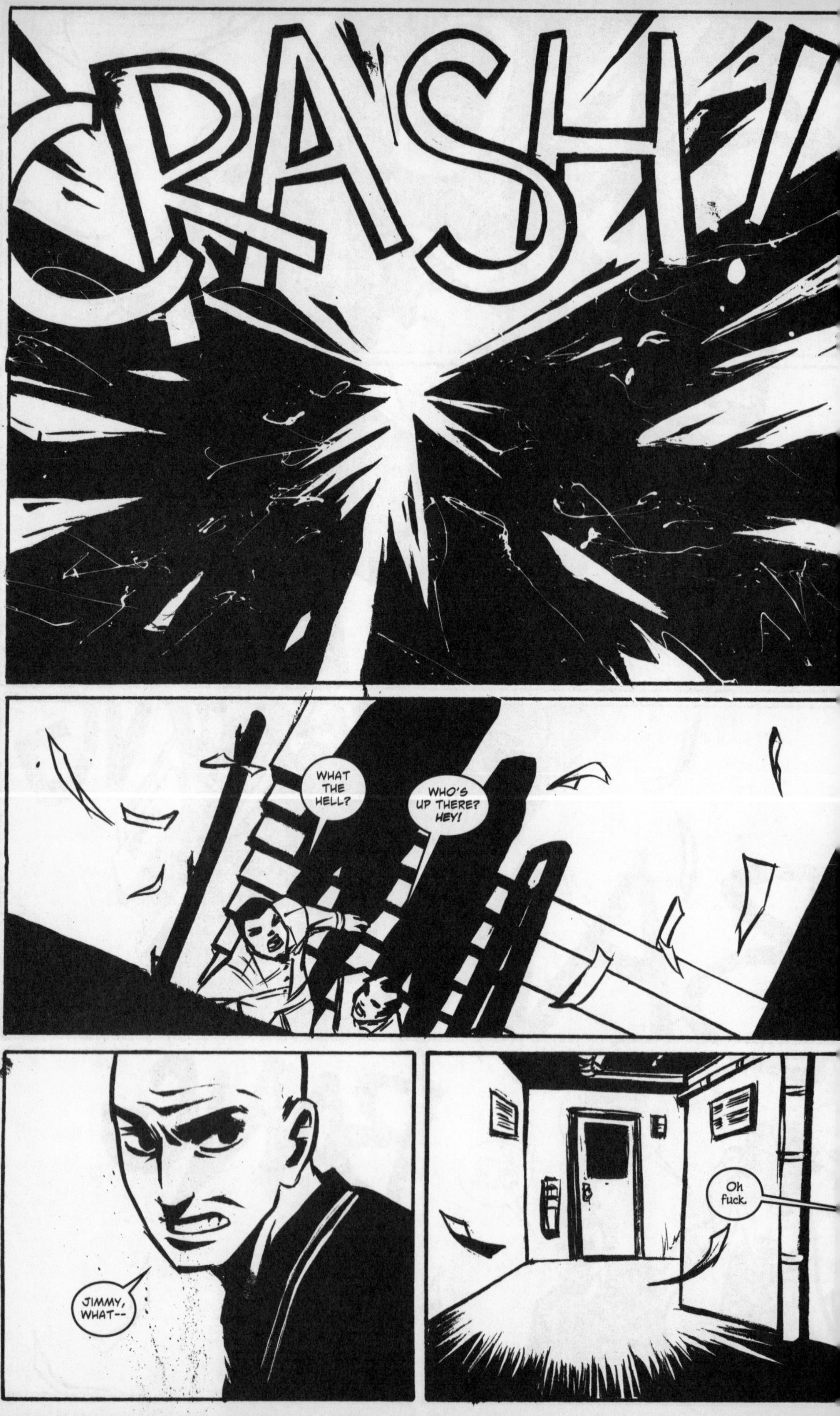
CRASH!
WHAT THE HELL?
WHO'S UP THERE? HEY!
JIMMY, WHAT--
Oh fuck.

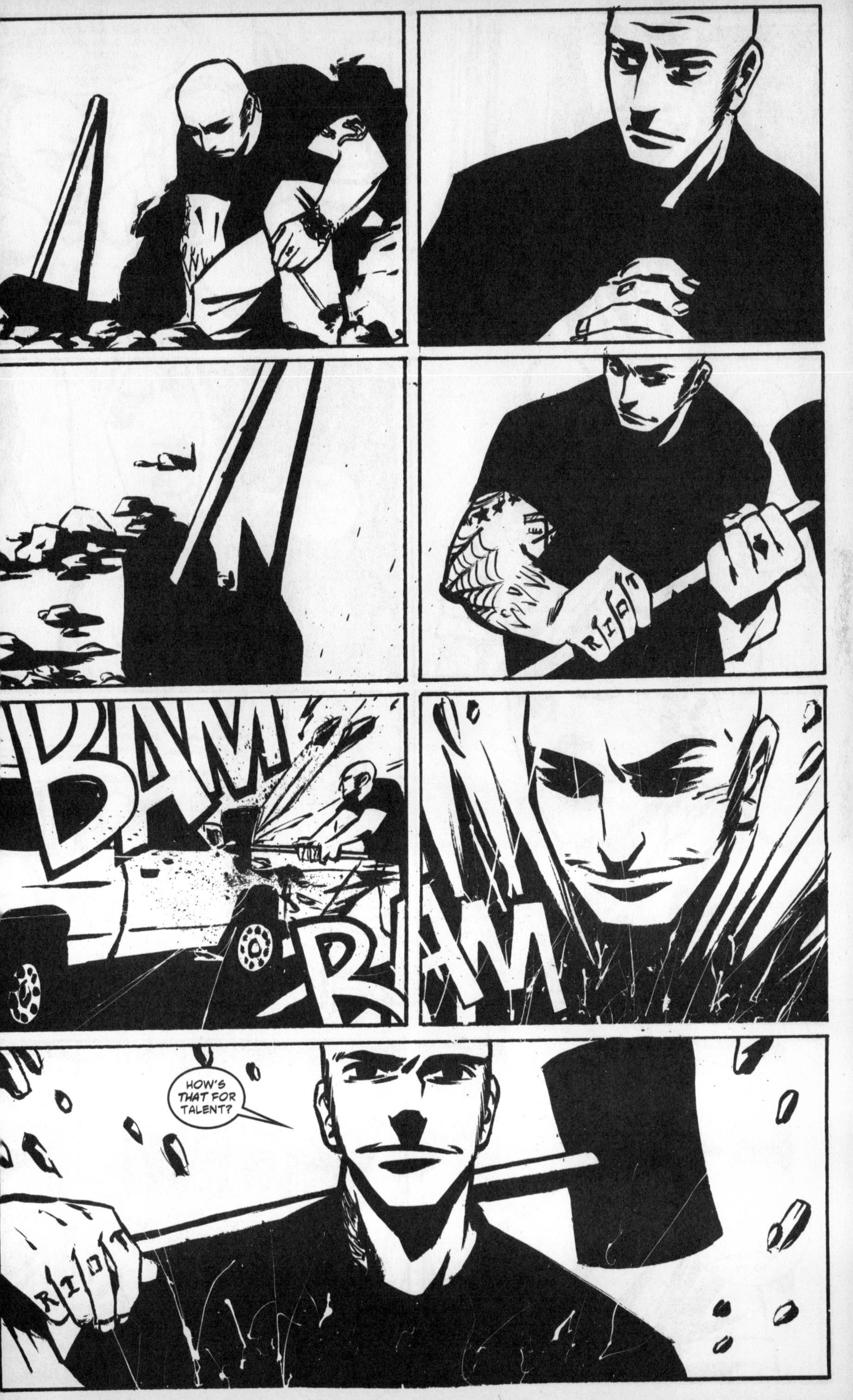
BAM
RIOT
BAM
HOW'S THAT FOR TALENT?
RIOT

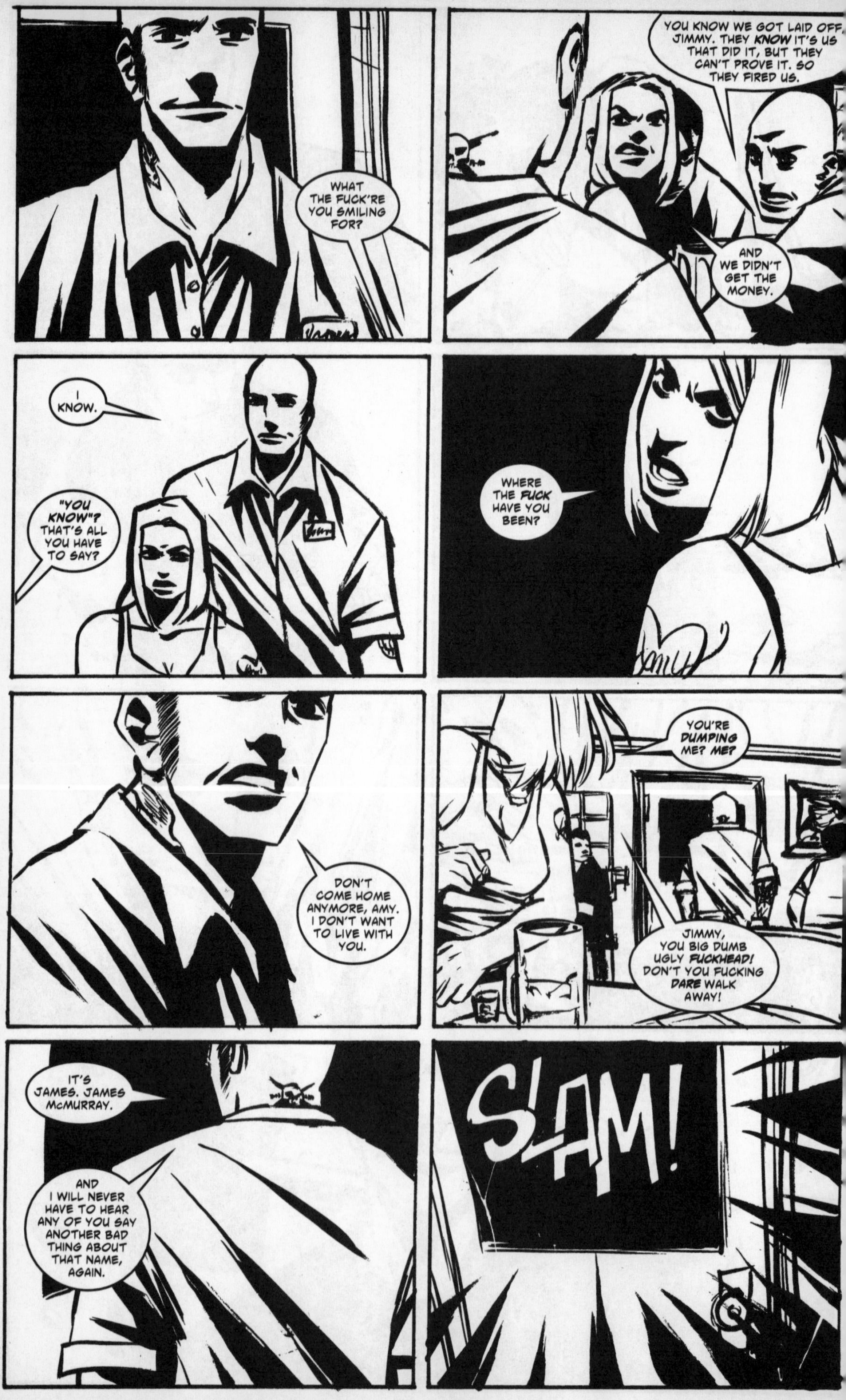
WHAT THE FUCK'RE YOU SMILING FOR?
YOU KNOW WE GOT LAID OFF, JIMMY. THEY KNOW IT'S US THAT DID IT, BUT THEY CAN'T PROVE IT. SO THEY FIRED US.
AND WE DIDN'T GET THE MONEY.
I KNOW.
"YOU KNOW"? THAT'S ALL YOU HAVE TO SAY?
WHERE THE FUCK HAVE YOU BEEN?
DON'T COME HOME ANYMORE, AMY. I DON'T WANT TO LIVE WITH YOU.
YOU'RE DUMPING ME? ME?
JIMMY, YOU BIG DUMB UGLY FUCKHEAD! DON'T YOU FUCKING DARE WALK AWAY!
IT'S JAMES. JAMES McMURRAY.
AND I WILL NEVER HAVE TO HEAR ANY OF YOU SAY ANOTHER BAD THING ABOUT THAT NAME, AGAIN.
SLAM!

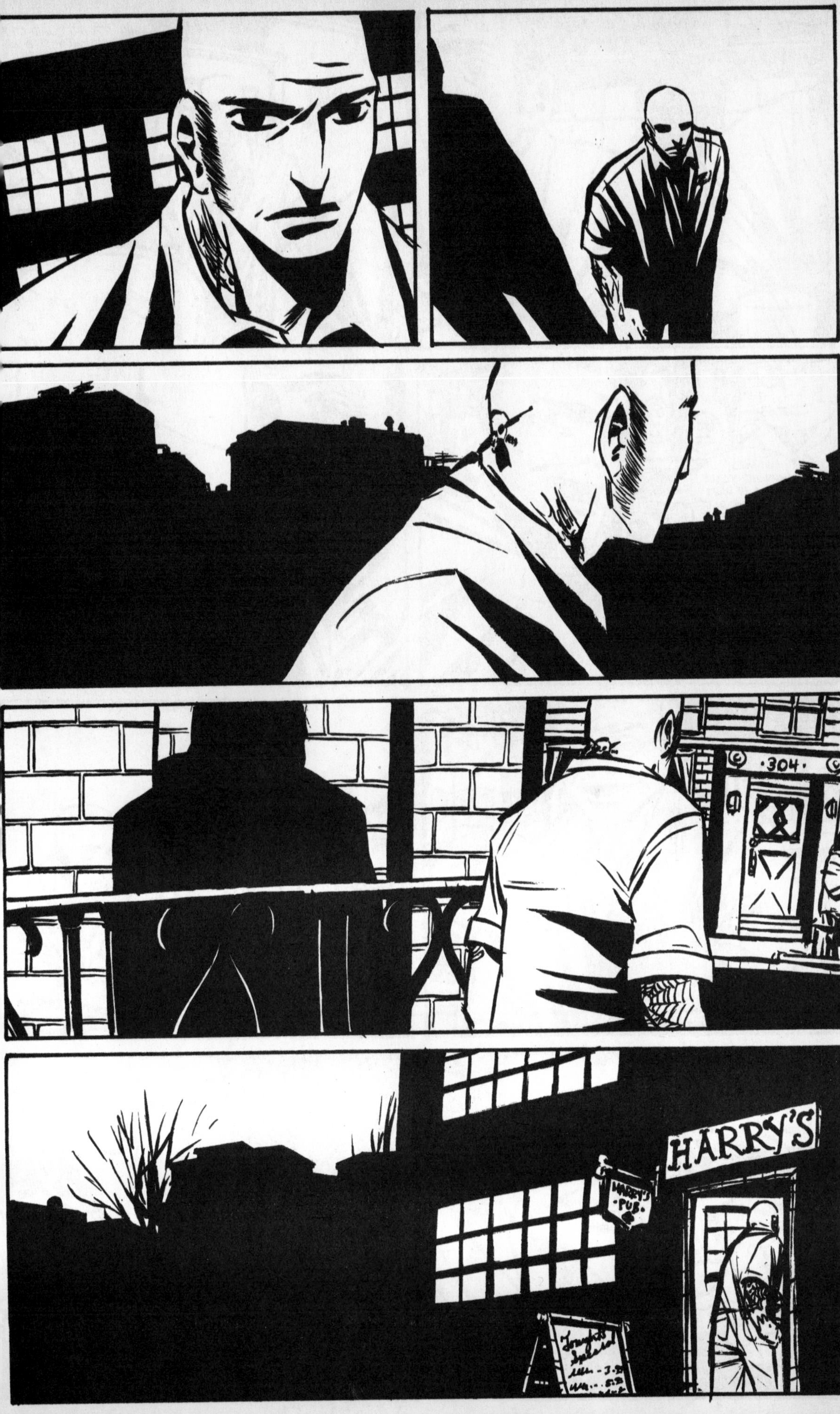
·304·
HARRY'S
HARRY'S PUB

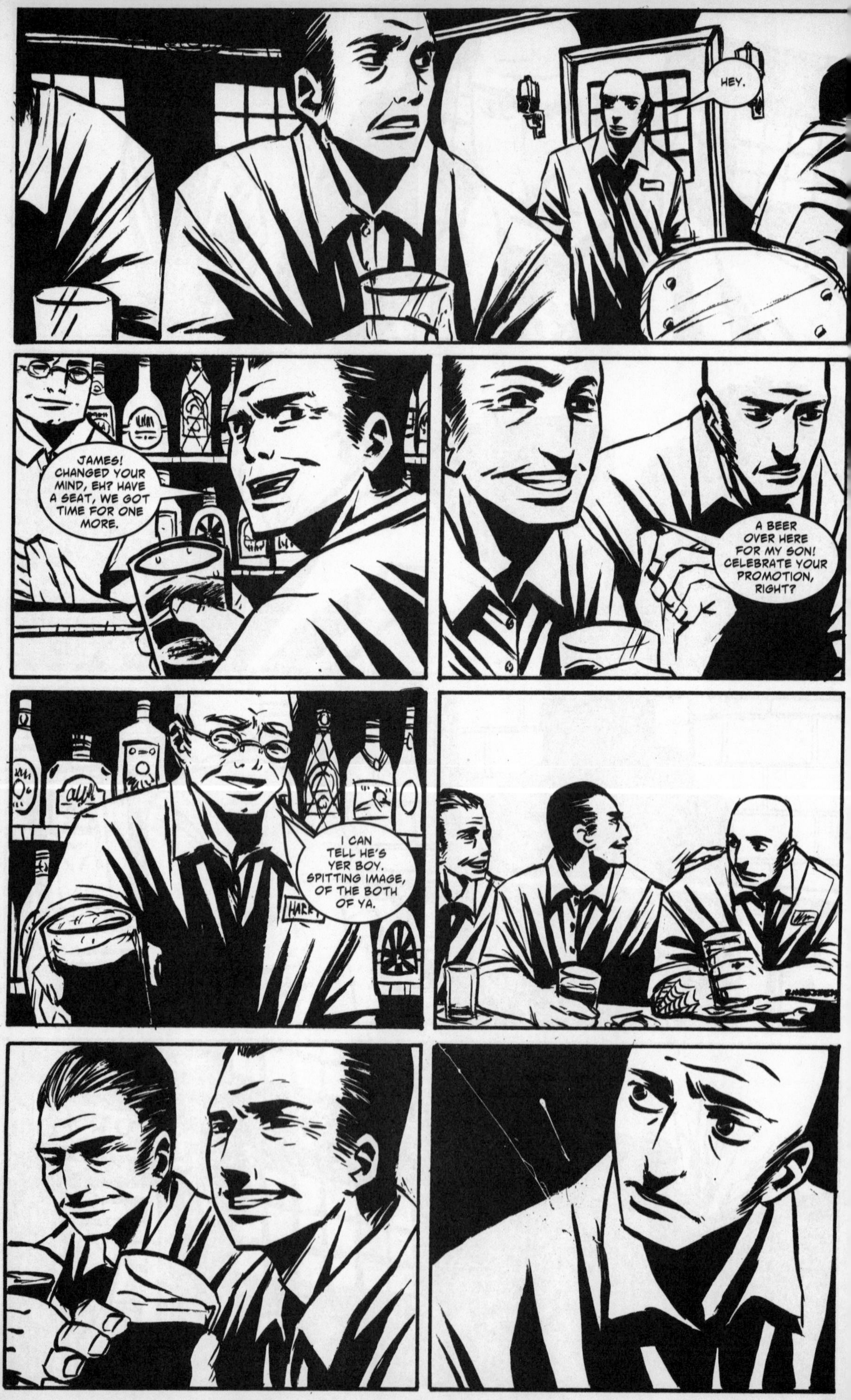
HEY.
JAMES! CHANGED YOUR MIND, EH? HAVE A SEAT, WE GOT TIME FOR ONE MORE.
A BEER OVER HERE FOR MY SON! CELEBRATE YOUR PROMOTION, RIGHT?
I CAN TELL HE'S YER BOY. SPITTING IMAGE, OF THE BOTH OF YA.

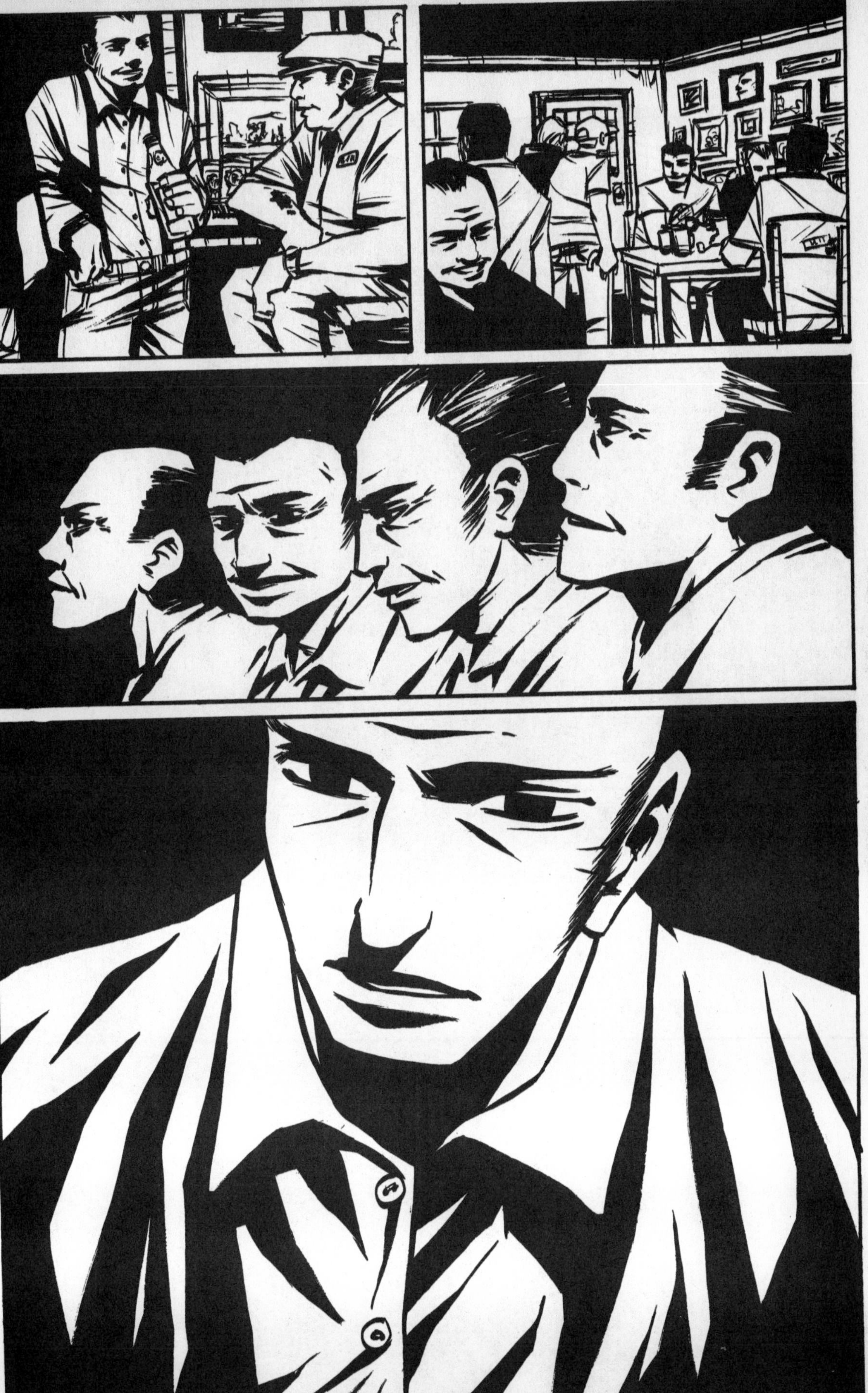

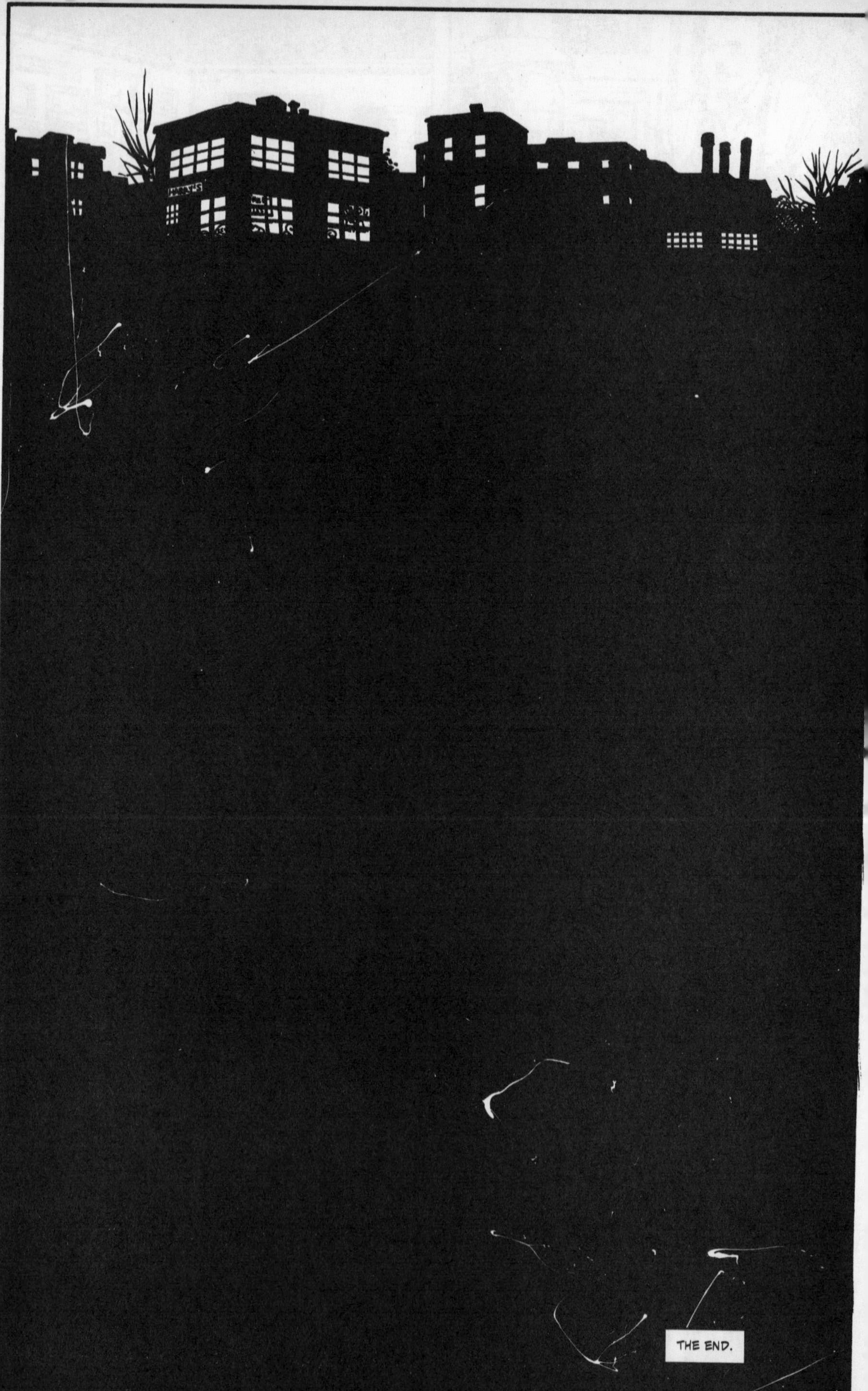

THE END.

5

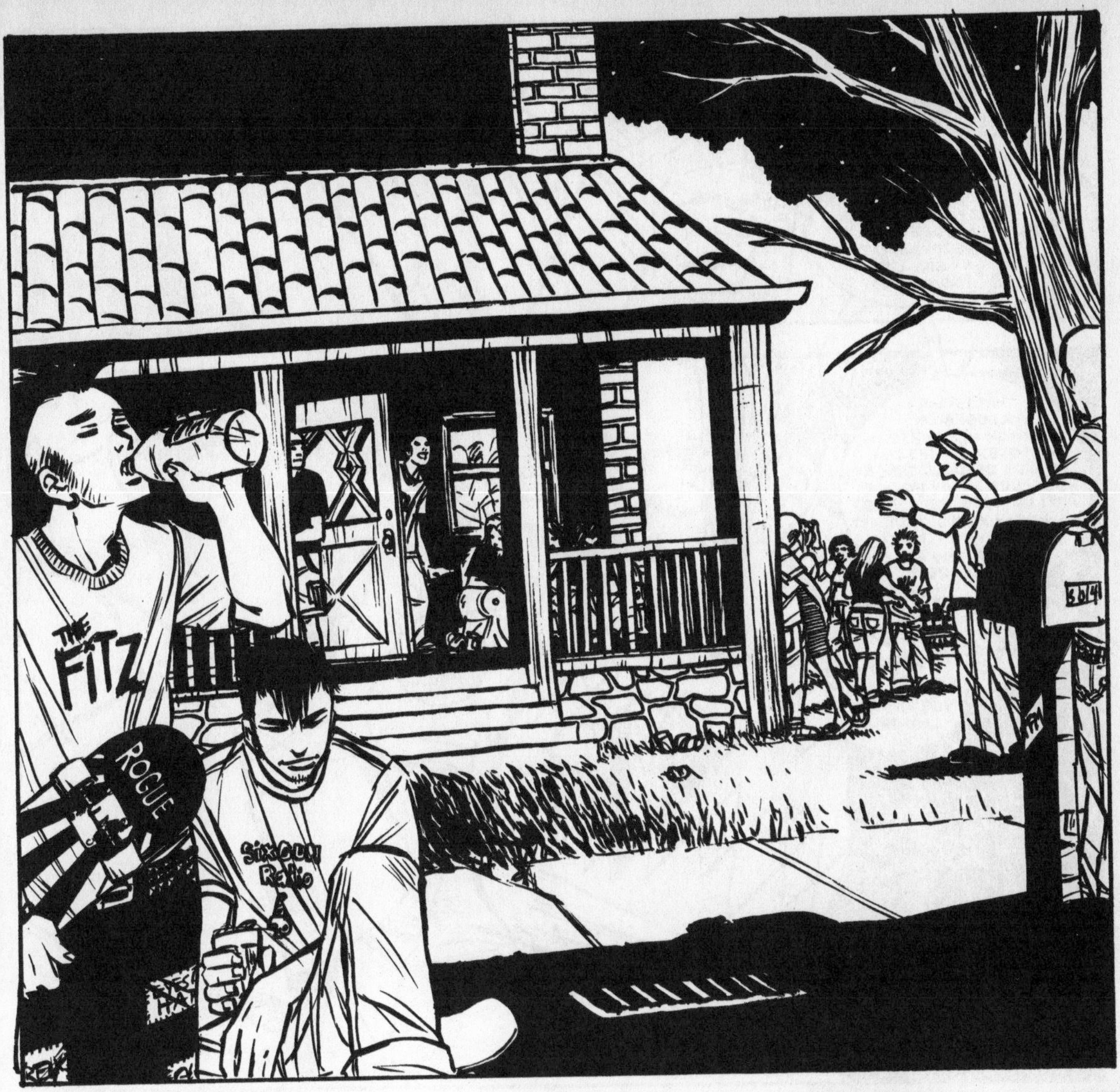
THE FITZ
ROGUE

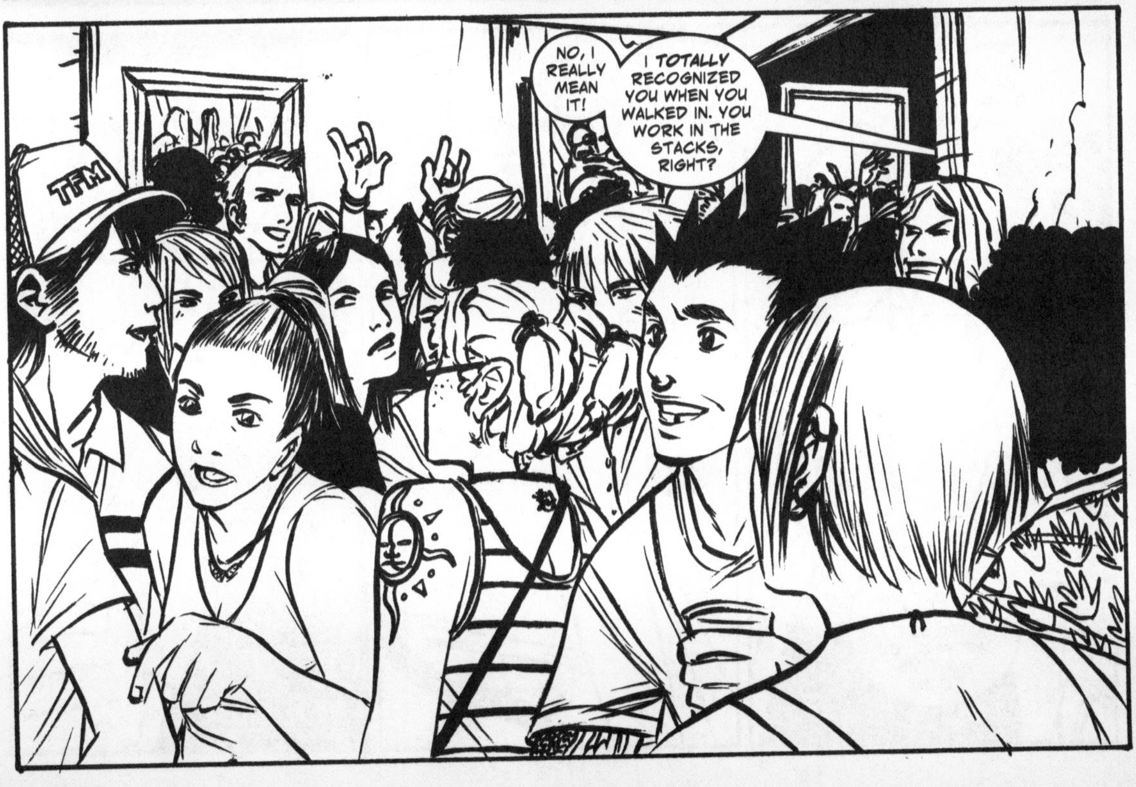
TFM
NO, I REALLY MEAN IT!
I TOTALLY RECOGNIZED YOU WHEN YOU WALKED IN. YOU WORK IN THE STACKS, RIGHT?

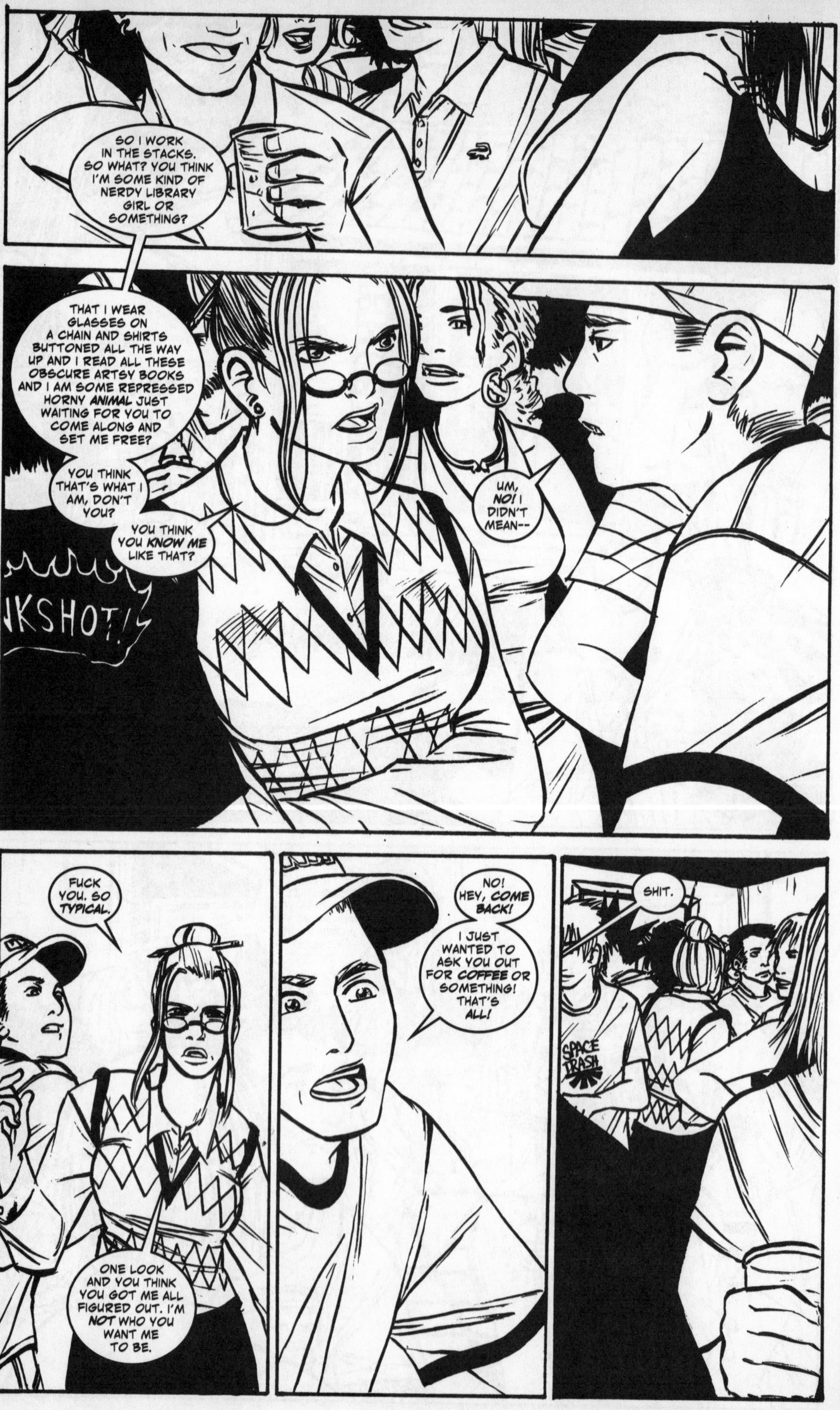
SO I WORK IN THE STACKS. SO WHAT? YOU THINK I'M SOME KIND OF NERDY LIBRARY GIRL OR SOMETHING?
THAT I WEAR GLASSES ON A CHAIN AND SHIRTS BUTTONED ALL THE WAY UP AND I READ ALL THESE OBSCURE ARTSY BOOKS AND I AM SOME REPRESSED HORNY ANIMAL JUST WAITING FOR YOU TO COME ALONG AND SET ME FREE?
YOU THINK THAT'S WHAT I AM, DON'T YOU?
YOU THINK YOU KNOW ME LIKE THAT?
UM, NO! I DIDN'T MEAN--
NKSHOT!
FUCK YOU. SO TYPICAL.
ONE LOOK AND YOU THINK YOU GOT ME ALL FIGURED OUT. I'M NOT WHO YOU WANT ME TO BE.
NO! HEY, COME BACK!
I JUST WANTED TO ASK YOU OUT FOR COFFEE OR SOMETHING! THAT'S ALL!
SHIT.
SPACE TRASH

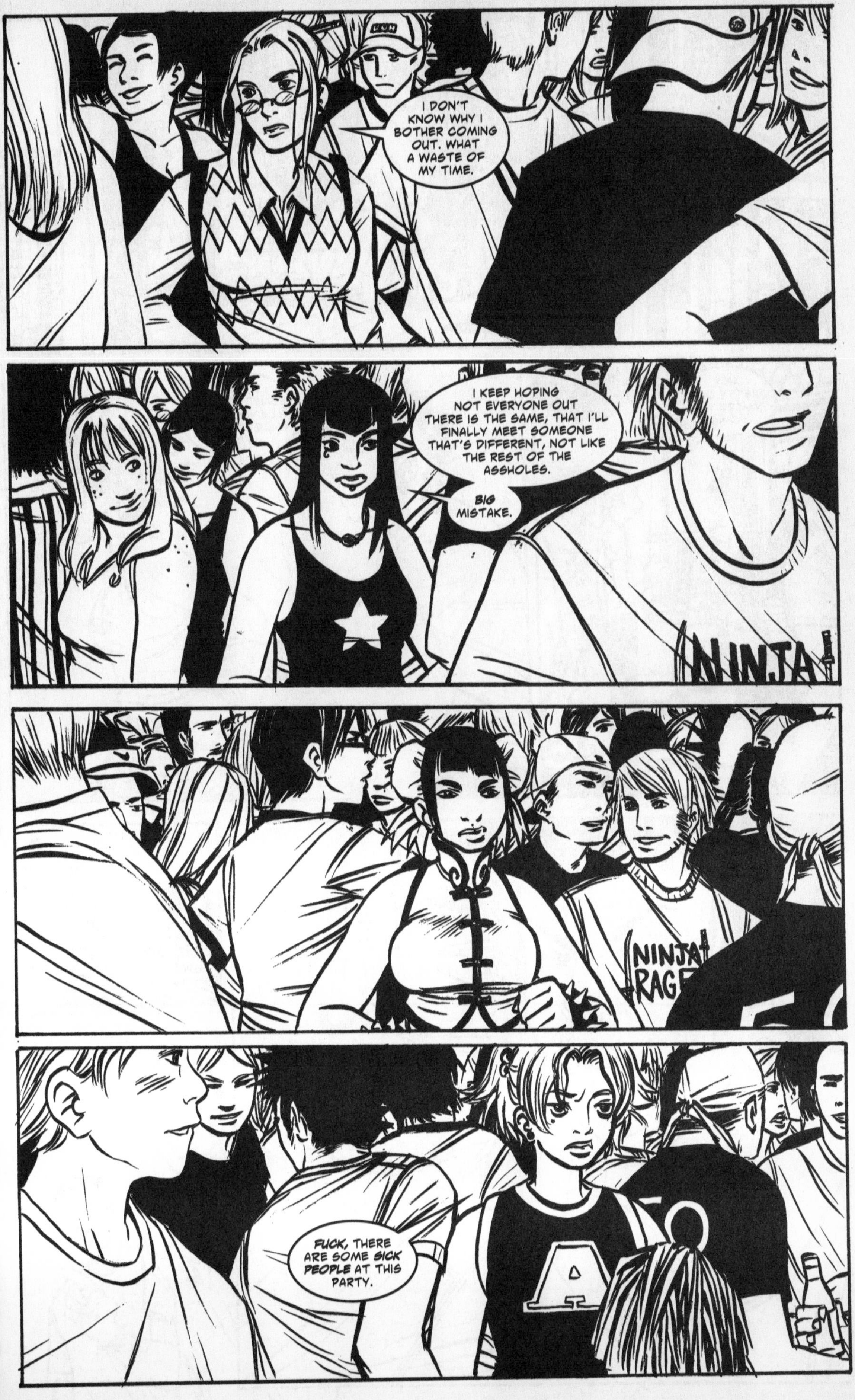
I DON'T KNOW WHY I BOTHER COMING OUT. WHAT A WASTE OF MY TIME.
I KEEP HOPING NOT EVERYONE OUT THERE IS THE SAME, THAT I'LL FINALLY MEET SOMEONE THAT'S DIFFERENT, NOT LIKE THE REST OF THE ASSHOLES.
BIG MISTAKE.
NINJA
FUCK, THERE ARE SOME SICK PEOPLE AT THIS PARTY.

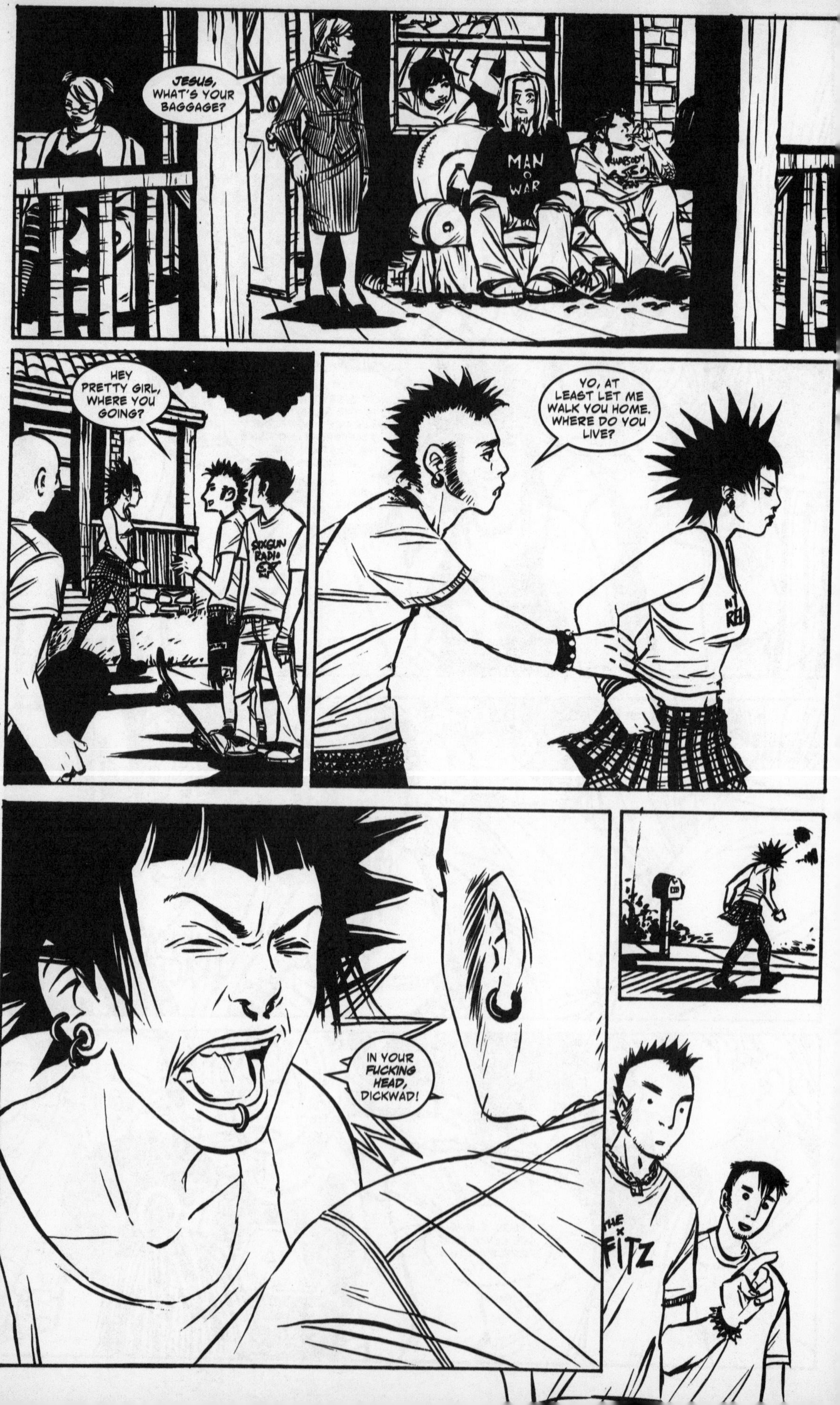
JESUS, WHAT'S YOUR BAGGAGE?
MAN O WAR
HEY PRETTY GIRL, WHERE YOU GOING?
SIXGUN RADIO
YO, AT LEAST LET ME WALK YOU HOME. WHERE DO YOU LIVE?
IN YOUR FUCKING HEAD, DICKWAD!
THE FITZ

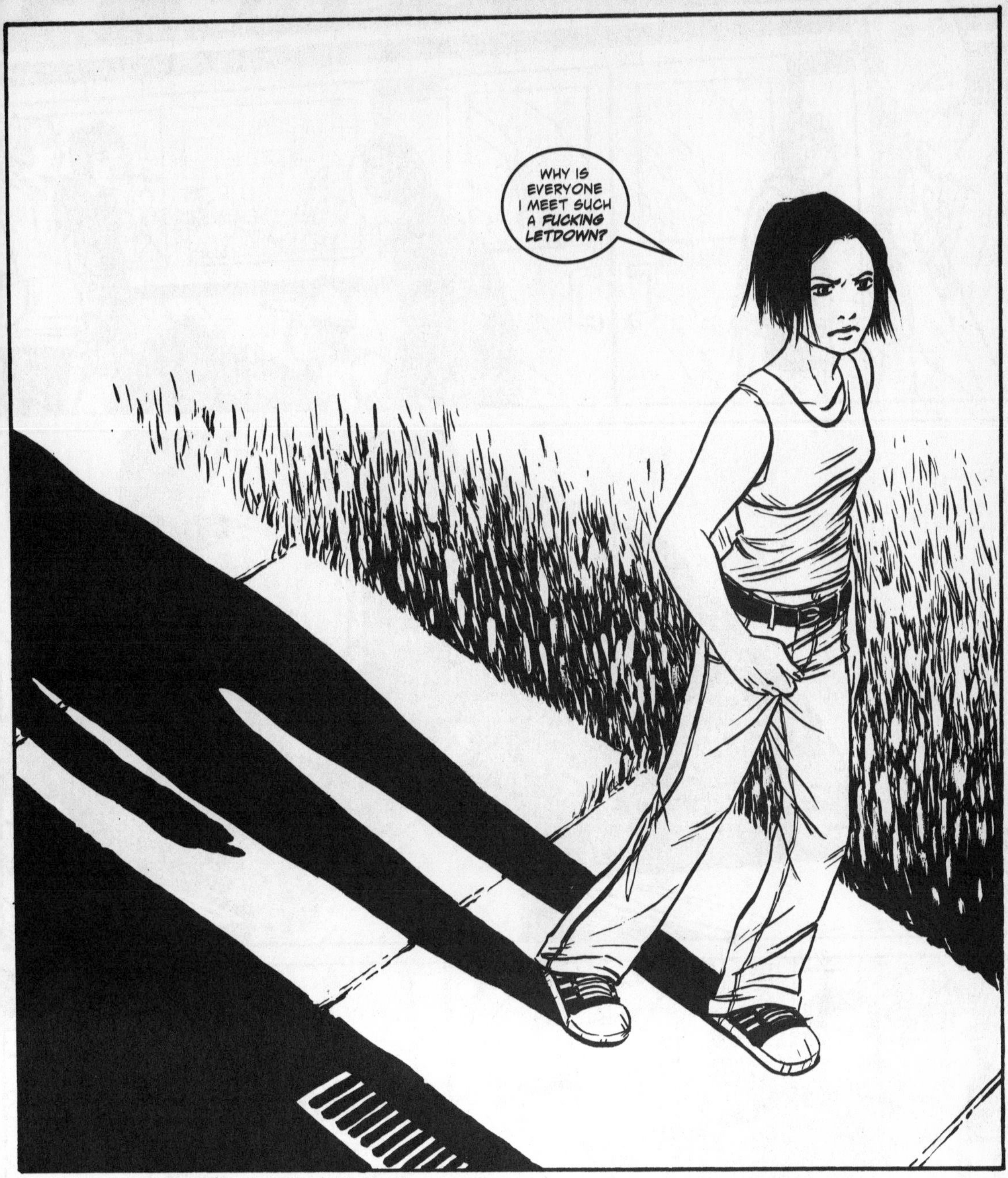
WHY IS EVERYONE I MEET SUCH A FUCKING LETDOWN?

"Girl You Want"

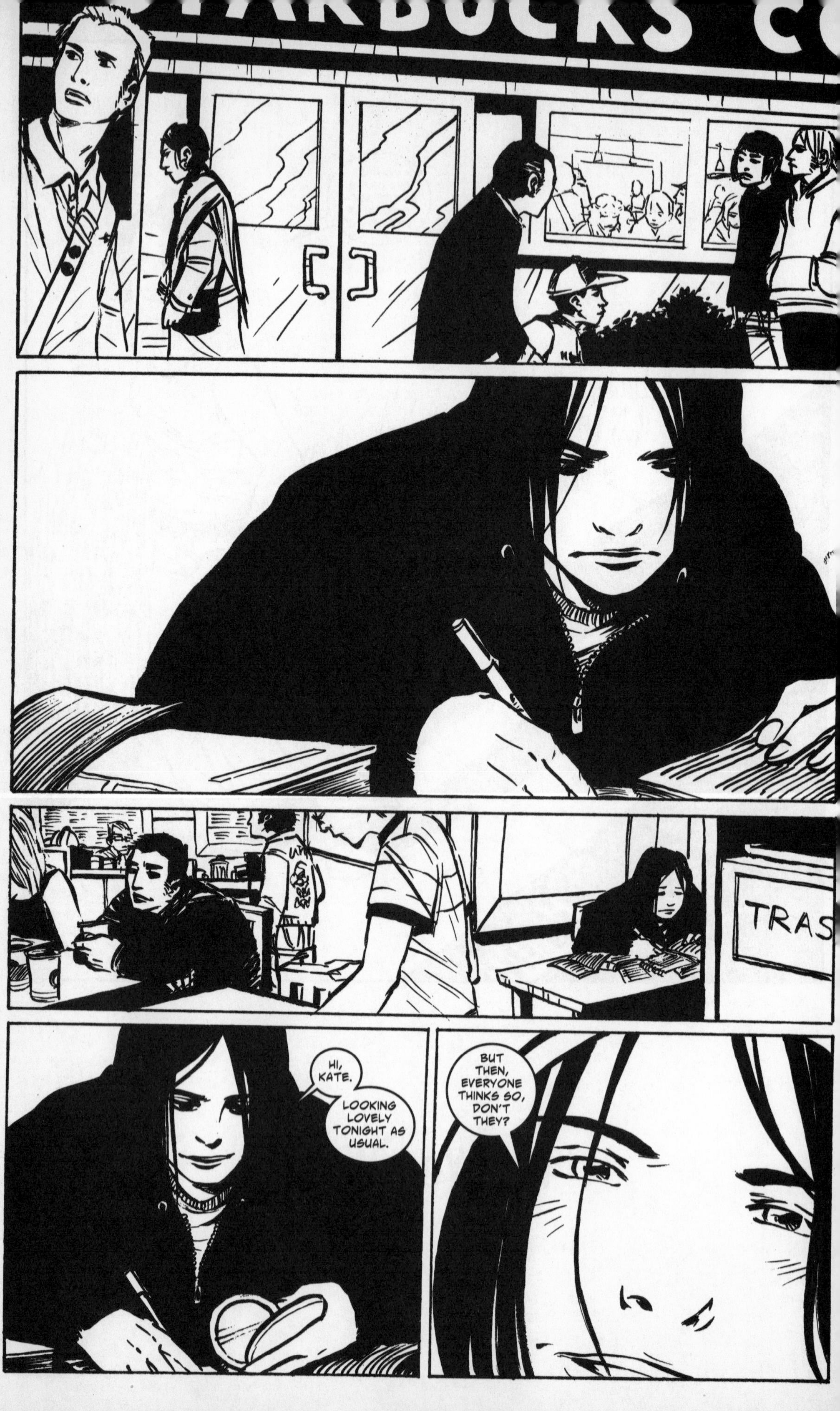
HI, KATE.
LOOKING LOVELY TONIGHT AS USUAL.
BUT THEN, EVERYONE THINKS SO, DON'T THEY?

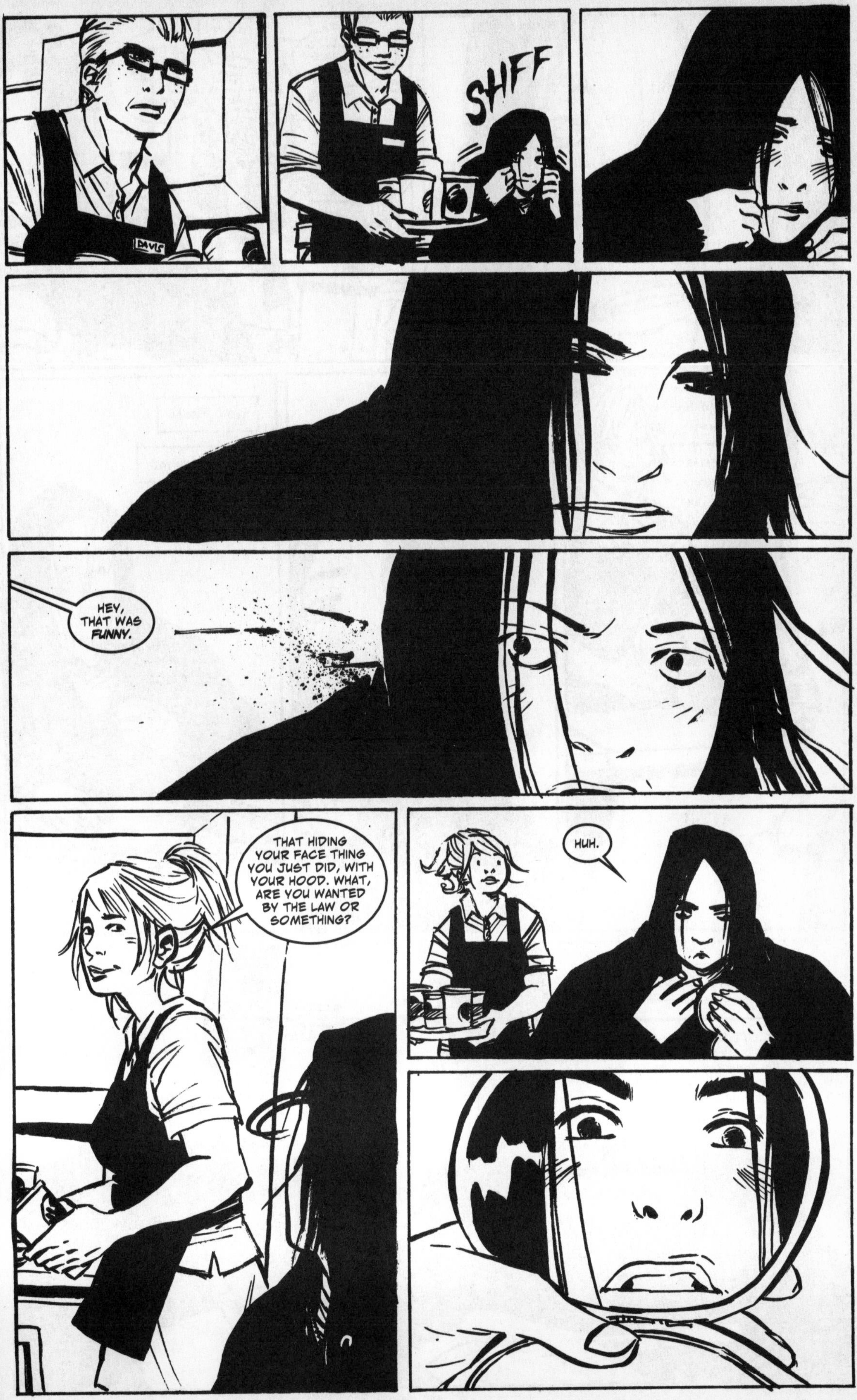
DAVIS
SHFF
HEY, THAT WAS FUNNY.
THAT HIDING YOUR FACE THING YOU JUST DID, WITH YOUR HOOD. WHAT, ARE YOU WANTED BY THE LAW OR SOMETHING?
HUH.

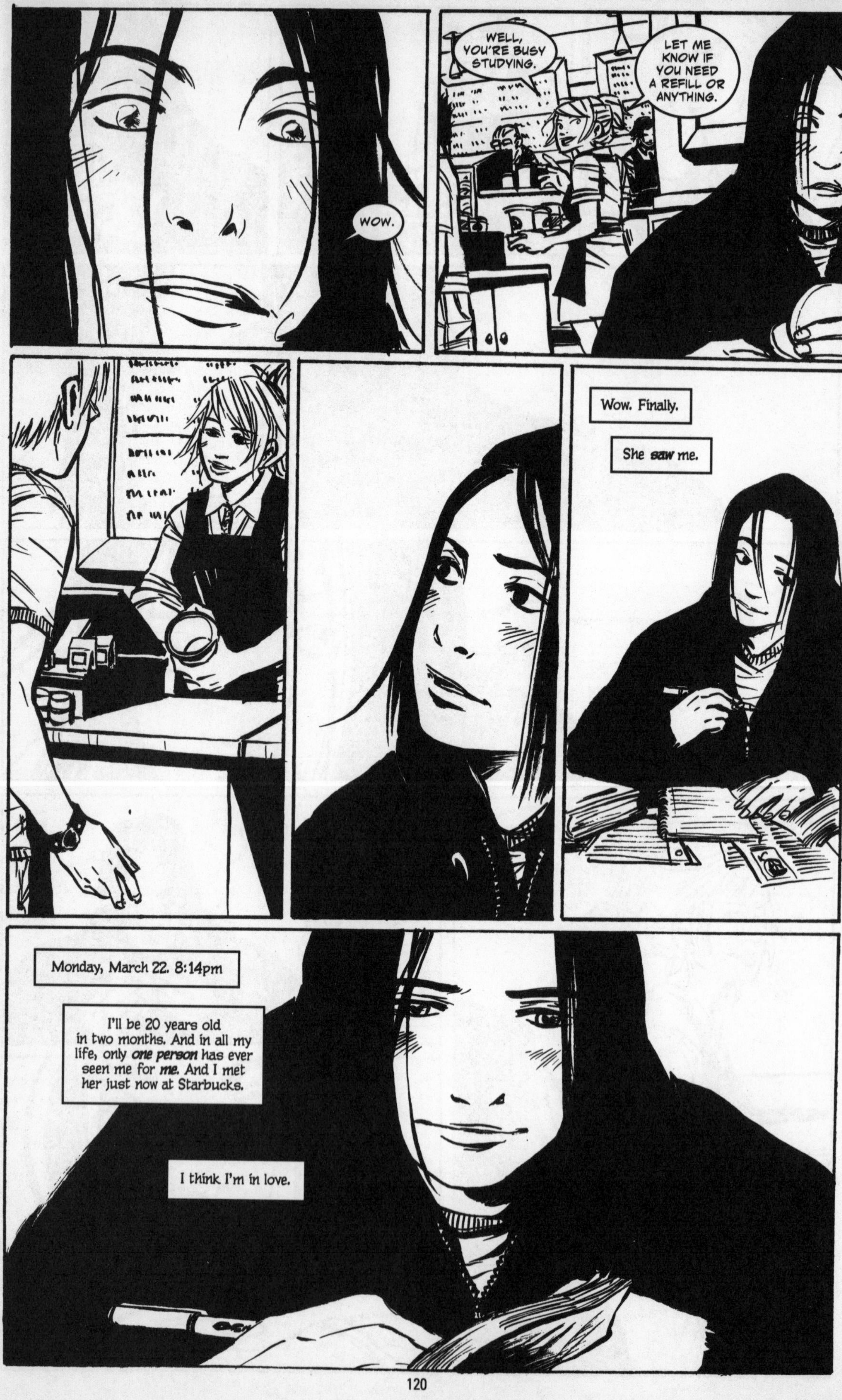
WOW.
WELL, YOU'RE BUSY STUDYING.
LET ME KNOW IF YOU NEED A REFILL OR ANYTHING.
Wow. Finally.
She *saw* me.
Monday, March 22. 8:14pm
I'll be 20 years old in two months. And in all my life, only *one person* has ever seen me for *me*. And I met her just now at Starbucks.
I think I'm in love.

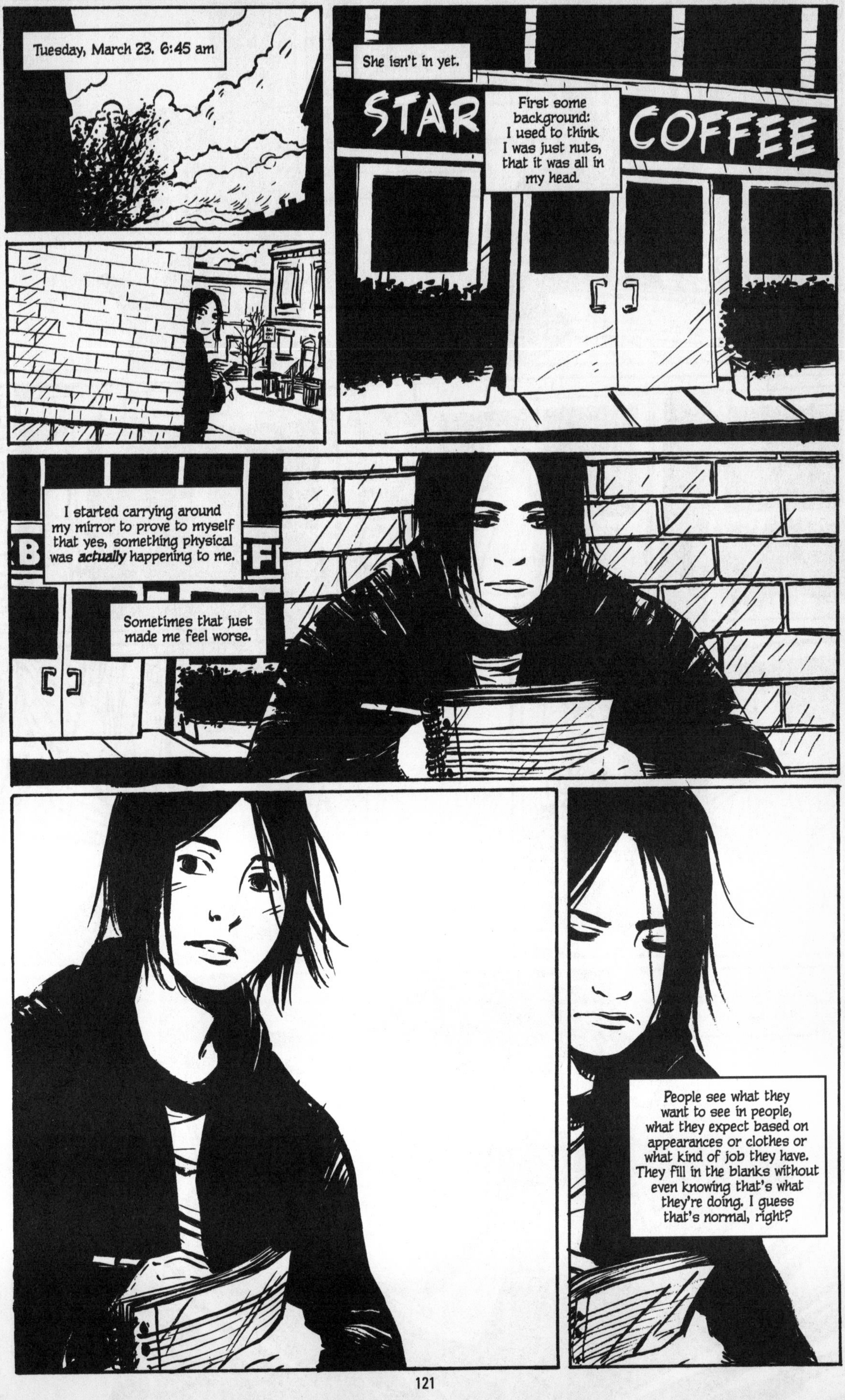
Tuesday, March 23. 6:45 am
She isn't in yet.
STAR COFFEE
First some background: I used to think I was just nuts, that it was all in my head.
I started carrying around my mirror to prove to myself that yes, something physical was *actually* happening to me.
Sometimes that just made me feel worse.
People see what they want to see in people, what they expect based on appearances or clothes or what kind of job they have. They fill in the blanks without even knowing that's what they're doing. I guess that's normal, right?

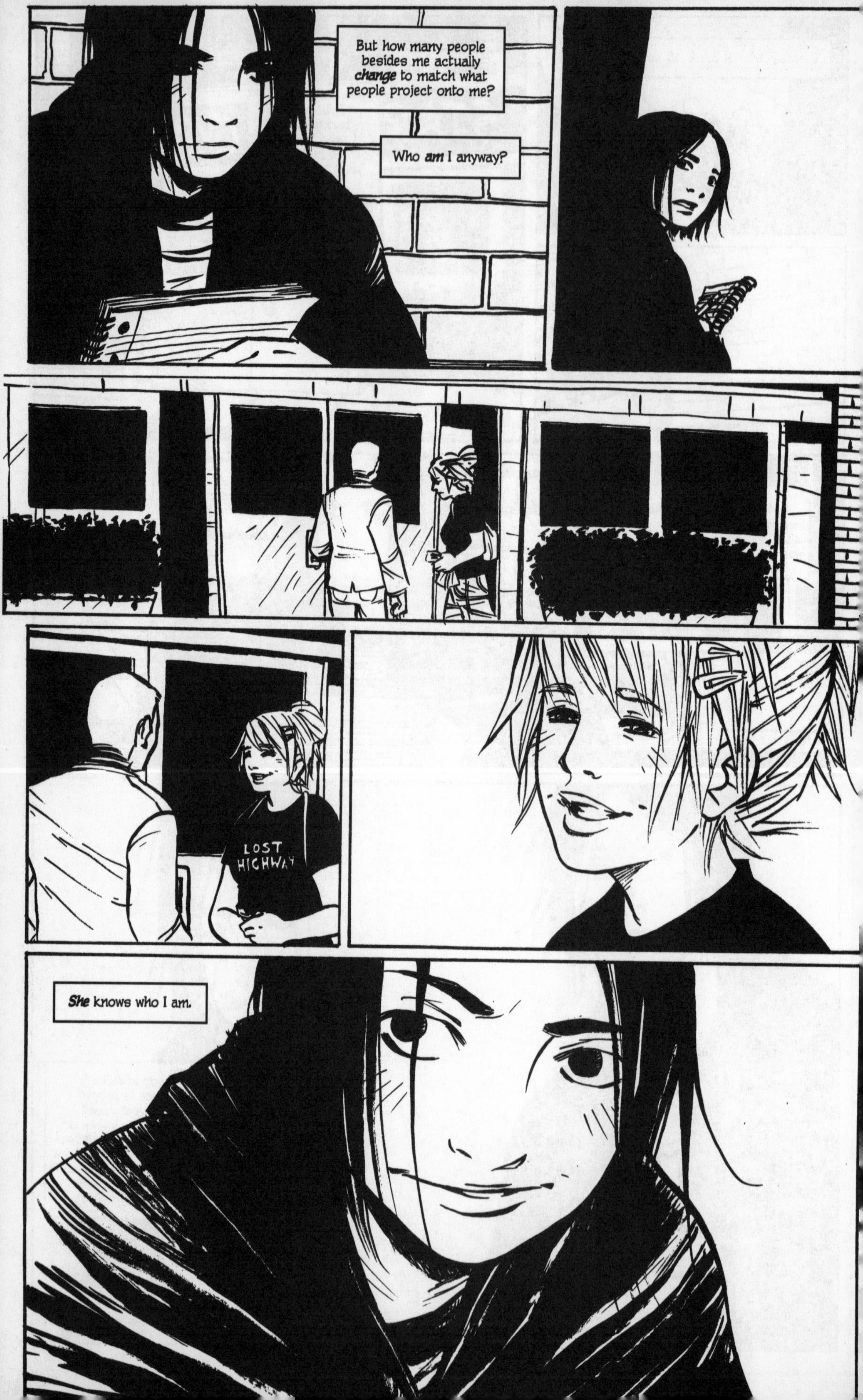
But how many people besides me actually *change* to match what people project onto me?
Who *am* I anyway?
LOST HIGHWAY
She knows who I am.

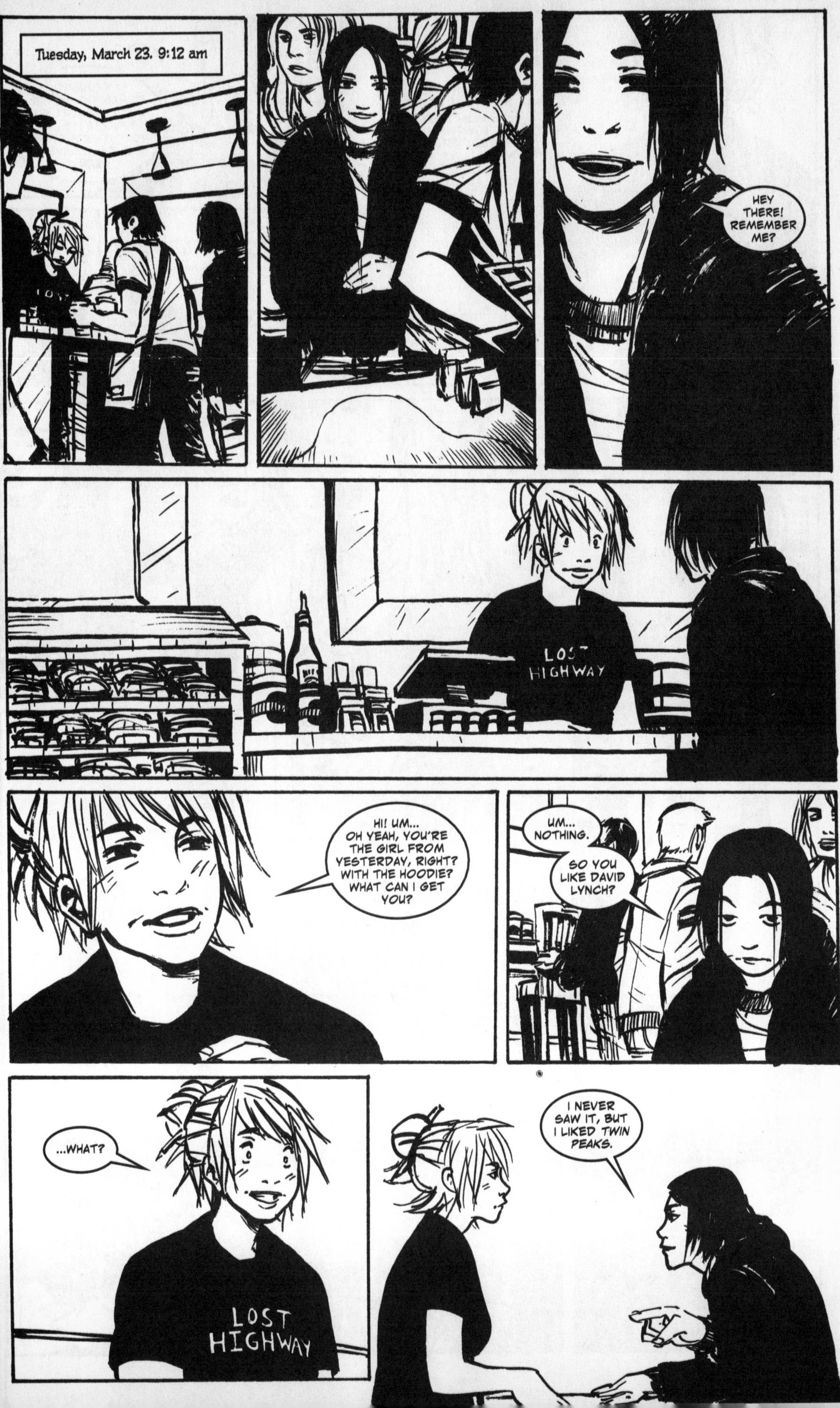
Tuesday, March 23. 9:12 am
HEY THERE! REMEMBER ME?
LOST HIGHWAY
HI! UM... OH YEAH, YOU'RE THE GIRL FROM YESTERDAY, RIGHT? WITH THE HOODIE? WHAT CAN I GET YOU?
UM... NOTHING.
SO YOU LIKE DAVID LYNCH?
...WHAT?
LOST HIGHWAY
I NEVER SAW IT, BUT I LIKED TWIN PEAKS.

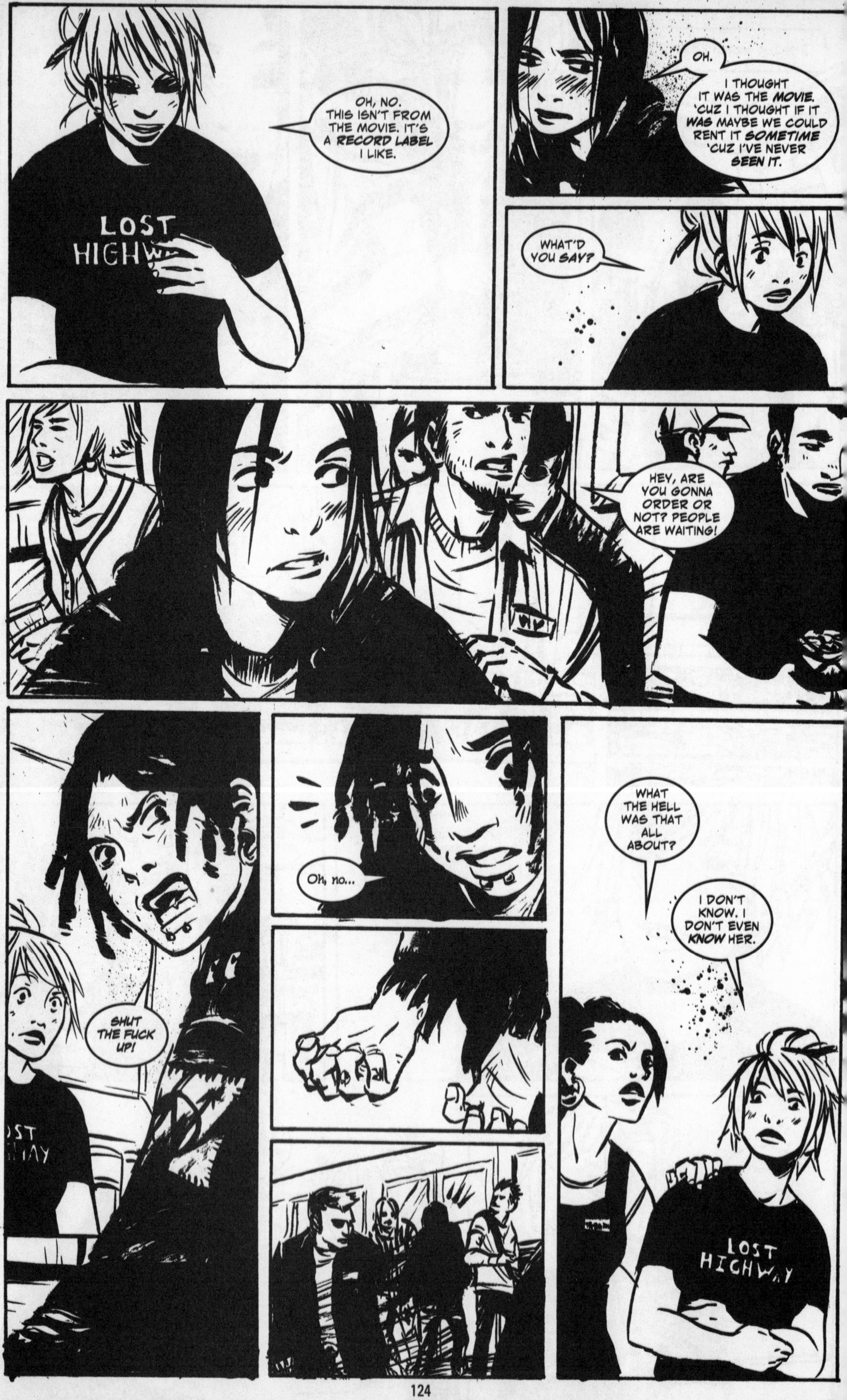
OH, NO. THIS ISN'T FROM THE MOVIE. IT'S A RECORD LABEL I LIKE.
LOST HIGHW
OH.
I THOUGHT IT WAS THE MOVIE. 'CUZ I THOUGHT IF IT WAS MAYBE WE COULD RENT IT SOMETIME 'CUZ I'VE NEVER SEEN IT.
WHAT'D YOU SAY?
HEY, ARE YOU GONNA ORDER OR NOT? PEOPLE ARE WAITING!
SHUT THE FUCK UP!
Oh, no...
WHAT THE HELL WAS THAT ALL ABOUT?
I DON'T KNOW. I DON'T EVEN KNOW HER.
LOST HIGHWAY

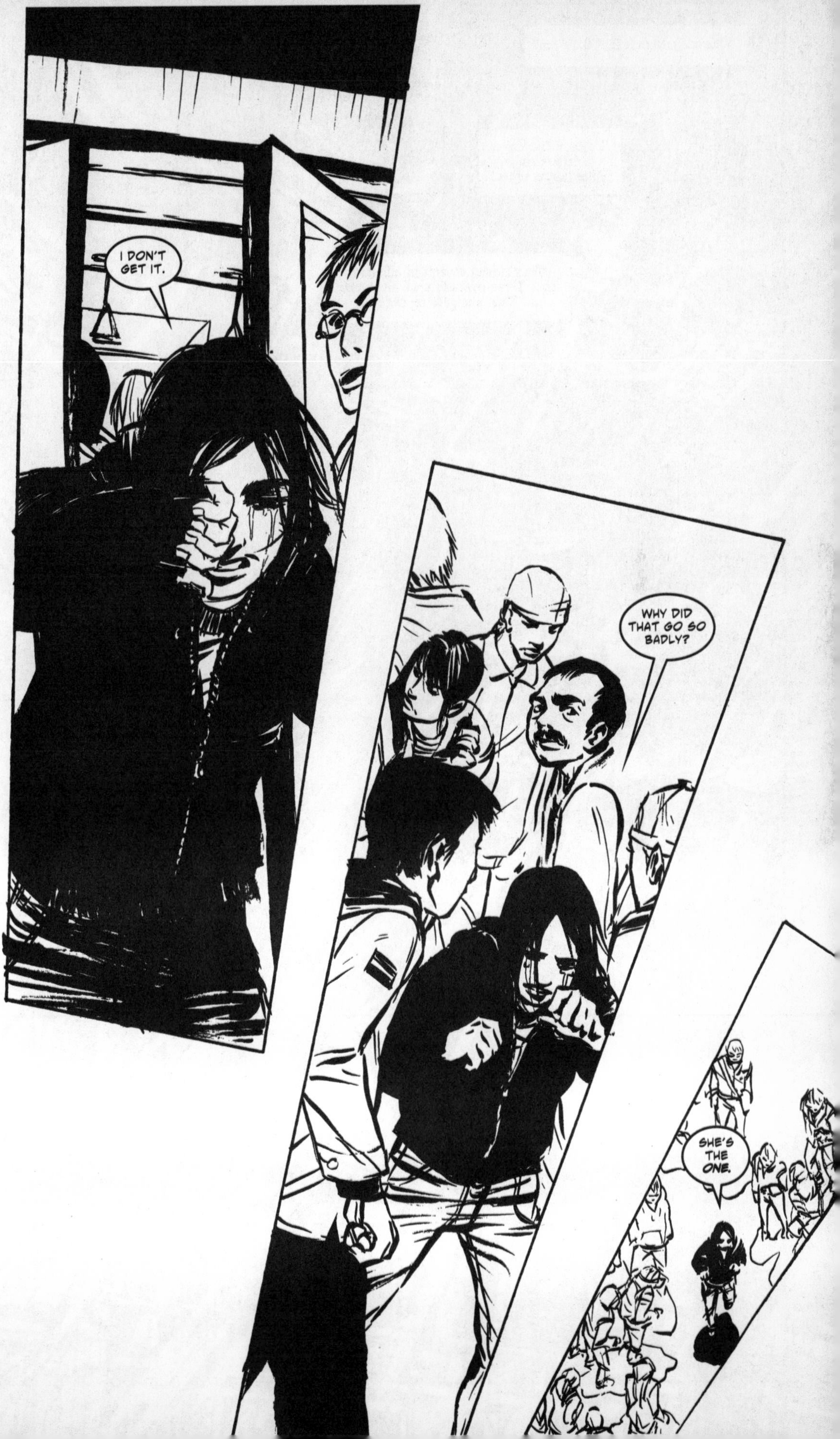
I DON'T GET IT.
WHY DID THAT GO SO BADLY?
SHE'S THE ONE.

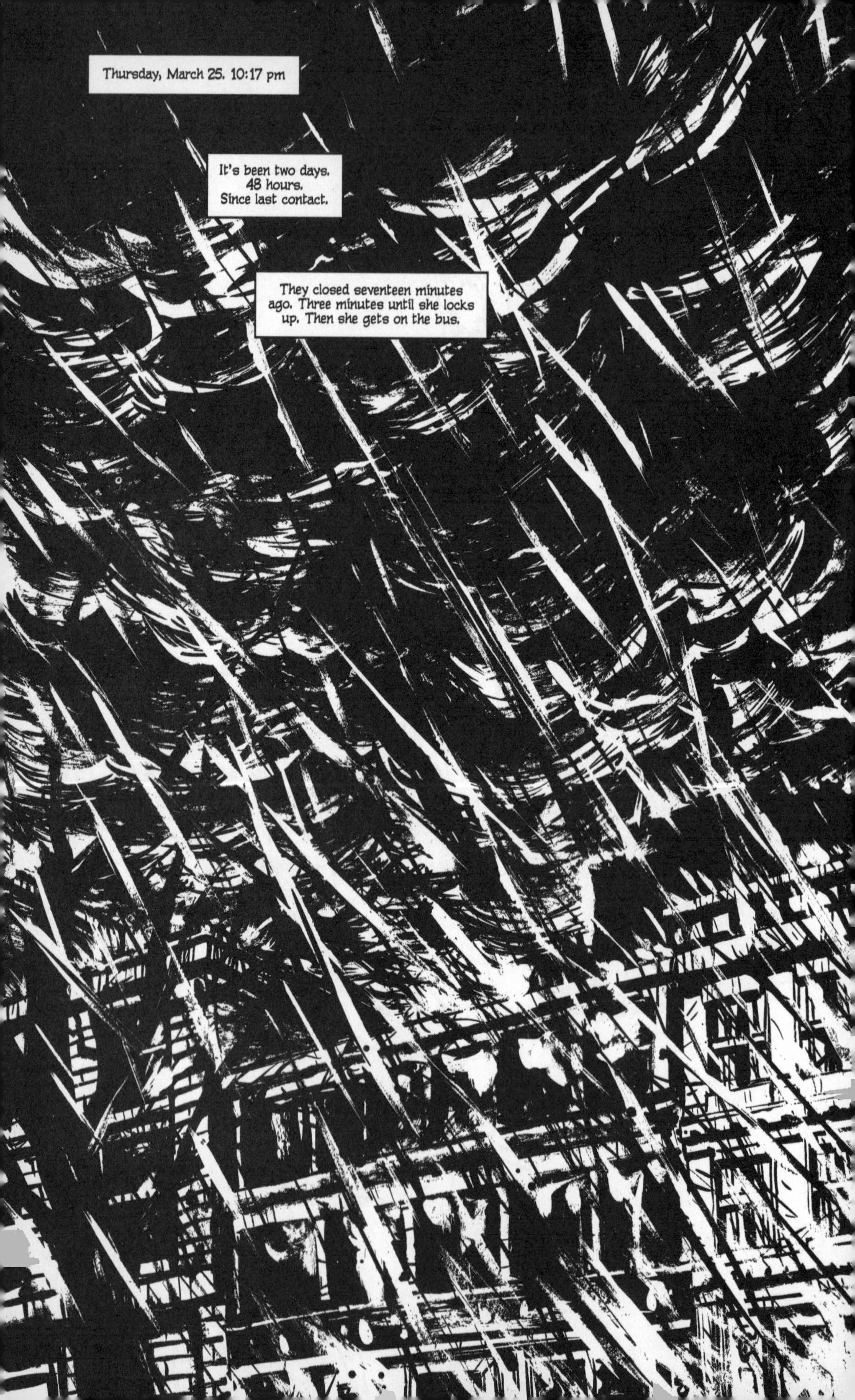
Thursday, March 25. 10:17 pm
It's been two days. 48 hours. Since last contact.
They closed seventeen minutes ago. Three minutes until she locks up. Then she gets on the bus.

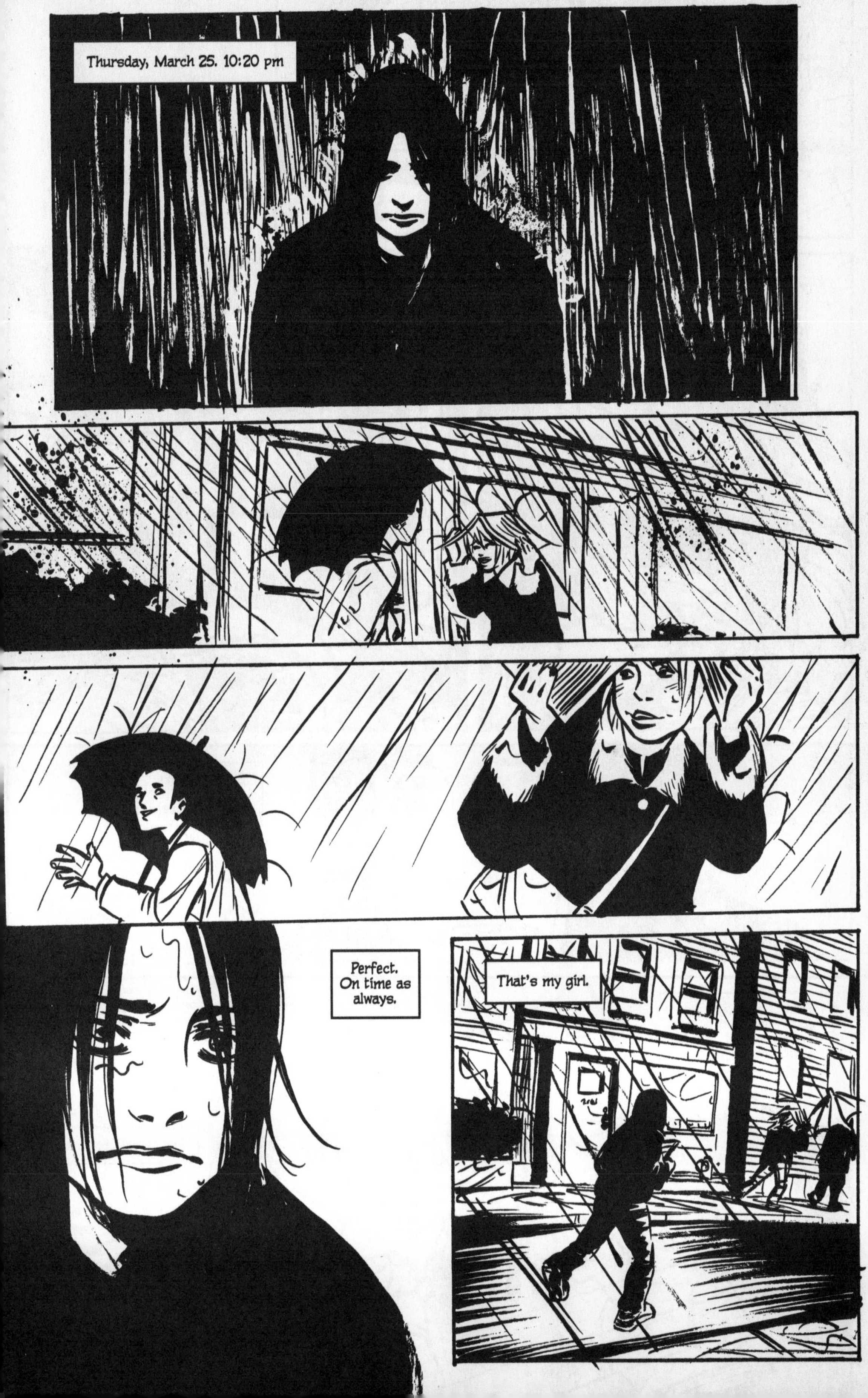
Thursday, March 25. 10:20 pm
Perfect. On time as always.
That's my girl.

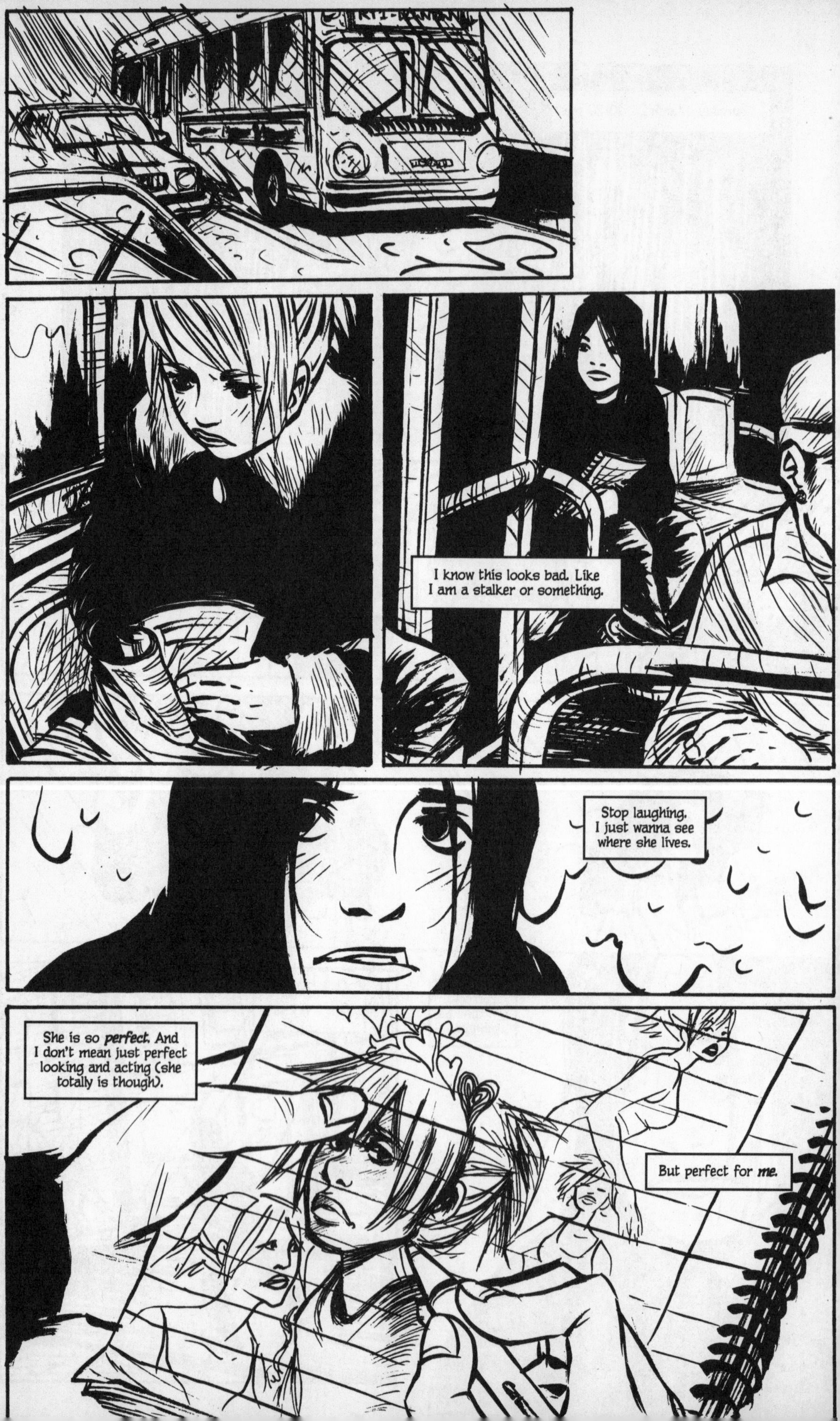
I know this looks bad. Like I am a stalker or something.
Stop laughing. I just wanna see where she lives.
She is so *perfect*. And I don't mean just perfect looking and acting (she totally is though).
But perfect for *me*.

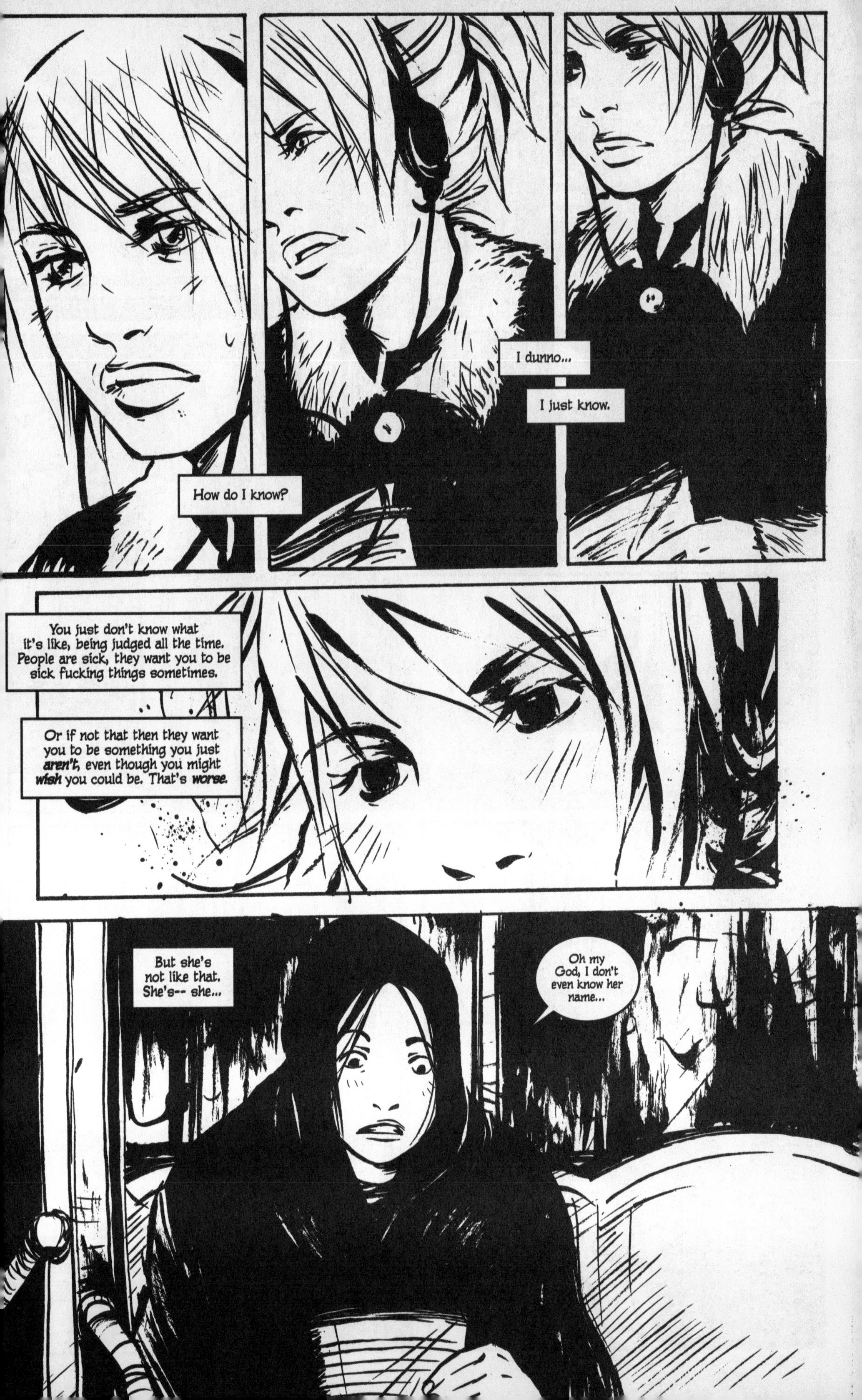
How do I know?
I dunno...
I just know.
You just don't know what it's like, being judged all the time. People are sick, they want you to be sick fucking things sometimes.
Or if not that then they want you to be something you just *aren't*, even though you might *wish* you could be. That's *worse*.
But she's not like that. She's-- she...
Oh my God, I don't even know her name...

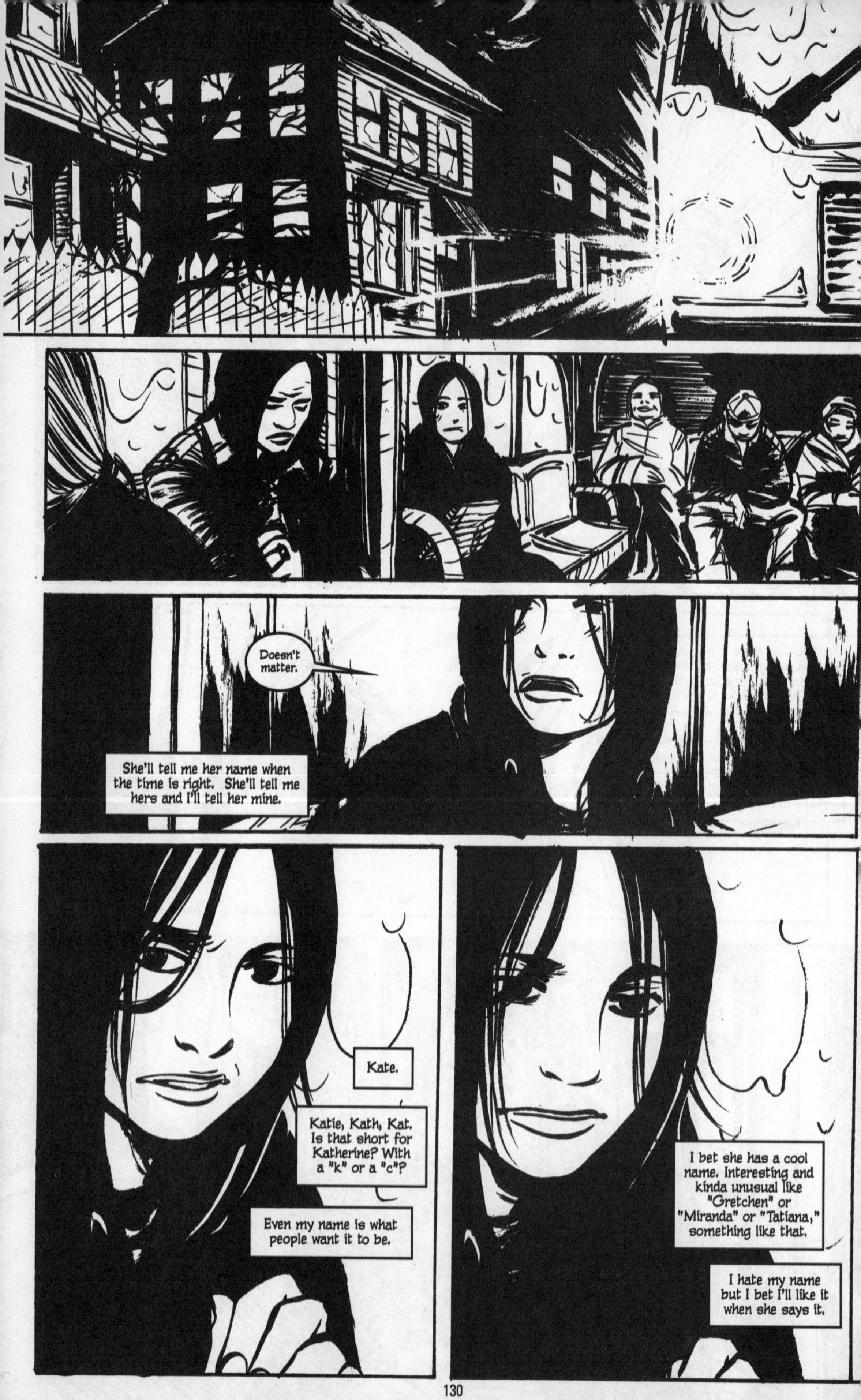
Doesn't matter.
She'll tell me her name when the time is right. She'll tell me hers and I'll tell her mine.
Kate.
Katie, Kath, Kat. Is that short for Katherine? With a "k" or a "c"?
Even my name is what people want it to be.
I bet she has a cool name. Interesting and kinda unusual like "Gretchen" or "Miranda" or "Tatiana," something like that.
I hate my name but I bet I'll like it when she says it.

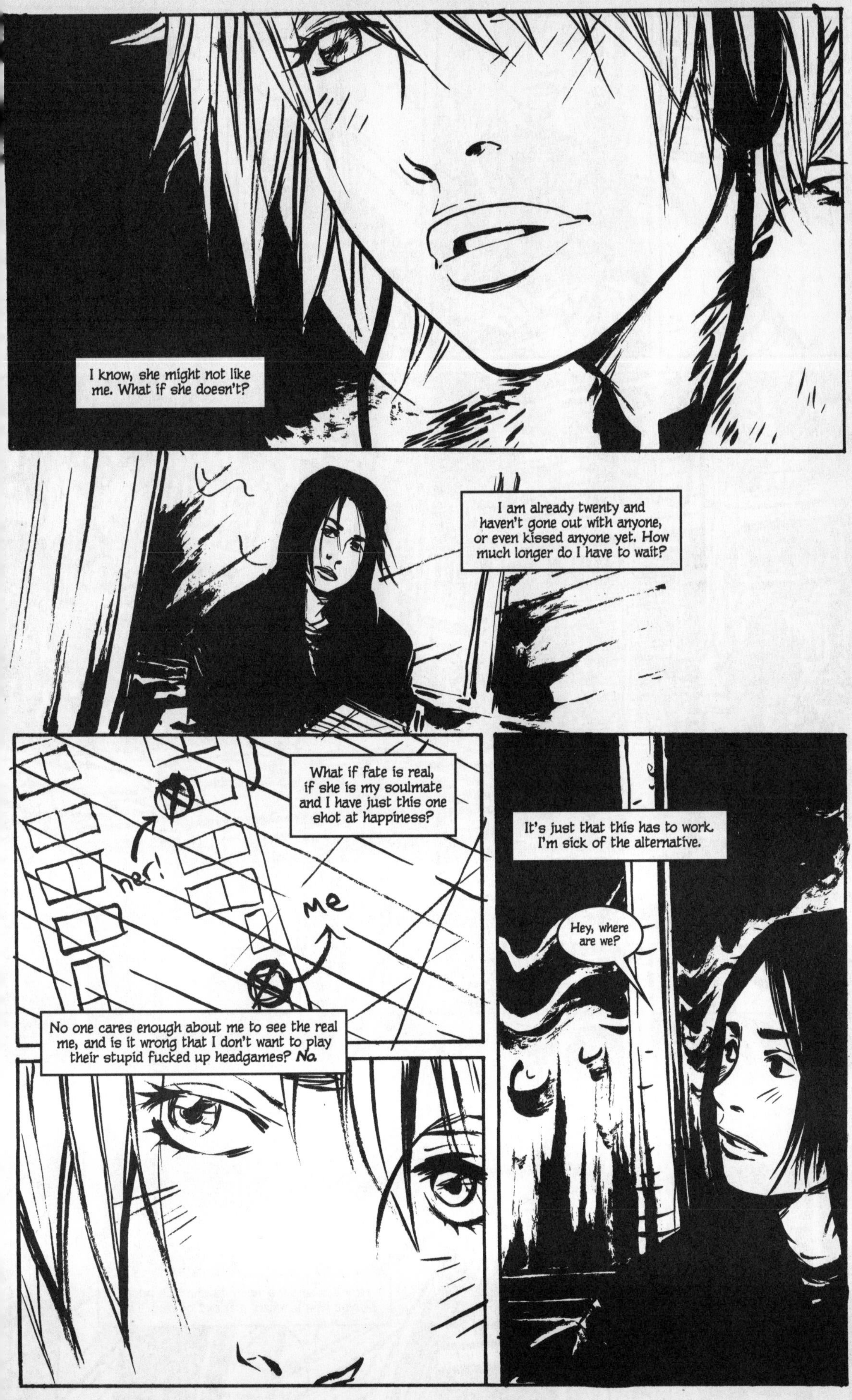
I know, she might not like me. What if she doesn't?
I am already twenty and haven't gone out with anyone, or even kissed anyone yet. How much longer do I have to wait?
What if fate is real, if she is my soulmate and I have just this one shot at happiness?
her!
me
No one cares enough about me to see the real me, and is it wrong that I don't want to play their stupid fucked up headgames? No.
It's just that this has to work. I'm sick of the alternative.
Hey, where are we?

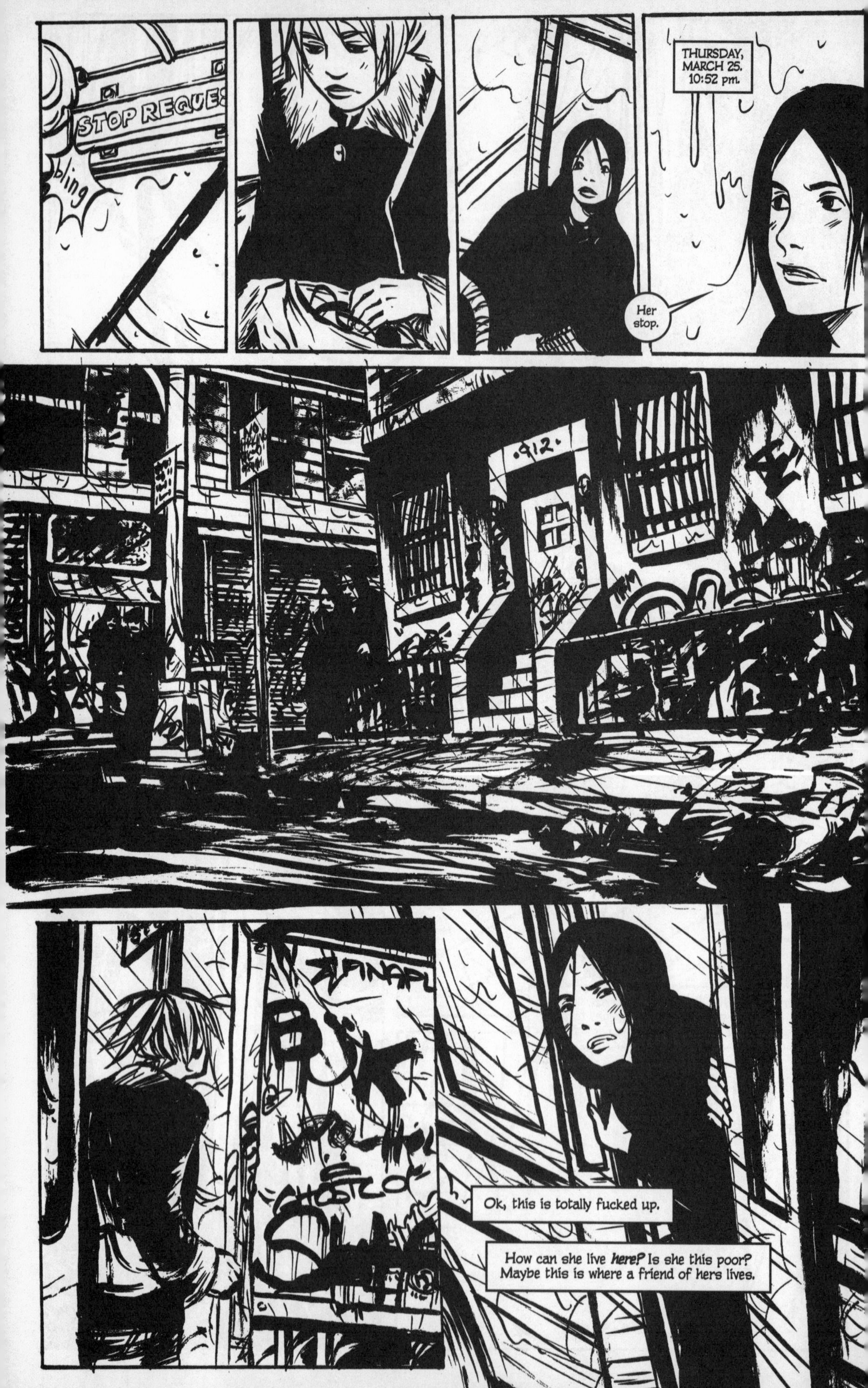
STOP REQUES
bling
THURSDAY, MARCH 25. 10:52 pm.
Her stop.
912
Ok, this is totally fucked up.
How can she live **here?** Is she this poor? Maybe this is where a friend of hers lives.

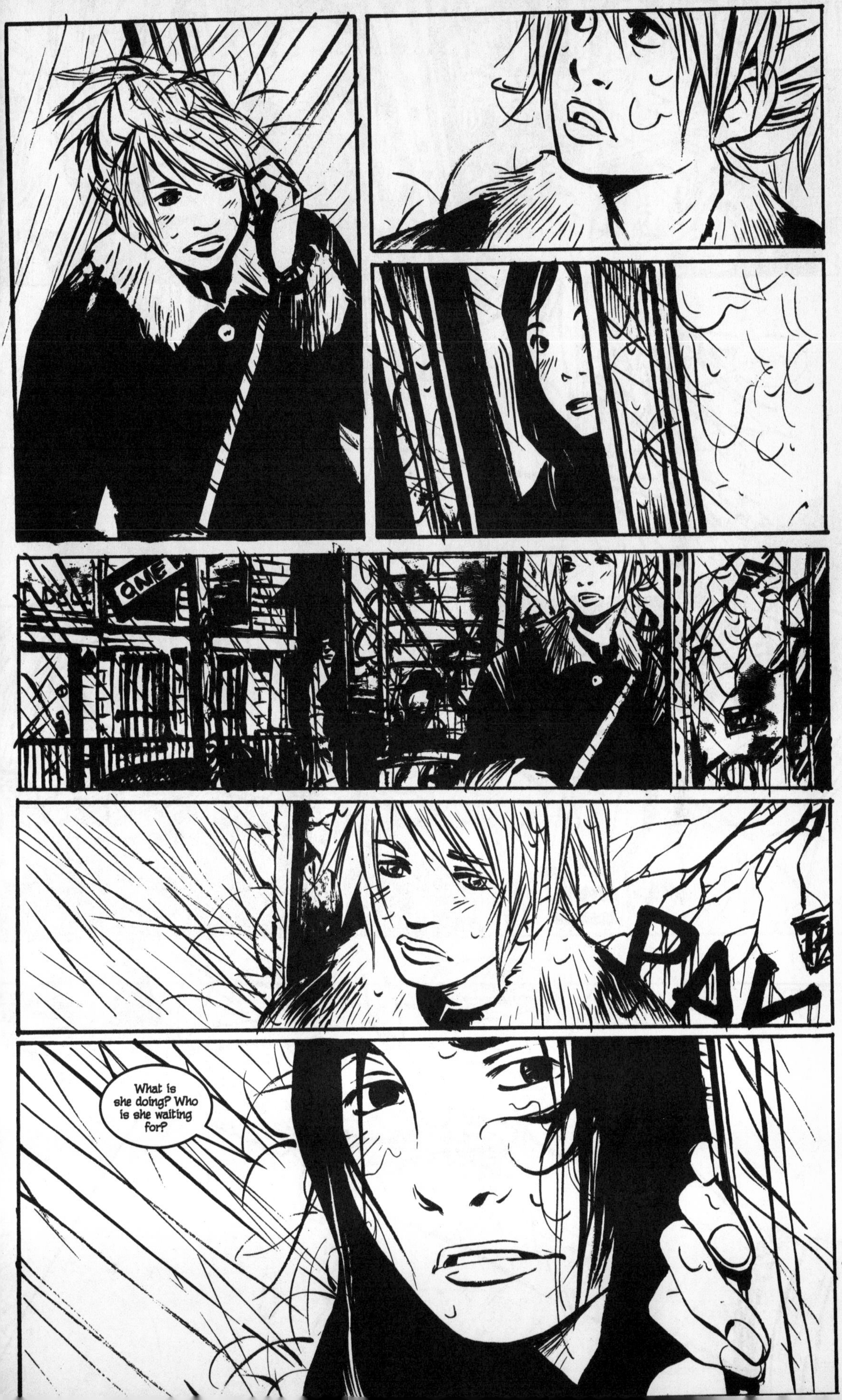
ONE
PAL
What is she doing? Who is she waiting for?

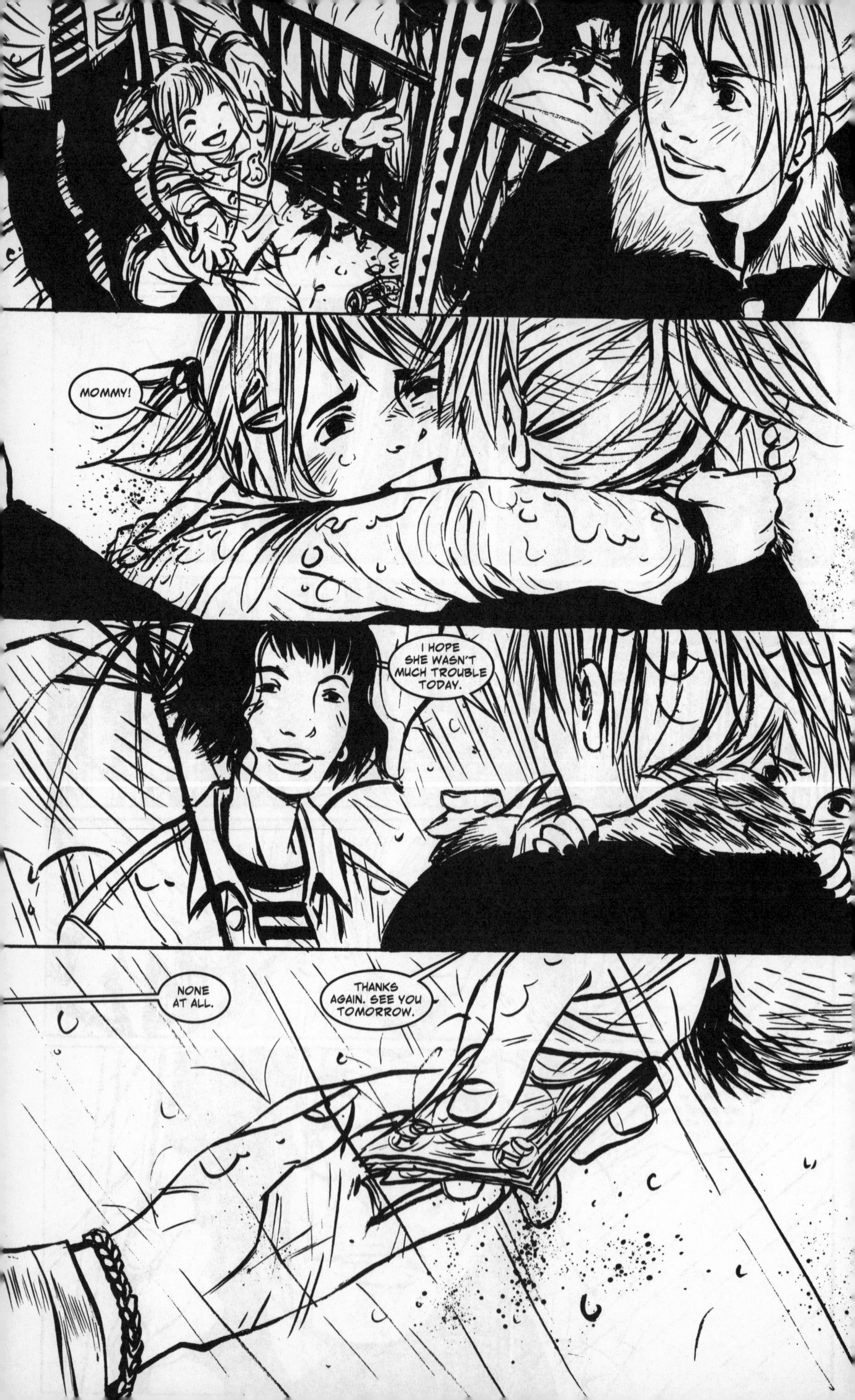
MOMMY!
I HOPE SHE WASN'T MUCH TROUBLE TODAY.
NONE AT ALL.
THANKS AGAIN. SEE YOU TOMORROW.

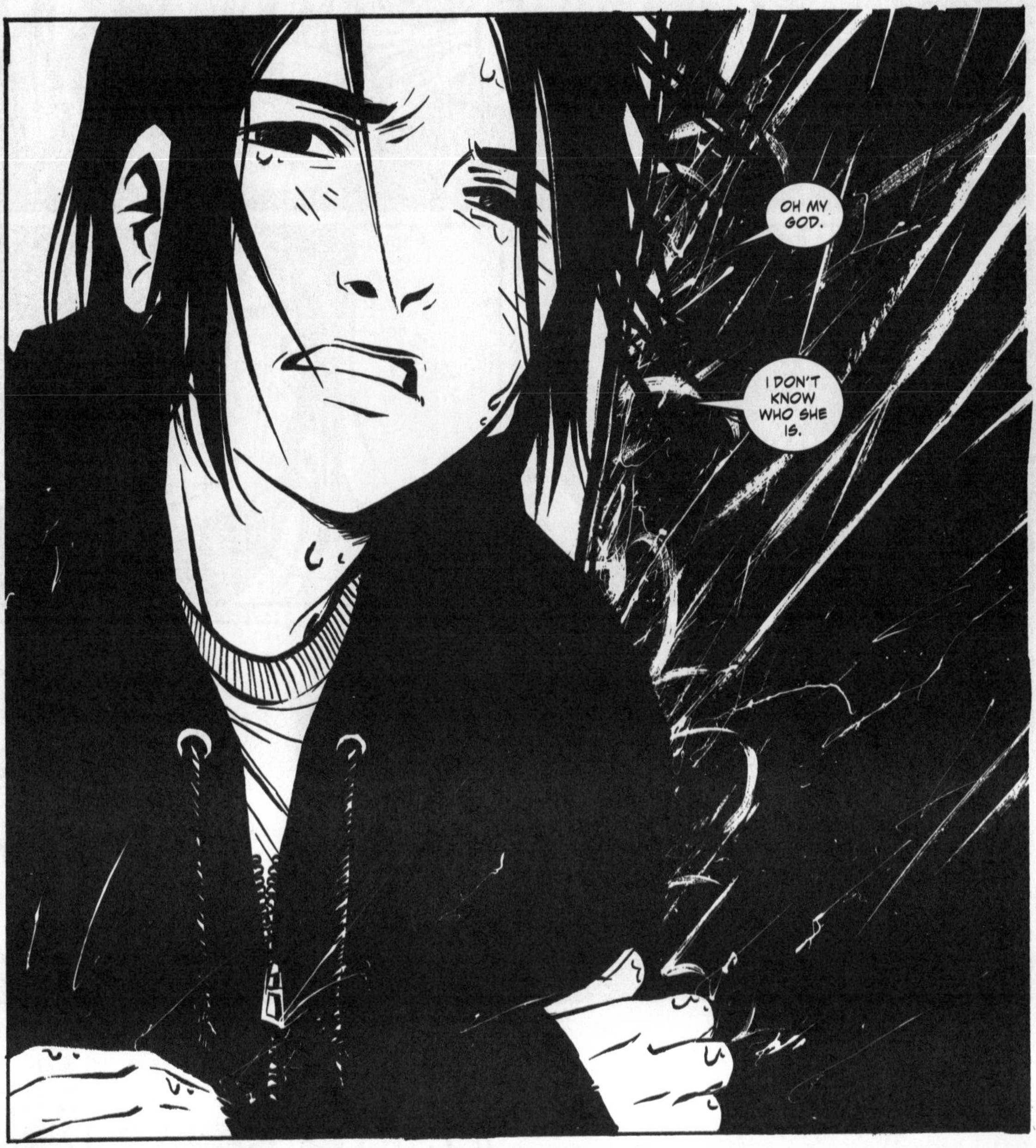
OH MY GOD.
I DON'T KNOW WHO SHE IS.

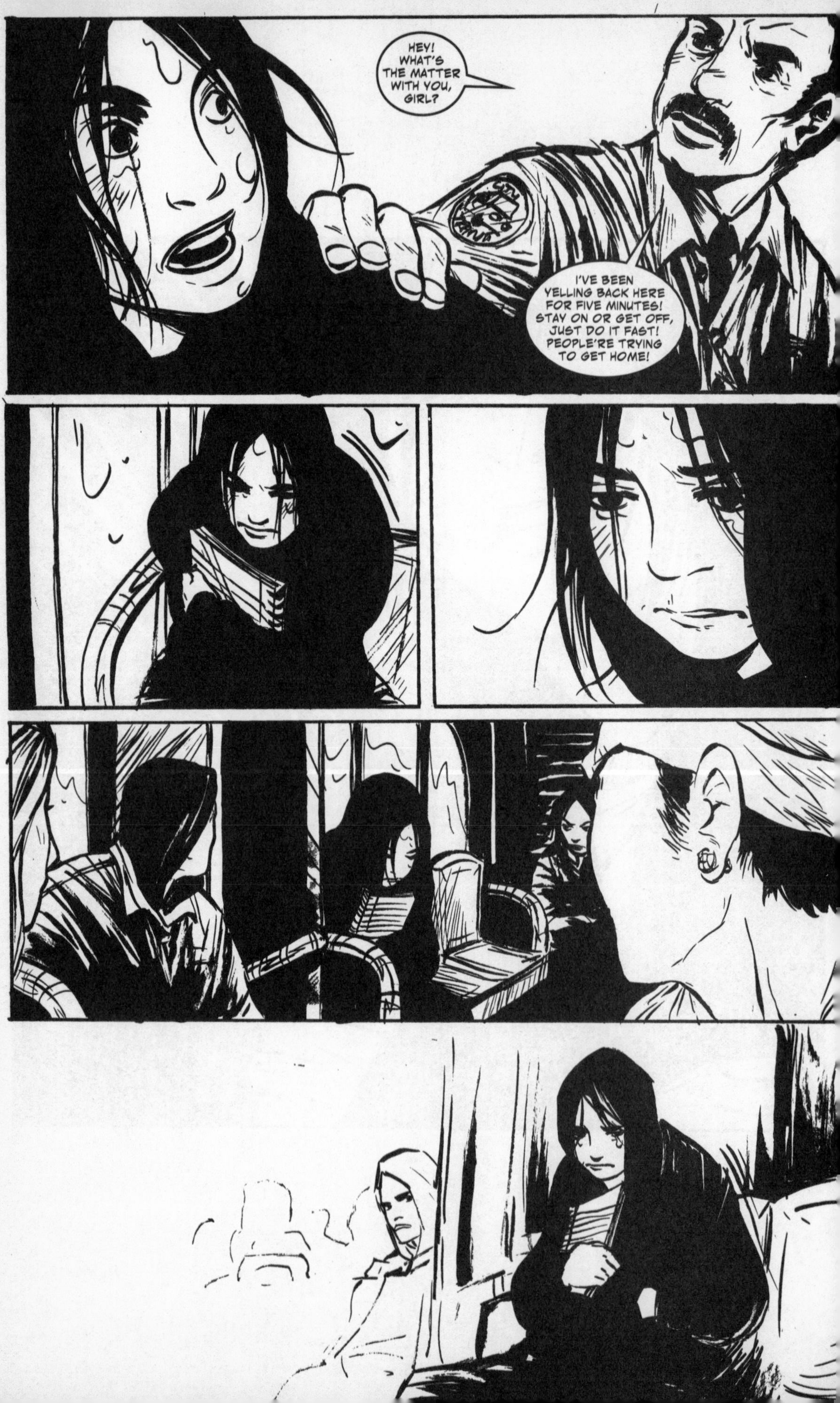
HEY! WHAT'S THE MATTER WITH YOU, GIRL?
I'VE BEEN YELLING BACK HERE FOR FIVE MINUTES! STAY ON OR GET OFF, JUST DO IT FAST! PEOPLE'RE TRYING TO GET HOME!

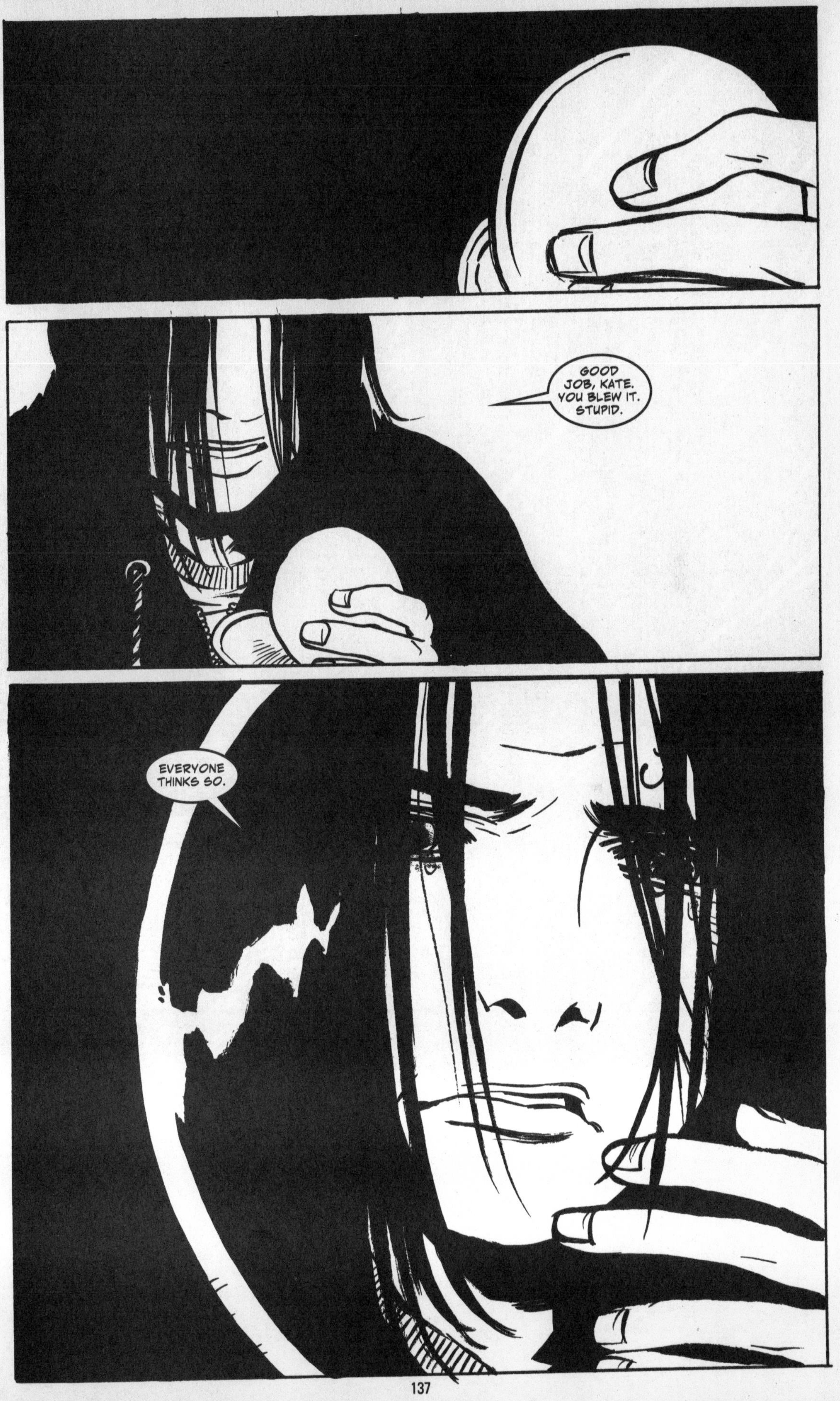
GOOD JOB, KATE. YOU BLEW IT. STUPID.
EVERYONE THINKS SO.

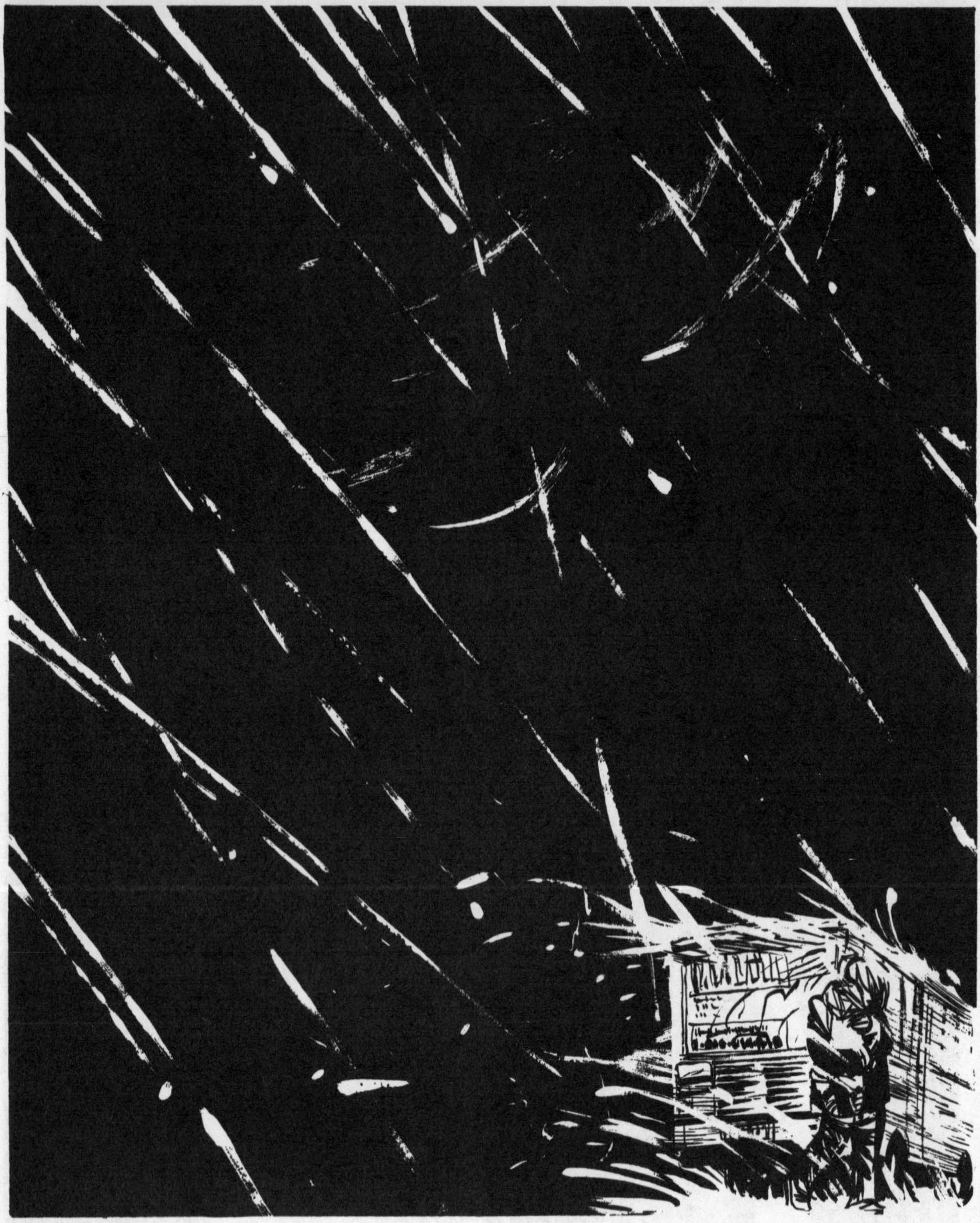

THE END

6

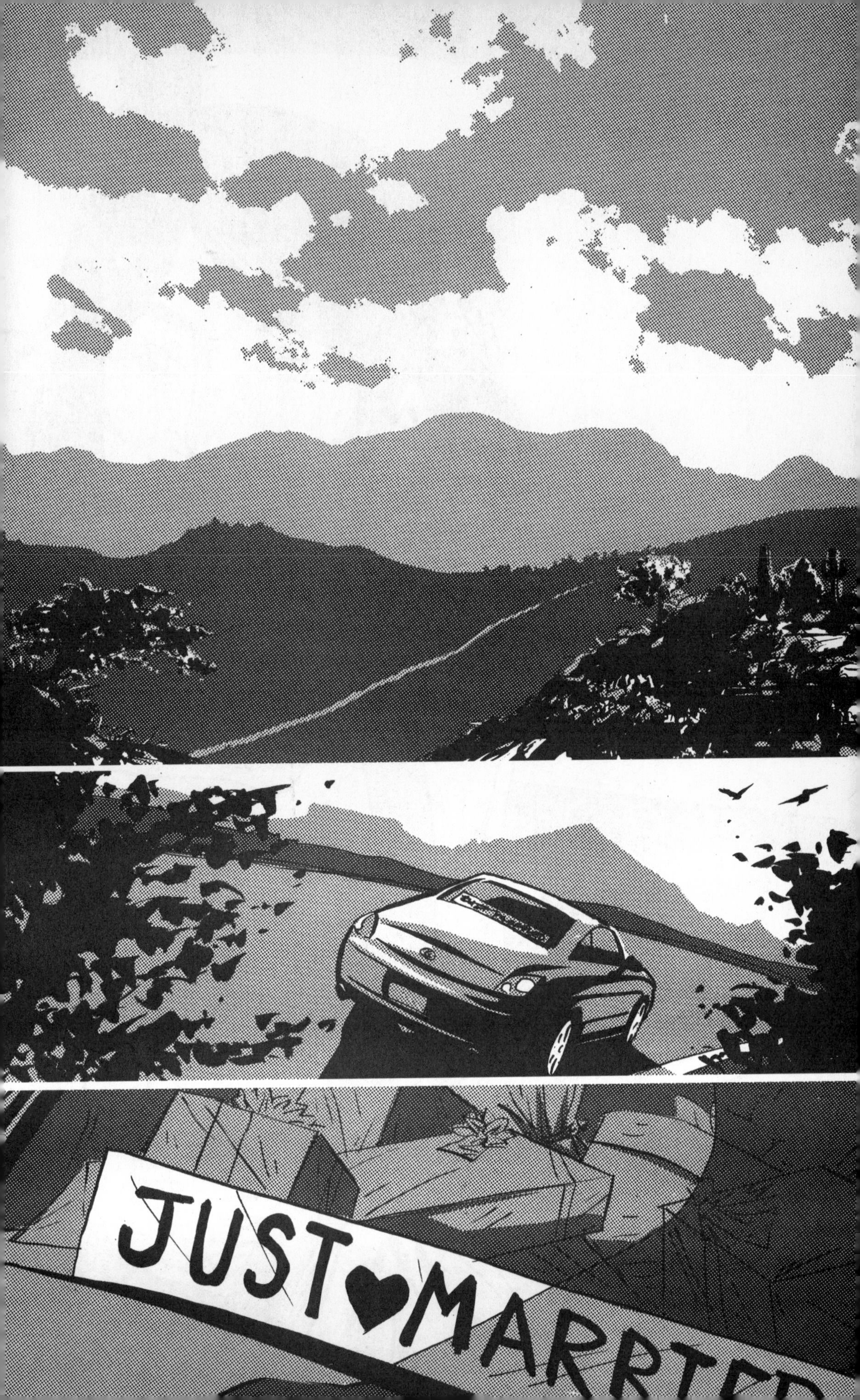
JUST♥MARRIE

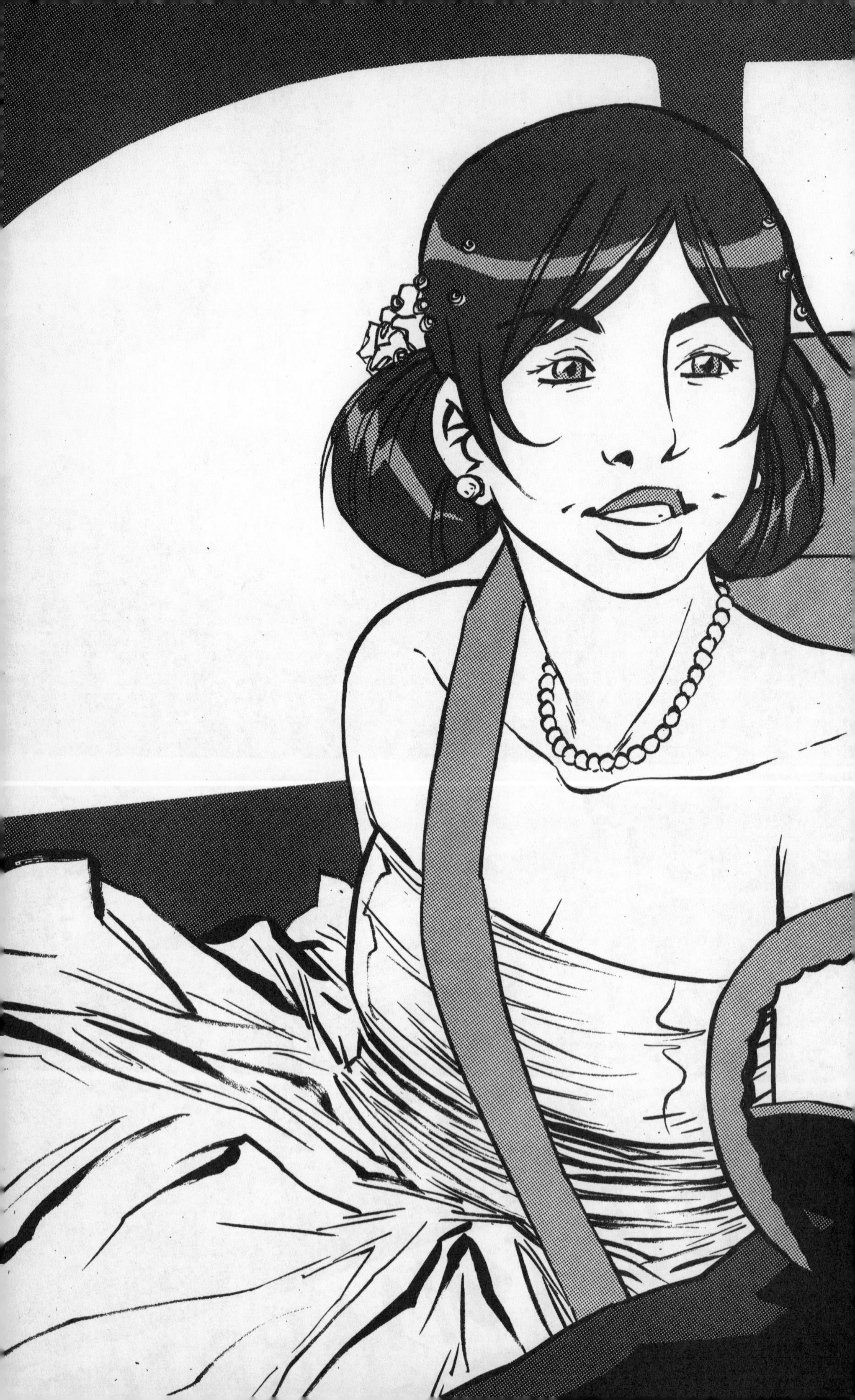

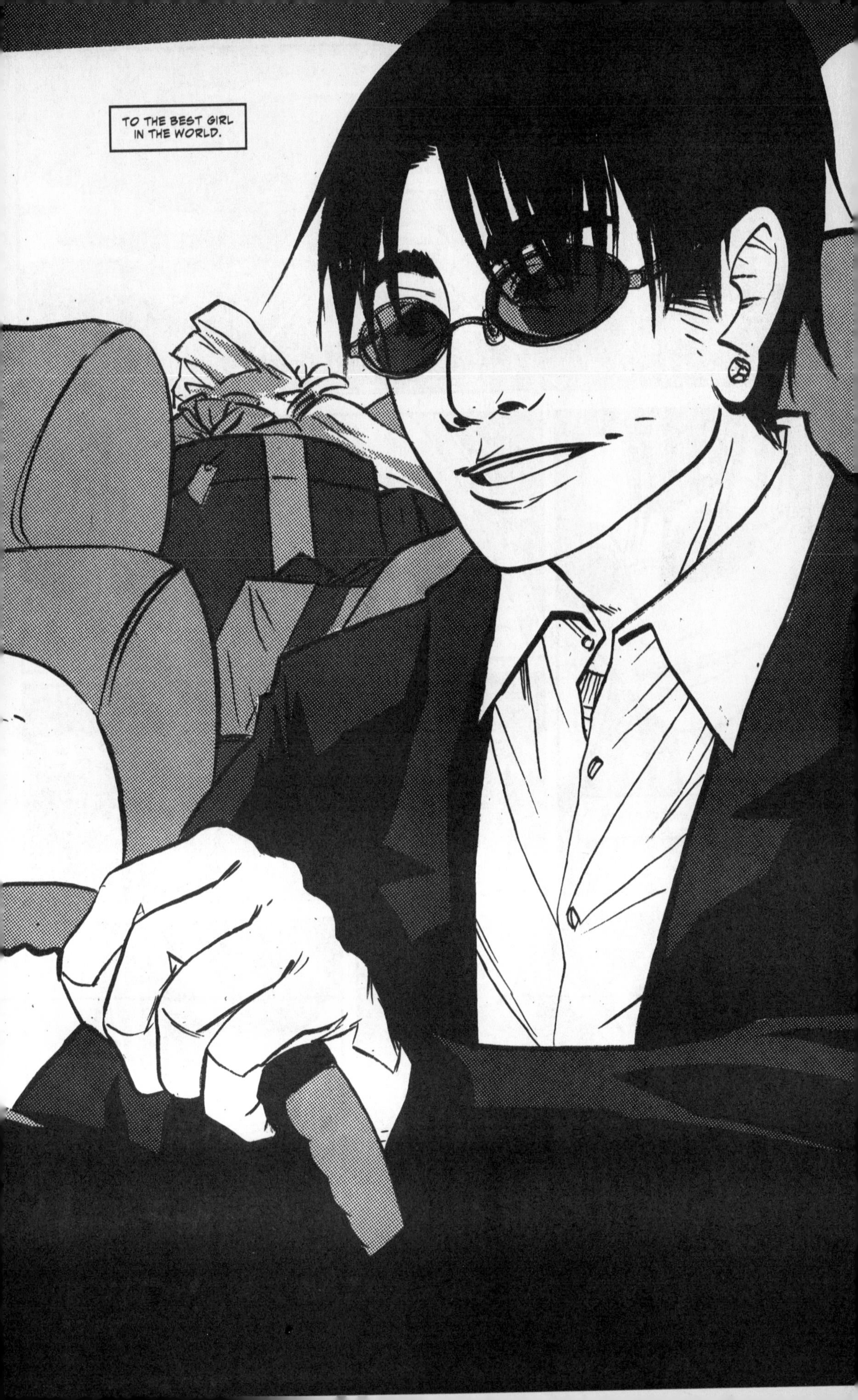
TO THE BEST GIRL IN THE WORLD.

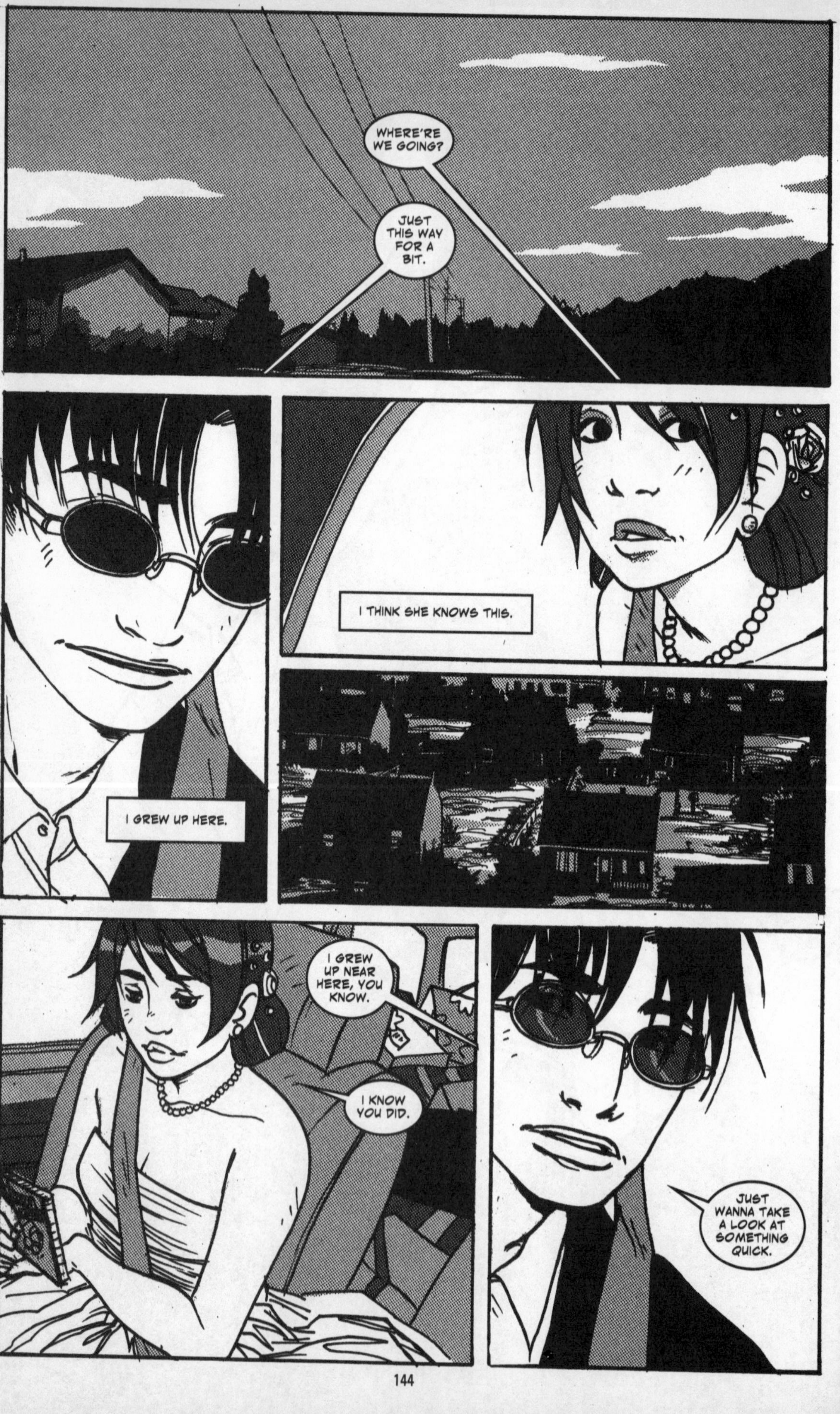
WHERE'RE WE GOING?
JUST THIS WAY FOR A BIT.
I GREW UP HERE.
I THINK SHE KNOWS THIS.
I GREW UP NEAR HERE, YOU KNOW.
I KNOW YOU DID.
JUST WANNA TAKE A LOOK AT SOMETHING QUICK.

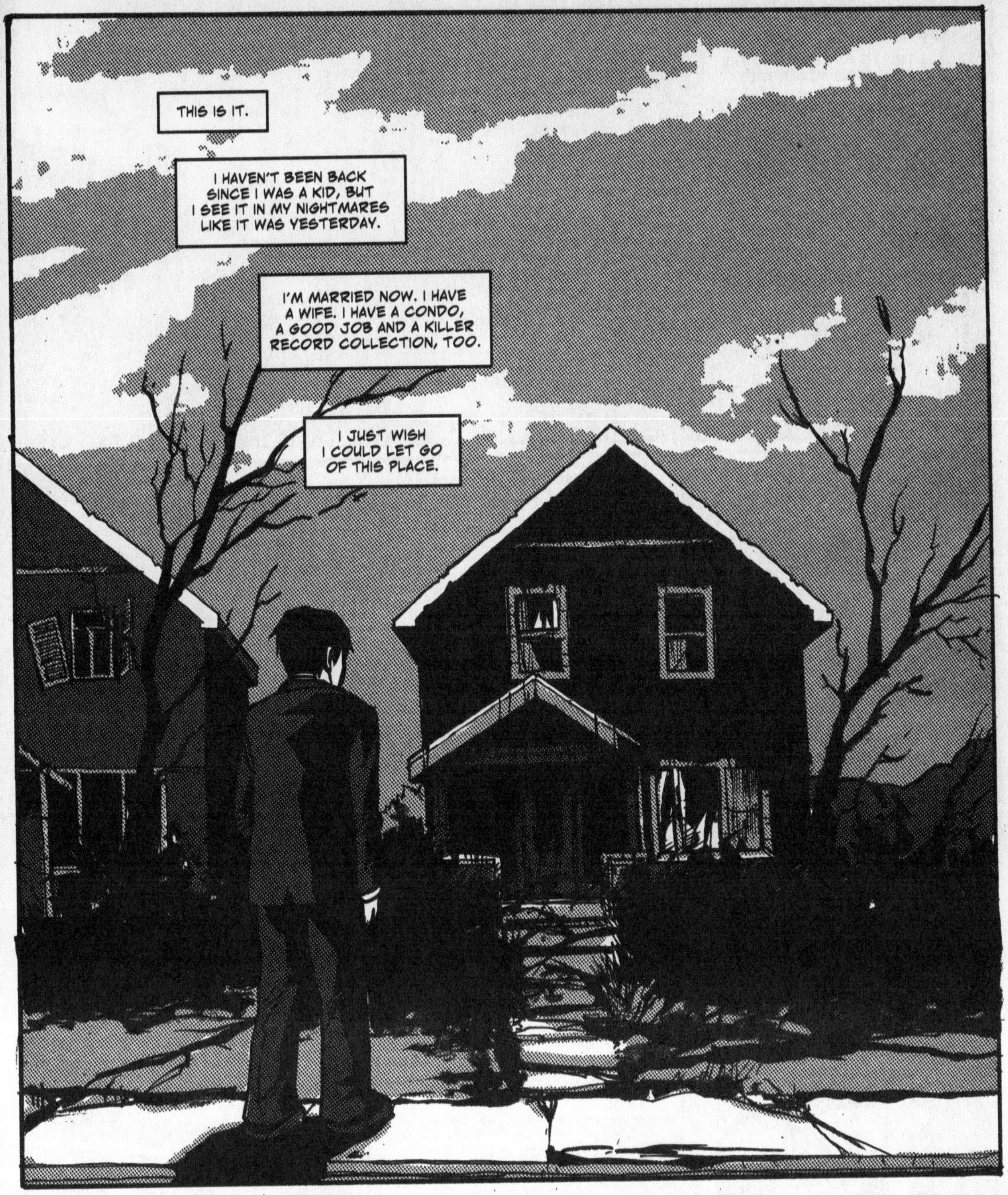
THIS IS IT.
I HAVEN'T BEEN BACK SINCE I WAS A KID, BUT I SEE IT IN MY NIGHTMARES LIKE IT WAS YESTERDAY.
I'M MARRIED NOW. I HAVE A WIFE. I HAVE A CONDO, A GOOD JOB AND A KILLER RECORD COLLECTION, TOO.
I JUST WISH I COULD LET GO OF THIS PLACE.

"What You Wish For"

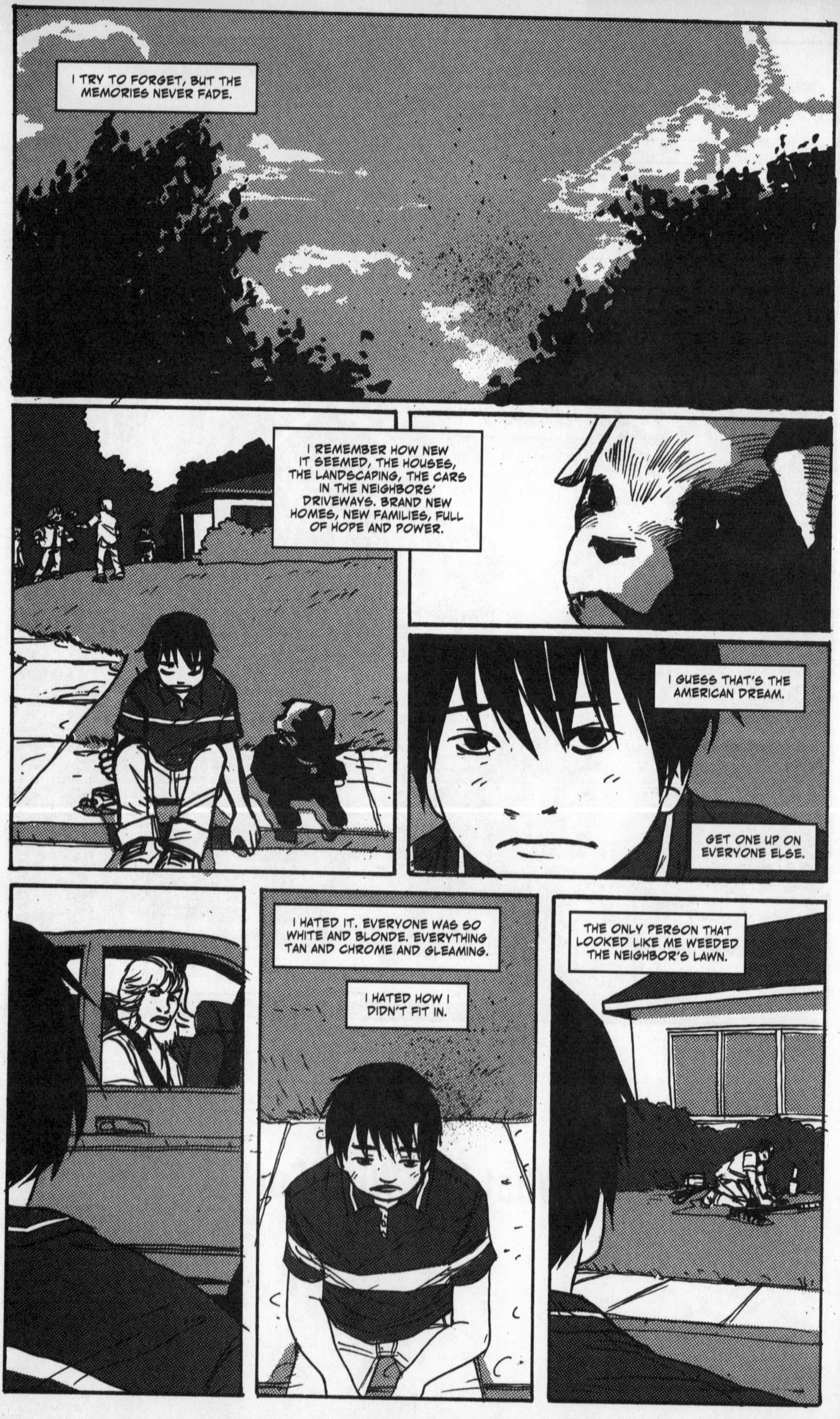
I TRY TO FORGET, BUT THE MEMORIES NEVER FADE.
I REMEMBER HOW NEW IT SEEMED, THE HOUSES, THE LANDSCAPING, THE CARS IN THE NEIGHBORS' DRIVEWAYS. BRAND NEW HOMES, NEW FAMILIES, FULL OF HOPE AND POWER.
I GUESS THAT'S THE AMERICAN DREAM.
GET ONE UP ON EVERYONE ELSE.
I HATED IT. EVERYONE WAS SO WHITE AND BLONDE. EVERYTHING TAN AND CHROME AND GLEAMING.
I HATED HOW I DIDN'T FIT IN.
THE ONLY PERSON THAT LOOKED LIKE ME WEEDED THE NEIGHBOR'S LAWN.

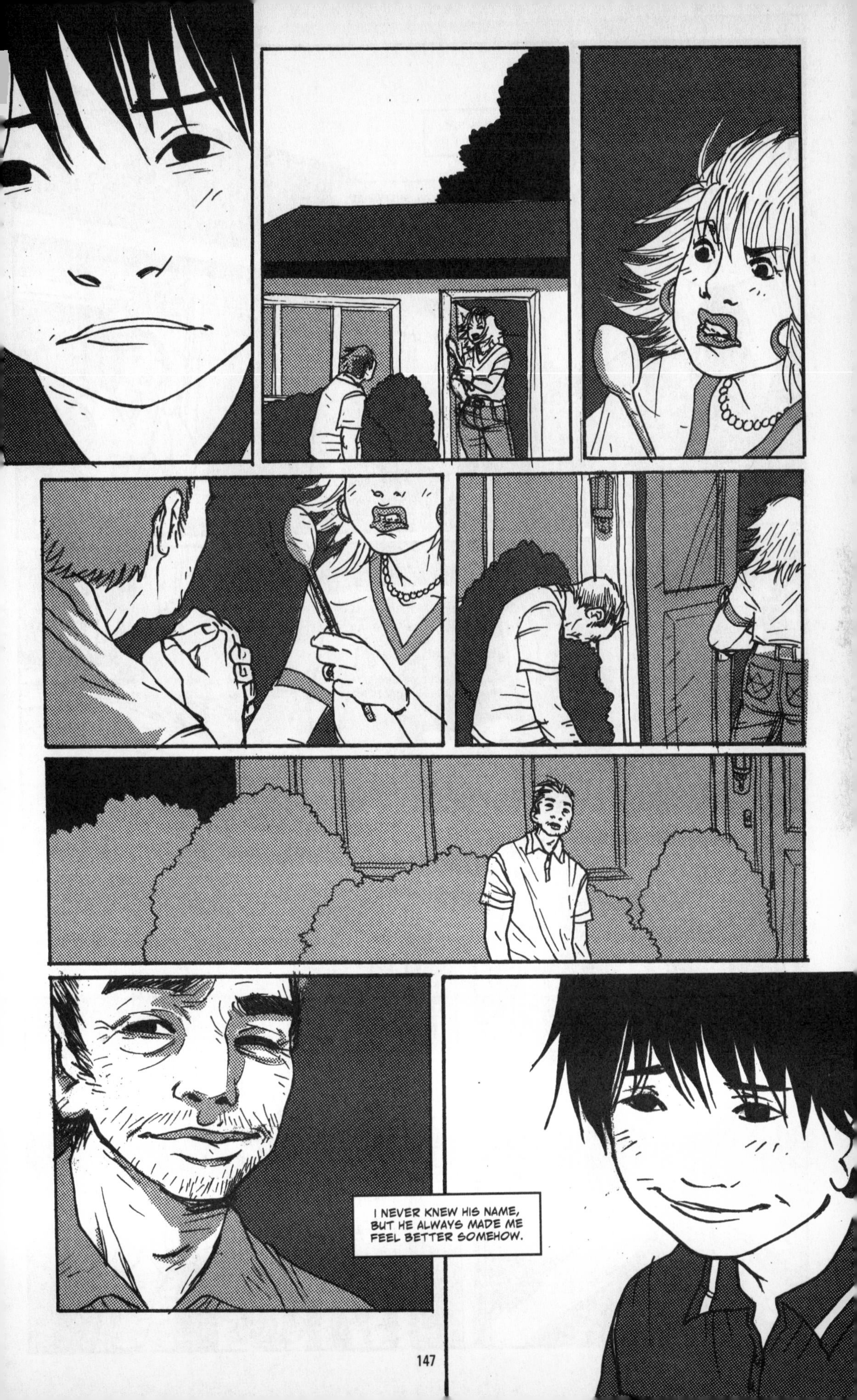
I NEVER KNEW HIS NAME, BUT HE ALWAYS MADE ME FEEL BETTER SOMEHOW.

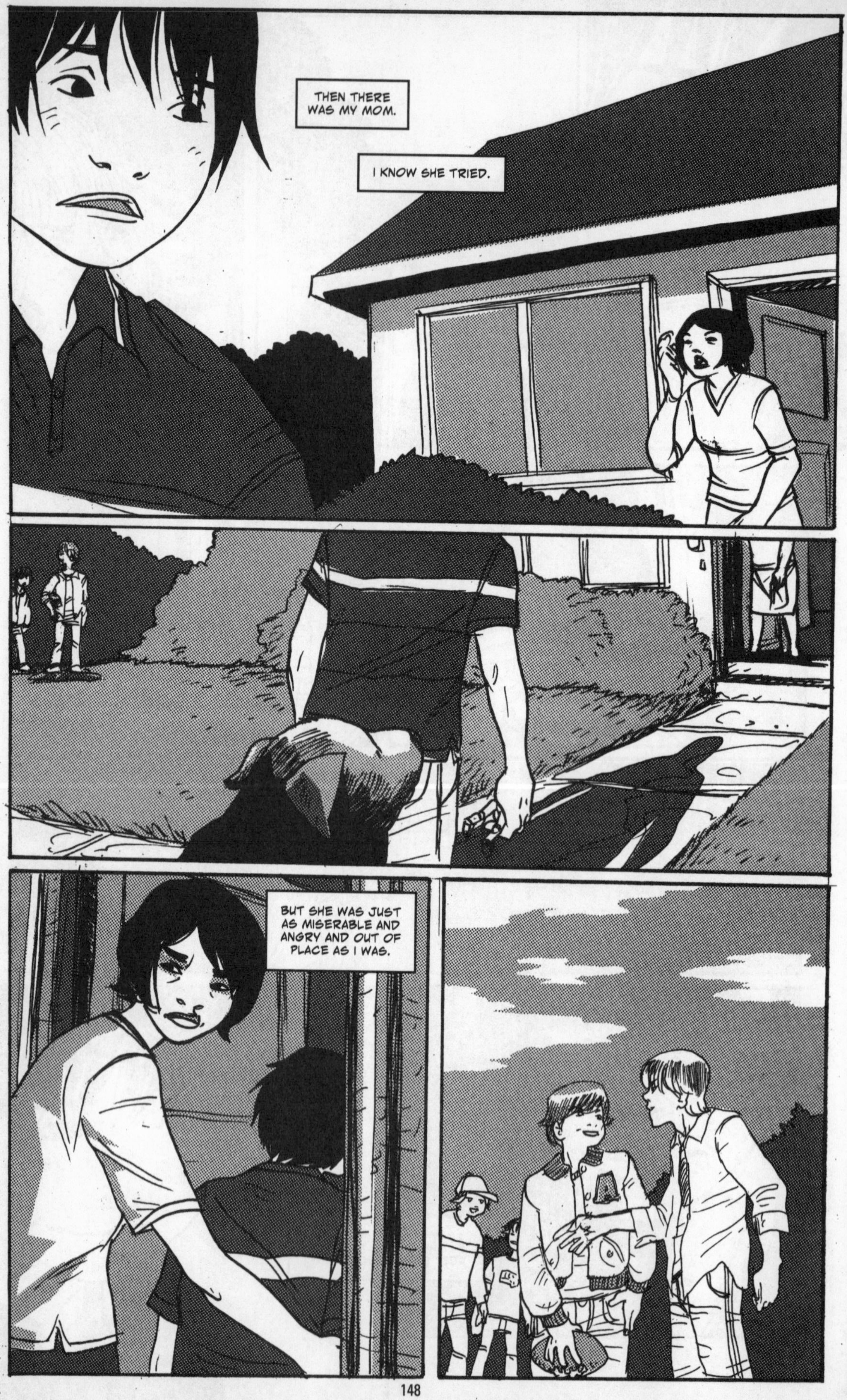
THEN THERE WAS MY MOM.
I KNOW SHE TRIED.
BUT SHE WAS JUST AS MISERABLE AND ANGRY AND OUT OF PLACE AS I WAS.

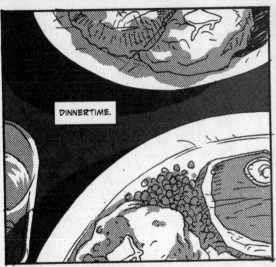

DINNERTIME.

DAD TALKING ABOUT HIS BORING JOB.

AGAIN.

DAD WAS OK.

HE WAS IN THE NAVY AND MET MY MOM OVERSEAS.

WE GOT ALONG GREAT, I JUST WONDER IF HE KNEW WHAT HE WAS GETTING INTO WHEN HE MARRIED HER.

BUT I KNOW DAD TRIED TOO.

hee hee

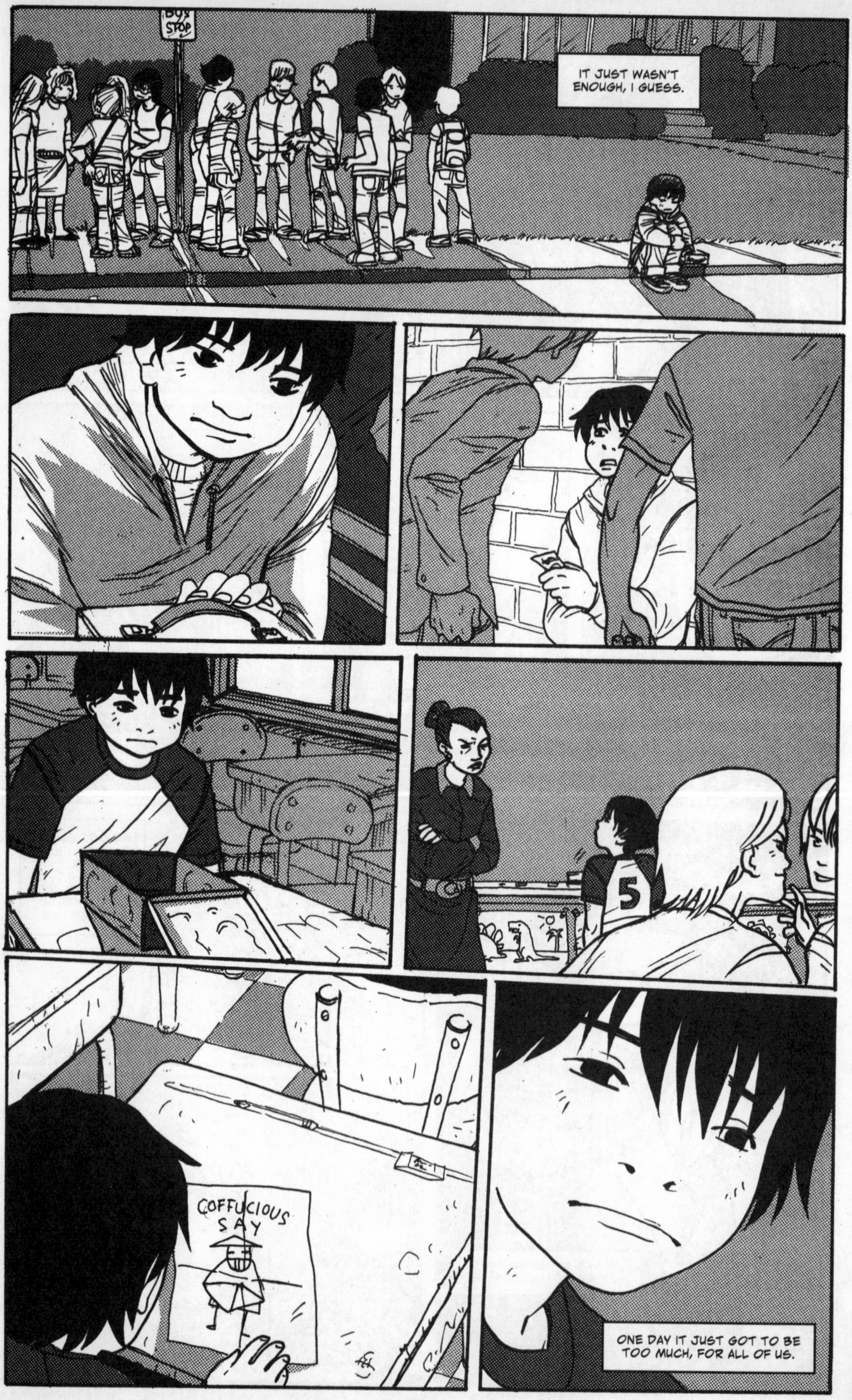
BUS
STOP
IT JUST WASN'T ENOUGH, I GUESS.
5
COFFUCIOUS SAY
ONE DAY IT JUST GOT TO BE TOO MUCH, FOR ALL OF US.

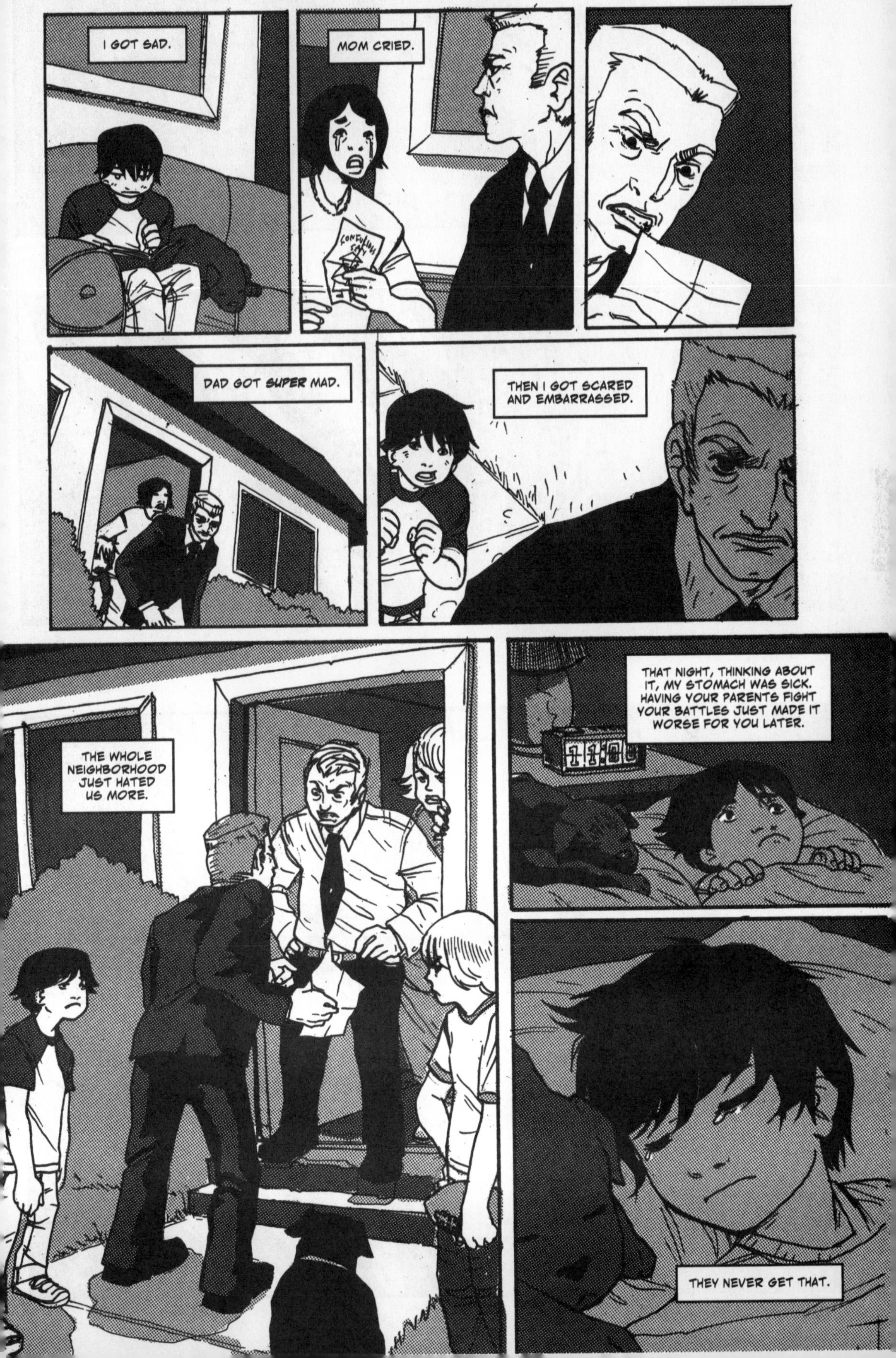
I GOT SAD.
MOM CRIED.
DAD GOT SUPER MAD.
THEN I GOT SCARED AND EMBARRASSED.
THE WHOLE NEIGHBORHOOD JUST HATED US MORE.
THAT NIGHT, THINKING ABOUT IT, MY STOMACH WAS SICK. HAVING YOUR PARENTS FIGHT YOUR BATTLES JUST MADE IT WORSE FOR YOU LATER.
THEY NEVER GET THAT.

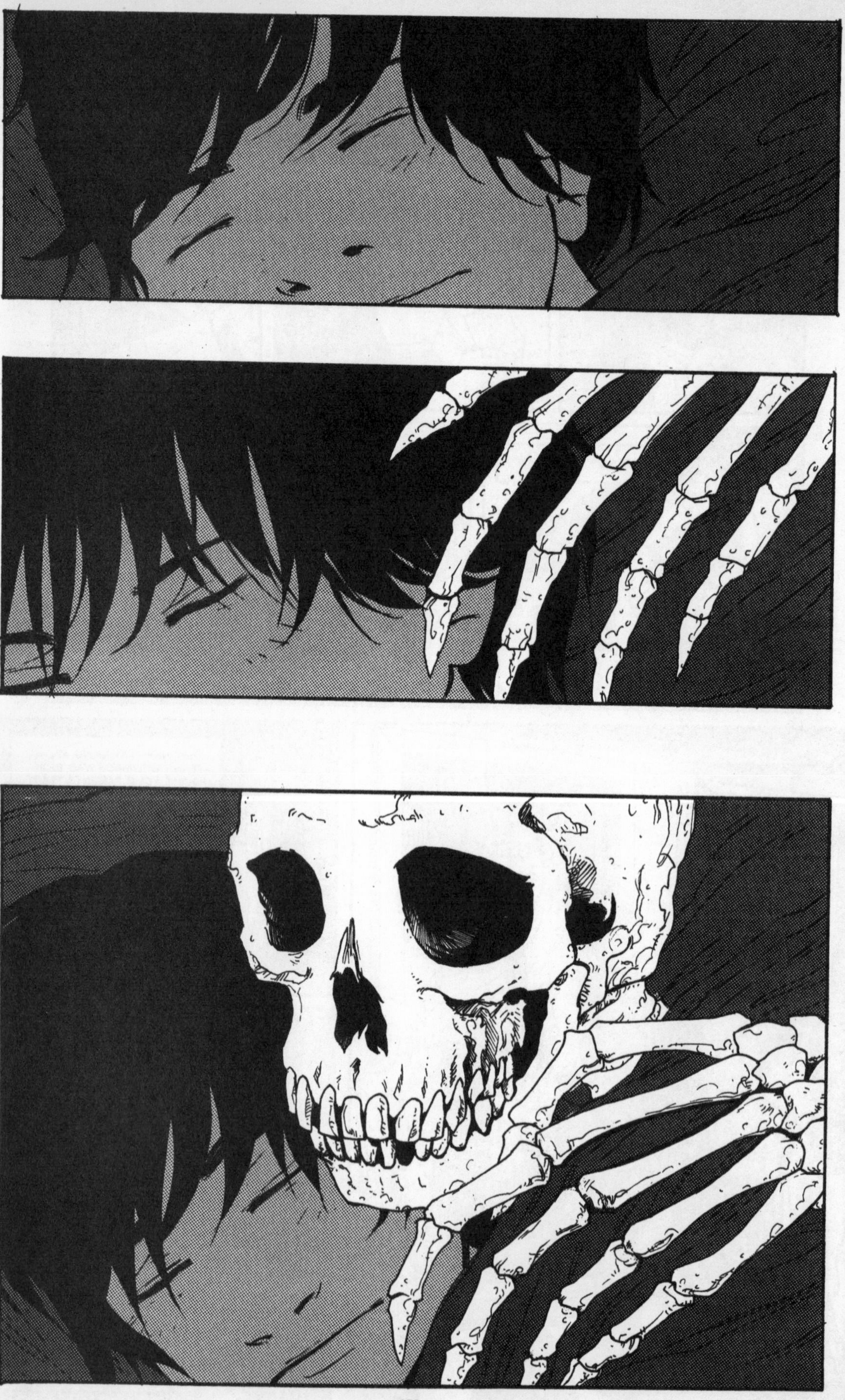

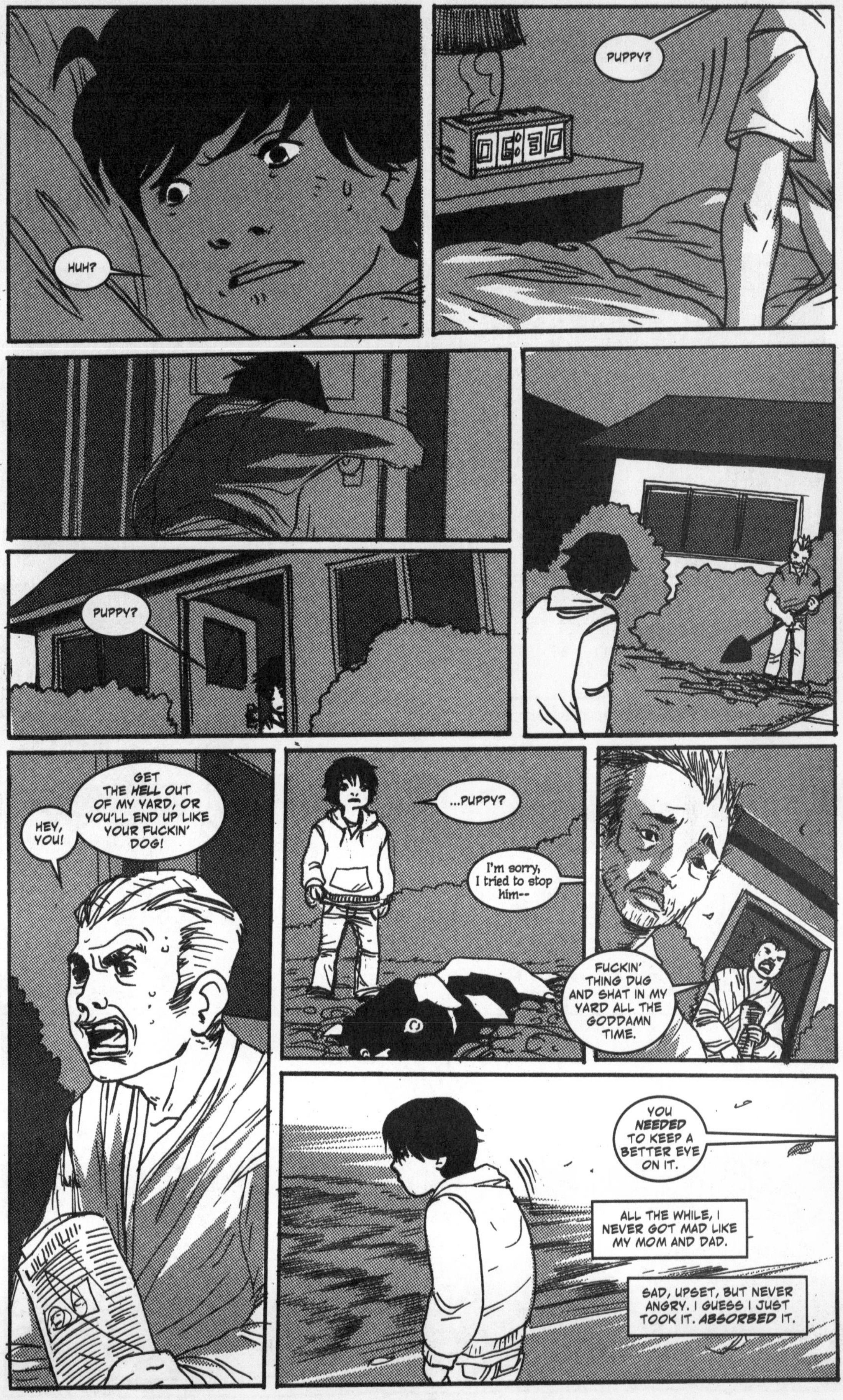
HUH?
PUPPY?
PUPPY?
HEY, YOU!
GET THE HELL OUT OF MY YARD, OR YOU'LL END UP LIKE YOUR FUCKIN' DOG!
...PUPPY?
I'm sorry, I tried to stop him--
FUCKIN' THING DUG AND SHAT IN MY YARD ALL THE GODDAMN TIME.
YOU NEEDED TO KEEP A BETTER EYE ON IT.
ALL THE WHILE, I NEVER GOT MAD LIKE MY MOM AND DAD.
SAD, UPSET, BUT NEVER ANGRY. I GUESS I JUST TOOK IT. ABSORBED IT.

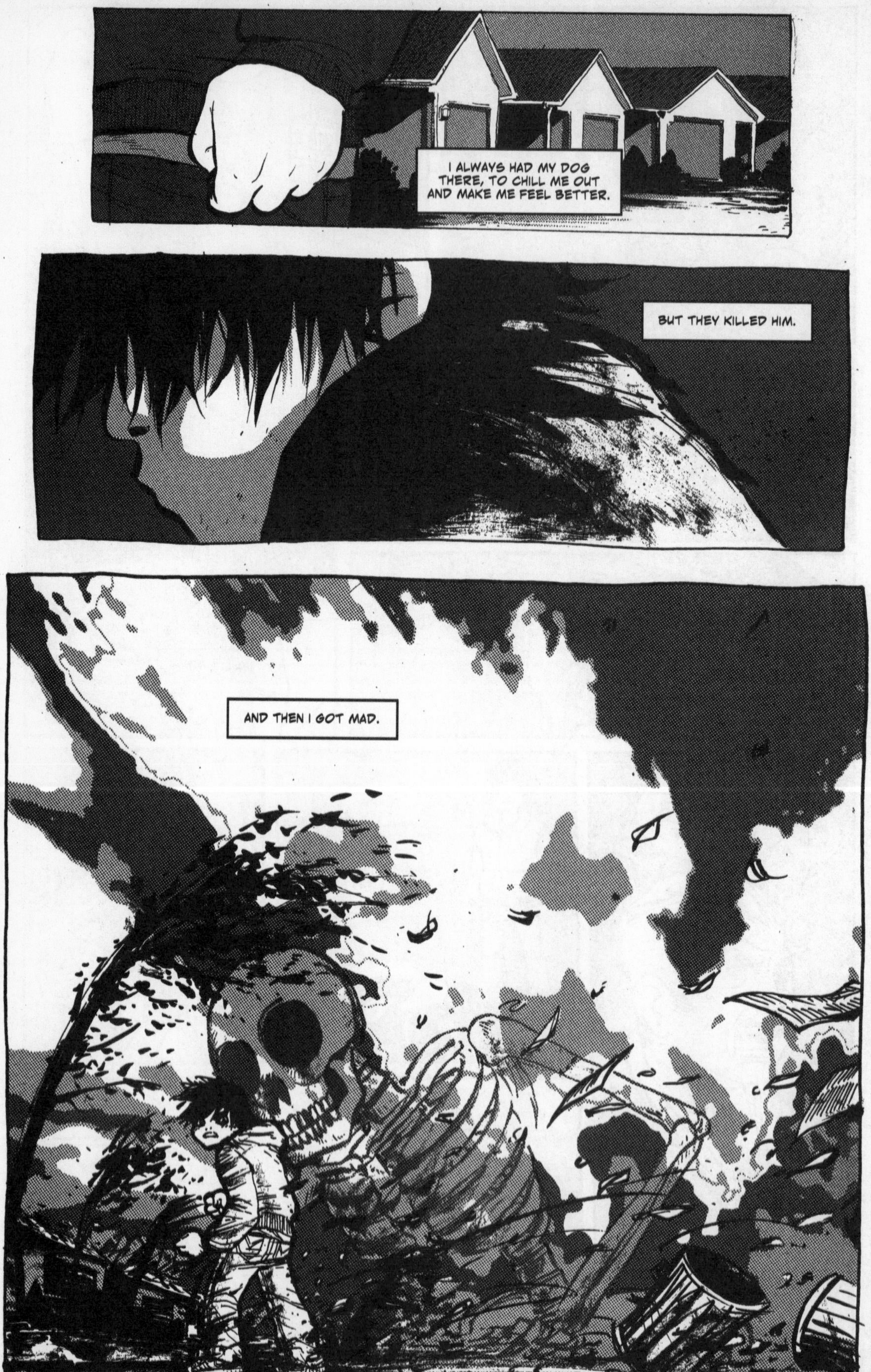
I ALWAYS HAD MY DOG THERE, TO CHILL ME OUT AND MAKE ME FEEL BETTER.
BUT THEY KILLED HIM.
AND THEN I GOT MAD.

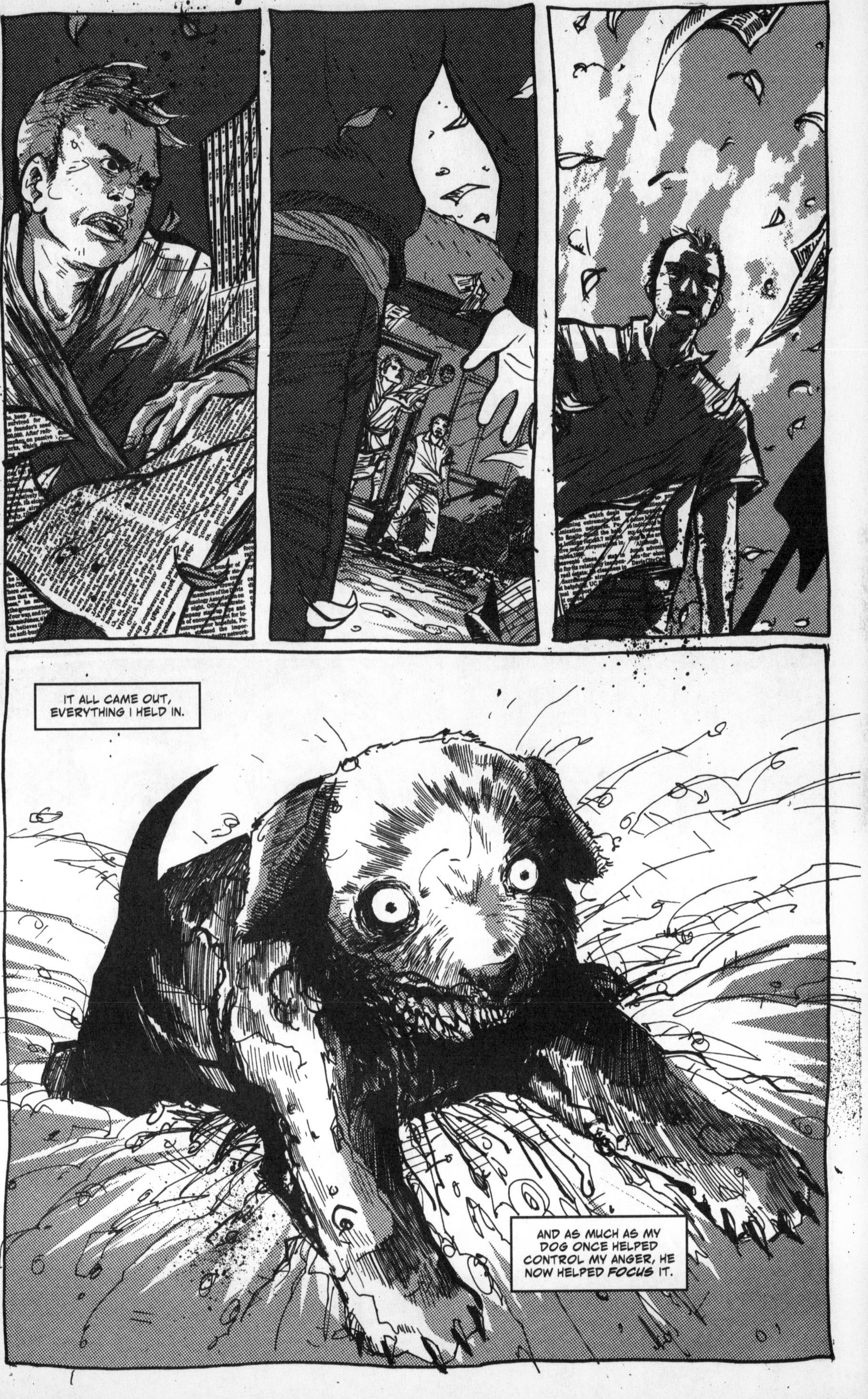
IT ALL CAME OUT, EVERYTHING I HELD IN.
AND AS MUCH AS MY DOG ONCE HELPED CONTROL MY ANGER, HE NOW HELPED *FOCUS* IT.

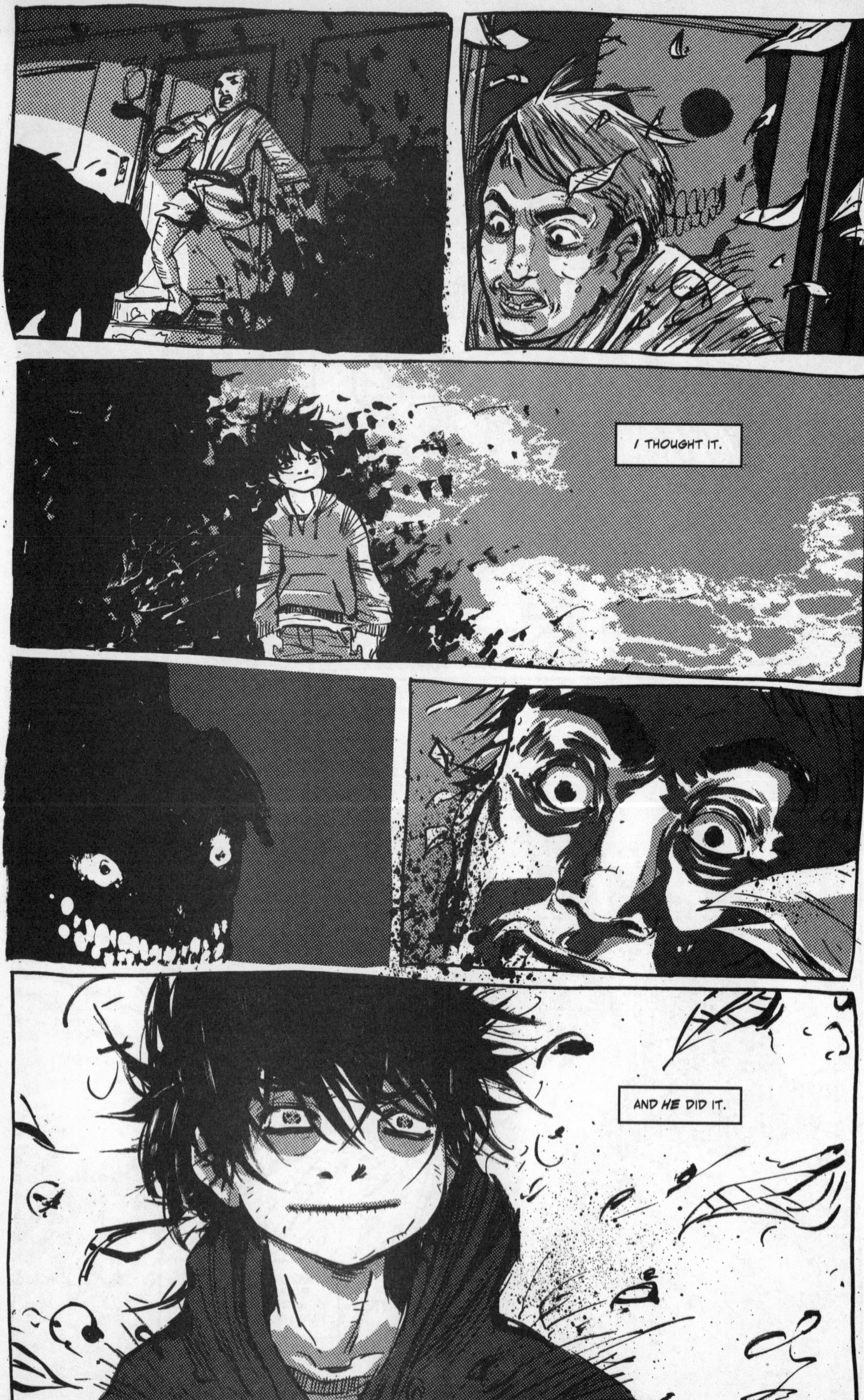
I THOUGHT IT.
AND HE DID IT.

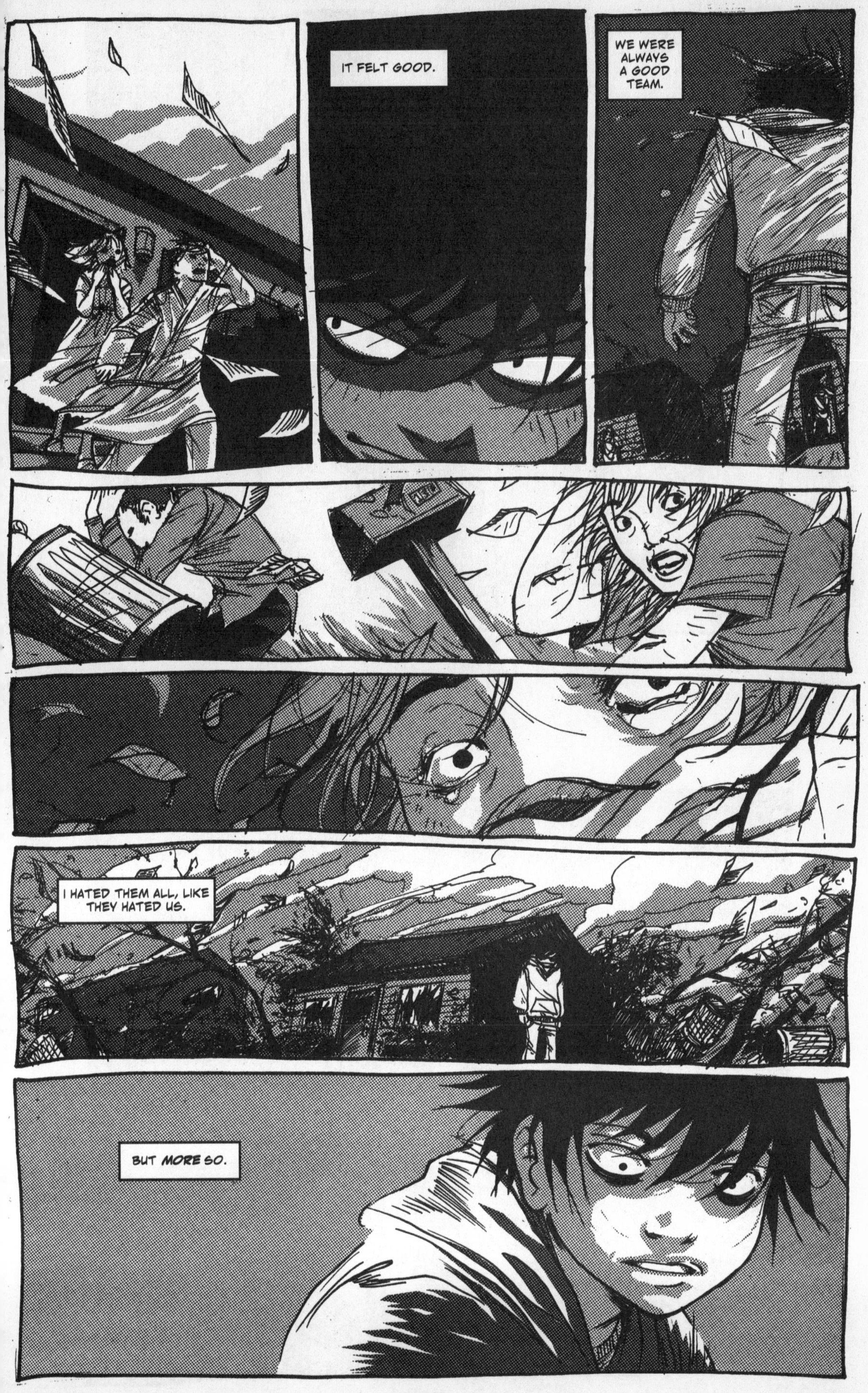
IT FELT GOOD.
WE WERE ALWAYS A GOOD TEAM.
I HATED THEM ALL, LIKE THEY HATED US.
BUT *MORE* SO.

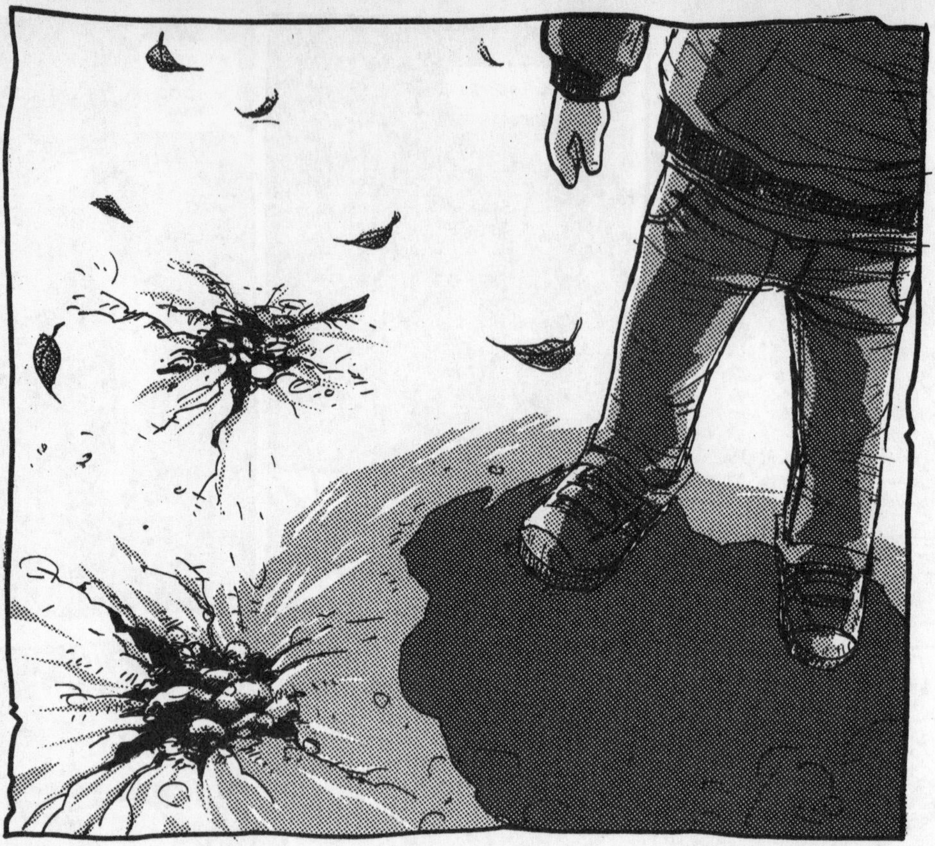

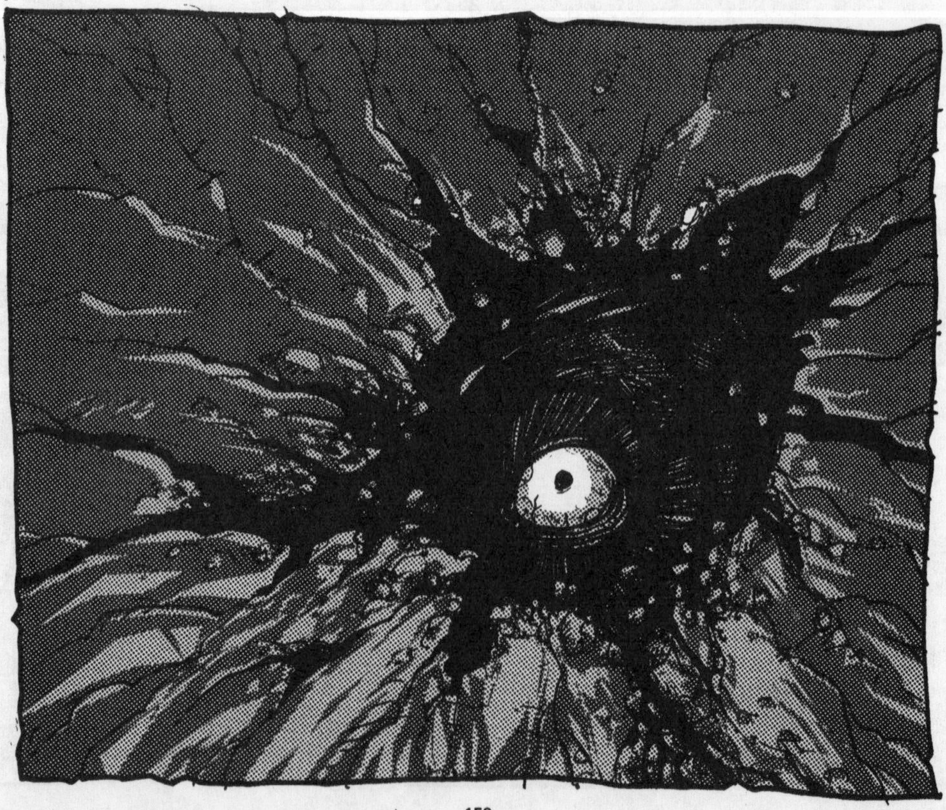

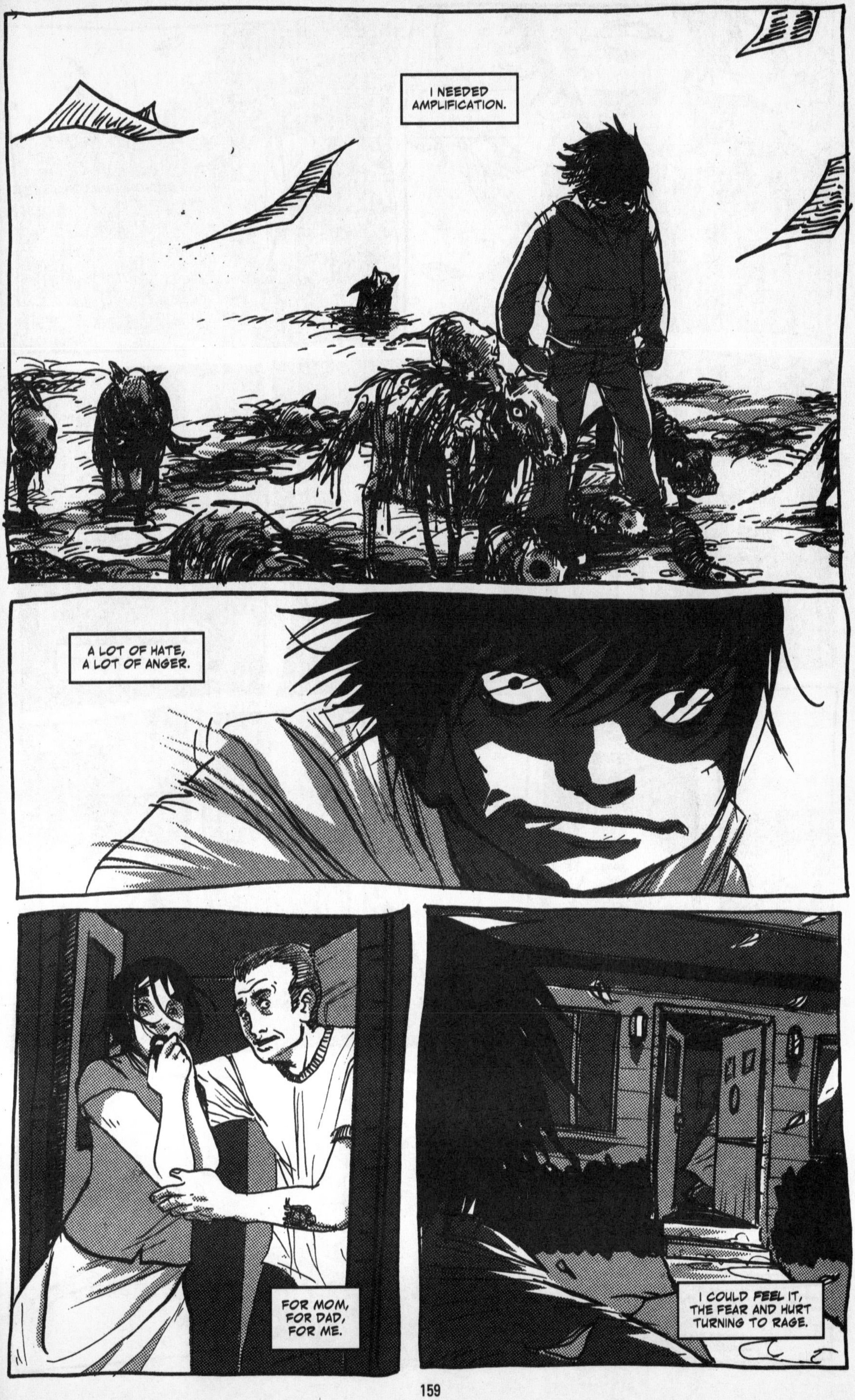
I NEEDED AMPLIFICATION.
A LOT OF HATE, A LOT OF ANGER.
FOR MOM, FOR DAD, FOR ME.
I COULD FEEL IT, THE FEAR AND HURT TURNING TO RAGE.

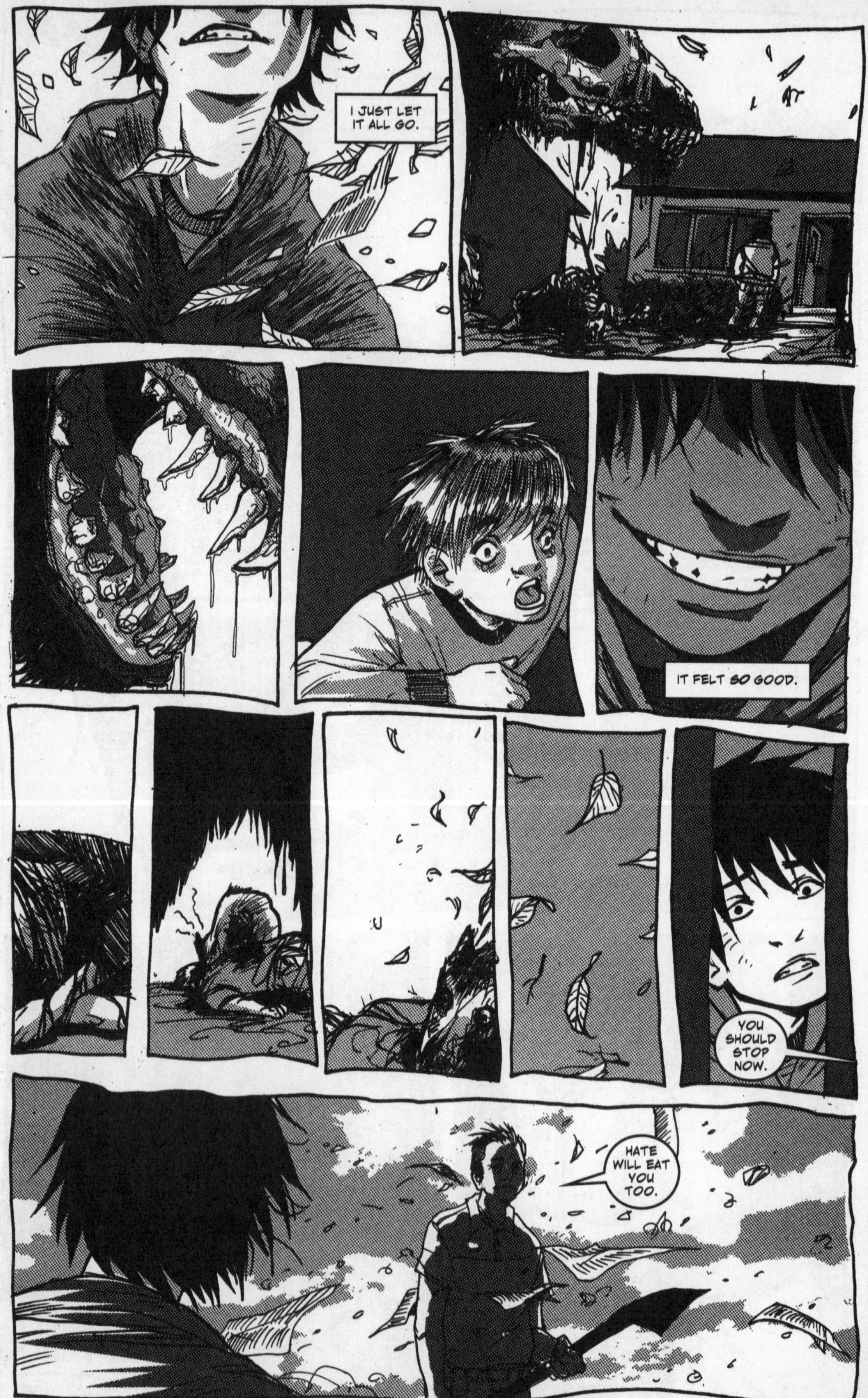
I JUST LET IT ALL GO.
IT FELT SO GOOD.
YOU SHOULD STOP NOW.
HATE WILL EAT YOU TOO.

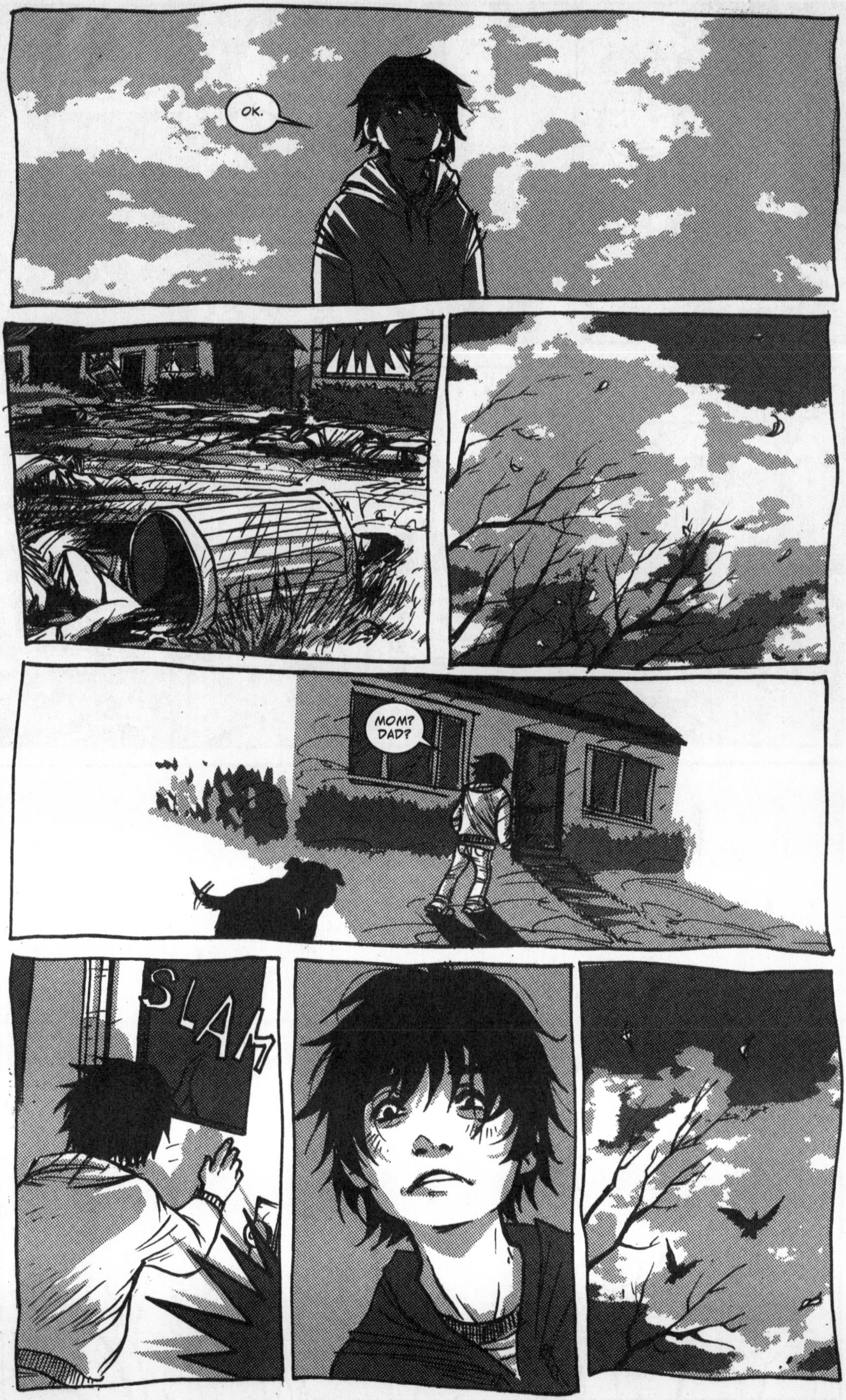
OK.
MOM? DAD?
SLAM

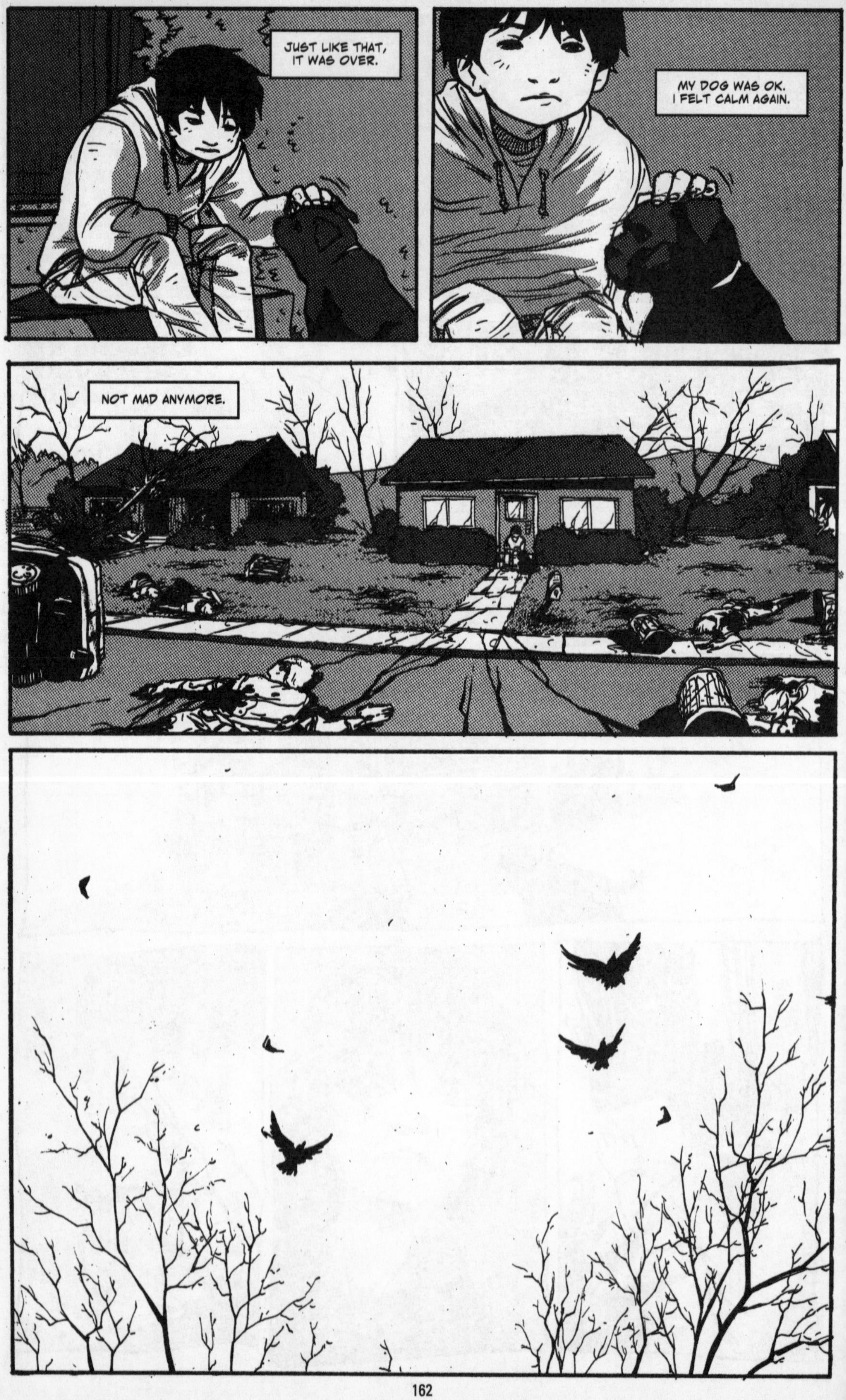
JUST LIKE THAT, IT WAS OVER.
MY DOG WAS OK. I FELT CALM AGAIN.
NOT MAD ANYMORE.

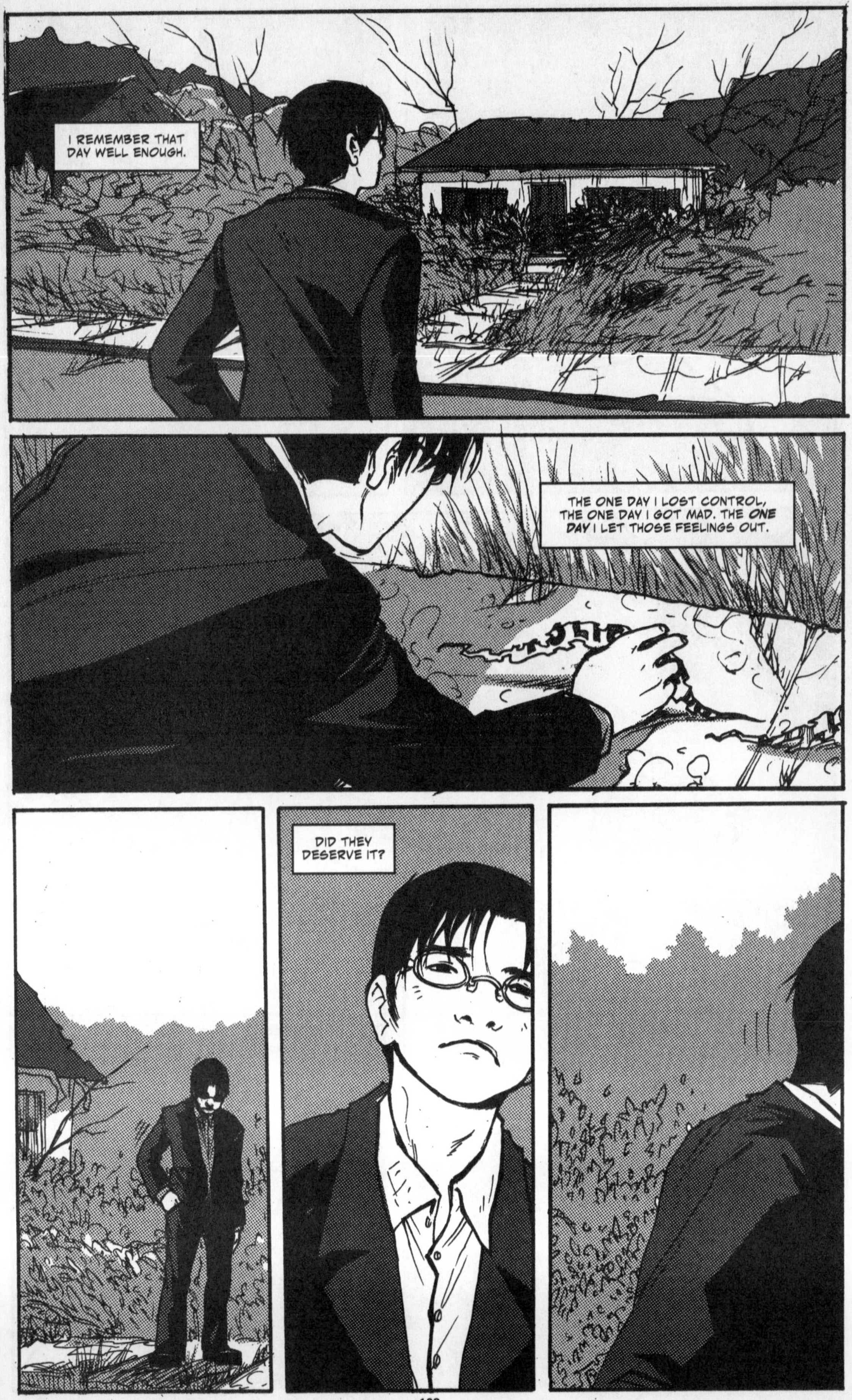
I REMEMBER THAT DAY WELL ENOUGH.
THE ONE DAY I LOST CONTROL, THE ONE DAY I GOT MAD. THE ONE DAY I LET THOSE FEELINGS OUT.
DID THEY DESERVE IT?

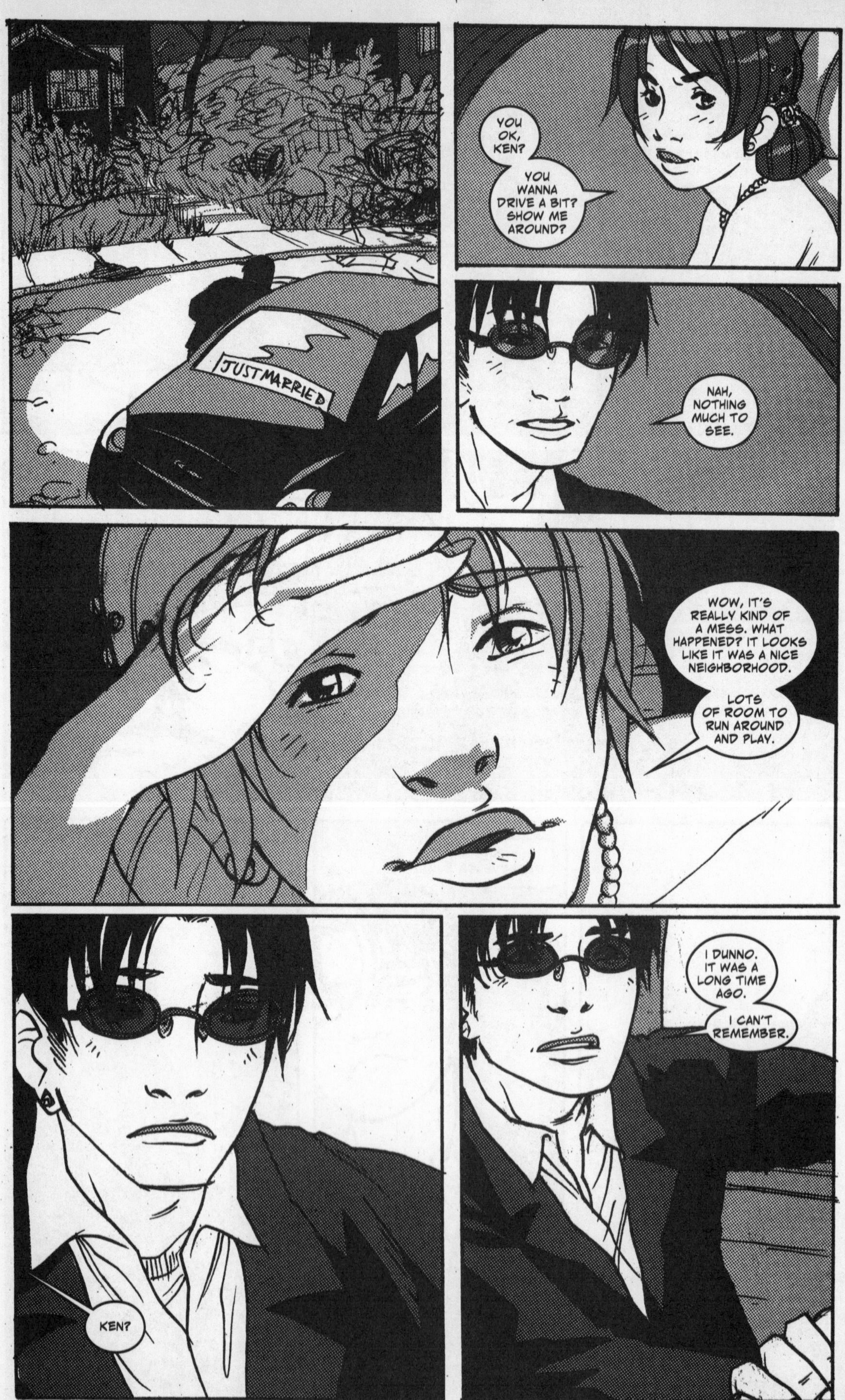
JUST MARRIED
YOU OK, KEN?
YOU WANNA DRIVE A BIT? SHOW ME AROUND?
NAH, NOTHING MUCH TO SEE.
WOW, IT'S REALLY KIND OF A MESS. WHAT HAPPENED? IT LOOKS LIKE IT WAS A NICE NEIGHBORHOOD.
LOTS OF ROOM TO RUN AROUND AND PLAY.
KEN?
I DUNNO. IT WAS A LONG TIME AGO.
I CAN'T REMEMBER.

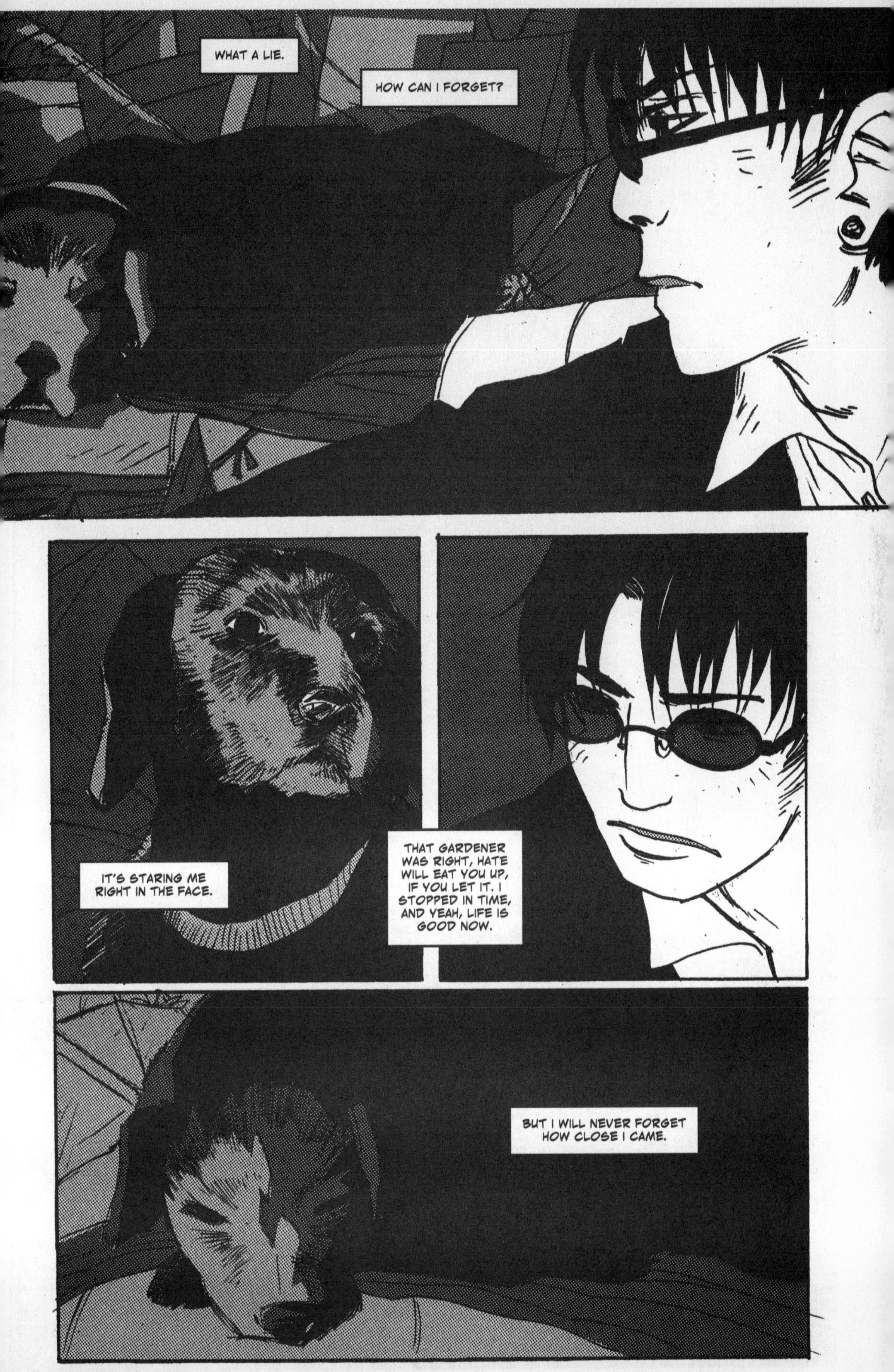
WHAT A LIE.
HOW CAN I FORGET?
IT'S STARING ME RIGHT IN THE FACE.
THAT GARDENER WAS RIGHT, HATE WILL EAT YOU UP, IF YOU LET IT. I STOPPED IN TIME, AND YEAH, LIFE IS GOOD NOW.
BUT I WILL NEVER FORGET HOW CLOSE I CAME.

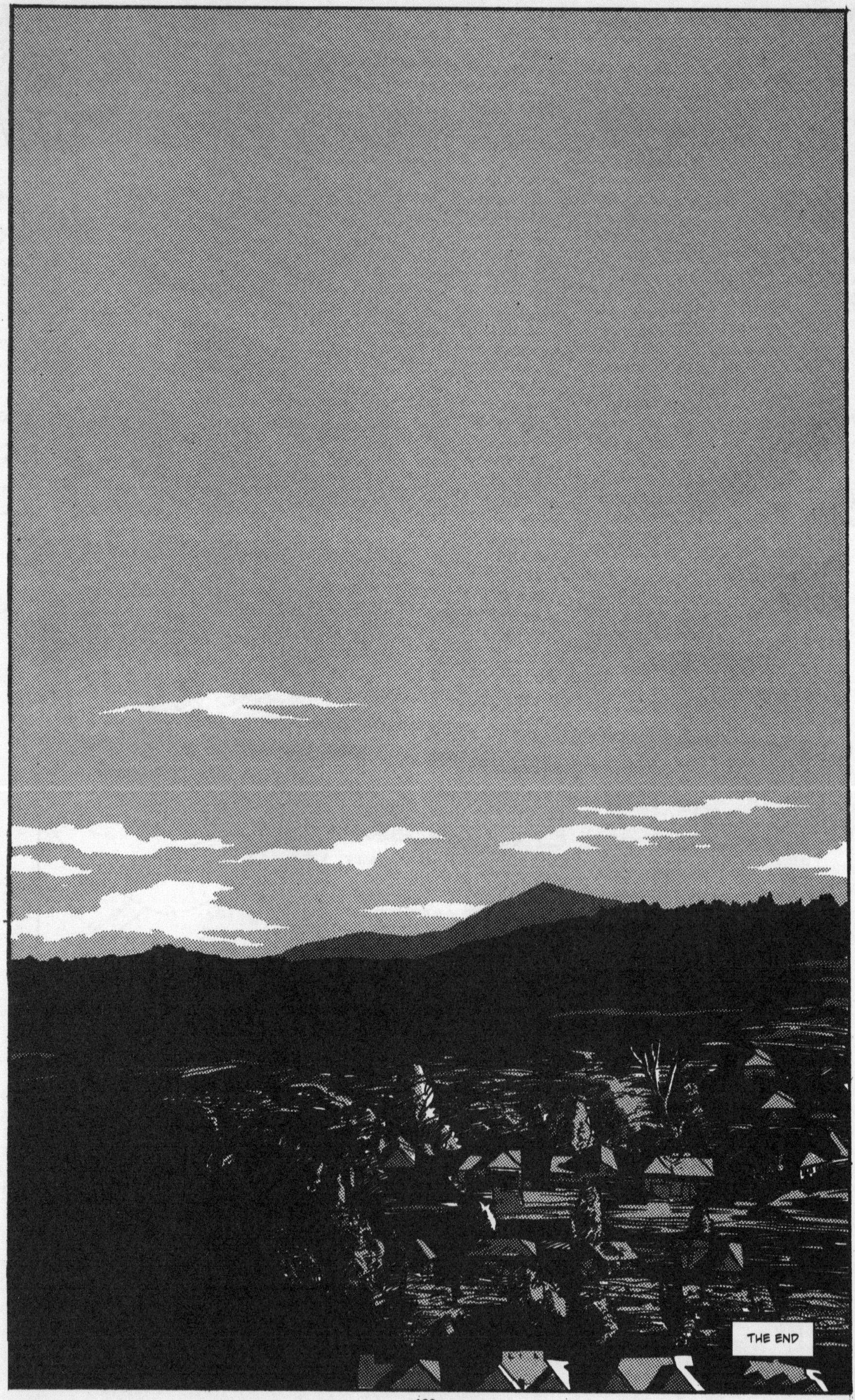
THE END

7

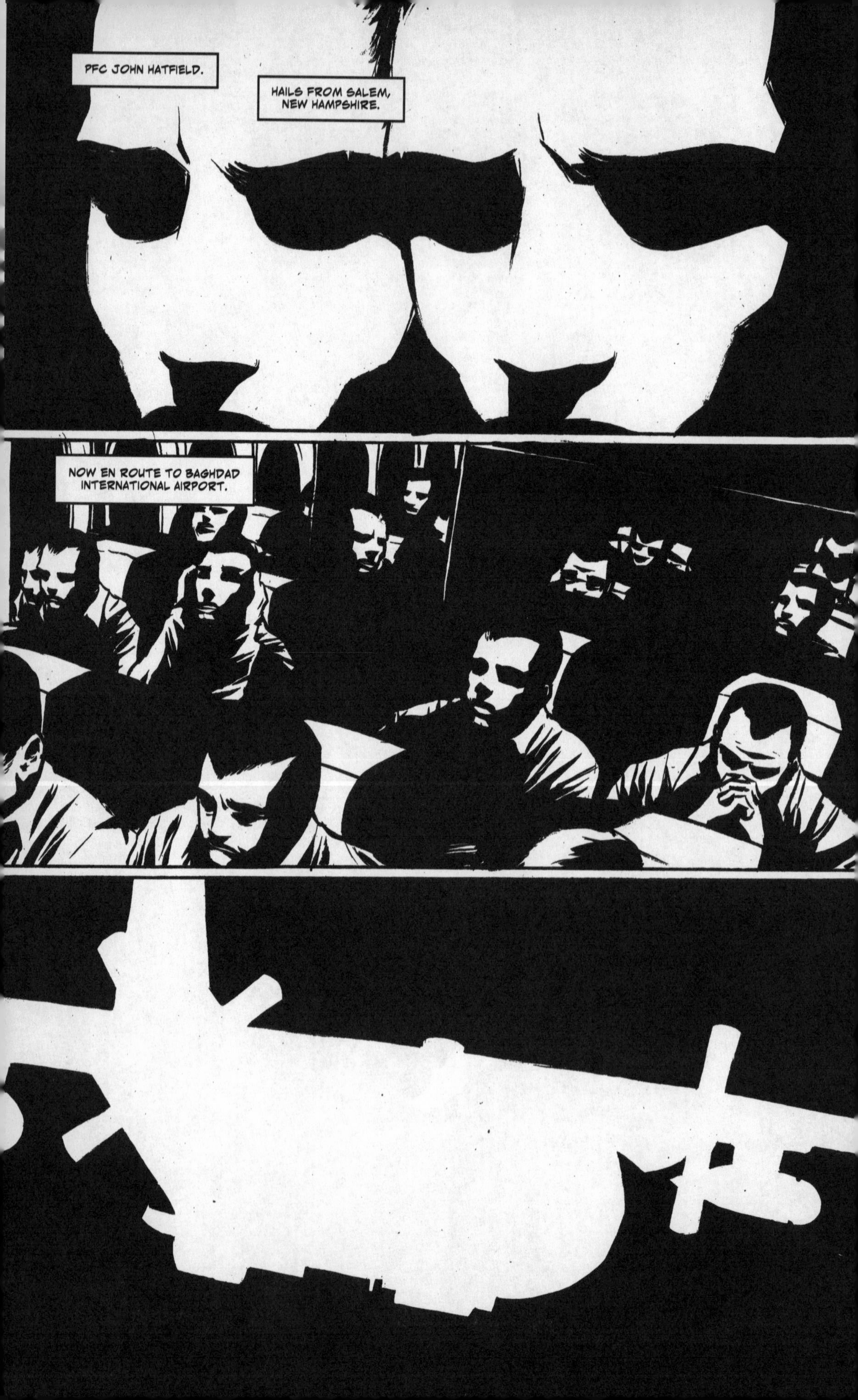
PFC JOHN HATFIELD.
HAILS FROM SALEM, NEW HAMPSHIRE.
NOW EN ROUTE TO BAGHDAD INTERNATIONAL AIRPORT.

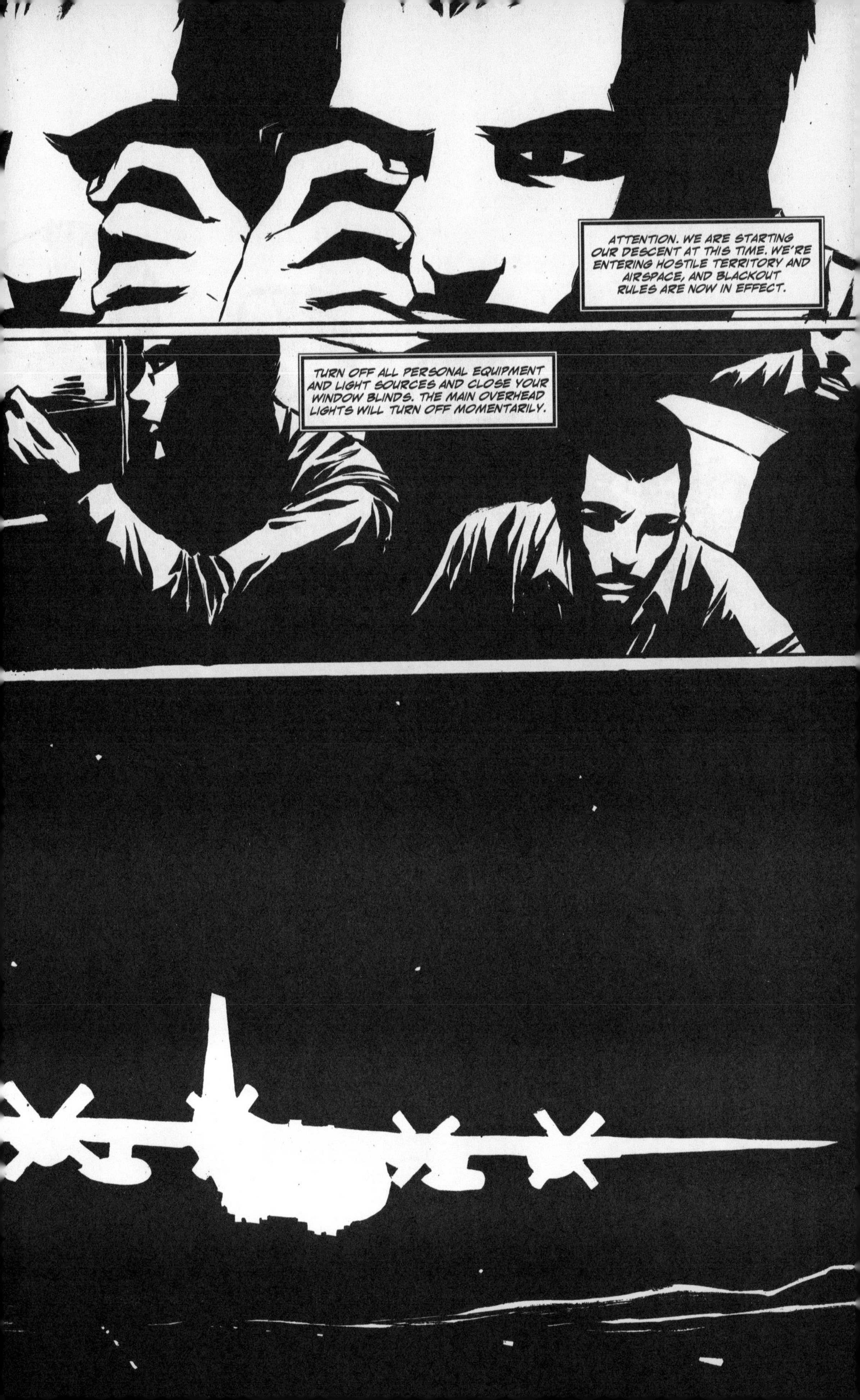
ATTENTION. WE ARE STARTING OUR DESCENT AT THIS TIME. WE'RE ENTERING HOSTILE TERRITORY AND AIRSPACE, AND BLACKOUT RULES ARE NOW IN EFFECT.
TURN OFF ALL PERSONAL EQUIPMENT AND LIGHT SOURCES AND CLOSE YOUR WINDOW BLINDS. THE MAIN OVERHEAD LIGHTS WILL TURN OFF MOMENTARILY.

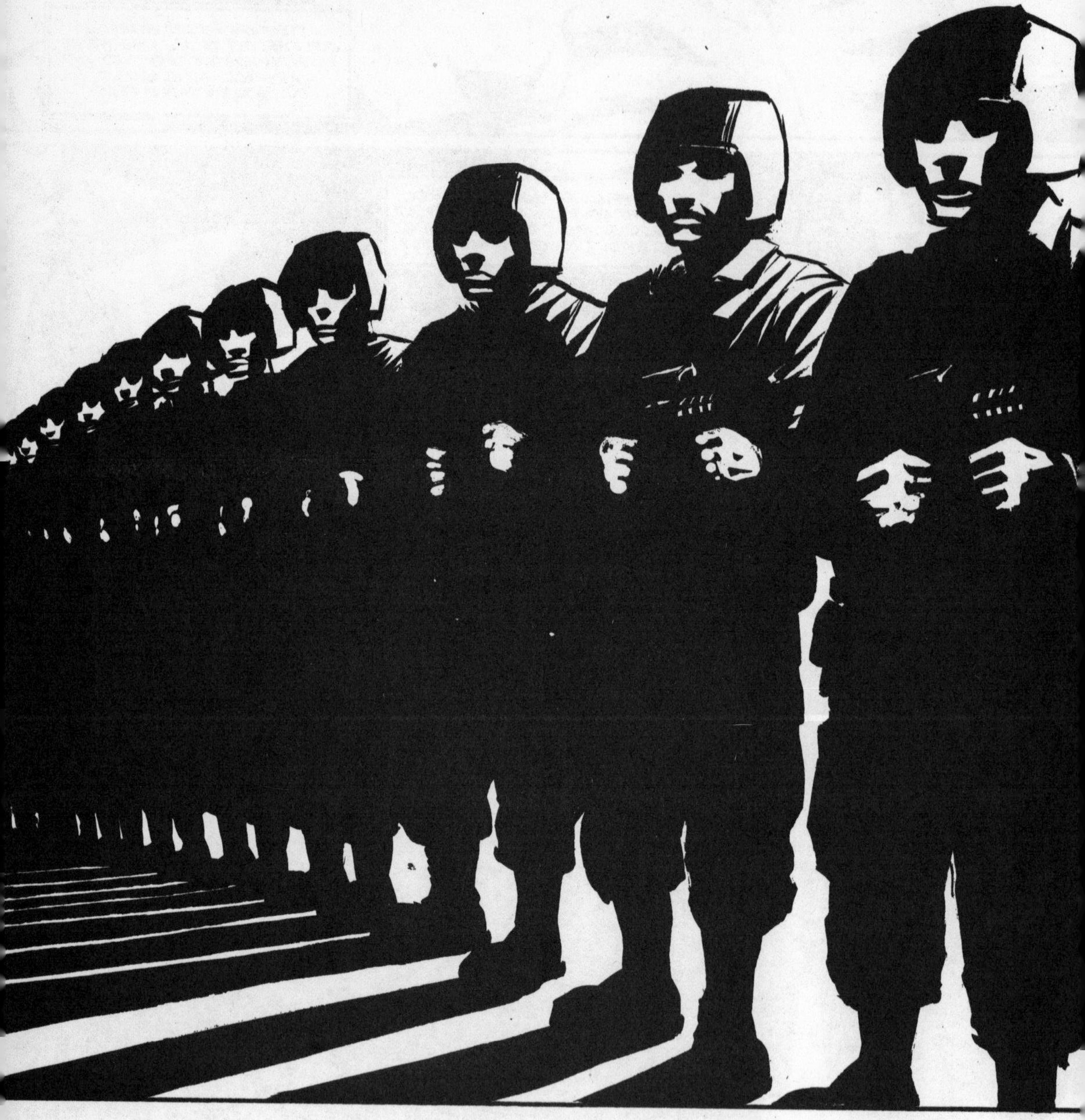

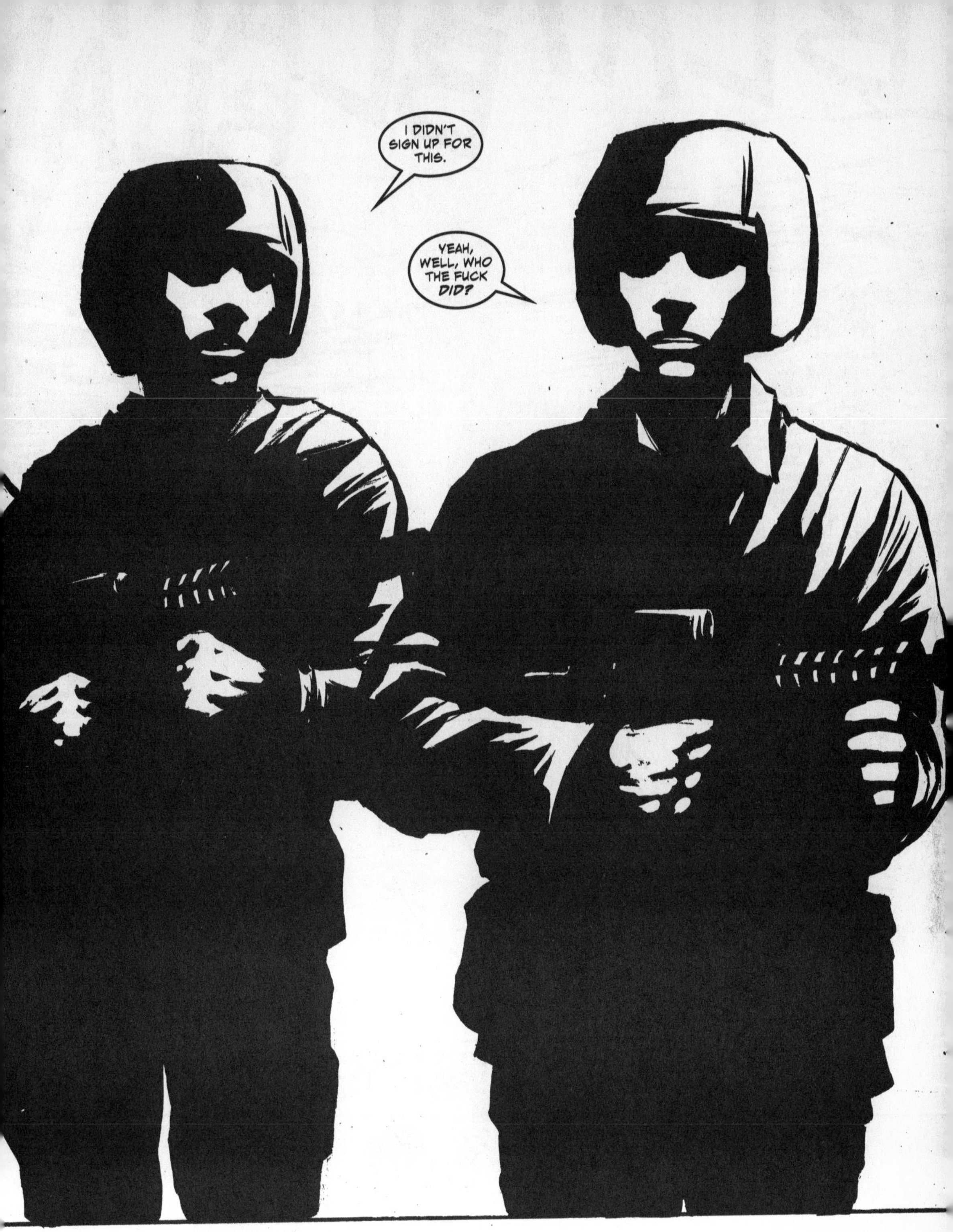
I DIDN'T SIGN UP FOR THIS.
YEAH, WELL, WHO THE FUCK *DID?*

"One Shot, Don't Miss"

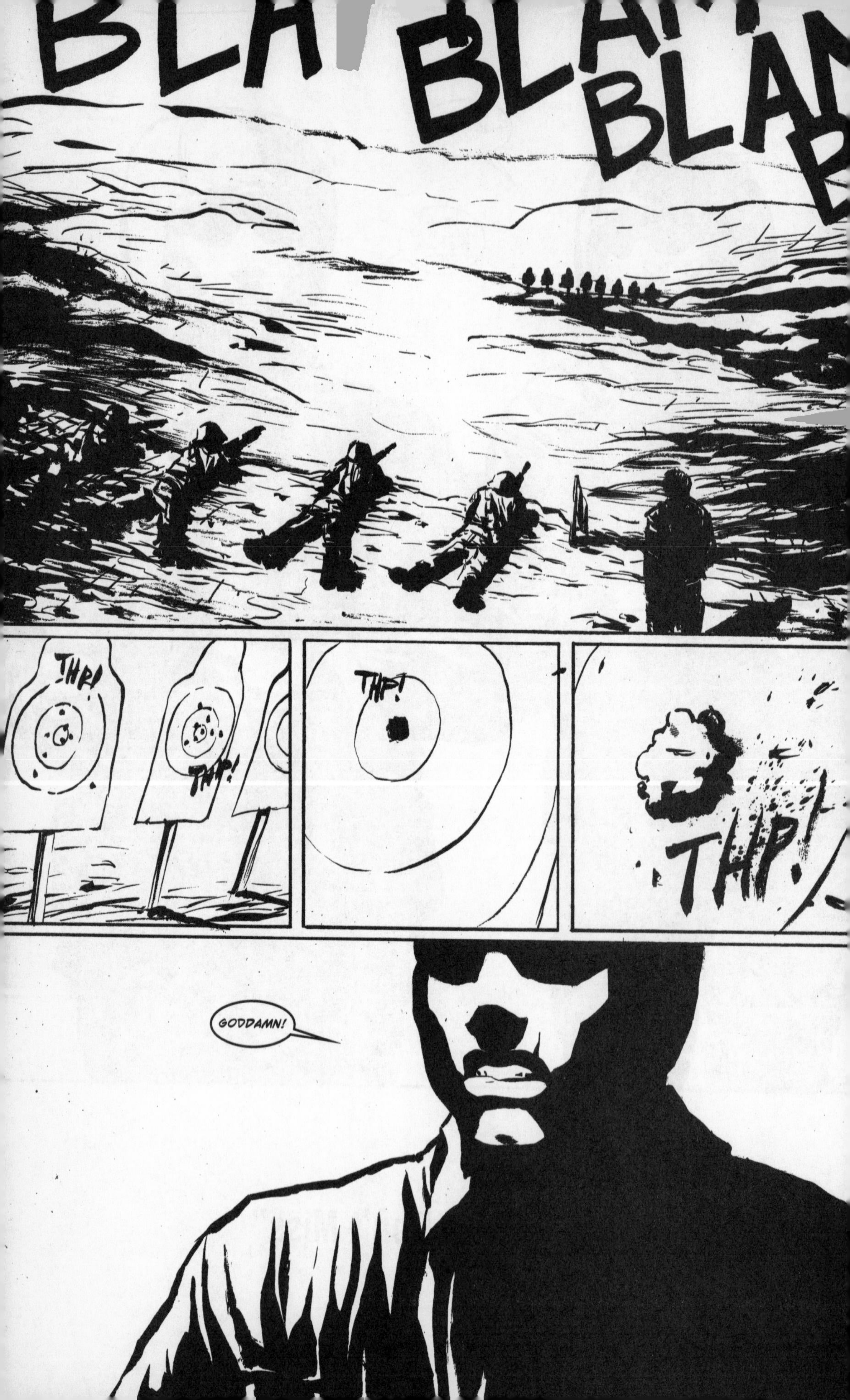
BLAM
BLAM
BLAM
THP!
THP!
THP!
THP!
GODDAMN!

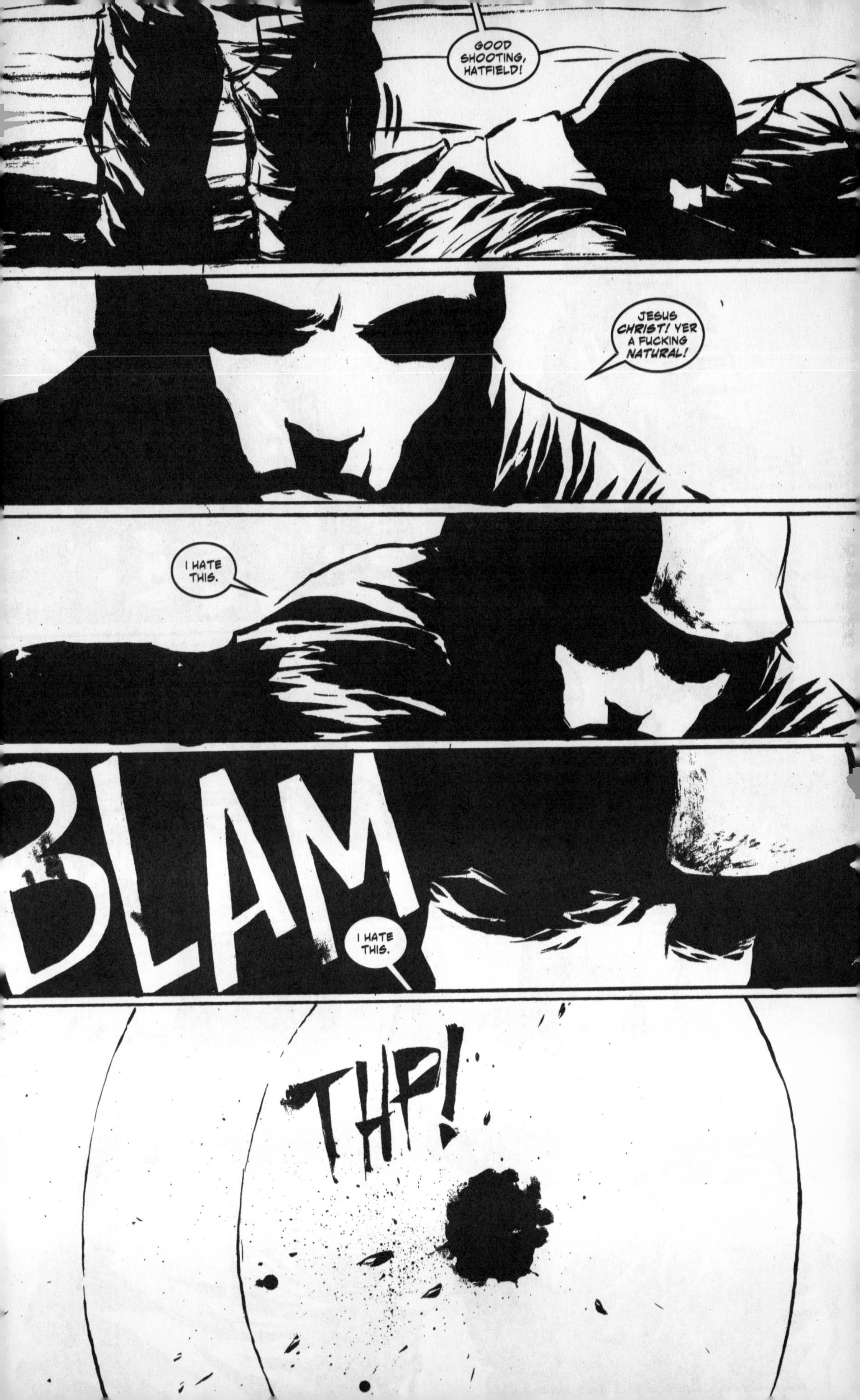
GOOD SHOOTING, HATFIELD!
JESUS CHRIST! YER A FUCKING NATURAL!
I HATE THIS.
BLAM
I HATE THIS.
THP!

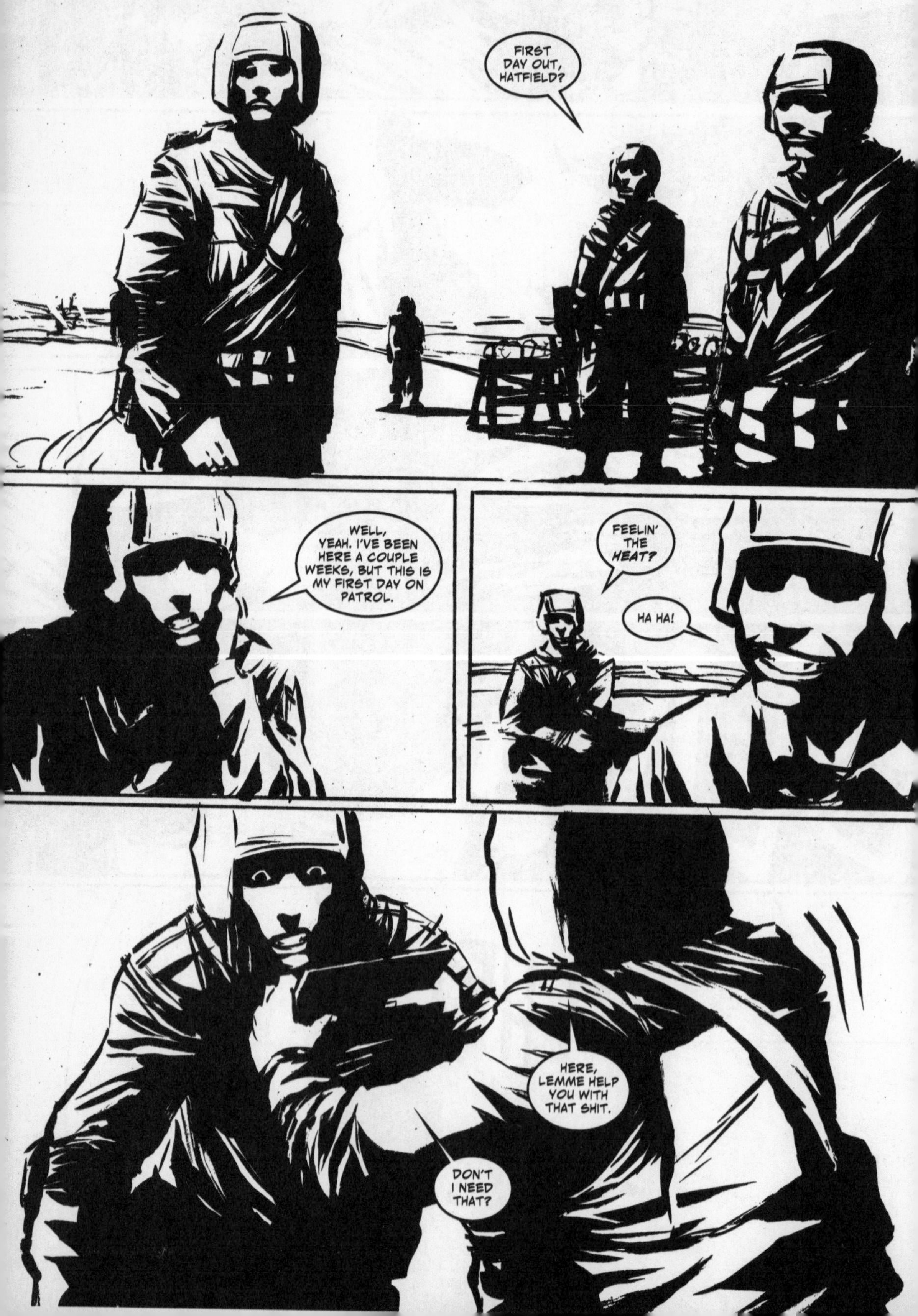
FIRST DAY OUT, HATFIELD?
WELL, YEAH. I'VE BEEN HERE A COUPLE WEEKS, BUT THIS IS MY FIRST DAY ON PATROL.
FEELIN' THE *HEAT?*
HA HA!
HERE, LEMME HELP YOU WITH THAT SHIT.
DON'T I NEED THAT?

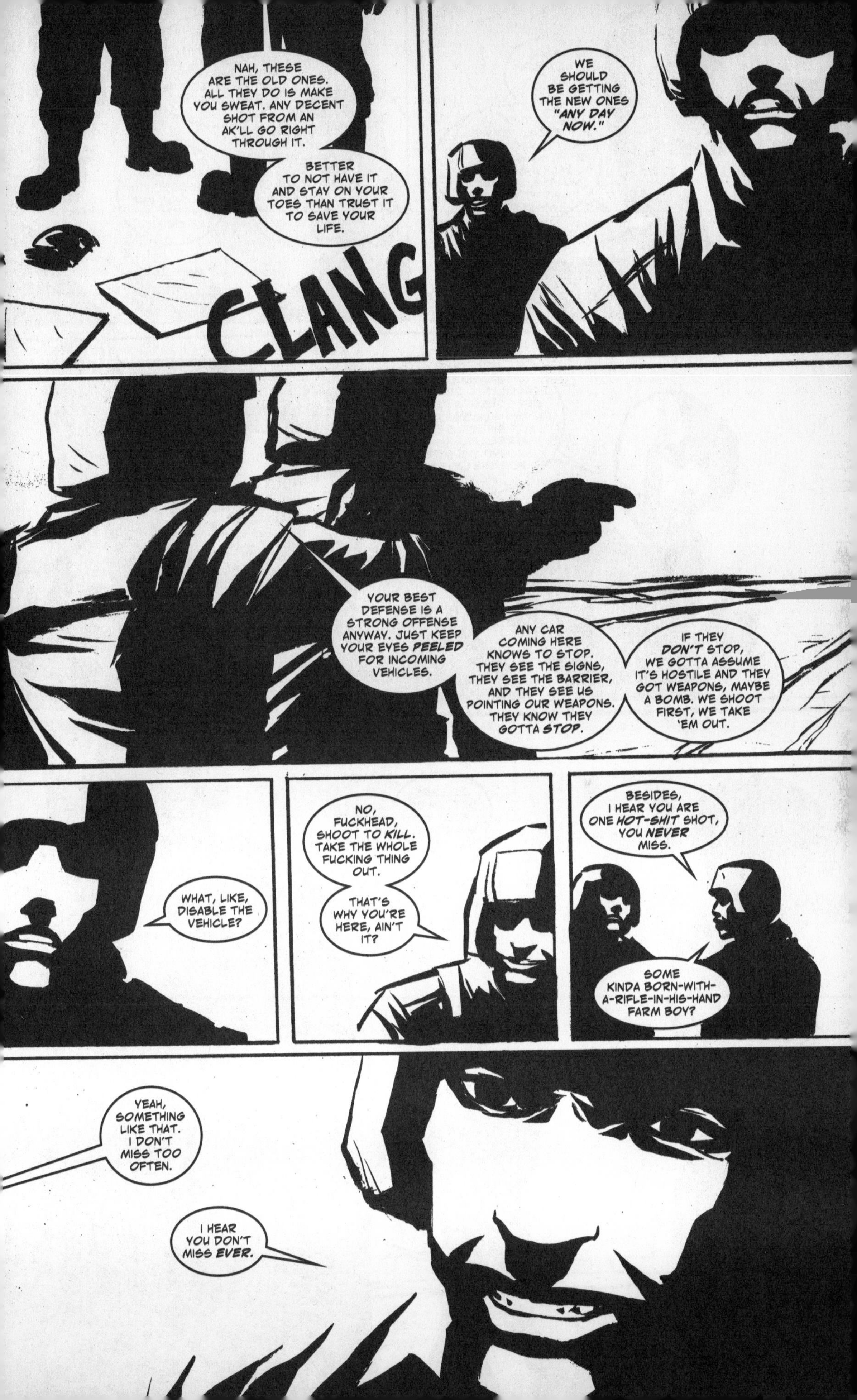
NAH, THESE ARE THE OLD ONES. ALL THEY DO IS MAKE YOU SWEAT. ANY DECENT SHOT FROM AN AK'LL GO RIGHT THROUGH IT.
BETTER TO NOT HAVE IT AND STAY ON YOUR TOES THAN TRUST IT TO SAVE YOUR LIFE.
CLANG
WE SHOULD BE GETTING THE NEW ONES "ANY DAY NOW."
YOUR BEST DEFENSE IS A STRONG OFFENSE ANYWAY. JUST KEEP YOUR EYES PEELED FOR INCOMING VEHICLES.
ANY CAR COMING HERE KNOWS TO STOP. THEY SEE THE SIGNS, THEY SEE THE BARRIER, AND THEY SEE US POINTING OUR WEAPONS. THEY KNOW THEY GOTTA STOP.
IF THEY DON'T STOP, WE GOTTA ASSUME IT'S HOSTILE AND THEY GOT WEAPONS, MAYBE A BOMB. WE SHOOT FIRST, WE TAKE 'EM OUT.
WHAT, LIKE, DISABLE THE VEHICLE?
NO, FUCKHEAD, SHOOT TO KILL. TAKE THE WHOLE FUCKING THING OUT.
THAT'S WHY YOU'RE HERE, AIN'T IT?
BESIDES, I HEAR YOU ARE ONE HOT-SHIT SHOT, YOU NEVER MISS.
SOME KINDA BORN-WITH-A-RIFLE-IN-HIS-HAND FARM BOY?
YEAH, SOMETHING LIKE THAT. I DON'T MISS TOO OFTEN.
I HEAR YOU DON'T MISS EVER.

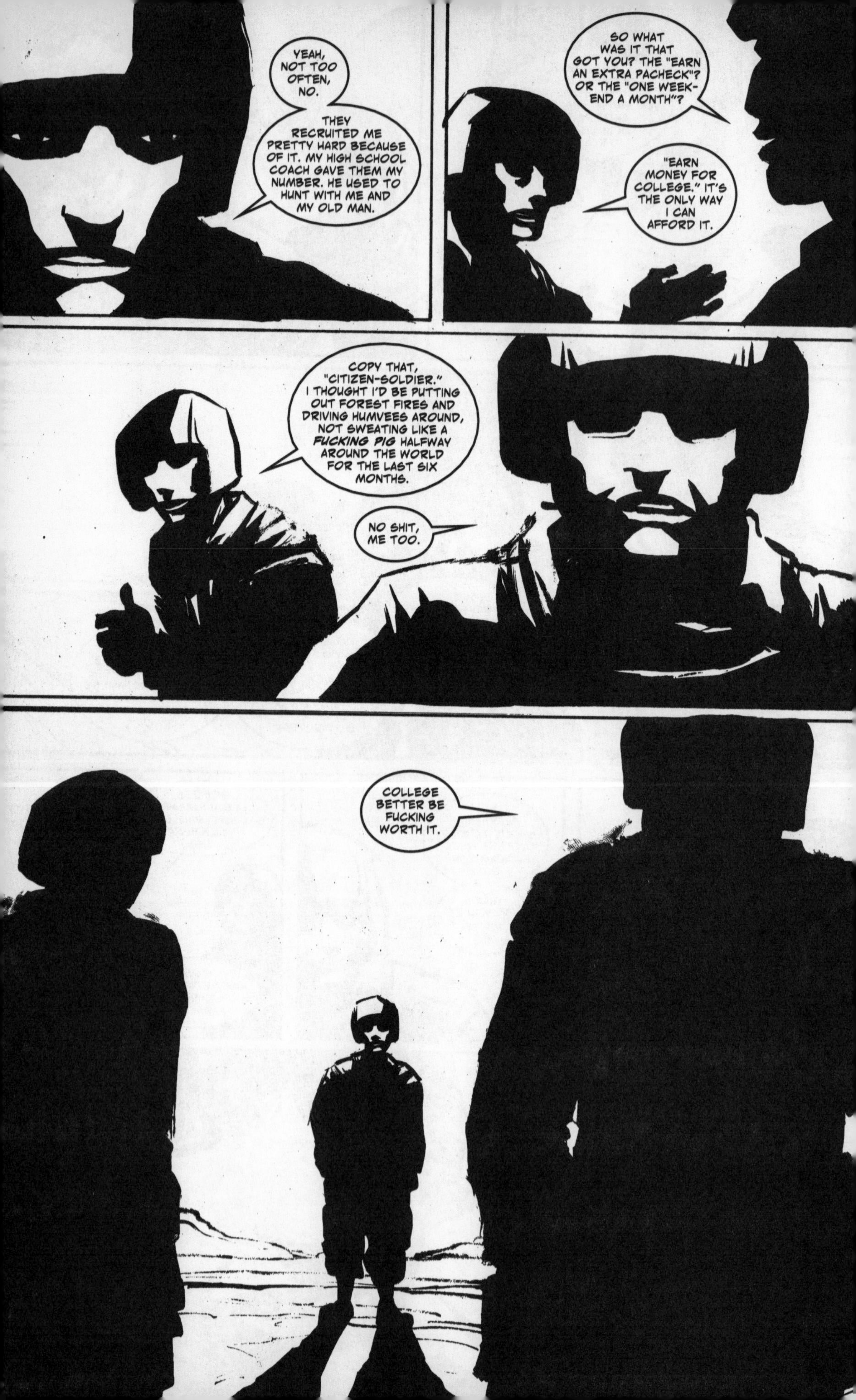
YEAH, NOT TOO OFTEN, NO.
THEY RECRUITED ME PRETTY HARD BECAUSE OF IT. MY HIGH SCHOOL COACH GAVE THEM MY NUMBER. HE USED TO HUNT WITH ME AND MY OLD MAN.
SO WHAT WAS IT THAT GOT YOU? THE "EARN AN EXTRA PACHECK"? OR THE "ONE WEEK-END A MONTH"?
"EARN MONEY FOR COLLEGE." IT'S THE ONLY WAY I CAN AFFORD IT.
COPY THAT, "CITIZEN-SOLDIER." I THOUGHT I'D BE PUTTING OUT FOREST FIRES AND DRIVING HUMVEES AROUND, NOT SWEATING LIKE A *FUCKING PIG* HALFWAY AROUND THE WORLD FOR THE LAST SIX MONTHS.
NO SHIT, ME TOO.
COLLEGE BETTER BE FUCKING WORTH IT.

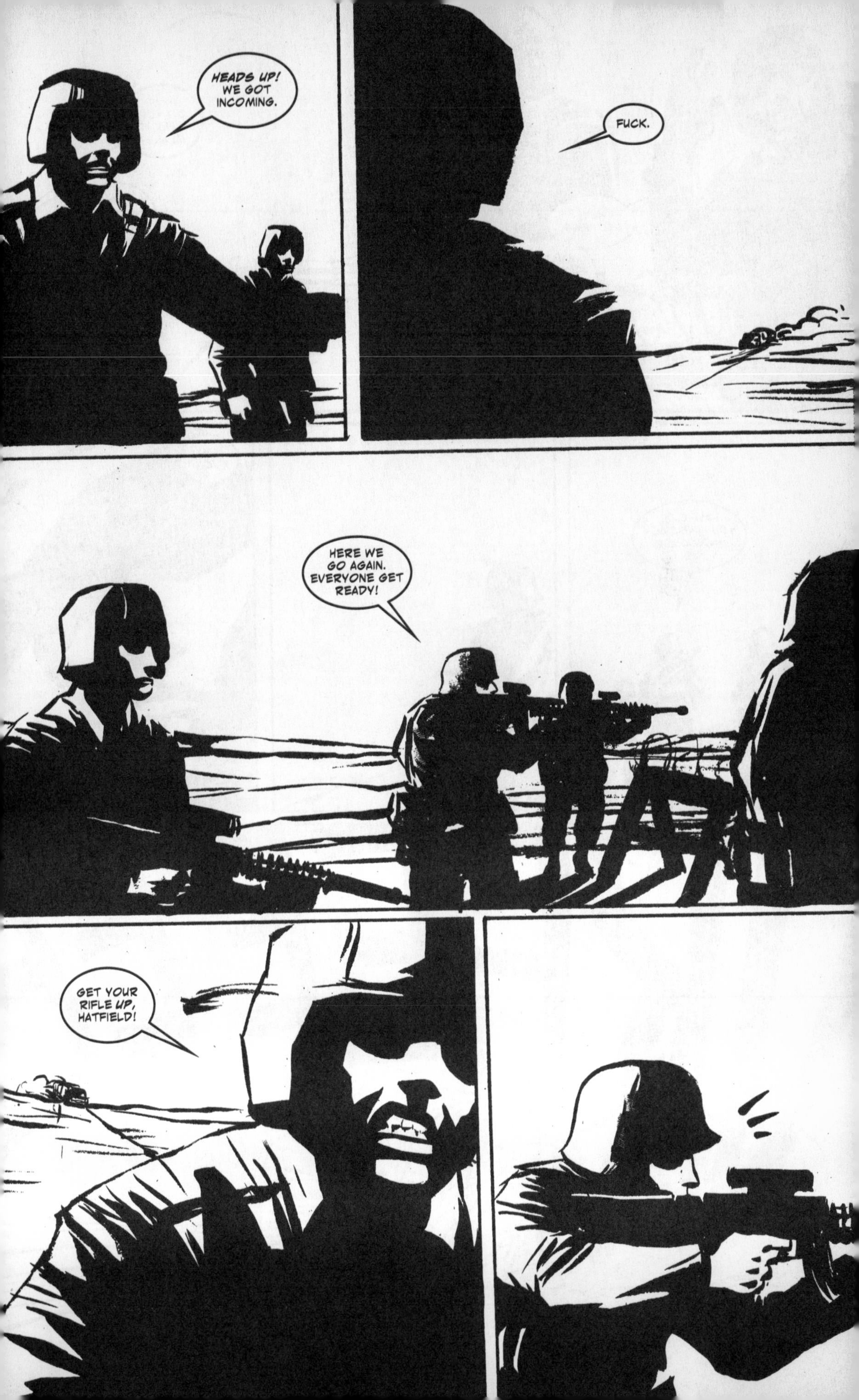
HEADS UP! WE GOT INCOMING.
FUCK.
HERE WE GO AGAIN. EVERYONE GET READY!
GET YOUR RIFLE UP, HATFIELD!

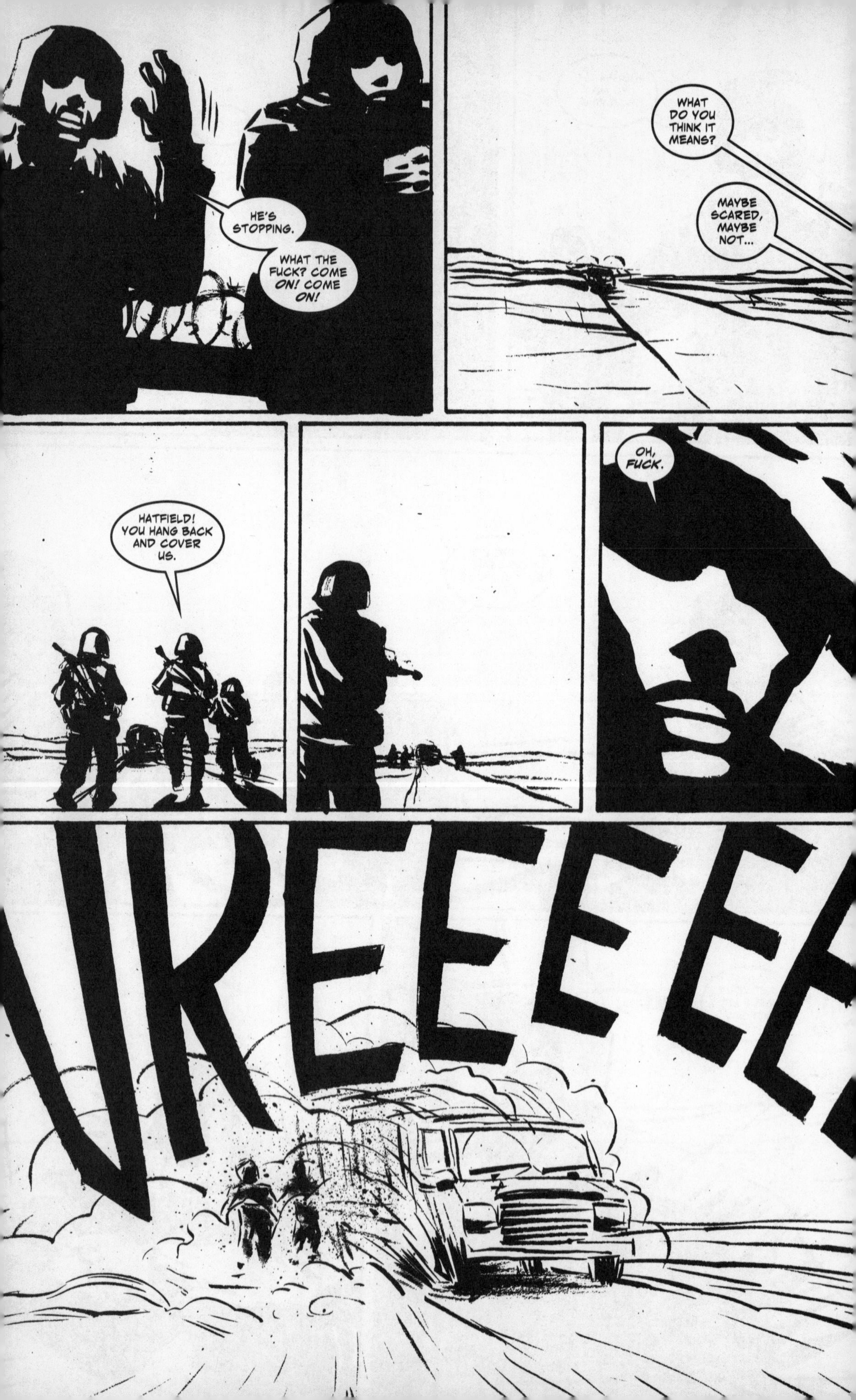
HE'S STOPPING.
WHAT THE FUCK? COME ON! COME ON!
WHAT DO YOU THINK IT MEANS?
MAYBE SCARED, MAYBE NOT...
HATFIELD! YOU HANG BACK AND COVER US.
OH, FUCK.
VREEEEE

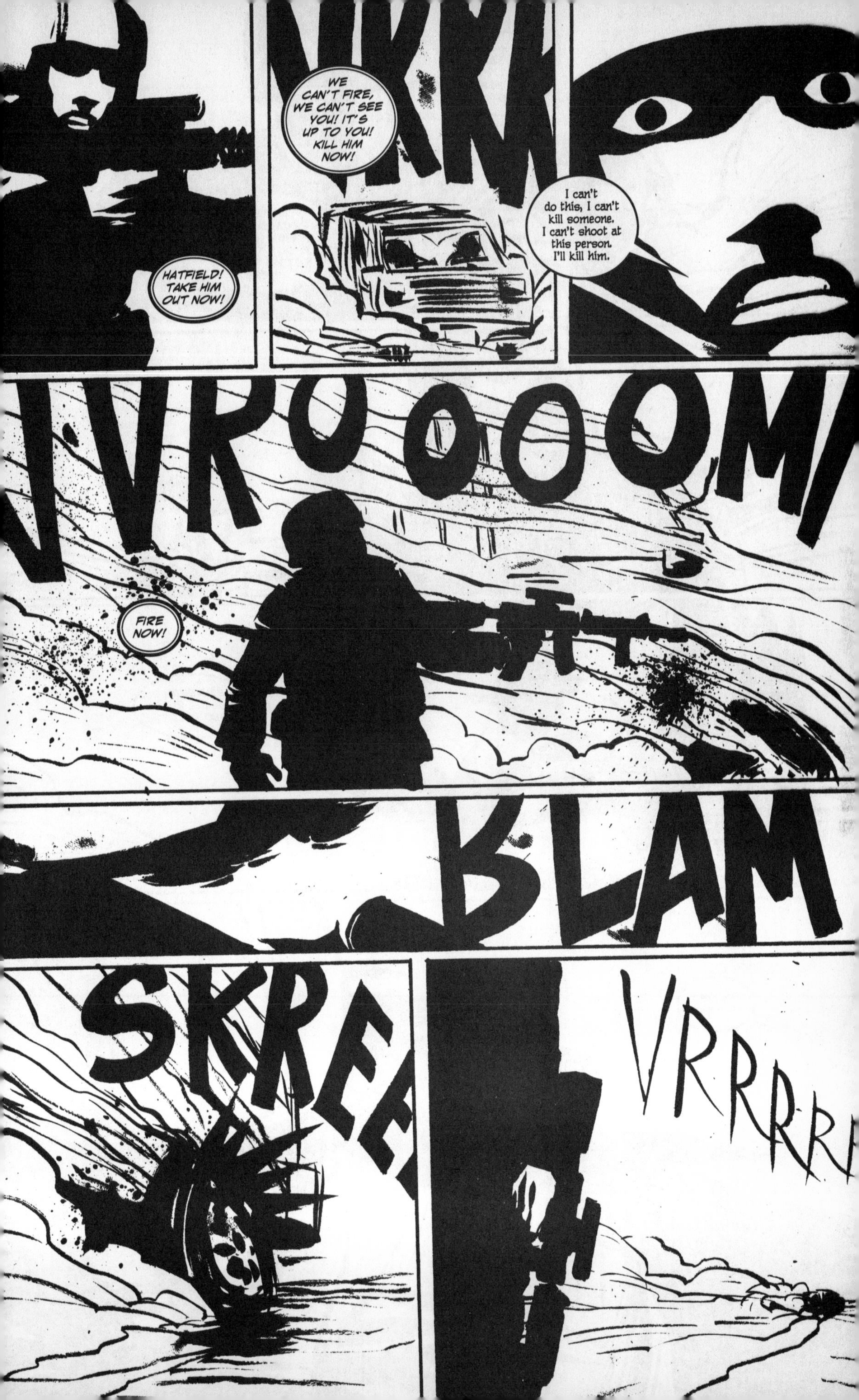
NKKH
WE CAN'T FIRE, WE CAN'T SEE YOU! IT'S UP TO YOU! KILL HIM NOW!
HATFIELD! TAKE HIM OUT NOW!
I can't do this, I can't kill someone. I can't shoot at this person. I'll kill him.
VROOOOM
FIRE NOW!
BLAM
SKREE
VRRRR

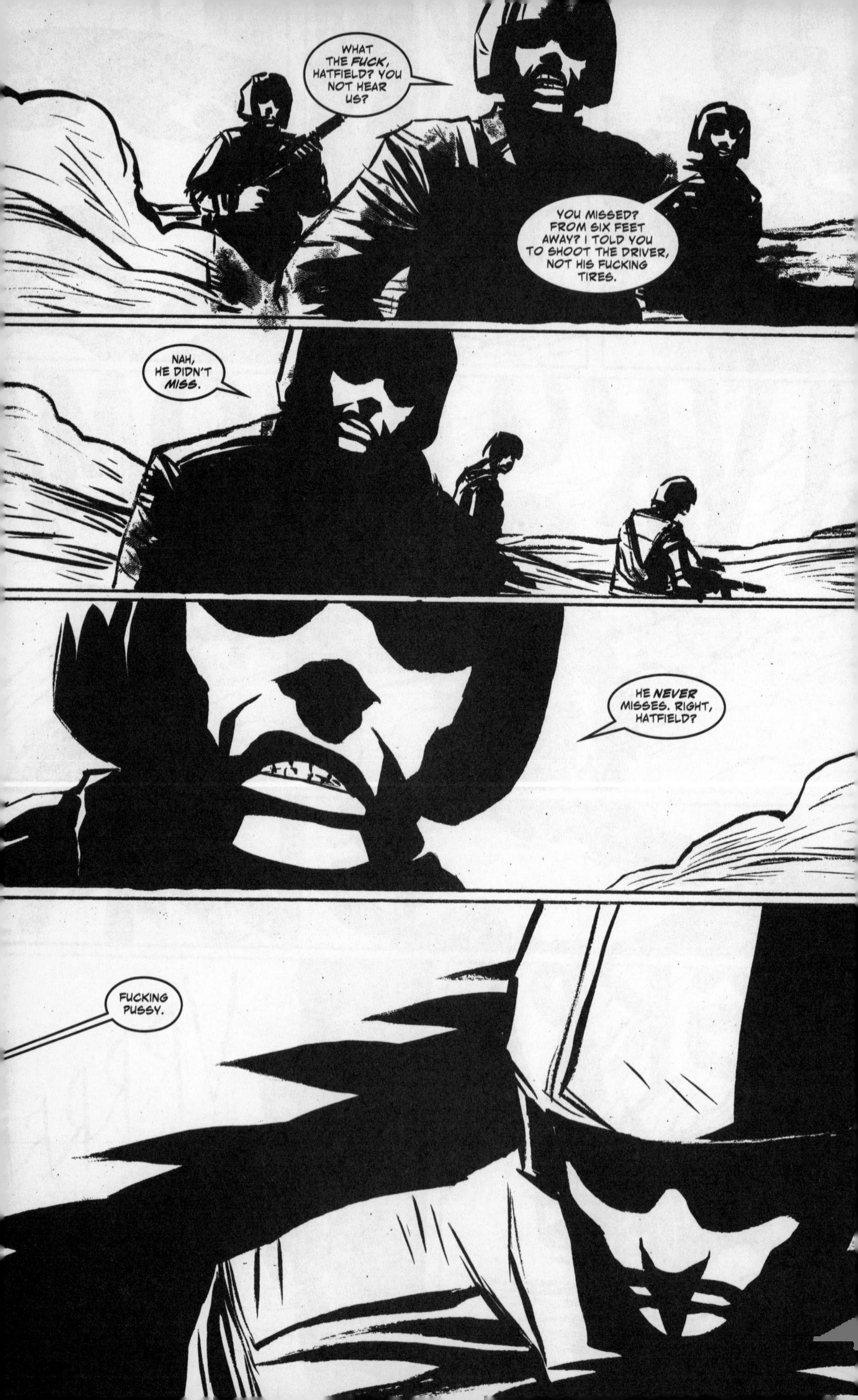
WHAT THE FUCK, HATFIELD? YOU NOT HEAR US?
YOU MISSED? FROM SIX FEET AWAY? I TOLD YOU TO SHOOT THE DRIVER, NOT HIS FUCKING TIRES.
NAH, HE DIDN'T MISS.
HE NEVER MISSES. RIGHT, HATFIELD?
FUCKING PUSSY.

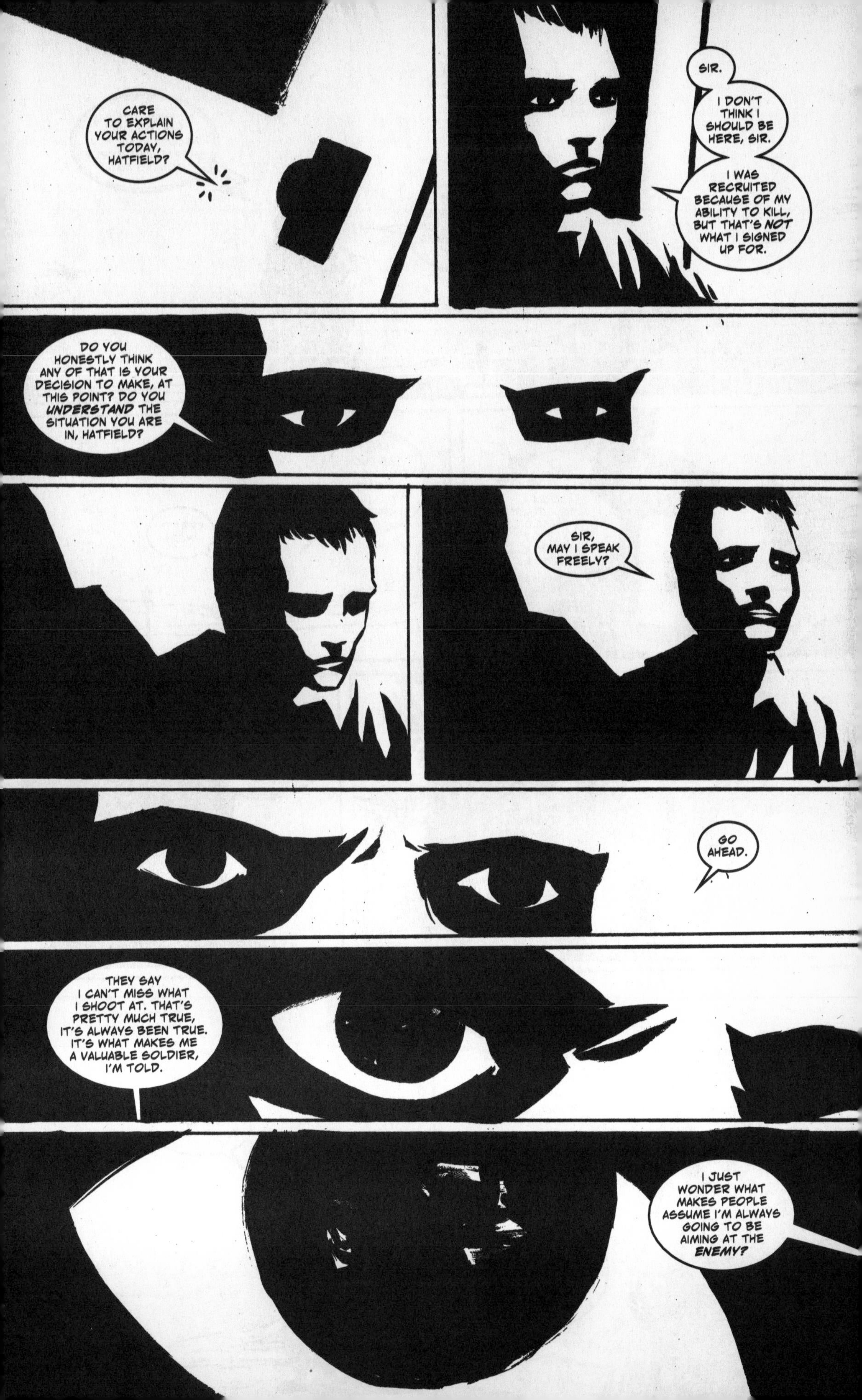
CARE TO EXPLAIN YOUR ACTIONS TODAY, HATFIELD?
SIR.
I DON'T THINK I SHOULD BE HERE, SIR.
I WAS RECRUITED BECAUSE OF MY ABILITY TO KILL, BUT THAT'S NOT WHAT I SIGNED UP FOR.
DO YOU HONESTLY THINK ANY OF THAT IS YOUR DECISION TO MAKE, AT THIS POINT? DO YOU UNDERSTAND THE SITUATION YOU ARE IN, HATFIELD?
SIR, MAY I SPEAK FREELY?
GO AHEAD.
THEY SAY I CAN'T MISS WHAT I SHOOT AT. THAT'S PRETTY MUCH TRUE, IT'S ALWAYS BEEN TRUE. IT'S WHAT MAKES ME A VALUABLE SOLDIER, I'M TOLD.
I JUST WONDER WHAT MAKES PEOPLE ASSUME I'M ALWAYS GOING TO BE AIMING AT THE ENEMY?

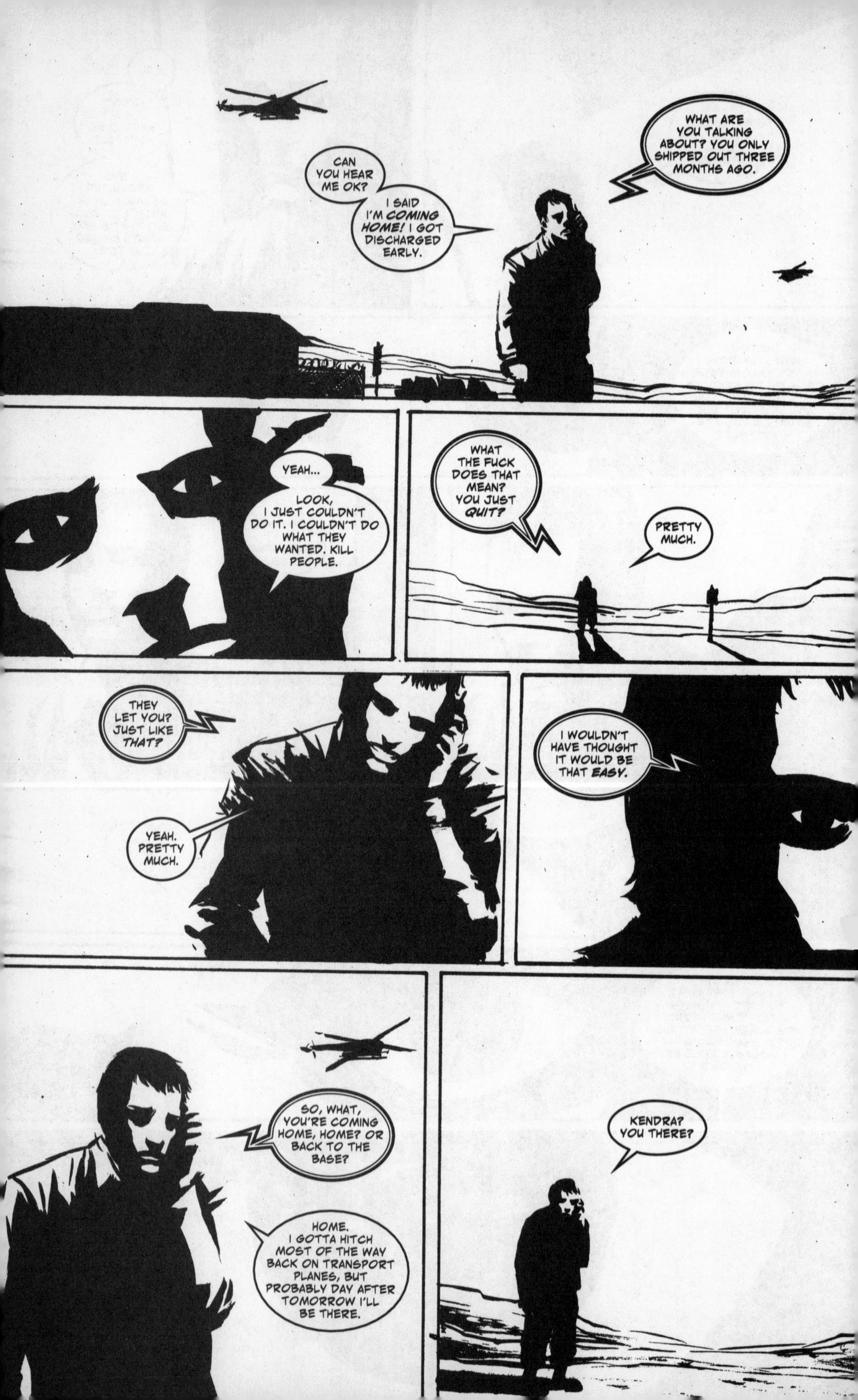
CAN YOU HEAR ME OK?
I SAID I'M COMING HOME! I GOT DISCHARGED EARLY.
WHAT ARE YOU TALKING ABOUT? YOU ONLY SHIPPED OUT THREE MONTHS AGO.
YEAH...
LOOK, I JUST COULDN'T DO IT. I COULDN'T DO WHAT THEY WANTED. KILL PEOPLE.
WHAT THE FUCK DOES THAT MEAN? YOU JUST QUIT?
PRETTY MUCH.
THEY LET YOU? JUST LIKE THAT?
YEAH. PRETTY MUCH.
I WOULDN'T HAVE THOUGHT IT WOULD BE THAT EASY.
SO, WHAT, YOU'RE COMING HOME, HOME? OR BACK TO THE BASE?
HOME. I GOTTA HITCH MOST OF THE WAY BACK ON TRANSPORT PLANES, BUT PROBABLY DAY AFTER TOMORROW I'LL BE THERE.
KENDRA? YOU THERE?

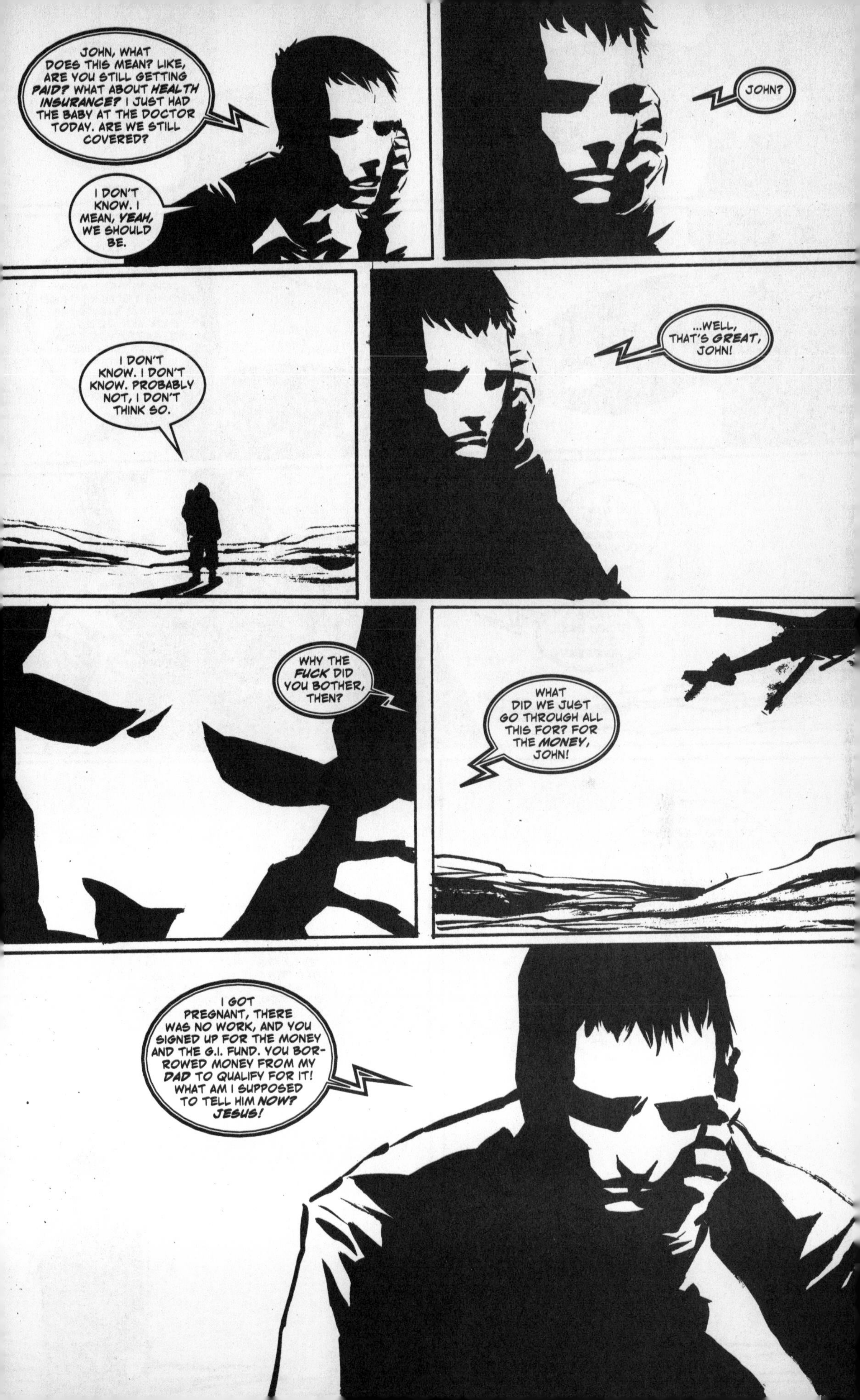
JOHN, WHAT DOES THIS MEAN? LIKE, ARE YOU STILL GETTING PAID? WHAT ABOUT HEALTH INSURANCE? I JUST HAD THE BABY AT THE DOCTOR TODAY. ARE WE STILL COVERED?
I DON'T KNOW. I MEAN, YEAH, WE SHOULD BE.
JOHN?
I DON'T KNOW. I DON'T KNOW. PROBABLY NOT, I DON'T THINK SO.
...WELL, THAT'S GREAT, JOHN!
WHY THE FUCK DID YOU BOTHER, THEN?
WHAT DID WE JUST GO THROUGH ALL THIS FOR? FOR THE MONEY, JOHN!
I GOT PREGNANT, THERE WAS NO WORK, AND YOU SIGNED UP FOR THE MONEY AND THE G.I. FUND. YOU BORROWED MONEY FROM MY DAD TO QUALIFY FOR IT! WHAT AM I SUPPOSED TO TELL HIM NOW? JESUS!

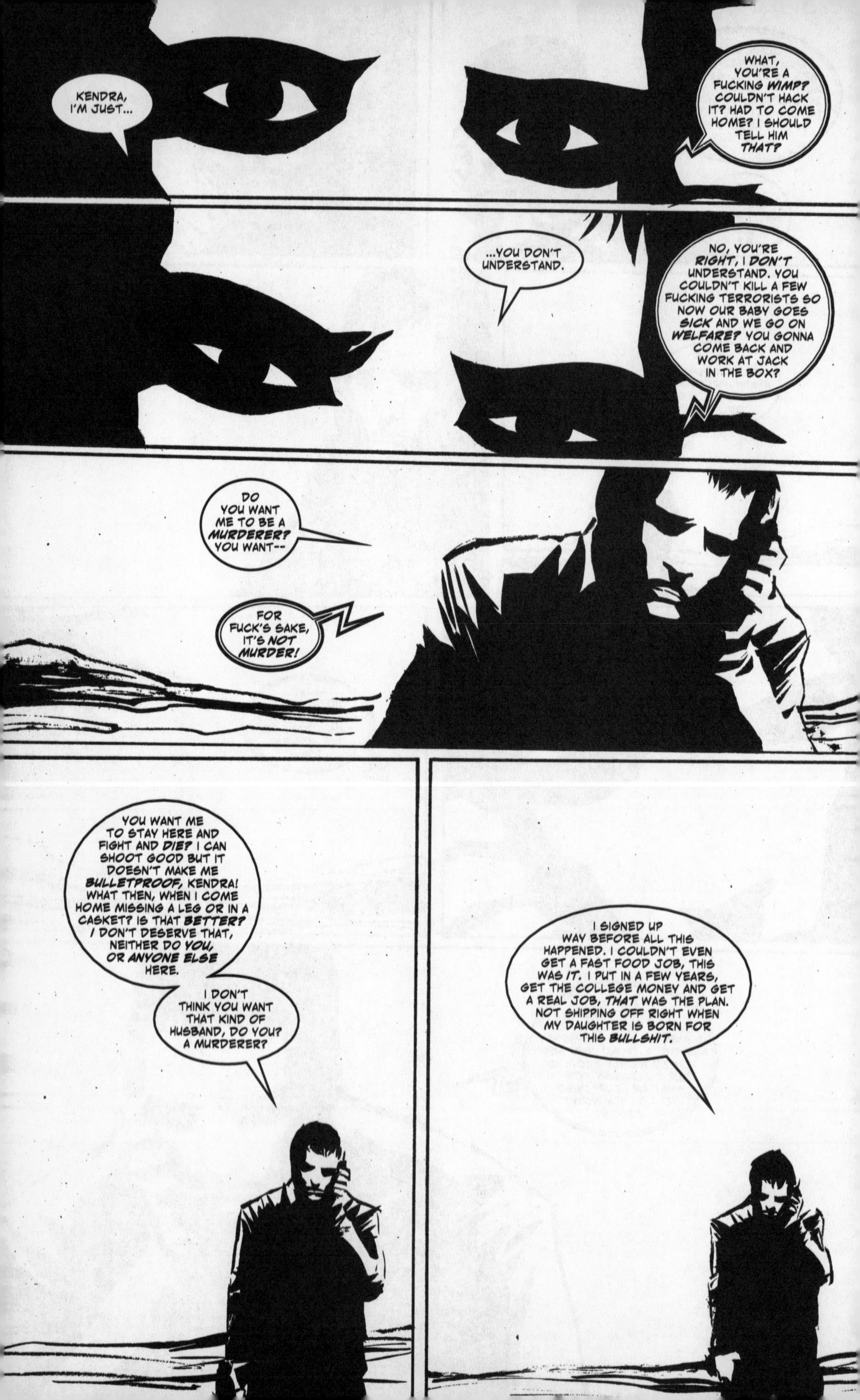
KENDRA, I'M JUST...
WHAT, YOU'RE A FUCKING WIMP? COULDN'T HACK IT? HAD TO COME HOME? I SHOULD TELL HIM THAT?
...YOU DON'T UNDERSTAND.
NO, YOU'RE RIGHT, I DON'T UNDERSTAND. YOU COULDN'T KILL A FEW FUCKING TERRORISTS SO NOW OUR BABY GOES SICK AND WE GO ON WELFARE? YOU GONNA COME BACK AND WORK AT JACK IN THE BOX?
DO YOU WANT ME TO BE A MURDERER? YOU WANT--
FOR FUCK'S SAKE, IT'S NOT MURDER!
YOU WANT ME TO STAY HERE AND FIGHT AND DIE? I CAN SHOOT GOOD BUT IT DOESN'T MAKE ME BULLETPROOF, KENDRA! WHAT THEN, WHEN I COME HOME MISSING A LEG OR IN A CASKET? IS THAT BETTER? I DON'T DESERVE THAT, NEITHER DO YOU, OR ANYONE ELSE HERE.
I DON'T THINK YOU WANT THAT KIND OF HUSBAND, DO YOU? A MURDERER?
I SIGNED UP WAY BEFORE ALL THIS HAPPENED. I COULDN'T EVEN GET A FAST FOOD JOB, THIS WAS IT. I PUT IN A FEW YEARS, GET THE COLLEGE MONEY AND GET A REAL JOB, THAT WAS THE PLAN. NOT SHIPPING OFF RIGHT WHEN MY DAUGHTER IS BORN FOR THIS BULLSHIT.

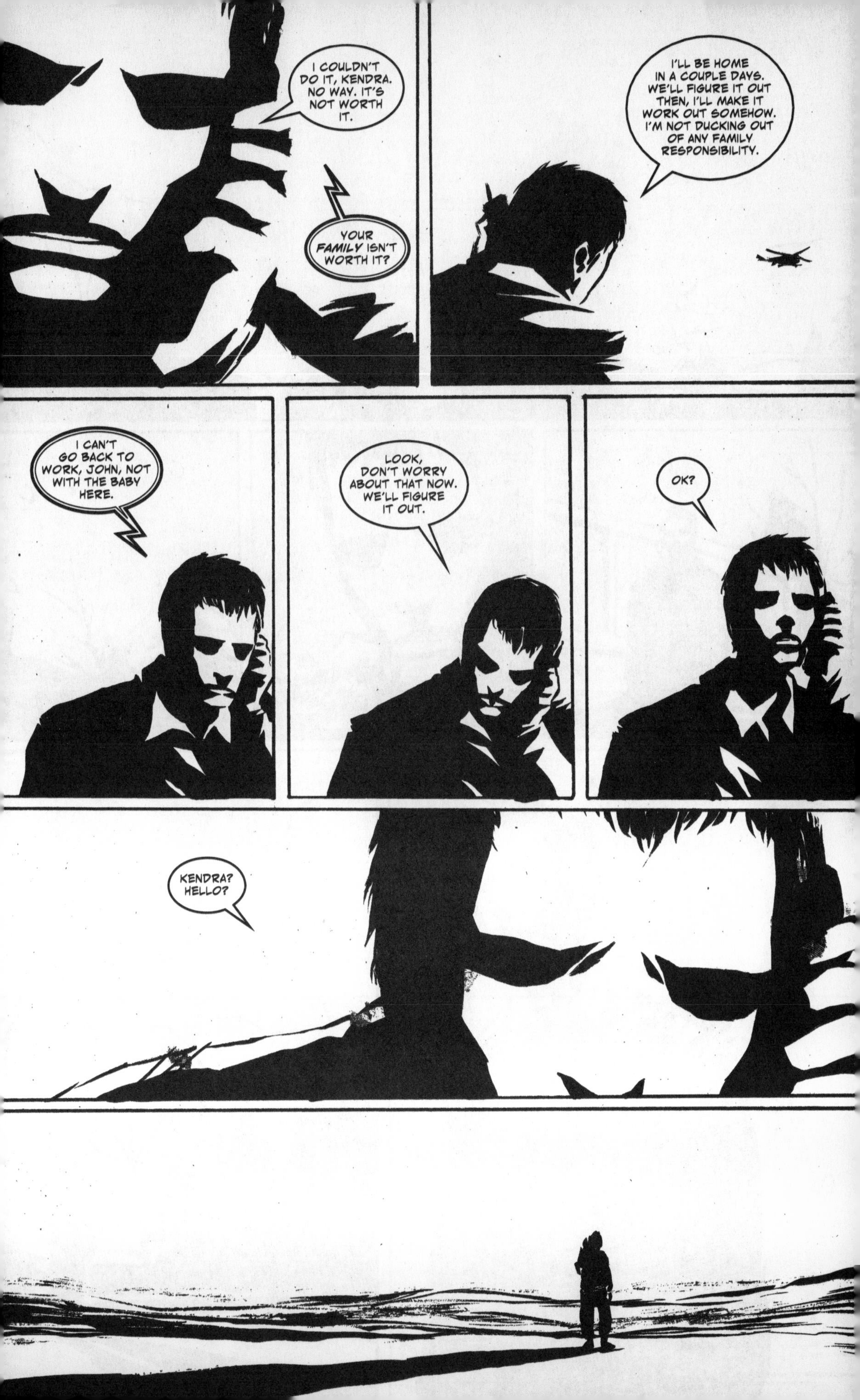
I COULDN'T DO IT, KENDRA. NO WAY. IT'S NOT WORTH IT.
YOUR *FAMILY* ISN'T WORTH IT?
I'LL BE HOME IN A COUPLE DAYS. WE'LL FIGURE IT OUT THEN, I'LL MAKE IT WORK OUT SOMEHOW. I'M NOT DUCKING OUT OF ANY FAMILY RESPONSIBILITY.
I CAN'T GO BACK TO WORK, JOHN, NOT WITH THE BABY HERE.
LOOK, DON'T WORRY ABOUT THAT NOW. WE'LL FIGURE IT OUT.
OK?
KENDRA? HELLO?

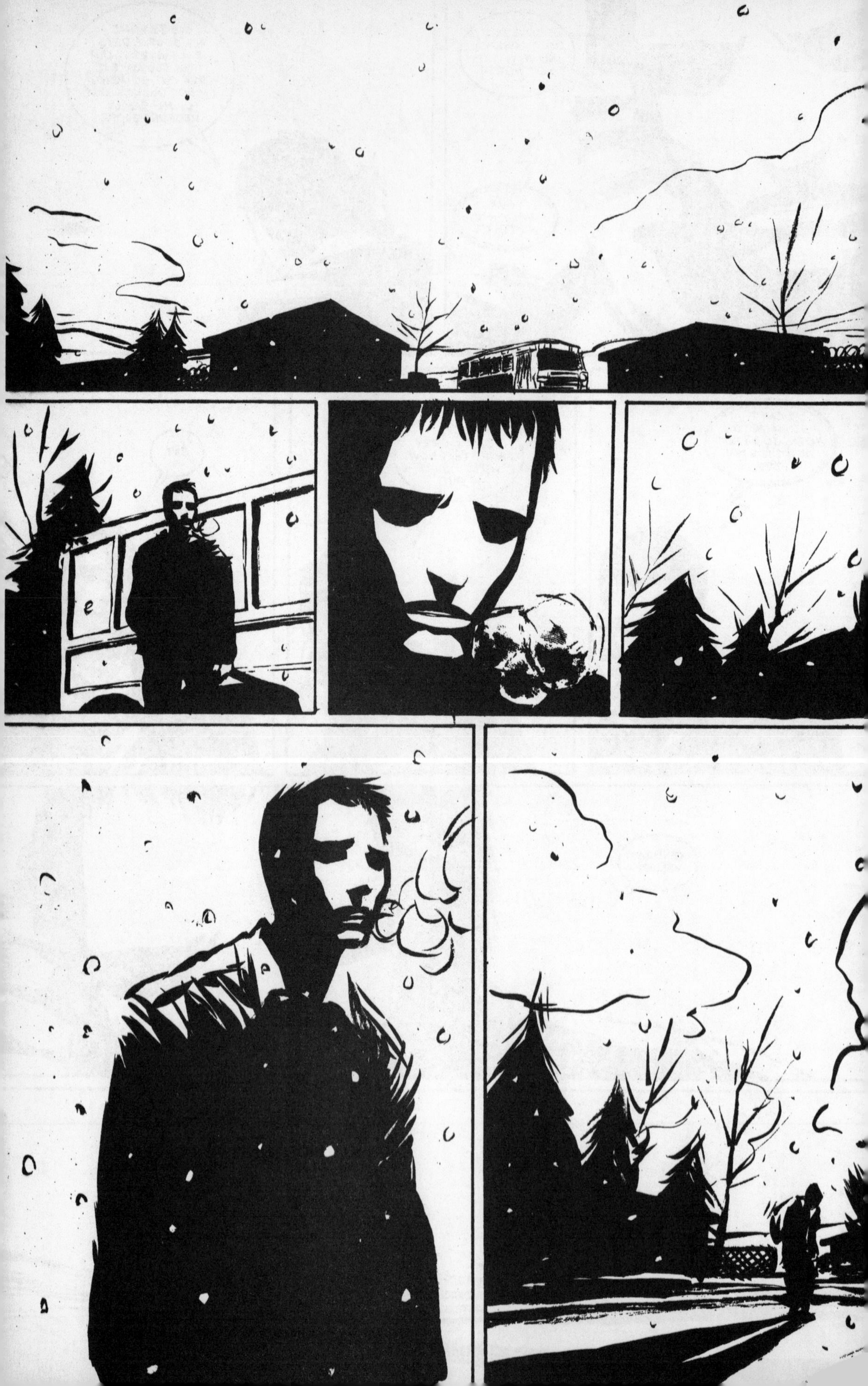

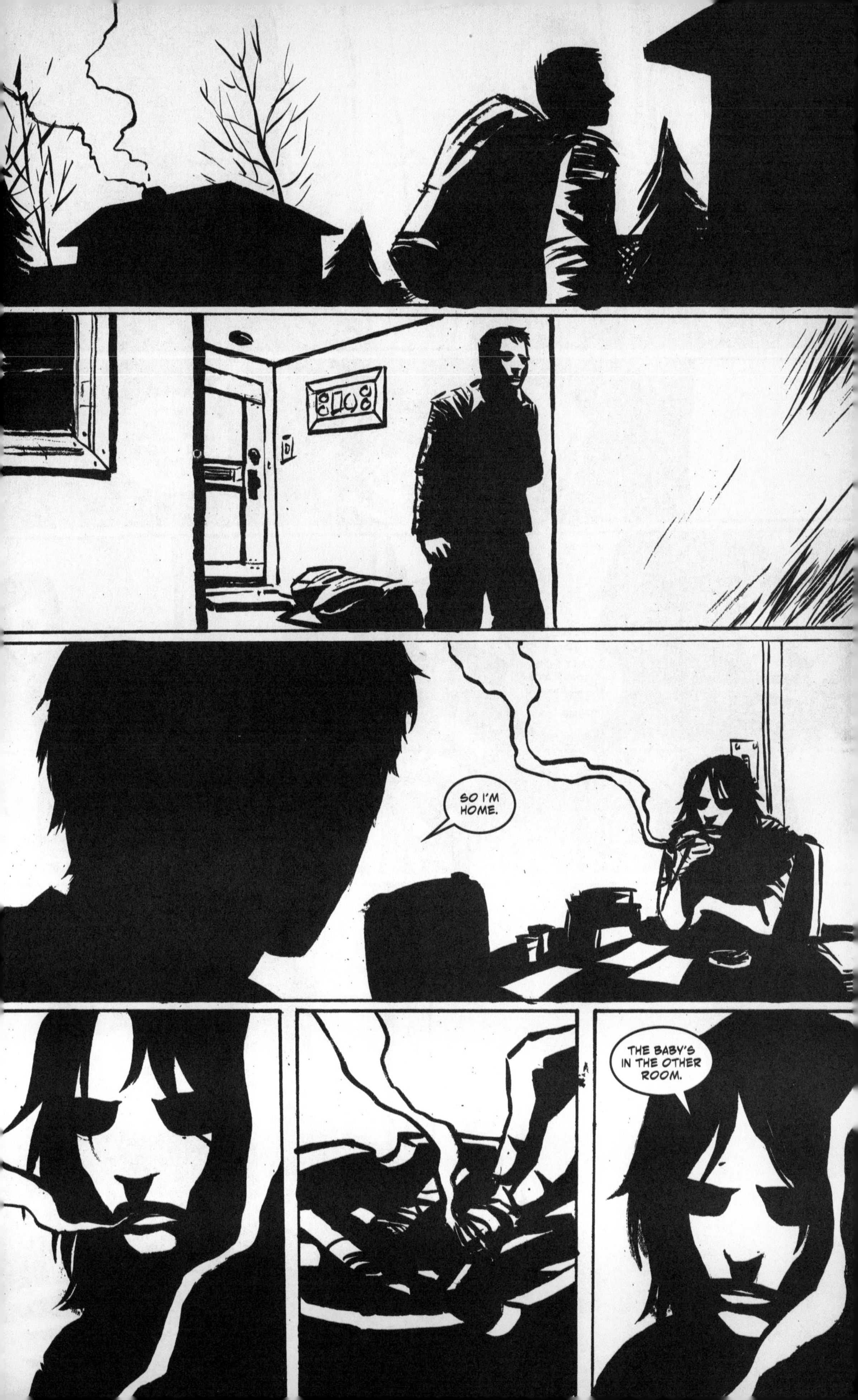
SO I'M HOME.
THE BABY'S IN THE OTHER ROOM.

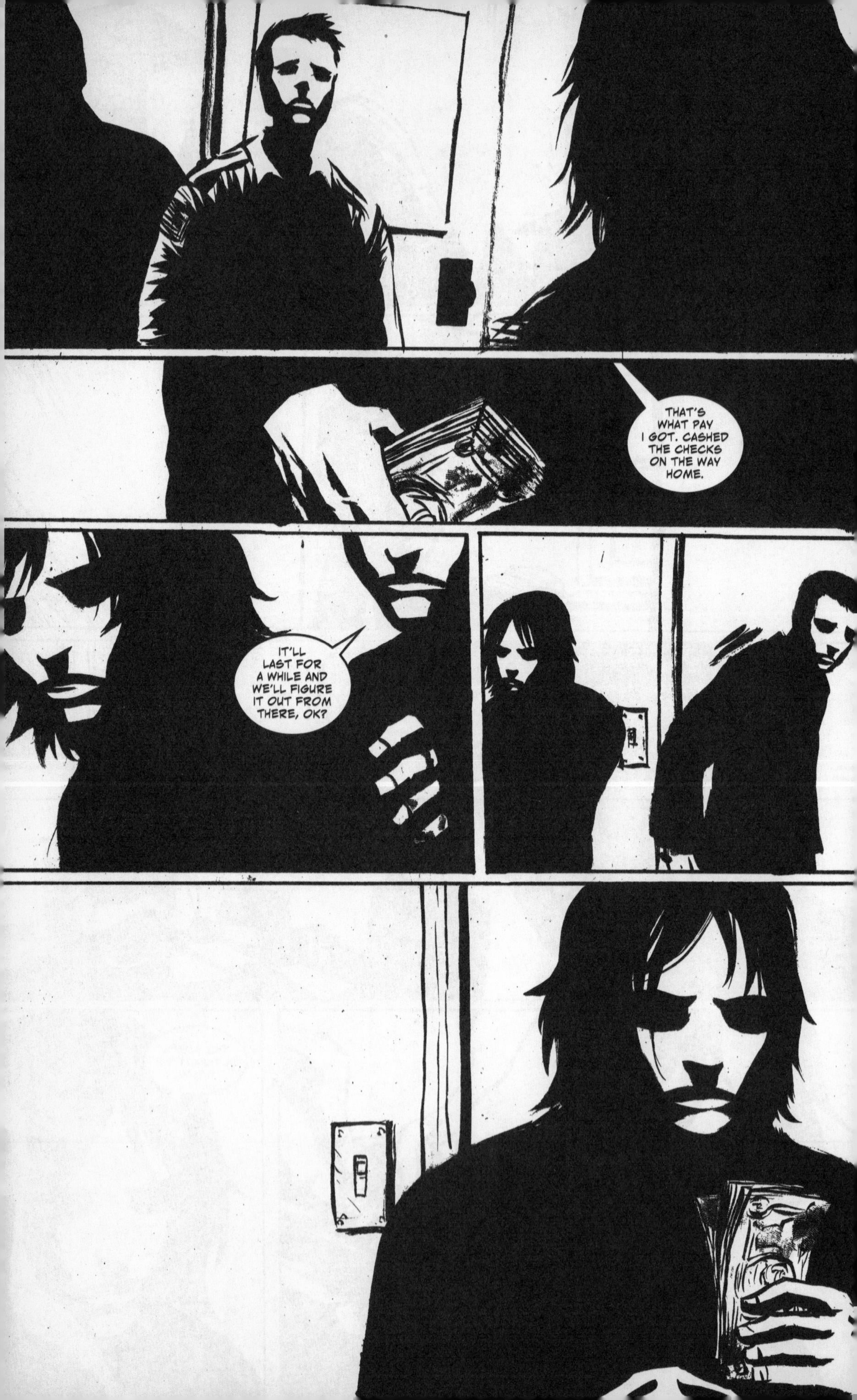
THAT'S WHAT PAY I GOT. CASHED THE CHECKS ON THE WAY HOME.
IT'LL LAST FOR A WHILE AND WE'LL FIGURE IT OUT FROM THERE, OK?

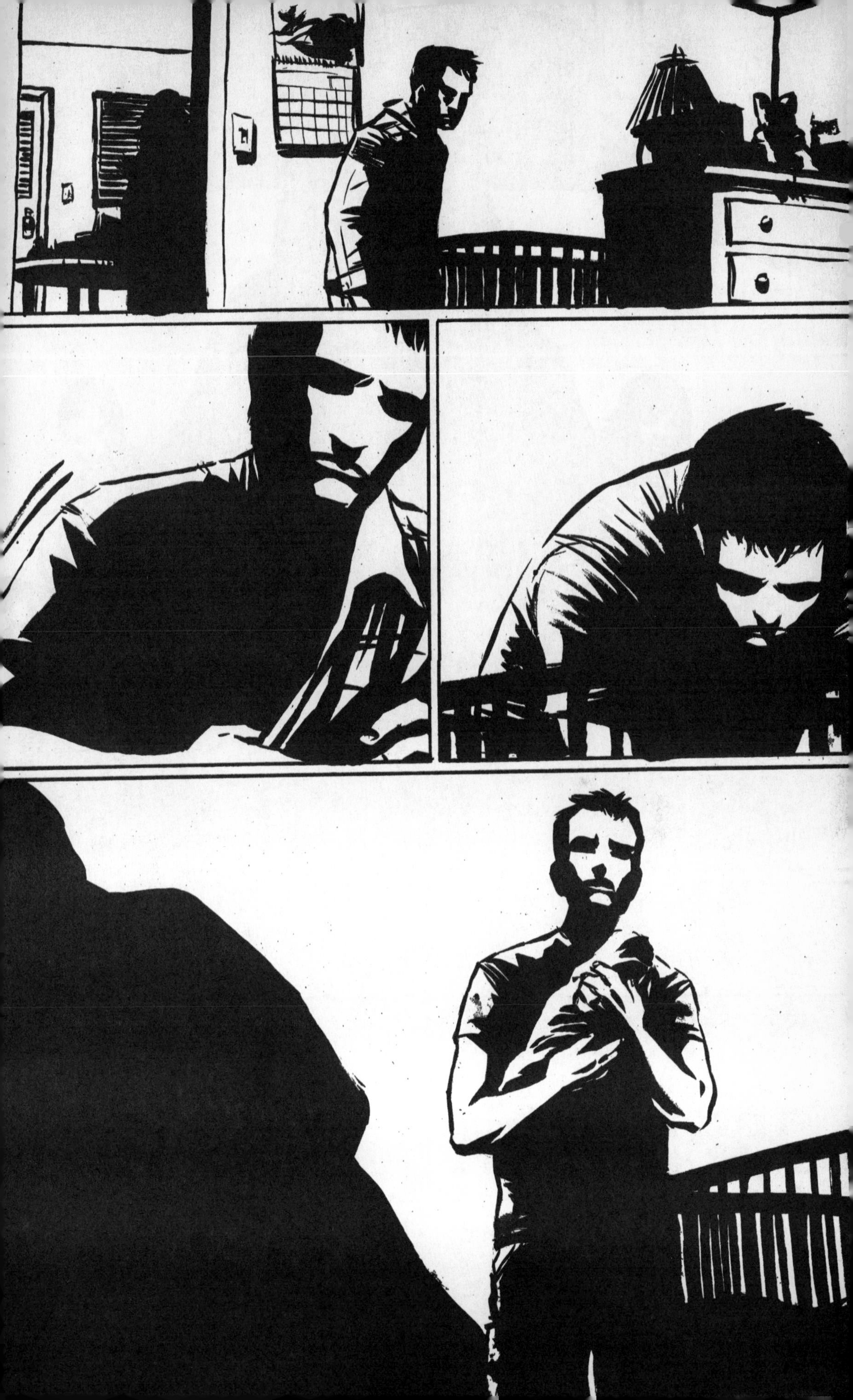

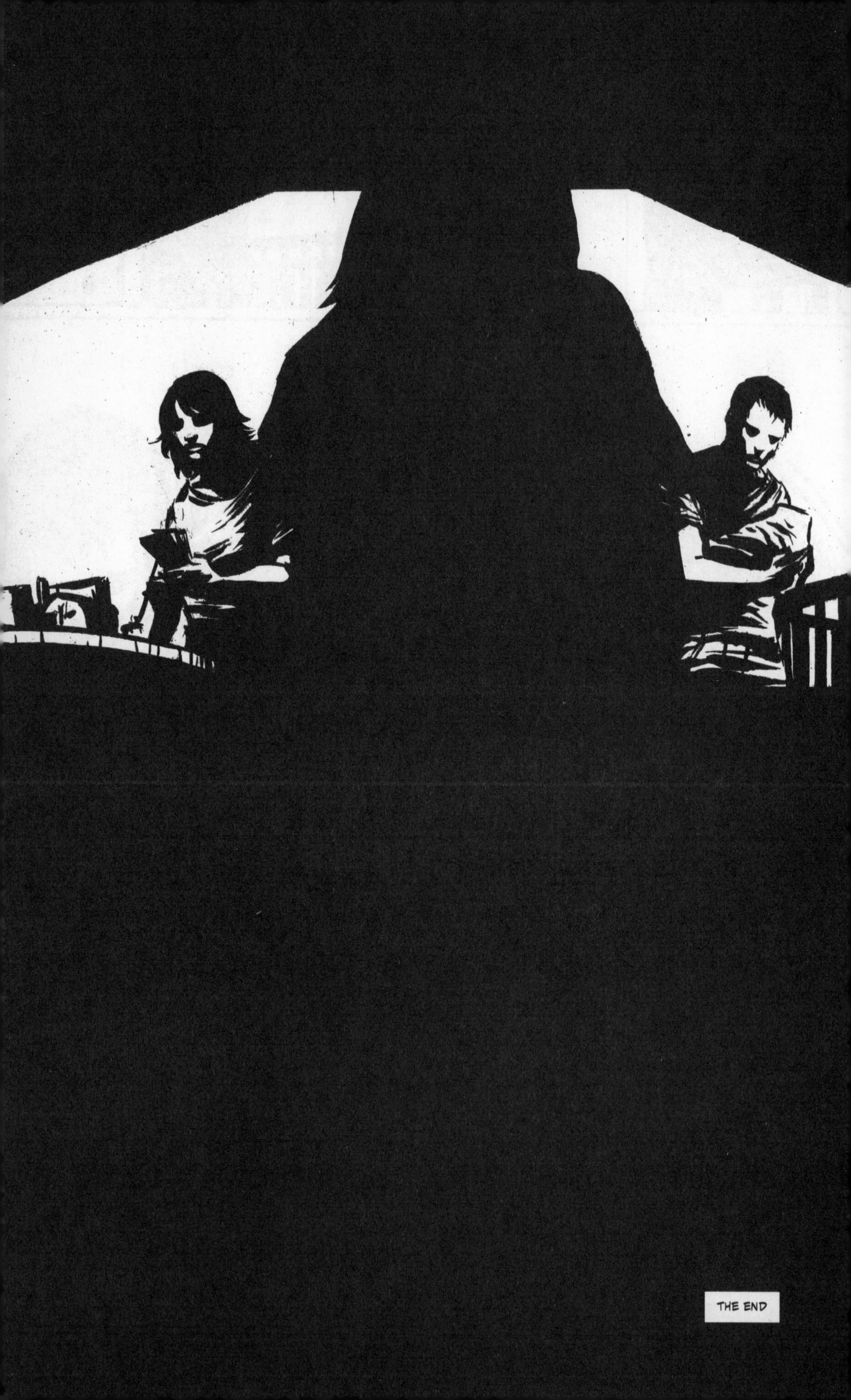
THE END

8

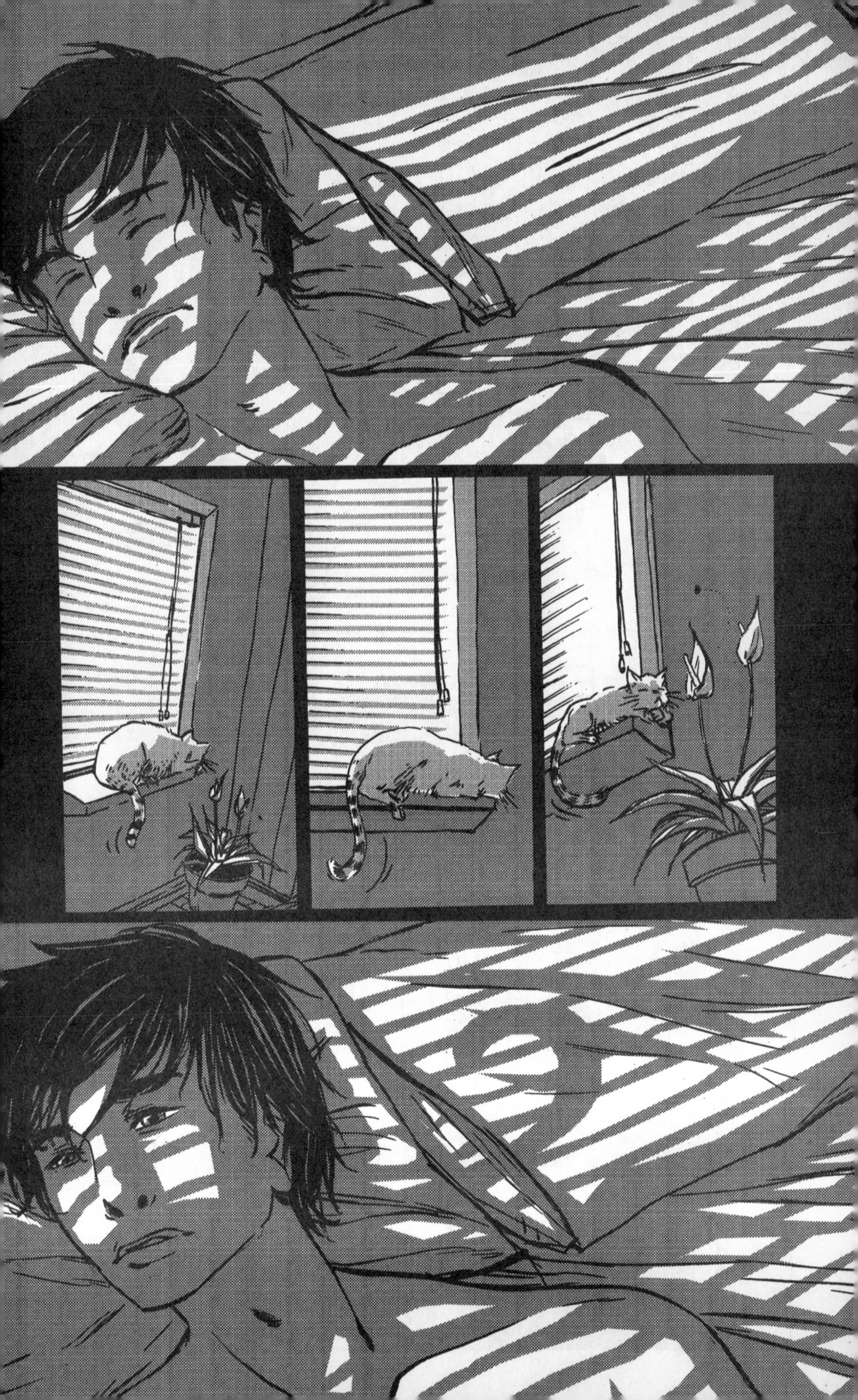

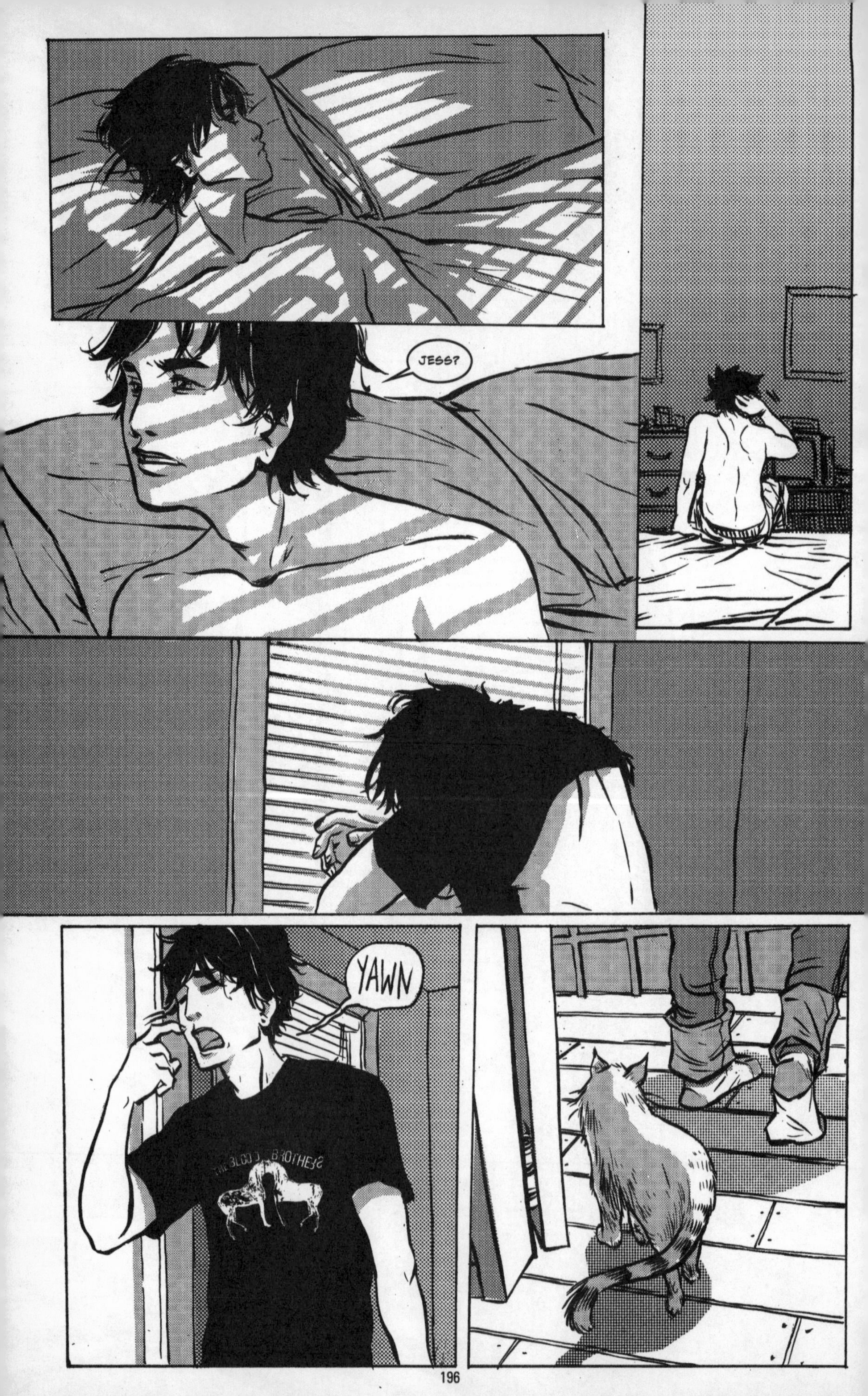
JESS?
YAWN
THE BLOOD BROTHERS

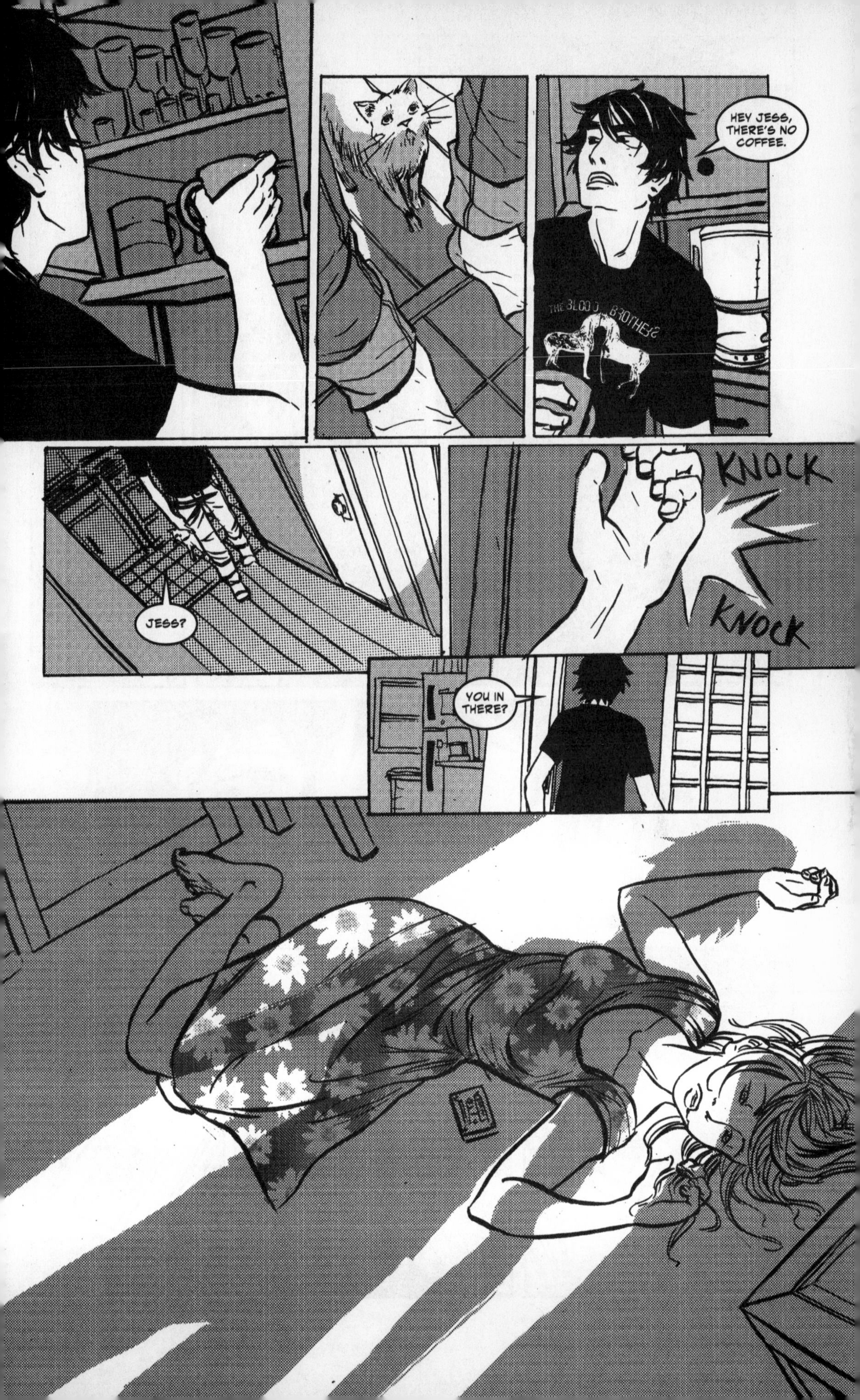
HEY JESS, THERE'S NO COFFEE.
JESS?
KNOCK
KNOCK
YOU IN THERE?

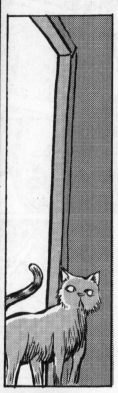

THE BLOOD BROTHERS

Oh my
god.

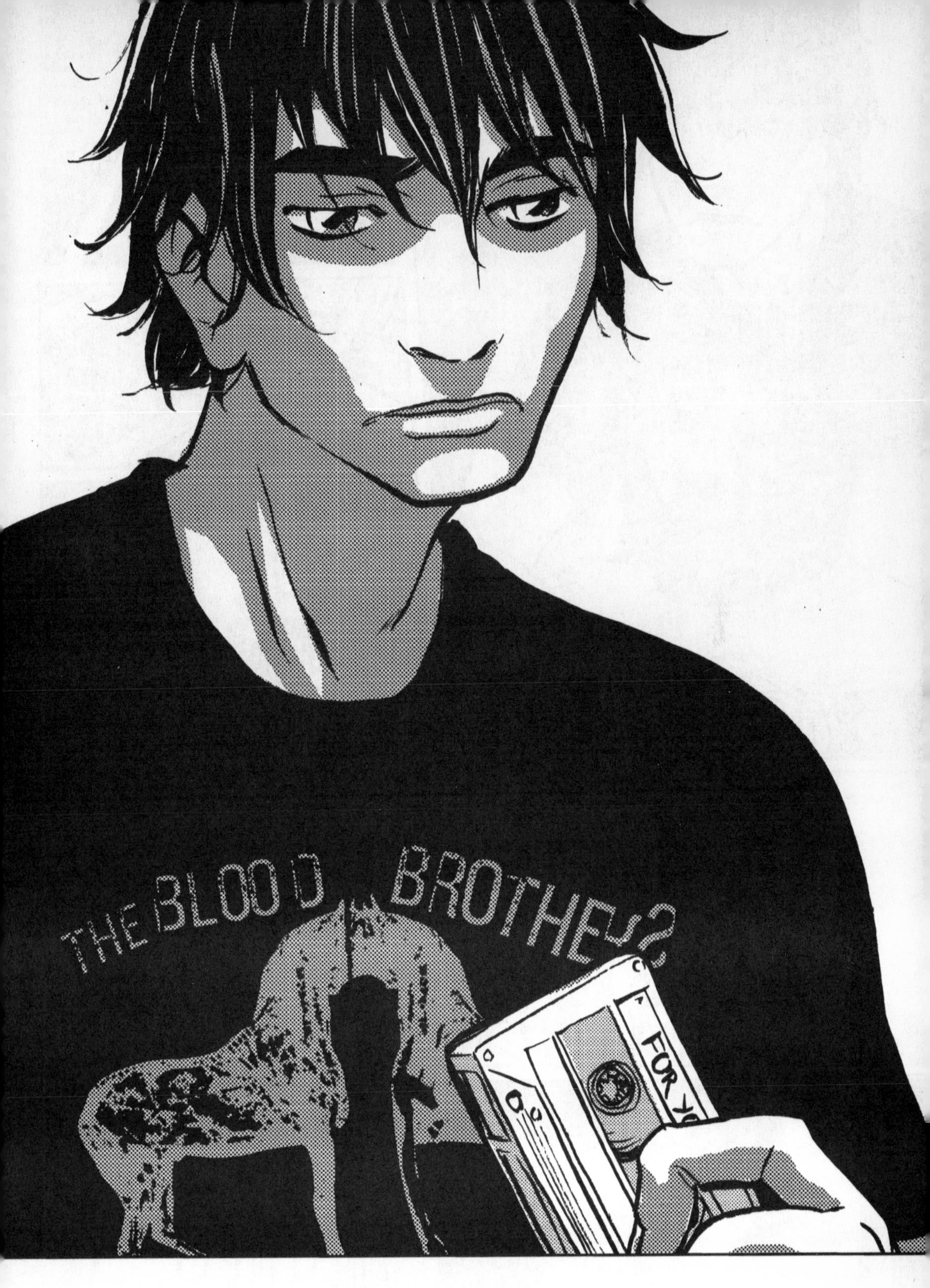
THE BLOOD

“Mixtape”

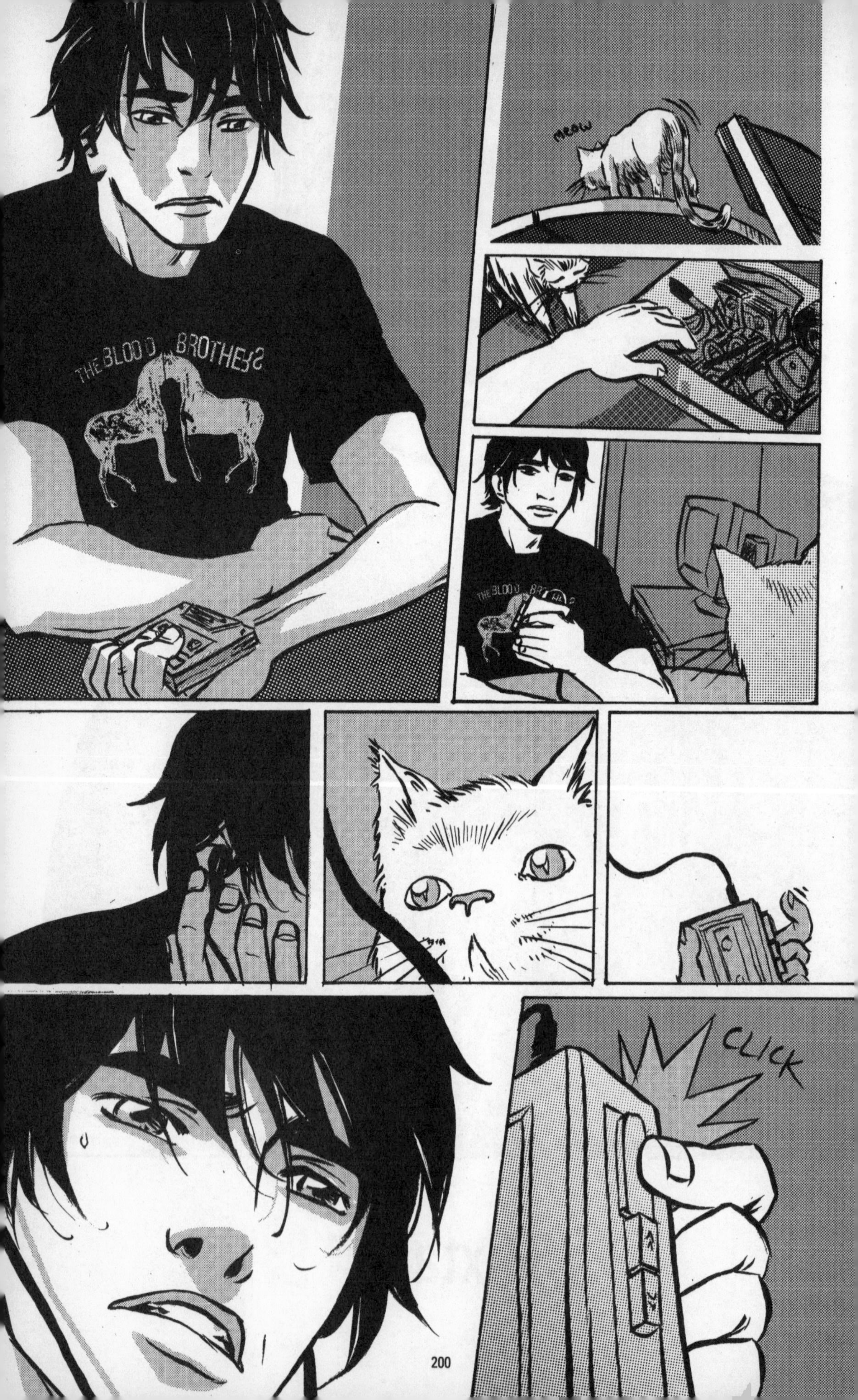
MEOW
THE BLOOD BROTHERS
CLICK

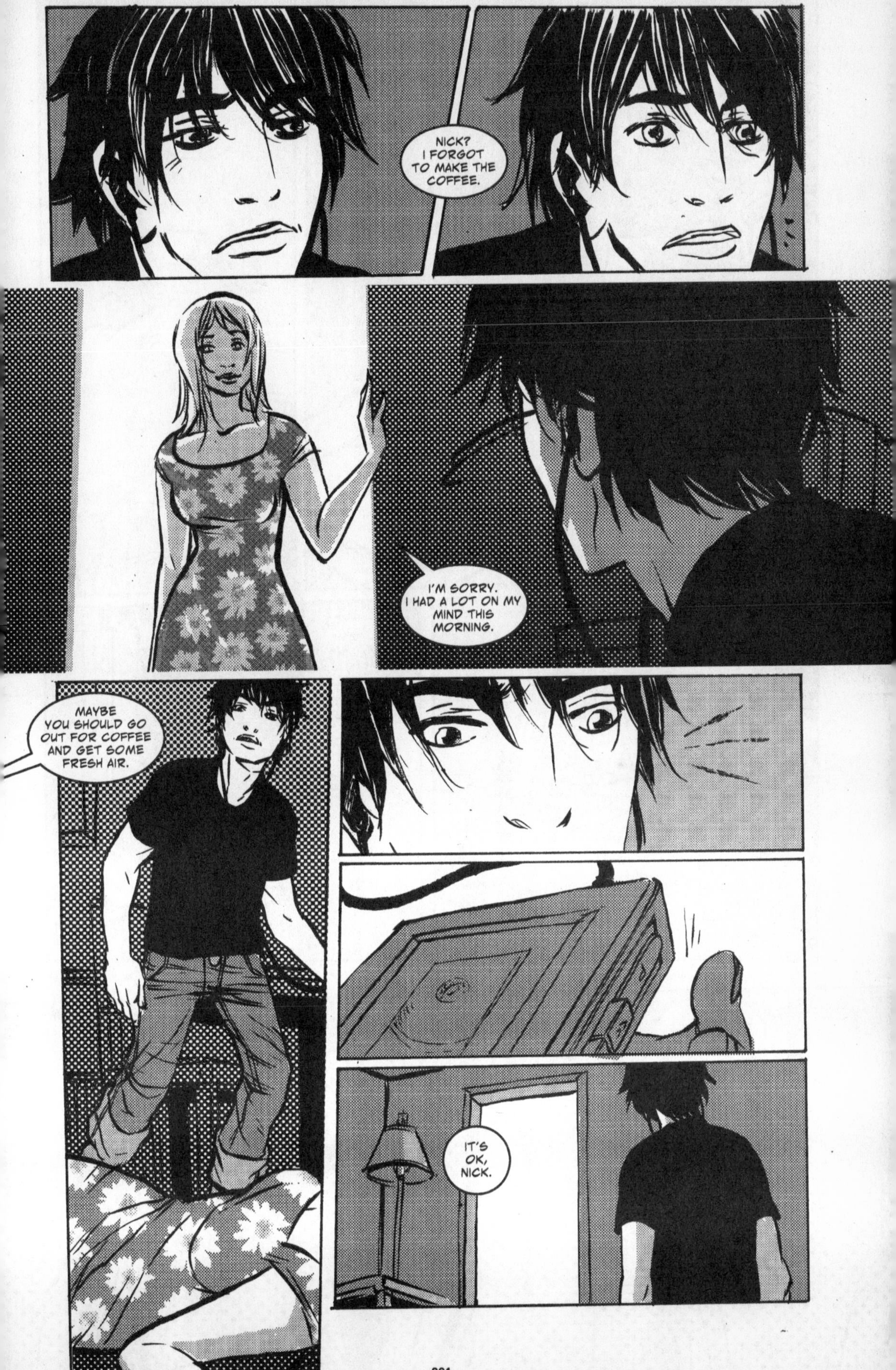
NICK? I FORGOT TO MAKE THE COFFEE.
I'M SORRY. I HAD A LOT ON MY MIND THIS MORNING.
MAYBE YOU SHOULD GO OUT FOR COFFEE AND GET SOME FRESH AIR.
IT'S OK, NICK.

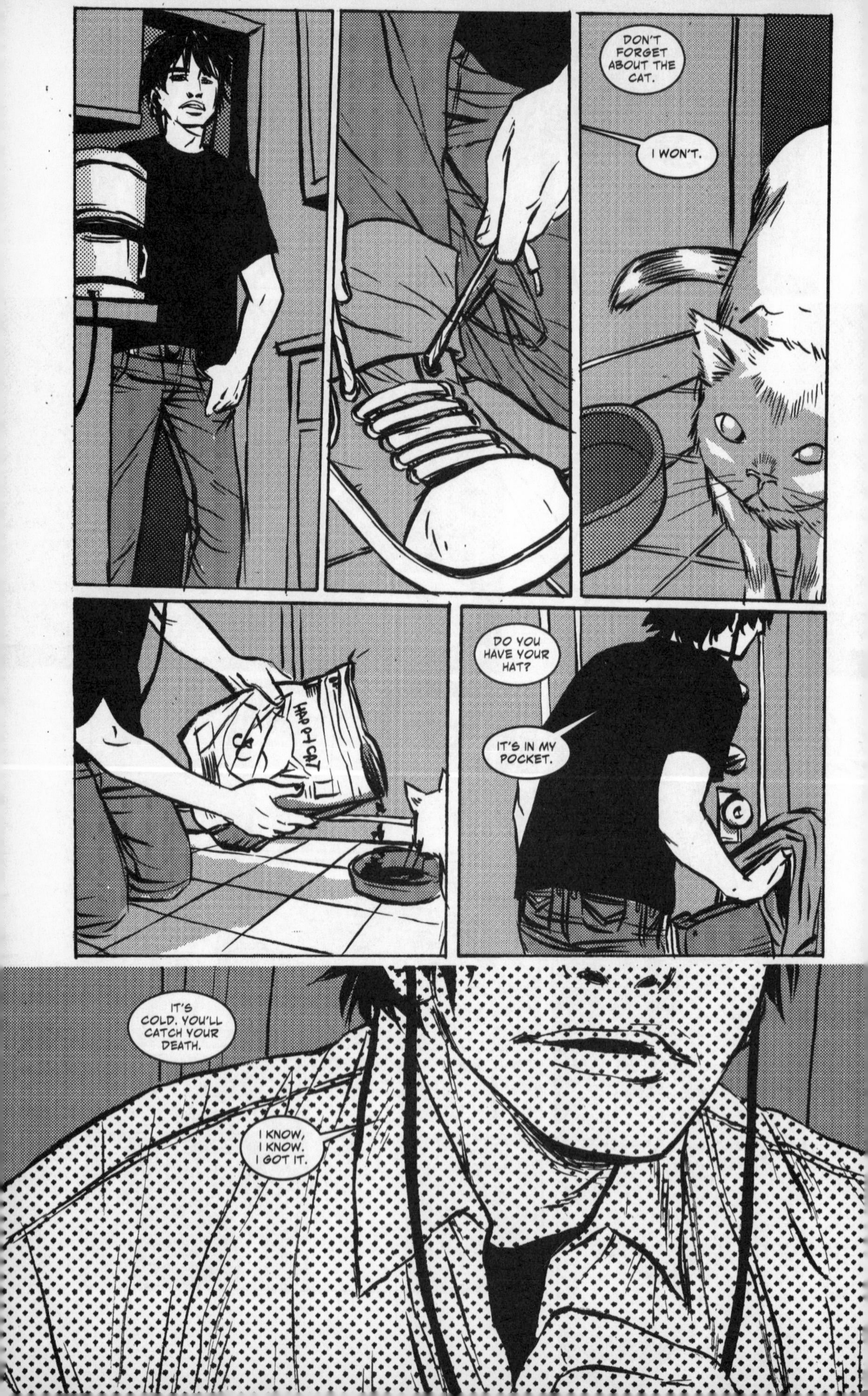
DON'T FORGET ABOUT THE CAT.
I WON'T.
HAPPY CAT
DO YOU HAVE YOUR HAT?
IT'S IN MY POCKET.
IT'S COLD. YOU'LL CATCH YOUR DEATH.
I KNOW, I KNOW. I GOT IT.

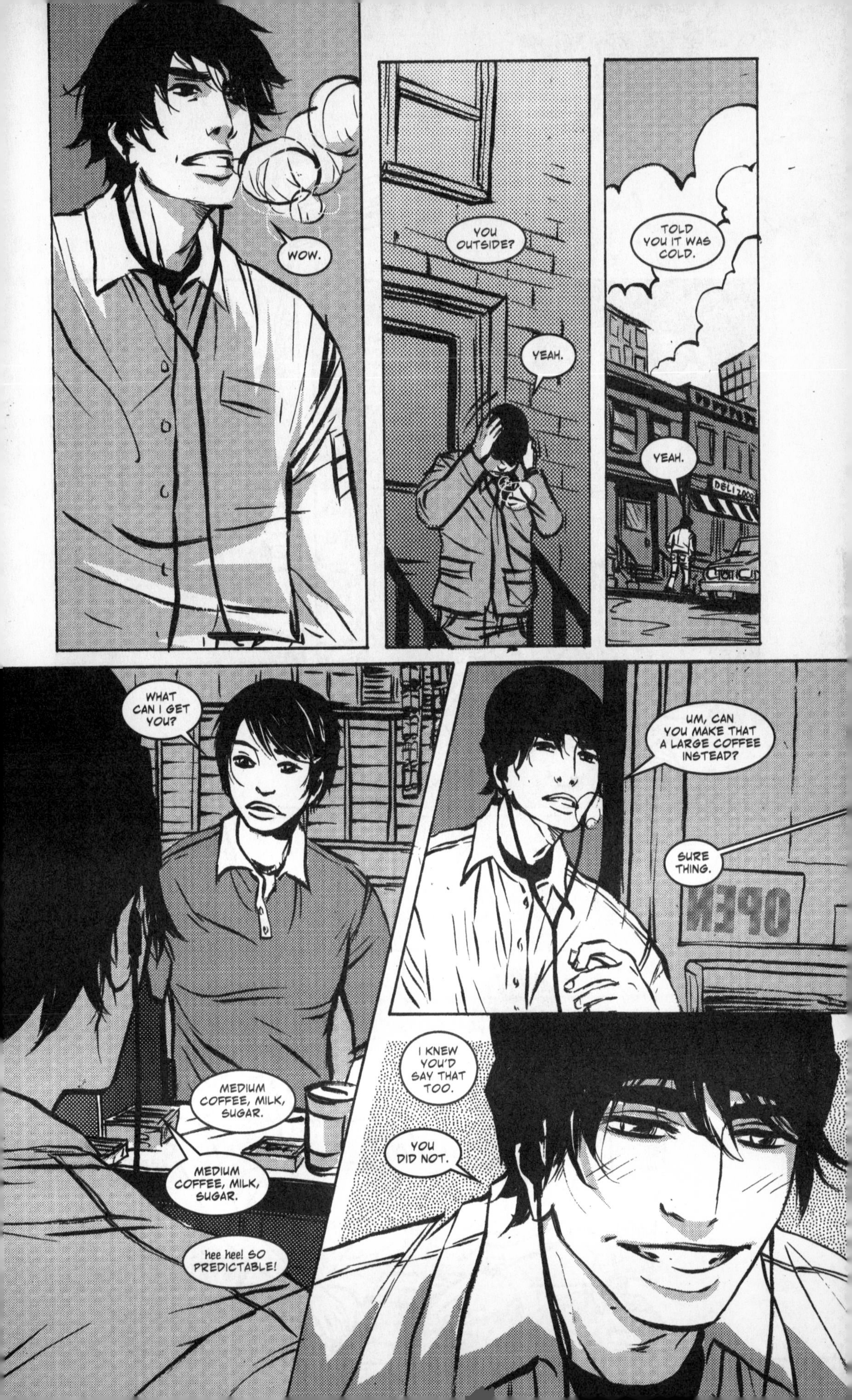
WOW.
YOU OUTSIDE?
YEAH.
TOLD YOU IT WAS COLD.
YEAH.
DELI
WHAT CAN I GET YOU?
UM, CAN YOU MAKE THAT A LARGE COFFEE INSTEAD?
SURE THING.
OPEN
MEDIUM COFFEE, MILK, SUGAR.
MEDIUM COFFEE, MILK, SUGAR.
hee hee! SO PREDICTABLE!
I KNEW YOU'D SAY THAT TOO.
YOU DID NOT.

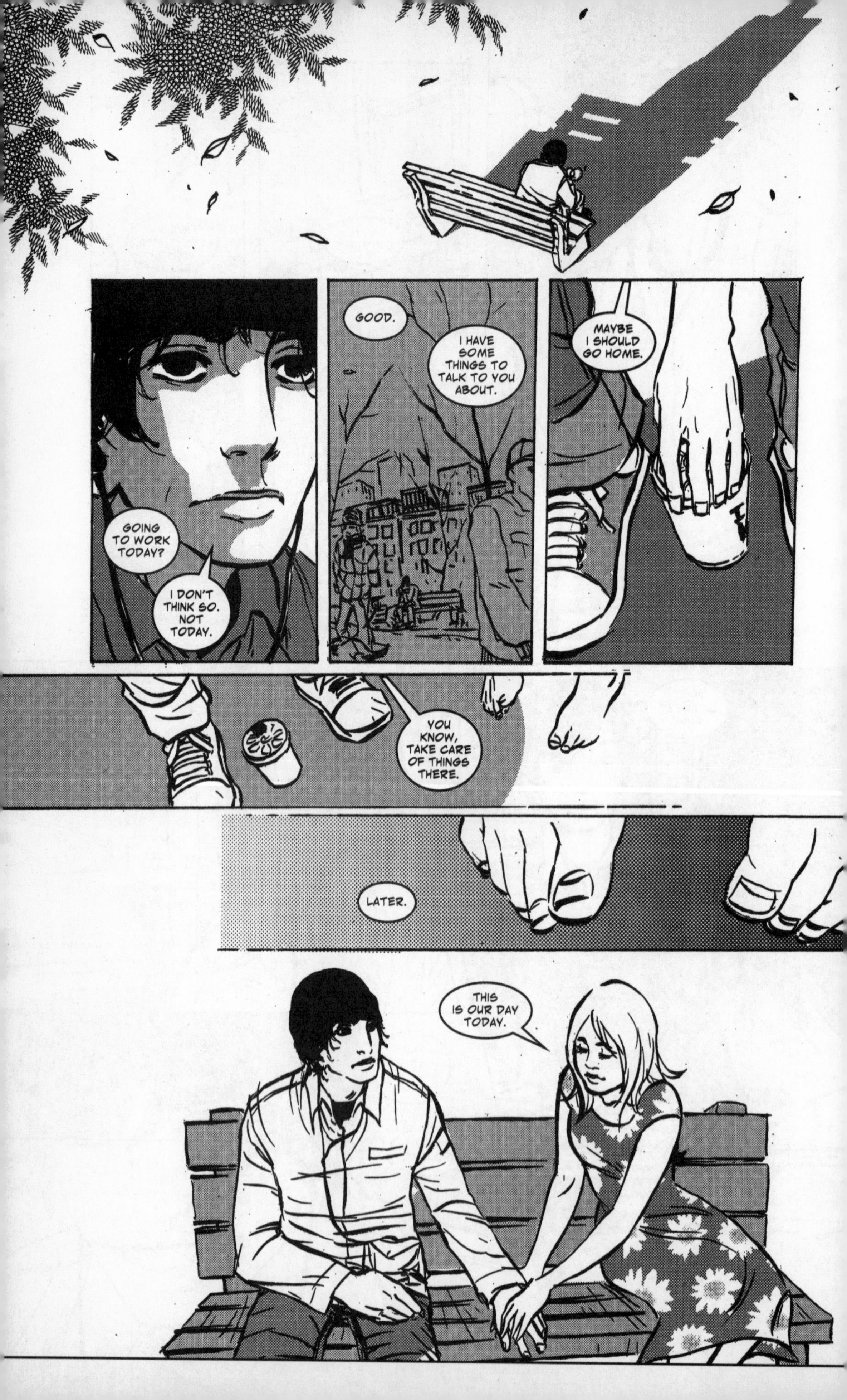
GOING TO WORK TODAY?
I DON'T THINK SO. NOT TODAY.
GOOD.
I HAVE SOME THINGS TO TALK TO YOU ABOUT.
MAYBE I SHOULD GO HOME.
YOU KNOW, TAKE CARE OF THINGS THERE.
LATER.
THIS IS OUR DAY TODAY.

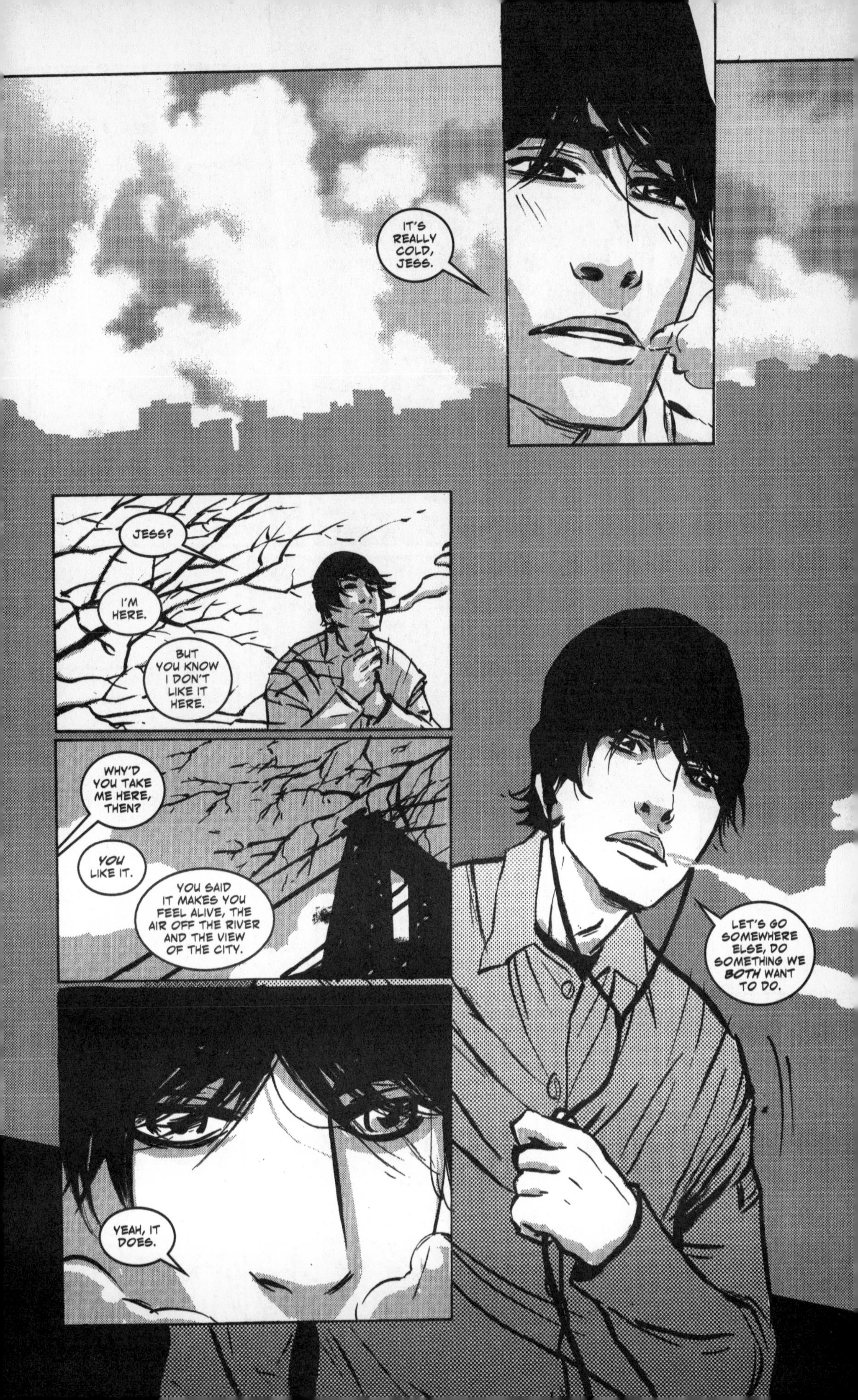
IT'S REALLY COLD, JESS.
JESS?
I'M HERE.
BUT YOU KNOW I DON'T LIKE IT HERE.
WHY'D YOU TAKE ME HERE, THEN?
YOU LIKE IT.
YOU SAID IT MAKES YOU FEEL ALIVE, THE AIR OFF THE RIVER AND THE VIEW OF THE CITY.
YEAH, IT DOES.
LET'S GO SOMEWHERE ELSE, DO SOMETHING WE BOTH WANT TO DO.

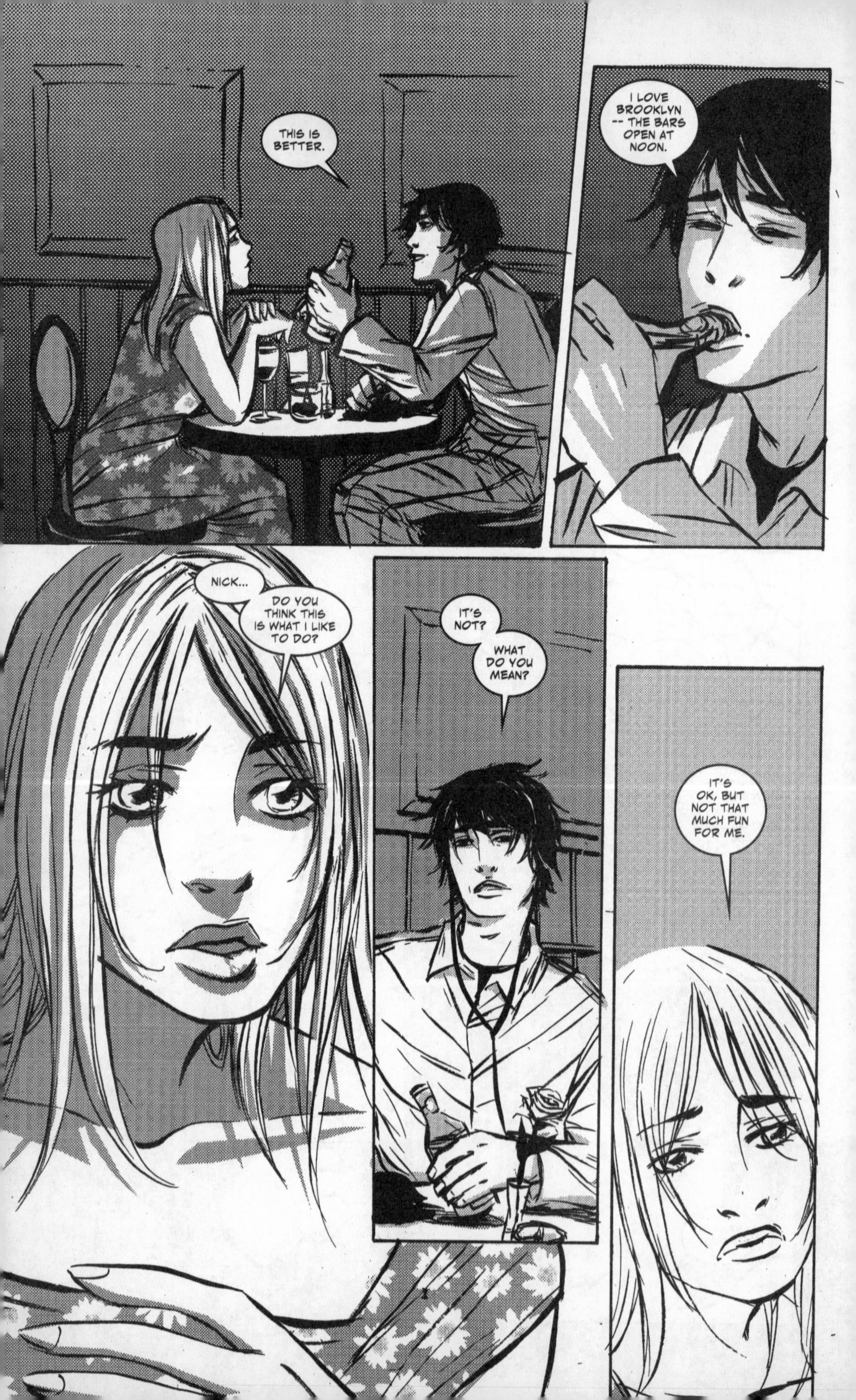
THIS IS BETTER.
I LOVE BROOKLYN -- THE BARS OPEN AT NOON.
NICK...
DO YOU THINK THIS IS WHAT I LIKE TO DO?
IT'S NOT?
WHAT DO YOU MEAN?
IT'S OK, BUT NOT THAT MUCH FUN FOR ME.

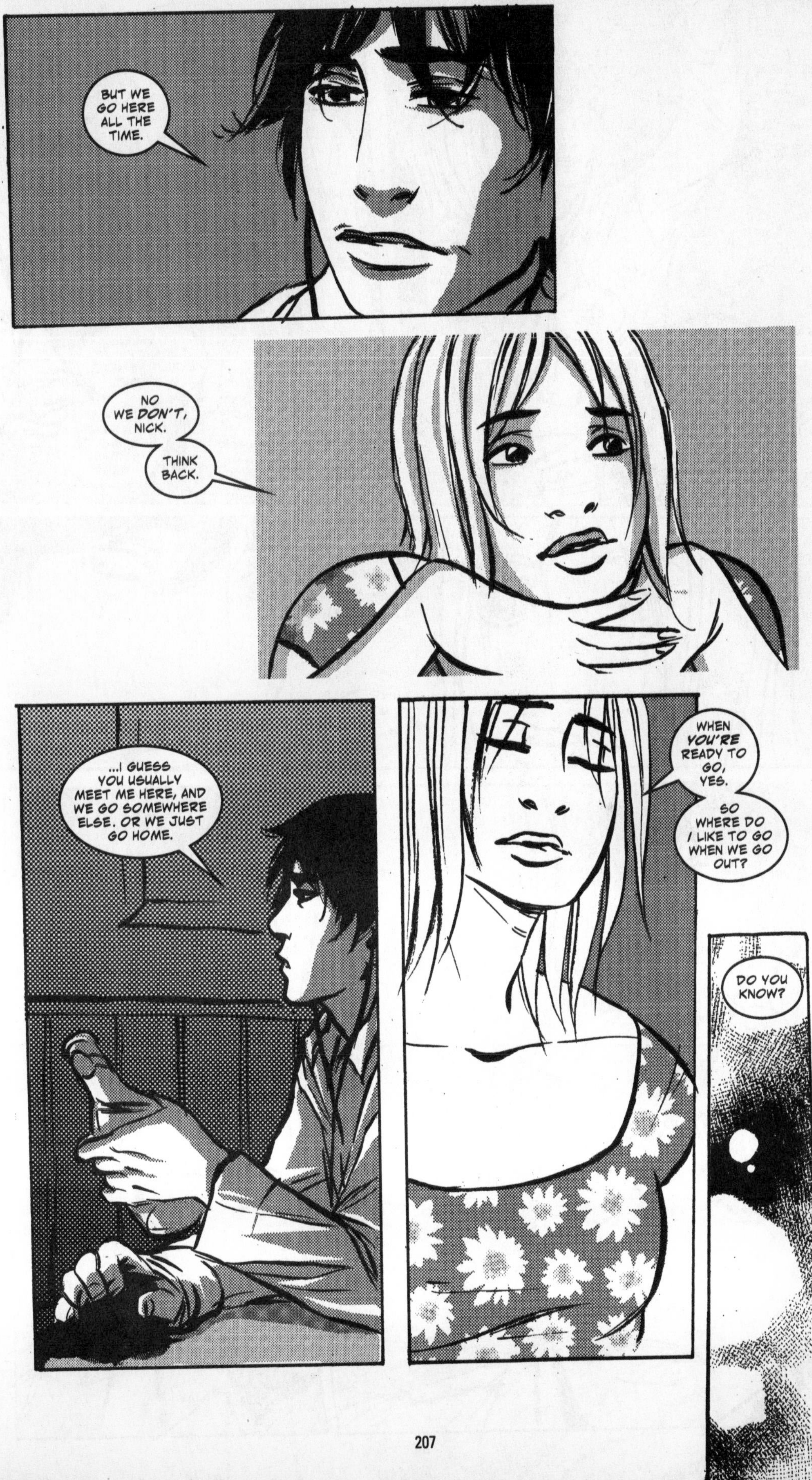
BUT WE GO HERE ALL THE TIME.
NO WE *DON'T*, NICK.
THINK BACK.
...I GUESS YOU USUALLY MEET ME HERE, AND WE GO SOMEWHERE ELSE. OR WE JUST GO HOME.
WHEN *YOU'RE* READY TO GO, YES.
SO WHERE DO *I* LIKE TO GO WHEN WE GO OUT?
DO YOU KNOW?

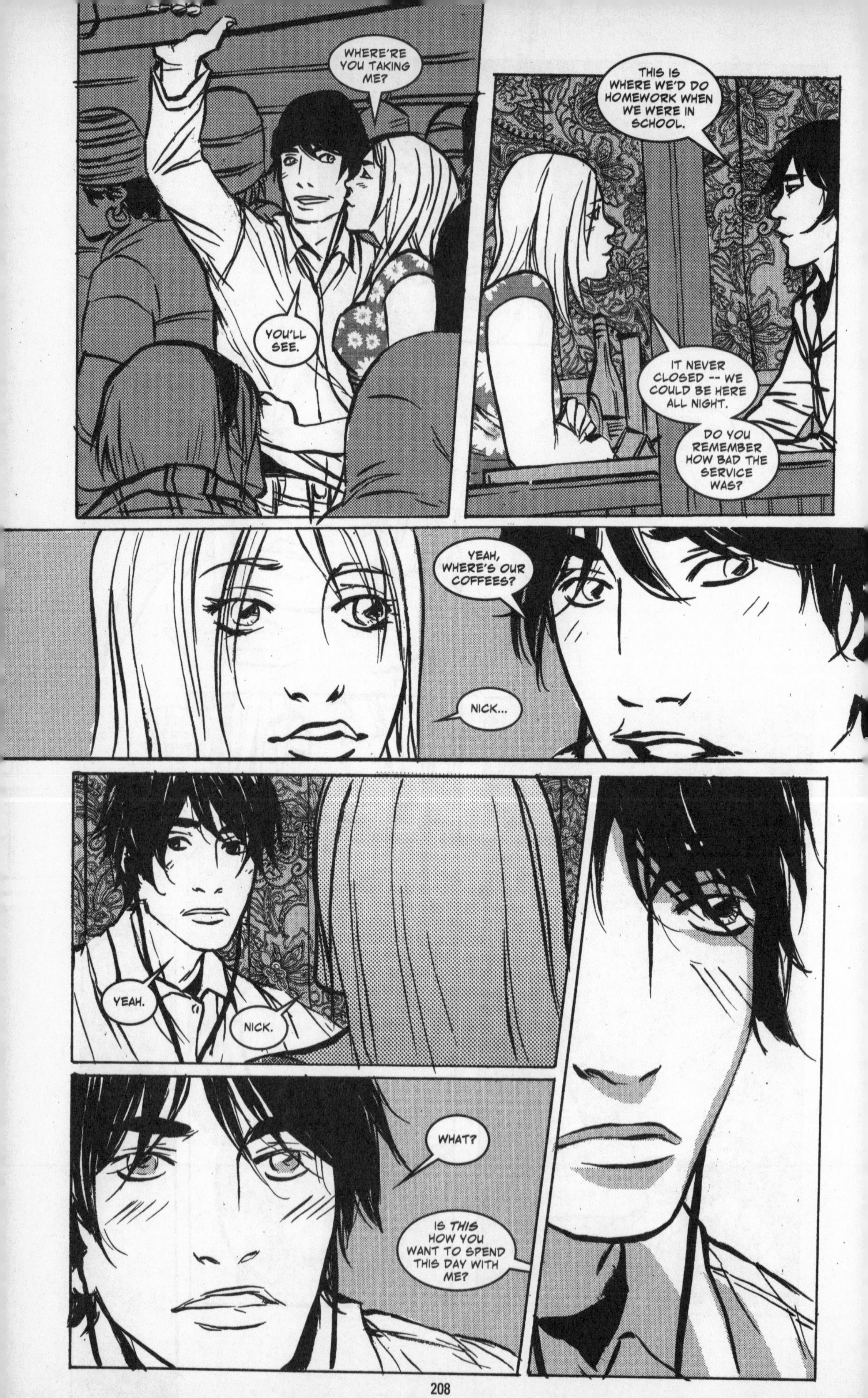
WHERE'RE YOU TAKING ME?
YOU'LL SEE.
THIS IS WHERE WE'D DO HOMEWORK WHEN WE WERE IN SCHOOL.
IT NEVER CLOSED -- WE COULD BE HERE ALL NIGHT.
DO YOU REMEMBER HOW BAD THE SERVICE WAS?
YEAH, WHERE'S OUR COFFEES?
NICK...
YEAH.
NICK.
WHAT?
IS *THIS* HOW YOU WANT TO SPEND THIS DAY WITH ME?

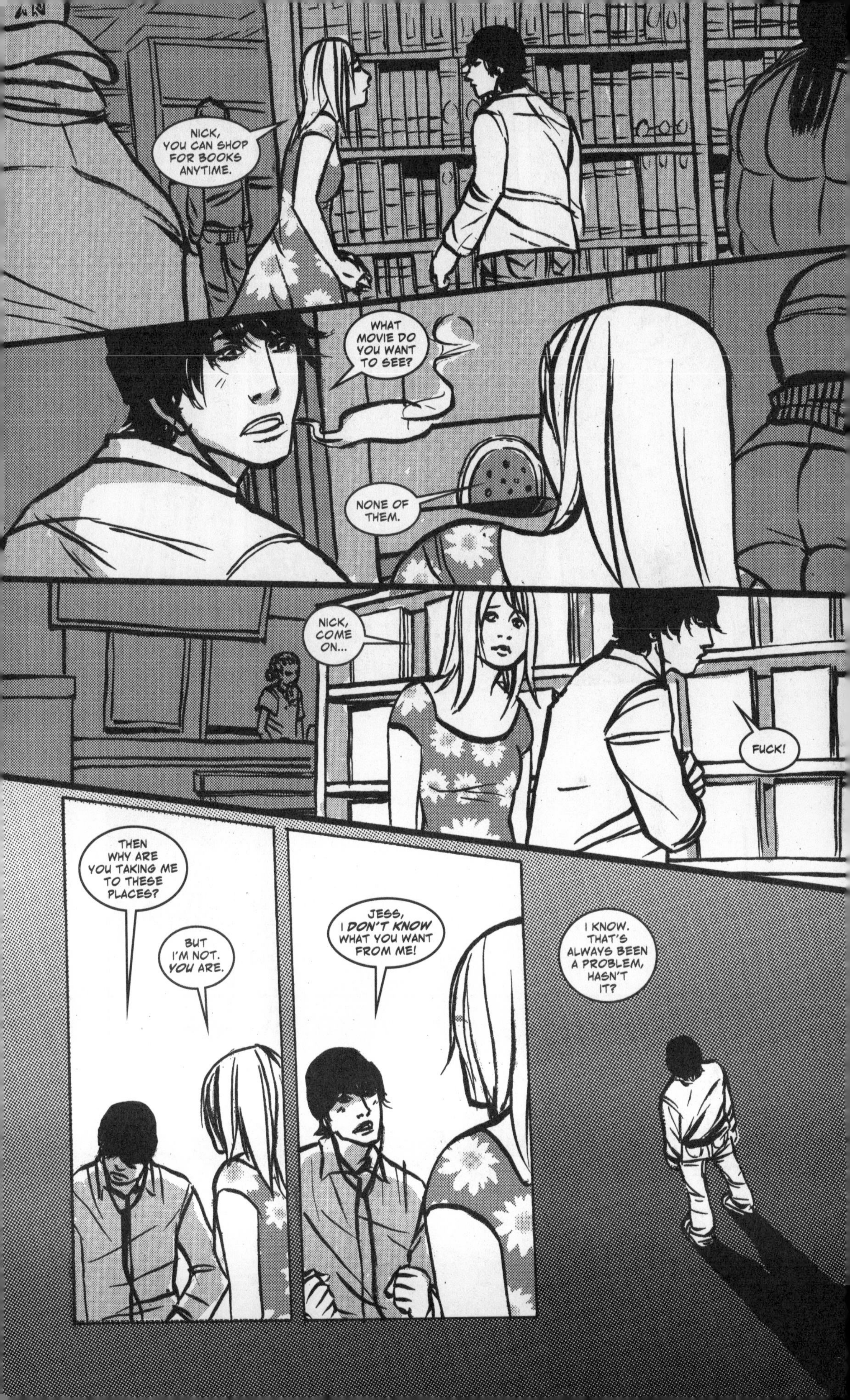
NICK, YOU CAN SHOP FOR BOOKS ANYTIME.
WHAT MOVIE DO YOU WANT TO SEE?
NONE OF THEM.
NICK, COME ON...
FUCK!
THEN WHY ARE YOU TAKING ME TO THESE PLACES?
BUT I'M NOT. *YOU* ARE.
JESS, I *DON'T KNOW* WHAT YOU WANT FROM ME!
I KNOW. THAT'S ALWAYS BEEN A PROBLEM, HASN'T IT?

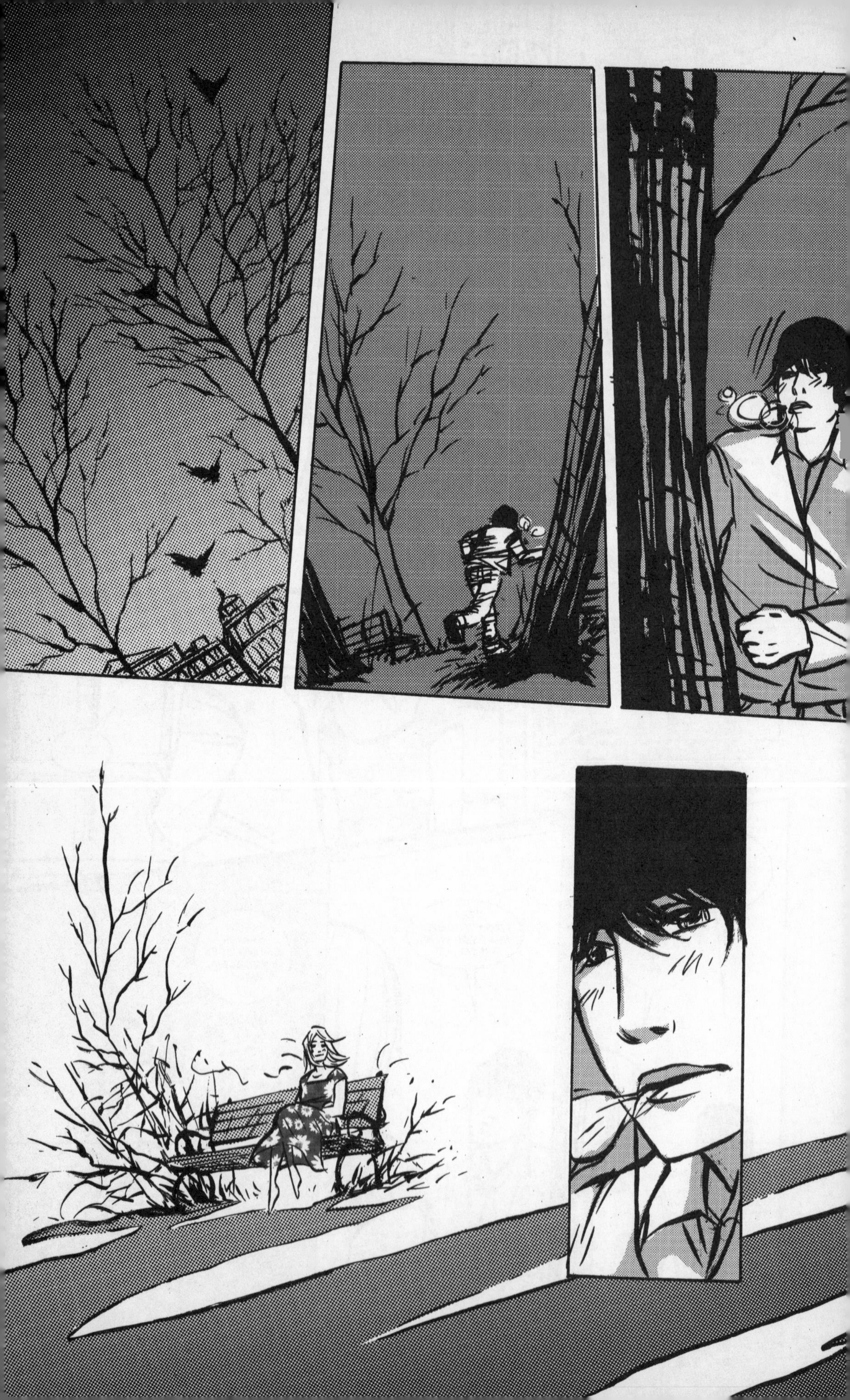

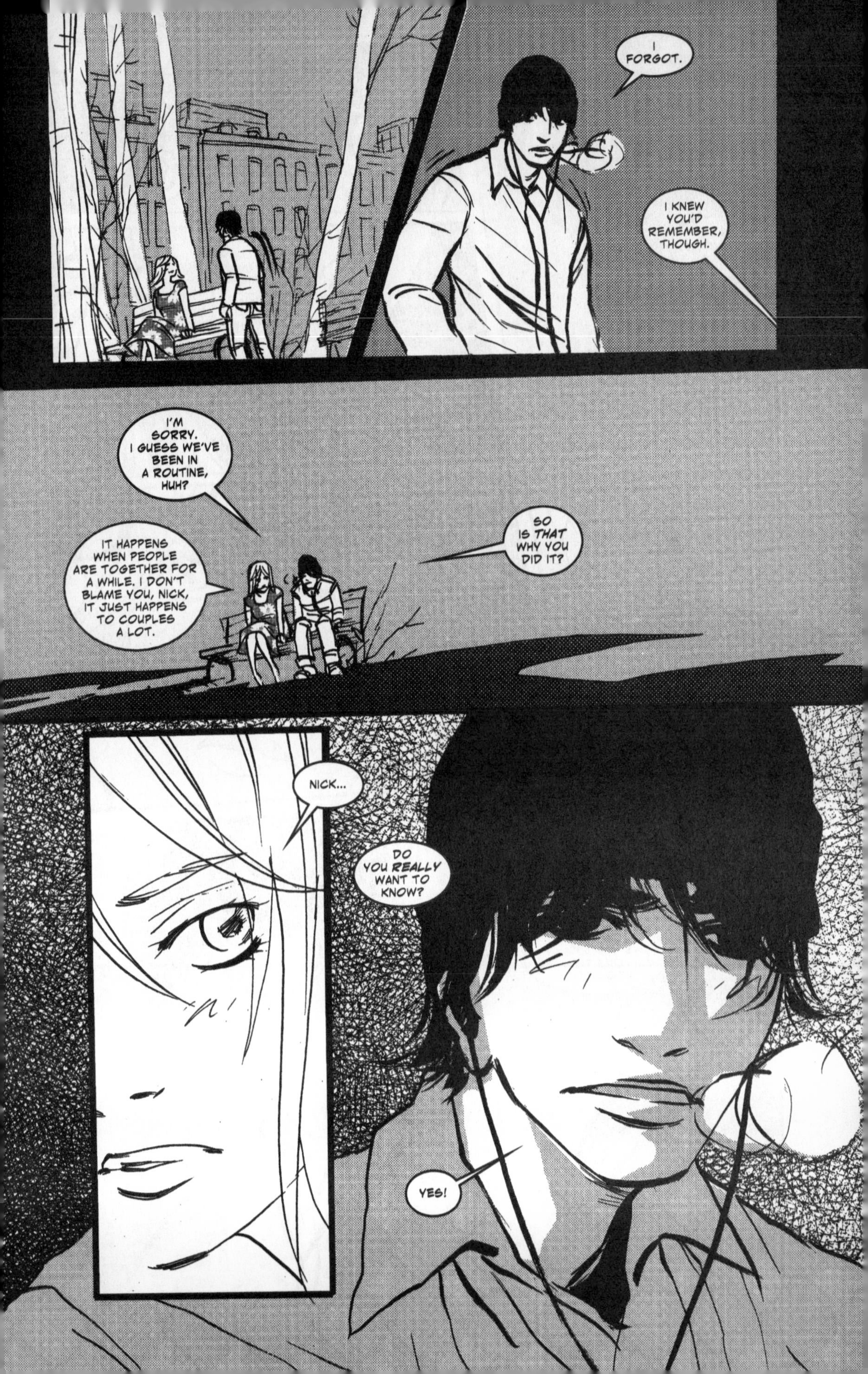
I FORGOT.
I KNEW YOU'D REMEMBER, THOUGH.
I'M SORRY. I GUESS WE'VE BEEN IN A ROUTINE, HUH?
IT HAPPENS WHEN PEOPLE ARE TOGETHER FOR A WHILE. I DON'T BLAME YOU, NICK, IT JUST HAPPENS TO COUPLES A LOT.
SO IS *THAT* WHY YOU DID IT?
NICK...
DO YOU *REALLY* WANT TO KNOW?
YES!

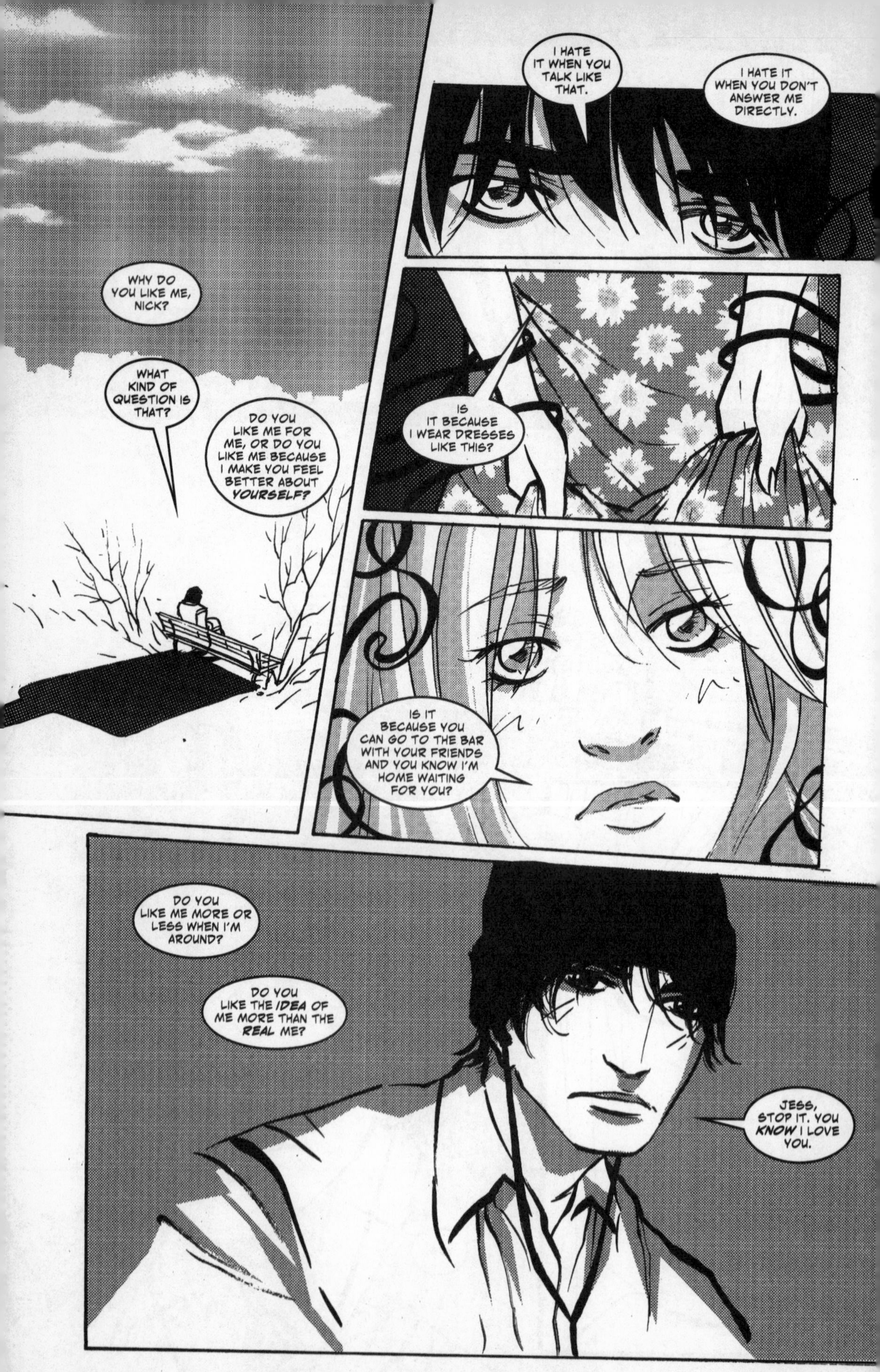
WHY DO YOU LIKE ME, NICK?
WHAT KIND OF QUESTION IS THAT?
DO YOU LIKE ME FOR ME, OR DO YOU LIKE ME BECAUSE I MAKE YOU FEEL BETTER ABOUT *YOURSELF?*
I HATE IT WHEN YOU TALK LIKE THAT.
I HATE IT WHEN YOU DON'T ANSWER ME DIRECTLY.
IS IT BECAUSE I WEAR DRESSES LIKE THIS?
IS IT BECAUSE YOU CAN GO TO THE BAR WITH YOUR FRIENDS AND YOU KNOW I'M HOME WAITING FOR YOU?
DO YOU LIKE ME MORE OR LESS WHEN I'M AROUND?
DO YOU LIKE THE *IDEA* OF ME MORE THAN THE *REAL* ME?
JESS, STOP IT. YOU *KNOW* I LOVE YOU.

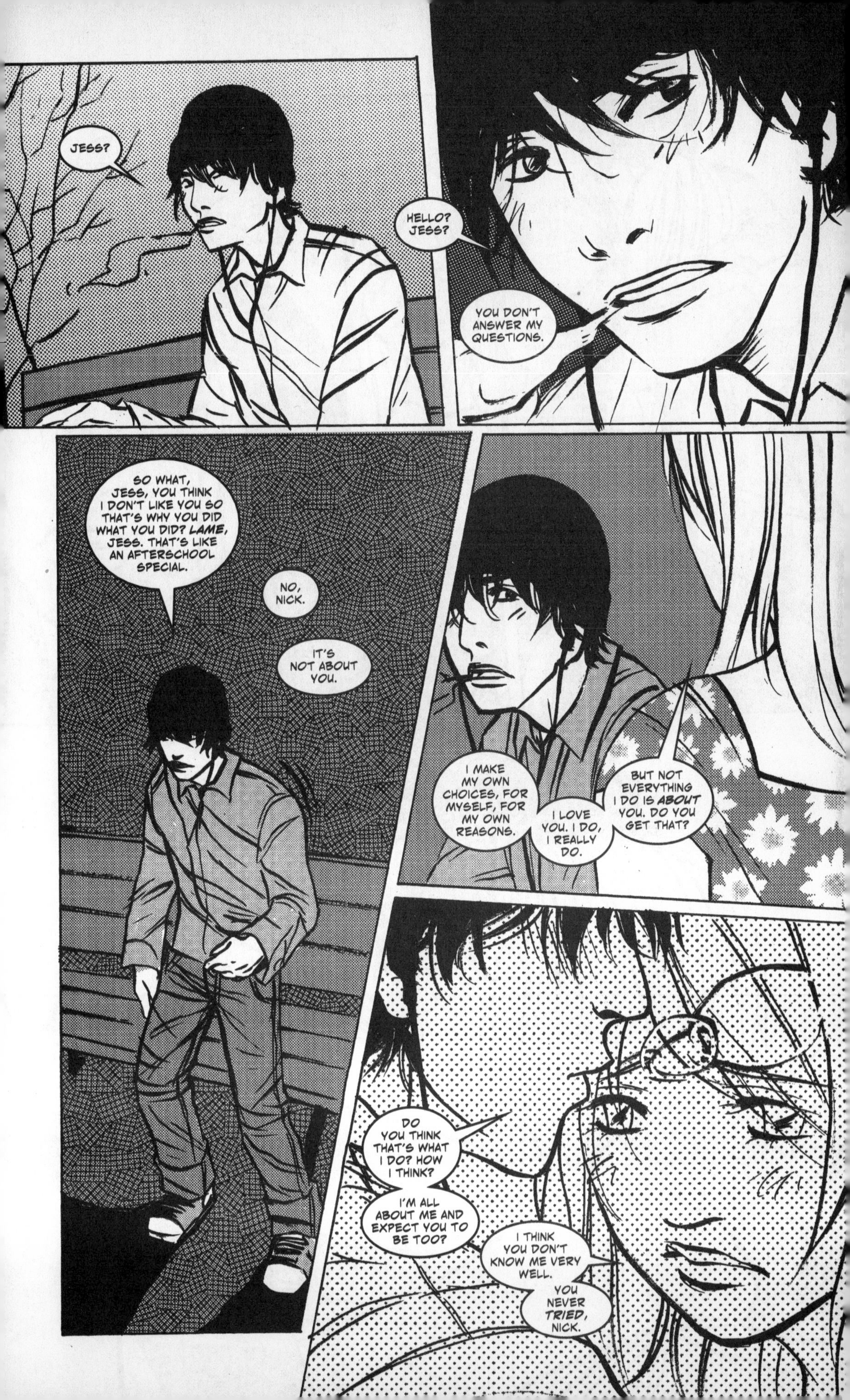
JESS?
HELLO? JESS?
YOU DON'T ANSWER MY QUESTIONS.
SO WHAT, JESS, YOU THINK I DON'T LIKE YOU SO THAT'S WHY YOU DID WHAT YOU DID? LAME, JESS. THAT'S LIKE AN AFTERSCHOOL SPECIAL.
NO, NICK.
IT'S NOT ABOUT YOU.
I MAKE MY OWN CHOICES, FOR MYSELF, FOR MY OWN REASONS.
I LOVE YOU. I DO, I REALLY DO.
BUT NOT EVERYTHING I DO IS ABOUT YOU. DO YOU GET THAT?
DO YOU THINK THAT'S WHAT I DO? HOW I THINK?
I'M ALL ABOUT ME AND EXPECT YOU TO BE TOO?
I THINK YOU DON'T KNOW ME VERY WELL.
YOU NEVER TRIED, NICK.

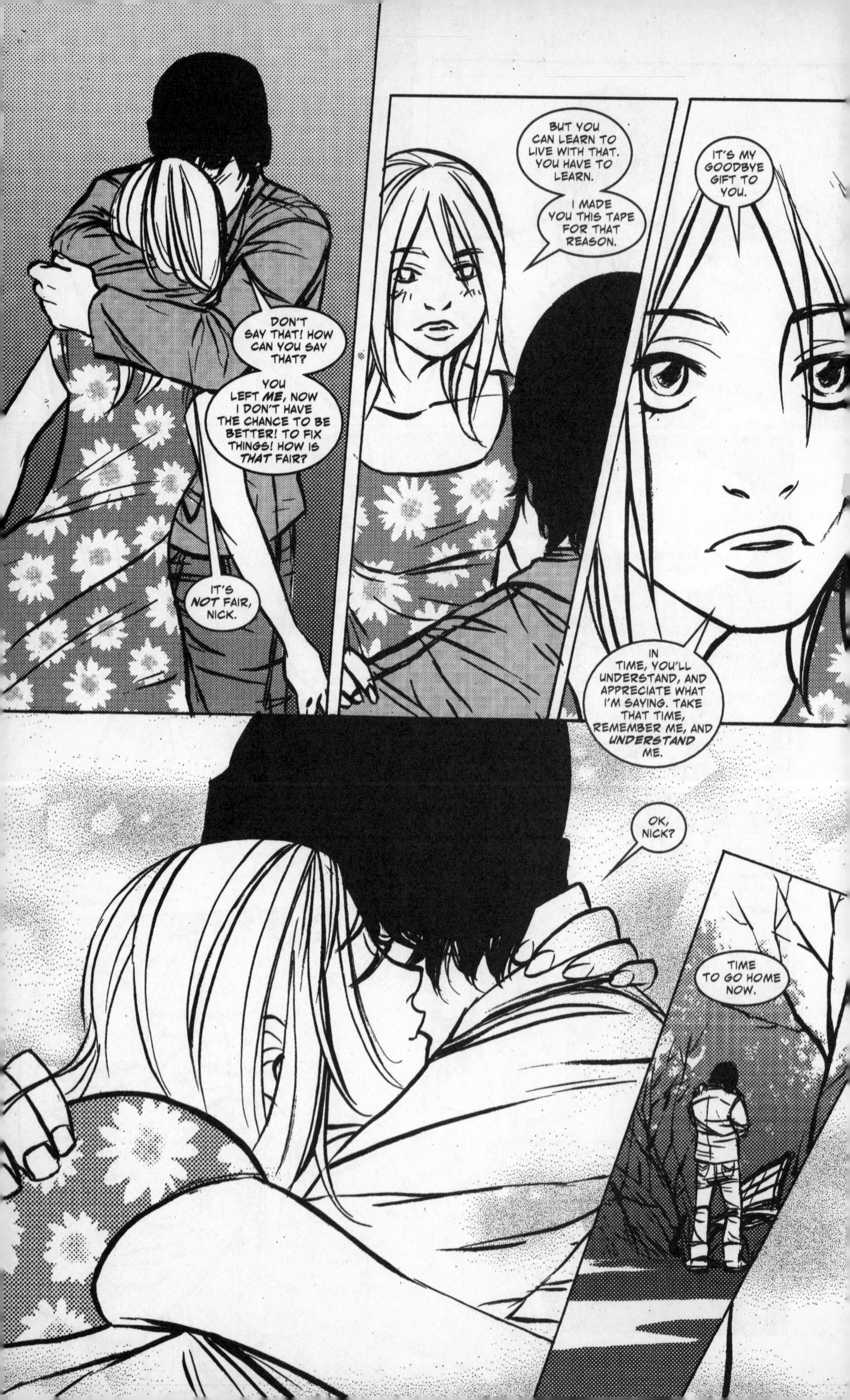
DON'T SAY THAT! HOW CAN YOU SAY THAT?
YOU LEFT *ME*, NOW I DON'T HAVE THE CHANCE TO BE BETTER! TO FIX THINGS! HOW IS *THAT* FAIR?
IT'S *NOT* FAIR, NICK.
BUT YOU CAN LEARN TO LIVE WITH THAT. YOU HAVE TO LEARN.
I MADE YOU THIS TAPE FOR THAT REASON.
IT'S MY GOODBYE GIFT TO YOU.
IN TIME, YOU'LL UNDERSTAND, AND APPRECIATE WHAT I'M SAYING. TAKE THAT TIME, REMEMBER ME, AND ***UNDERSTAND*** ME.
OK, NICK?
TIME TO GO HOME NOW.

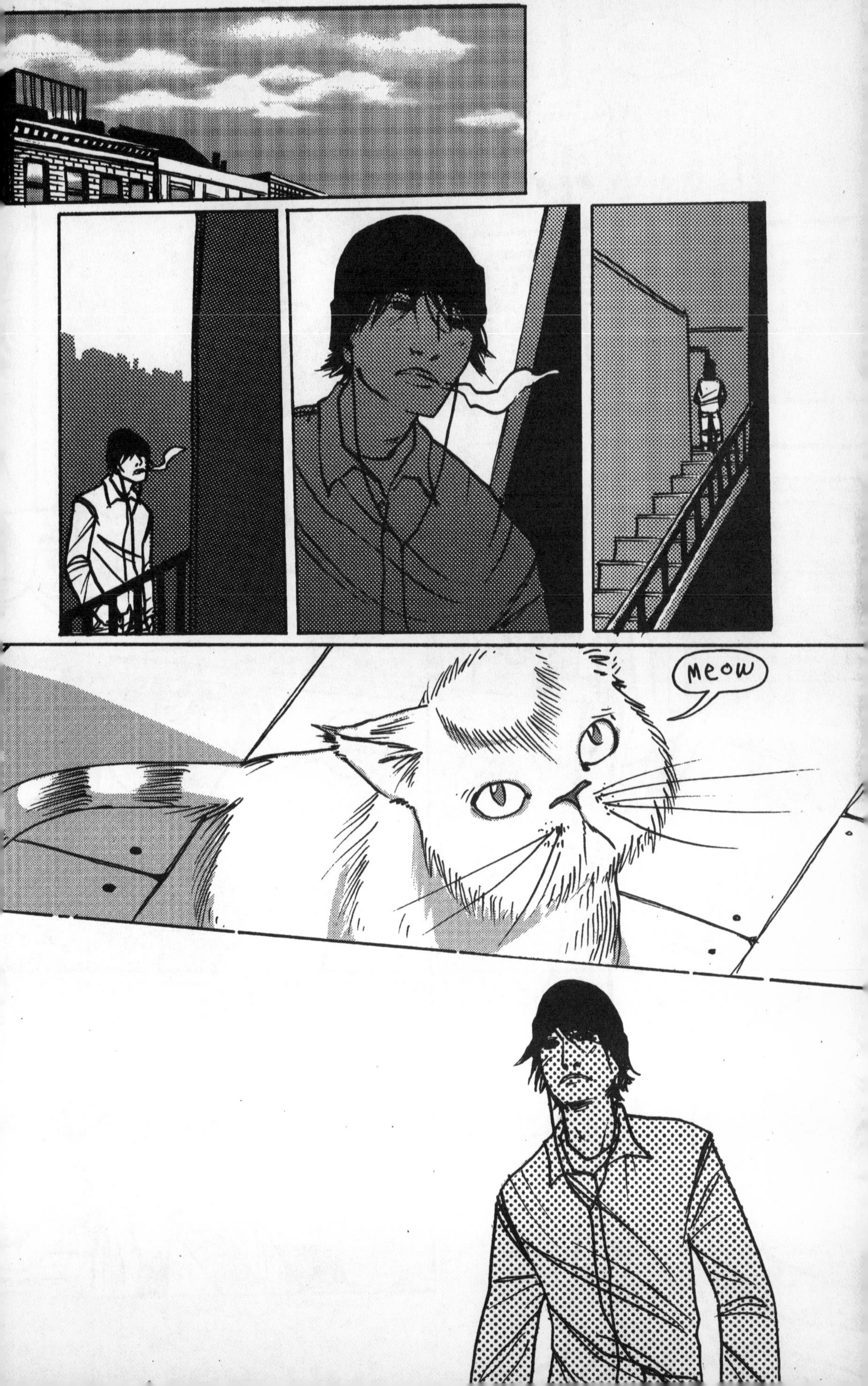
MEOW

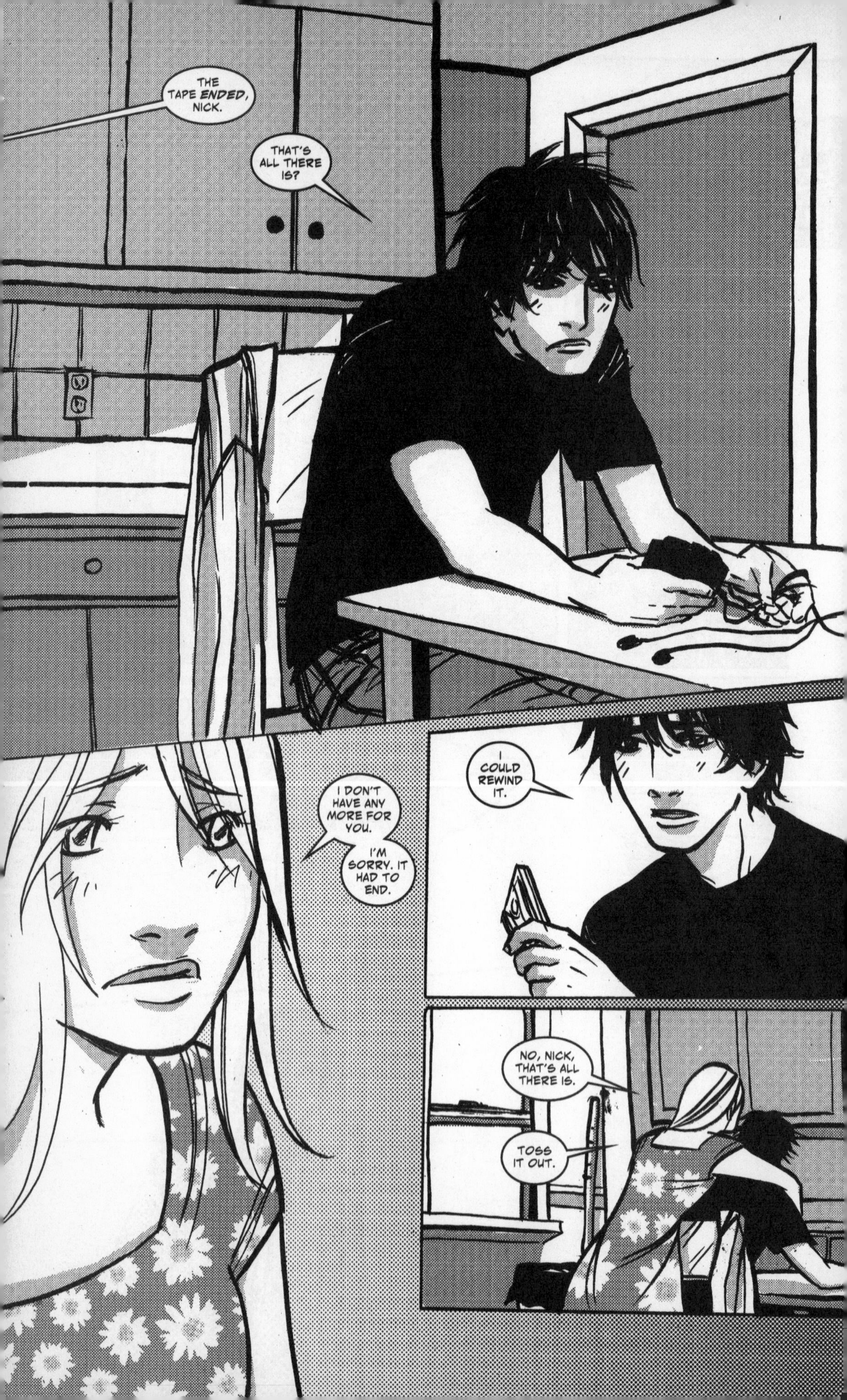
THE TAPE *ENDED*, NICK.
THAT'S ALL THERE IS?
I COULD REWIND IT.
I DON'T HAVE ANY MORE FOR YOU.
I'M SORRY. IT HAD TO END.
NO, NICK, THAT'S ALL THERE IS.
TOSS IT OUT.

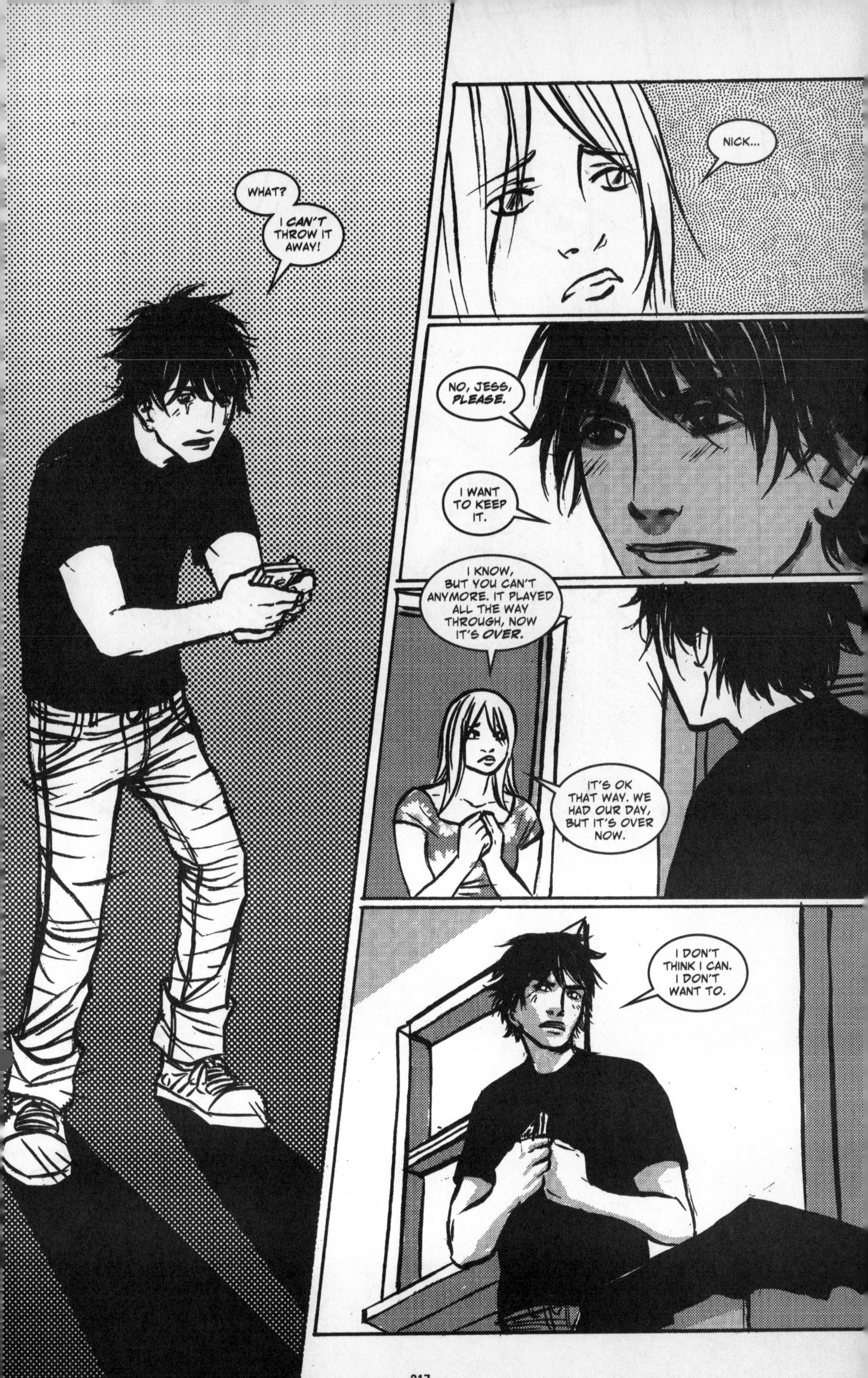
WHAT?
I CAN'T THROW IT AWAY!
NICK...
NO, JESS, PLEASE.
I WANT TO KEEP IT.
I KNOW, BUT YOU CAN'T ANYMORE. IT PLAYED ALL THE WAY THROUGH, NOW IT'S OVER.
IT'S OK THAT WAY. WE HAD OUR DAY, BUT IT'S OVER NOW.
I DON'T THINK I CAN. I DON'T WANT TO.

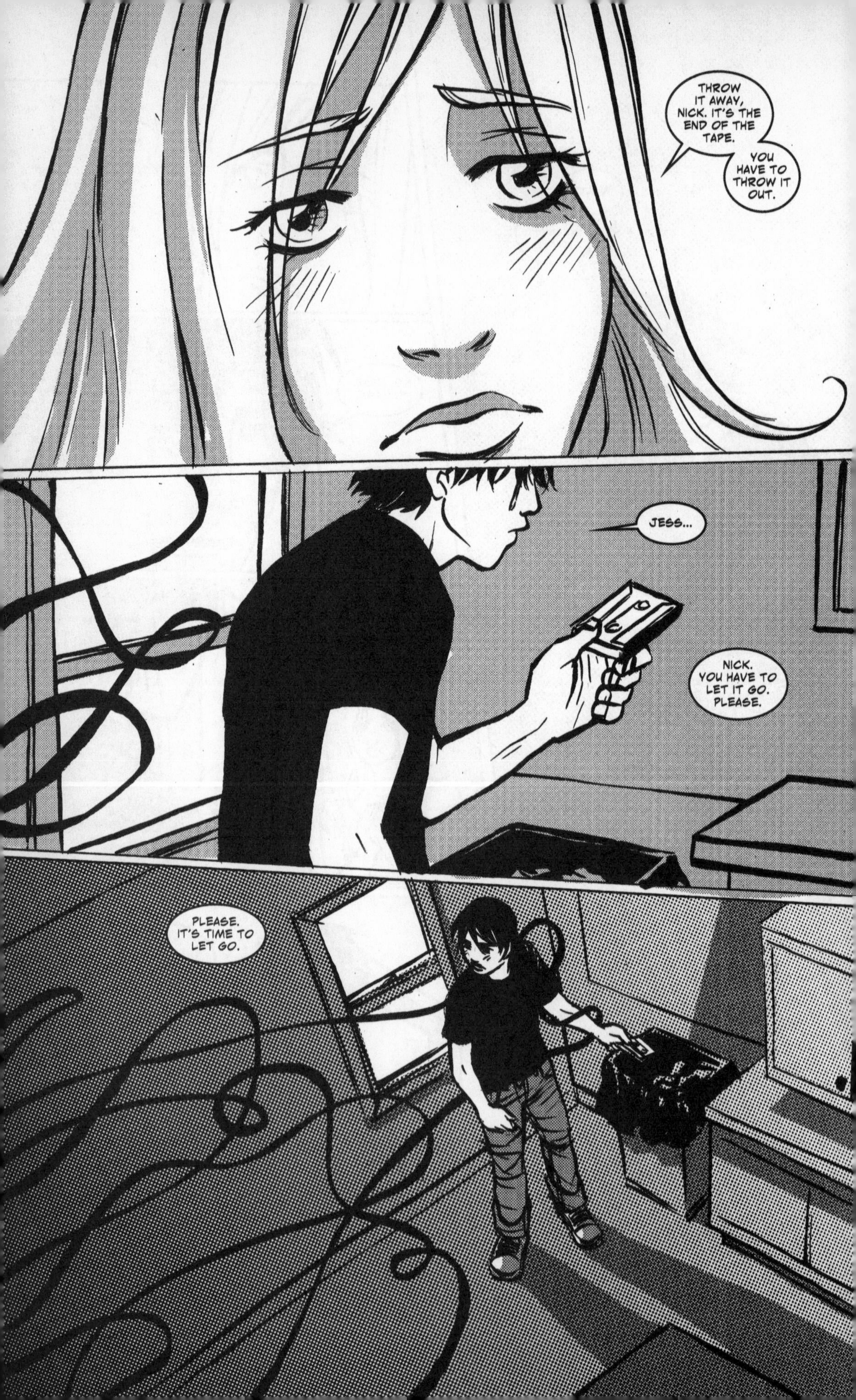
THROW IT AWAY, NICK. IT'S THE END OF THE TAPE.
YOU HAVE TO THROW IT OUT.
JESS...
NICK. YOU HAVE TO LET IT GO. PLEASE.
PLEASE. IT'S TIME TO LET GO.

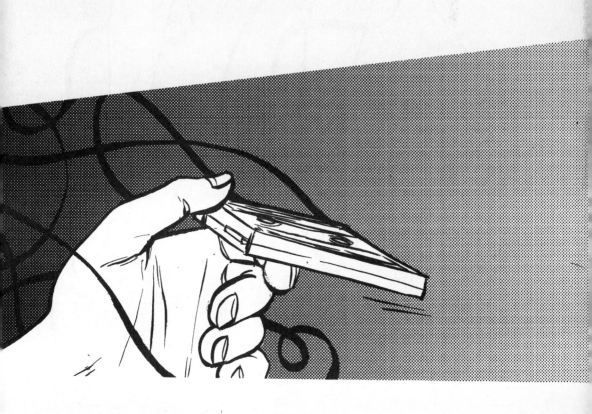

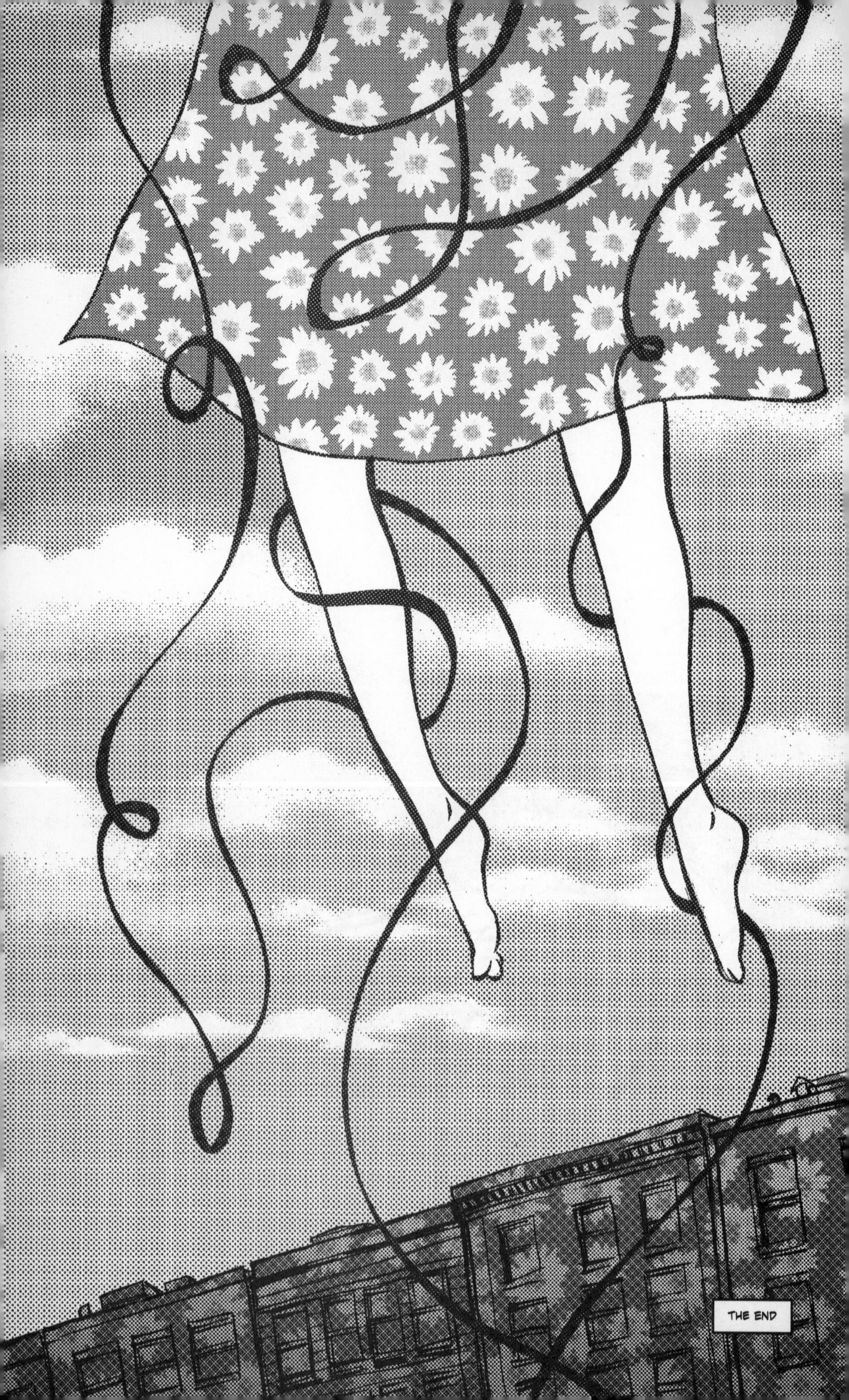
THE END

9

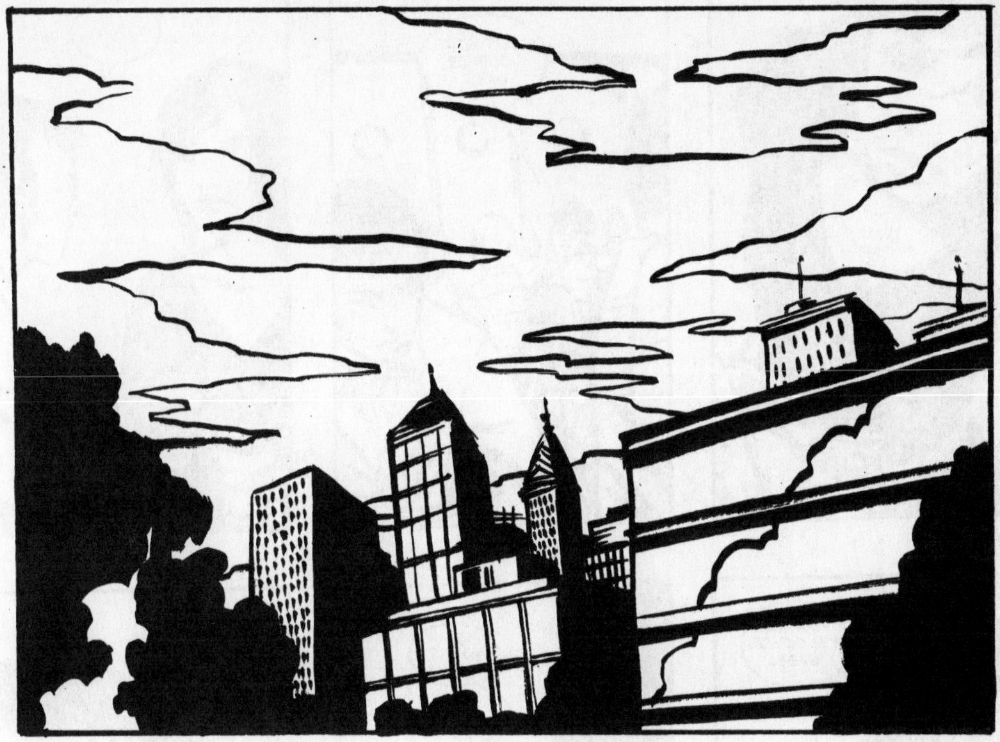

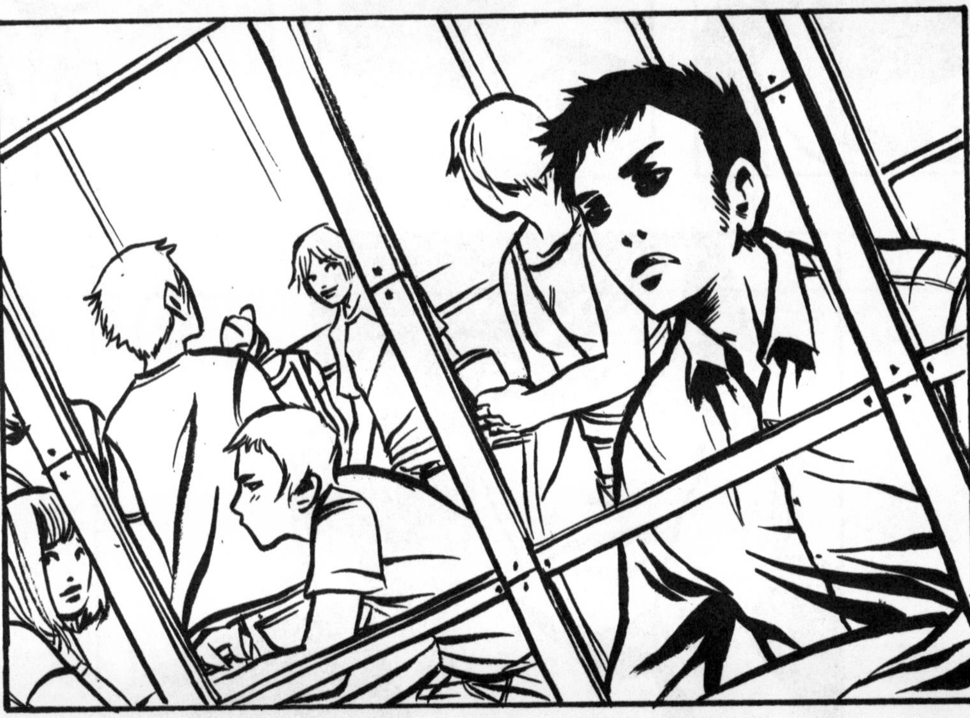

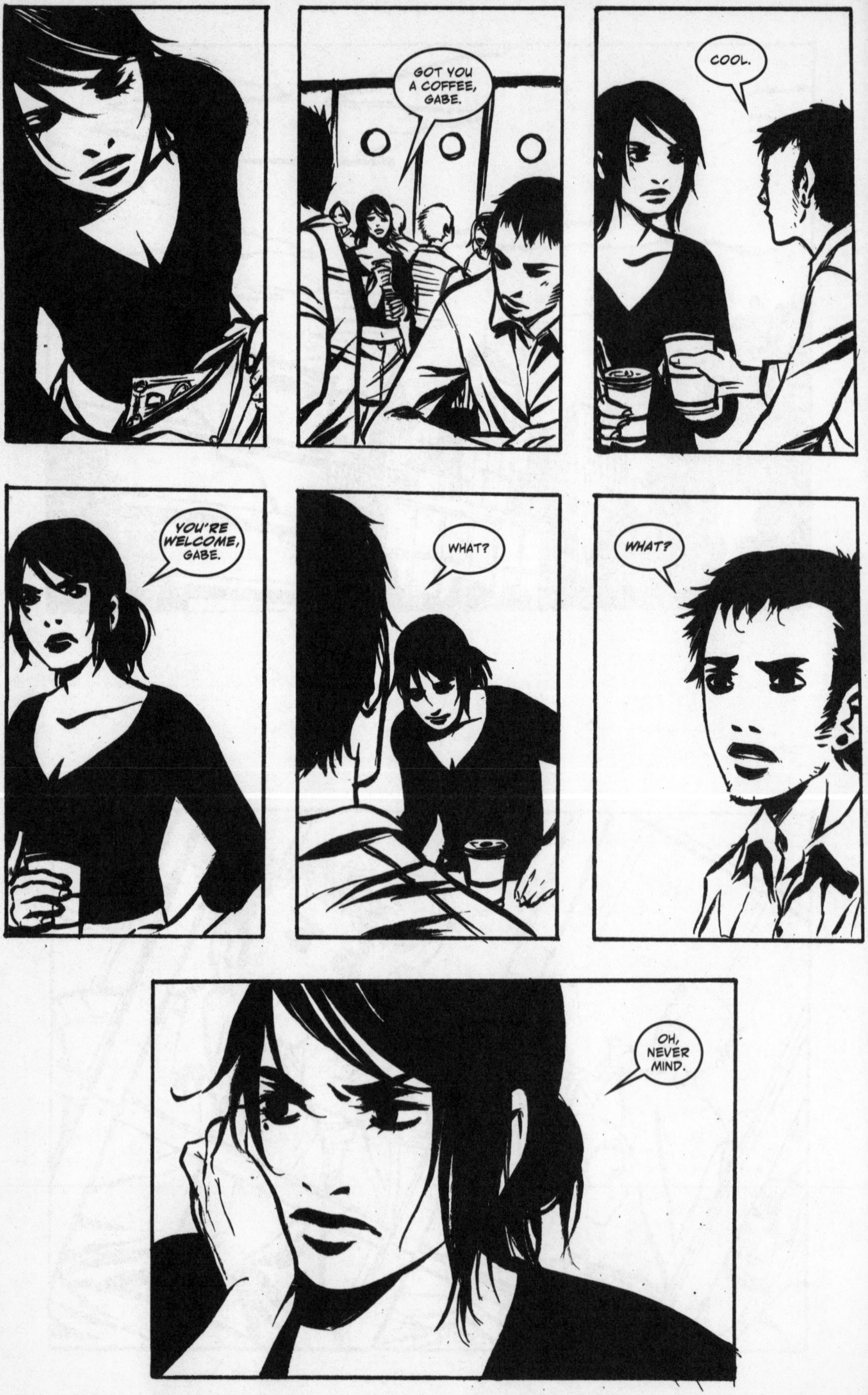
GOT YOU A COFFEE, GABE.
COOL.
YOU'RE WELCOME, GABE.
WHAT?
WHAT?
OH, NEVER MIND.

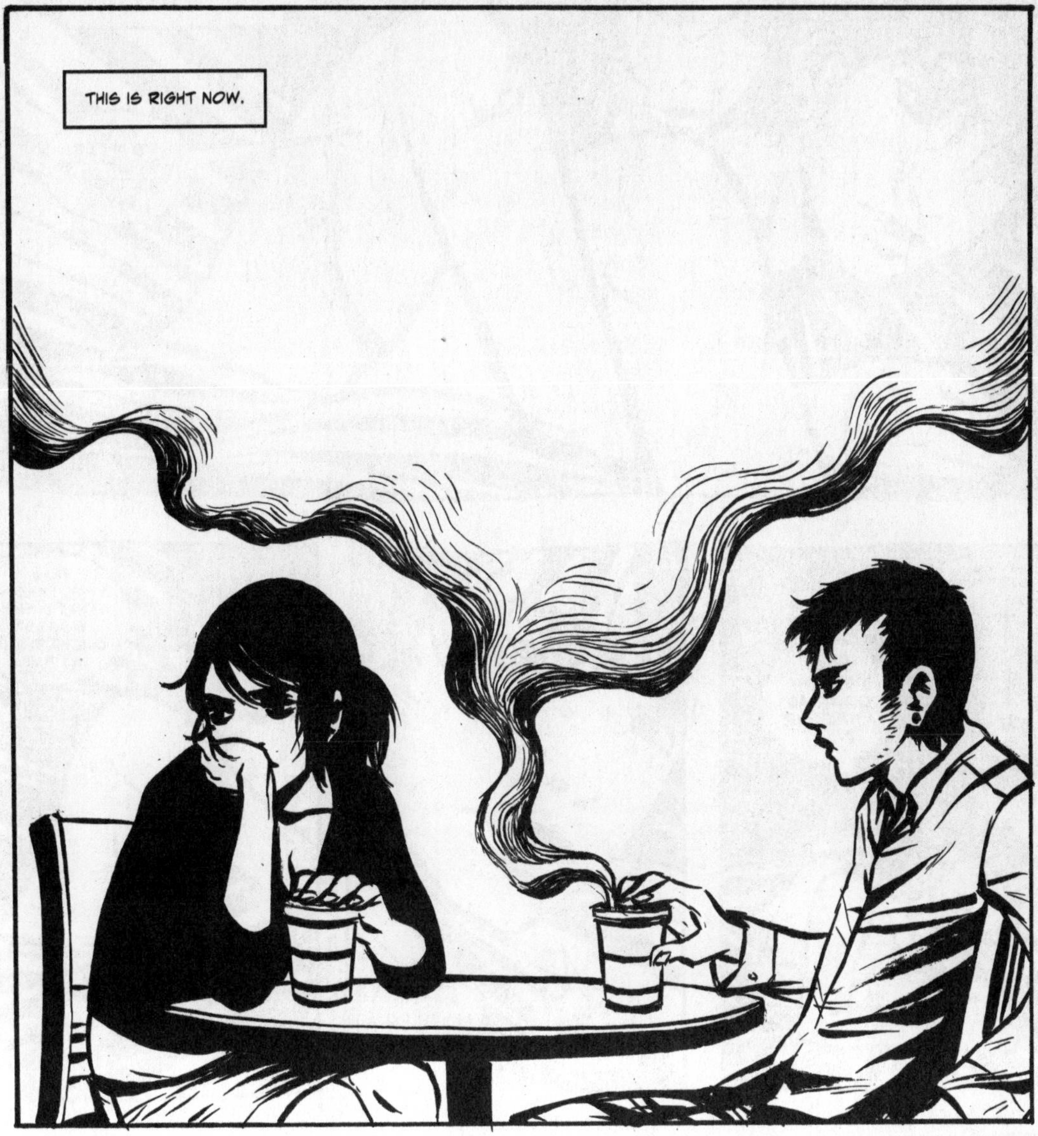
THIS IS RIGHT NOW.

"Breaking Up"

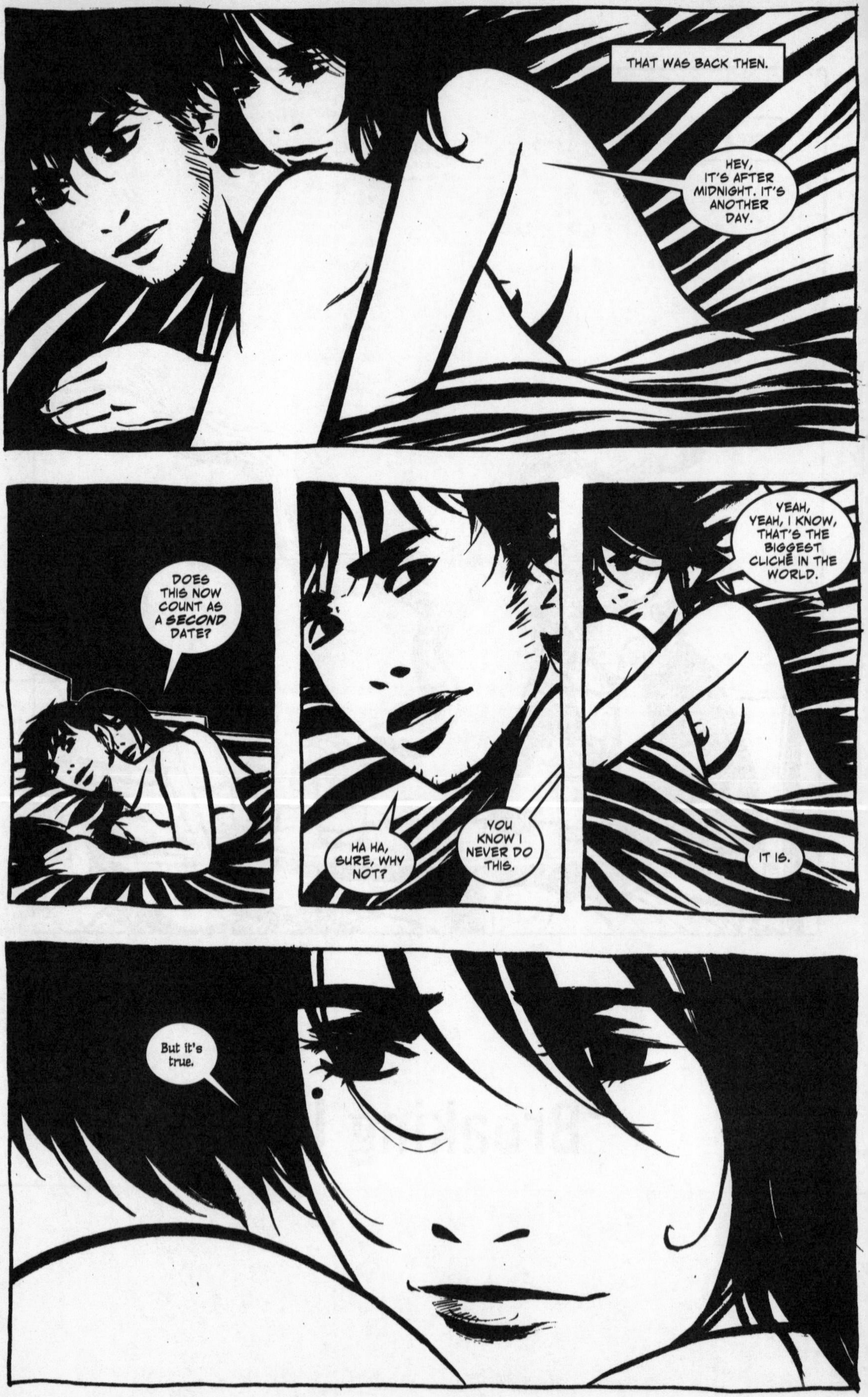

THAT WAS BACK THEN.
HEY, IT'S AFTER MIDNIGHT. IT'S ANOTHER DAY.
DOES THIS NOW COUNT AS A SECOND DATE?
HA HA, SURE, WHY NOT?
YOU KNOW I NEVER DO THIS.
YEAH, YEAH, I KNOW, THAT'S THE BIGGEST CLICHÉ IN THE WORLD.
IT IS.
But it's true.

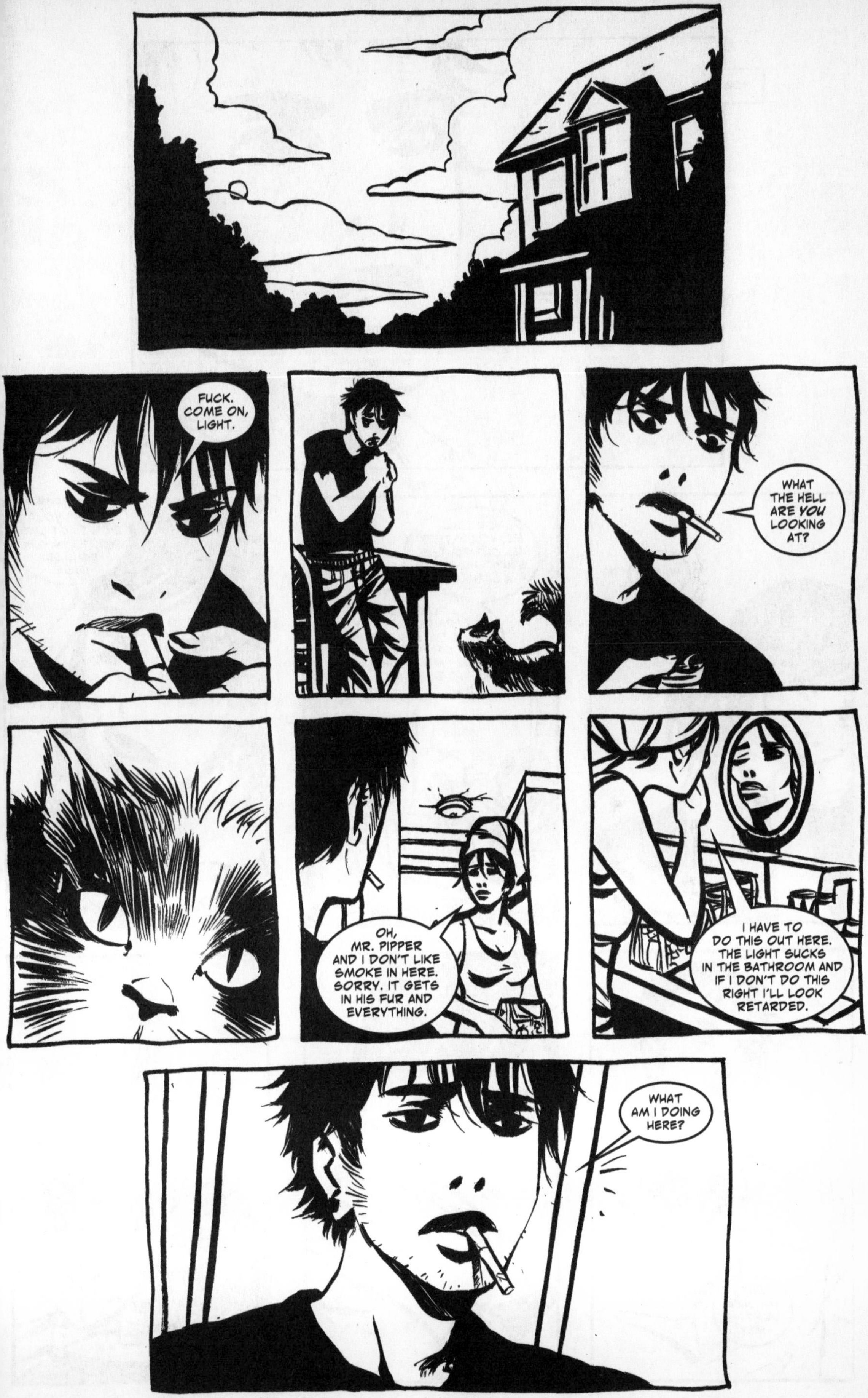
FUCK. COME ON, LIGHT.
WHAT THE HELL ARE *YOU* LOOKING AT?
OH, MR. PIPPER AND I DON'T LIKE SMOKE IN HERE. SORRY. IT GETS IN HIS FUR AND EVERYTHING.
I HAVE TO DO THIS OUT HERE. THE LIGHT SUCKS IN THE BATHROOM AND IF I DON'T DO THIS RIGHT I'LL LOOK RETARDED.
WHAT AM I DOING HERE?

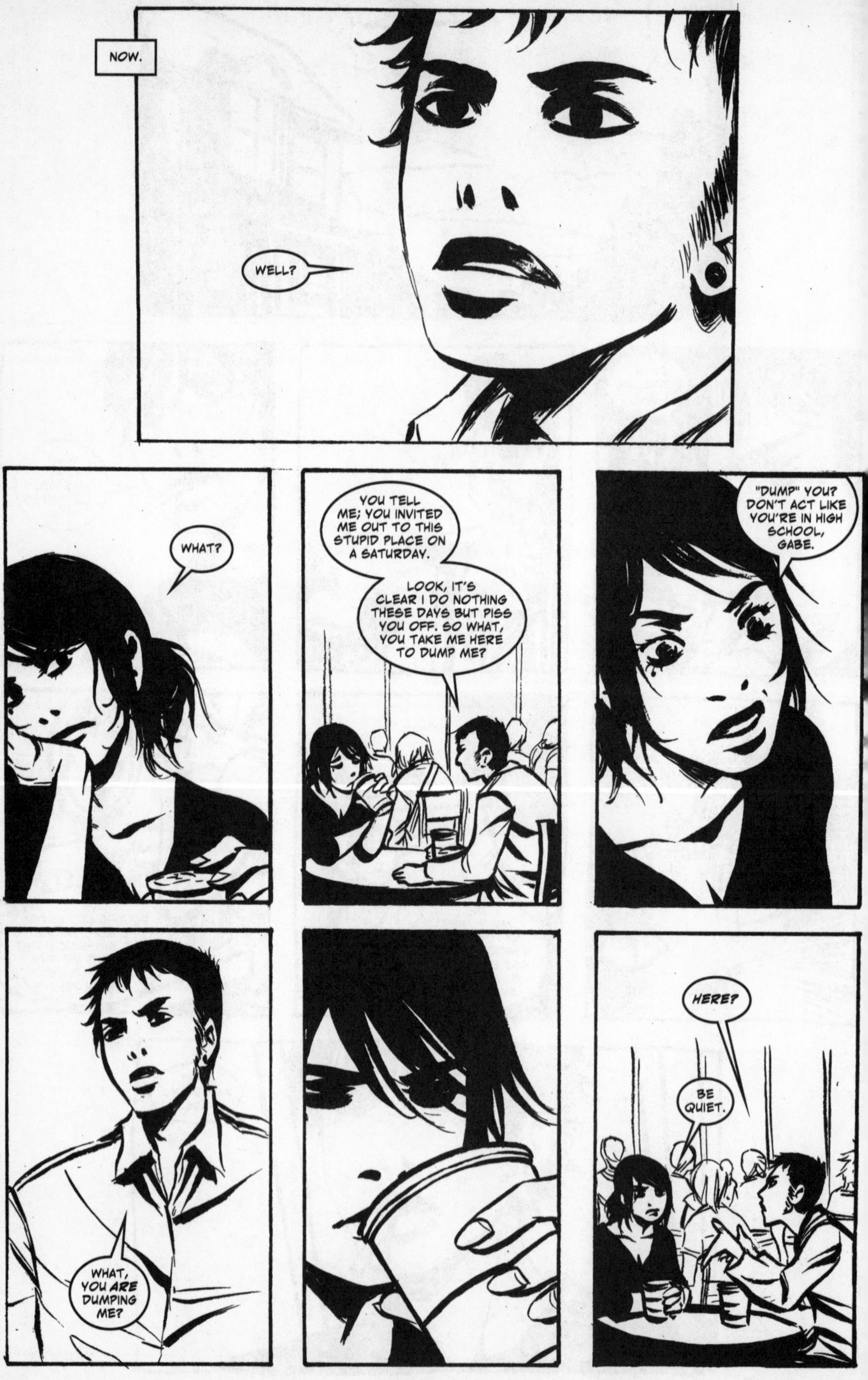
NOW.
WELL?
WHAT?
YOU TELL ME; YOU INVITED ME OUT TO THIS STUPID PLACE ON A SATURDAY.
LOOK, IT'S CLEAR I DO NOTHING THESE DAYS BUT PISS YOU OFF. SO WHAT, YOU TAKE ME HERE TO DUMP ME?
"DUMP" YOU? DON'T ACT LIKE YOU'RE IN HIGH SCHOOL, GABE.
WHAT, YOU ARE DUMPING ME?
HERE?
BE QUIET.

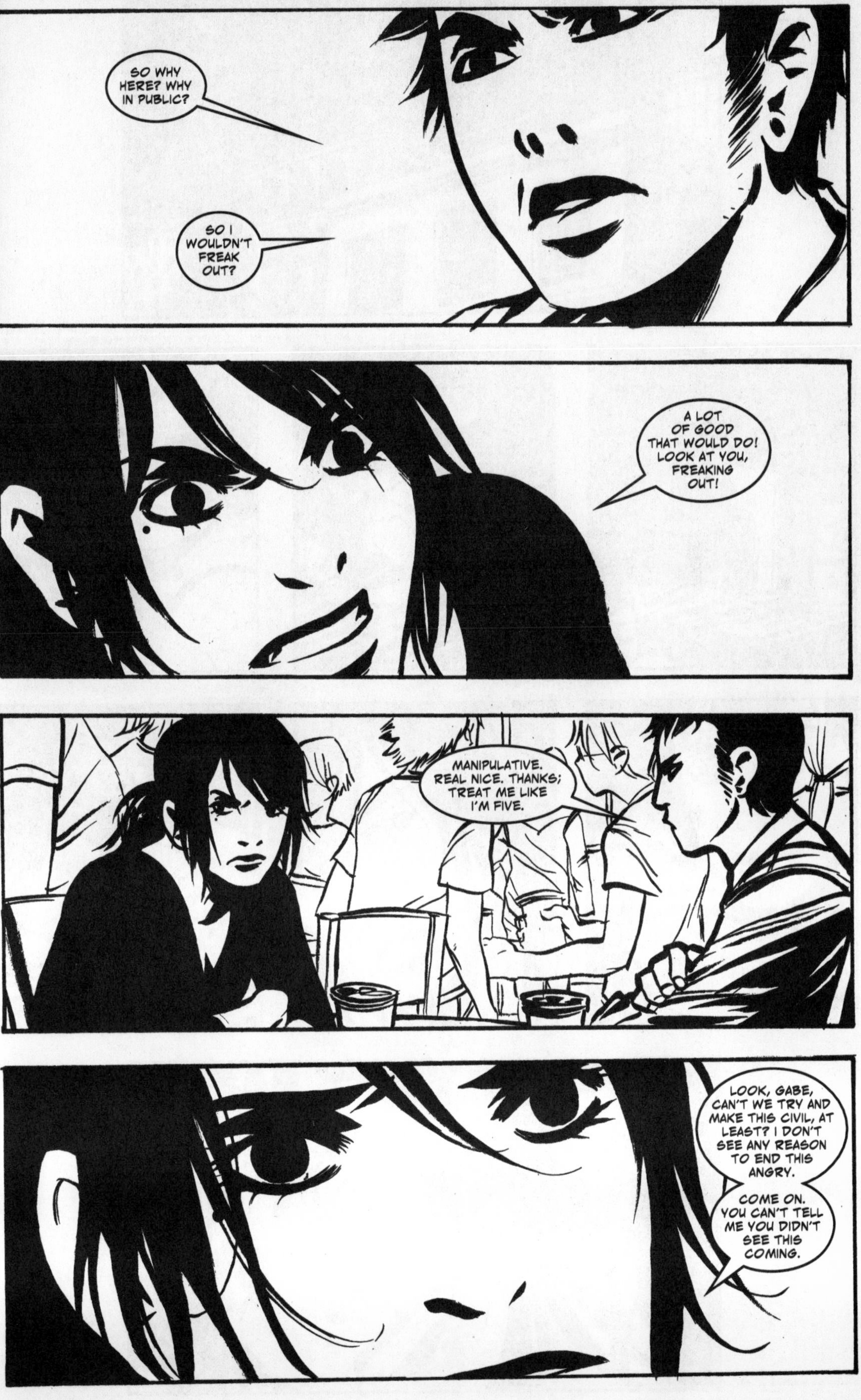
SO WHY HERE? WHY IN PUBLIC?
SO I WOULDN'T FREAK OUT?
A LOT OF GOOD THAT WOULD DO! LOOK AT YOU, FREAKING OUT!
MANIPULATIVE. REAL NICE. THANKS; TREAT ME LIKE I'M FIVE.
LOOK, GABE, CAN'T WE TRY AND MAKE THIS CIVIL, AT LEAST? I DON'T SEE ANY REASON TO END THIS ANGRY.
COME ON. YOU CAN'T TELL ME YOU DIDN'T SEE THIS COMING.

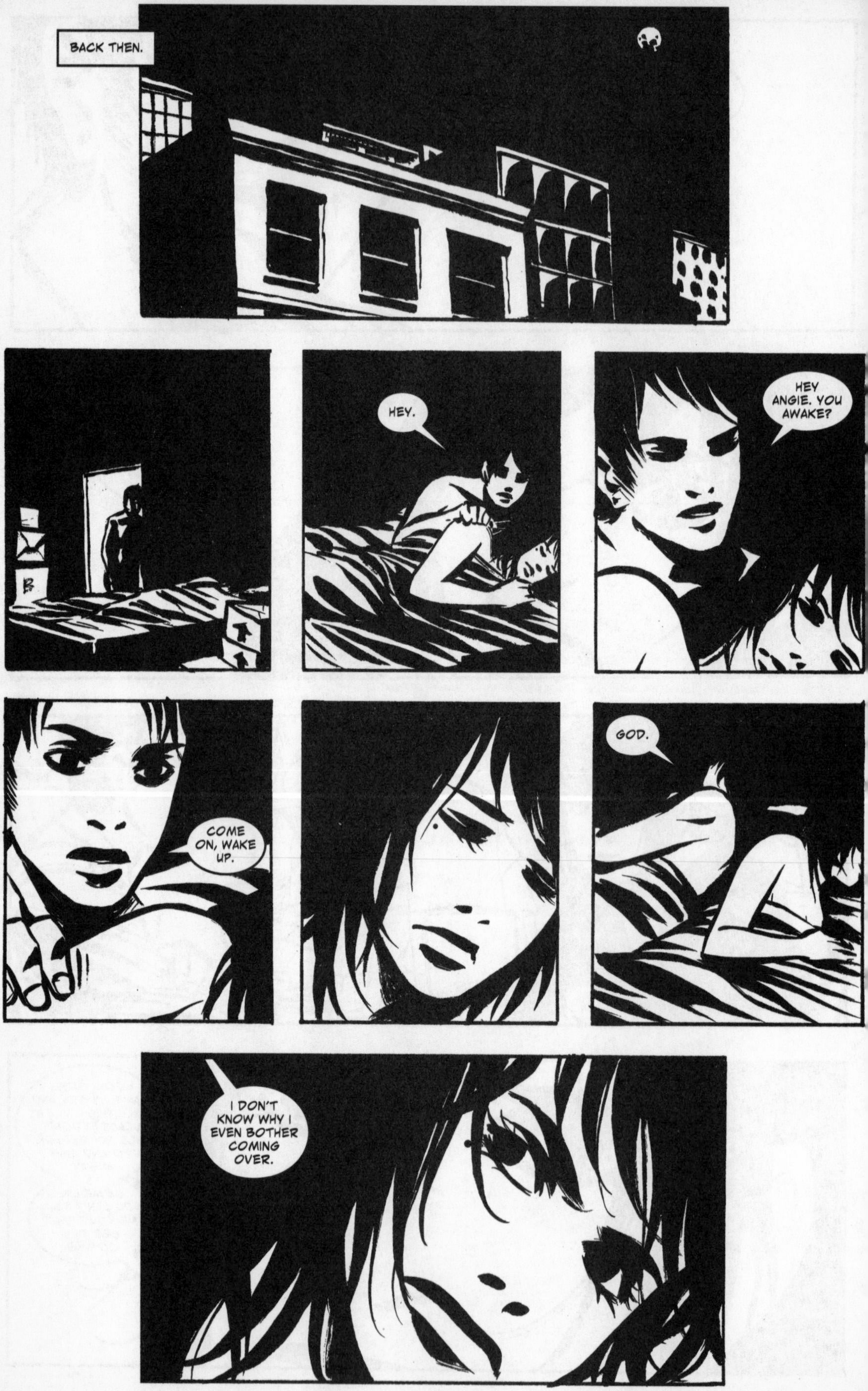
BACK THEN.
HEY.
HEY ANGIE. YOU AWAKE?
COME ON, WAKE UP.
GOD.
I DON'T KNOW WHY I EVEN BOTHER COMING OVER.

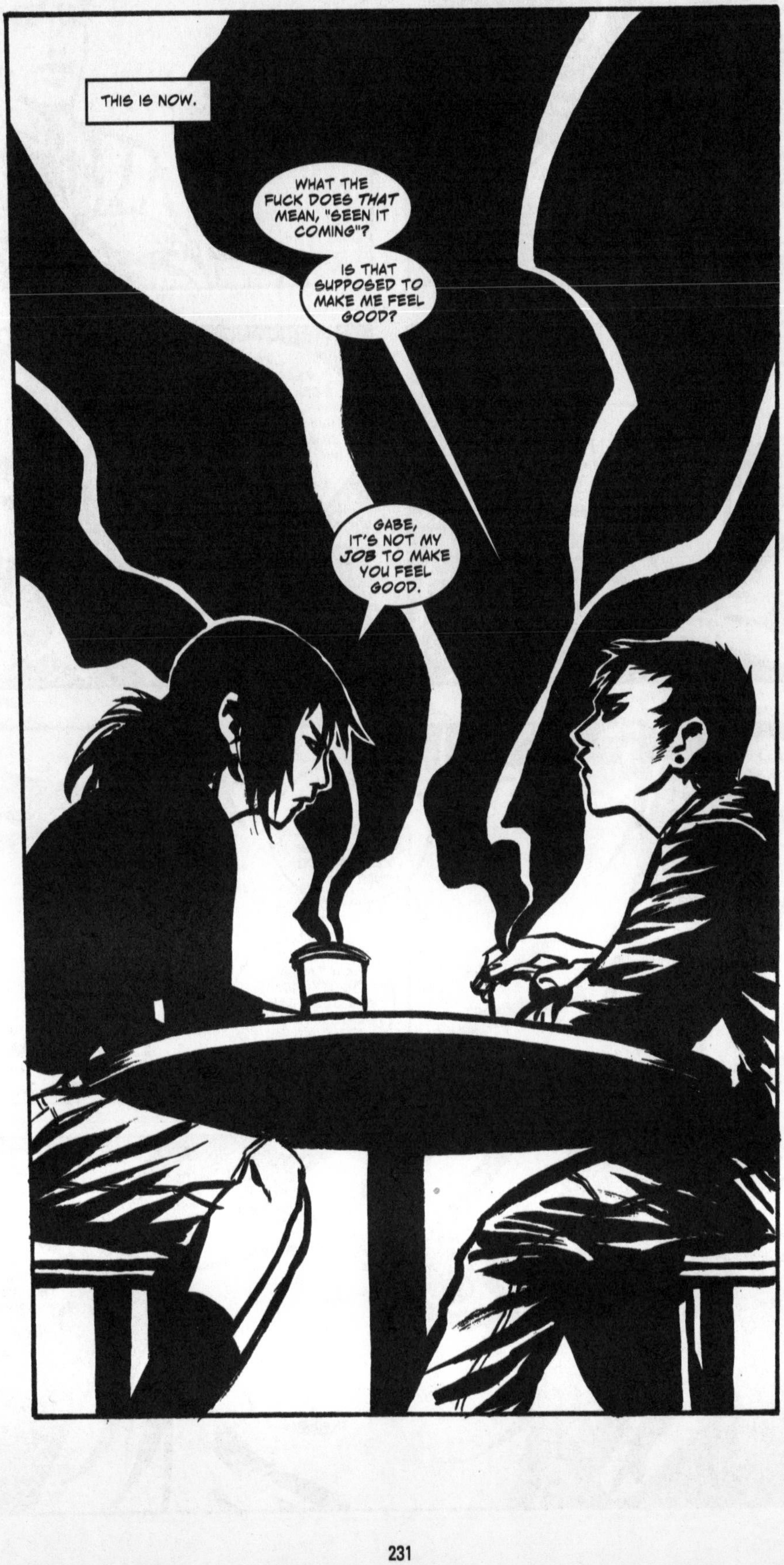
THIS IS NOW.
WHAT THE FUCK DOES *THAT* MEAN, "SEEN IT COMING"?
IS THAT SUPPOSED TO MAKE ME FEEL GOOD?
GABE, IT'S NOT MY *JOB* TO MAKE YOU FEEL GOOD.

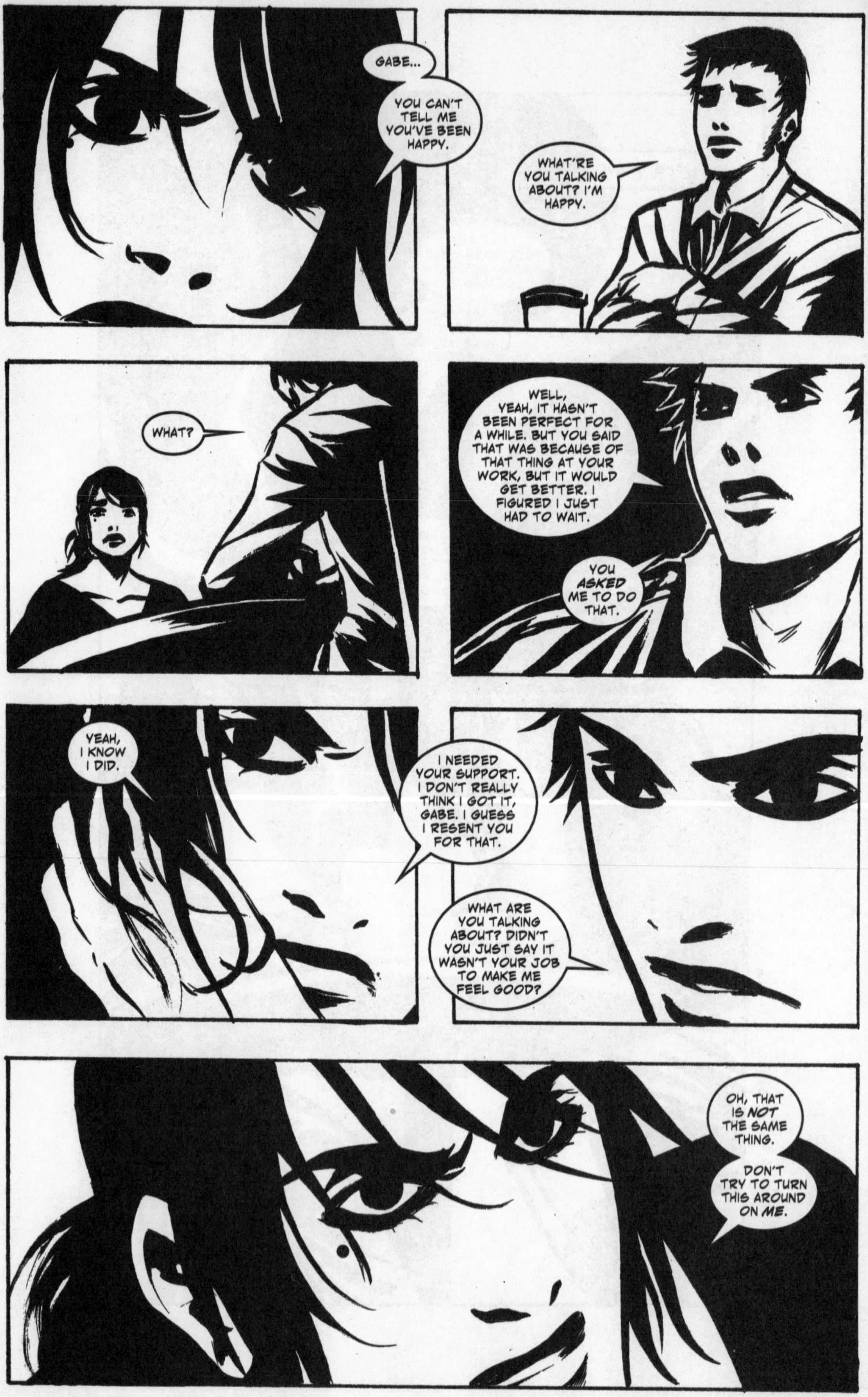
GABE...
YOU CAN'T TELL ME YOU'VE BEEN HAPPY.
WHAT'RE YOU TALKING ABOUT? I'M HAPPY.
WHAT?
WELL, YEAH, IT HASN'T BEEN PERFECT FOR A WHILE. BUT YOU SAID THAT WAS BECAUSE OF THAT THING AT YOUR WORK, BUT IT WOULD GET BETTER. I FIGURED I JUST HAD TO WAIT.
YOU *ASKED* ME TO DO THAT.
YEAH, I KNOW I DID.
I NEEDED YOUR SUPPORT. I DON'T REALLY THINK I GOT IT, GABE. I GUESS I RESENT YOU FOR THAT.
WHAT ARE YOU TALKING ABOUT? DIDN'T YOU JUST SAY IT WASN'T YOUR JOB TO MAKE ME FEEL GOOD?
OH, THAT IS *NOT* THE SAME THING.
DON'T TRY TO TURN THIS AROUND ON *ME*.

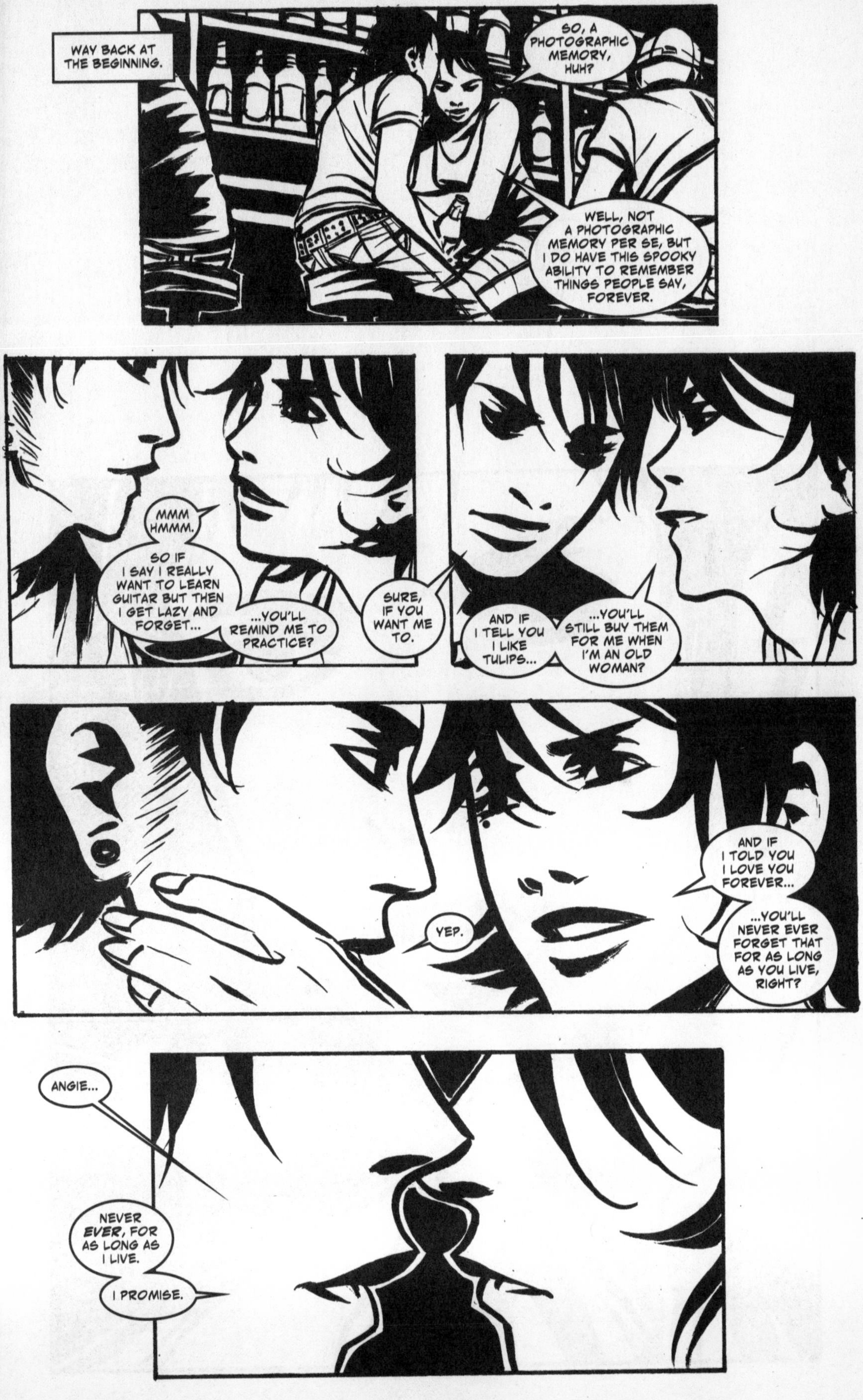
WAY BACK AT THE BEGINNING.
SO, A PHOTOGRAPHIC MEMORY, HUH?
WELL, NOT A PHOTOGRAPHIC MEMORY PER SE, BUT I DO HAVE THIS SPOOKY ABILITY TO REMEMBER THINGS PEOPLE SAY, FOREVER.
MMM HMMM.
SO IF I SAY I REALLY WANT TO LEARN GUITAR BUT THEN I GET LAZY AND FORGET...
...YOU'LL REMIND ME TO PRACTICE?
SURE, IF YOU WANT ME TO.
AND IF I TELL YOU I LIKE TULIPS...
...YOU'LL STILL BUY THEM FOR ME WHEN I'M AN OLD WOMAN?
AND IF I TOLD YOU I LOVE YOU FOREVER...
...YOU'LL NEVER EVER FORGET THAT FOR AS LONG AS YOU LIVE, RIGHT?
YEP.
ANGIE...
NEVER *EVER*, FOR AS LONG AS I LIVE.
I PROMISE.

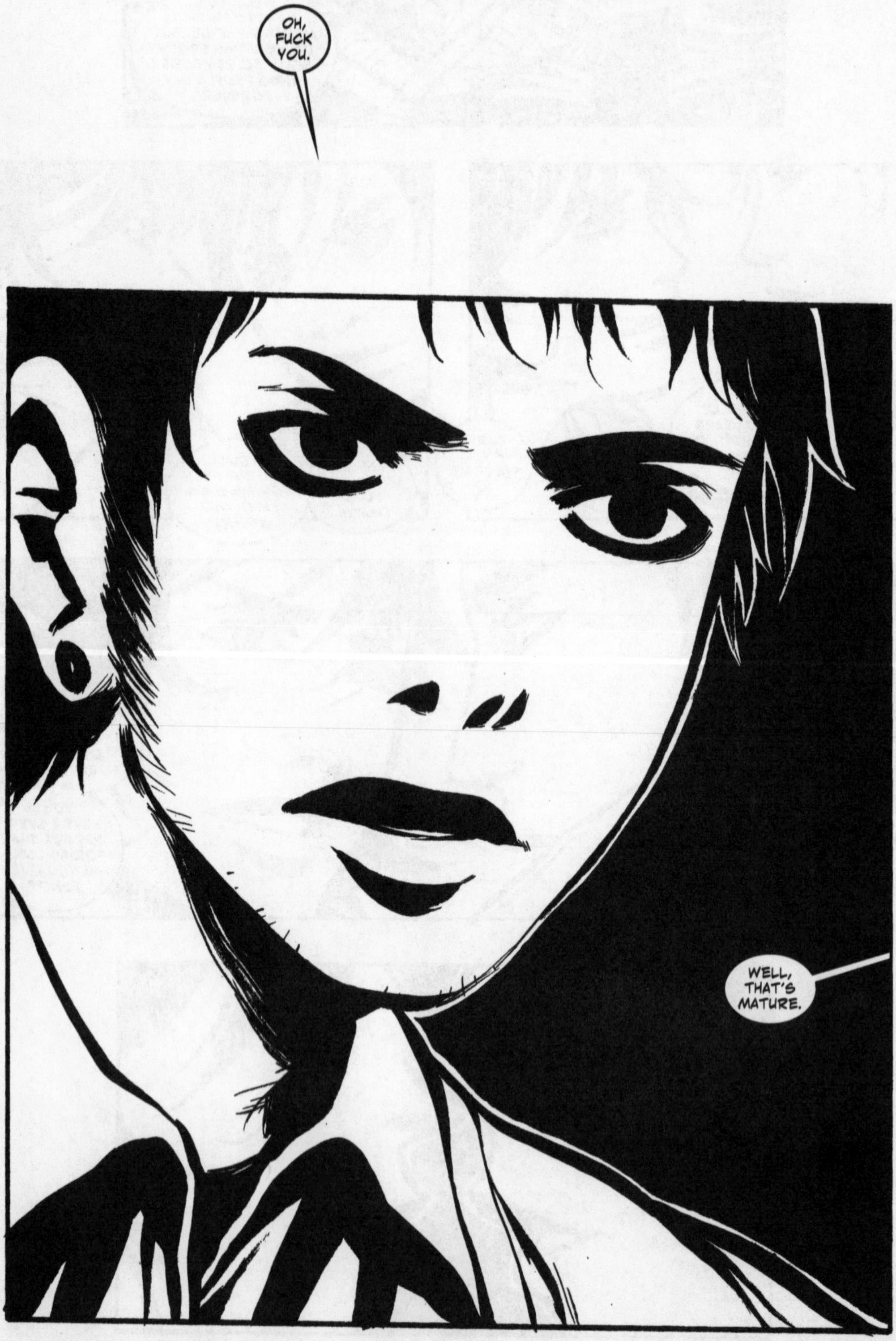
OH, FUCK YOU.
WELL, THAT'S MATURE.

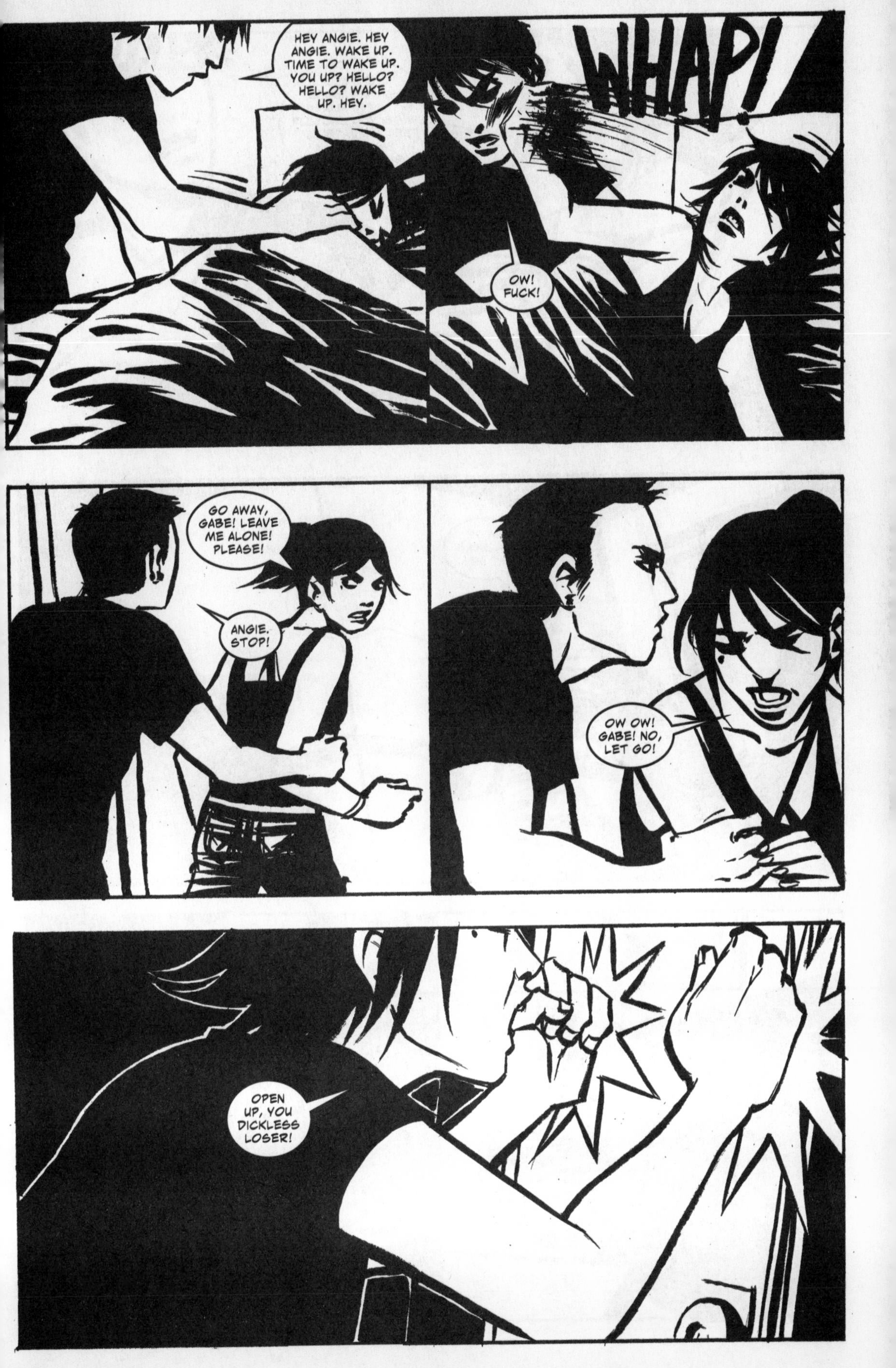
HEY ANGIE. HEY ANGIE. WAKE UP. TIME TO WAKE UP. YOU UP? HELLO? HELLO? WAKE UP. HEY.
WHAP!
OW! FUCK!
GO AWAY, GABE! LEAVE ME ALONE! PLEASE!
ANGIE. STOP!
OW OW! GABE! NO, LET GO!
OPEN UP, YOU DICKLESS LOSER!

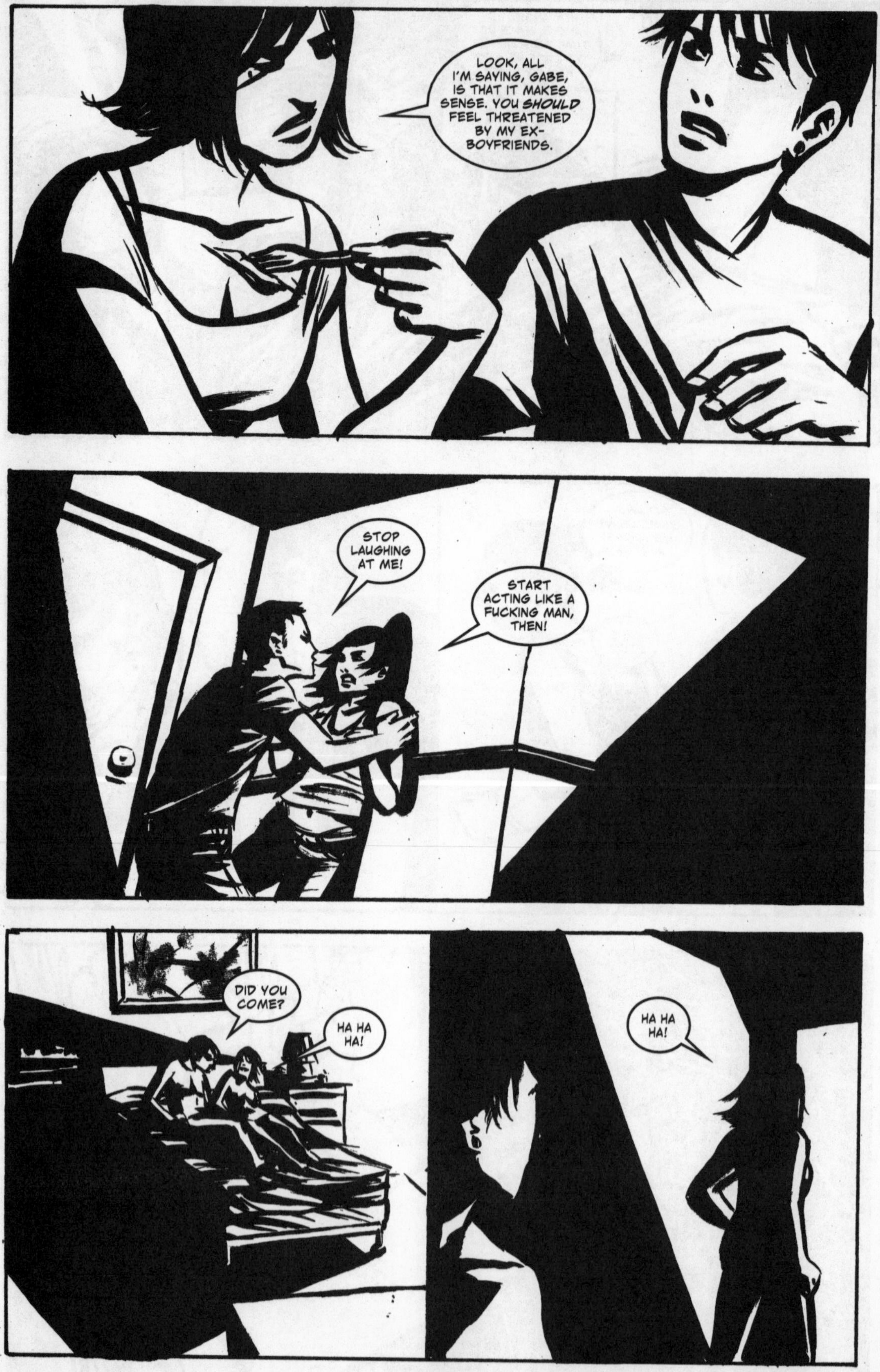
LOOK, ALL I'M SAYING, GABE, IS THAT IT MAKES SENSE. YOU *SHOULD* FEEL THREATENED BY MY EX-BOYFRIENDS.
STOP LAUGHING AT ME!
START ACTING LIKE A FUCKING MAN, THEN!
DID YOU COME?
HA HA HA!
HA HA HA!

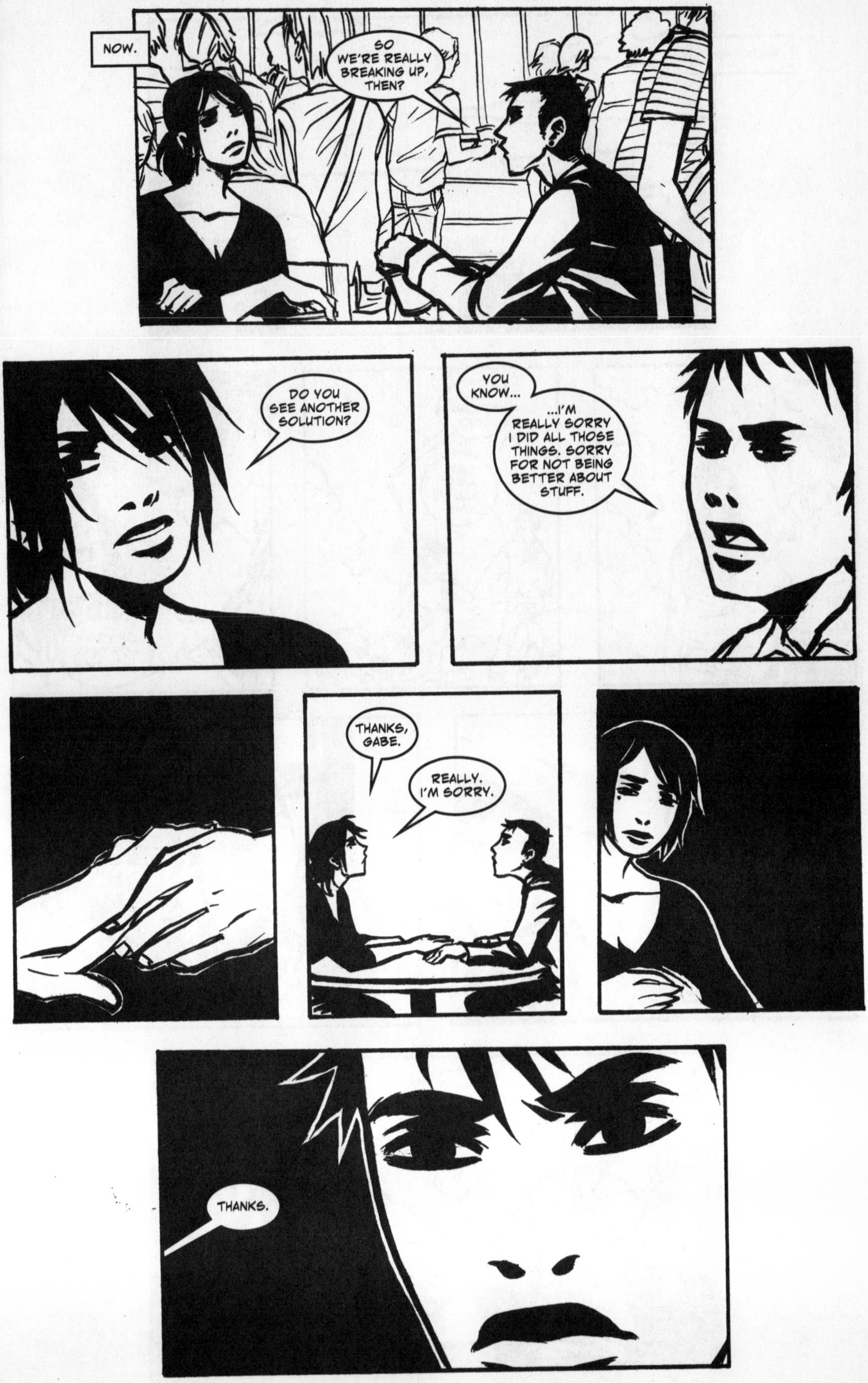
NOW.
SO WE'RE REALLY BREAKING UP, THEN?
DO YOU SEE ANOTHER SOLUTION?
YOU KNOW...
...I'M REALLY SORRY I DID ALL THOSE THINGS. SORRY FOR NOT BEING BETTER ABOUT STUFF.
THANKS, GABE.
REALLY. I'M SORRY.
THANKS.

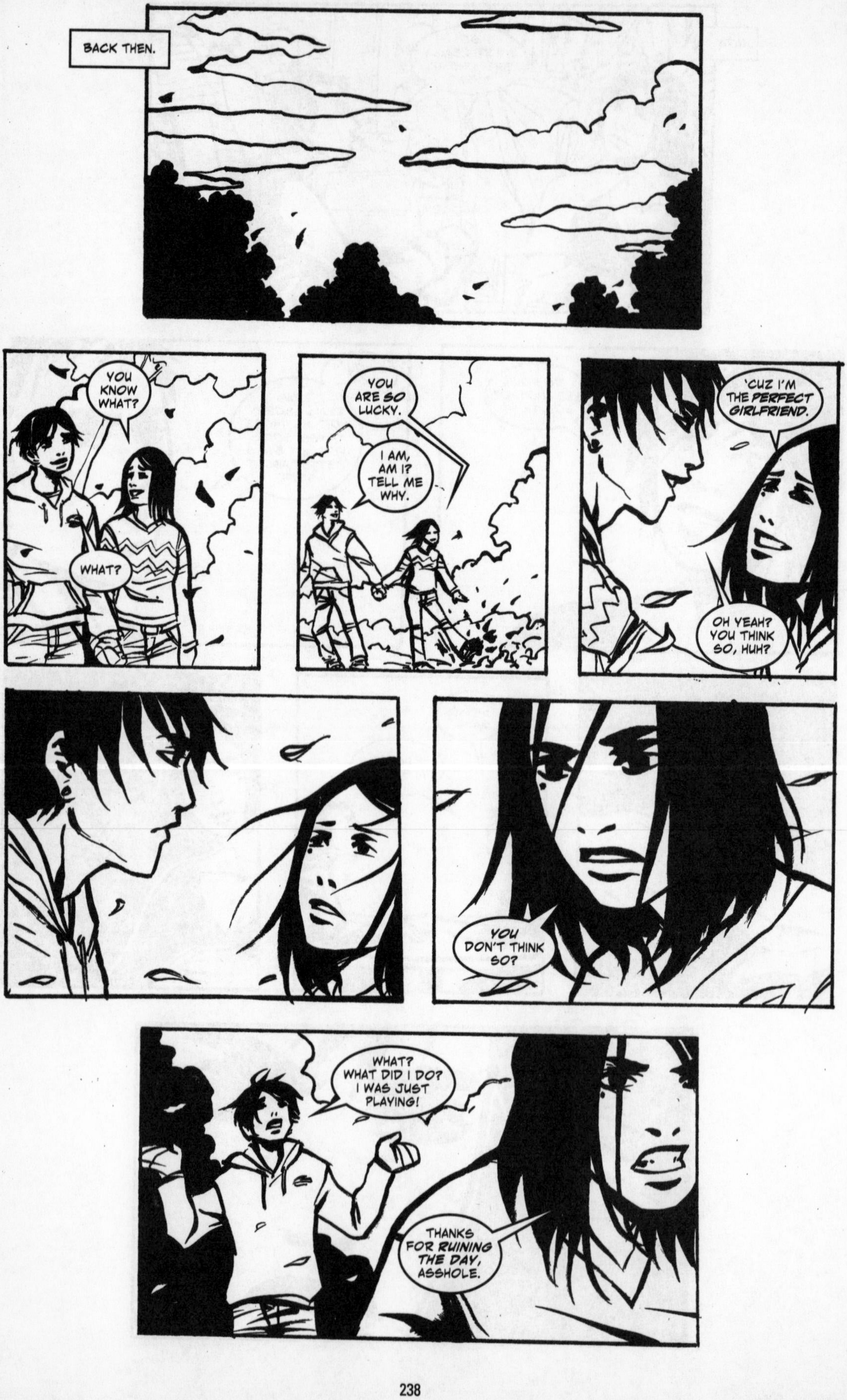
BACK THEN.
YOU KNOW WHAT?
WHAT?
YOU ARE SO LUCKY.
I AM, AM I? TELL ME WHY.
'CUZ I'M THE PERFECT GIRLFRIEND.
OH YEAH? YOU THINK SO, HUH?
YOU DON'T THINK SO?
WHAT? WHAT DID I DO? I WAS JUST PLAYING!
THANKS FOR RUINING THE DAY, ASSHOLE.

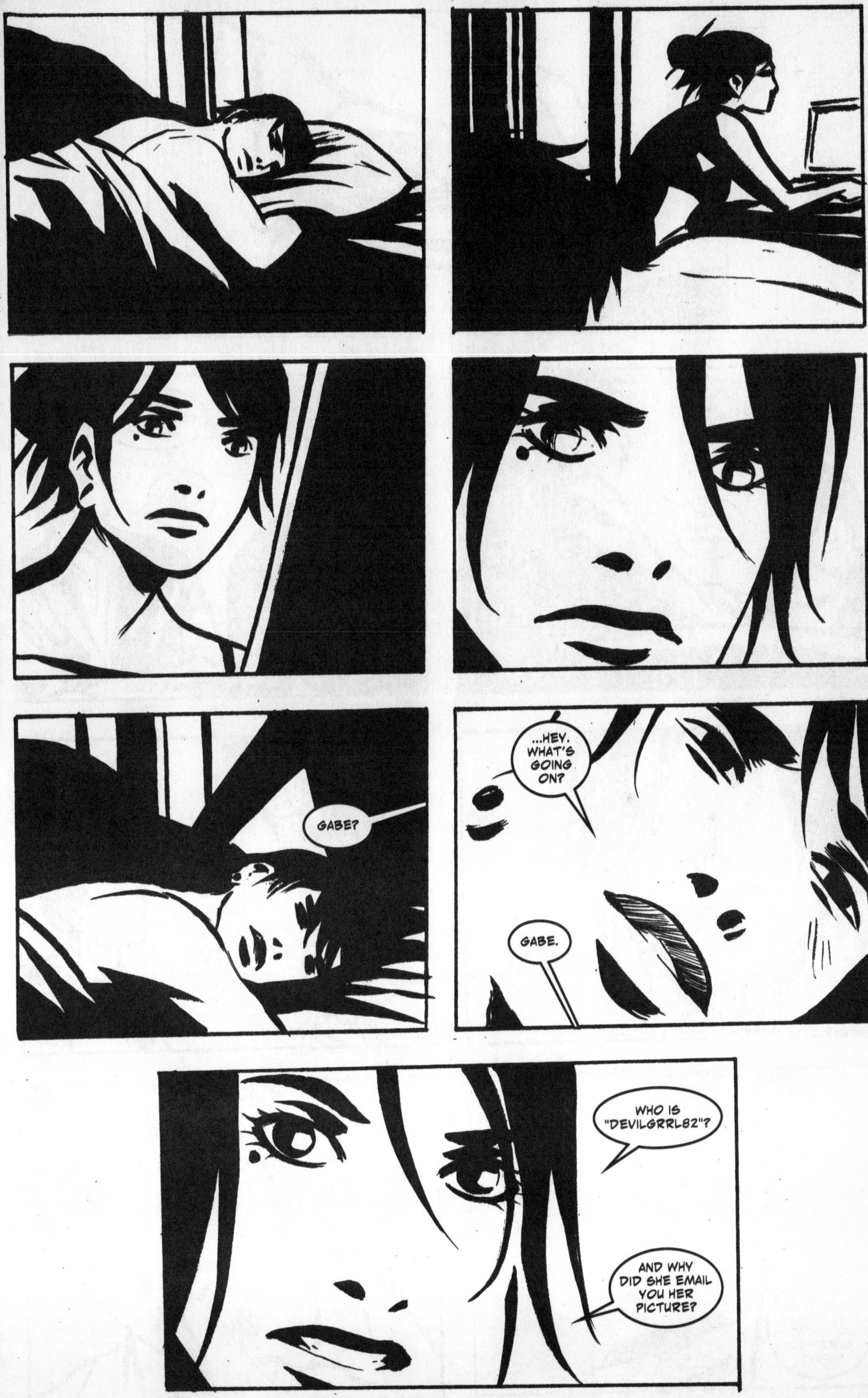
GABE?
...HEY. WHAT'S GOING ON?
GABE.
WHO IS "DEVILGRRL82"?
AND WHY DID SHE EMAIL YOU HER PICTURE?

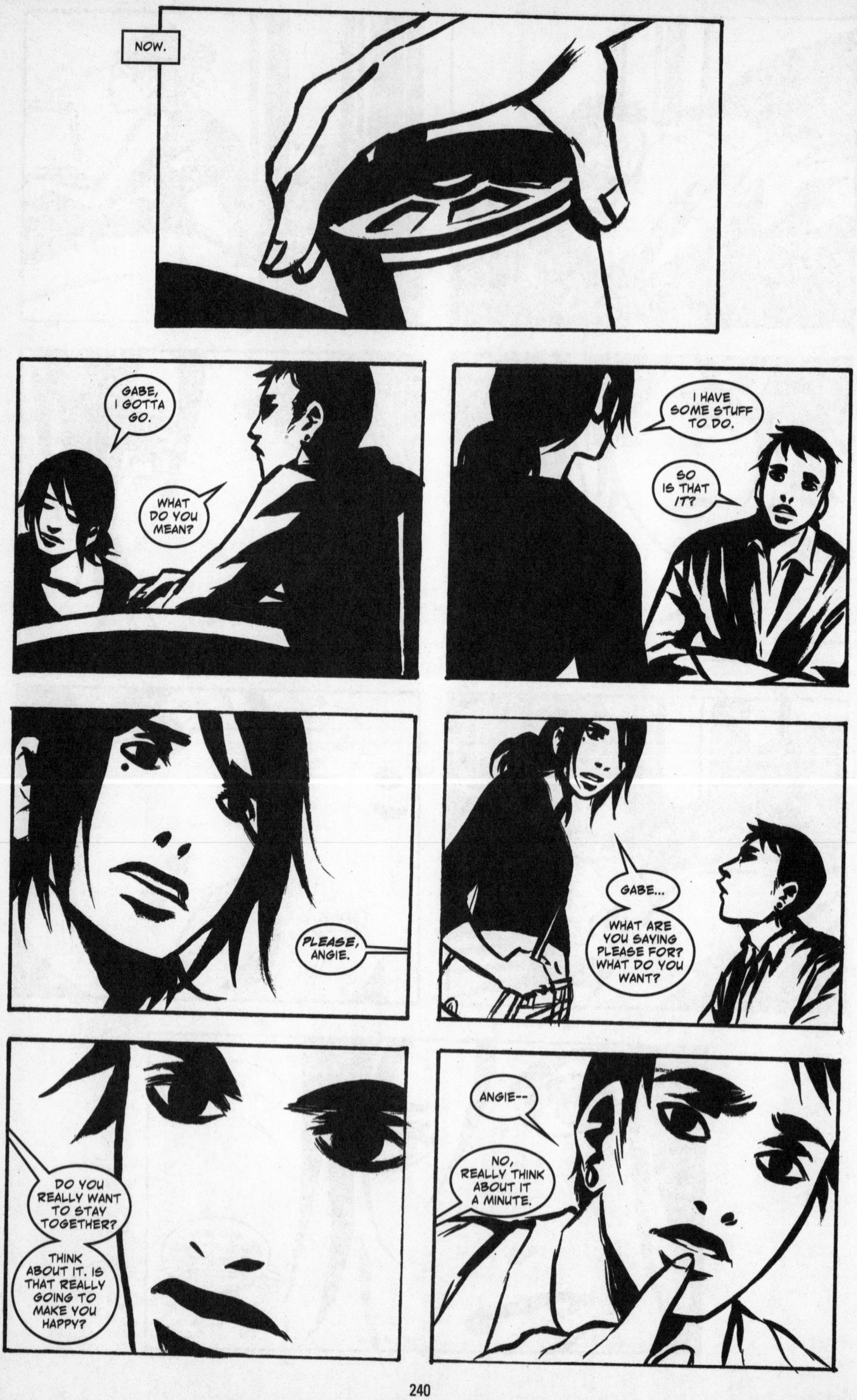
NOW.
GABE, I GOTTA GO.
WHAT DO YOU MEAN?
I HAVE SOME STUFF TO DO.
SO IS THAT IT?
PLEASE, ANGIE.
GABE...
WHAT ARE YOU SAYING PLEASE FOR? WHAT DO YOU WANT?
DO YOU REALLY WANT TO STAY TOGETHER?
THINK ABOUT IT. IS THAT REALLY GOING TO MAKE YOU HAPPY?
ANGIE--
NO, REALLY THINK ABOUT IT A MINUTE.

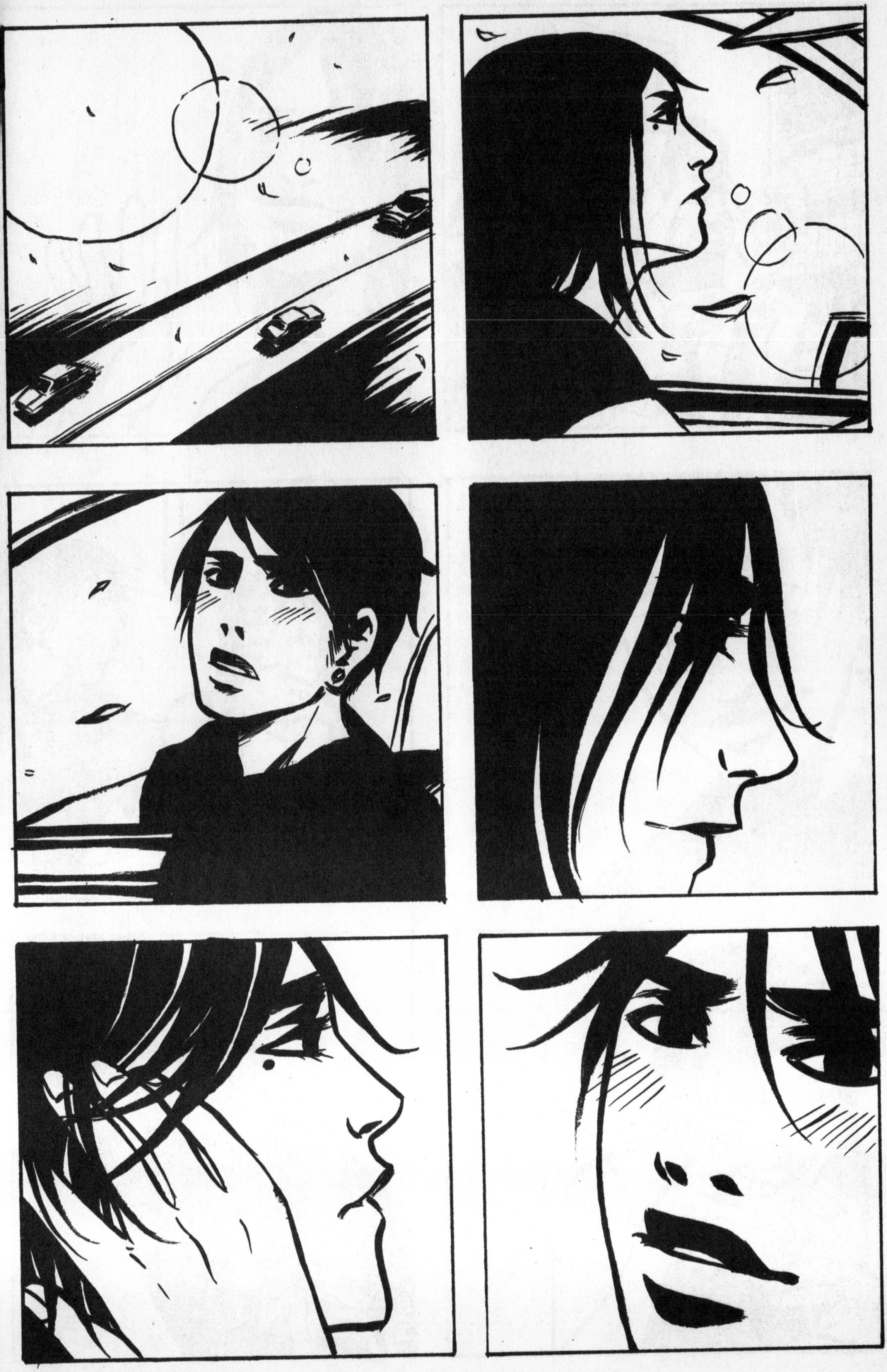

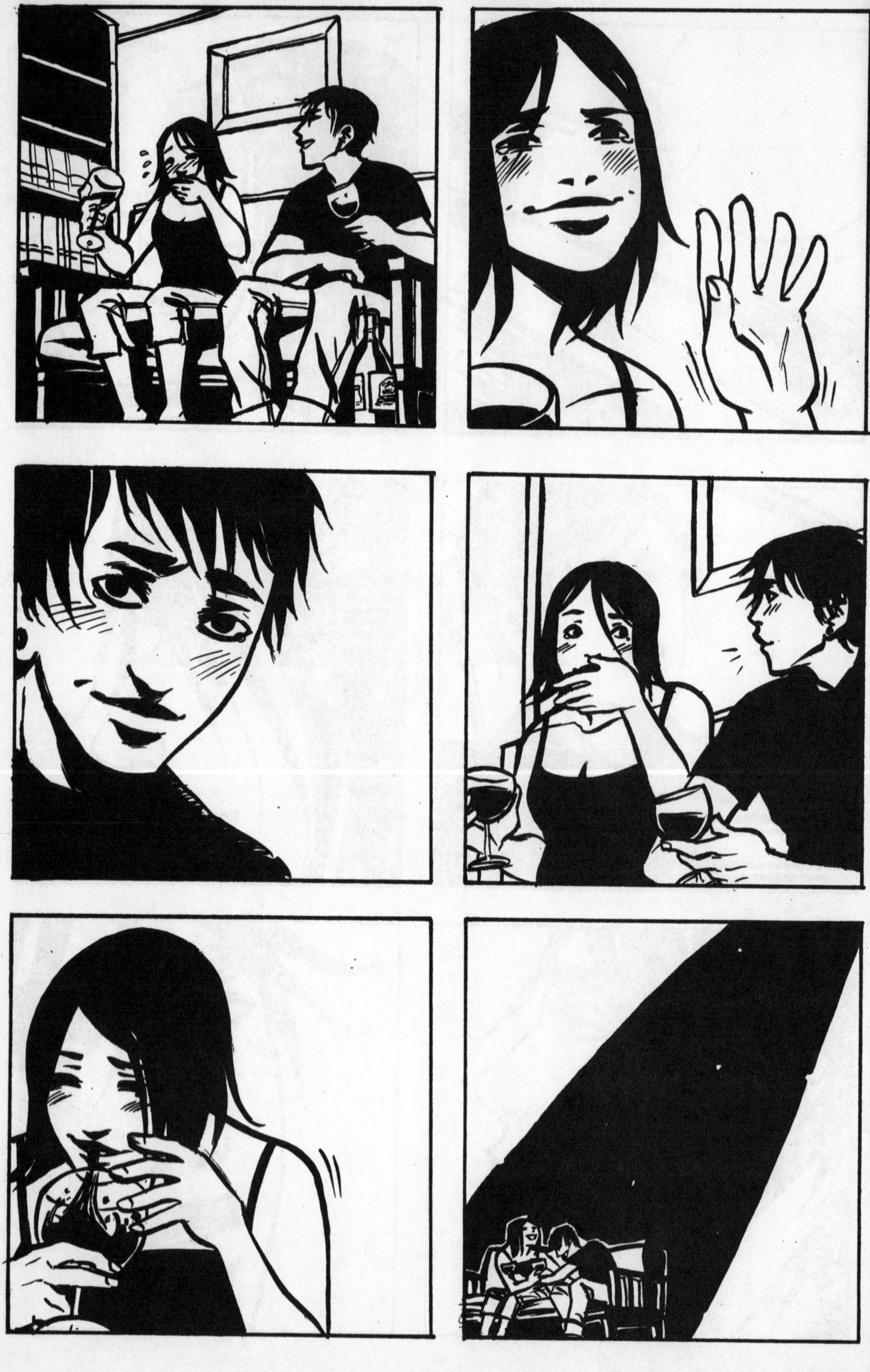

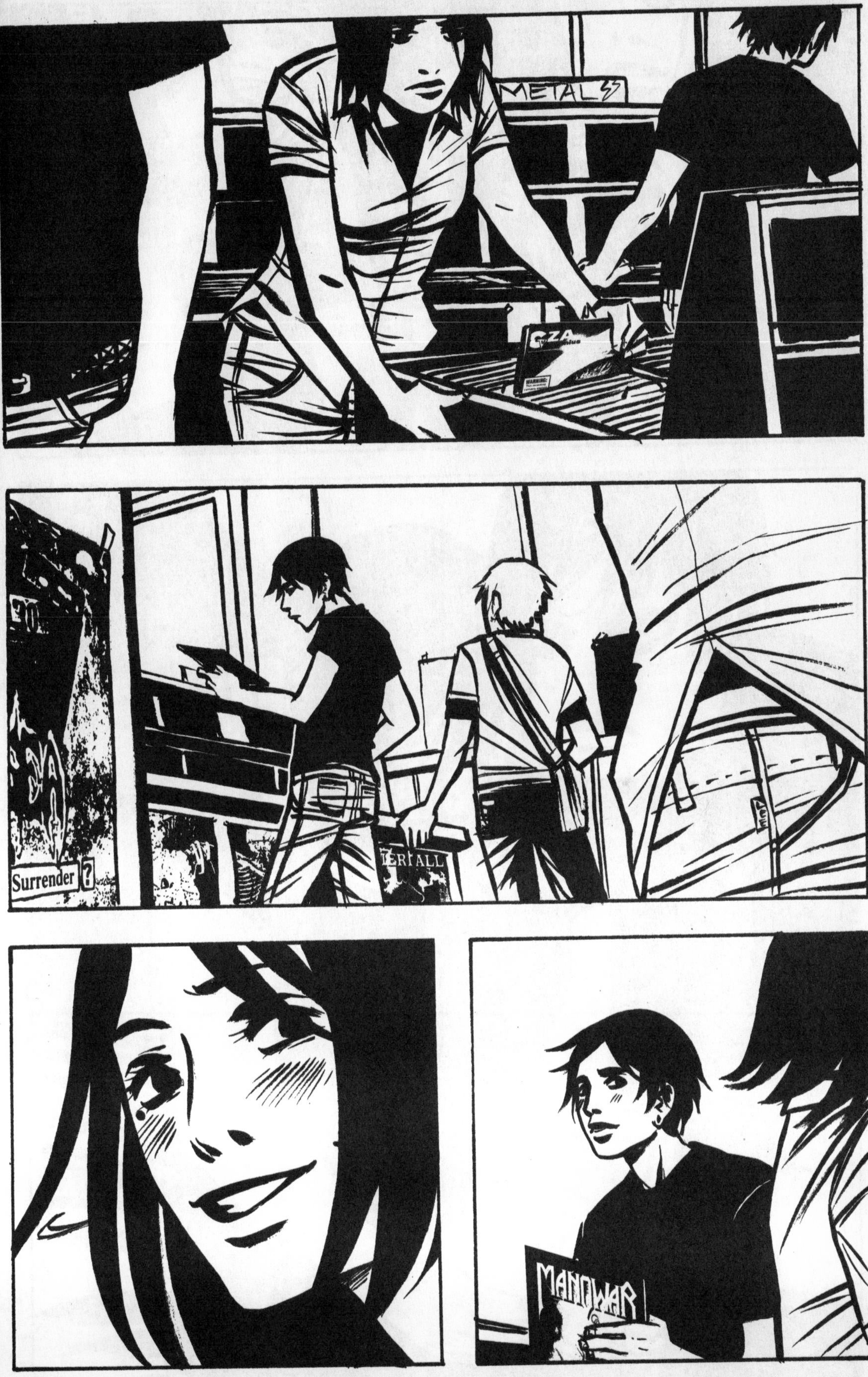
METAL
CZA
Surrender ?
MANOWAR

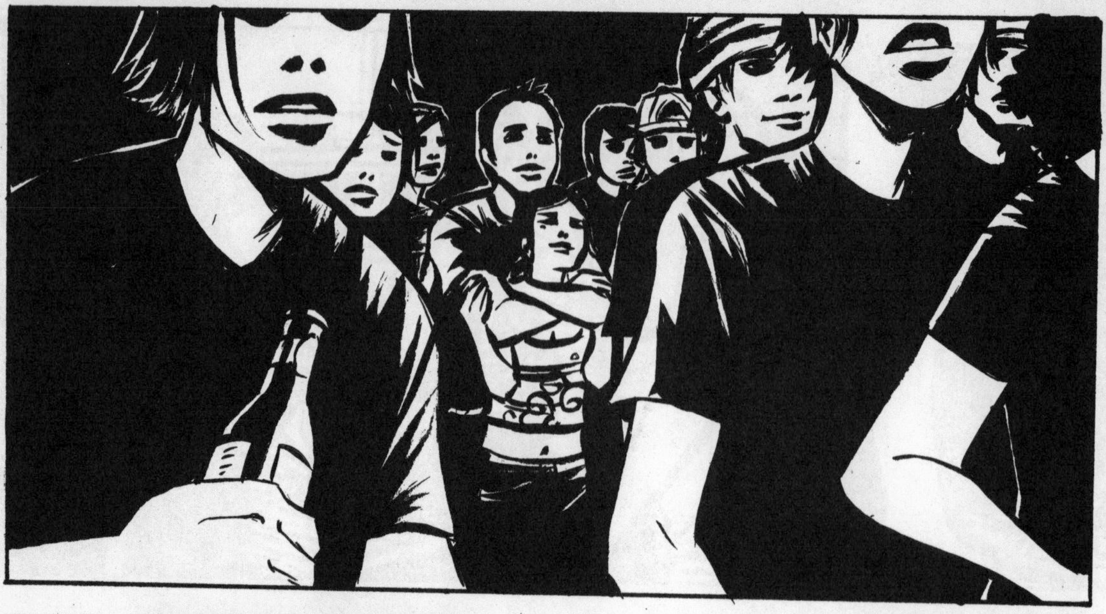

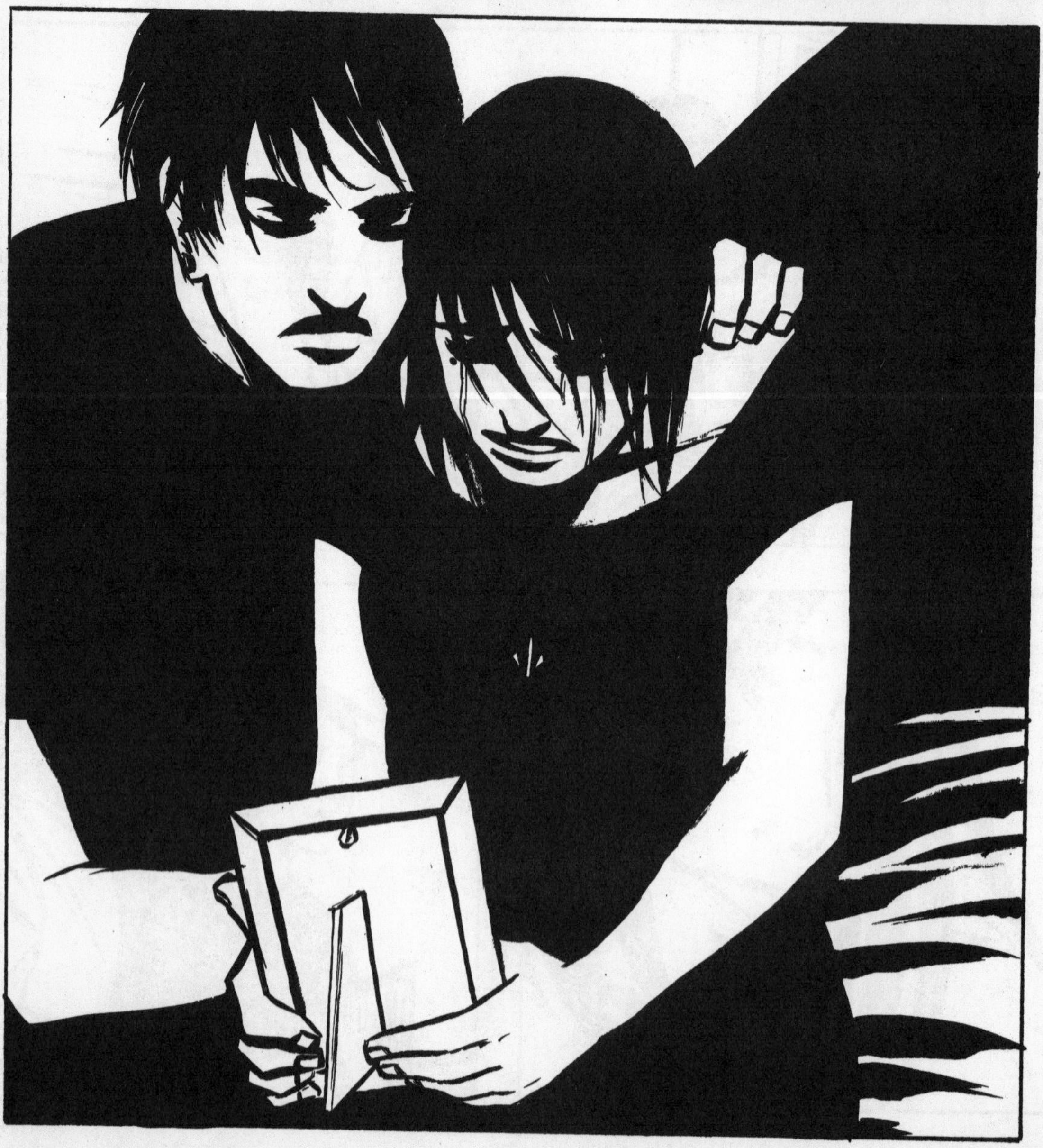

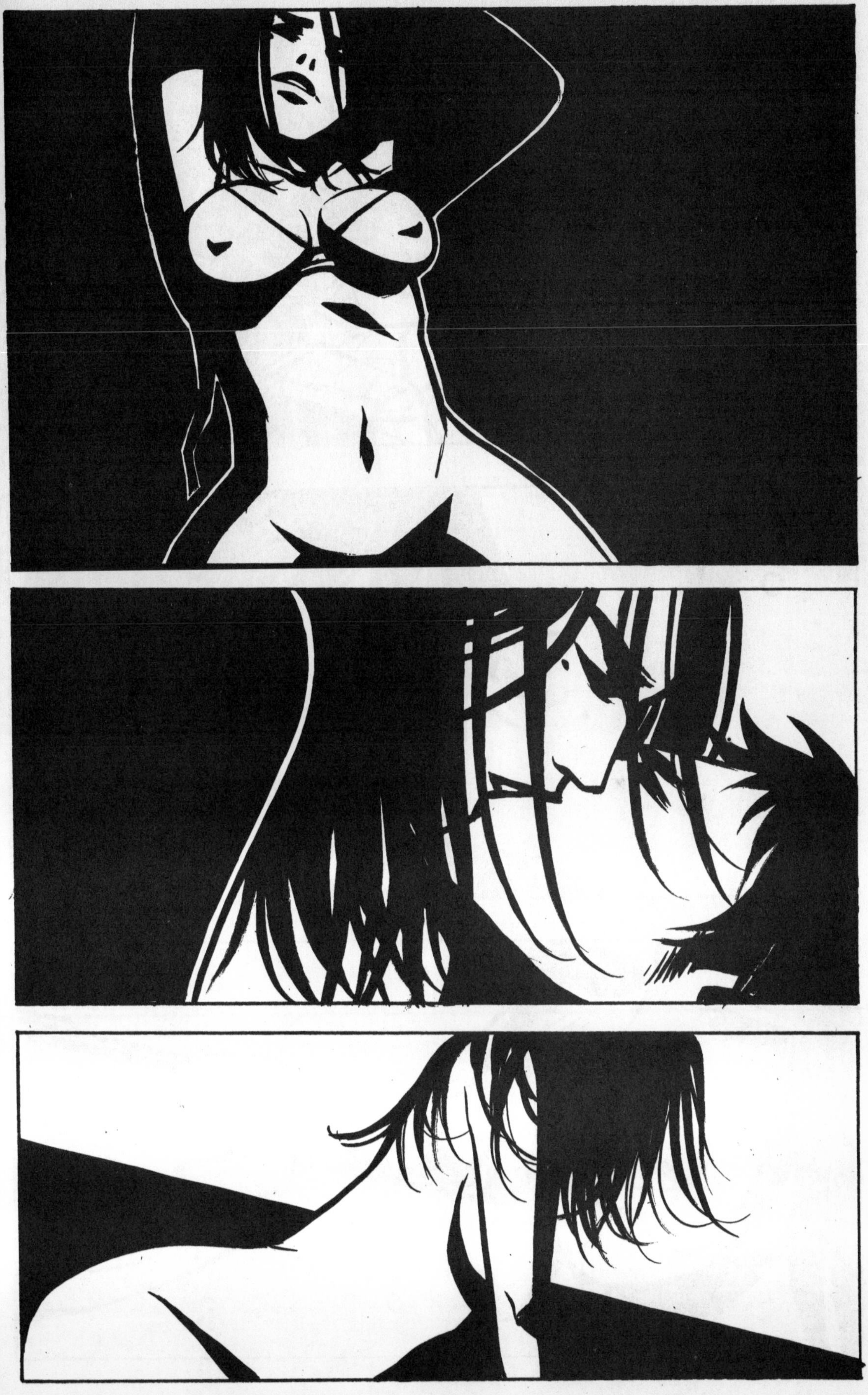

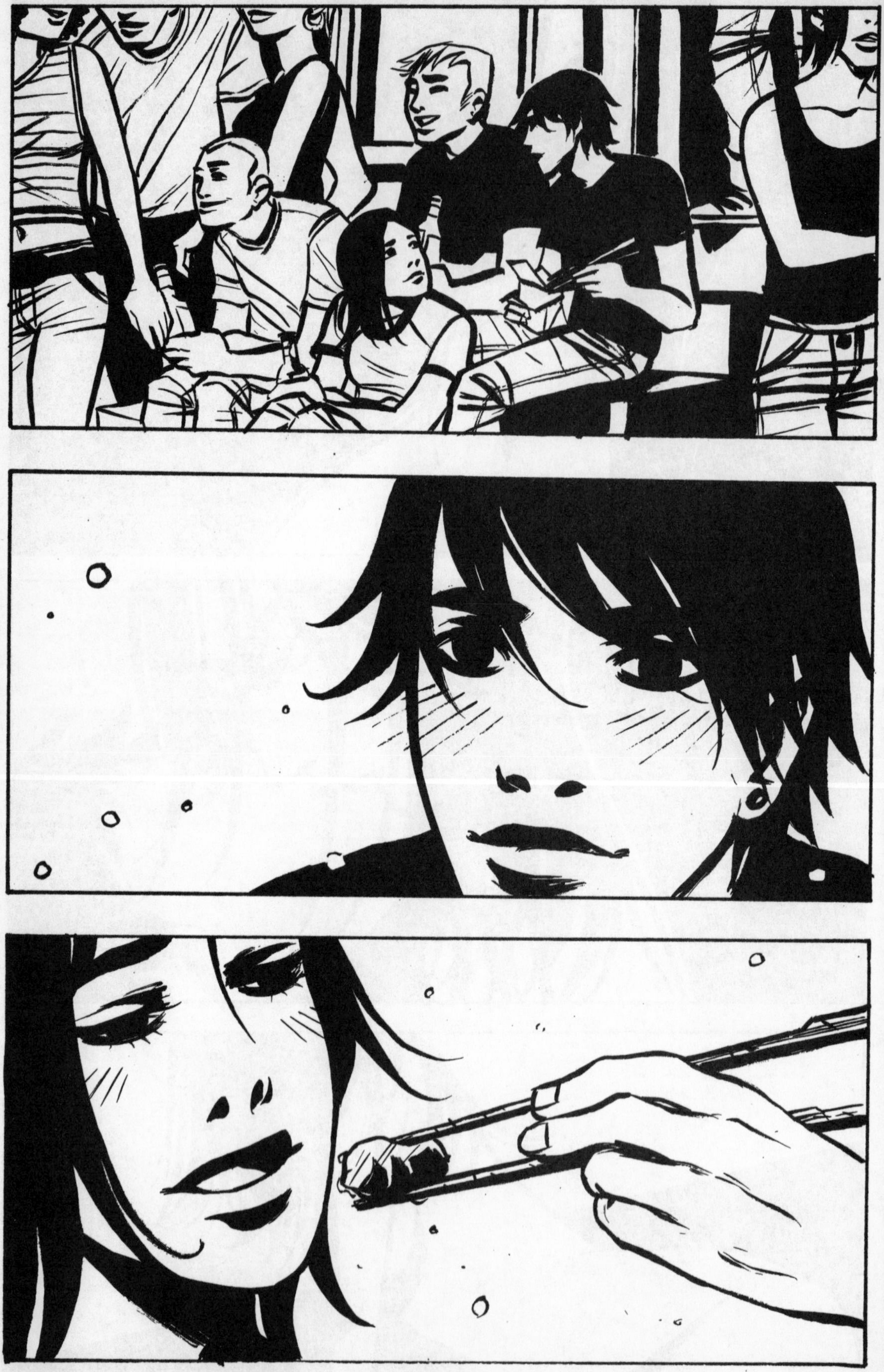

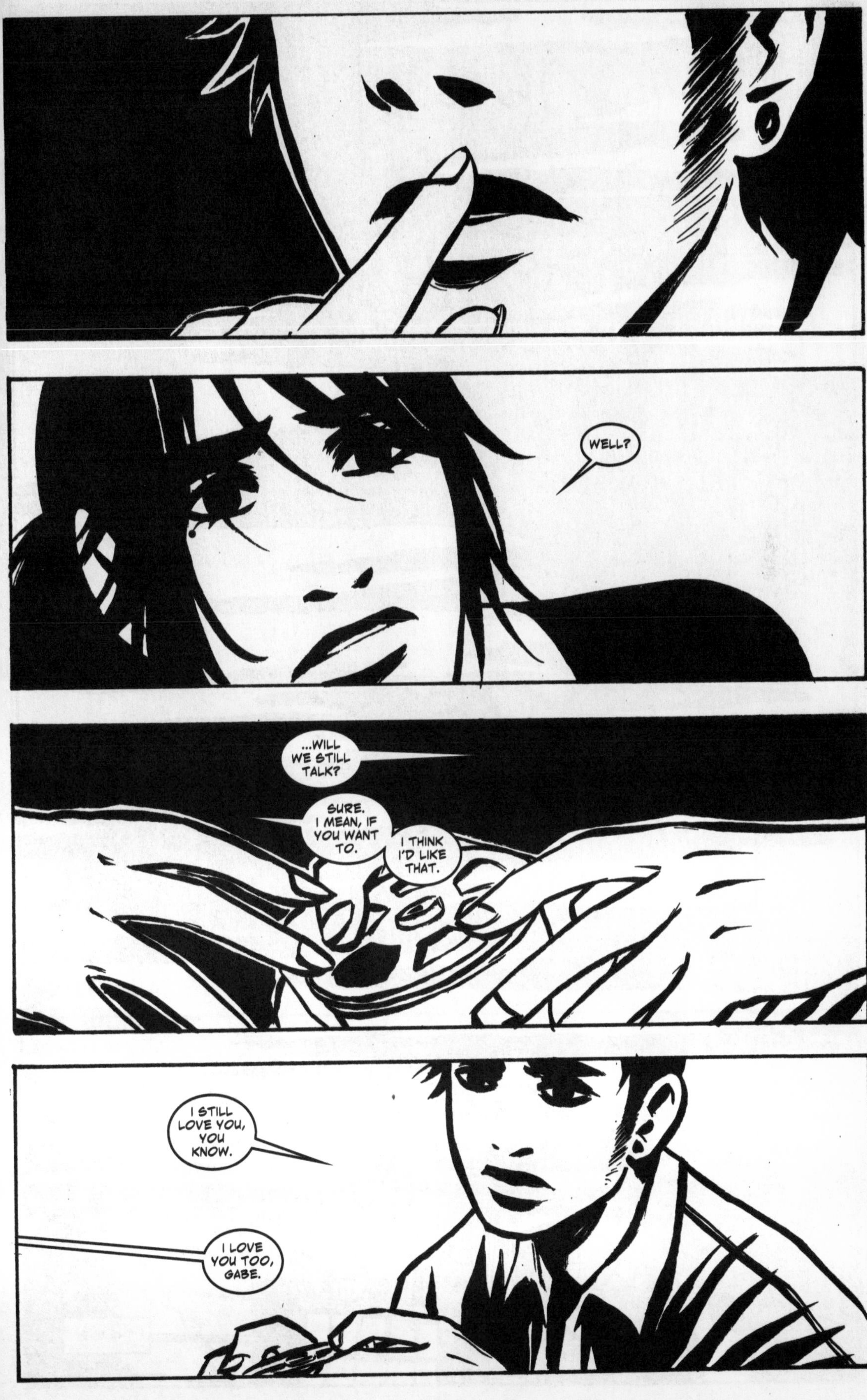
WELL?
...WILL WE STILL TALK?
SURE. I MEAN, IF YOU WANT TO.
I THINK I'D LIKE THAT.
I STILL LOVE YOU, YOU KNOW.
I LOVE YOU TOO, GABE.

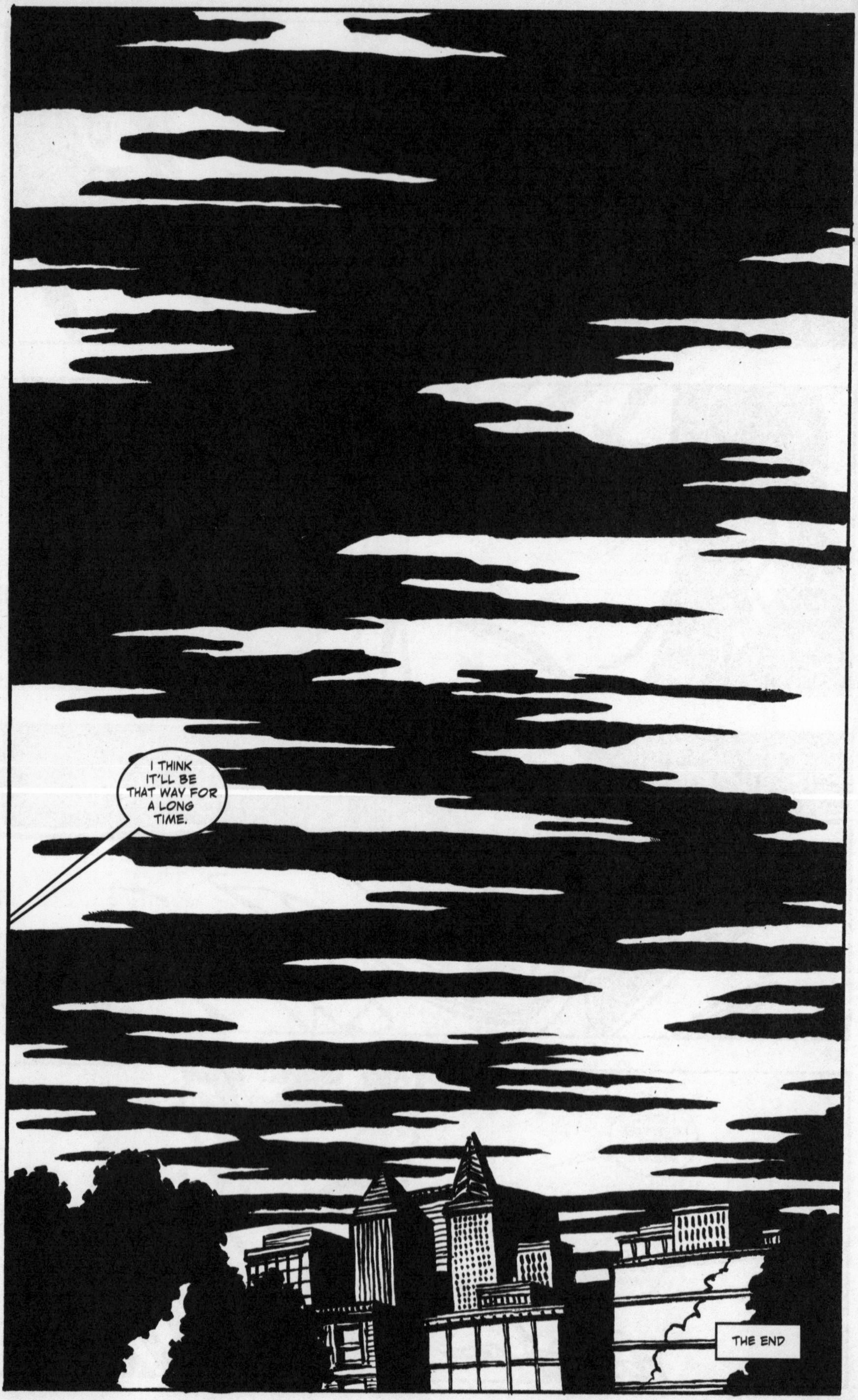
I THINK IT'LL BE THAT WAY FOR A LONG TIME.
THE END

10

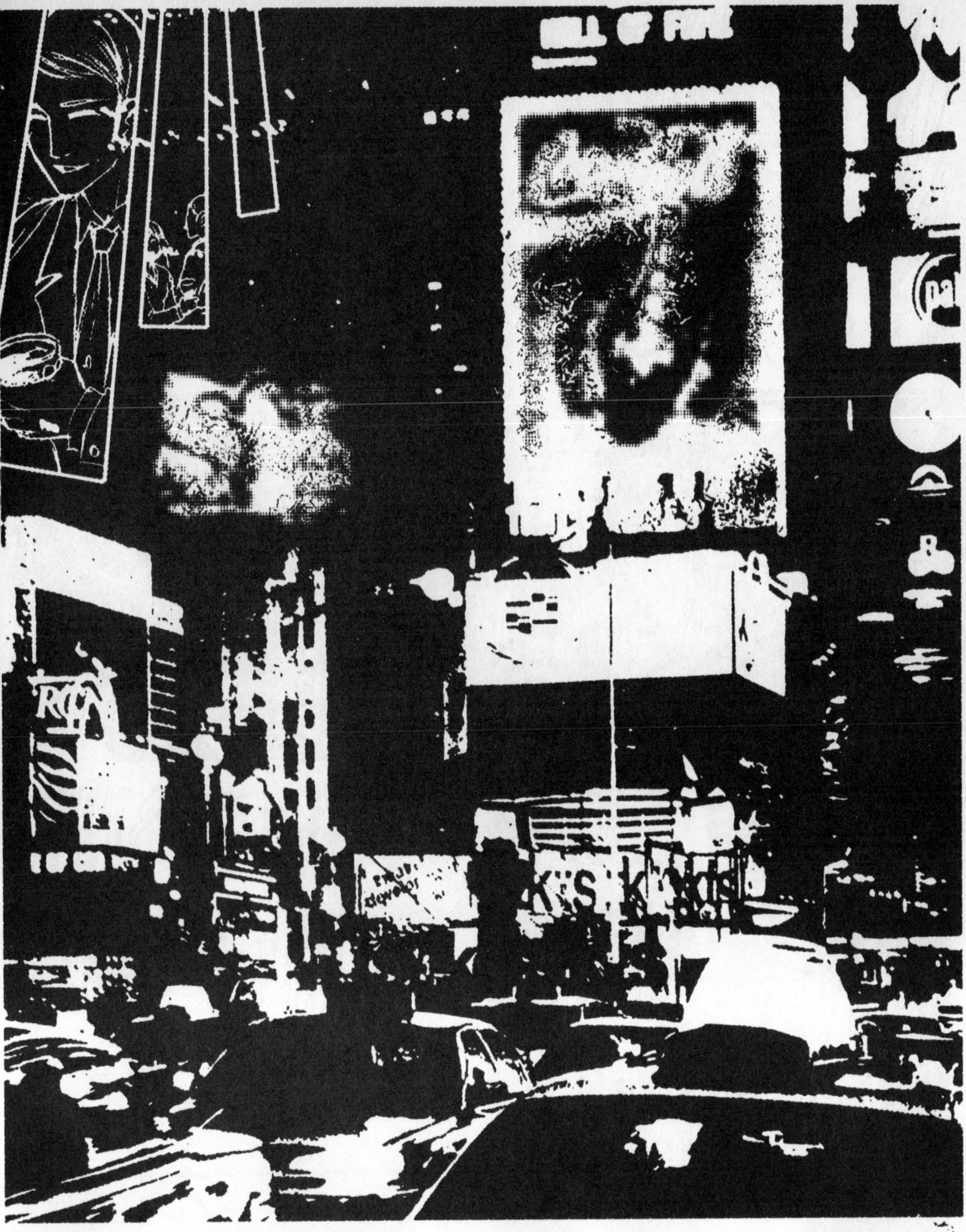

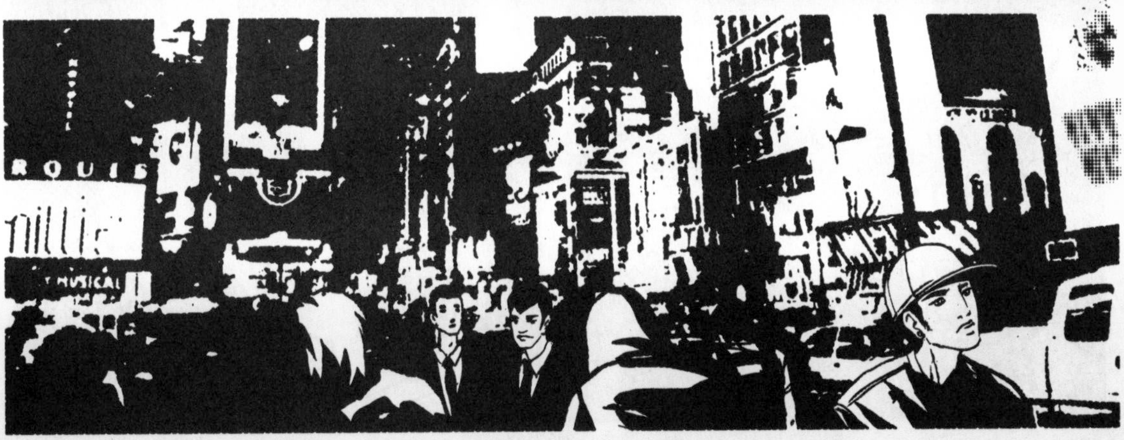
MUSICAL

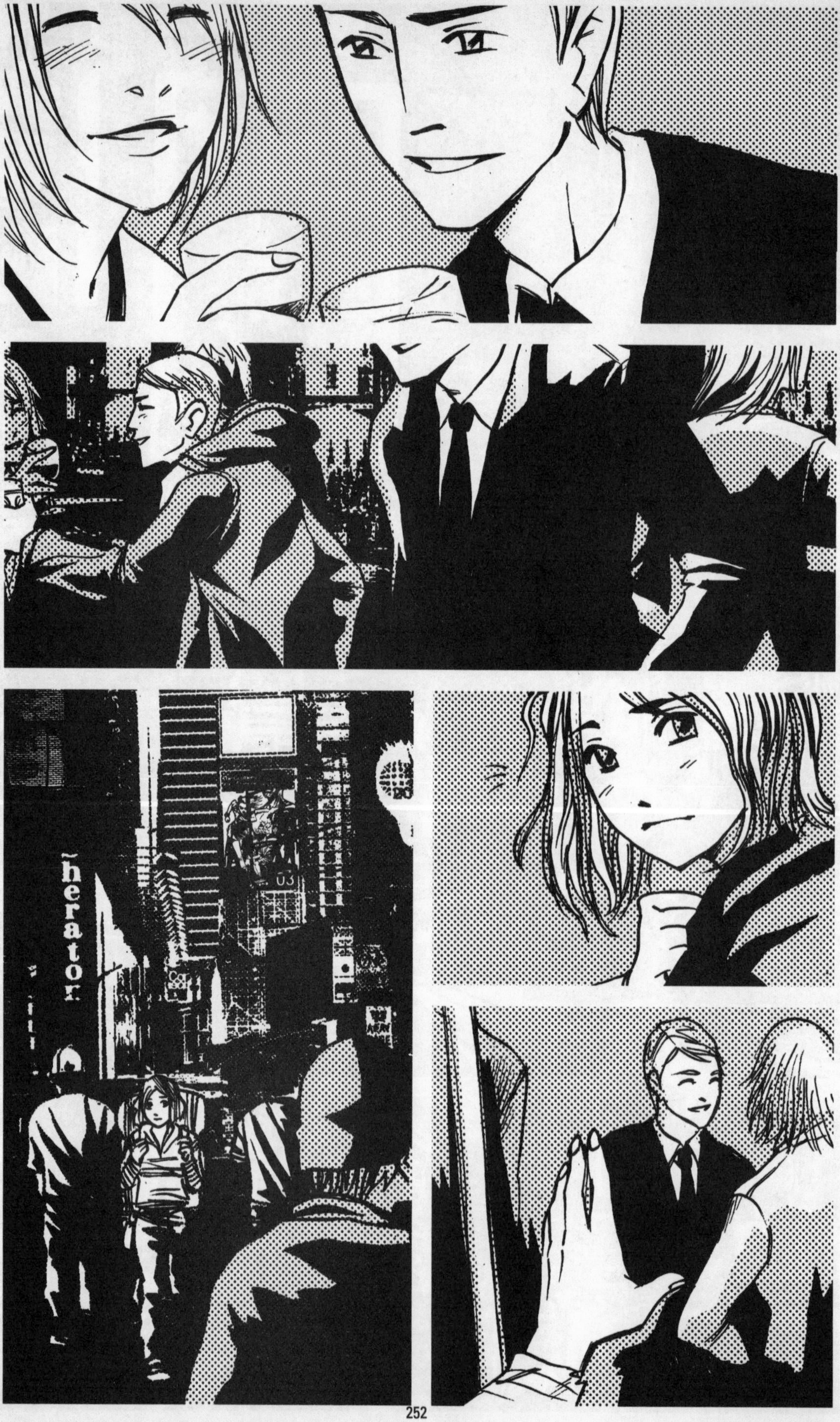
herator
03

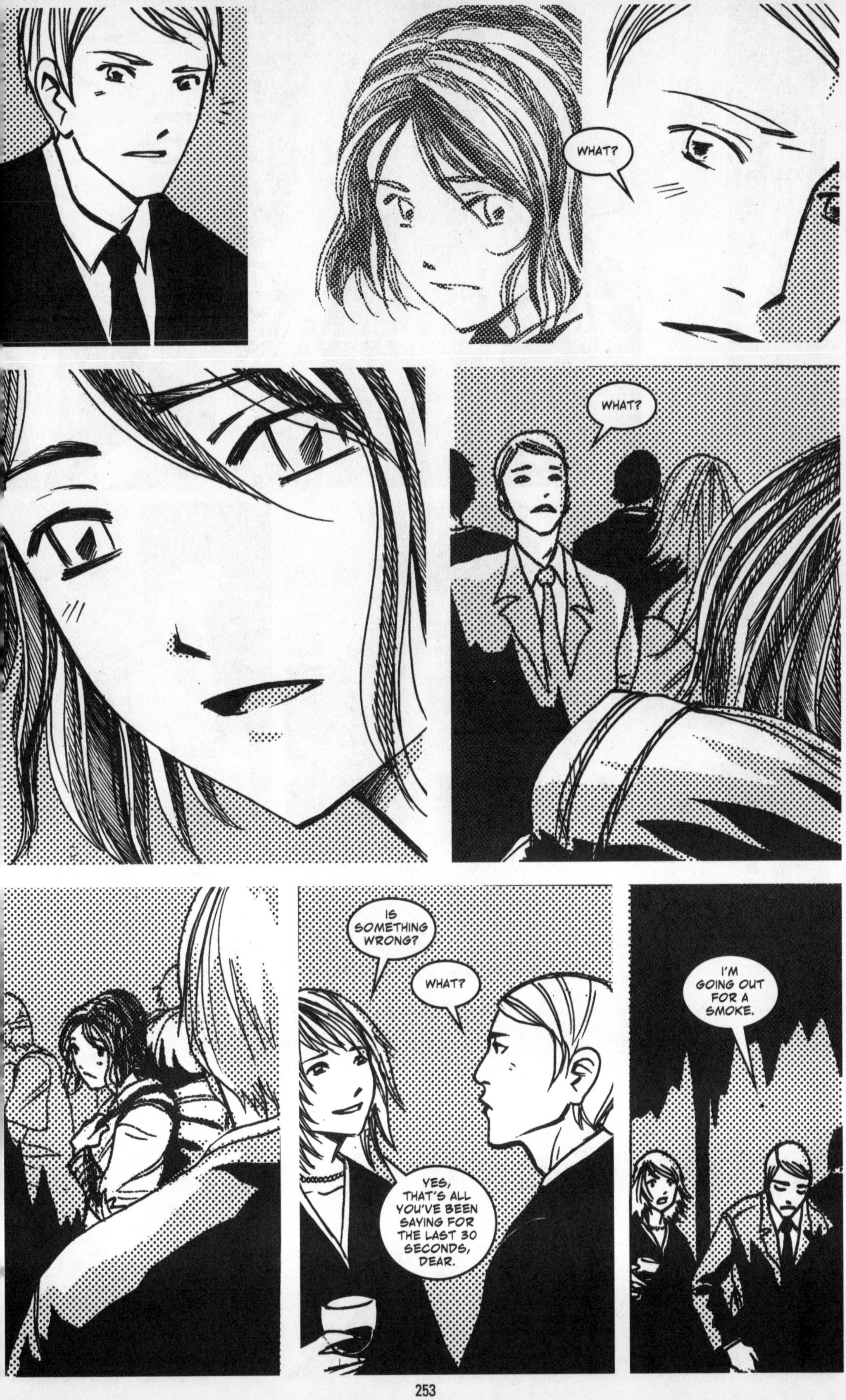
WHAT?
WHAT?
IS SOMETHING WRONG?
WHAT?
YES, THAT'S ALL YOU'VE BEEN SAYING FOR THE LAST 30 SECONDS, DEAR.
I'M GOING OUT FOR A SMOKE.

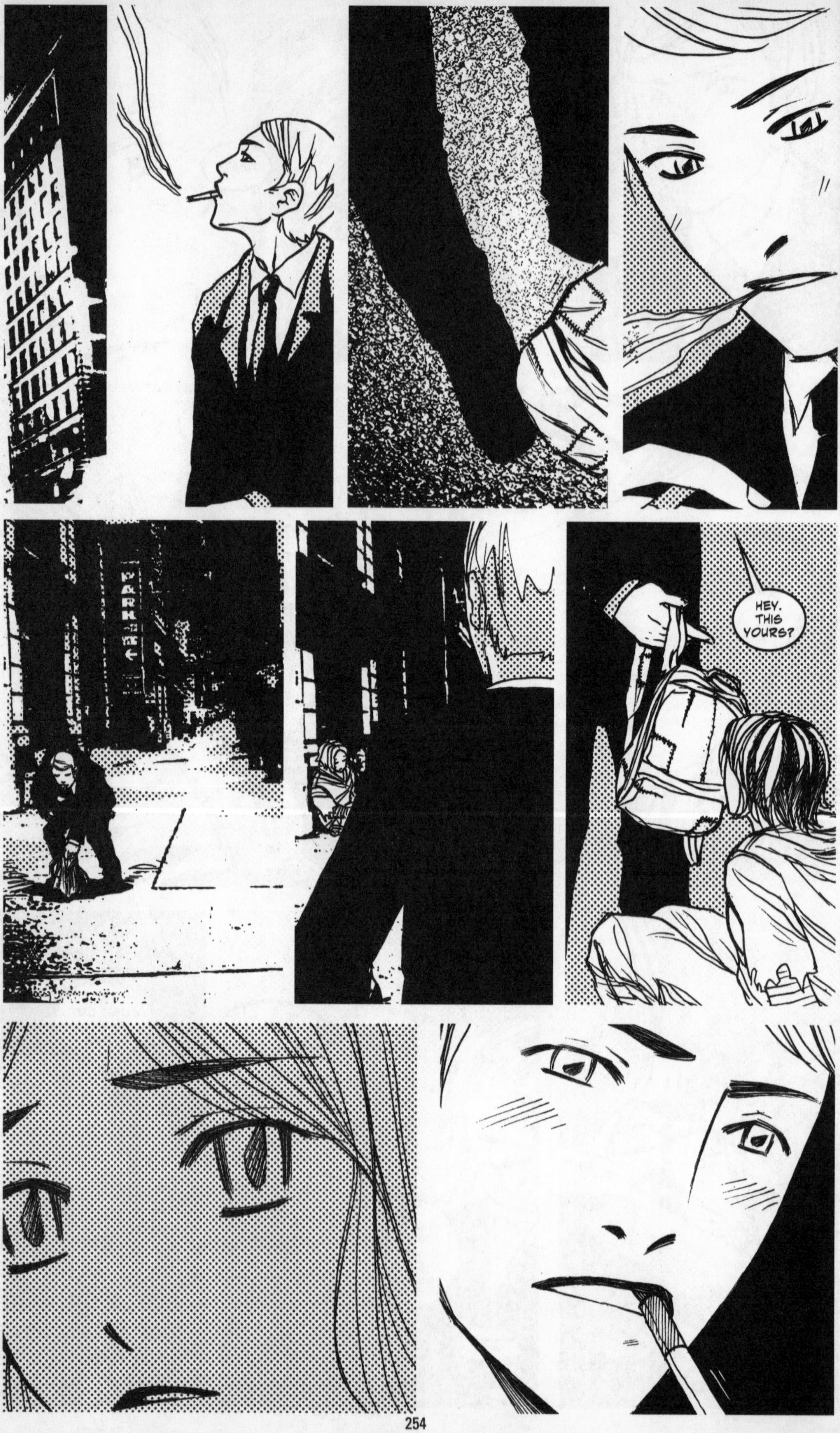
HEY. THIS YOURS?

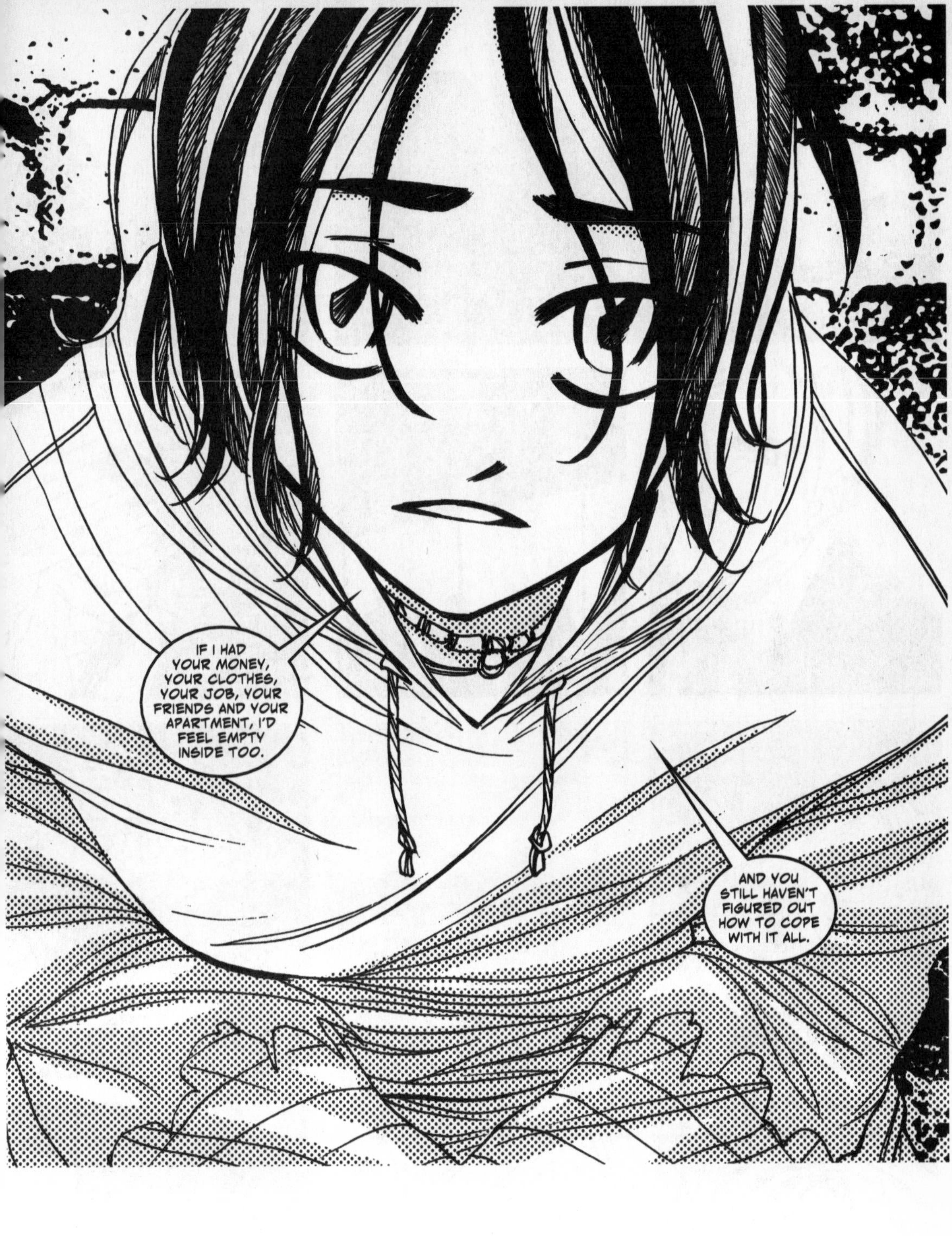
IF I HAD YOUR MONEY, YOUR CLOTHES, YOUR JOB, YOUR FRIENDS AND YOUR APARTMENT, I'D FEEL EMPTY INSIDE TOO.
AND YOU STILL HAVEN'T FIGURED OUT HOW TO COPE WITH IT ALL.

"Damaged"

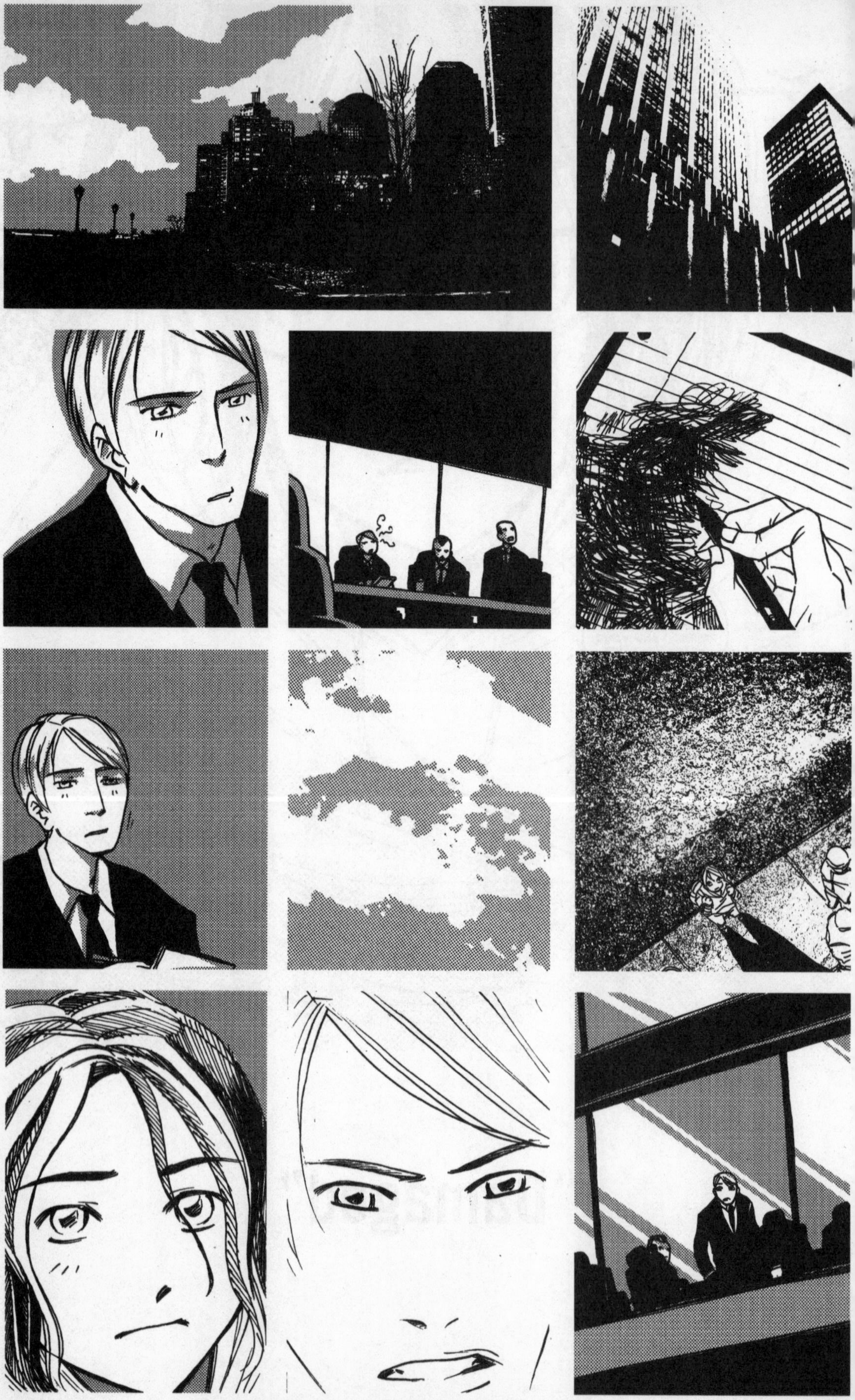

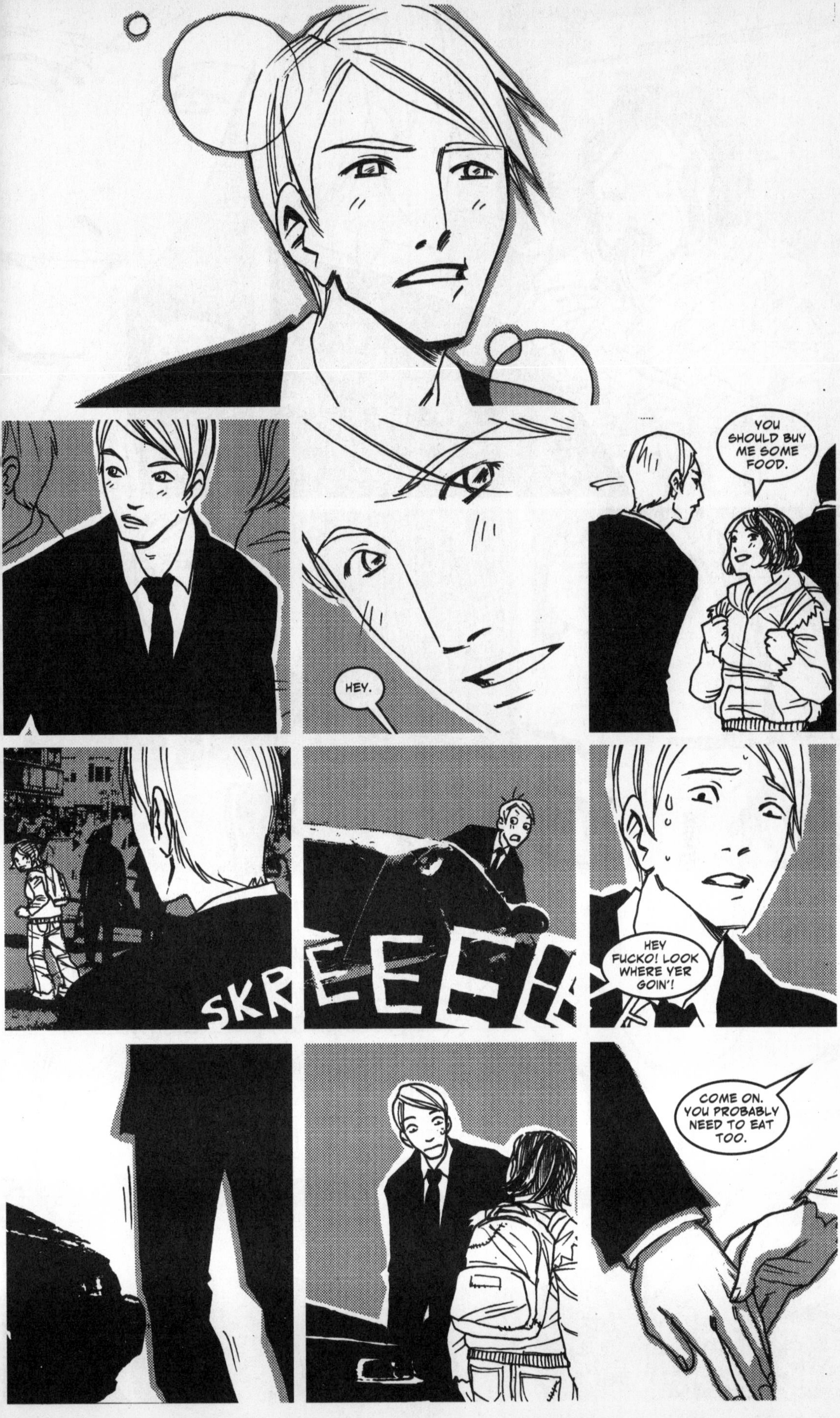
HEY.
YOU SHOULD BUY ME SOME FOOD.
SKREEEEE
HEY FUCKO! LOOK WHERE YER GOIN'!
COME ON. YOU PROBABLY NEED TO EAT TOO.

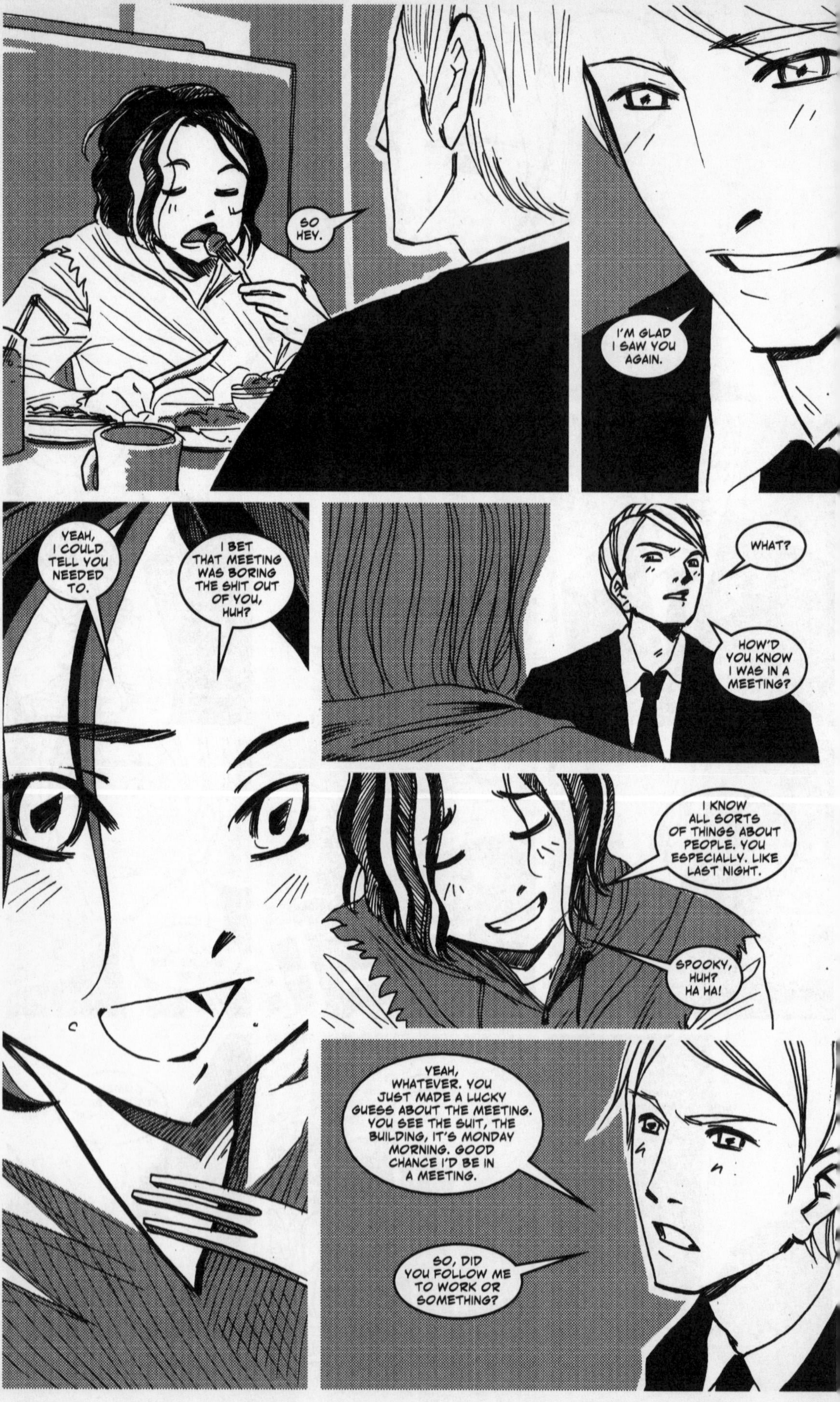
SO HEY.
I'M GLAD I SAW YOU AGAIN.
YEAH, I COULD TELL YOU NEEDED TO.
I BET THAT MEETING WAS BORING THE SHIT OUT OF YOU, HUH?
WHAT?
HOW'D YOU KNOW I WAS IN A MEETING?
I KNOW ALL SORTS OF THINGS ABOUT PEOPLE. YOU ESPECIALLY. LIKE LAST NIGHT.
SPOOKY, HUH? HA HA!
YEAH, WHATEVER. YOU JUST MADE A LUCKY GUESS ABOUT THE MEETING. YOU SEE THE SUIT, THE BUILDING, IT'S MONDAY MORNING. GOOD CHANCE I'D BE IN A MEETING.
SO, DID YOU FOLLOW ME TO WORK OR SOMETHING?

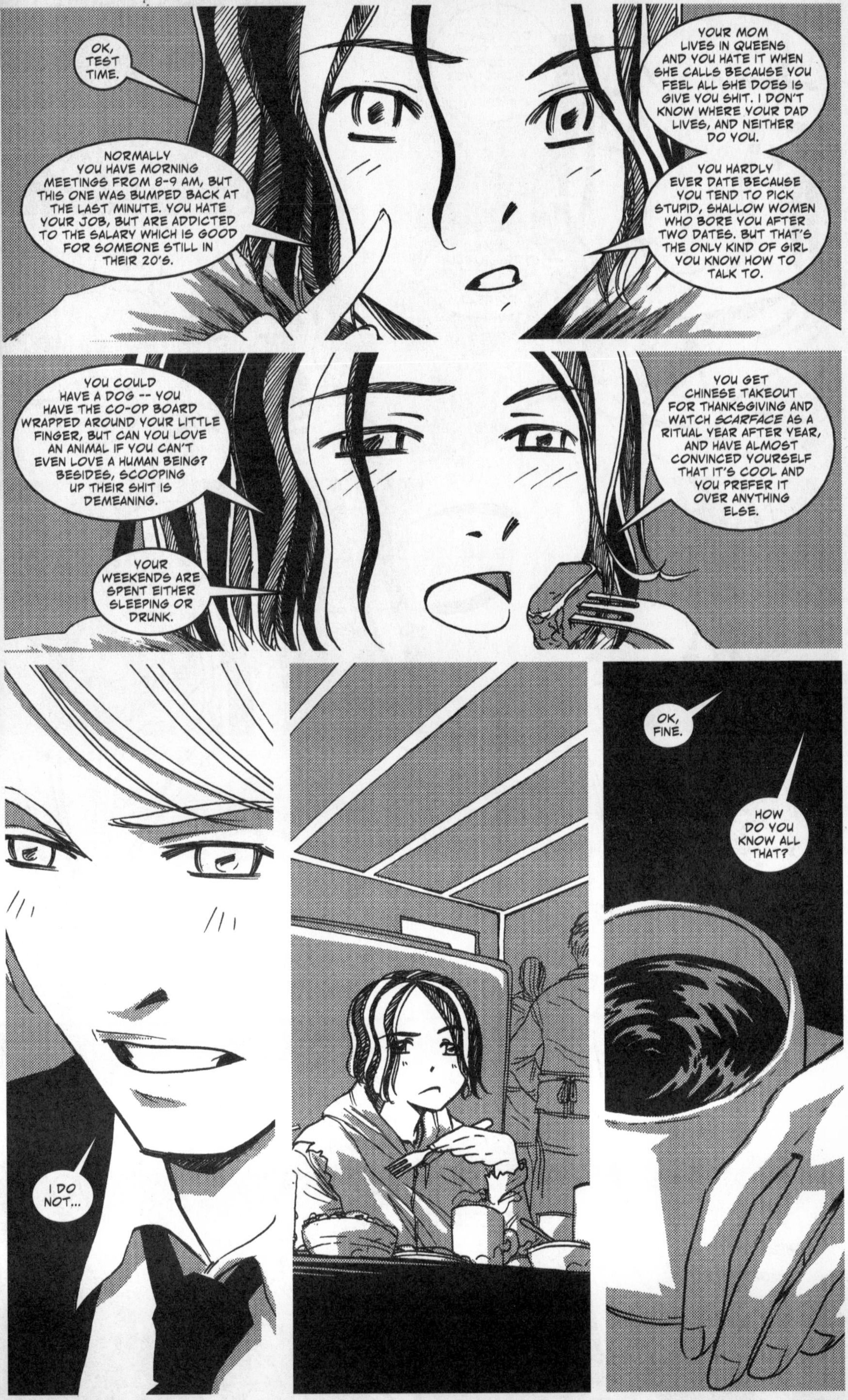
OK, TEST TIME.
YOUR MOM LIVES IN QUEENS AND YOU HATE IT WHEN SHE CALLS BECAUSE YOU FEEL ALL SHE DOES IS GIVE YOU SHIT. I DON'T KNOW WHERE YOUR DAD LIVES, AND NEITHER DO YOU.
NORMALLY YOU HAVE MORNING MEETINGS FROM 8-9 AM, BUT THIS ONE WAS BUMPED BACK AT THE LAST MINUTE. YOU HATE YOUR JOB, BUT ARE ADDICTED TO THE SALARY WHICH IS GOOD FOR SOMEONE STILL IN THEIR 20'S.
YOU HARDLY EVER DATE BECAUSE YOU TEND TO PICK STUPID, SHALLOW WOMEN WHO BORE YOU AFTER TWO DATES. BUT THAT'S THE ONLY KIND OF GIRL YOU KNOW HOW TO TALK TO.
YOU COULD HAVE A DOG -- YOU HAVE THE CO-OP BOARD WRAPPED AROUND YOUR LITTLE FINGER, BUT CAN YOU LOVE AN ANIMAL IF YOU CAN'T EVEN LOVE A HUMAN BEING? BESIDES, SCOOPING UP THEIR SHIT IS DEMEANING.
YOU GET CHINESE TAKEOUT FOR THANKSGIVING AND WATCH *SCARFACE* AS A RITUAL YEAR AFTER YEAR, AND HAVE ALMOST CONVINCED YOURSELF THAT IT'S COOL AND YOU PREFER IT OVER ANYTHING ELSE.
YOUR WEEKENDS ARE SPENT EITHER SLEEPING OR DRUNK.
I DO NOT...
OK, FINE.
HOW DO YOU KNOW ALL THAT?

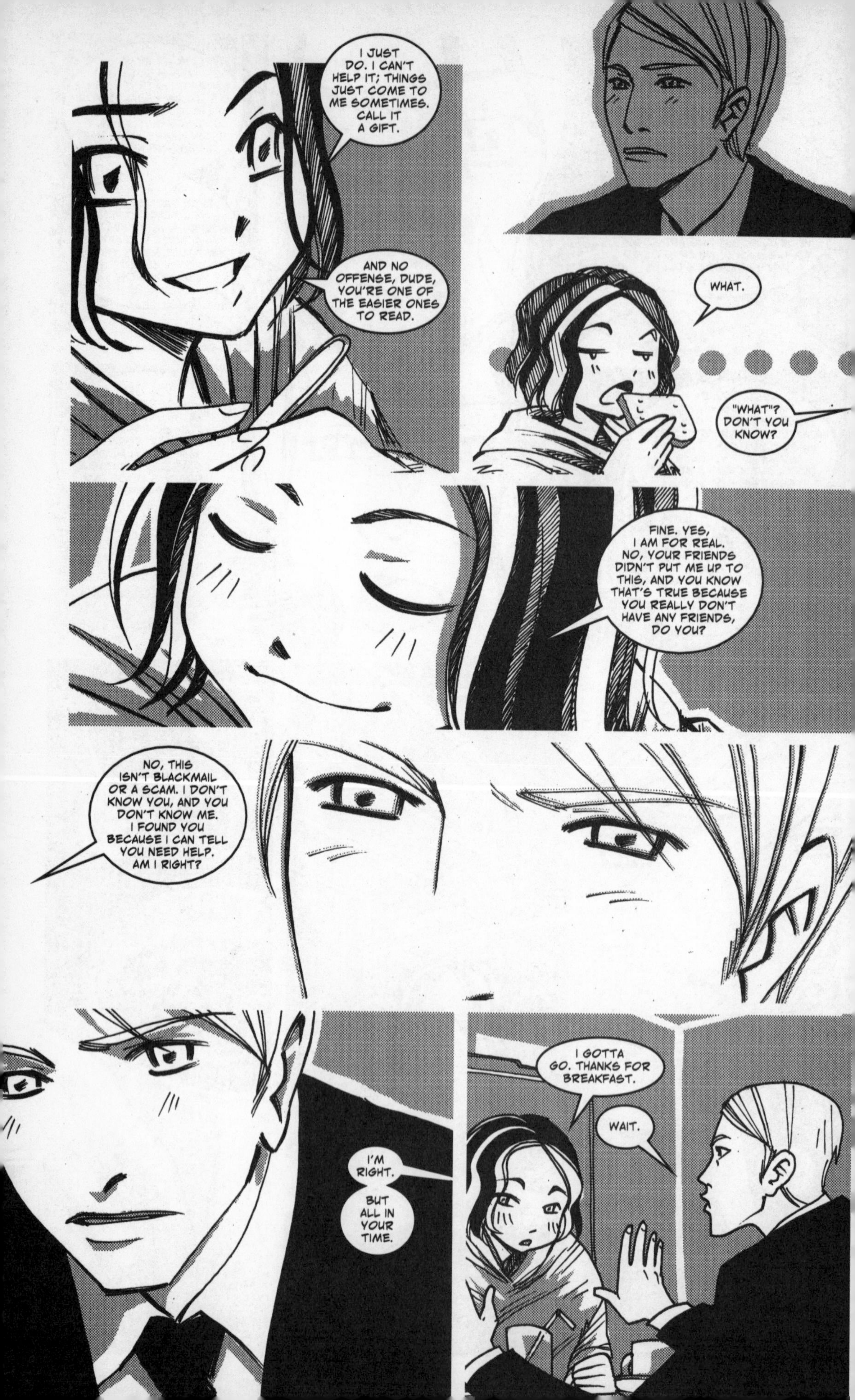
I JUST DO. I CAN'T HELP IT; THINGS JUST COME TO ME SOMETIMES. CALL IT A GIFT.
AND NO OFFENSE, DUDE, YOU'RE ONE OF THE EASIER ONES TO READ.
WHAT.
"WHAT"? DON'T YOU KNOW?
FINE. YES, I AM FOR REAL. NO, YOUR FRIENDS DIDN'T PUT ME UP TO THIS, AND YOU KNOW THAT'S TRUE BECAUSE YOU REALLY DON'T HAVE ANY FRIENDS, DO YOU?
NO, THIS ISN'T BLACKMAIL OR A SCAM. I DON'T KNOW YOU, AND YOU DON'T KNOW ME. I FOUND YOU BECAUSE I CAN TELL YOU NEED HELP. AM I RIGHT?
I'M RIGHT.
BUT ALL IN YOUR TIME.
I GOTTA GO. THANKS FOR BREAKFAST.
WAIT.

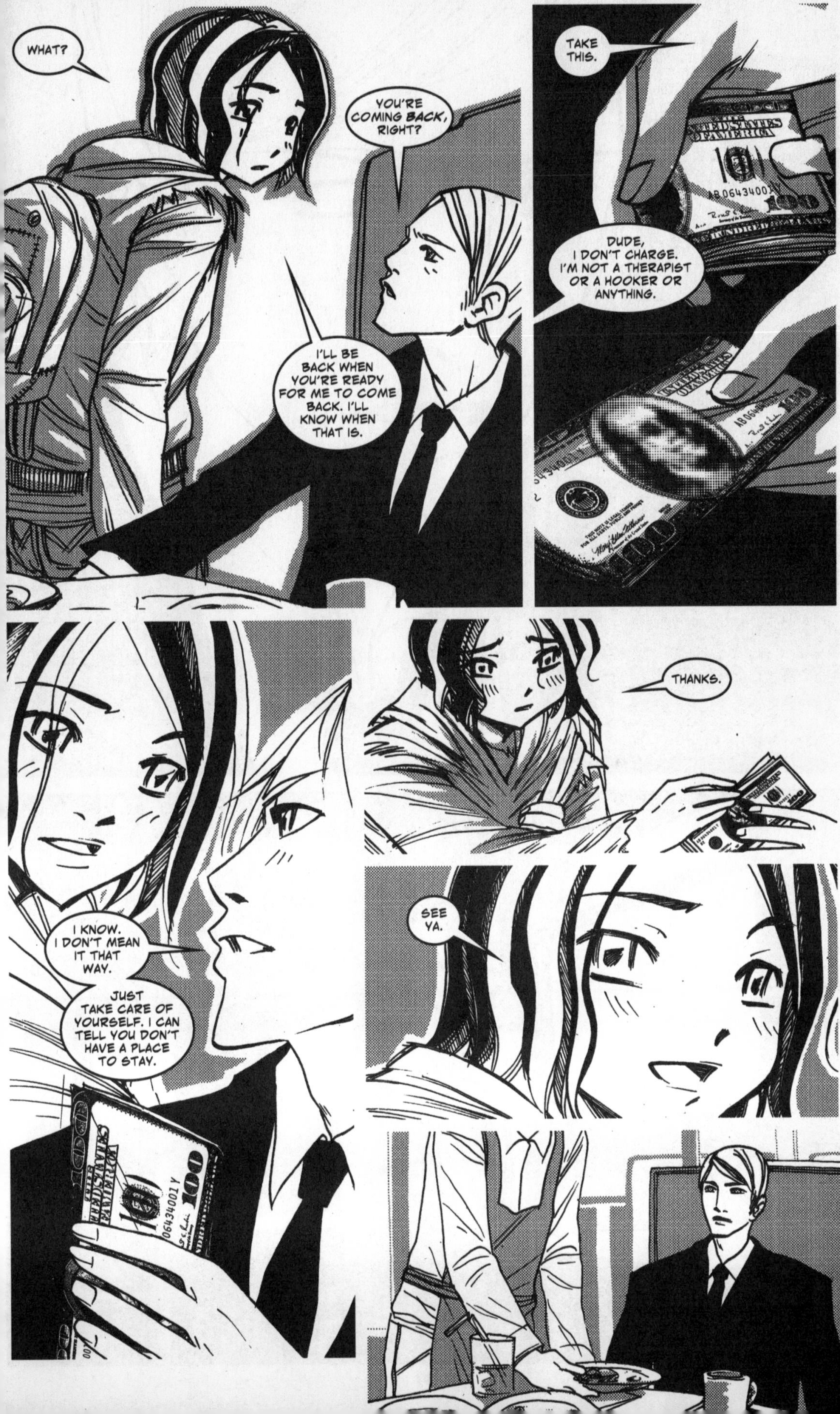
WHAT?
YOU'RE COMING BACK, RIGHT?
I'LL BE BACK WHEN YOU'RE READY FOR ME TO COME BACK. I'LL KNOW WHEN THAT IS.
TAKE THIS.
DUDE, I DON'T CHARGE. I'M NOT A THERAPIST OR A HOOKER OR ANYTHING.
I KNOW. I DON'T MEAN IT THAT WAY.
JUST TAKE CARE OF YOURSELF. I CAN TELL YOU DON'T HAVE A PLACE TO STAY.
THANKS.
SEE YA.

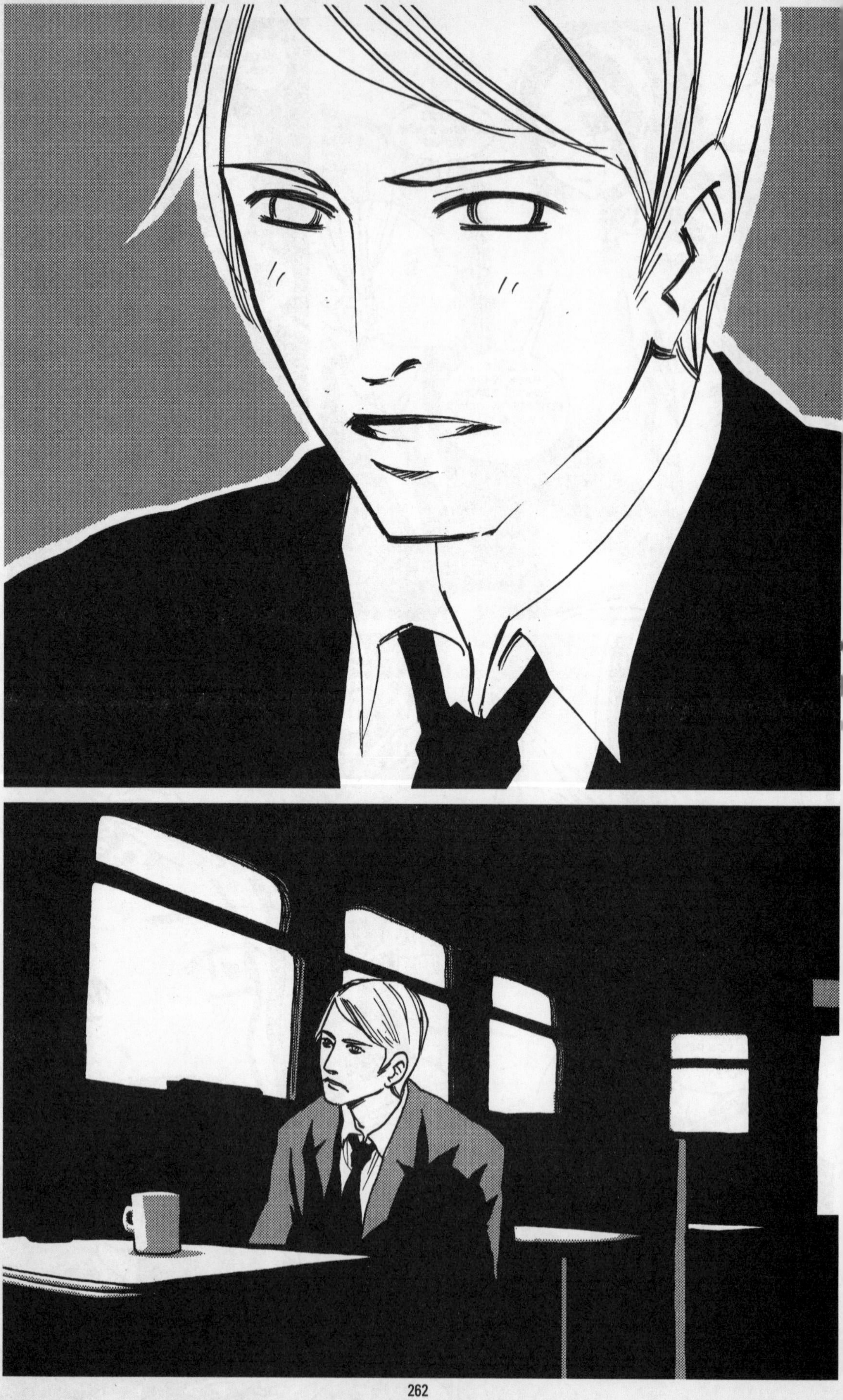

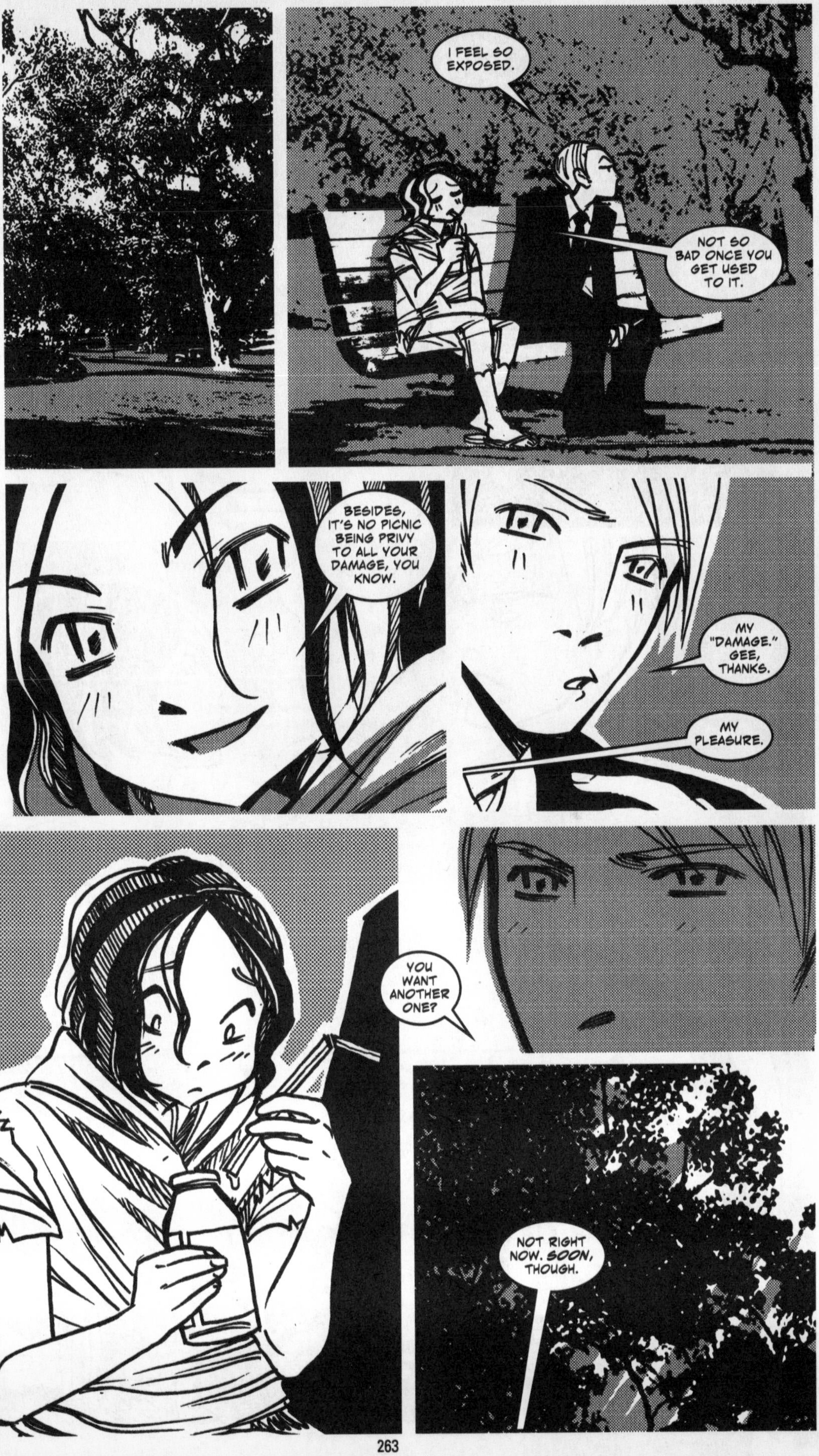
I FEEL SO EXPOSED.
NOT SO BAD ONCE YOU GET USED TO IT.
BESIDES, IT'S NO PICNIC BEING PRIVY TO ALL YOUR DAMAGE, YOU KNOW.
MY "DAMAGE." GEE, THANKS.
MY PLEASURE.
YOU WANT ANOTHER ONE?
NOT RIGHT NOW. *SOON,* THOUGH.

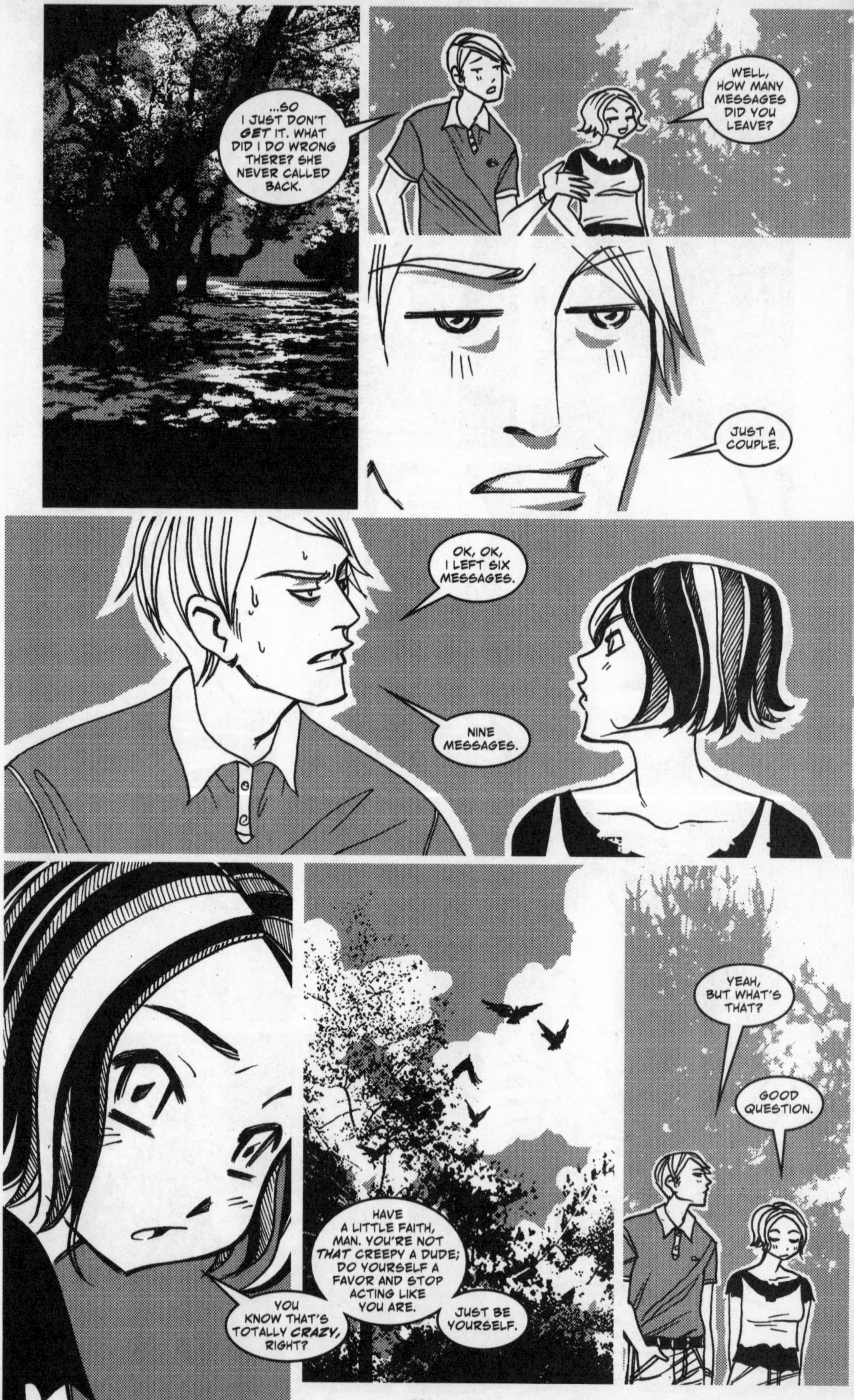
...SO I JUST DON'T GET IT. WHAT DID I DO WRONG THERE? SHE NEVER CALLED BACK.
WELL, HOW MANY MESSAGES DID YOU LEAVE?
JUST A COUPLE.
OK, OK, I LEFT SIX MESSAGES.
NINE MESSAGES.
YOU KNOW THAT'S TOTALLY CRAZY, RIGHT?
HAVE A LITTLE FAITH, MAN. YOU'RE NOT THAT CREEPY A DUDE; DO YOURSELF A FAVOR AND STOP ACTING LIKE YOU ARE.
JUST BE YOURSELF.
YEAH, BUT WHAT'S THAT?
GOOD QUESTION.

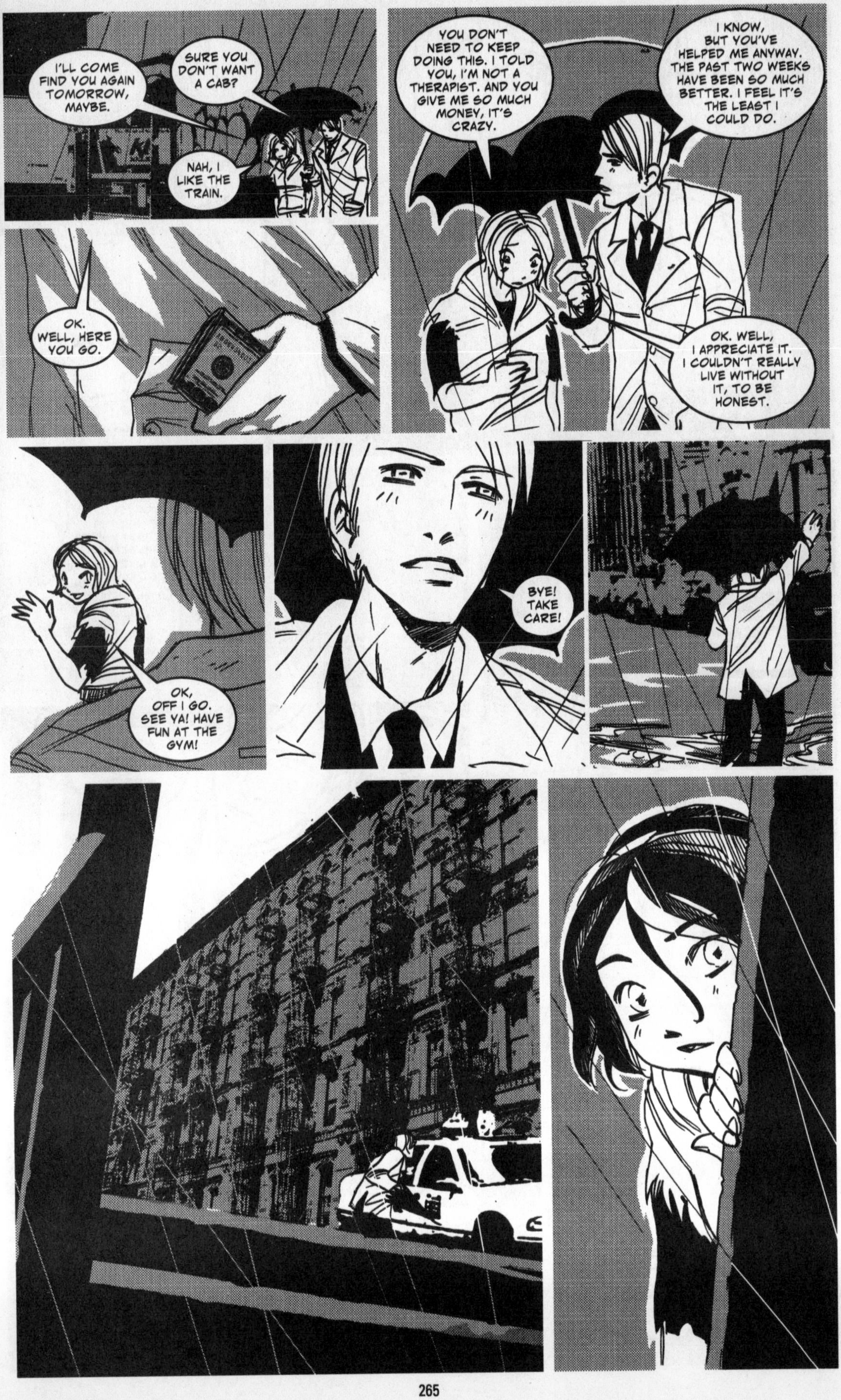
I'LL COME FIND YOU AGAIN TOMORROW, MAYBE.
SURE YOU DON'T WANT A CAB?
NAH, I LIKE THE TRAIN.
YOU DON'T NEED TO KEEP DOING THIS. I TOLD YOU, I'M NOT A THERAPIST. AND YOU GIVE ME SO MUCH MONEY, IT'S CRAZY.
I KNOW, BUT YOU'VE HELPED ME ANYWAY. THE PAST TWO WEEKS HAVE BEEN SO MUCH BETTER. I FEEL IT'S THE LEAST I COULD DO.
OK. WELL, HERE YOU GO.
OK. WELL, I APPRECIATE IT. I COULDN'T REALLY LIVE WITHOUT IT, TO BE HONEST.
OK, OFF I GO. SEE YA! HAVE FUN AT THE GYM!
BYE! TAKE CARE!

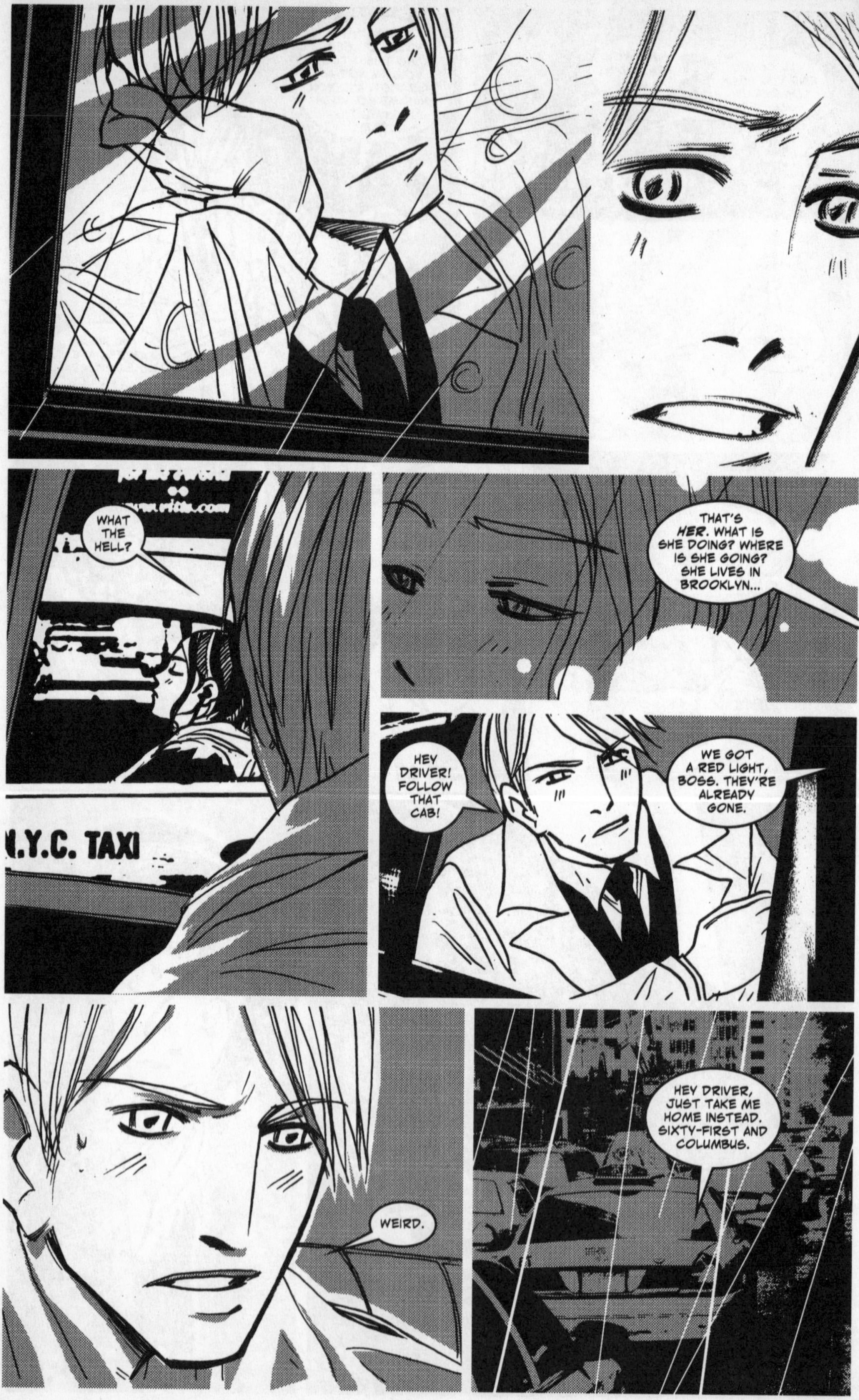
WHAT THE HELL?
N.Y.C. TAXI
THAT'S *HER*. WHAT IS SHE DOING? WHERE IS SHE GOING? SHE LIVES IN BROOKLYN...
HEY DRIVER! FOLLOW THAT CAB!
WE GOT A RED LIGHT, BOSS. THEY'RE ALREADY GONE.
WEIRD.
HEY DRIVER, JUST TAKE ME HOME INSTEAD. SIXTY-FIRST AND COLUMBUS.

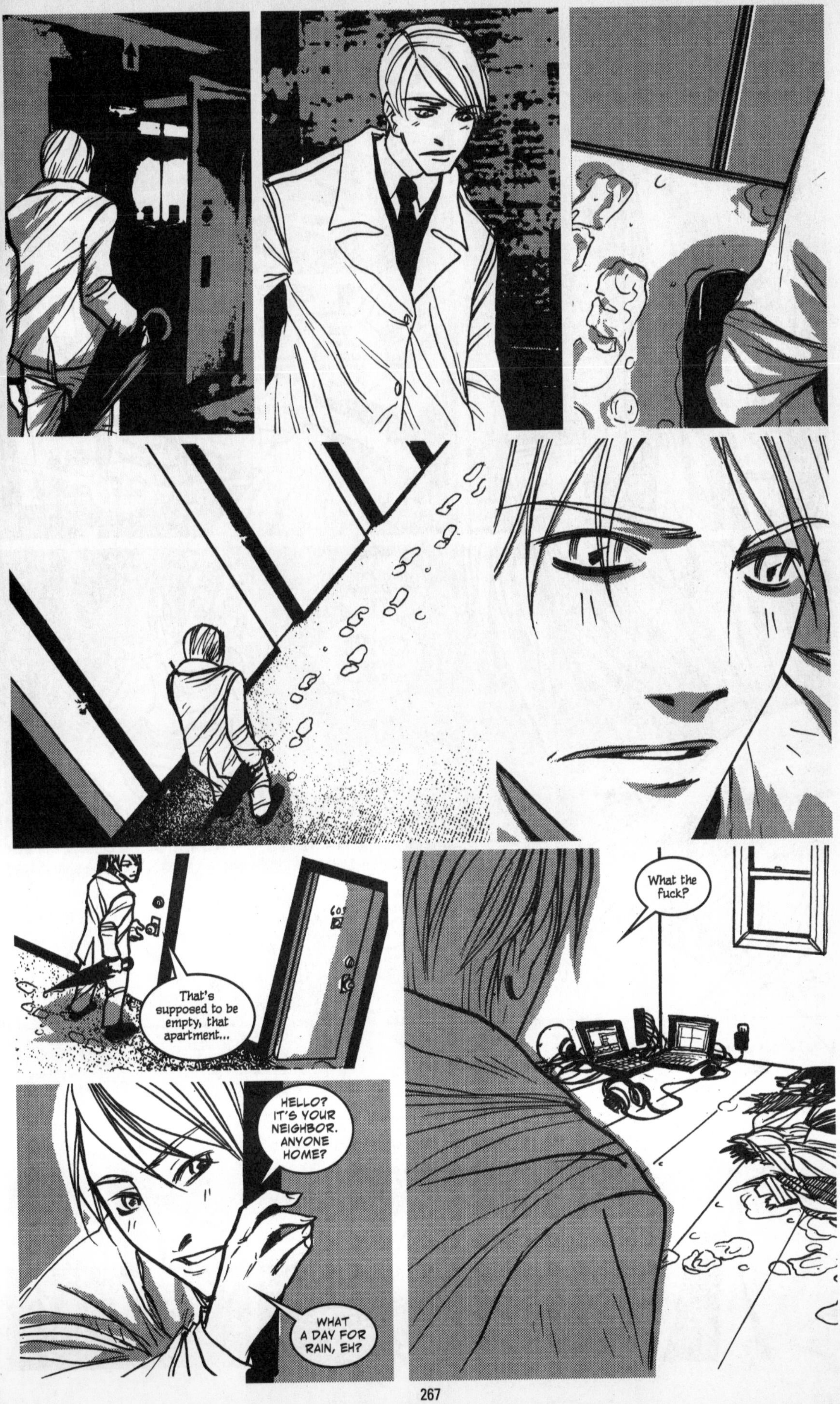
That's supposed to be empty, that apartment...
HELLO? IT'S YOUR NEIGHBOR. ANYONE HOME?
WHAT A DAY FOR RAIN, EH?
What the fuck?

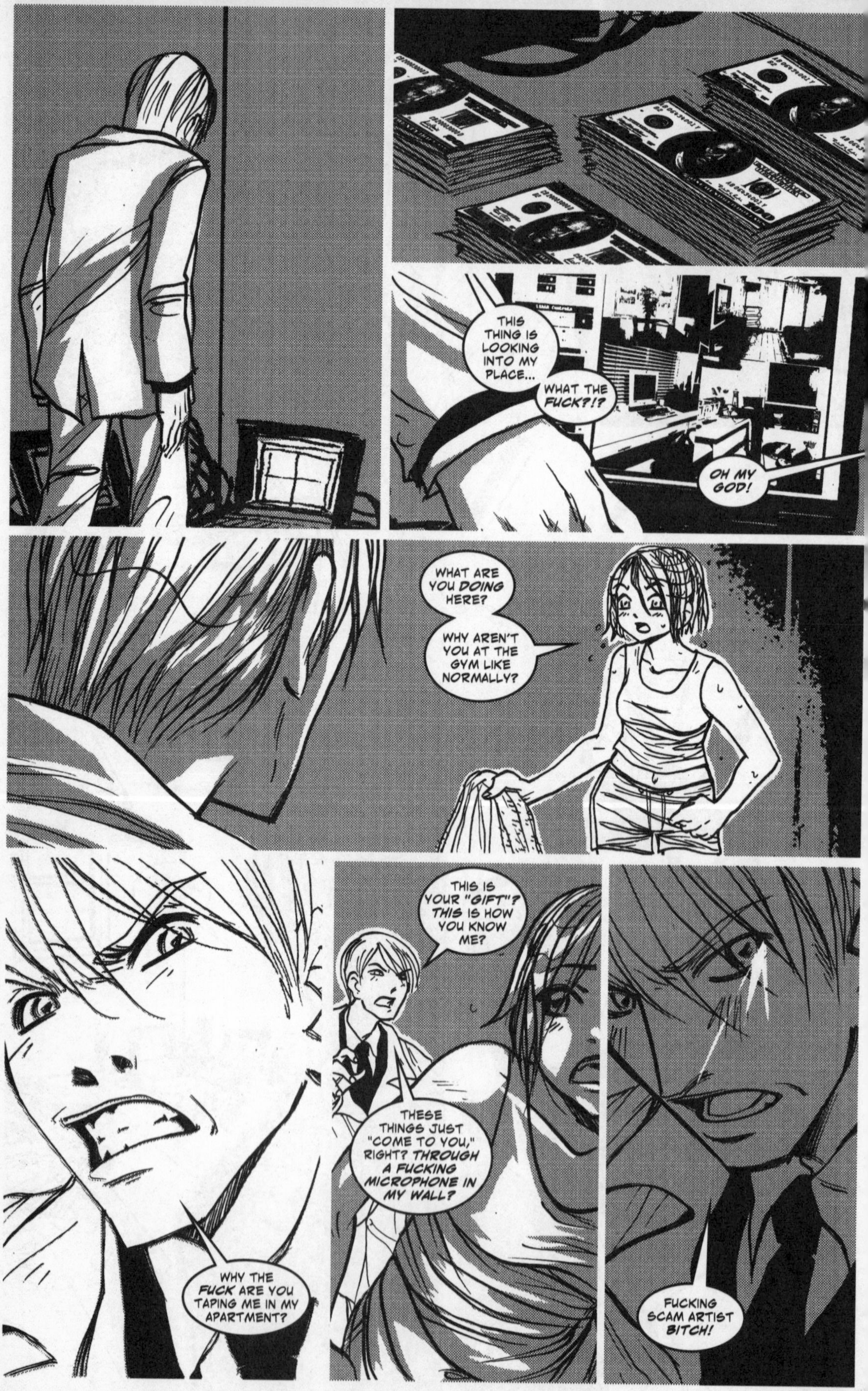
THIS THING IS LOOKING INTO MY PLACE...
WHAT THE FUCK?!?
OH MY GOD!
WHAT ARE YOU DOING HERE?
WHY AREN'T YOU AT THE GYM LIKE NORMALLY?
WHY THE FUCK ARE YOU TAPING ME IN MY APARTMENT?
THIS IS YOUR "GIFT"? THIS IS HOW YOU KNOW ME?
THESE THINGS JUST "COME TO YOU," RIGHT? THROUGH A FUCKING MICROPHONE IN MY WALL?
FUCKING SCAM ARTIST BITCH!

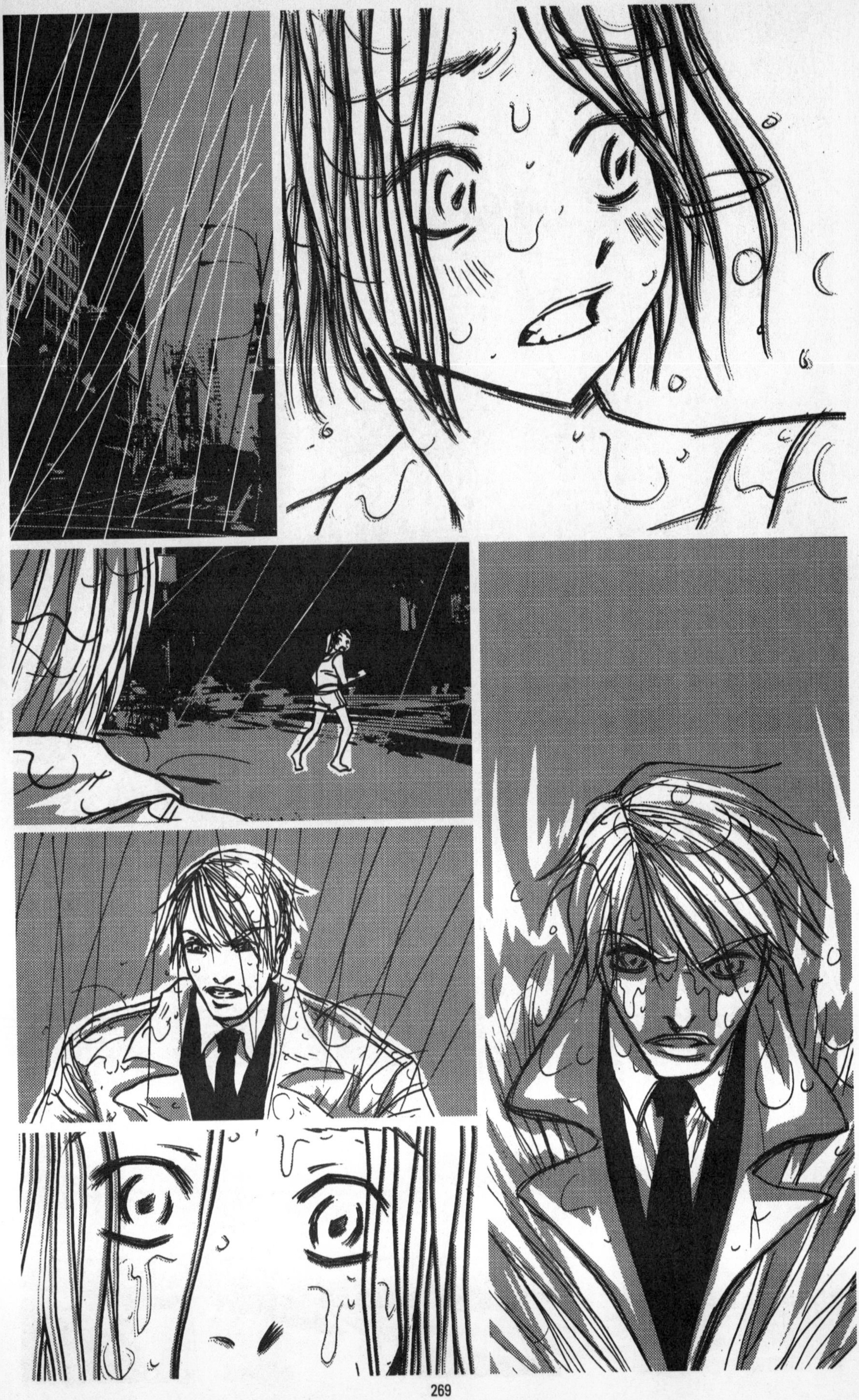

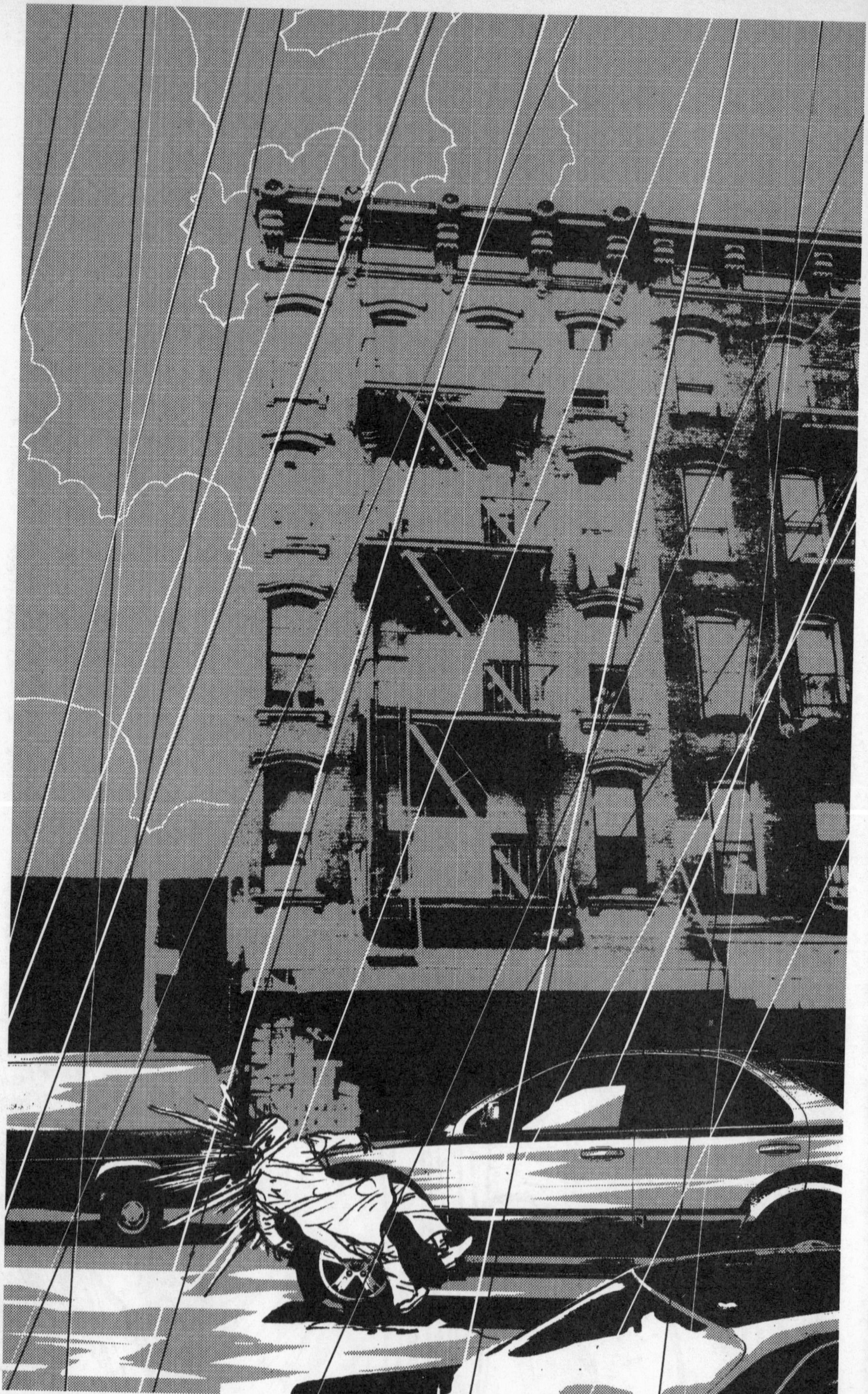

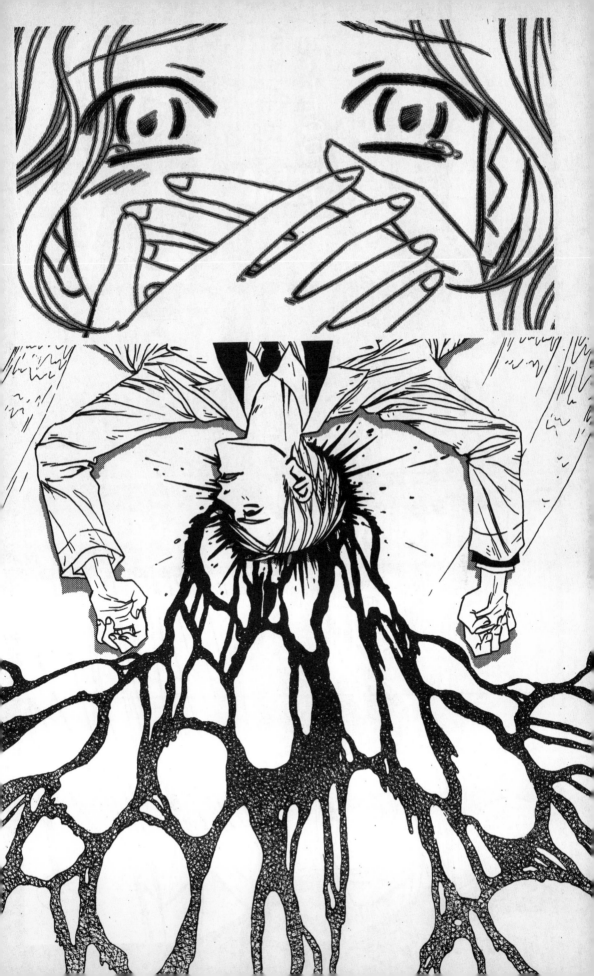

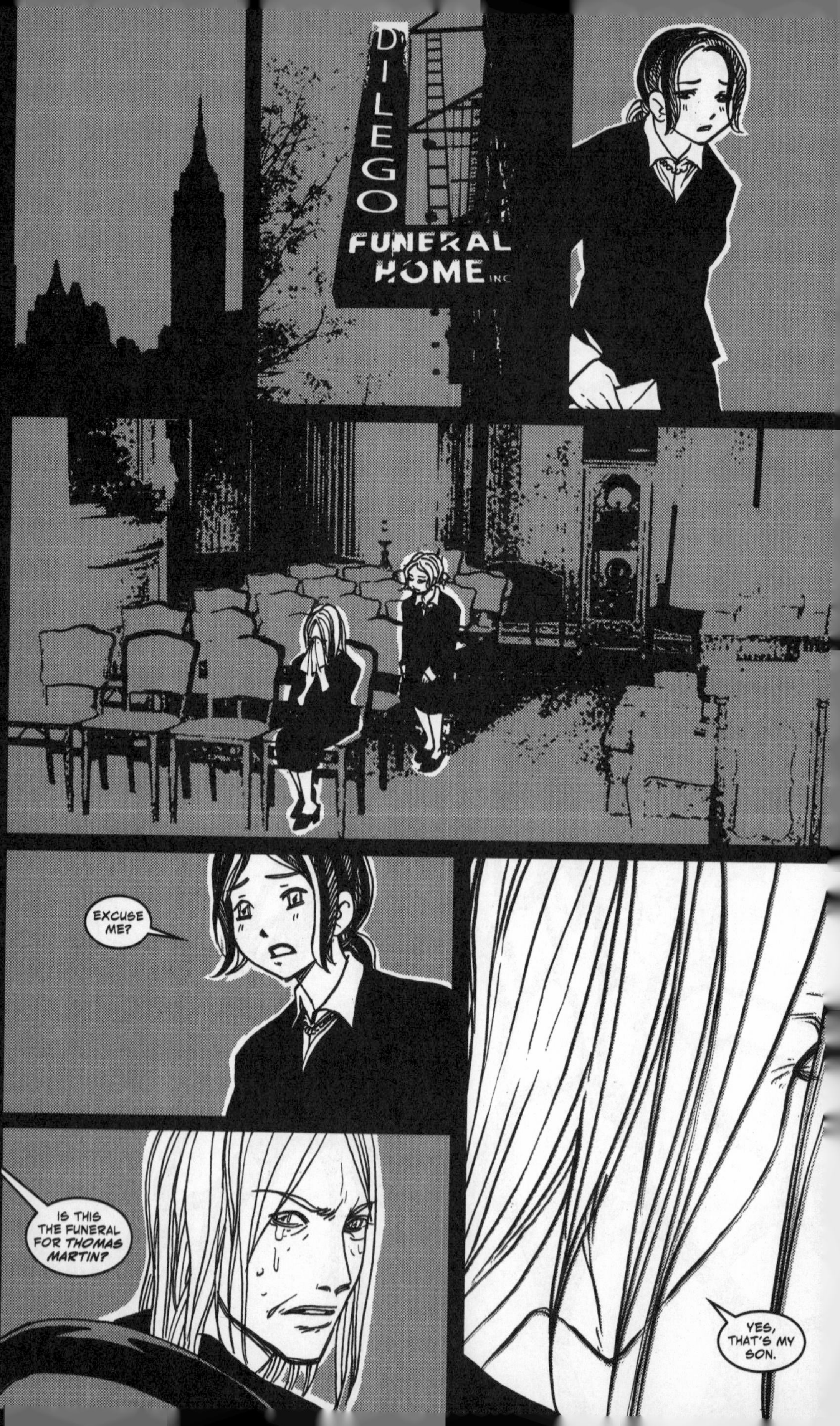
D'ILEGO
FUNERAL
HOME INC
EXCUSE ME?
IS THIS THE FUNERAL FOR *THOMAS MARTIN?*
YES, THAT'S MY SON.

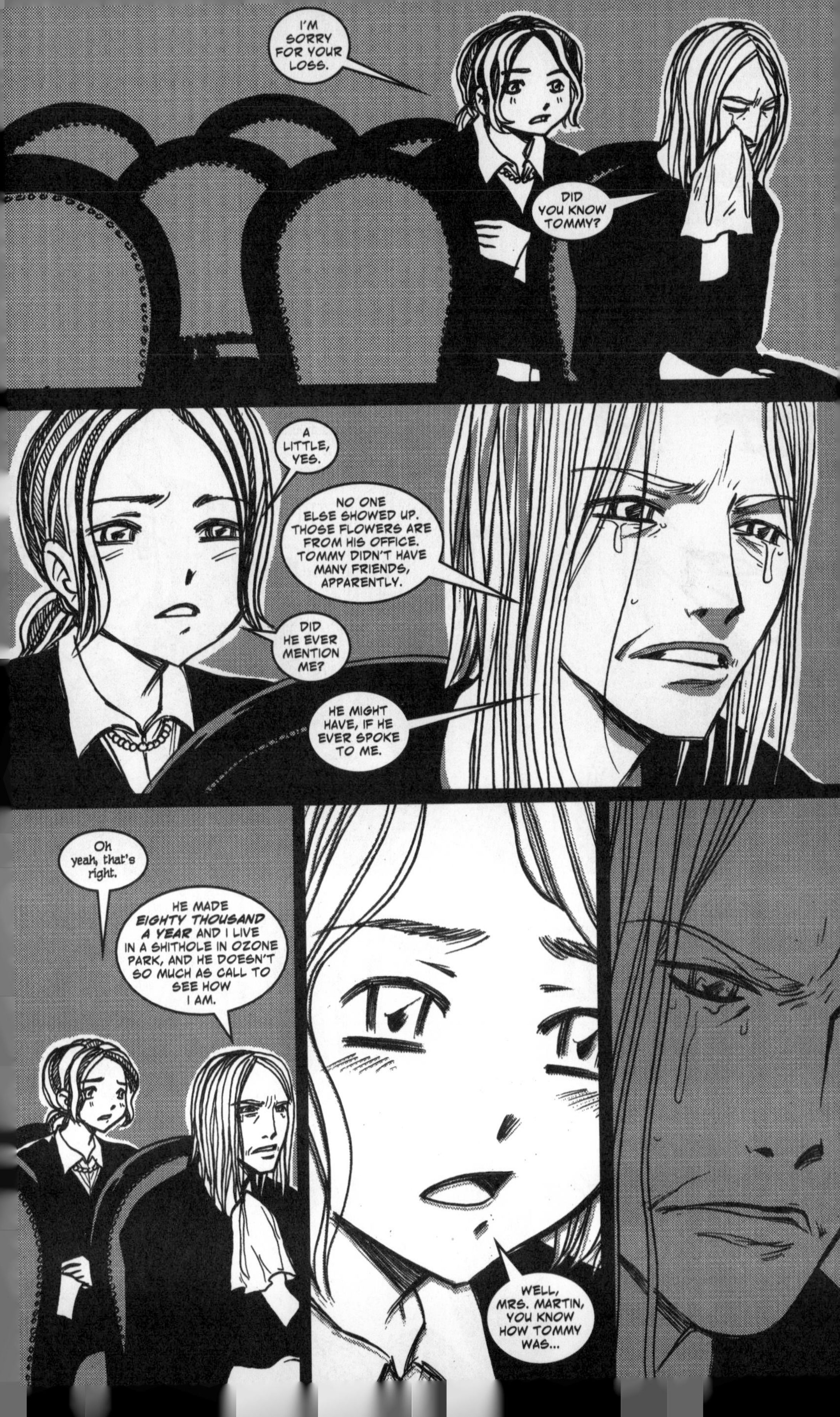
I'M SORRY FOR YOUR LOSS.
DID YOU KNOW TOMMY?
A LITTLE, YES.
NO ONE ELSE SHOWED UP. THOSE FLOWERS ARE FROM HIS OFFICE. TOMMY DIDN'T HAVE MANY FRIENDS, APPARENTLY.
DID HE EVER MENTION ME?
HE MIGHT HAVE, IF HE EVER SPOKE TO ME.
Oh yeah, that's right.
HE MADE EIGHTY THOUSAND A YEAR AND I LIVE IN A SHITHOLE IN OZONE PARK, AND HE DOESN'T SO MUCH AS CALL TO SEE HOW I AM.
WELL, MRS. MARTIN, YOU KNOW HOW TOMMY WAS...

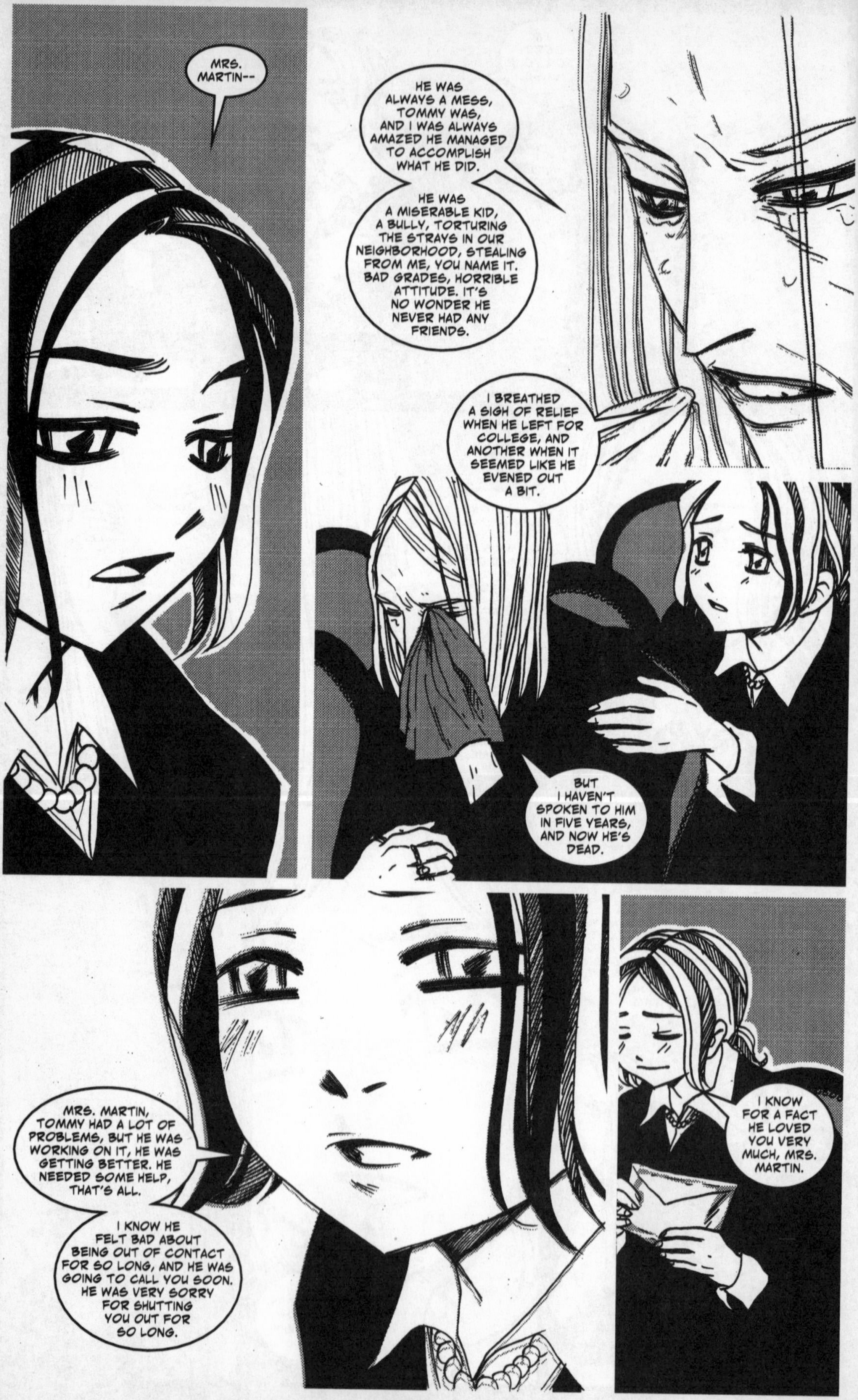

MRS. MARTIN--
HE WAS ALWAYS A MESS, TOMMY WAS, AND I WAS ALWAYS AMAZED HE MANAGED TO ACCOMPLISH WHAT HE DID.
HE WAS A MISERABLE KID, A BULLY, TORTURING THE STRAYS IN OUR NEIGHBORHOOD, STEALING FROM ME, YOU NAME IT. BAD GRADES, HORRIBLE ATTITUDE. IT'S NO WONDER HE NEVER HAD ANY FRIENDS.
I BREATHED A SIGH OF RELIEF WHEN HE LEFT FOR COLLEGE, AND ANOTHER WHEN IT SEEMED LIKE HE EVENED OUT A BIT.
BUT I HAVEN'T SPOKEN TO HIM IN FIVE YEARS, AND NOW HE'S DEAD.
MRS. MARTIN, TOMMY HAD A LOT OF PROBLEMS, BUT HE WAS WORKING ON IT, HE WAS GETTING BETTER. HE NEEDED SOME HELP, THAT'S ALL.
I KNOW HE FELT BAD ABOUT BEING OUT OF CONTACT FOR SO LONG, AND HE WAS GOING TO CALL YOU SOON. HE WAS VERY SORRY FOR SHUTTING YOU OUT FOR SO LONG.
I KNOW FOR A FACT HE LOVED YOU VERY MUCH, MRS. MARTIN.

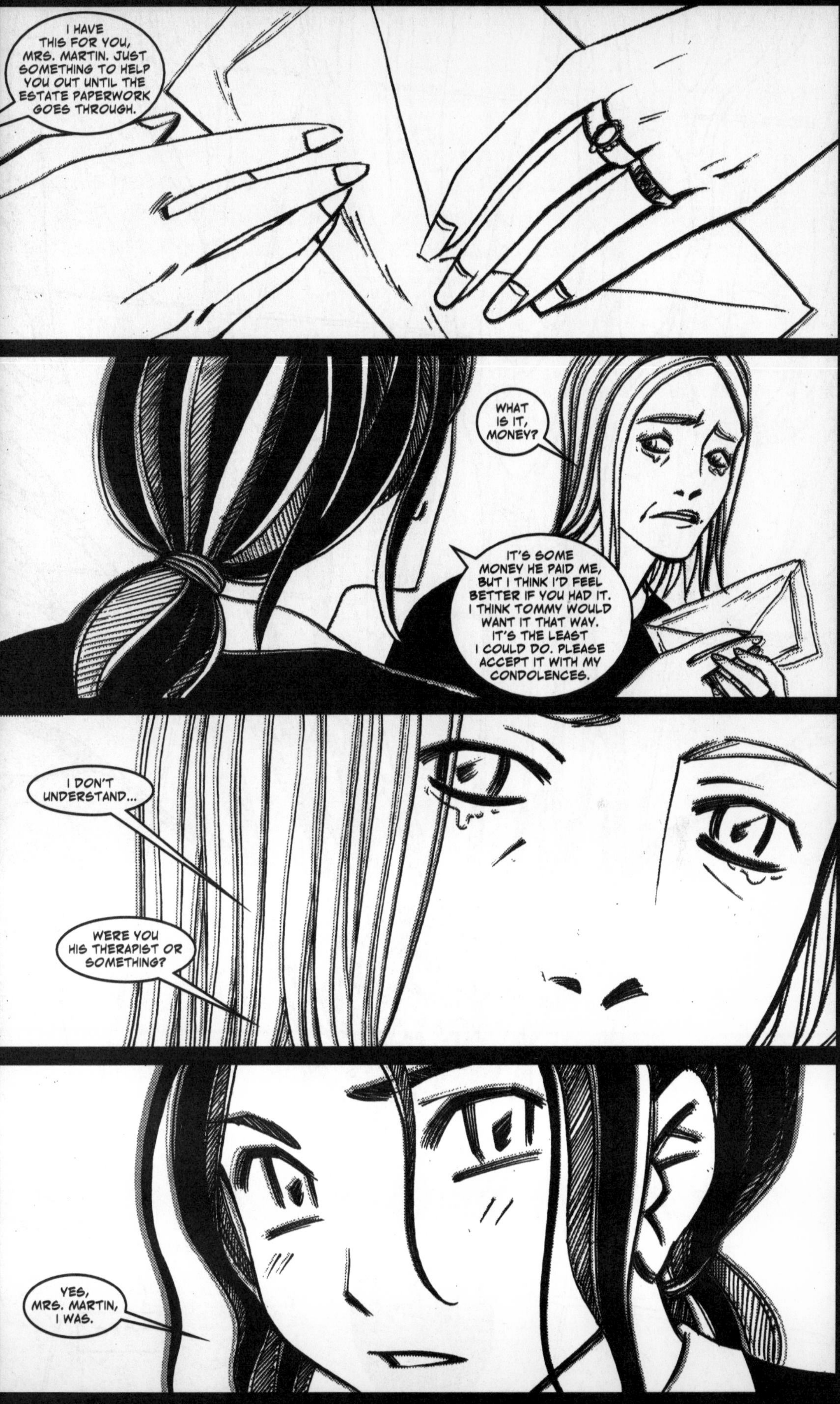
I HAVE THIS FOR YOU, MRS. MARTIN. JUST SOMETHING TO HELP YOU OUT UNTIL THE ESTATE PAPERWORK GOES THROUGH.
WHAT IS IT, MONEY?
IT'S SOME MONEY HE PAID ME, BUT I THINK I'D FEEL BETTER IF YOU HAD IT. I THINK TOMMY WOULD WANT IT THAT WAY. IT'S THE LEAST I COULD DO. PLEASE ACCEPT IT WITH MY CONDOLENCES.
I DON'T UNDERSTAND...
WERE YOU HIS THERAPIST OR SOMETHING?
YES, MRS. MARTIN, I WAS.

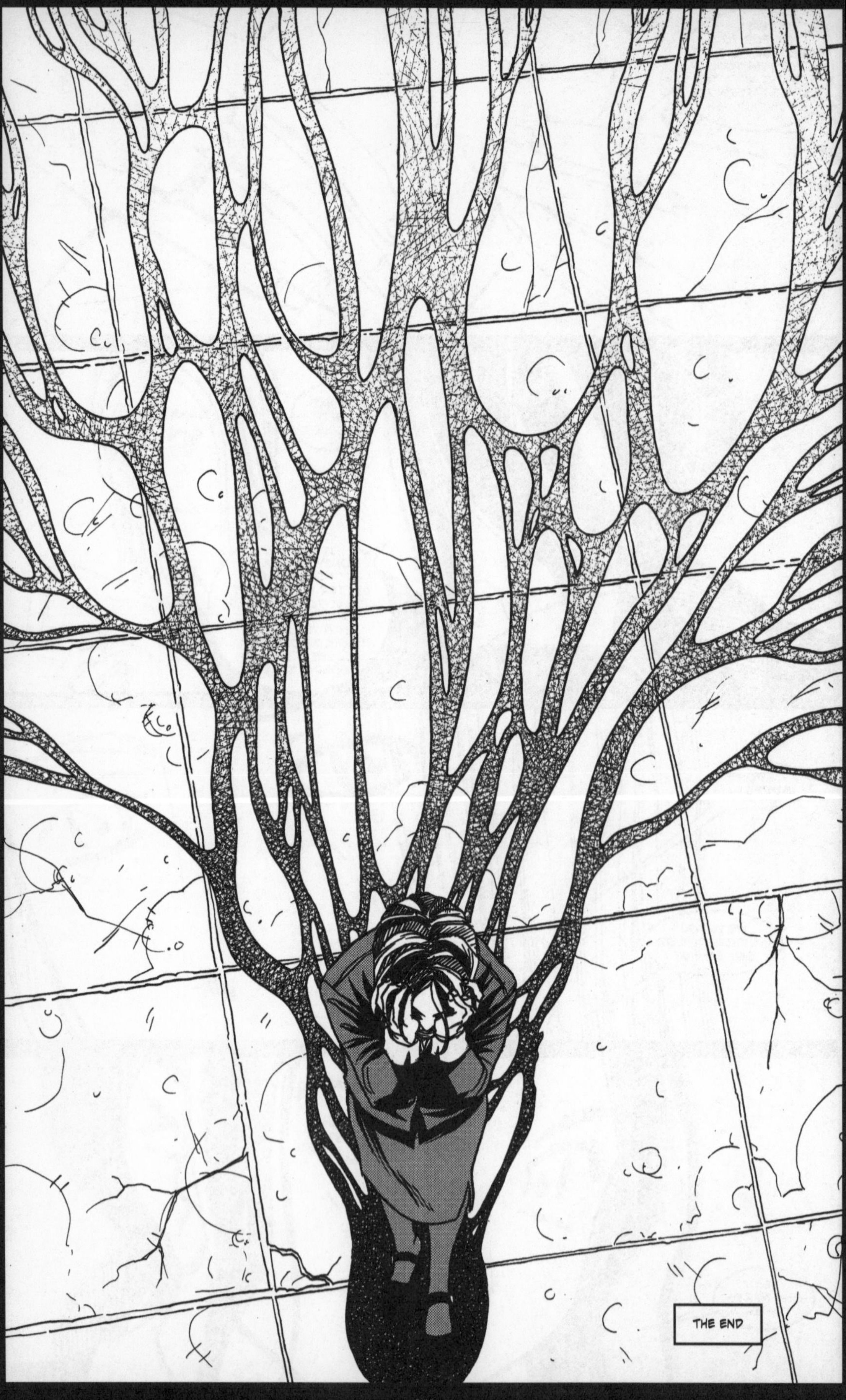
THE END

11

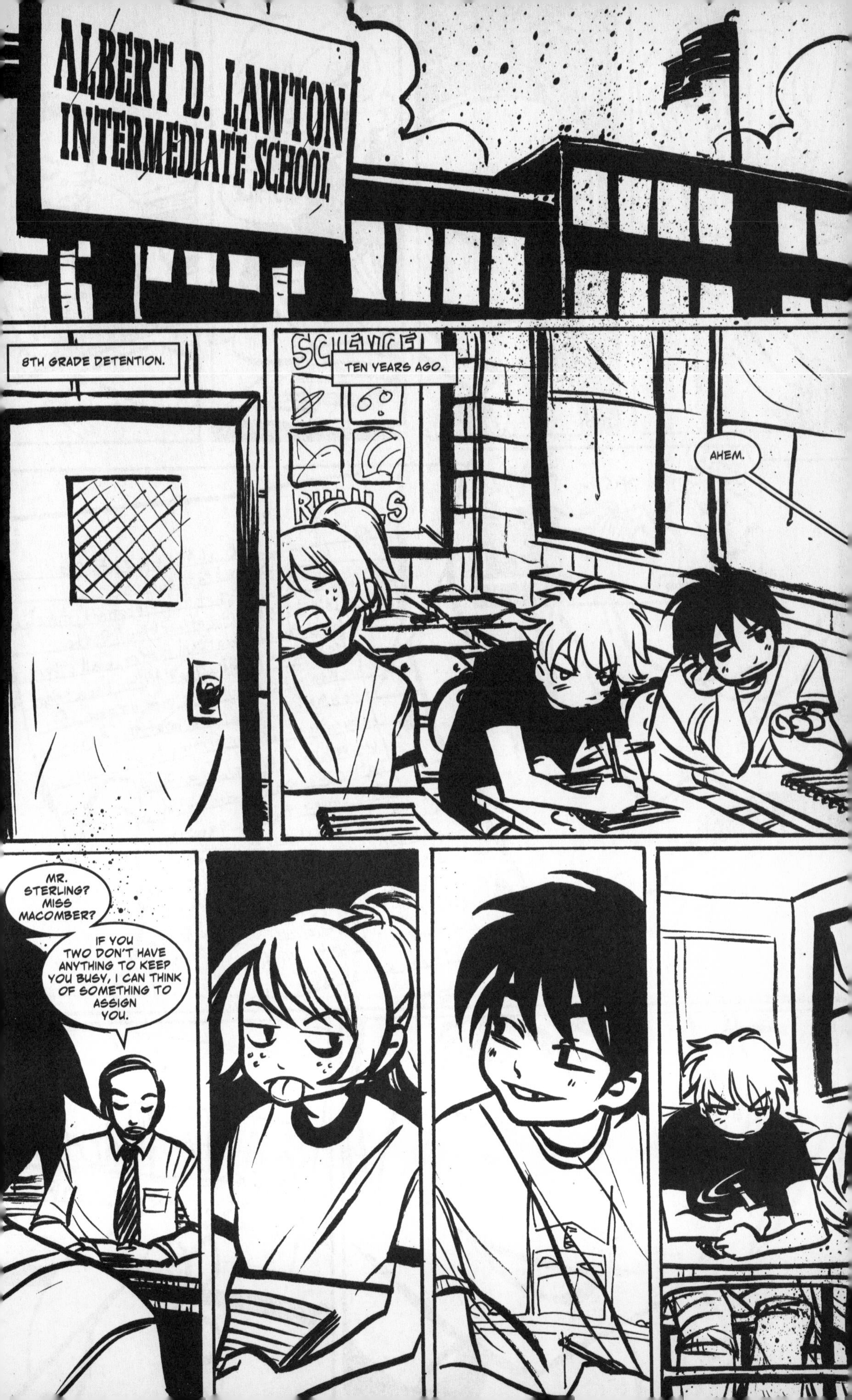
ALBERT D. LAWTON INTERMEDIATE SCHOOL
8TH GRADE DETENTION.
TEN YEARS AGO.
AHEM.
MR. STERLING? MISS MACOMBER?
IF YOU TWO DON'T HAVE ANYTHING TO KEEP YOU BUSY, I CAN THINK OF SOMETHING TO ASSIGN YOU.

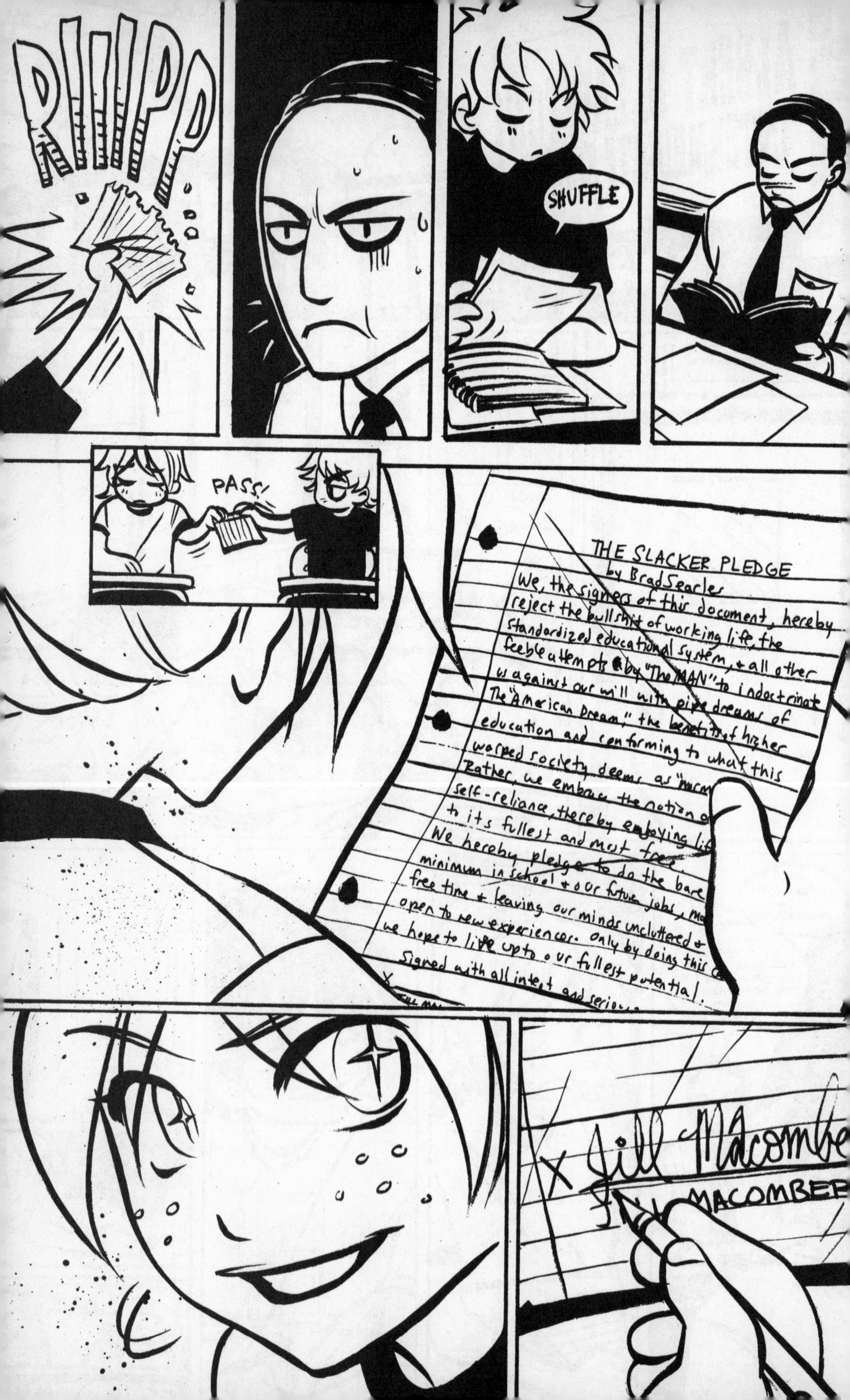
RIIIPP
SHUFFLE
PASS!
THE SLACKER PLEDGE
by Brad Searles
We, the signers of this document, hereby
reject the bullshit of working life, the
standardized educational system, & all other
feeble attempts by "The MAN" to indoctrinat
us against our will with pipe dreams of
The "American Dream," the benefits of higher
education and conforming to what this
warped society deems as
Rather, we embrace the notion
self-reliance, thereby enjoying
to its fullest and most free.
We hereby pledge to do the bare
minimum in school & our future jobs,
free time & leaving our minds uncluttered &
open to new experiences. Only by doing this
we hope to live up to our fullest potential.
Signed with all intent and
X Jill Macombe
MACOMBE

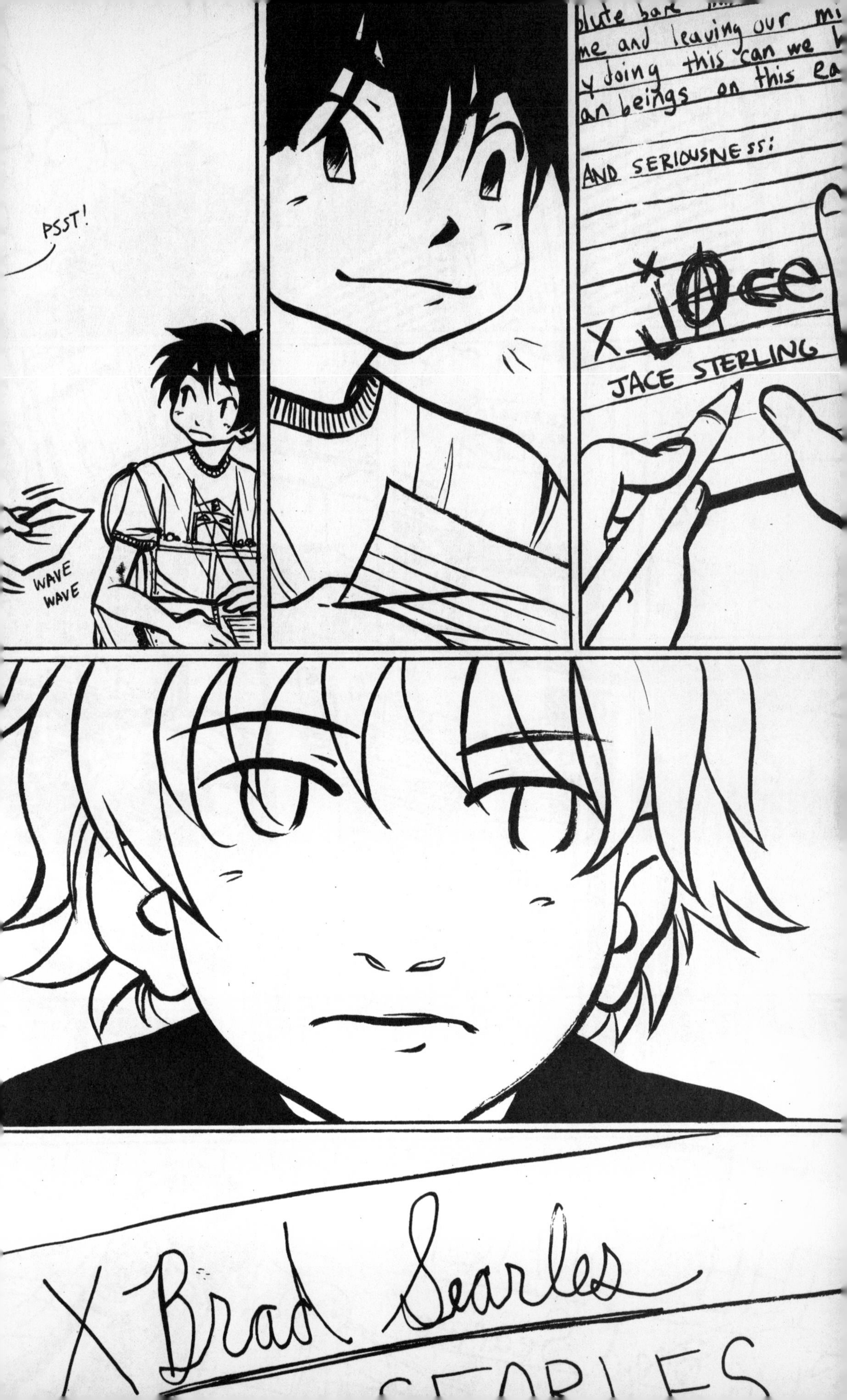
PSST!
WAVE WAVE
...blute bar...
...me and leaving our mi...
...y doing this can we b...
...an beings on this ea...
AND SERIOUSNESS:
X Jace
JACE STERLING
X Brad Searles
...SEARLES

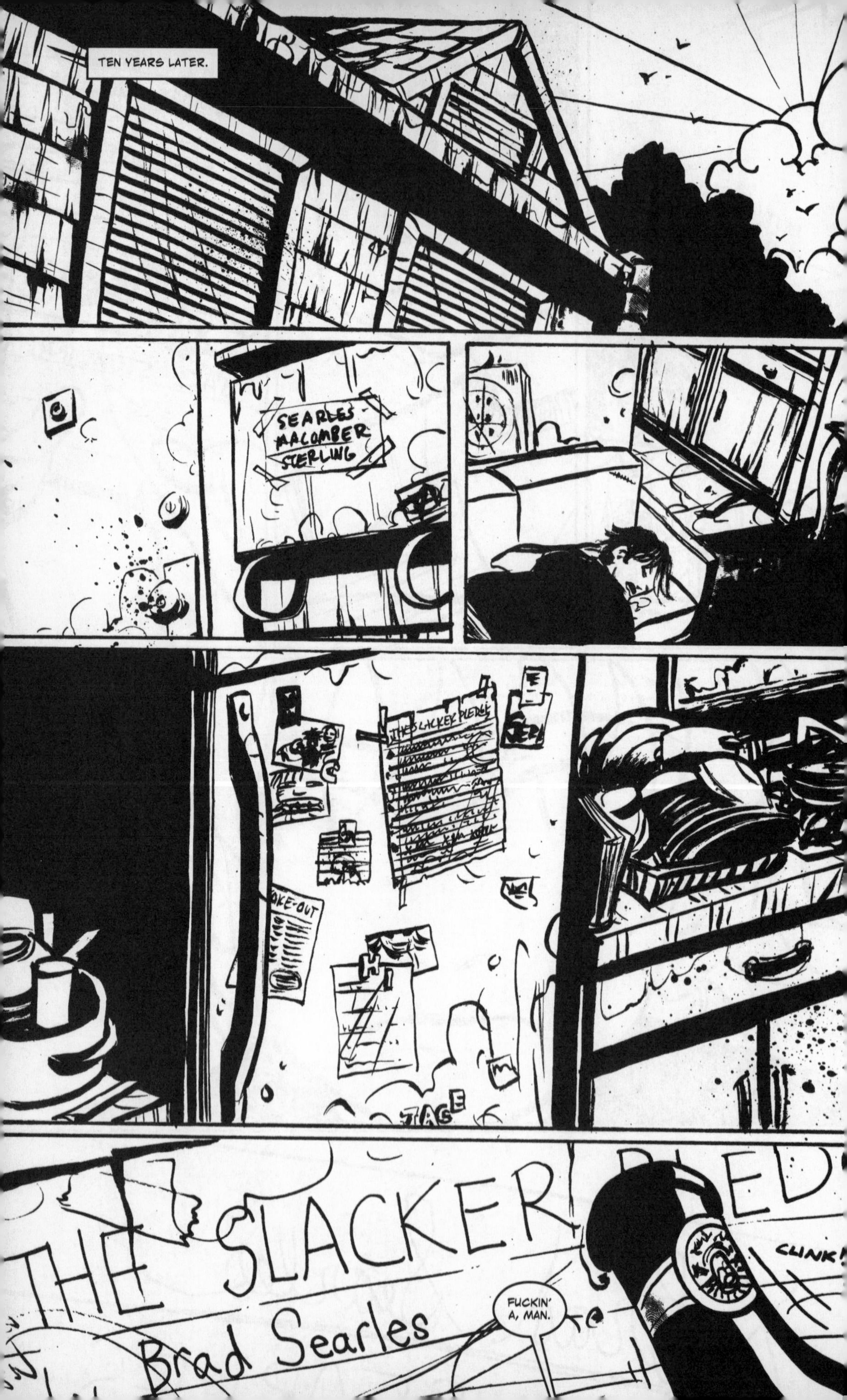
TEN YEARS LATER.
SEARLES
MACOMBER
STERLING
THE SLACKER PLEDGE
TAKE-OUT
THE SLACKER PLED
Brad Searles
FUCKIN' A, MAN.
CLINK!

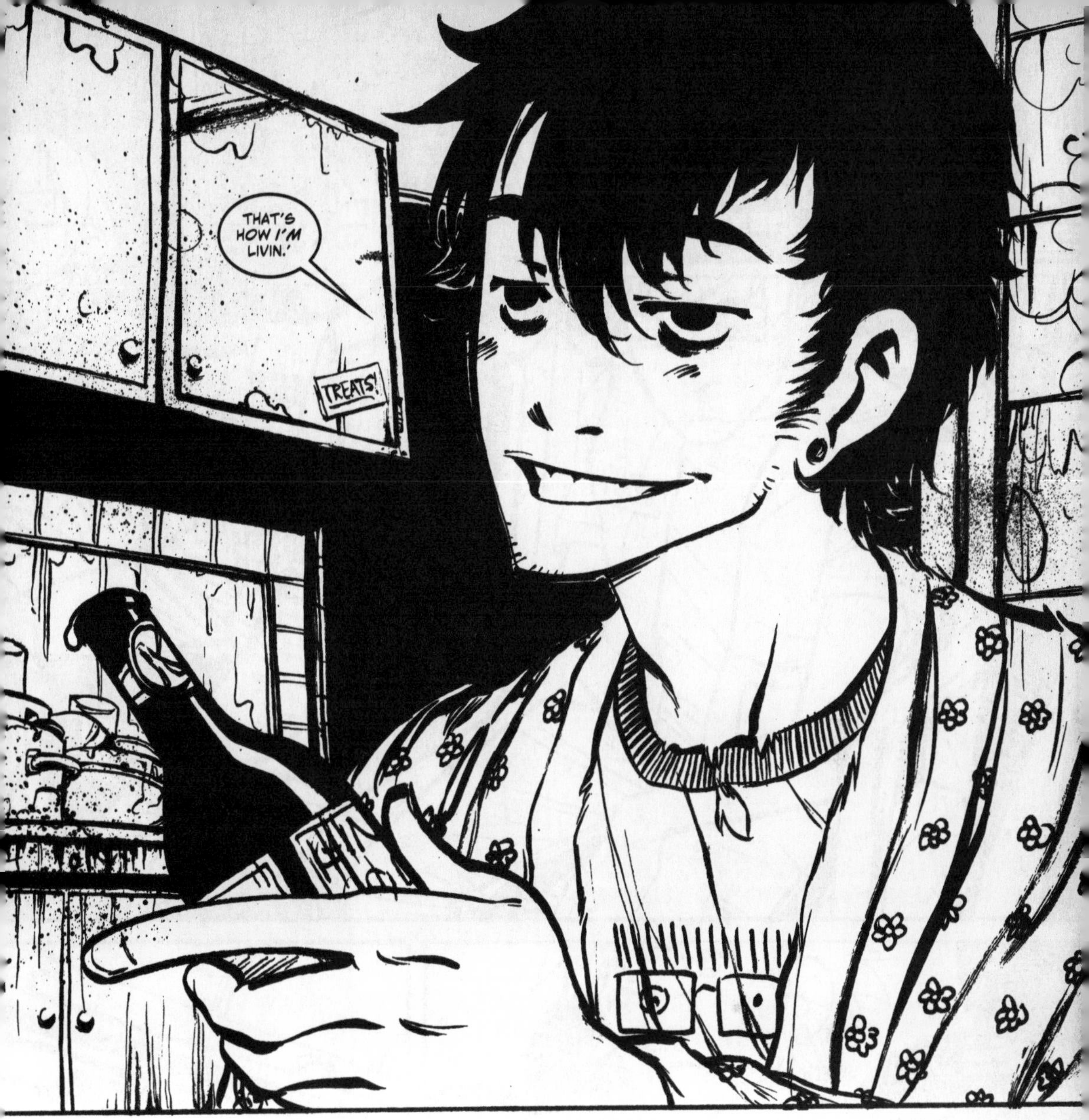
THAT'S HOW I'M LIVIN.'
TREATS!

“Midnight to Six”

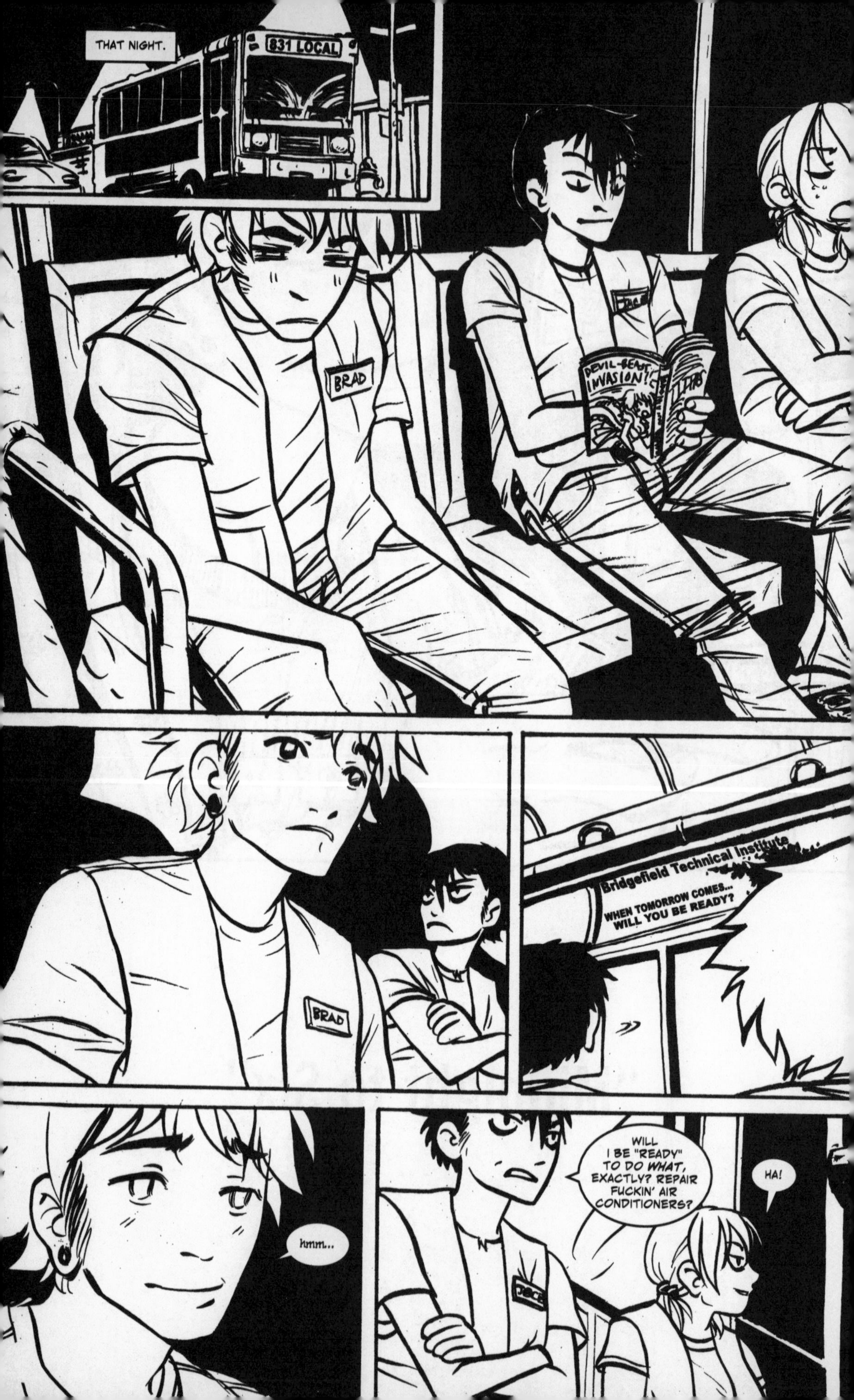
THAT NIGHT.
831 LOCAL
BRAD
DEVIL-BEAST INVASION!
BRAD
Bridgefield Technical Institute
WHEN TOMORROW COMES...
WILL YOU BE READY?
hmm...
WILL I BE "READY" TO DO WHAT, EXACTLY? REPAIR FUCKIN' AIR CONDITIONERS?
HA!

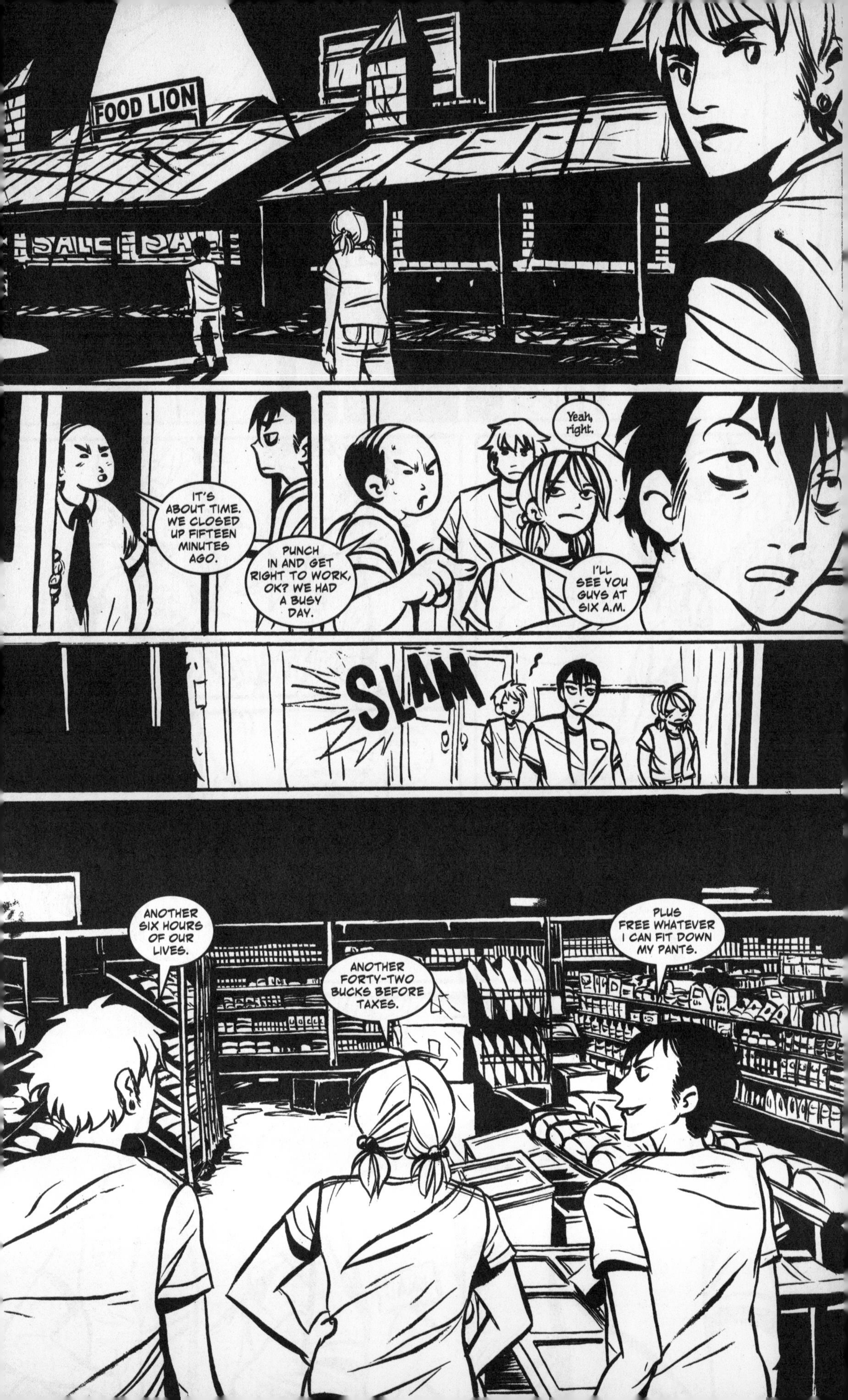
FOOD LION
SALE SALE
IT'S ABOUT TIME. WE CLOSED UP FIFTEEN MINUTES AGO.
PUNCH IN AND GET RIGHT TO WORK, OK? WE HAD A BUSY DAY.
Yeah, right.
I'LL SEE YOU GUYS AT SIX A.M.
SLAM
ANOTHER SIX HOURS OF OUR LIVES.
ANOTHER FORTY-TWO BUCKS BEFORE TAXES.
PLUS FREE WHATEVER I CAN FIT DOWN MY PANTS.

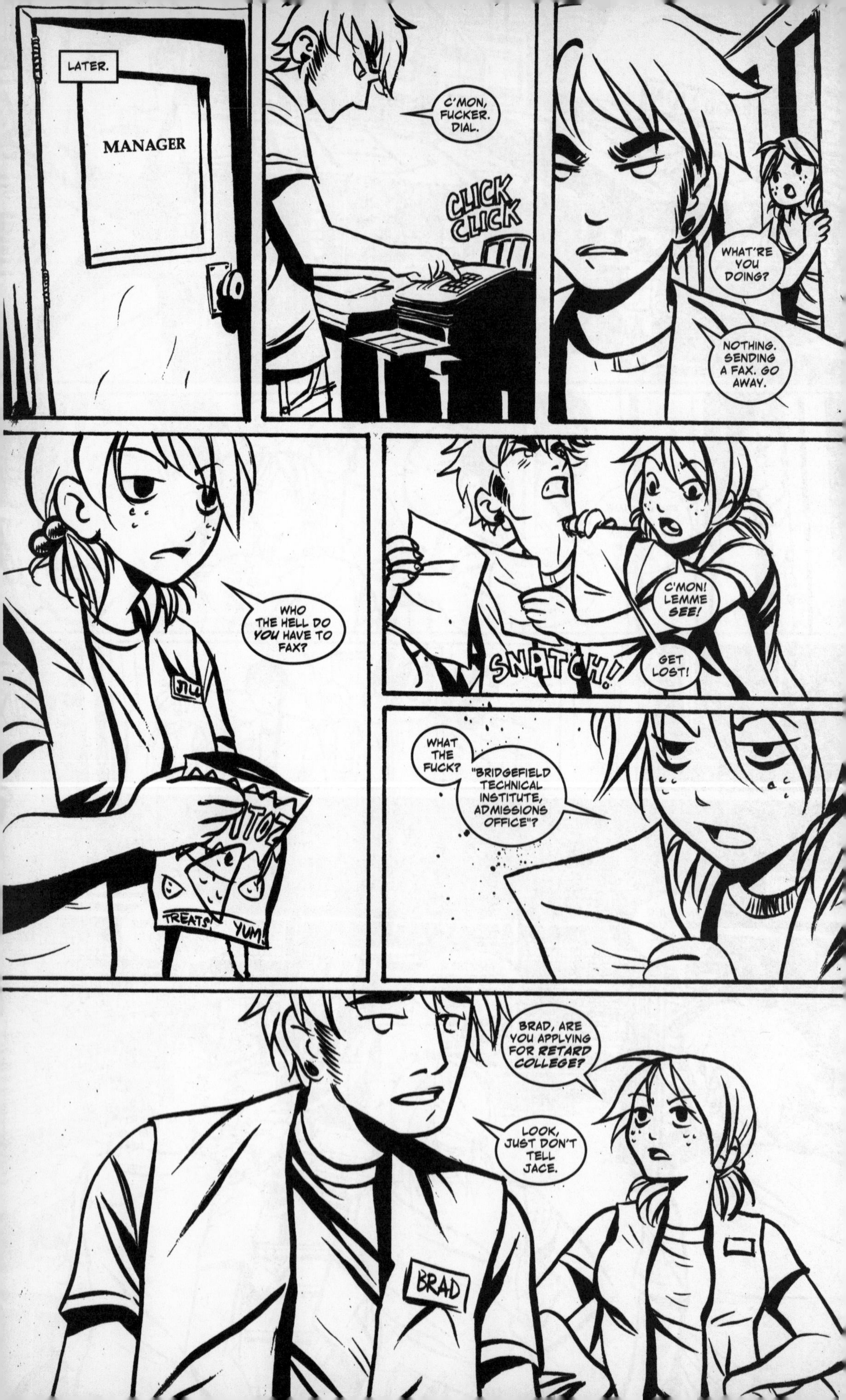
LATER.
MANAGER
C'MON, FUCKER. DIAL.
CLICK CLICK
WHAT'RE YOU DOING?
NOTHING. SENDING A FAX. GO AWAY.
WHO THE HELL DO *YOU* HAVE TO FAX?
TREATS
YUM!
C'MON! LEMME *SEE!*
SNATCH!
GET LOST!
WHAT THE FUCK?
"BRIDGEFIELD TECHNICAL INSTITUTE, ADMISSIONS OFFICE"?
BRAD, ARE YOU APPLYING FOR *RETARD COLLEGE?*
LOOK, JUST DON'T TELL JACE.
BRAD

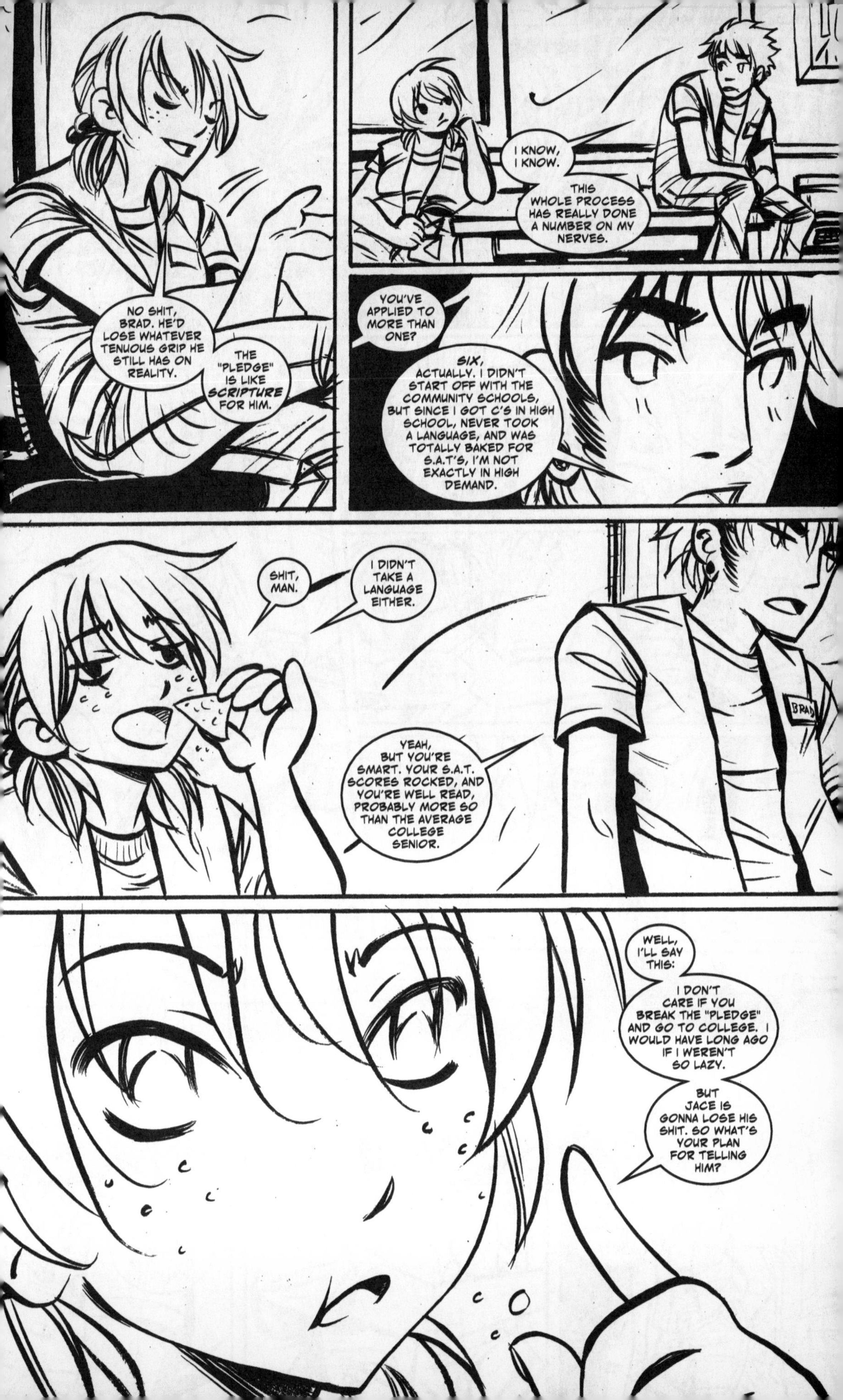
NO SHIT, BRAD. HE'D LOSE WHATEVER TENUOUS GRIP HE STILL HAS ON REALITY.
THE "PLEDGE" IS LIKE SCRIPTURE FOR HIM.
I KNOW, I KNOW.
THIS WHOLE PROCESS HAS REALLY DONE A NUMBER ON MY NERVES.
YOU'VE APPLIED TO MORE THAN ONE?
SIX, ACTUALLY. I DIDN'T START OFF WITH THE COMMUNITY SCHOOLS, BUT SINCE I GOT C'S IN HIGH SCHOOL, NEVER TOOK A LANGUAGE, AND WAS TOTALLY BAKED FOR S.A.T'S, I'M NOT EXACTLY IN HIGH DEMAND.
SHIT, MAN.
I DIDN'T TAKE A LANGUAGE EITHER.
BRAD
YEAH, BUT YOU'RE SMART. YOUR S.A.T. SCORES ROCKED, AND YOU'RE WELL READ, PROBABLY MORE SO THAN THE AVERAGE COLLEGE SENIOR.
WELL, I'LL SAY THIS:
I DON'T CARE IF YOU BREAK THE "PLEDGE" AND GO TO COLLEGE. I WOULD HAVE LONG AGO IF I WEREN'T SO LAZY.
BUT JACE IS GONNA LOSE HIS SHIT. SO WHAT'S YOUR PLAN FOR TELLING HIM?

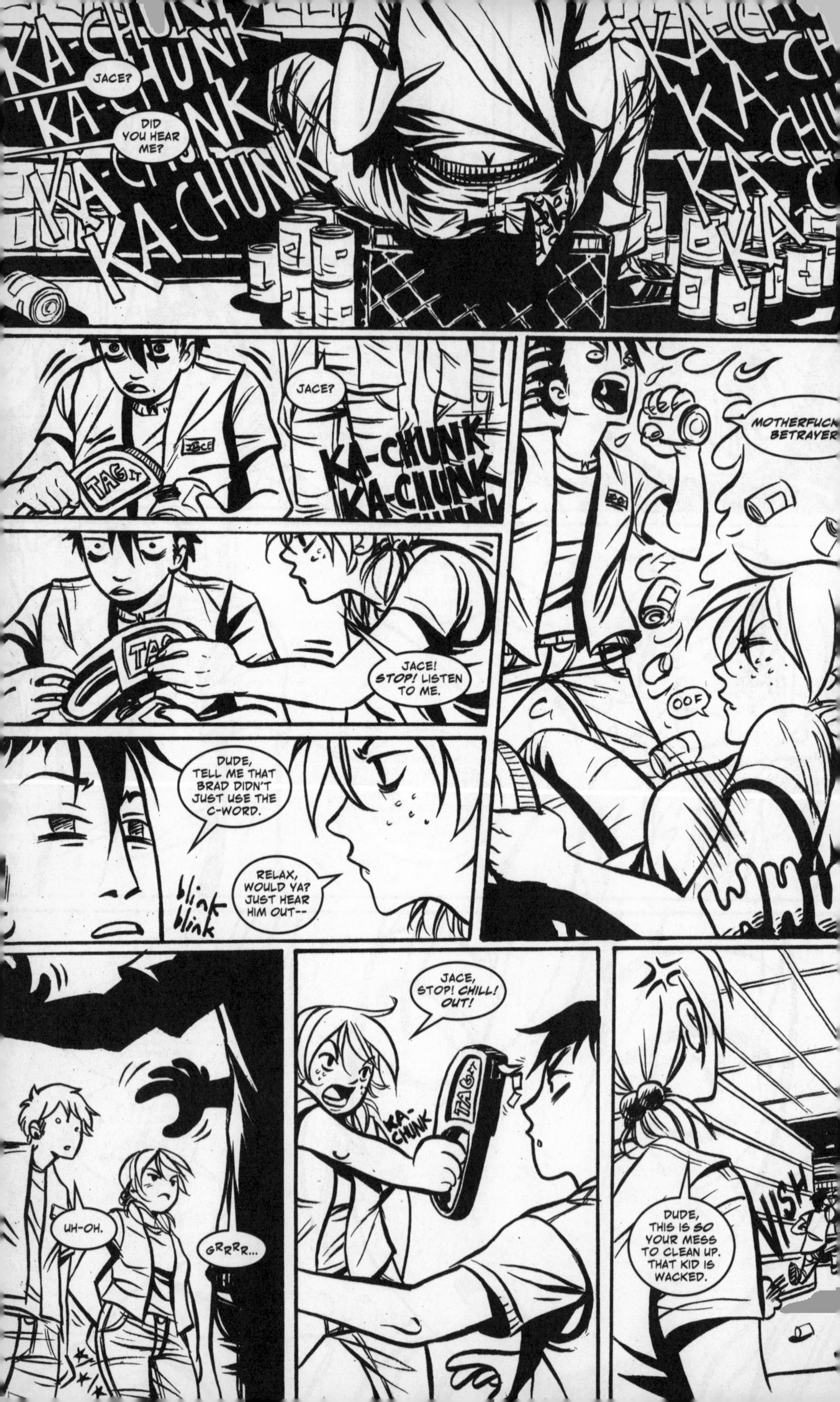
KA-CHUNK
JACE?
KA-CHUNK
DID YOU HEAR ME?
KA-CHUNK
KA-CHUNK
KA-CHUNK
JACE?
KA-CHUNK
KA-CHUNK
MOTHERFUCK BETRAYER
JACE! STOP! LISTEN TO ME.
OOF
DUDE, TELL ME THAT BRAD DIDN'T JUST USE THE C-WORD.
blink blink
RELAX, WOULD YA? JUST HEAR HIM OUT--
UH-OH.
GRRRR...
JACE, STOP! CHILL! OUT!
KA-CHUNK
DUDE, THIS IS SO YOUR MESS TO CLEAN UP. THAT KID IS WACKED.

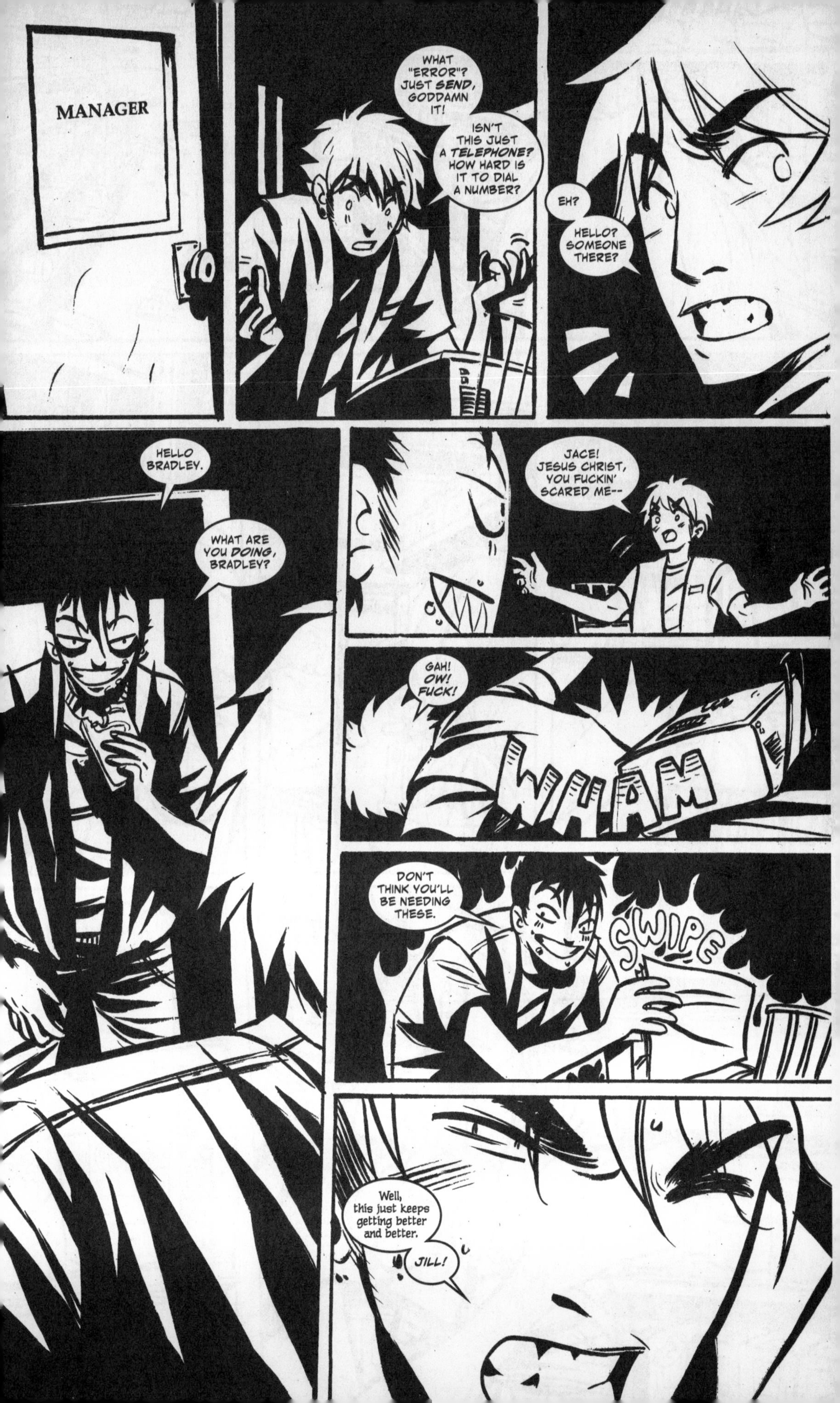

MANAGER
WHAT "ERROR"? JUST SEND, GODDAMN IT!
ISN'T THIS JUST A TELEPHONE? HOW HARD IS IT TO DIAL A NUMBER?
EH?
HELLO? SOMEONE THERE?
HELLO BRADLEY.
WHAT ARE YOU DOING, BRADLEY?
JACE! JESUS CHRIST, YOU FUCKIN' SCARED ME--
GAH! OW! FUCK!
WHAM
DON'T THINK YOU'LL BE NEEDING THESE.
SWIPE
Well, this just keeps getting better and better.
JILL!

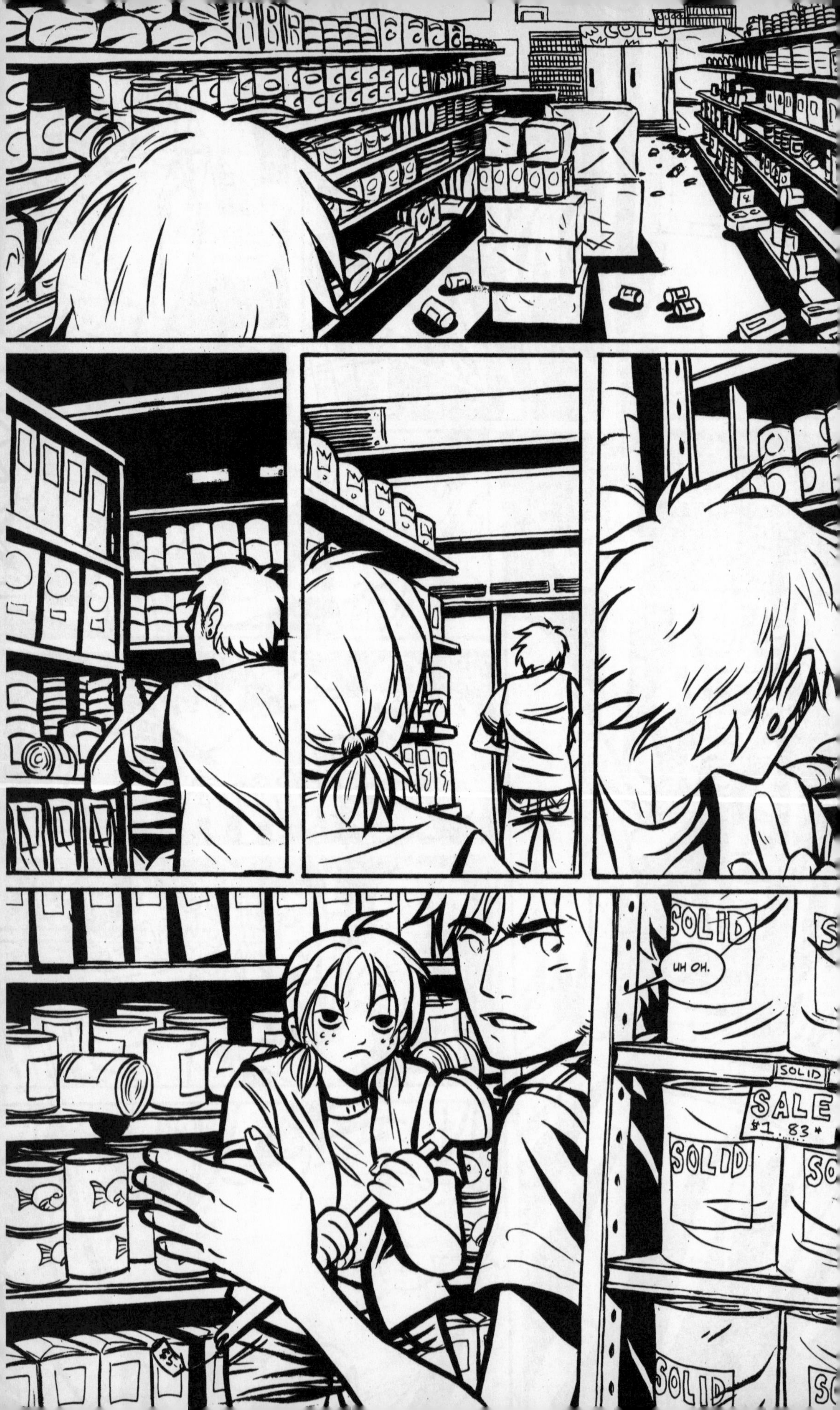
COLD
UH OH.
SOLID
SALE
$1.83*

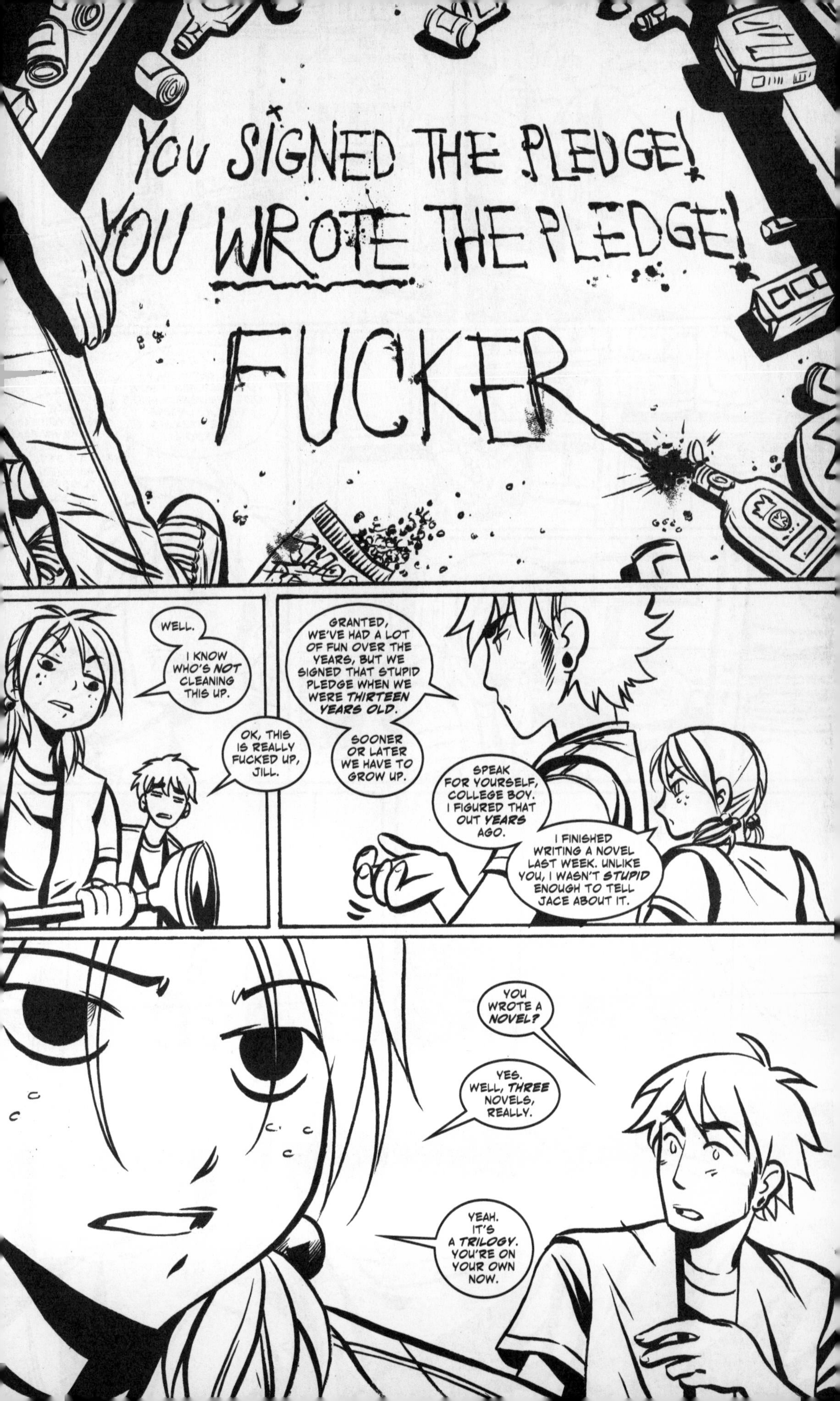

YOU SIGNED THE PLEDGE!
YOU WROTE THE PLEDGE!
FUCKER
WELL.
I KNOW WHO'S NOT CLEANING THIS UP.
OK, THIS IS REALLY FUCKED UP, JILL.
GRANTED, WE'VE HAD A LOT OF FUN OVER THE YEARS, BUT WE SIGNED THAT STUPID PLEDGE WHEN WE WERE THIRTEEN YEARS OLD.
SOONER OR LATER WE HAVE TO GROW UP.
SPEAK FOR YOURSELF, COLLEGE BOY. I FIGURED THAT OUT YEARS AGO.
I FINISHED WRITING A NOVEL LAST WEEK. UNLIKE YOU, I WASN'T STUPID ENOUGH TO TELL JACE ABOUT IT.
YOU WROTE A NOVEL?
YES. WELL, THREE NOVELS, REALLY.
YEAH. IT'S A TRILOGY. YOU'RE ON YOUR OWN NOW.

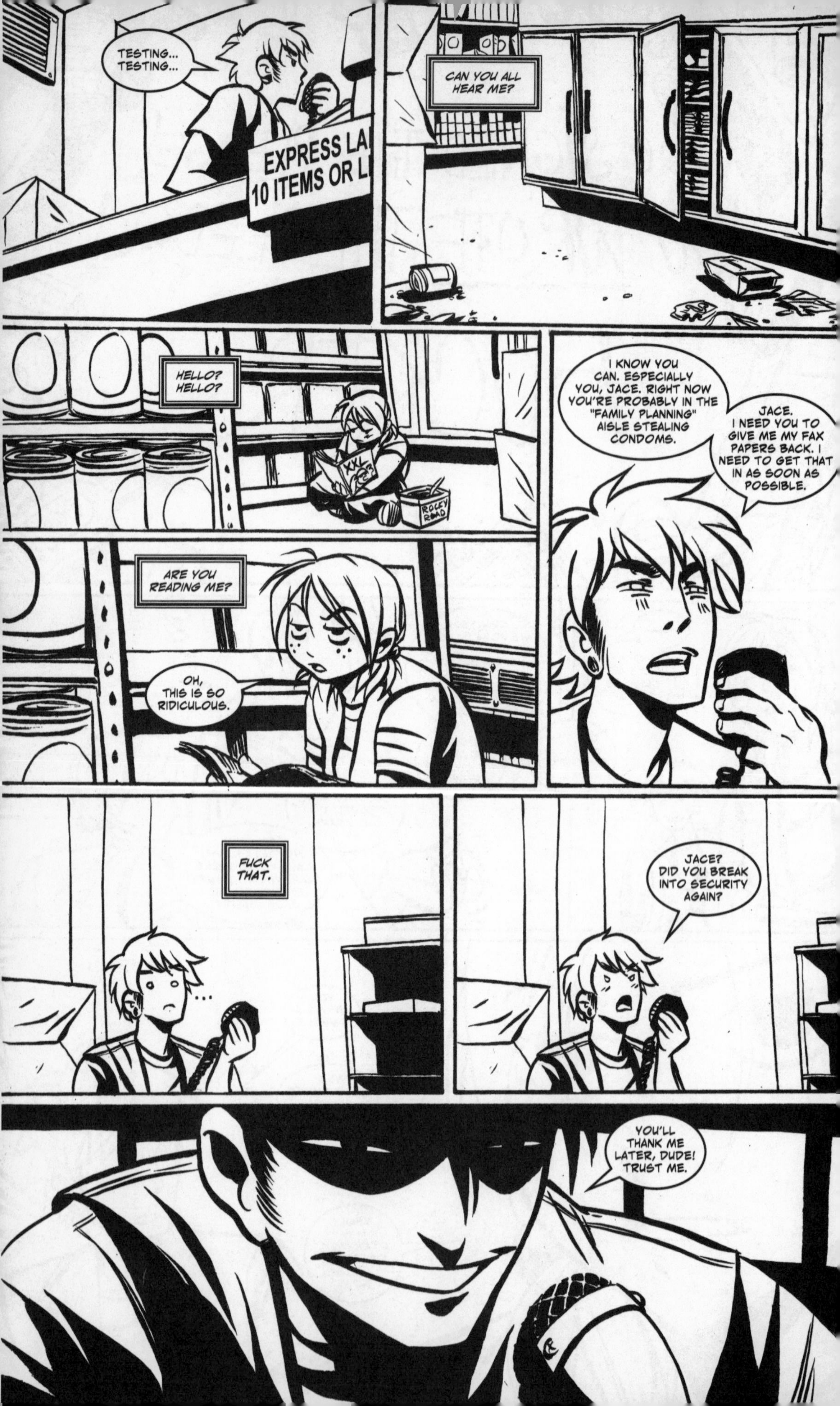

TESTING... TESTING...
EXPRESS LA
10 ITEMS OR L
CAN YOU ALL HEAR ME?
HELLO? HELLO?
XXL
ROCKY ROAD
I KNOW YOU CAN. ESPECIALLY YOU, JACE. RIGHT NOW YOU'RE PROBABLY IN THE "FAMILY PLANNING" AISLE STEALING CONDOMS.
JACE. I NEED YOU TO GIVE ME MY FAX PAPERS BACK. I NEED TO GET THAT IN AS SOON AS POSSIBLE.
ARE YOU READING ME?
OH, THIS IS SO RIDICULOUS.
FUCK THAT.
...
JACE? DID YOU BREAK INTO SECURITY AGAIN?
YOU'LL THANK ME LATER, DUDE! TRUST ME.

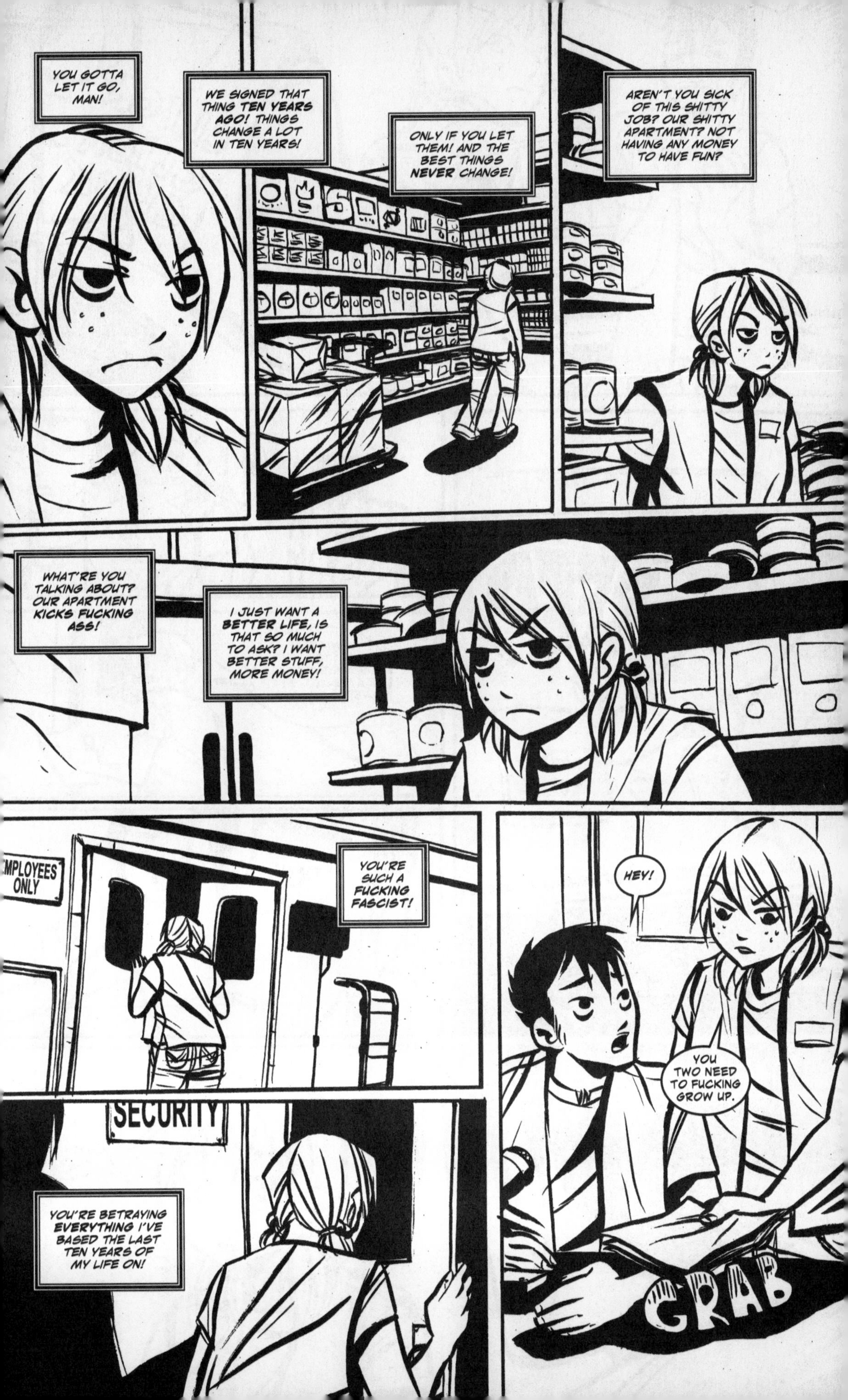
YOU GOTTA LET IT GO, MAN!
WE SIGNED THAT THING TEN YEARS AGO! THINGS CHANGE A LOT IN TEN YEARS!
ONLY IF YOU LET THEM! AND THE BEST THINGS NEVER CHANGE!
AREN'T YOU SICK OF THIS SHITTY JOB? OUR SHITTY APARTMENT? NOT HAVING ANY MONEY TO HAVE FUN?
WHAT'RE YOU TALKING ABOUT? OUR APARTMENT KICKS FUCKING ASS!
I JUST WANT A BETTER LIFE, IS THAT SO MUCH TO ASK? I WANT BETTER STUFF, MORE MONEY!
EMPLOYEES ONLY
YOU'RE SUCH A FUCKING FASCIST!
SECURITY
YOU'RE BETRAYING EVERYTHING I'VE BASED THE LAST TEN YEARS OF MY LIFE ON!
HEY!
YOU TWO NEED TO FUCKING GROW UP.
GRAB

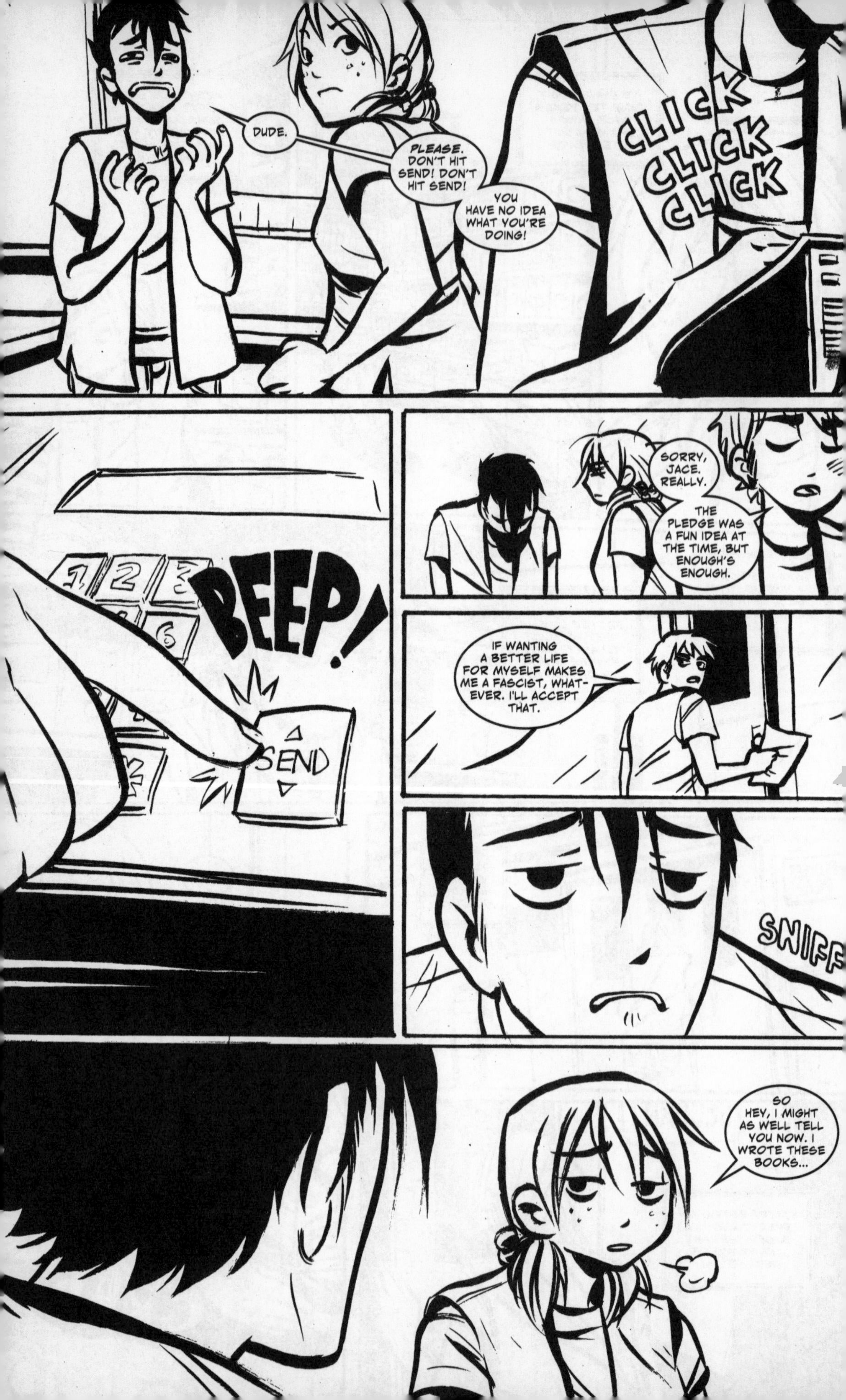
DUDE.
PLEASE. DON'T HIT SEND! DON'T HIT SEND!
YOU HAVE NO IDEA WHAT YOU'RE DOING!
CLICK CLICK CLICK
SEND
BEEP!
SORRY, JACE. REALLY.
THE PLEDGE WAS A FUN IDEA AT THE TIME, BUT ENOUGH'S ENOUGH.
IF WANTING A BETTER LIFE FOR MYSELF MAKES ME A FASCIST, WHAT-EVER. I'LL ACCEPT THAT.
SNIFF
SO HEY, I MIGHT AS WELL TELL YOU NOW. I WROTE THESE BOOKS...

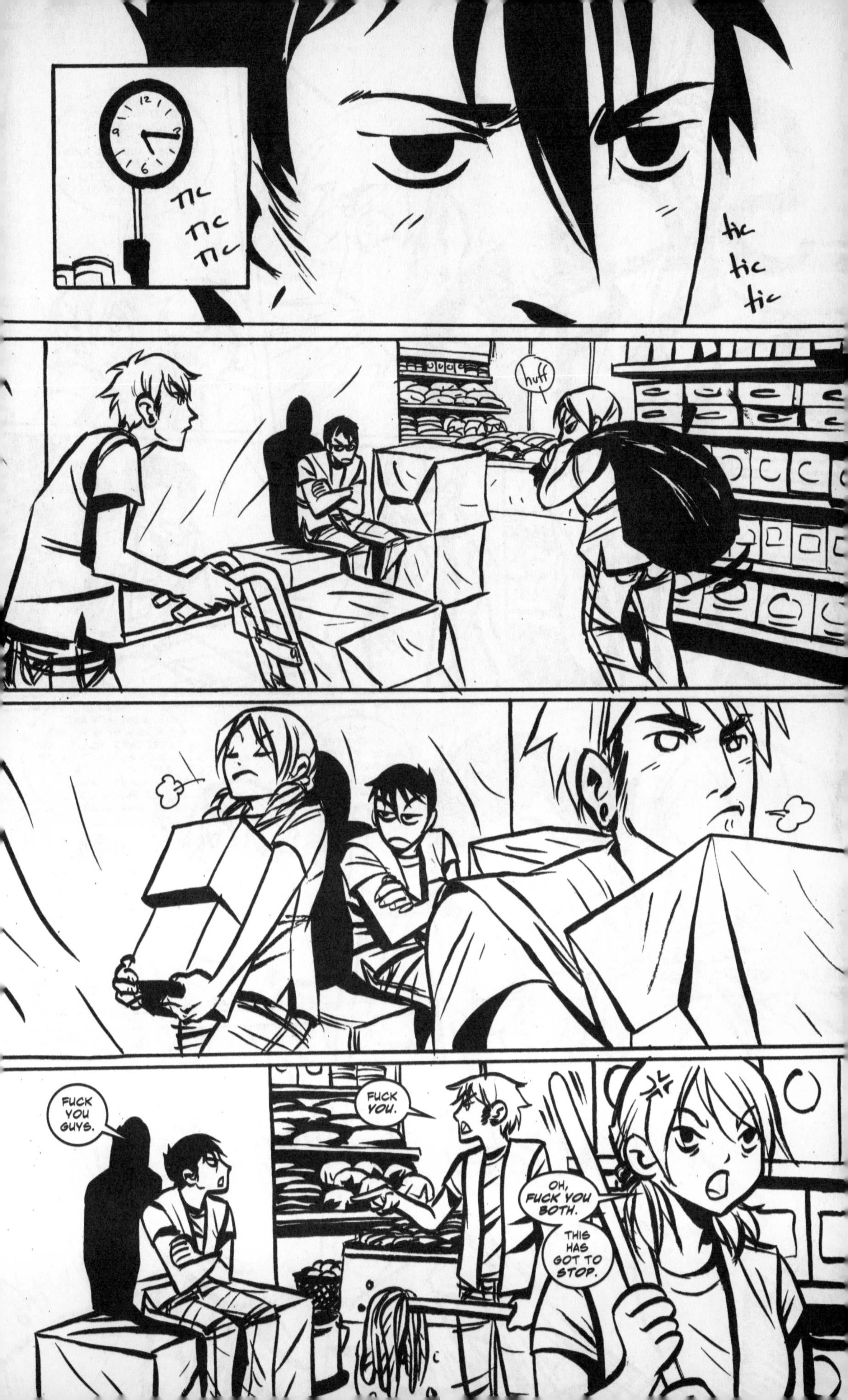
TIC
TIC
TIC
tic
tic
tic
huff
FUCK YOU GUYS.
FUCK YOU.
OH, FUCK YOU BOTH.
THIS HAS GOT TO STOP.

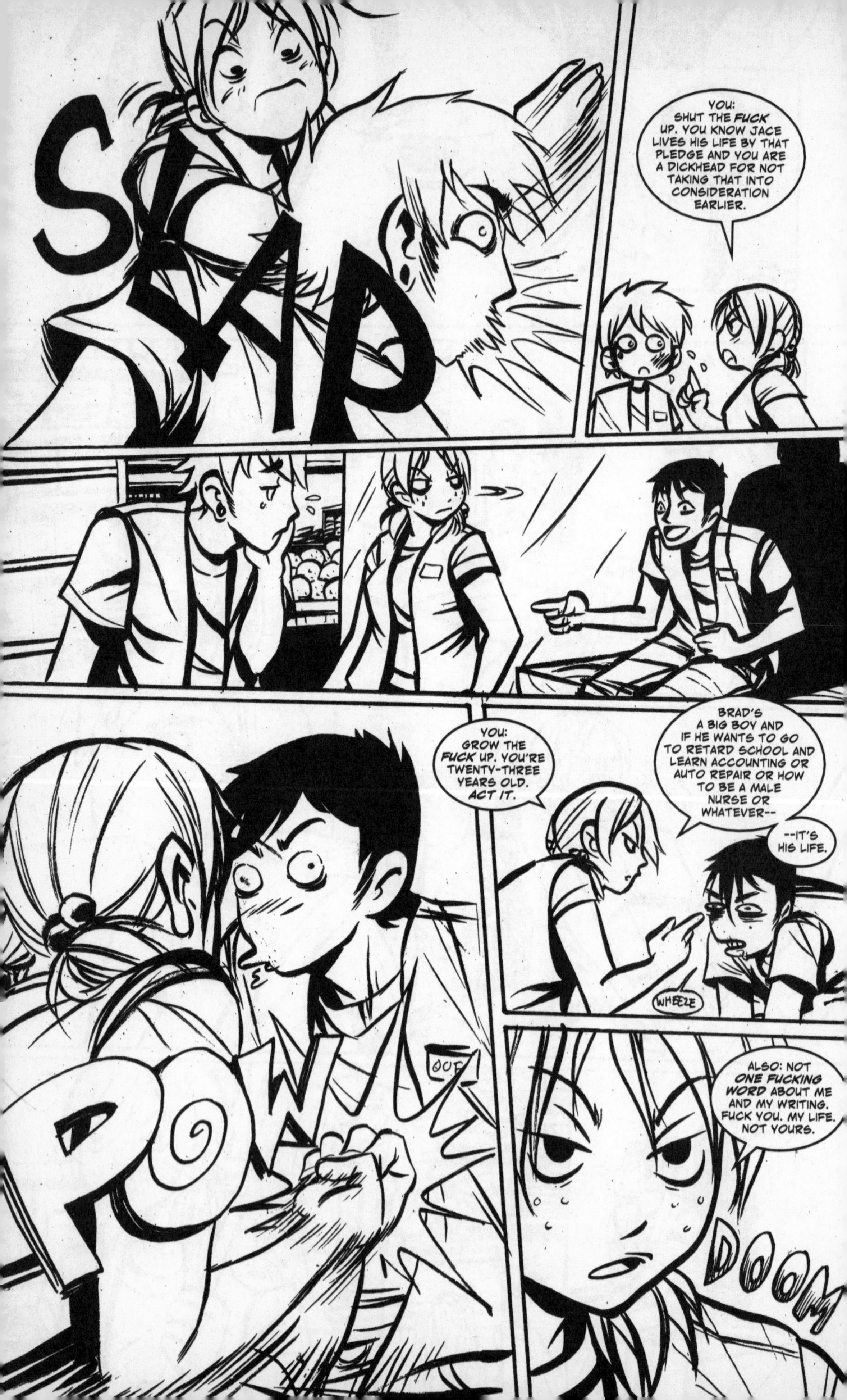
SLAP
YOU: SHUT THE FUCK UP. YOU KNOW JACE LIVES HIS LIFE BY THAT PLEDGE AND YOU ARE A DICKHEAD FOR NOT TAKING THAT INTO CONSIDERATION EARLIER.
YOU: GROW THE FUCK UP. YOU'RE TWENTY-THREE YEARS OLD. ACT IT.
POW
OOF
BRAD'S A BIG BOY AND IF HE WANTS TO GO TO RETARD SCHOOL AND LEARN ACCOUNTING OR AUTO REPAIR OR HOW TO BE A MALE NURSE OR WHATEVER--
--IT'S HIS LIFE.
WHEEZE
ALSO: NOT ONE FUCKING WORD ABOUT ME AND MY WRITING. FUCK YOU. MY LIFE. NOT YOURS.
DOOM

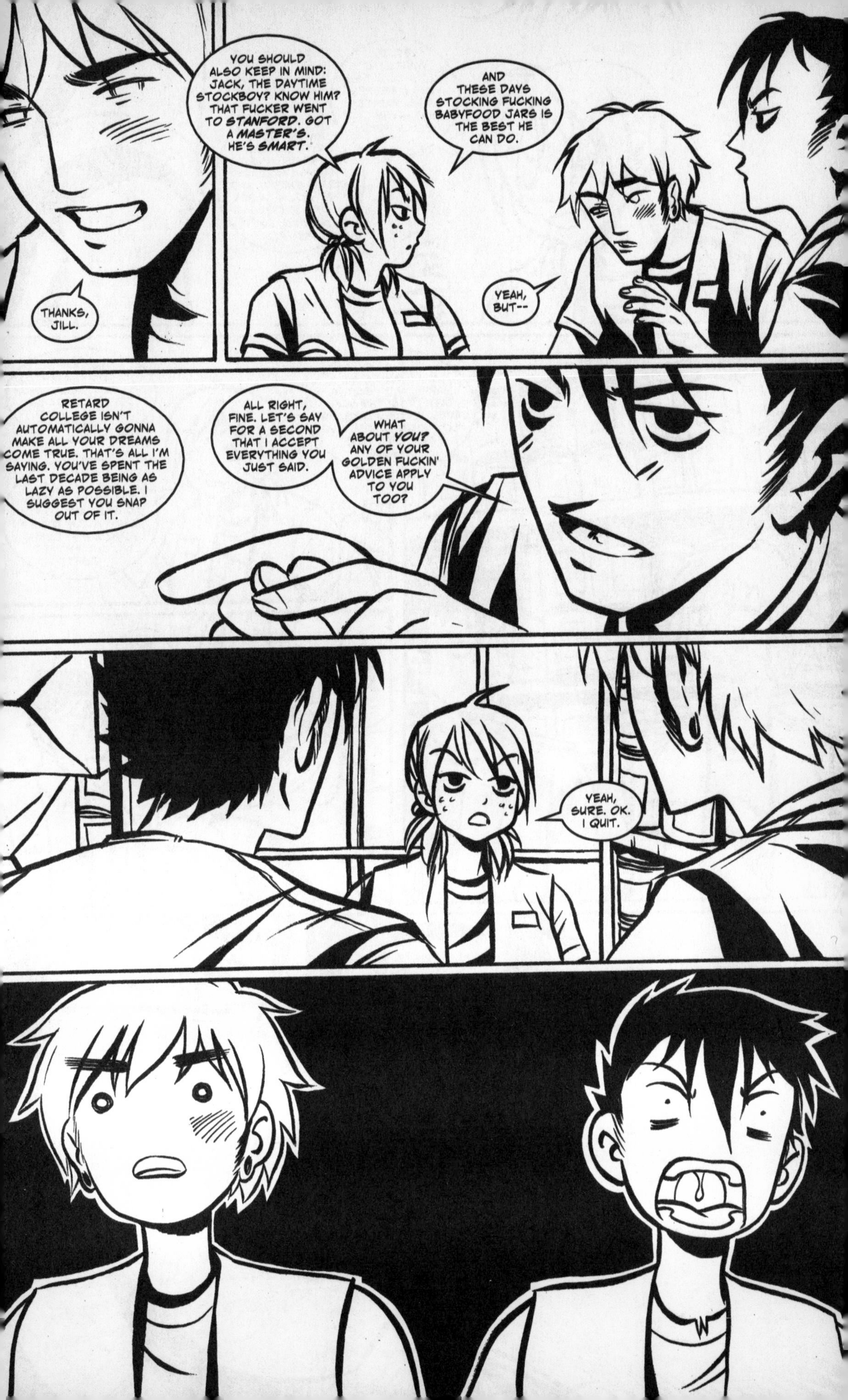
YOU SHOULD ALSO KEEP IN MIND: JACK, THE DAYTIME STOCKBOY? KNOW HIM? THAT FUCKER WENT TO STANFORD. GOT A MASTER'S. HE'S SMART.
AND THESE DAYS STOCKING FUCKING BABYFOOD JARS IS THE BEST HE CAN DO.
THANKS, JILL.
YEAH, BUT--
RETARD COLLEGE ISN'T AUTOMATICALLY GONNA MAKE ALL YOUR DREAMS COME TRUE. THAT'S ALL I'M SAYING. YOU'VE SPENT THE LAST DECADE BEING AS LAZY AS POSSIBLE. I SUGGEST YOU SNAP OUT OF IT.
ALL RIGHT, FINE. LET'S SAY FOR A SECOND THAT I ACCEPT EVERYTHING YOU JUST SAID.
WHAT ABOUT YOU? ANY OF YOUR GOLDEN FUCKIN' ADVICE APPLY TO YOU TOO?
YEAH, SURE. OK. I QUIT.

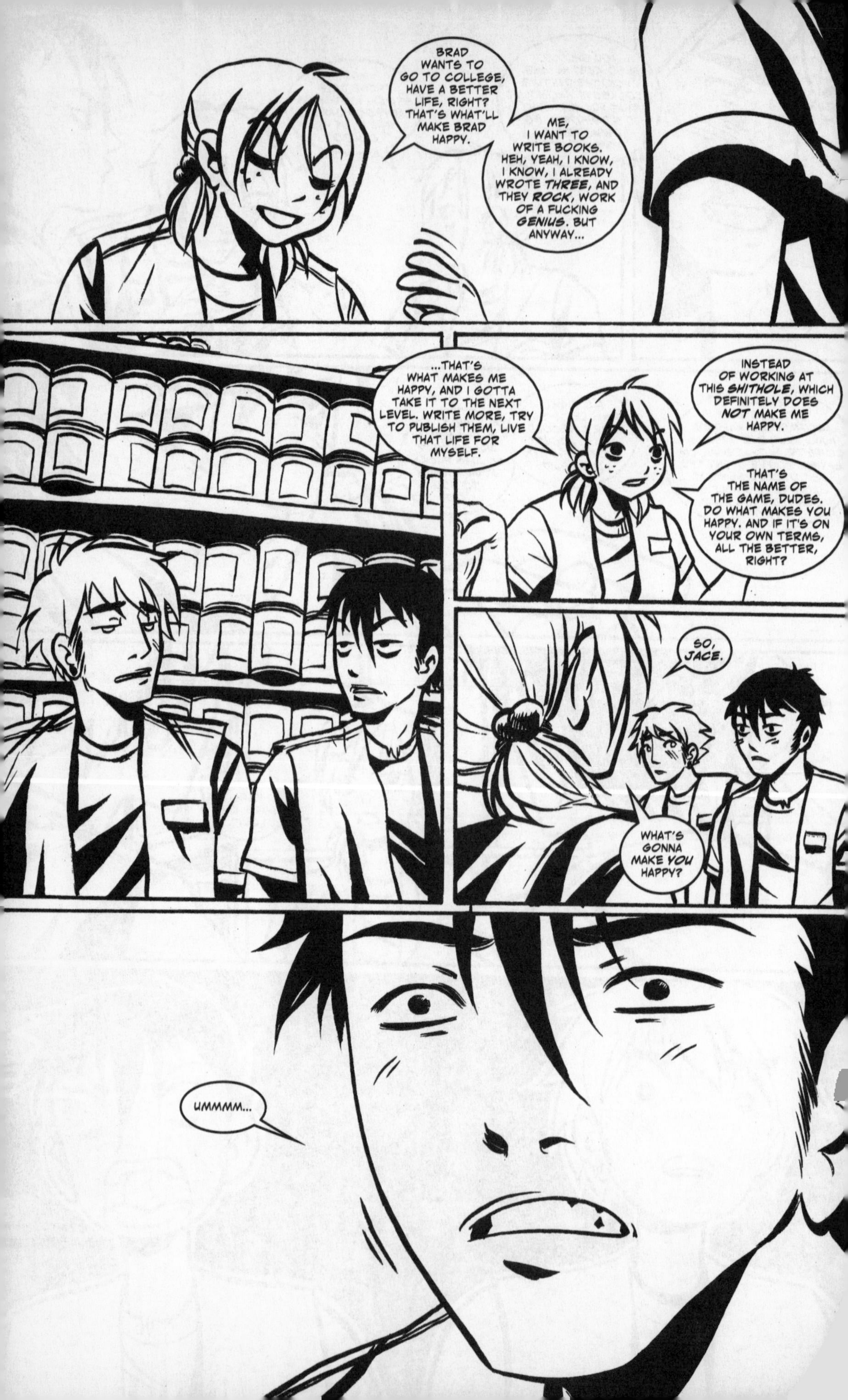
BRAD WANTS TO GO TO COLLEGE, HAVE A BETTER LIFE, RIGHT? THAT'S WHAT'LL MAKE BRAD HAPPY.
ME, I WANT TO WRITE BOOKS. HEH, YEAH, I KNOW, I KNOW, I ALREADY WROTE THREE, AND THEY ROCK, WORK OF A FUCKING GENIUS. BUT ANYWAY...
...THAT'S WHAT MAKES ME HAPPY, AND I GOTTA TAKE IT TO THE NEXT LEVEL. WRITE MORE, TRY TO PUBLISH THEM, LIVE THAT LIFE FOR MYSELF.
INSTEAD OF WORKING AT THIS SHITHOLE, WHICH DEFINITELY DOES NOT MAKE ME HAPPY.
THAT'S THE NAME OF THE GAME, DUDES. DO WHAT MAKES YOU HAPPY. AND IF IT'S ON YOUR OWN TERMS, ALL THE BETTER, RIGHT?
SO, JACE.
WHAT'S GONNA MAKE YOU HAPPY?
UMMMM...

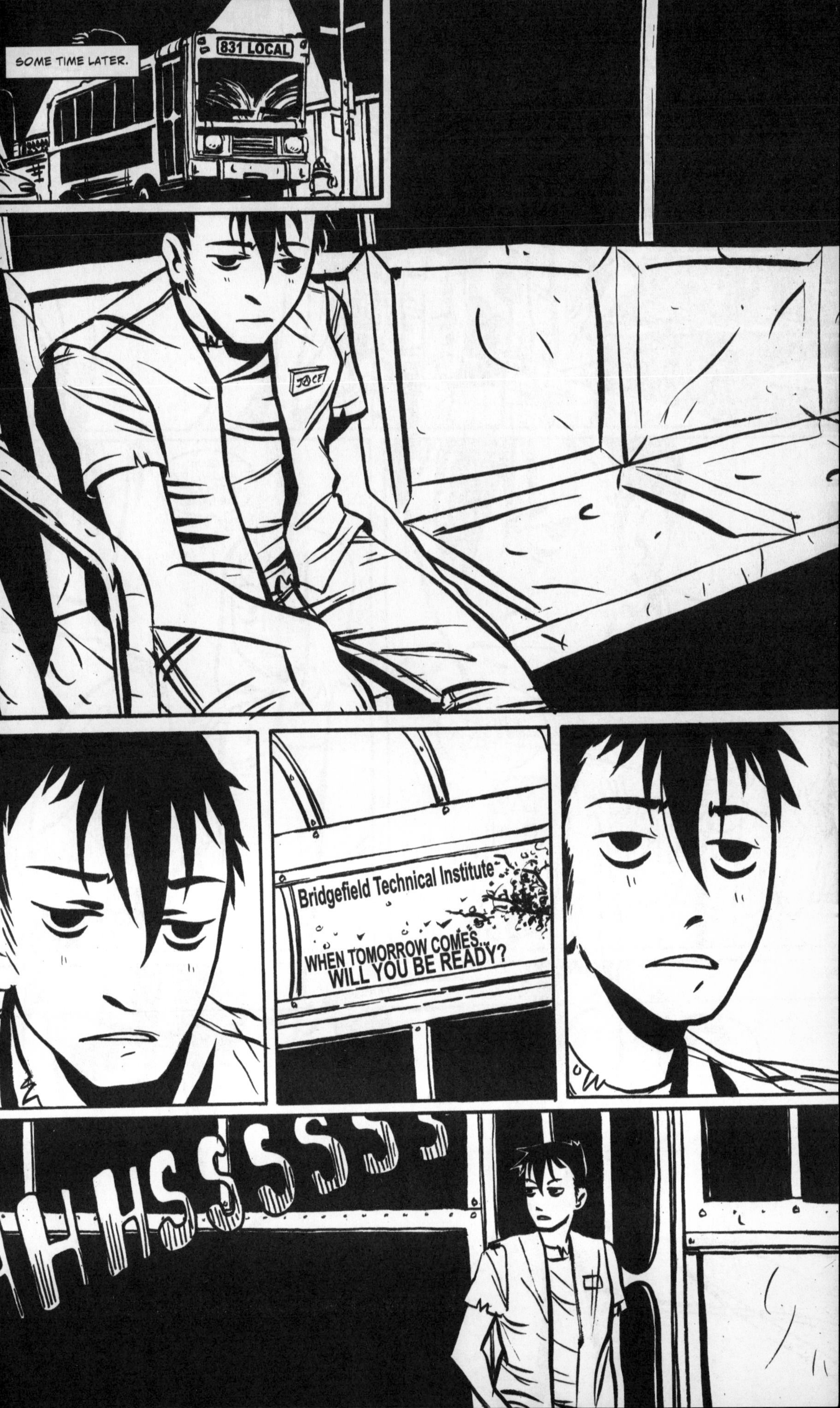
SOME TIME LATER.
831 LOCAL
JACE
Bridgefield Technical Institute
WHEN TOMORROW COMES...
WILL YOU BE READY?
HHSSSSSSS

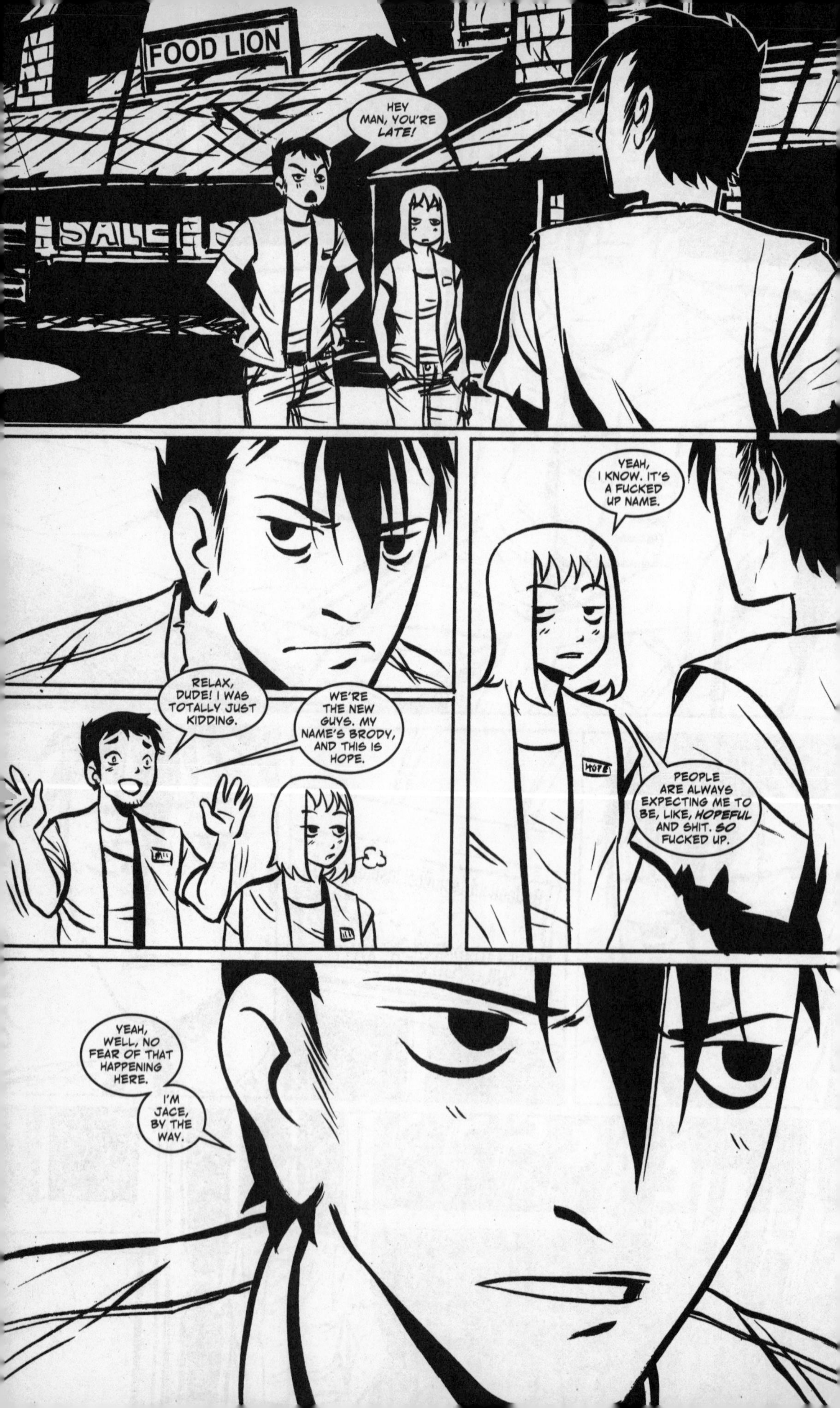
FOOD LION
SALE
HEY MAN, YOU'RE LATE!
YEAH, I KNOW. IT'S A FUCKED UP NAME.
RELAX, DUDE! I WAS TOTALLY JUST KIDDING.
WE'RE THE NEW GUYS. MY NAME'S BRODY, AND THIS IS HOPE.
HOPE
PEOPLE ARE ALWAYS EXPECTING ME TO BE, LIKE, HOPEFUL AND SHIT. SO FUCKED UP.
YEAH, WELL, NO FEAR OF THAT HAPPENING HERE.
I'M JACE, BY THE WAY.

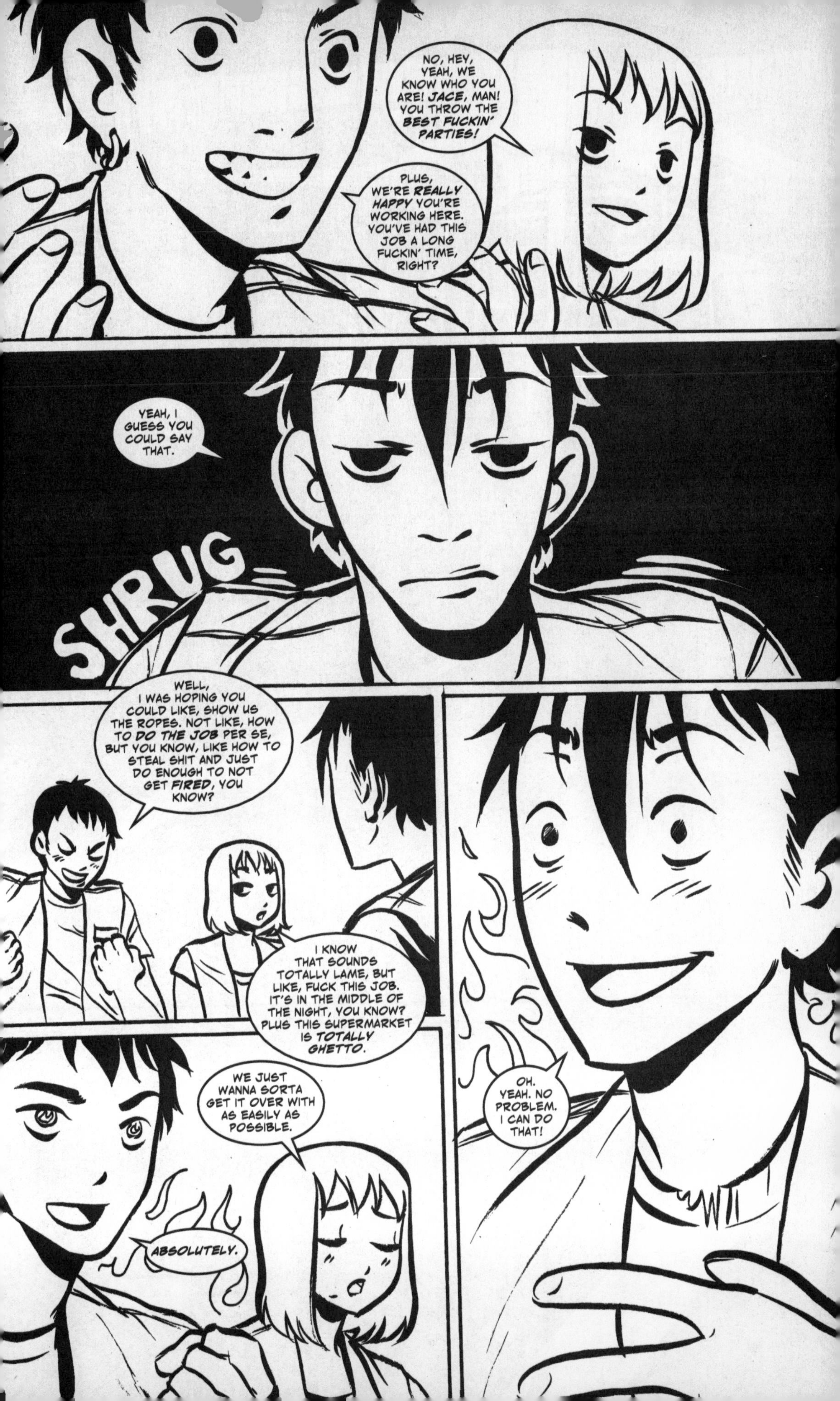
NO, HEY, YEAH, WE KNOW WHO YOU ARE! JACE, MAN! YOU THROW THE BEST FUCKIN' PARTIES!
PLUS, WE'RE REALLY HAPPY YOU'RE WORKING HERE. YOU'VE HAD THIS JOB A LONG FUCKIN' TIME, RIGHT?
YEAH, I GUESS YOU COULD SAY THAT.
SHRUG
WELL, I WAS HOPING YOU COULD LIKE, SHOW US THE ROPES. NOT LIKE, HOW TO DO THE JOB PER SE, BUT YOU KNOW, LIKE HOW TO STEAL SHIT AND JUST DO ENOUGH TO NOT GET FIRED, YOU KNOW?
I KNOW THAT SOUNDS TOTALLY LAME, BUT LIKE, FUCK THIS JOB. IT'S IN THE MIDDLE OF THE NIGHT, YOU KNOW? PLUS THIS SUPERMARKET IS TOTALLY GHETTO.
WE JUST WANNA SORTA GET IT OVER WITH AS EASILY AS POSSIBLE.
ABSOLUTELY.
OH. YEAH. NO PROBLEM. I CAN DO THAT!

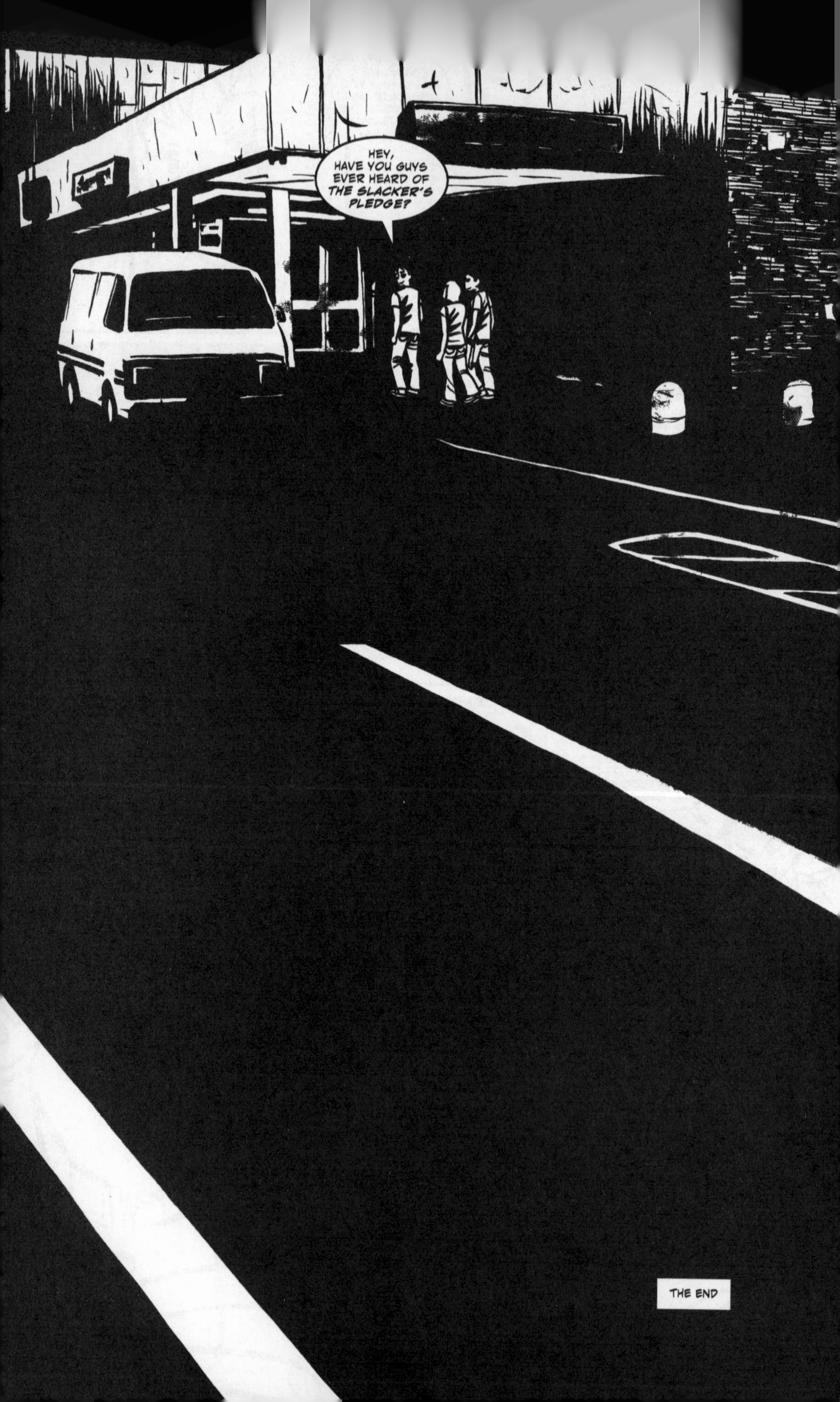
HEY,
HAVE YOU GUYS
EVER HEARD OF
THE SLACKER'S
PLEDGE?
THE END

12

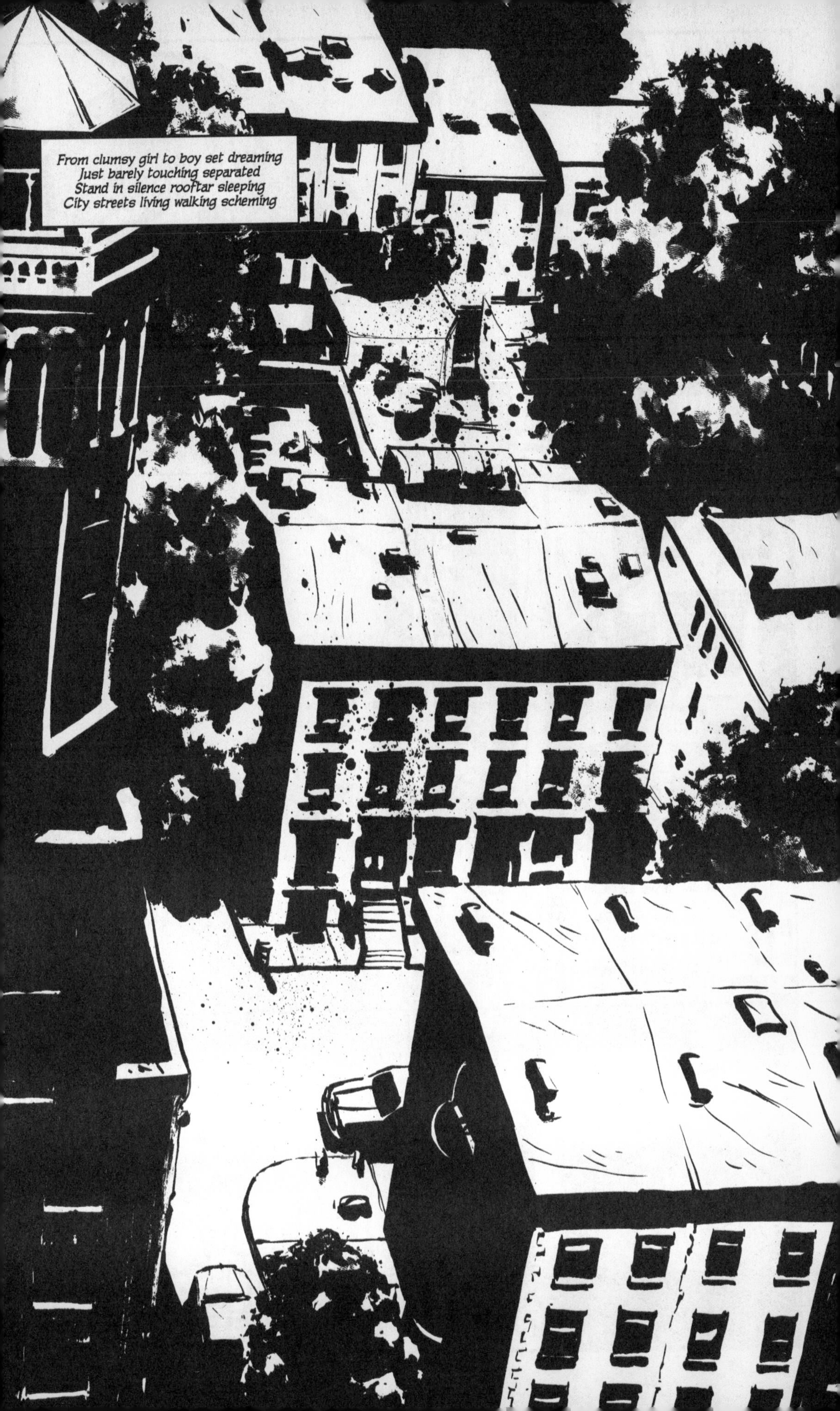
From clumsy girl to boy set dreaming
Just barely touching separated
Stand in silence rooftar sleeping
City streets living walking scheming

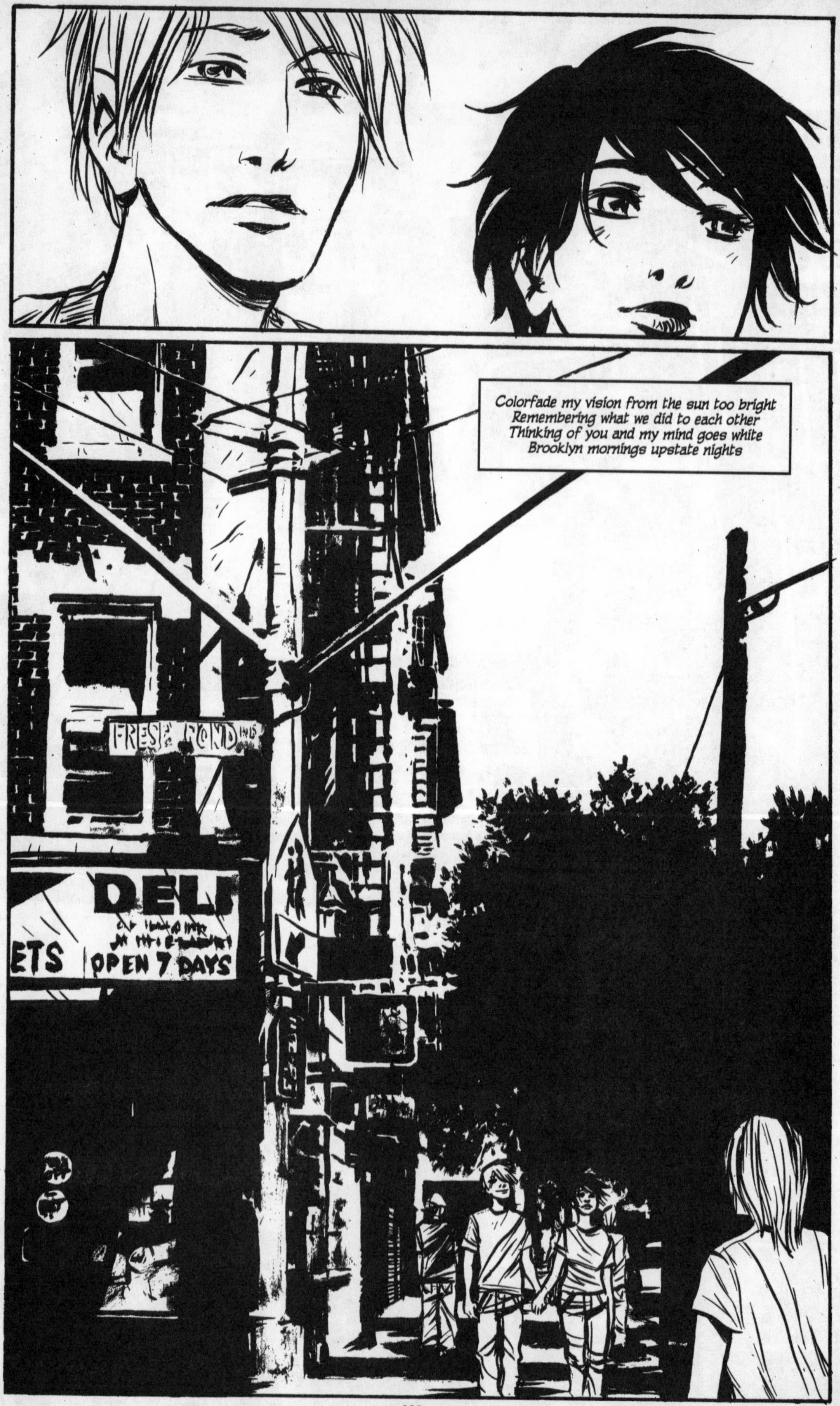
Colorfade my vision from the sun too bright
Remembering what we did to each other
Thinking of you and my mind goes white
Brooklyn mornings upstate nights
ETS
OPEN 7 DAYS

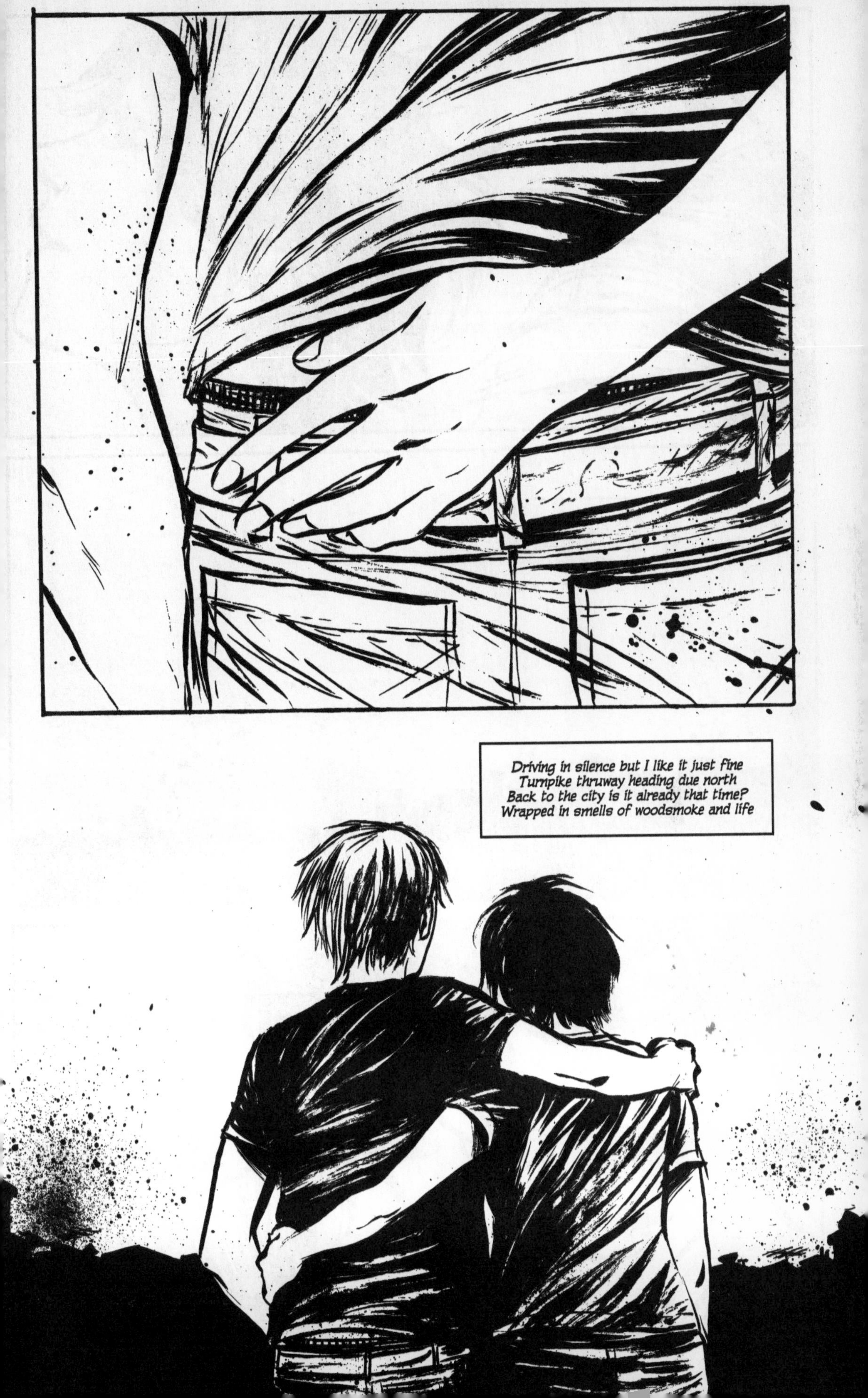
Driving in silence but I like it just fine
Turnpike thruway heading due north
Back to the city is it already that time?
Wrapped in smells of woodsmoke and life

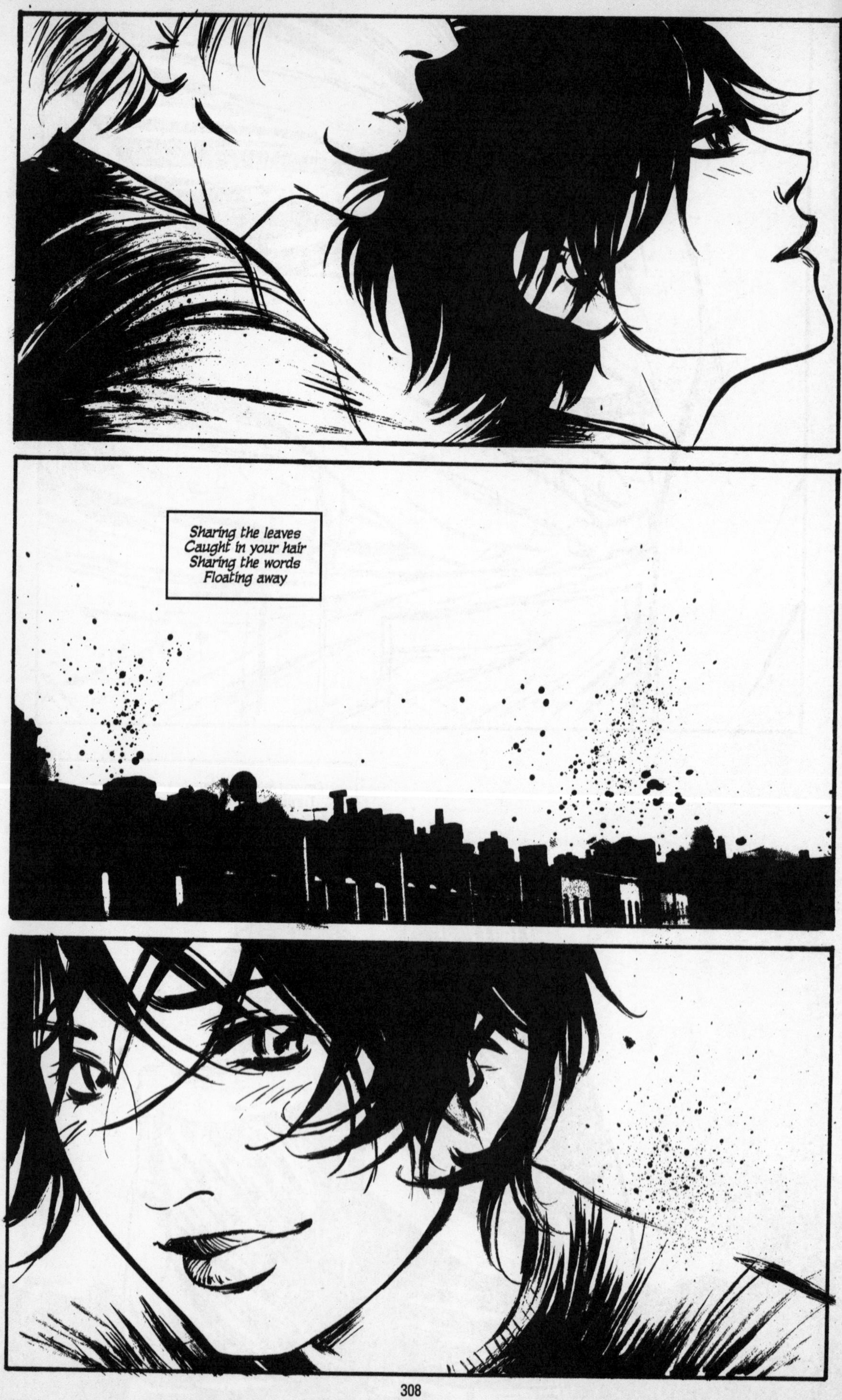
Sharing the leaves
Caught in your hair
Sharing the words
Floating away

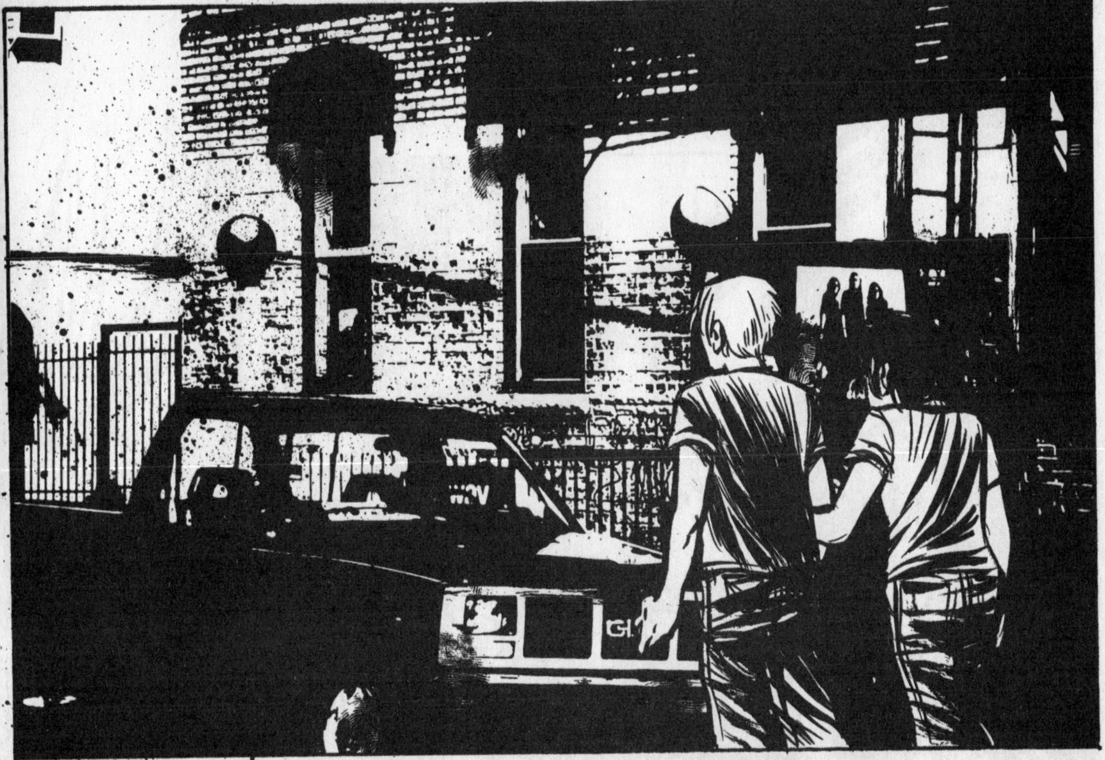

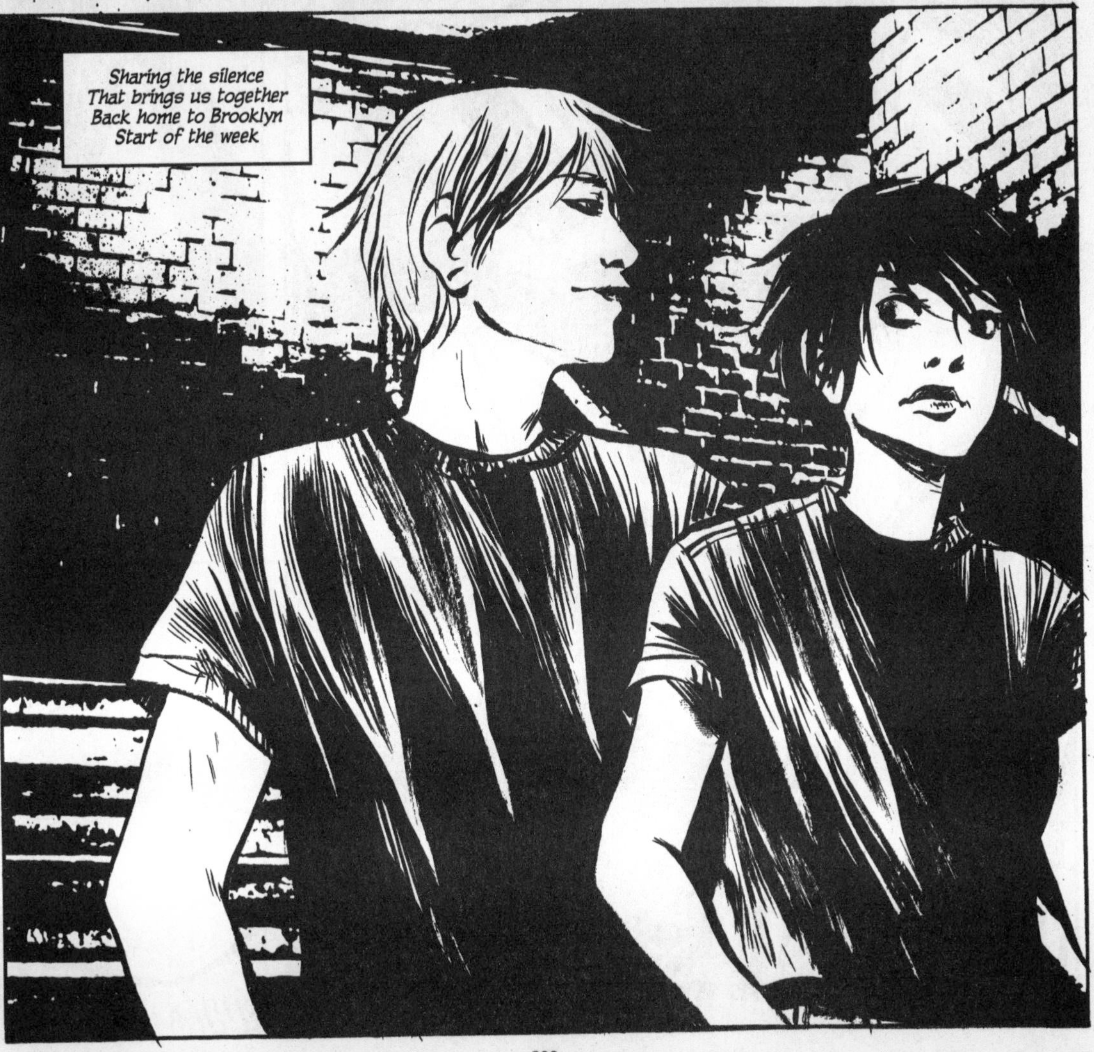
Sharing the silence
That brings us together
Back home to Brooklyn
Start of the week

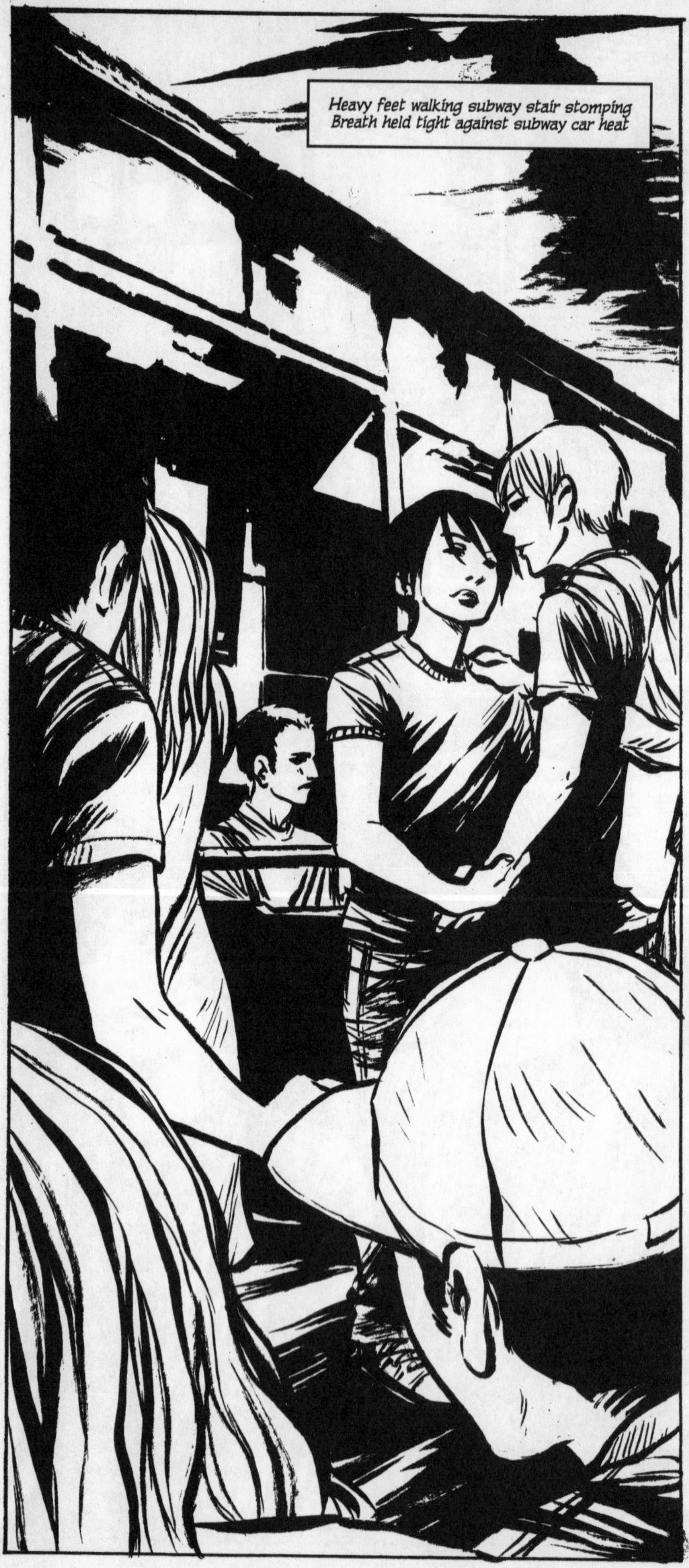
Heavy feet walking subway stair stomping
Breath held tight against subway car heat

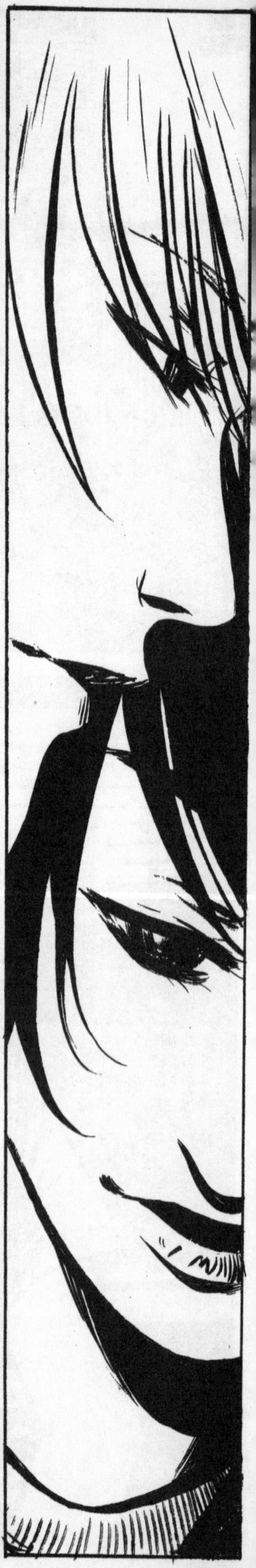

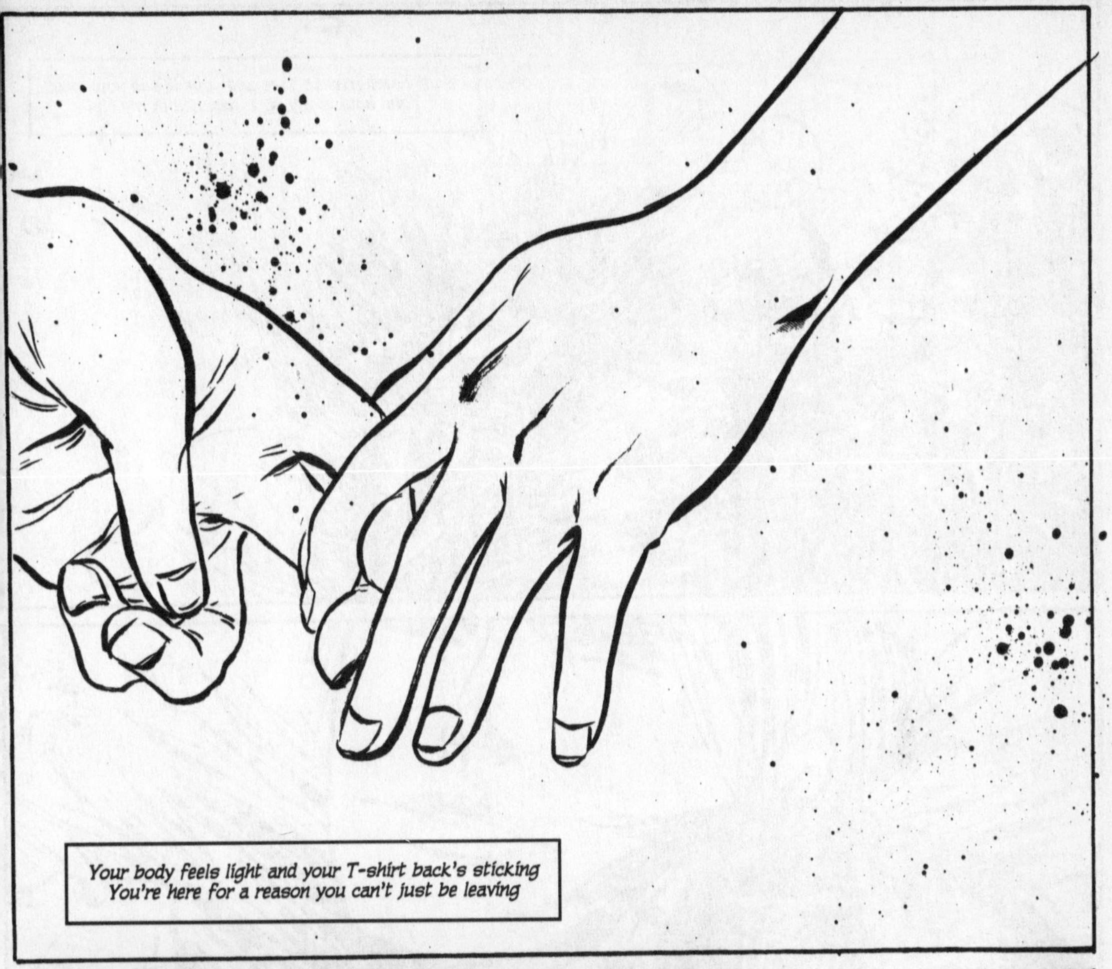
Your body feels light and your T-shirt back's sticking
You're here for a reason you can't just be leaving

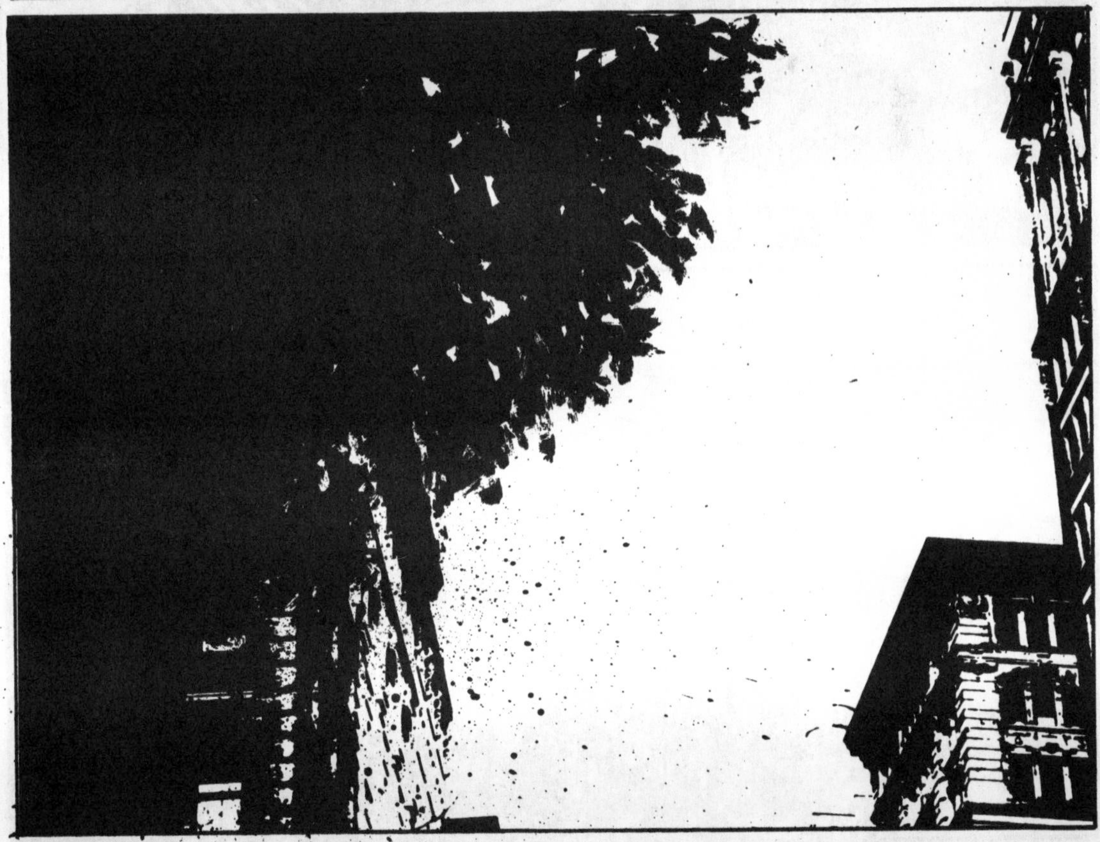

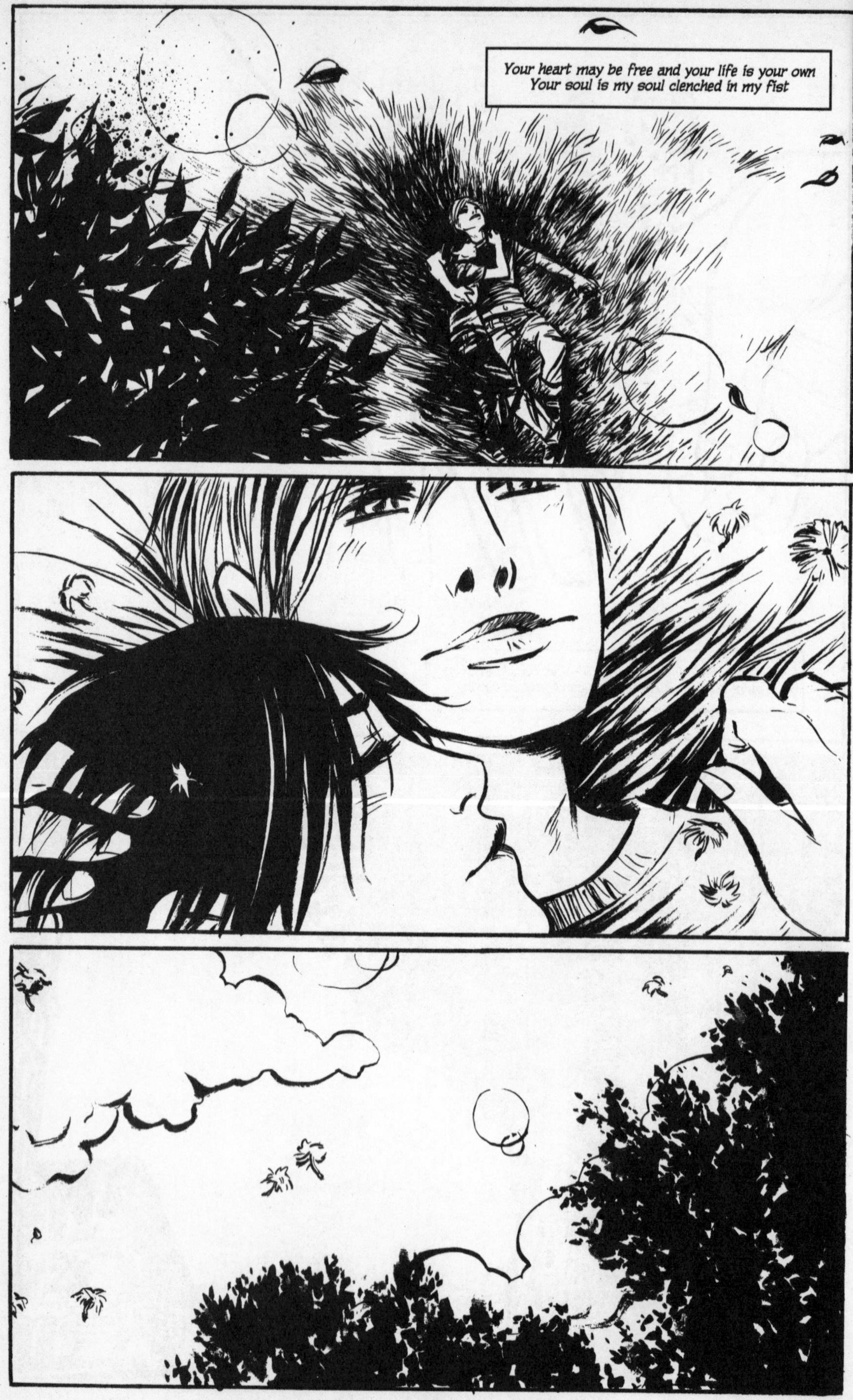
Your heart may be free and your life is your own
Your soul is my soul clenched in my fist

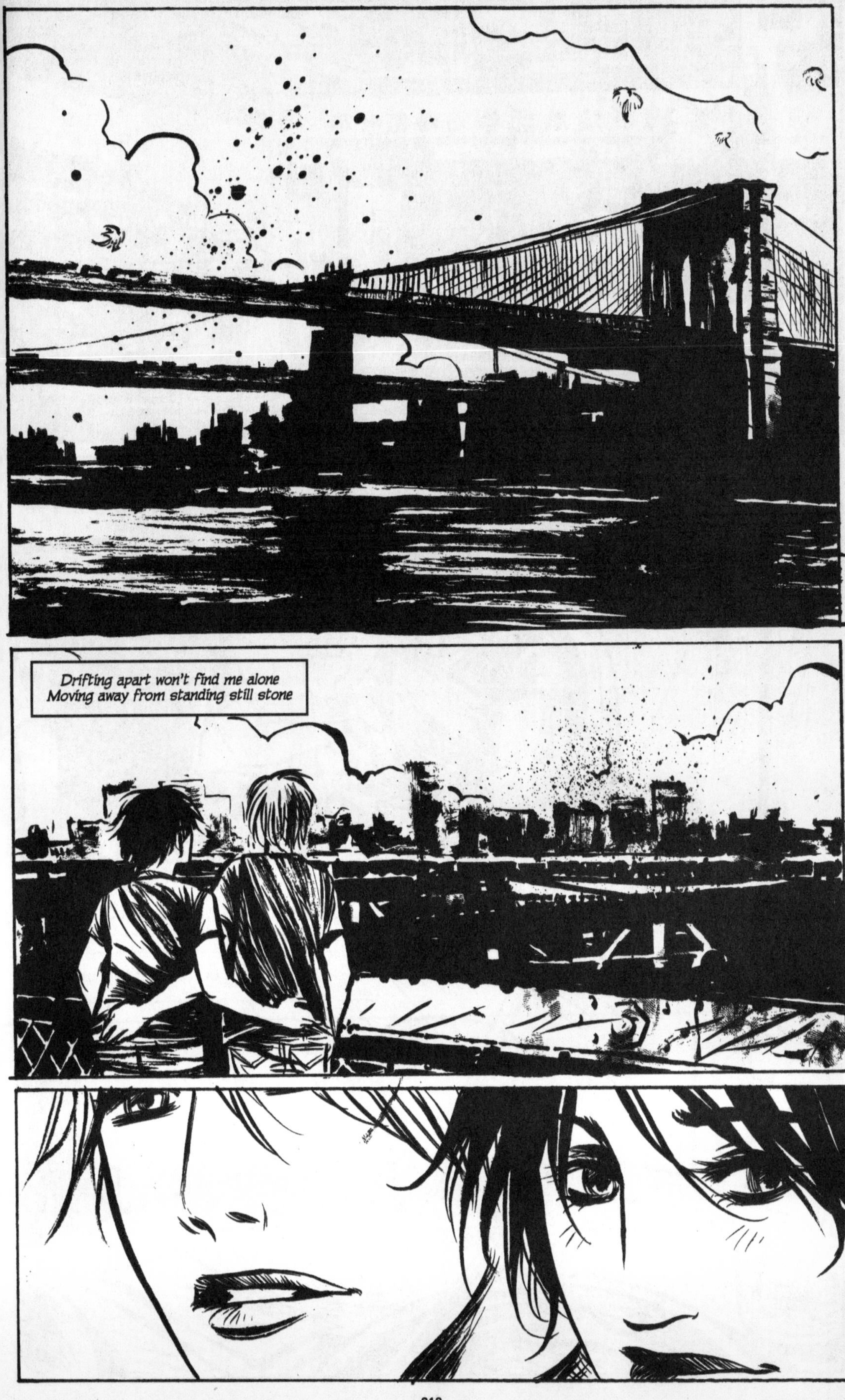
Drifting apart won't find me alone
Moving away from standing still stone

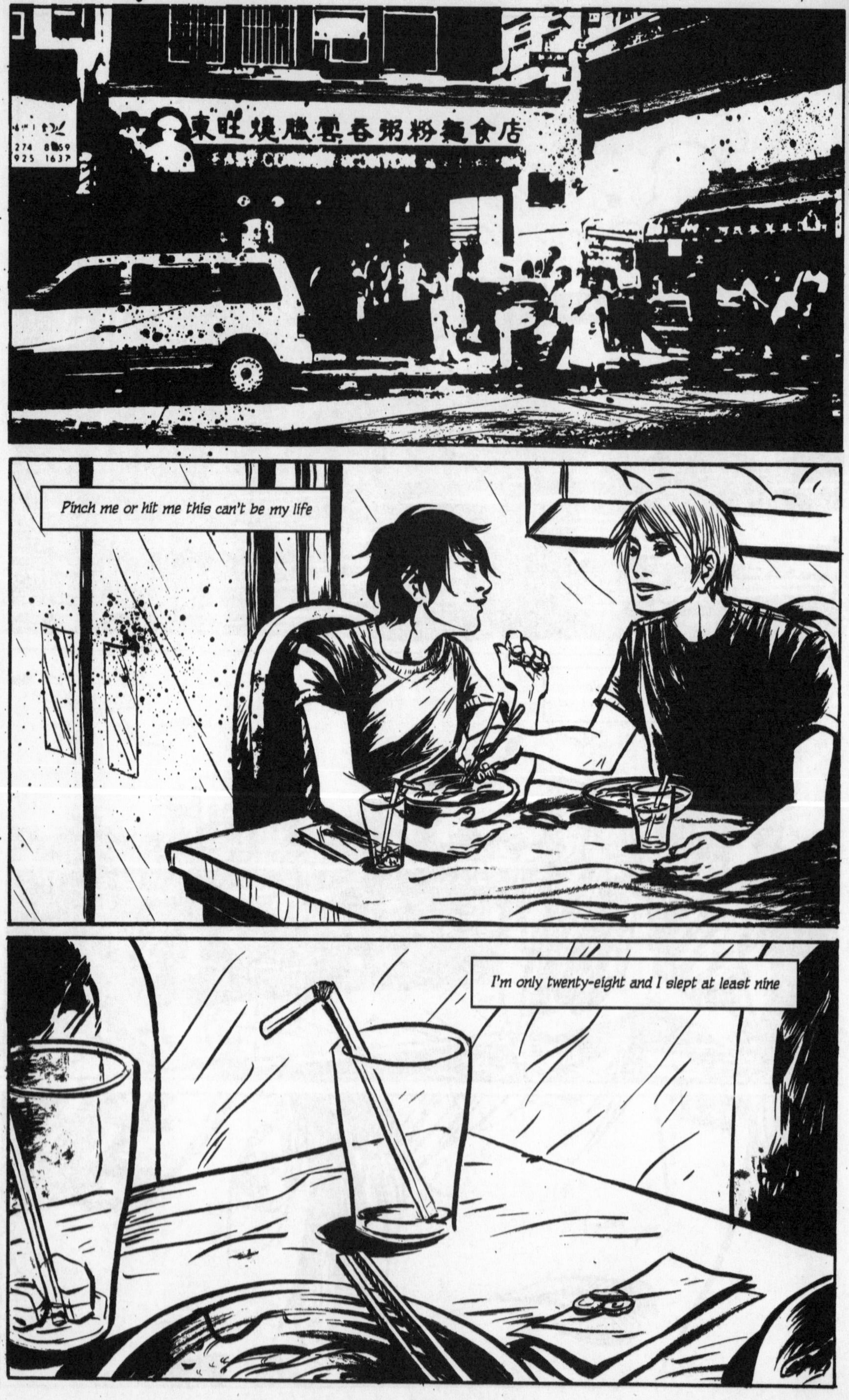
東旺燒臘雲吞粥粉麵食店
Pinch me or hit me this can't be my life
I'm only twenty-eight and I slept at least nine

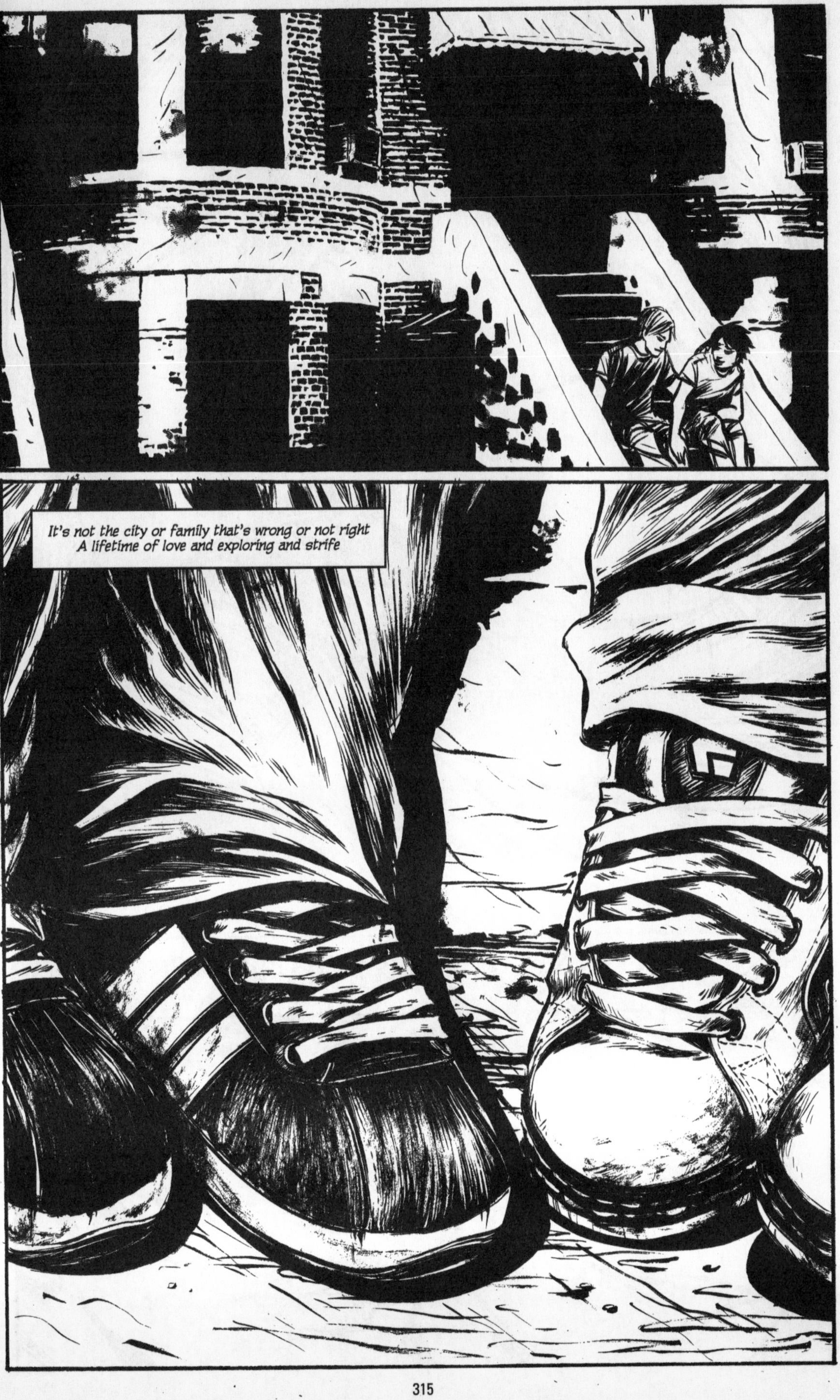
It's not the city or family that's wrong or not right
A lifetime of love and exploring and strife

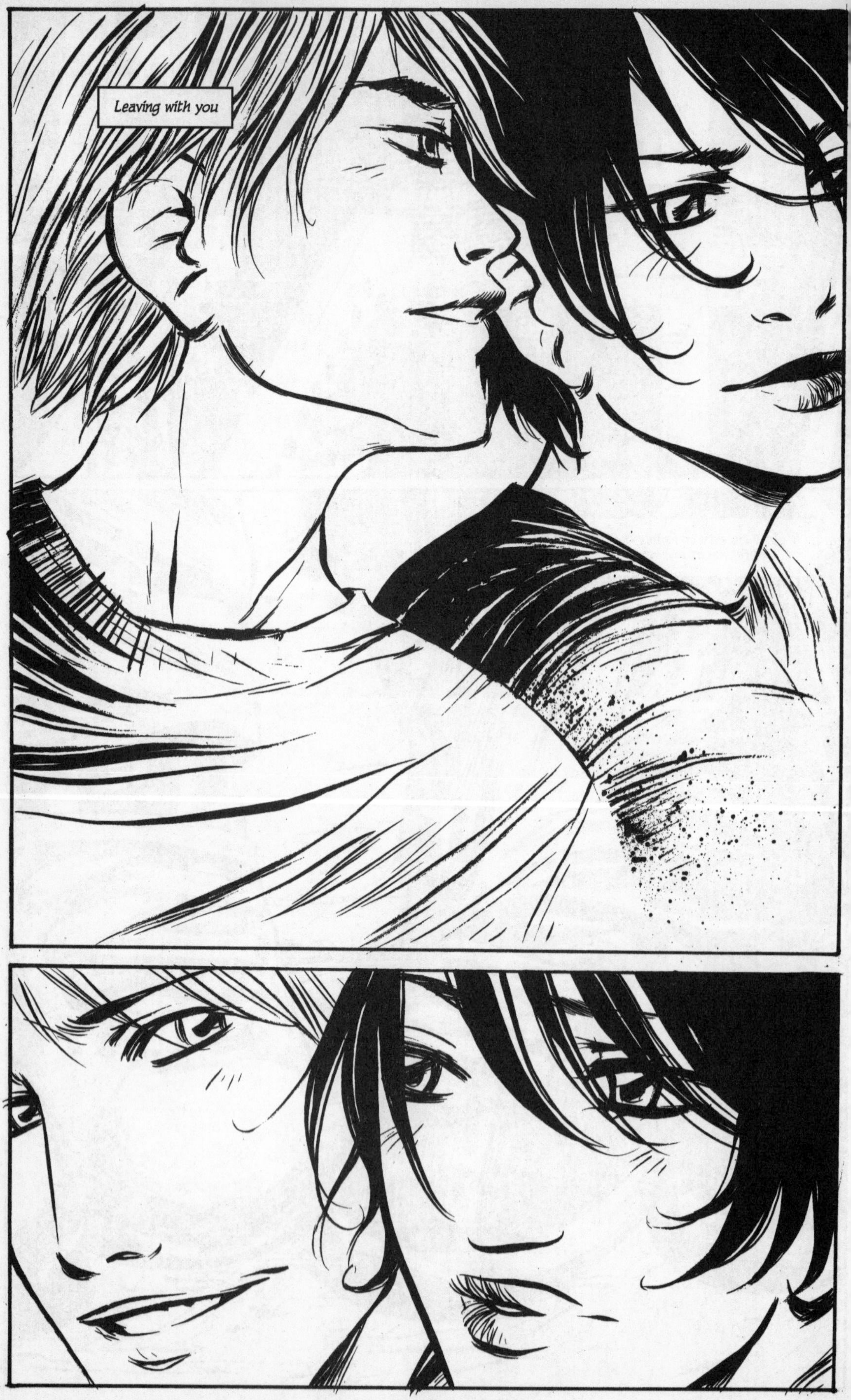
Leaving with you

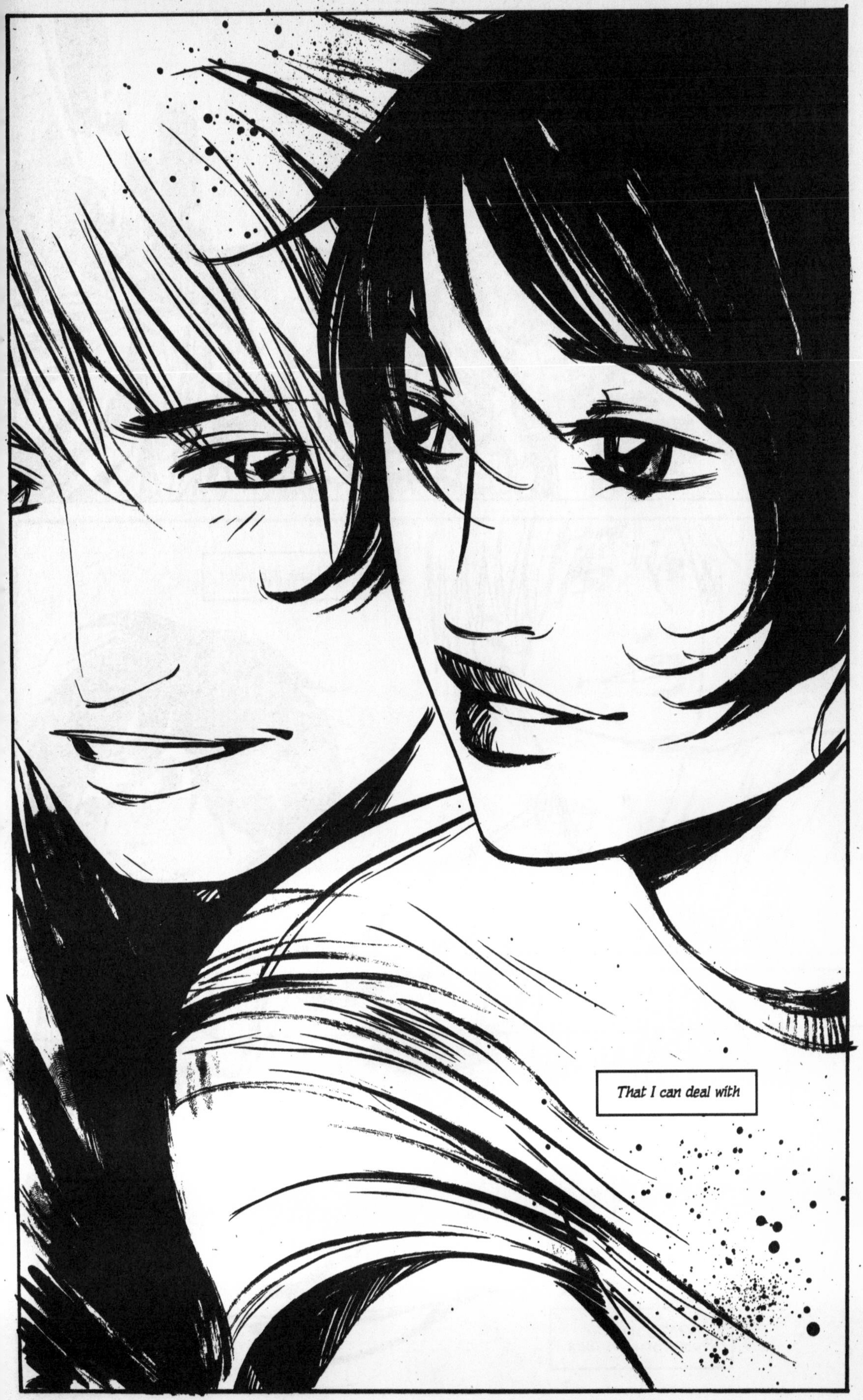
That I can deal with

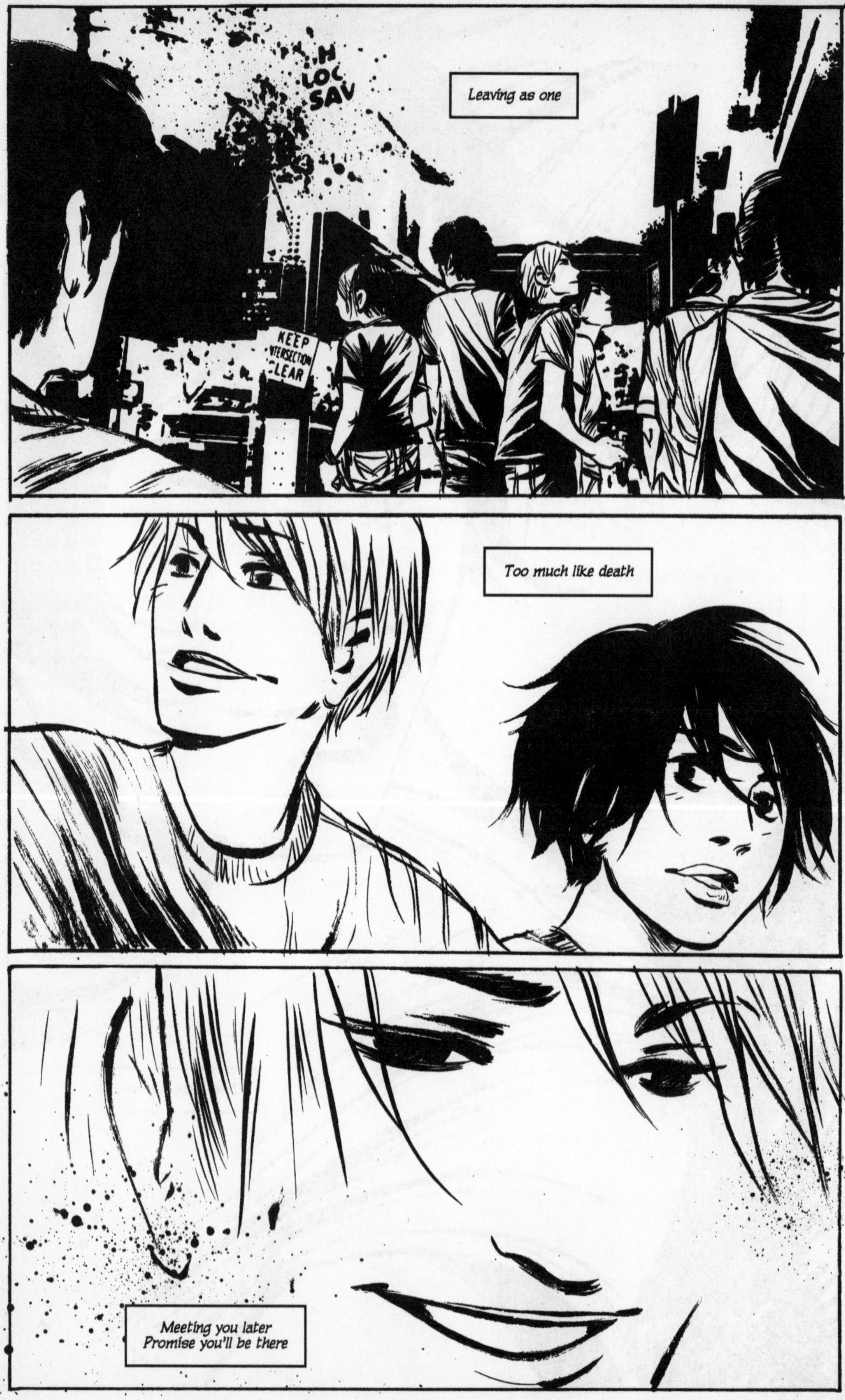
Leaving as one
KEEP
Too much like death
Meeting you later
Promise you'll be there

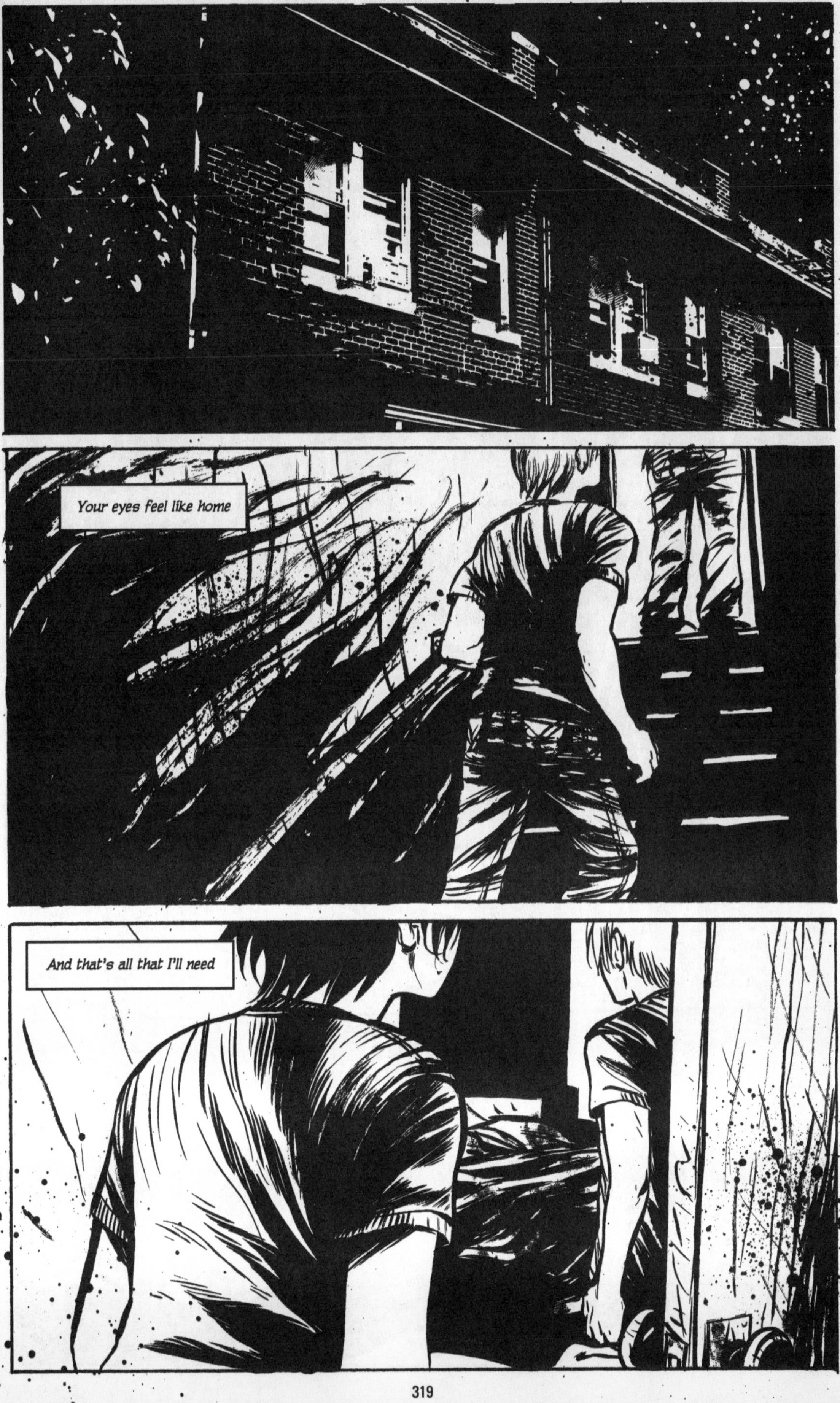
Your eyes feel like home
And that's all that I'll need

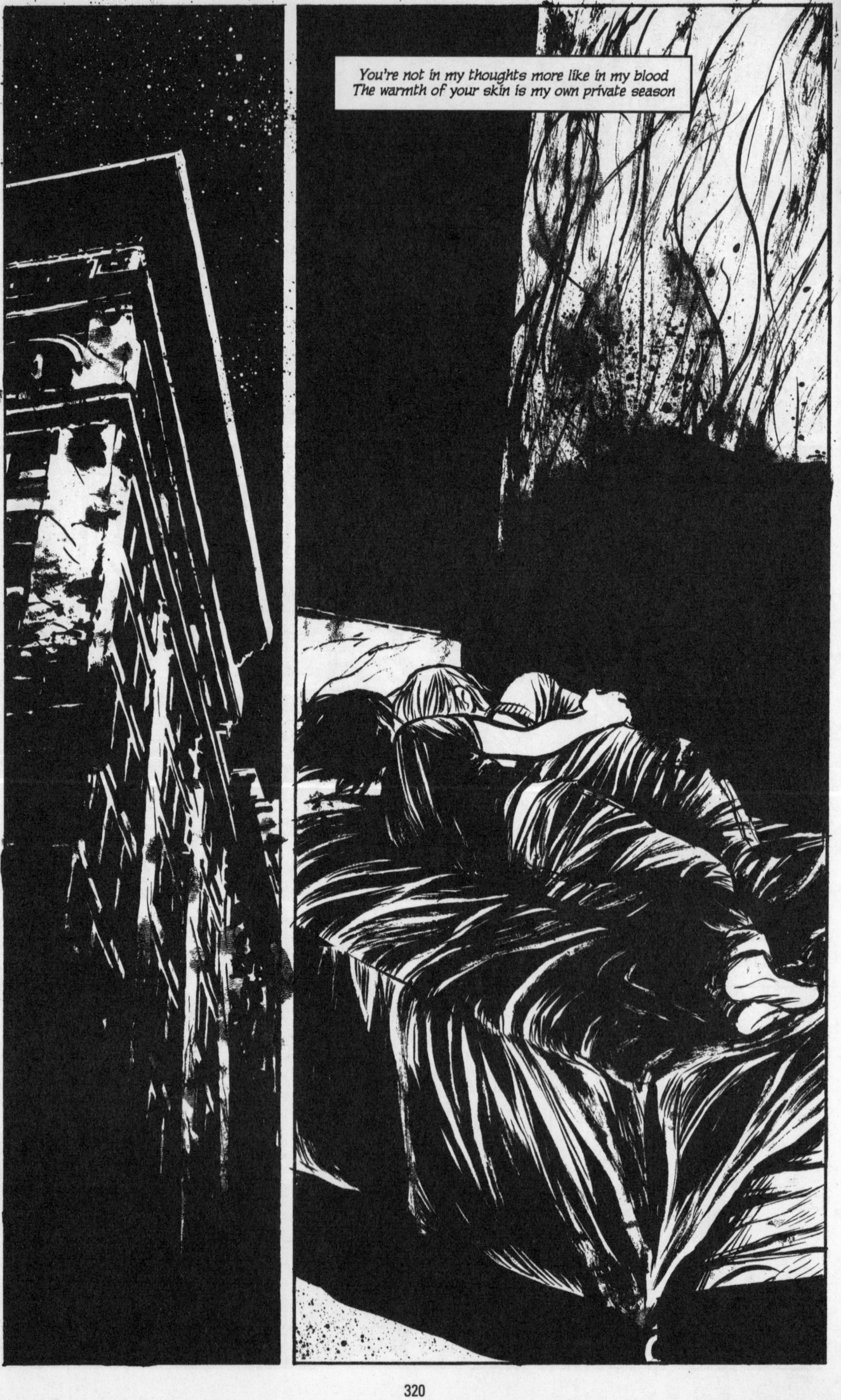
You're not in my thoughts more like in my blood
The warmth of your skin is my own private season

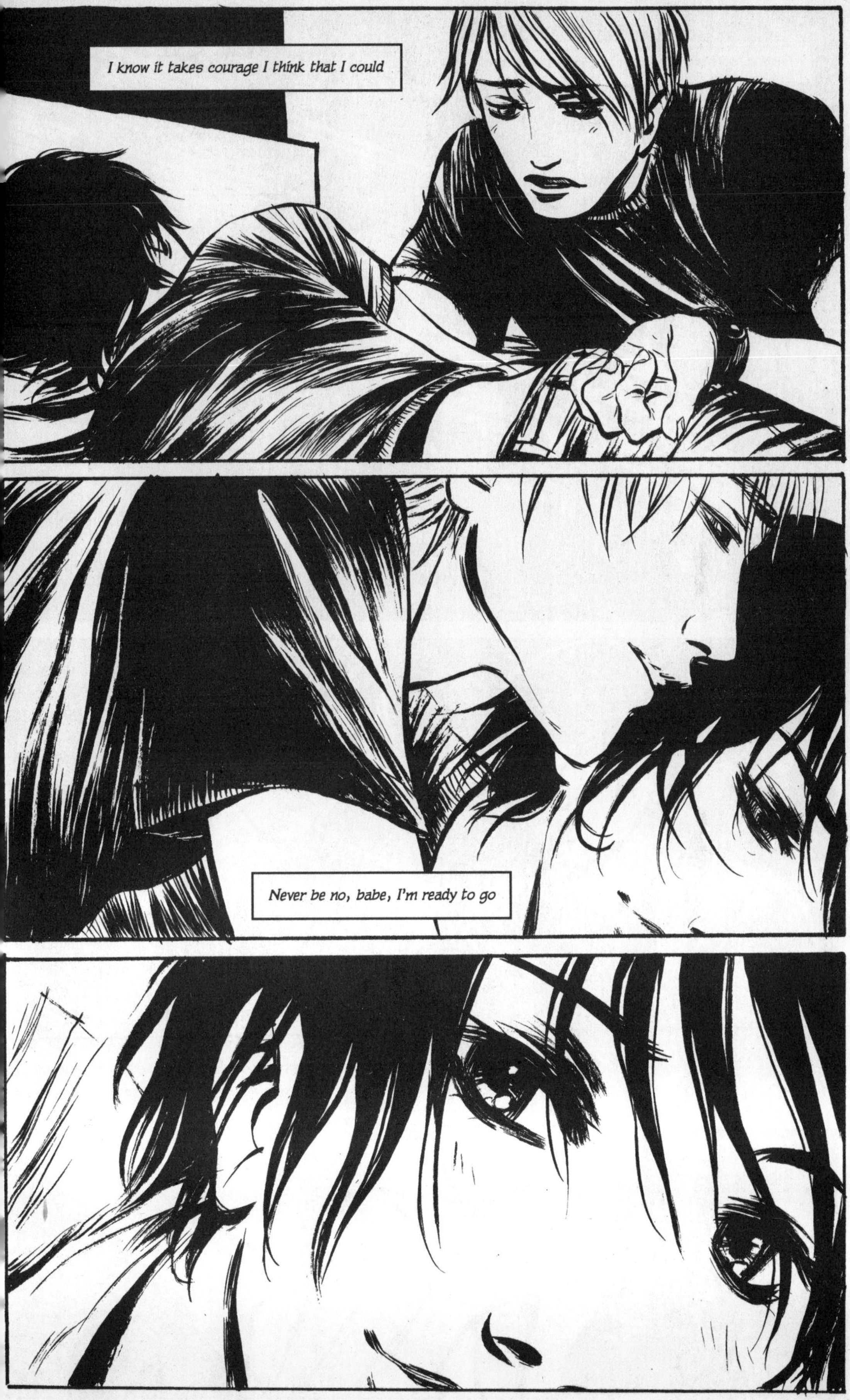
I know it takes courage I think that I could
Never be no, babe, I'm ready to go

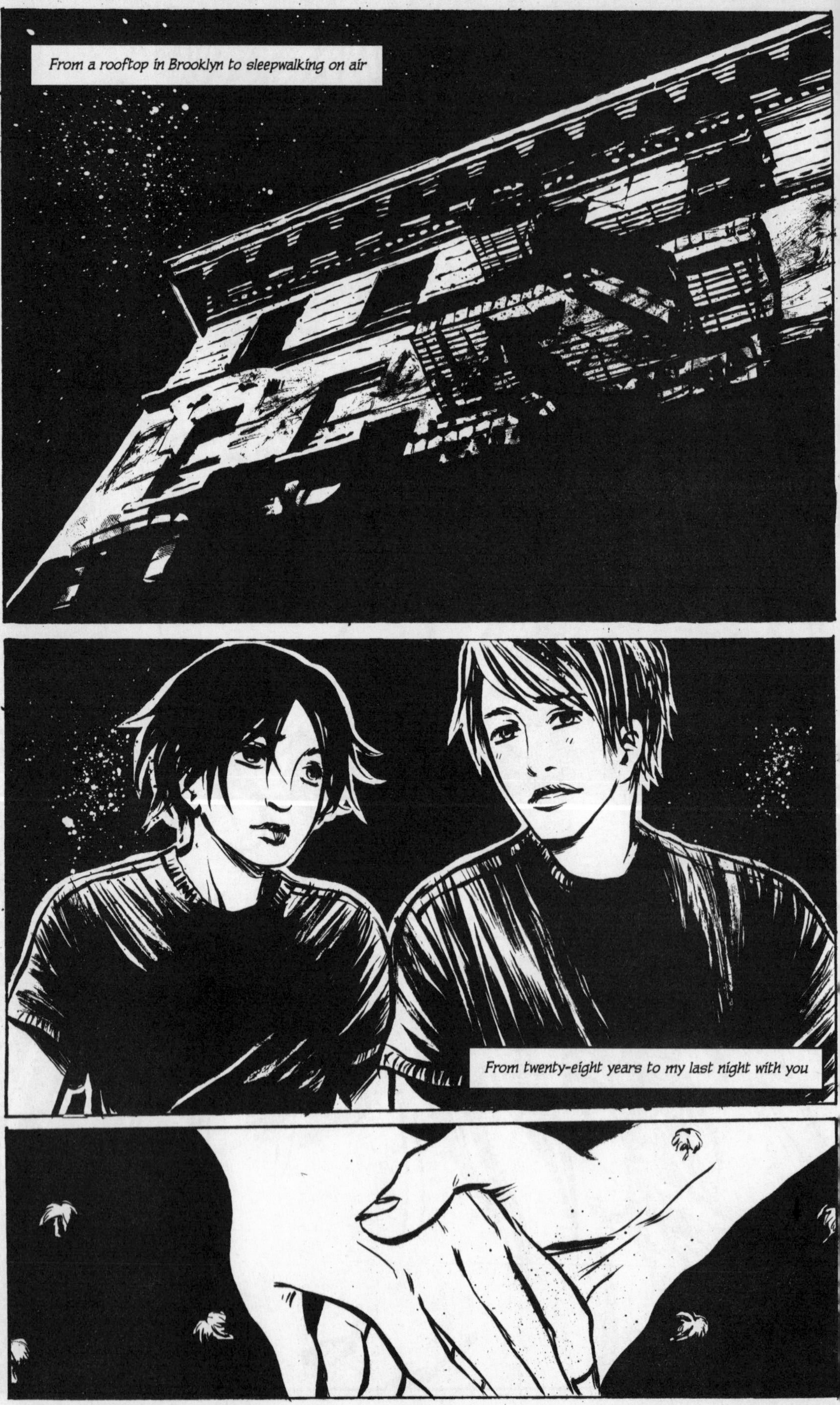
From a rooftop in Brooklyn to sleepwalking on air
From twenty-eight years to my last night with you

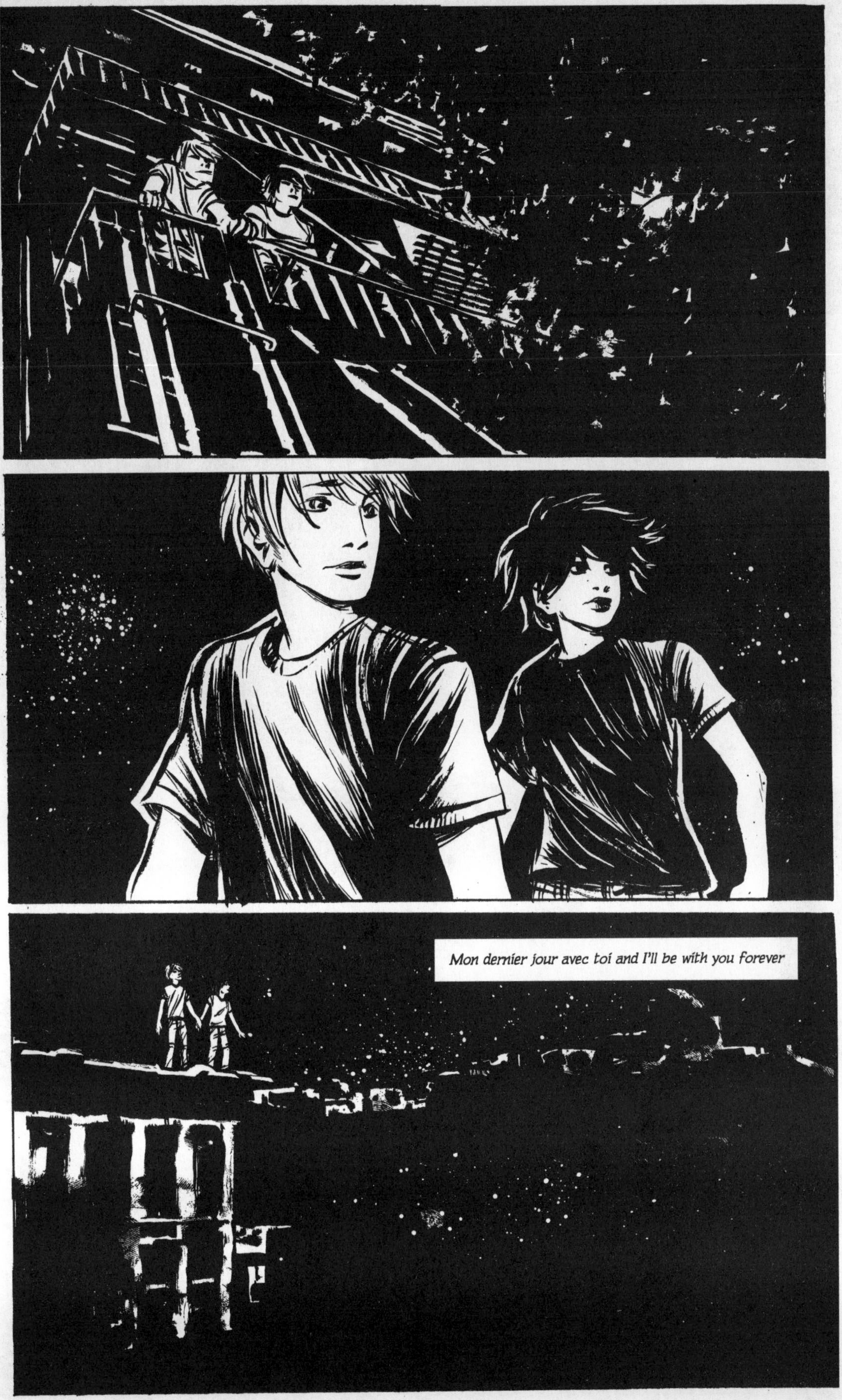
Mon dernier jour avec toi and I'll be with you forever

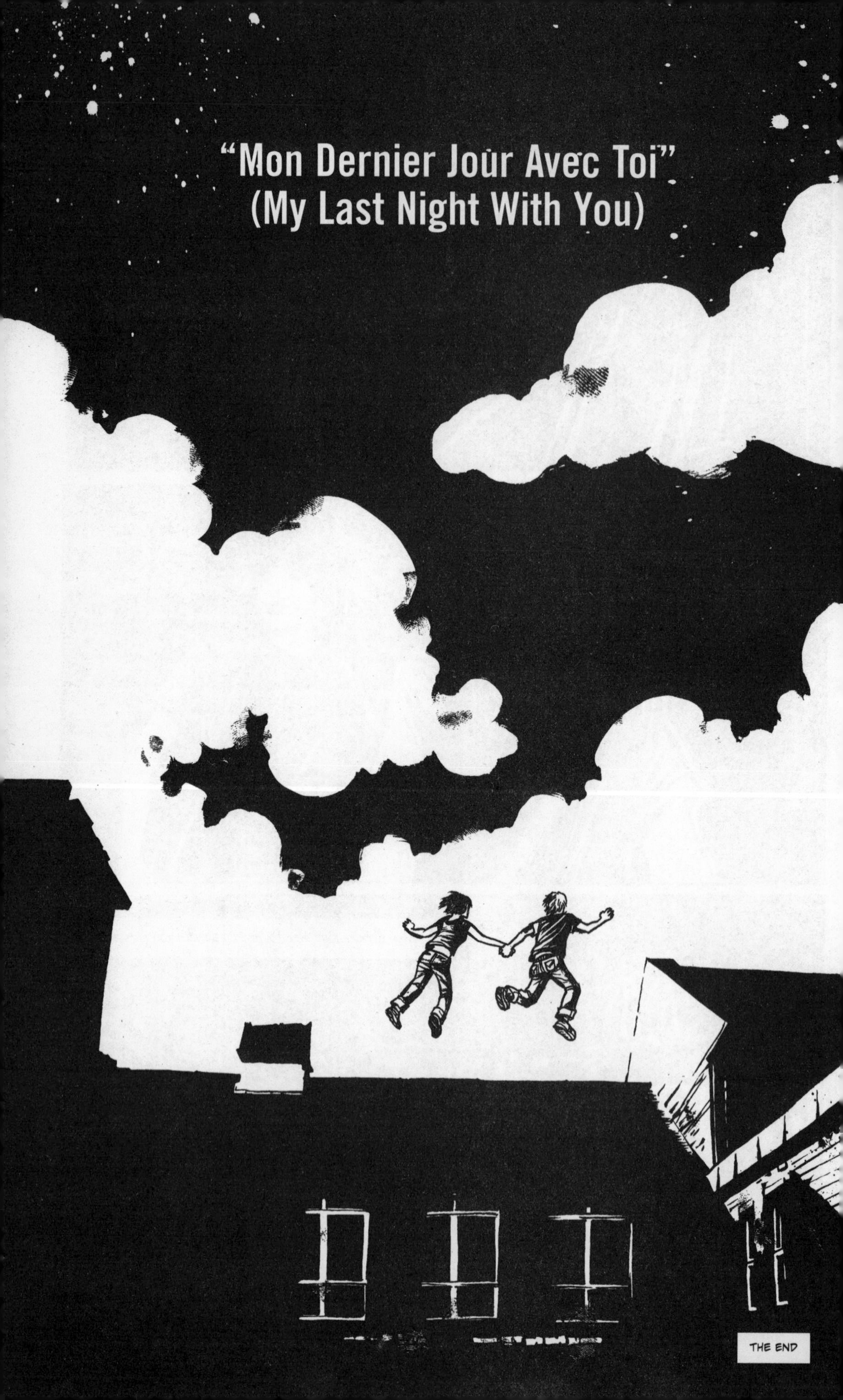
"Mon Dernier Jour Avec Toi"
(My Last Night With You)
THE END

I thought up DEMO back in 2002 in a car in upstate New York. I had spent some time a few years before writing teen superheroes for Marvel Comics, and I wanted to take a stab at something similar, but something I would have more control over, to interpret the concept of "young people with power" the way I wanted to. My first ideas weren't too far removed from standard comic book stereotypes, but as I sat down and began to write the scripts, the concept evolved. My definition of "superpowers" changed to more universal ideas about power and control, the characters grew up from rebellious teenagers to complex people in their twenties and thirties. Becky and I spent eighteen months with DEMO, ending the series with something completely different from when we started. This spontaneous creative evolution is one of my favorite things about DEMO.

The other would be Becky Cloonan's incredible range and versatility. She'll act nonchalant about it, but speaking as an illustrator myself, being able to switch styles as she did is a rare gift that few of us possess. I'll always feel honored to have her as a collaborator and a friend.

And even though DEMO was originally created as monthly serialized comics, collecting them into a single volume as short stories keeps them available for the long term, and if you're picking up DEMO for the first time, I hope you enjoy reading it as much as we did creating it.

Brian Wood

This book is a collection of 18 months of my life. It's so surreal; when I look back on each story I can remember exactly where I was and what I was feeling when I drew each page. I hope this collection brings back memories for everyone; the store that you bought a particular issue at, where you were when you read it, the people you lent your copies to and never got back...

I learned so much from working on this comic, and also from working with Brian. I learned things that stick with you, the kind of things that you will use for the rest of your life. I think of DEMO as a turning point, and I look back with fondness on every panel that I drew.

Becky Cloonan

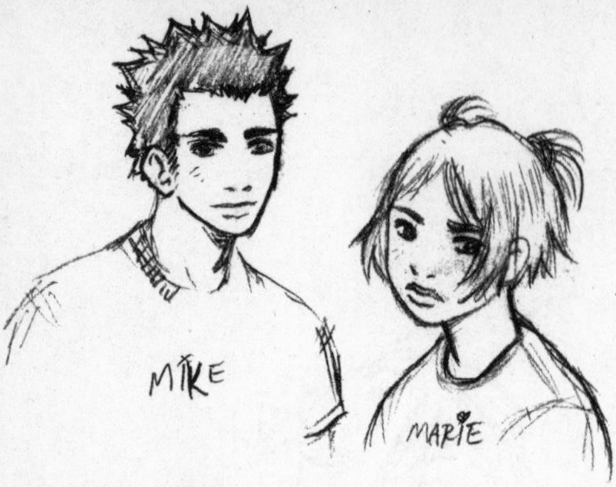
MIKE
MARIE

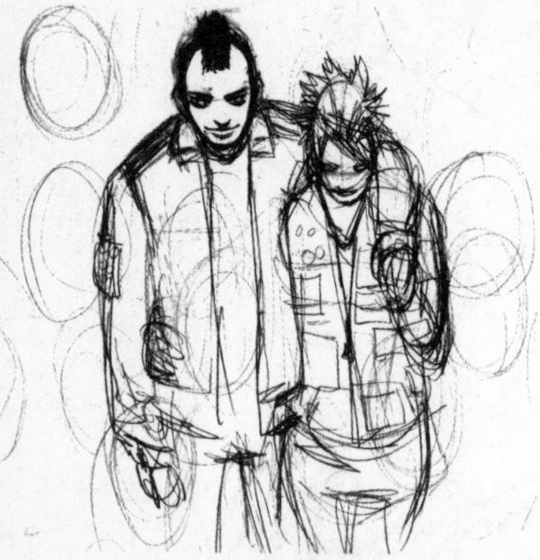

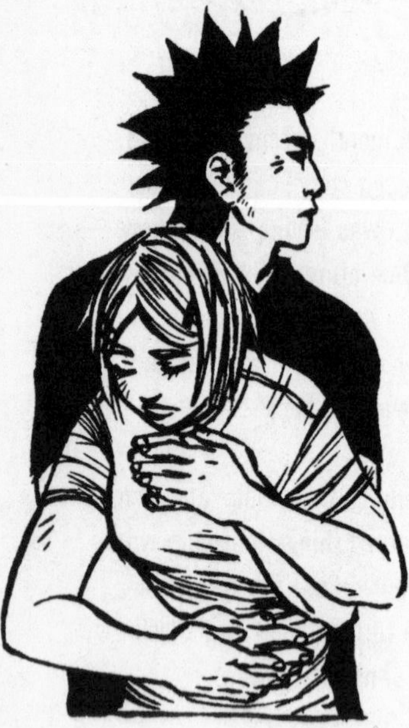

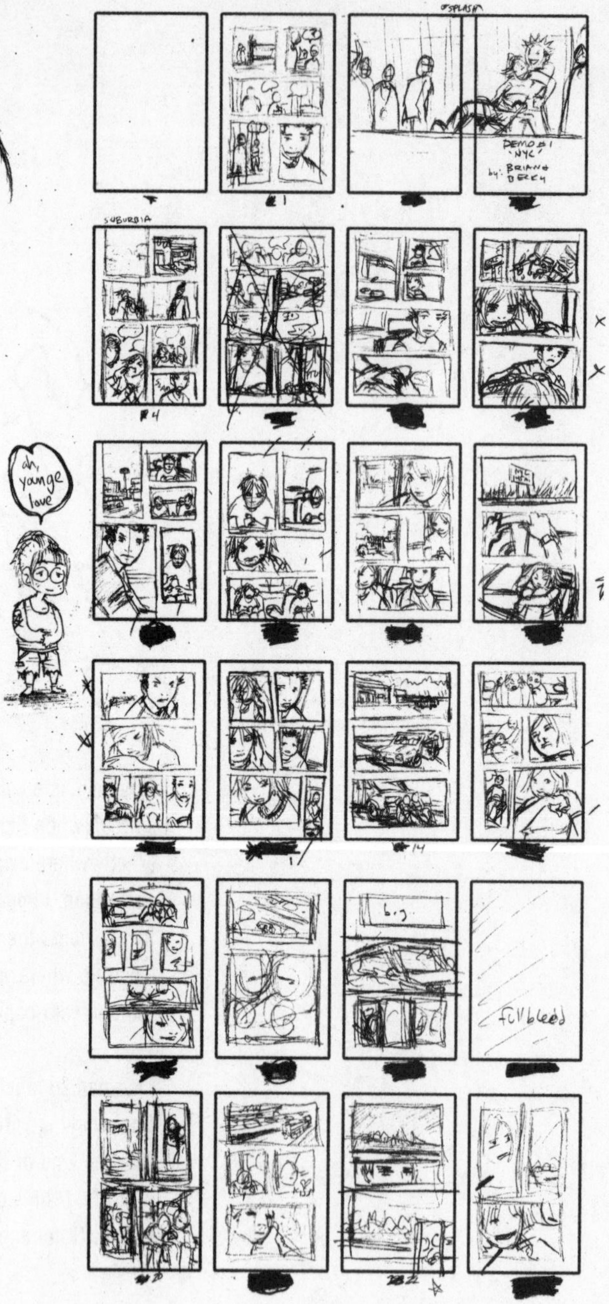
SPLASH
DEMO #1
'NYC'
by: BRIAN & BECKY
SUBURBIA
oh, younge love
b.g.
full bleed

1

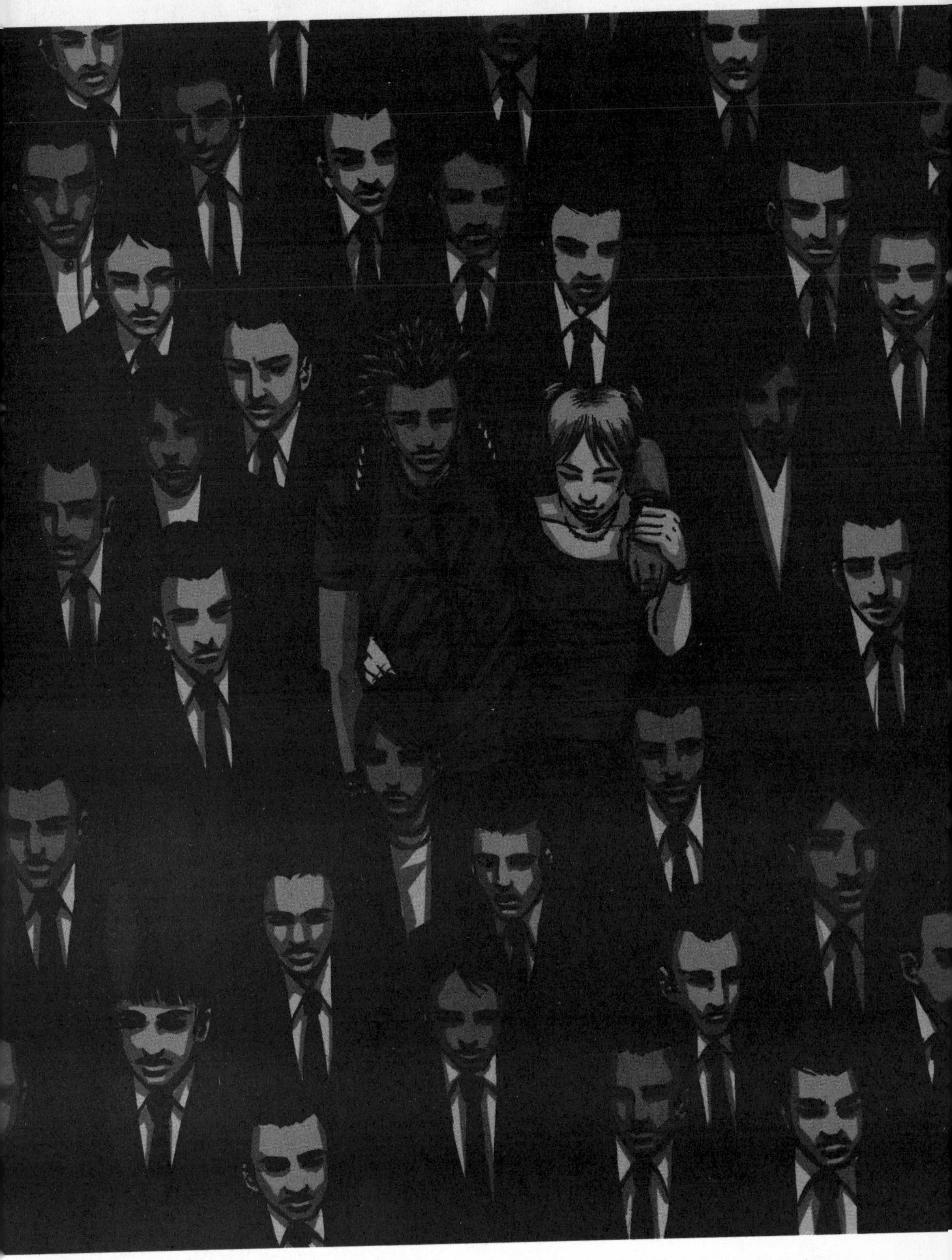

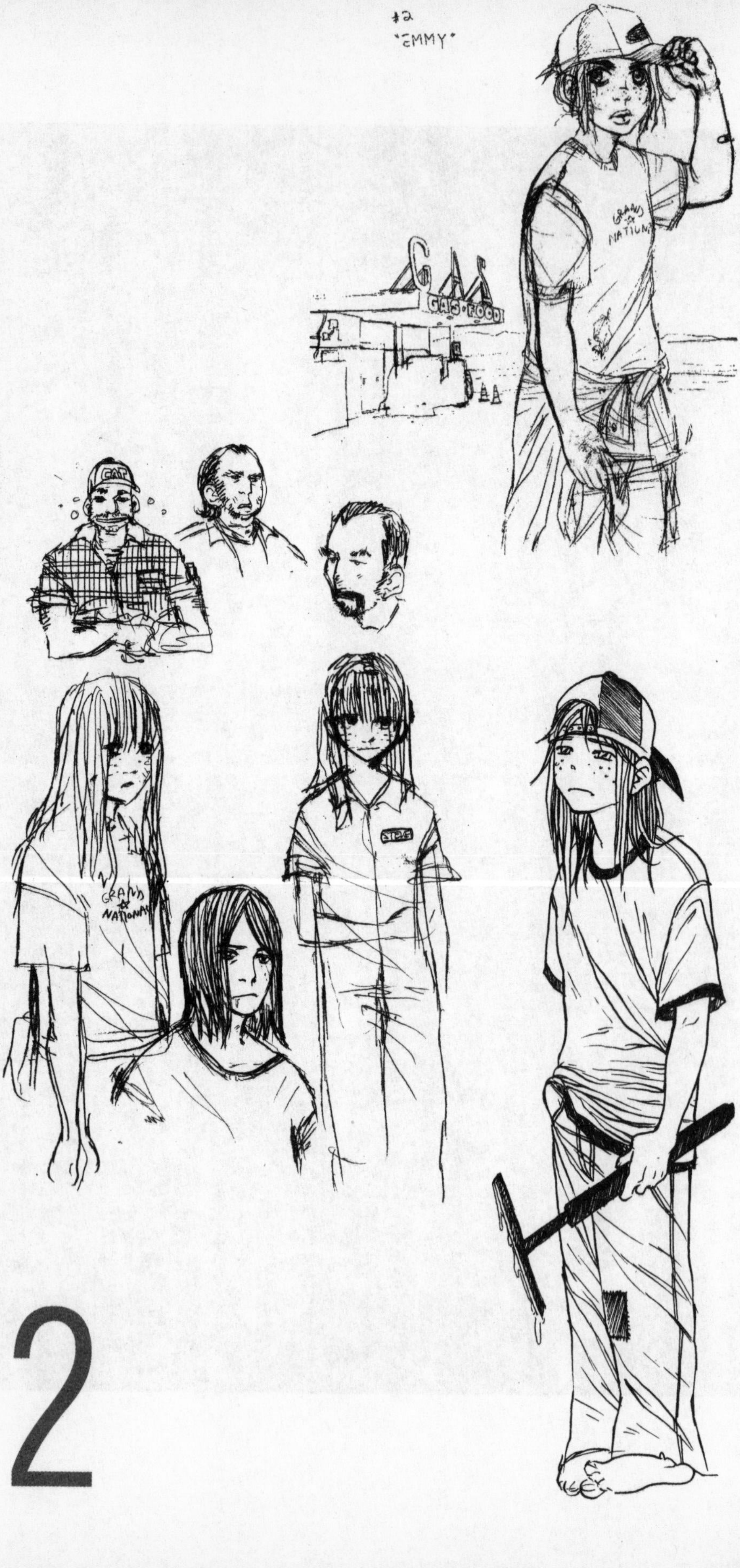
#2
"EMMY"
GAS
GAS·FOOD

2

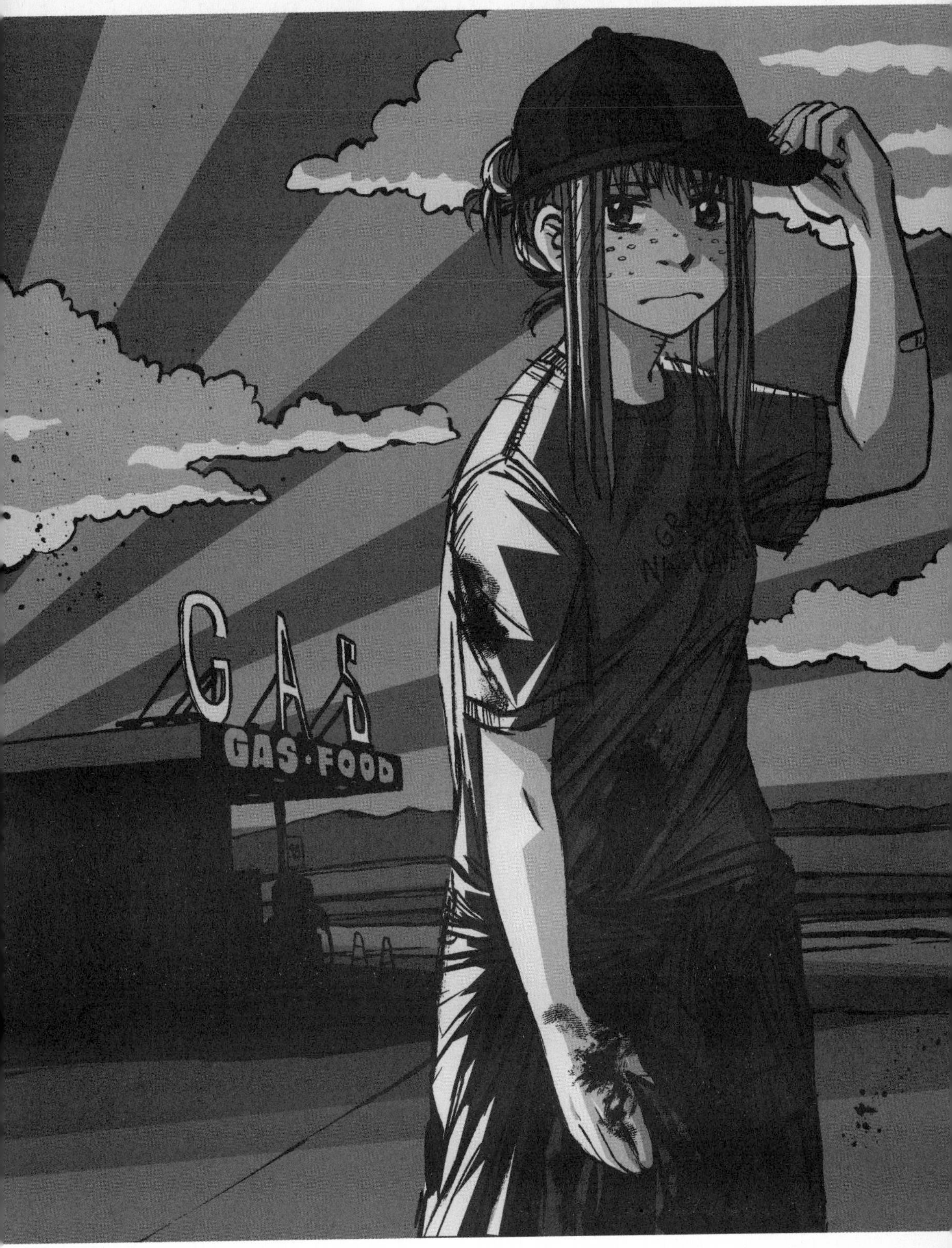
GAS
GAS · FOOD

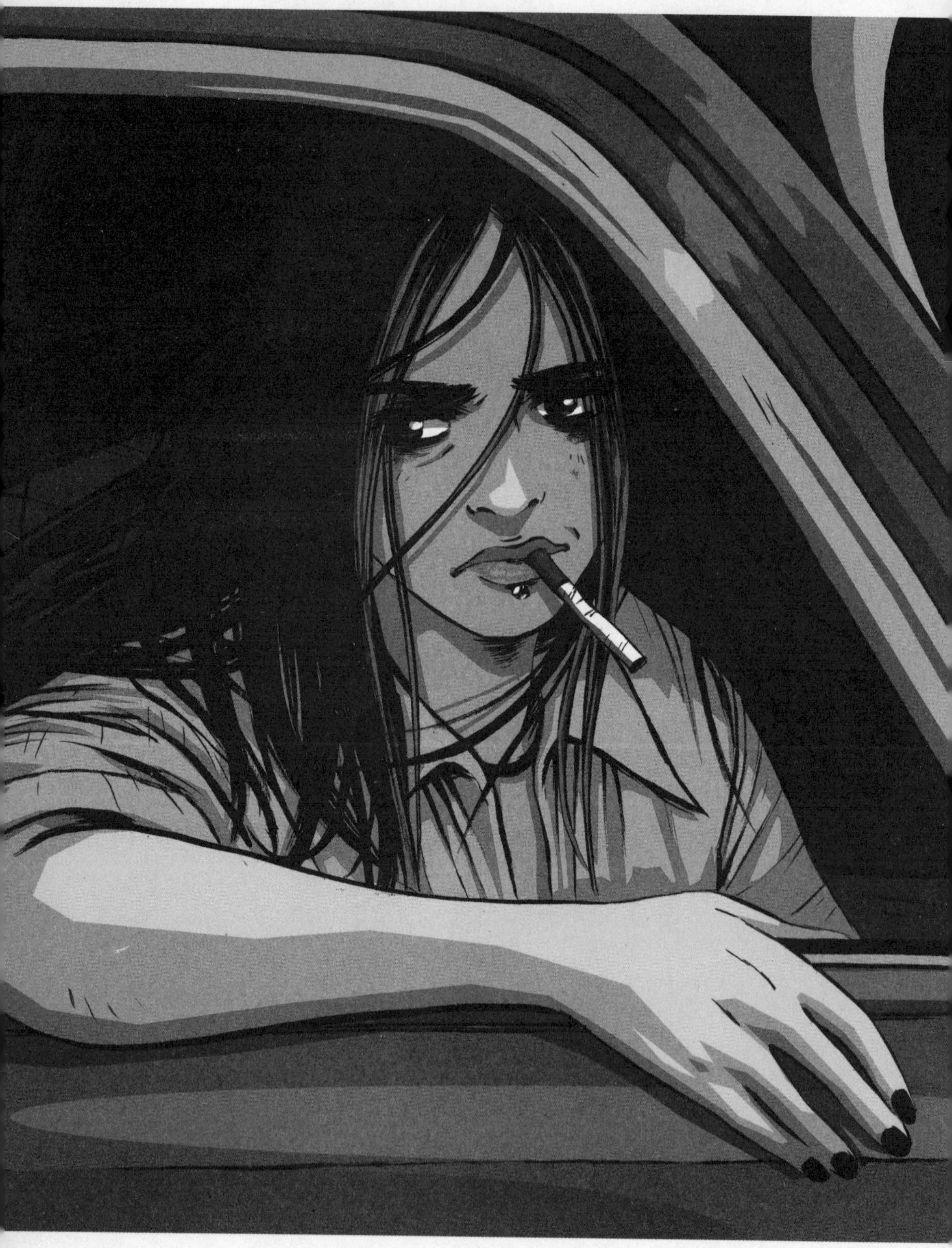

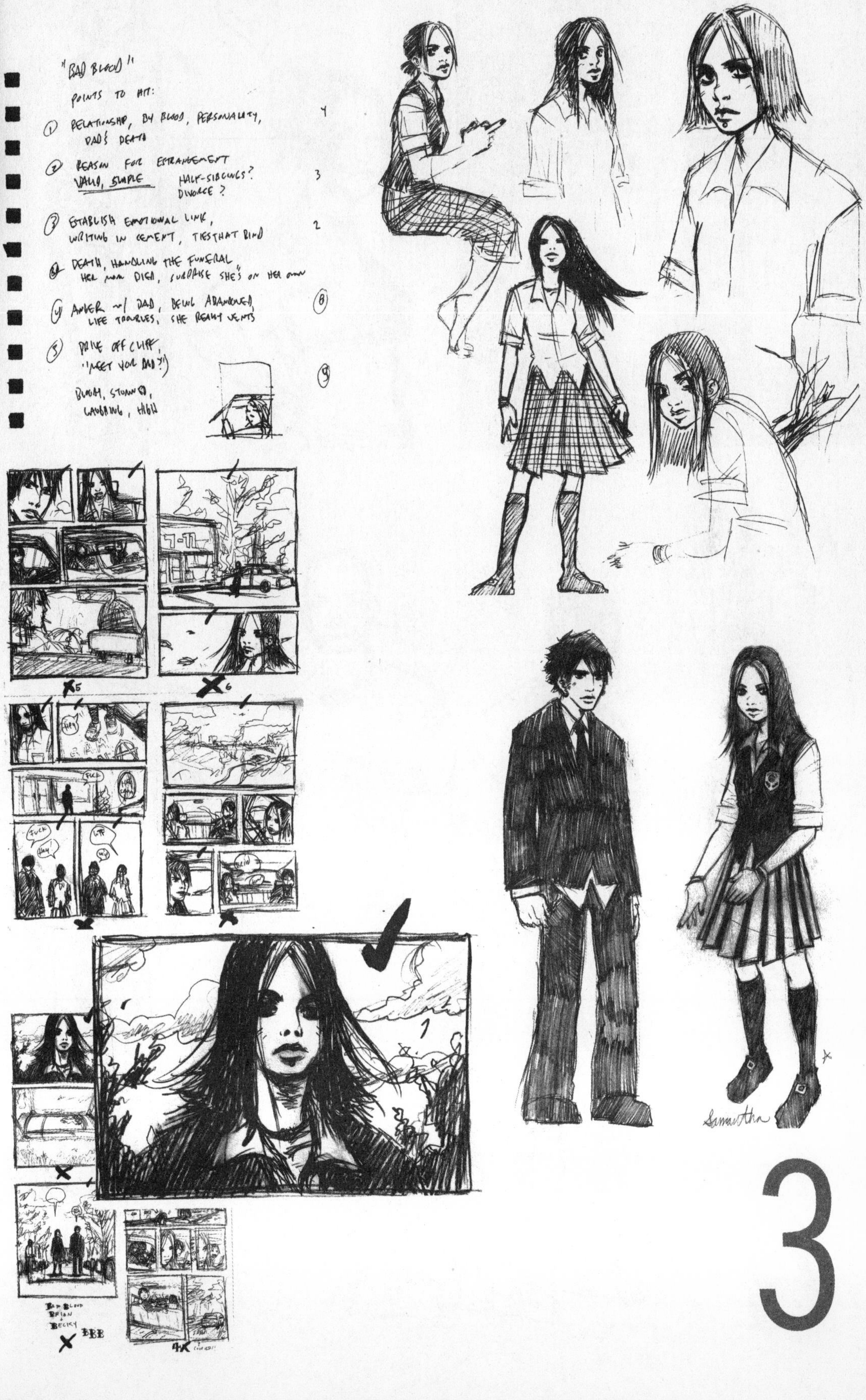
"BAD BLOOD"
POINTS TO HIT:
① RELATIONSHIP, BY BLOOD, PERSONALITY, DAD'S DEATH
② REASON FOR ESTRANGEMENT
VALID, SIMPLE
HALF-SIBLINGS? DIVORCE?
③ ESTABLISH EMOTIONAL LINK, WRITING IN CEMENT, TIES THAT BIND
DEATH, HANDLING THE FUNERAL HER MOM DIED, SURPRISE SHE'S ON HER OWN
④ ANGER w/ DAD, BEING ABANDONED, LIFE TROUBLES, SHE REALLY VENTS
⑤ DRIVE OFF CLIFF, "MEET YOUR DAD?!"
BLOOM, STUNNED, LAUGHING, HIGH
4
3
2
8
9
7-11
BAD BLOOD
BRIAN + BECKY
BBB
Samantha

3

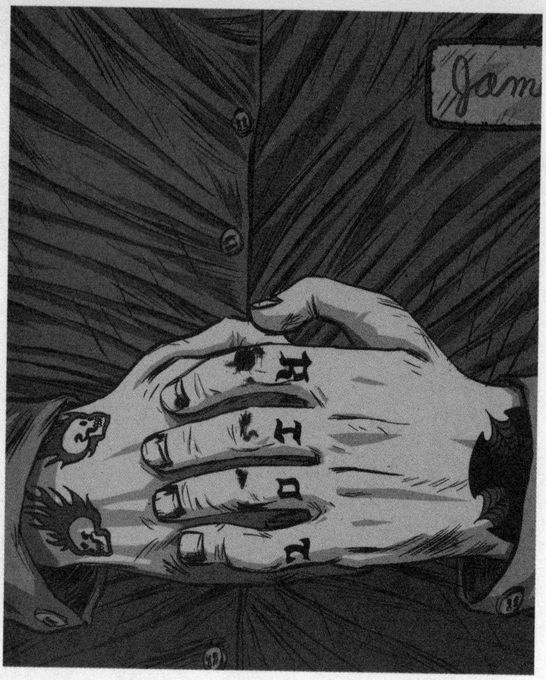
Jam

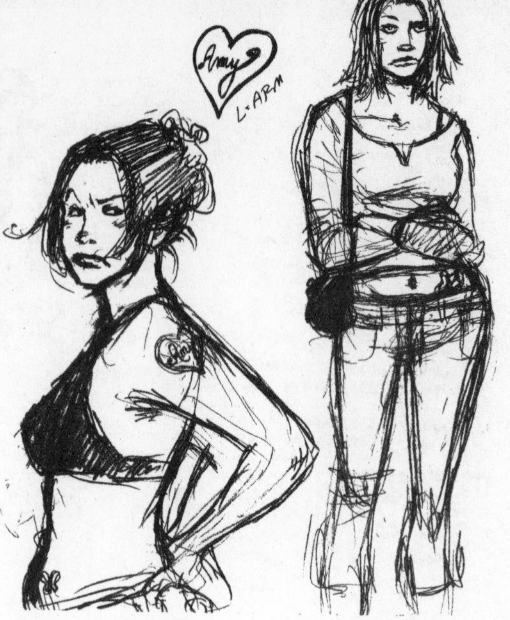
Amy
L-ARM

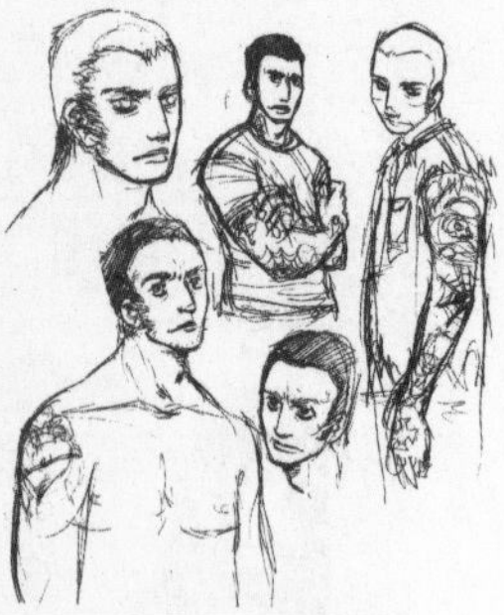

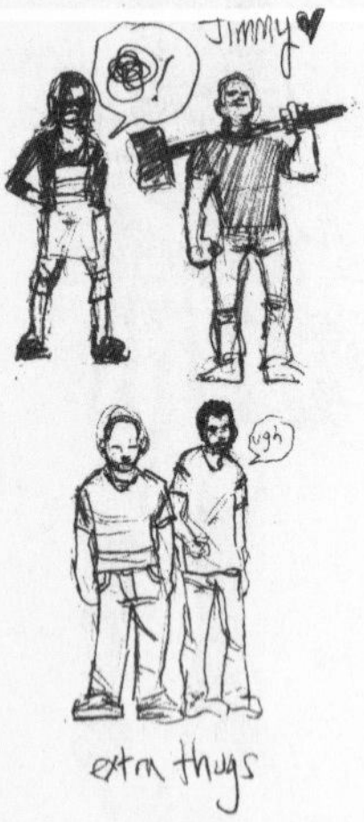
Jimmy♥
ugh
extra thugs

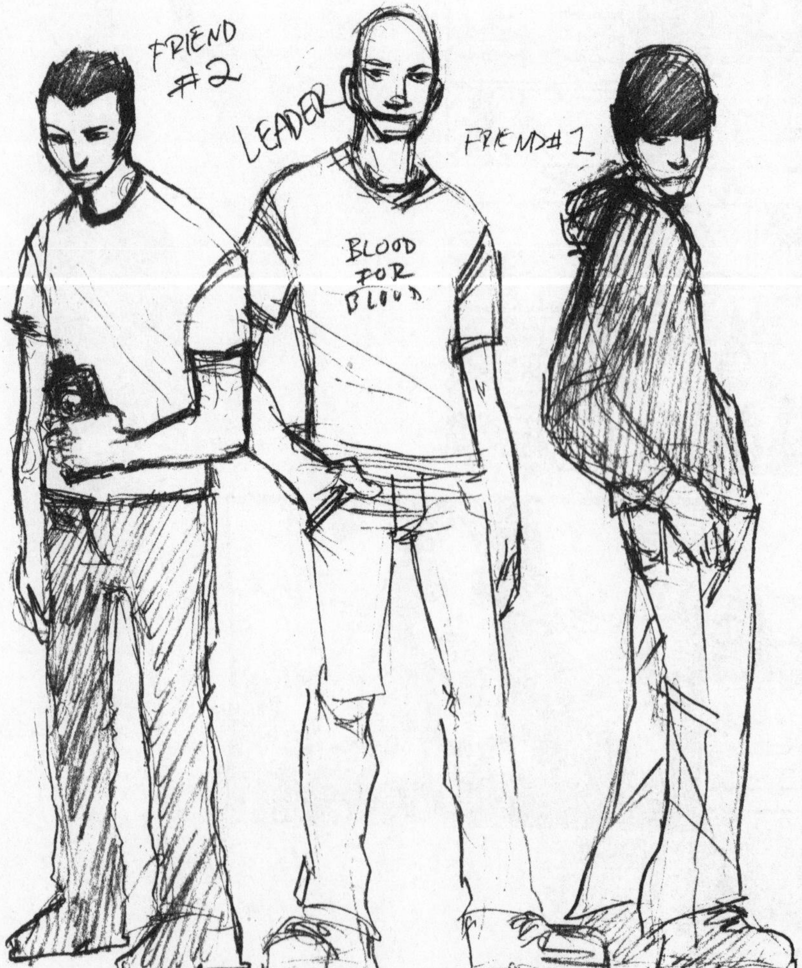
FRIEND #2
LEADER
FRIEND#1
BLOOD FOR BLOOD

4

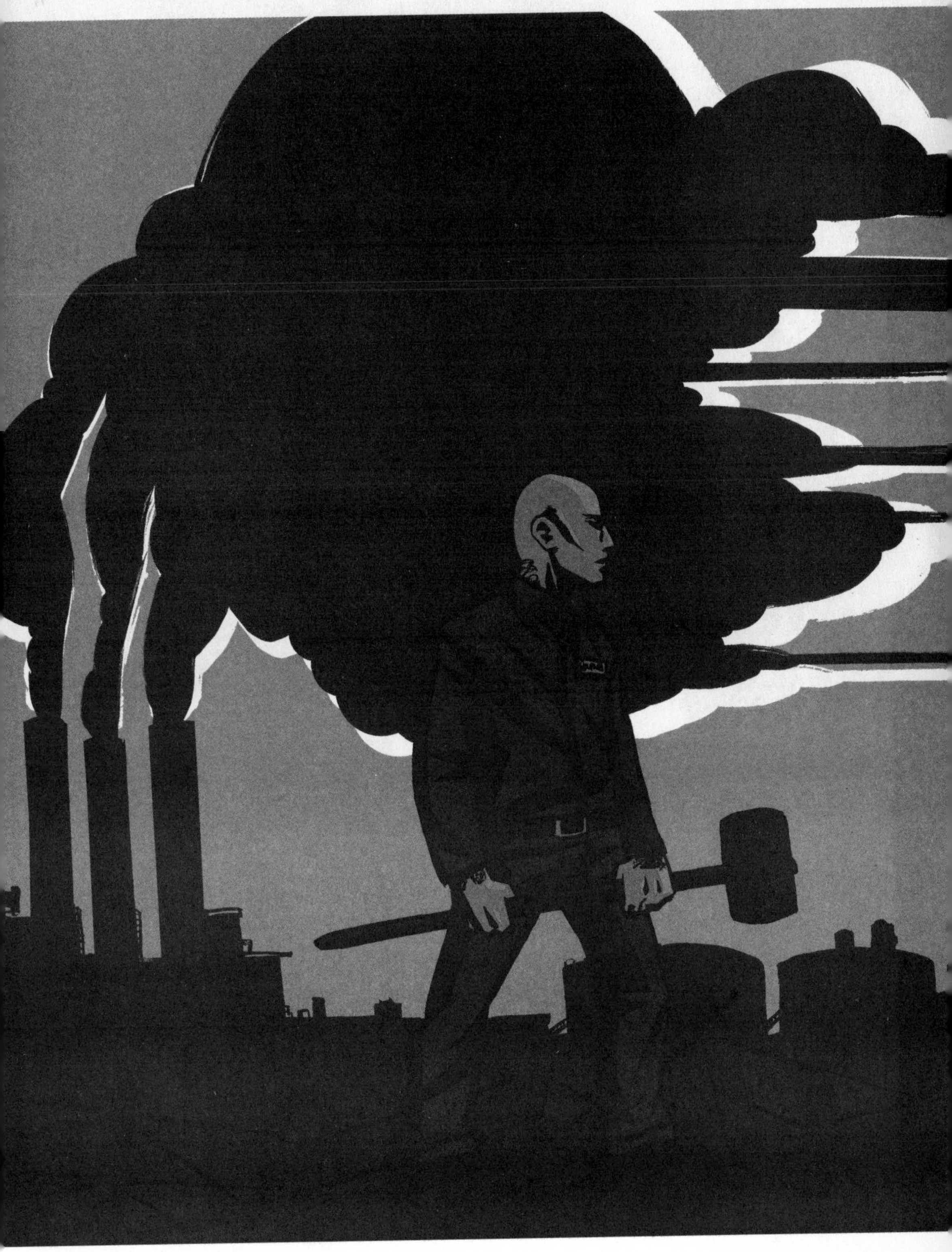

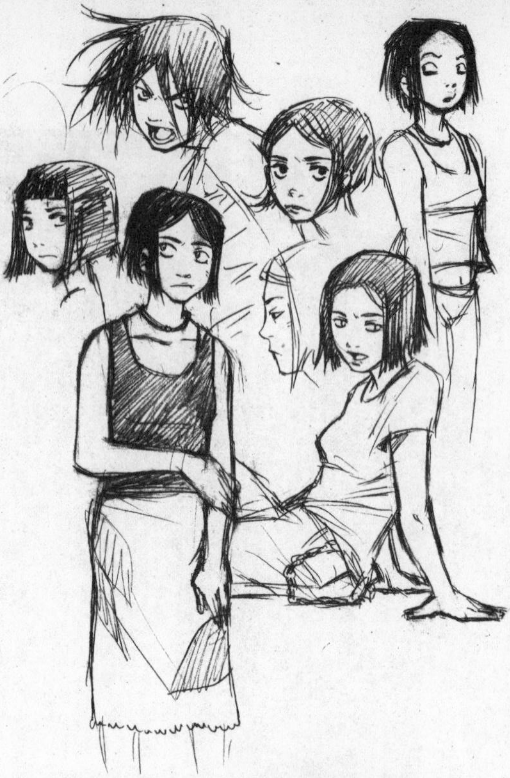

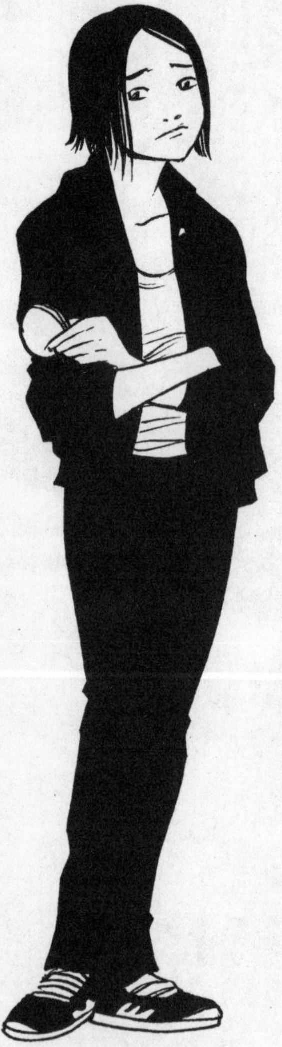

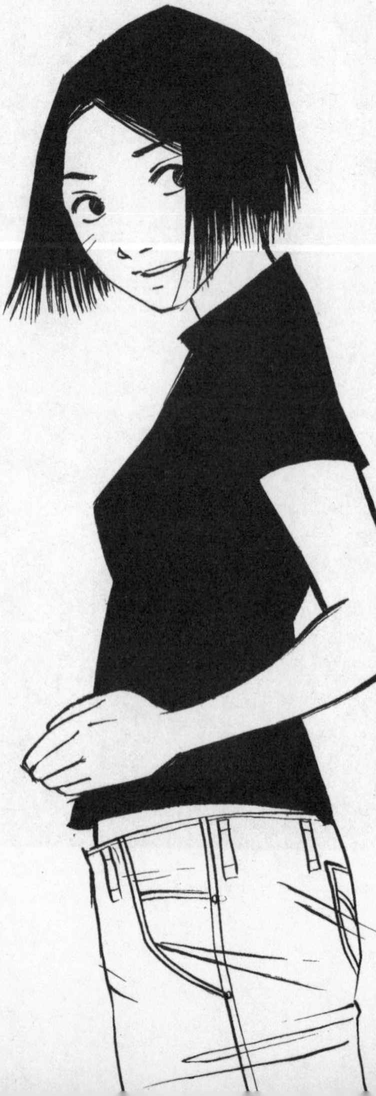

5

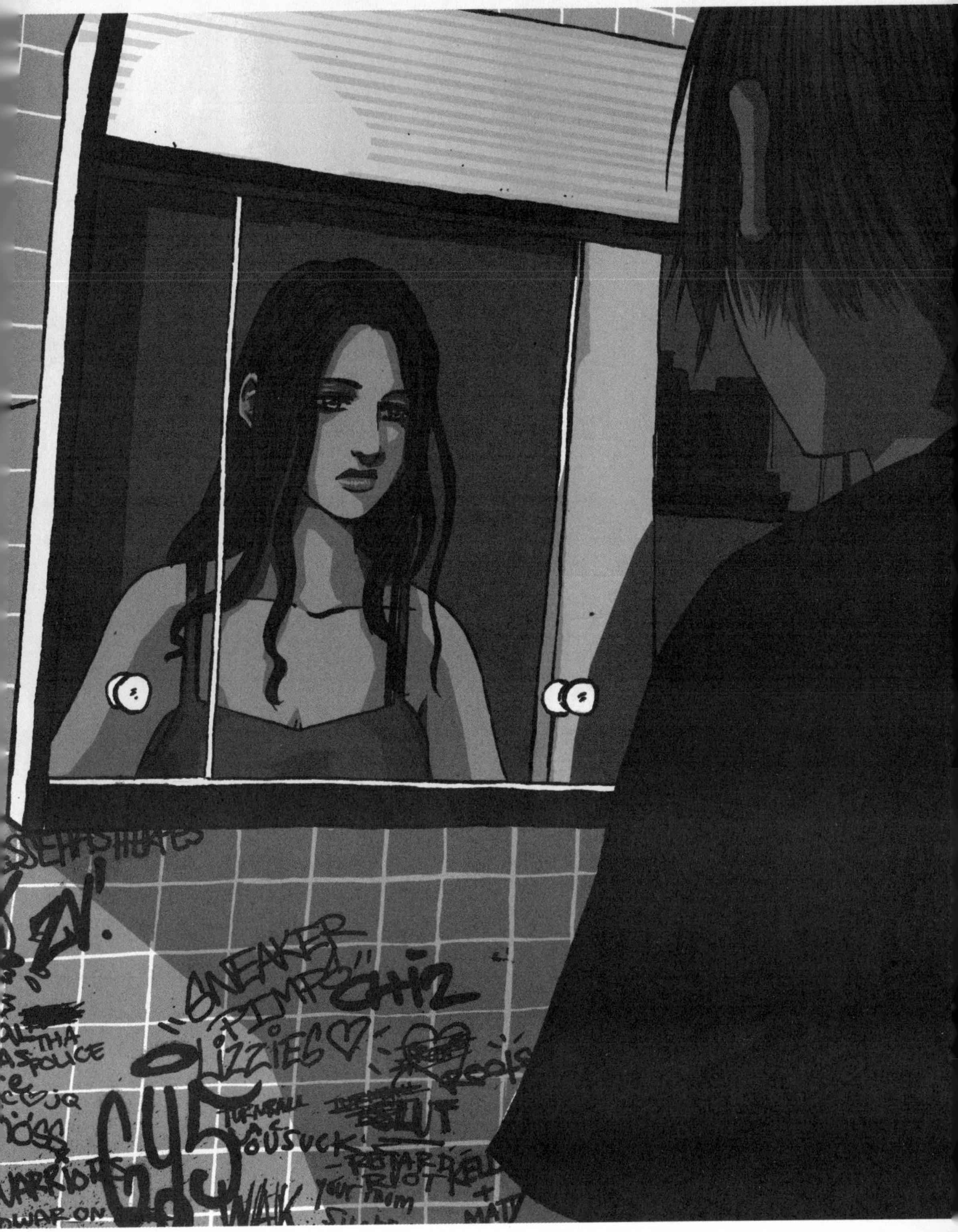
SNEAKER PIMPS
CHIZ
THA
POLICE
YOUSUCK
SLUT
WARRIORS
WAR ON

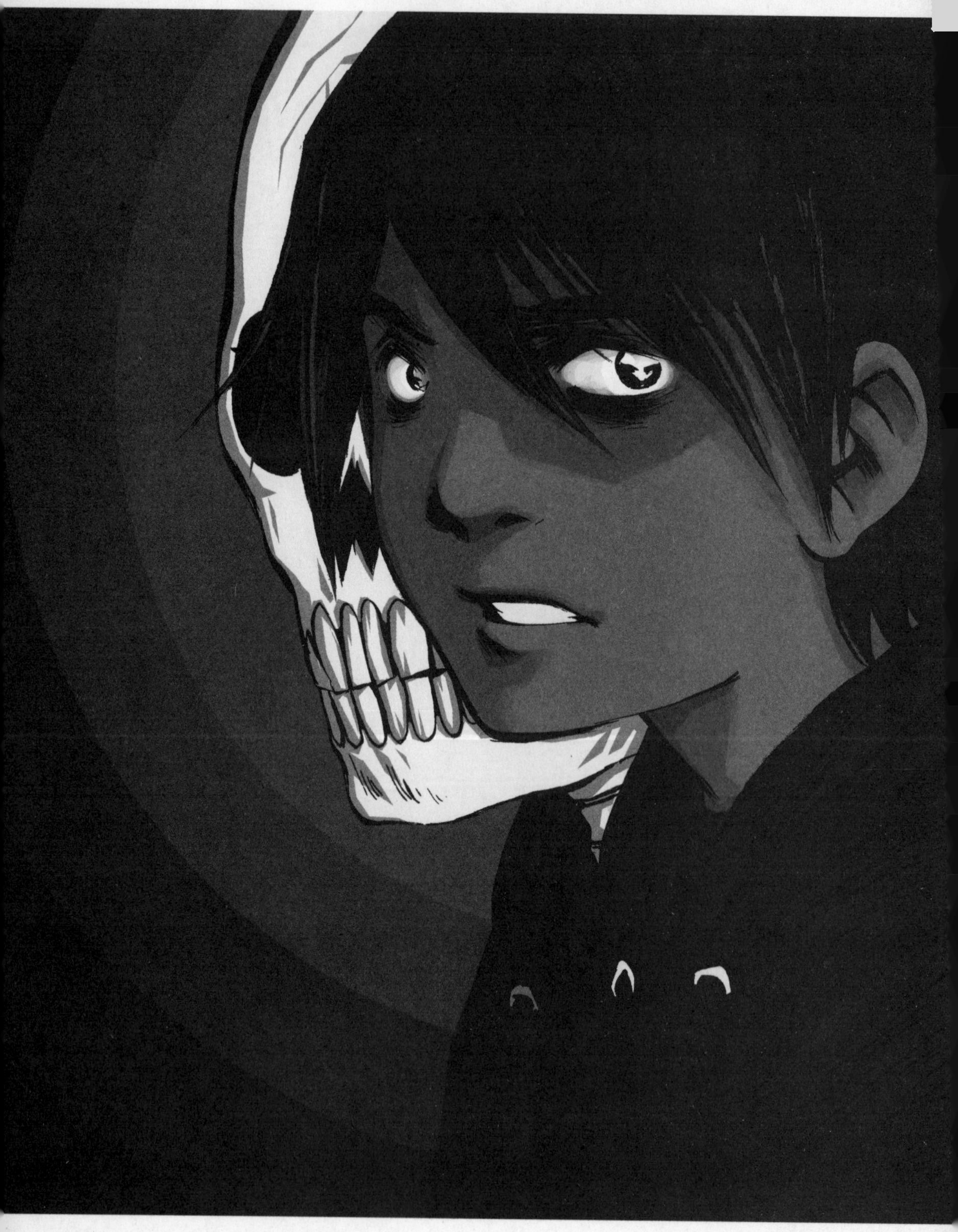

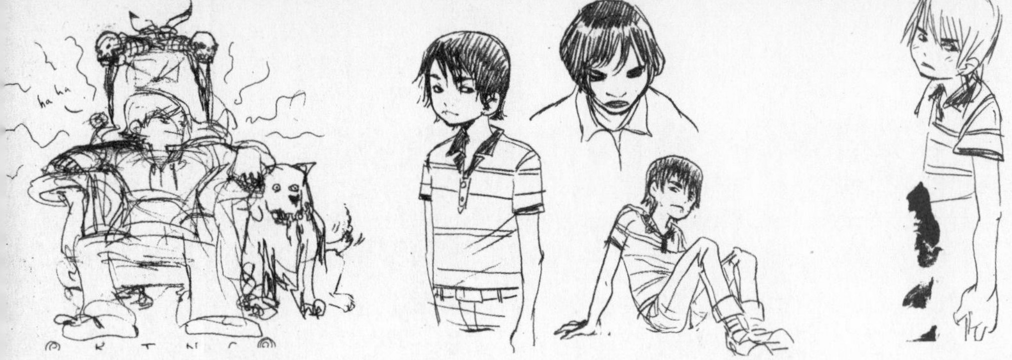
ha ha

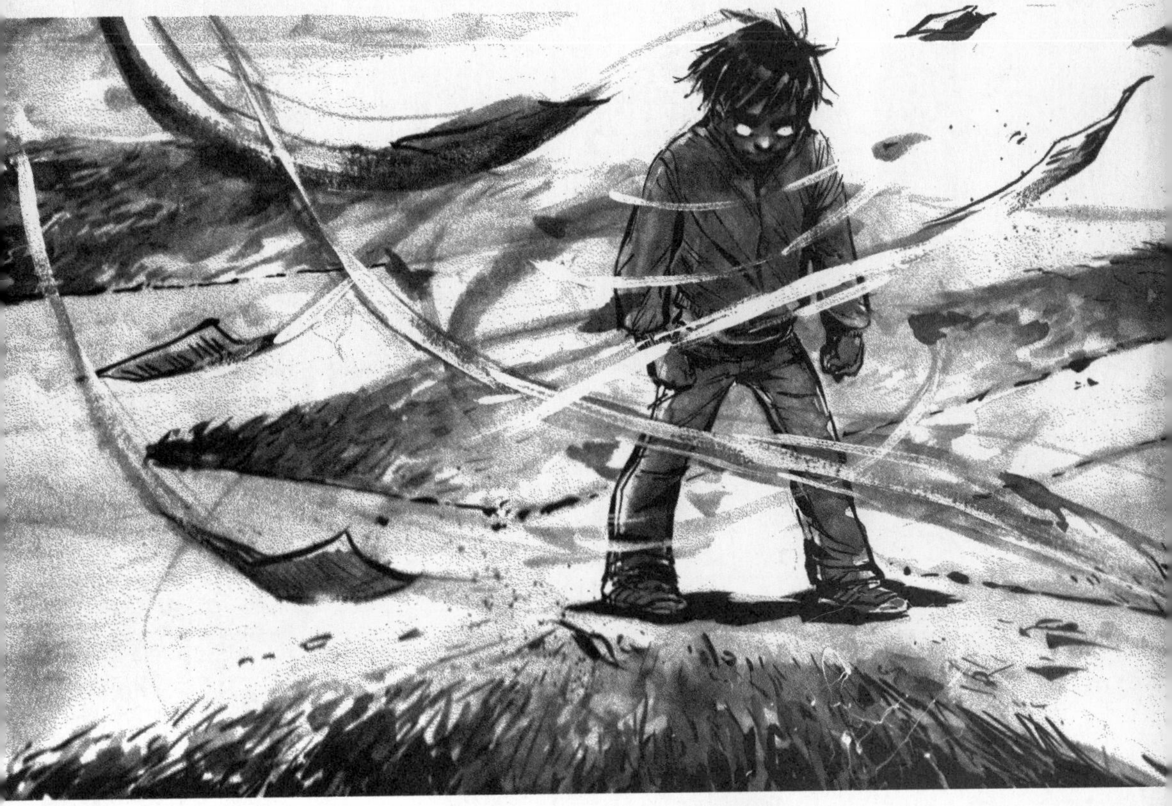

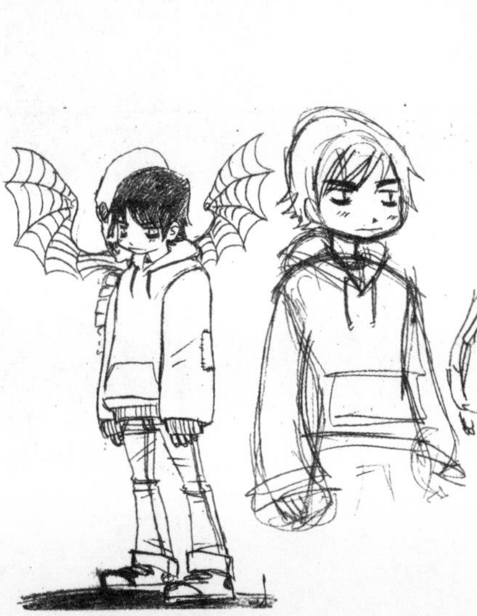

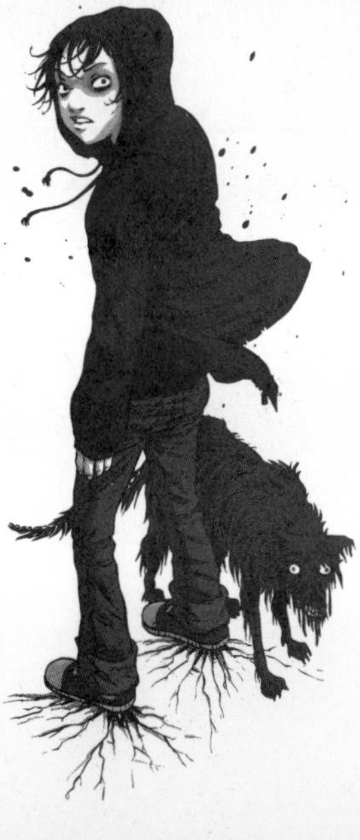

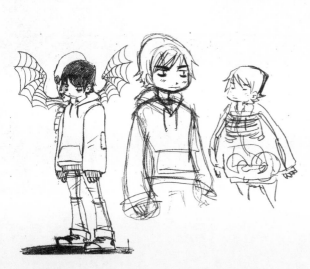

6

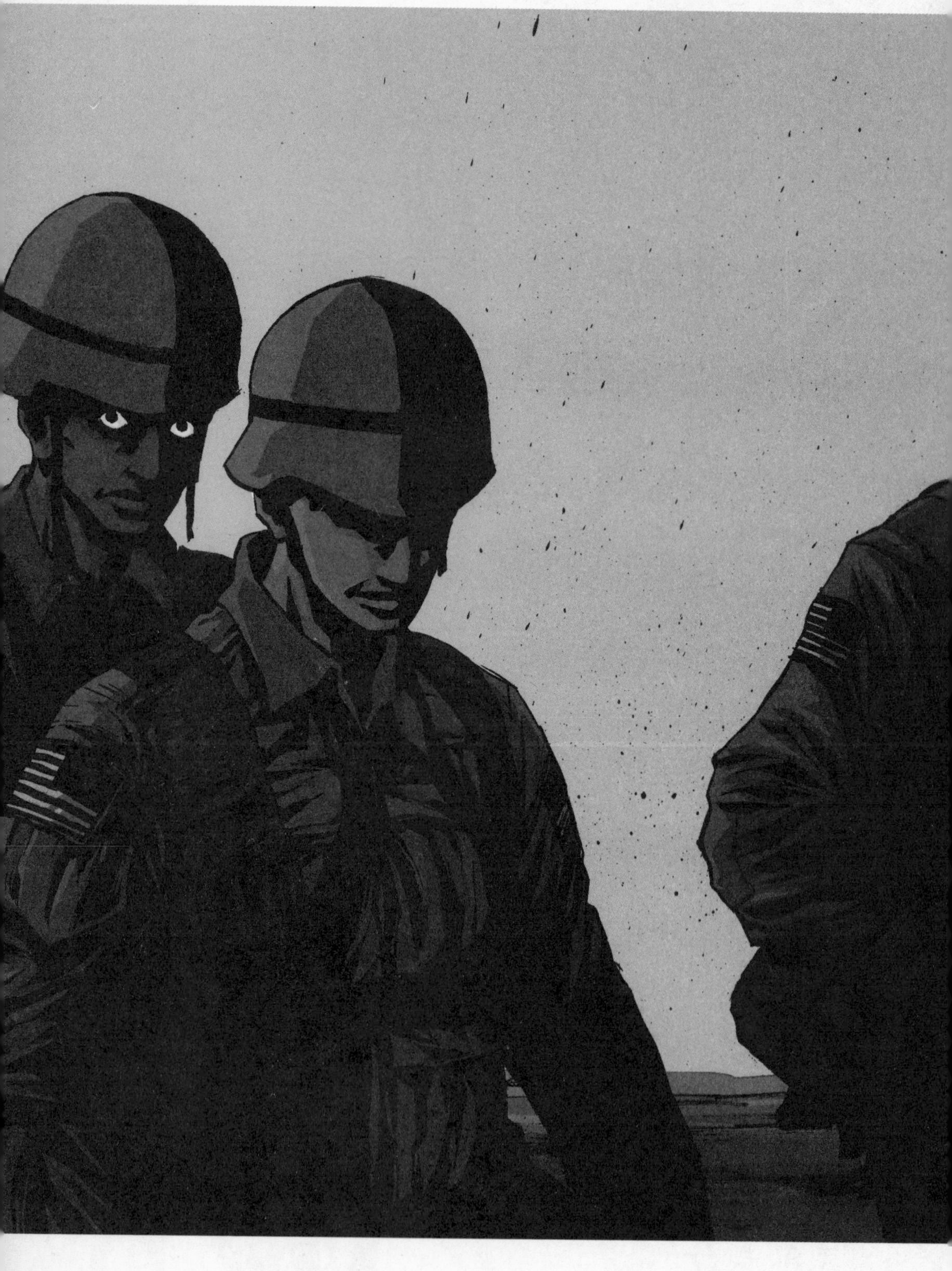

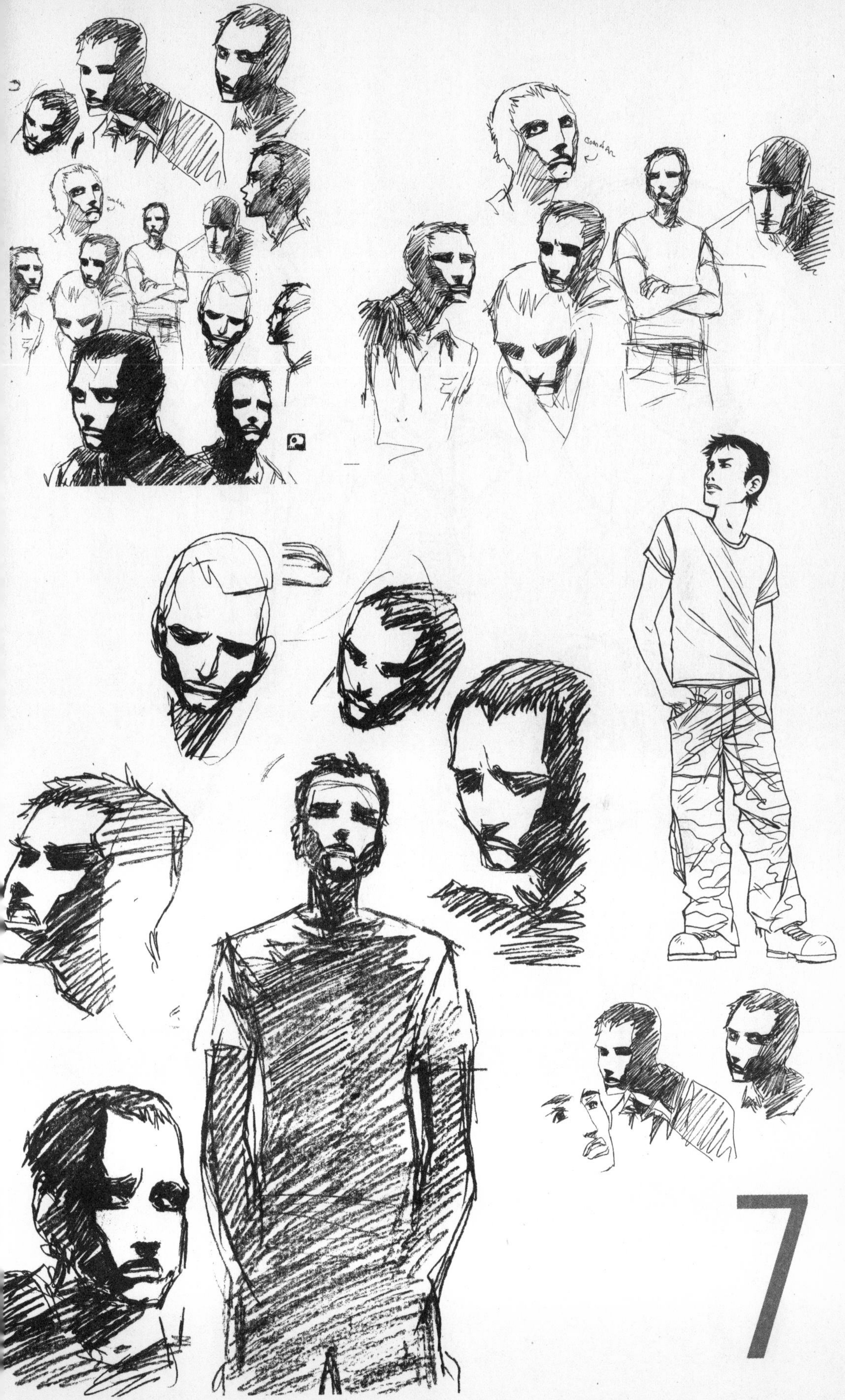

7

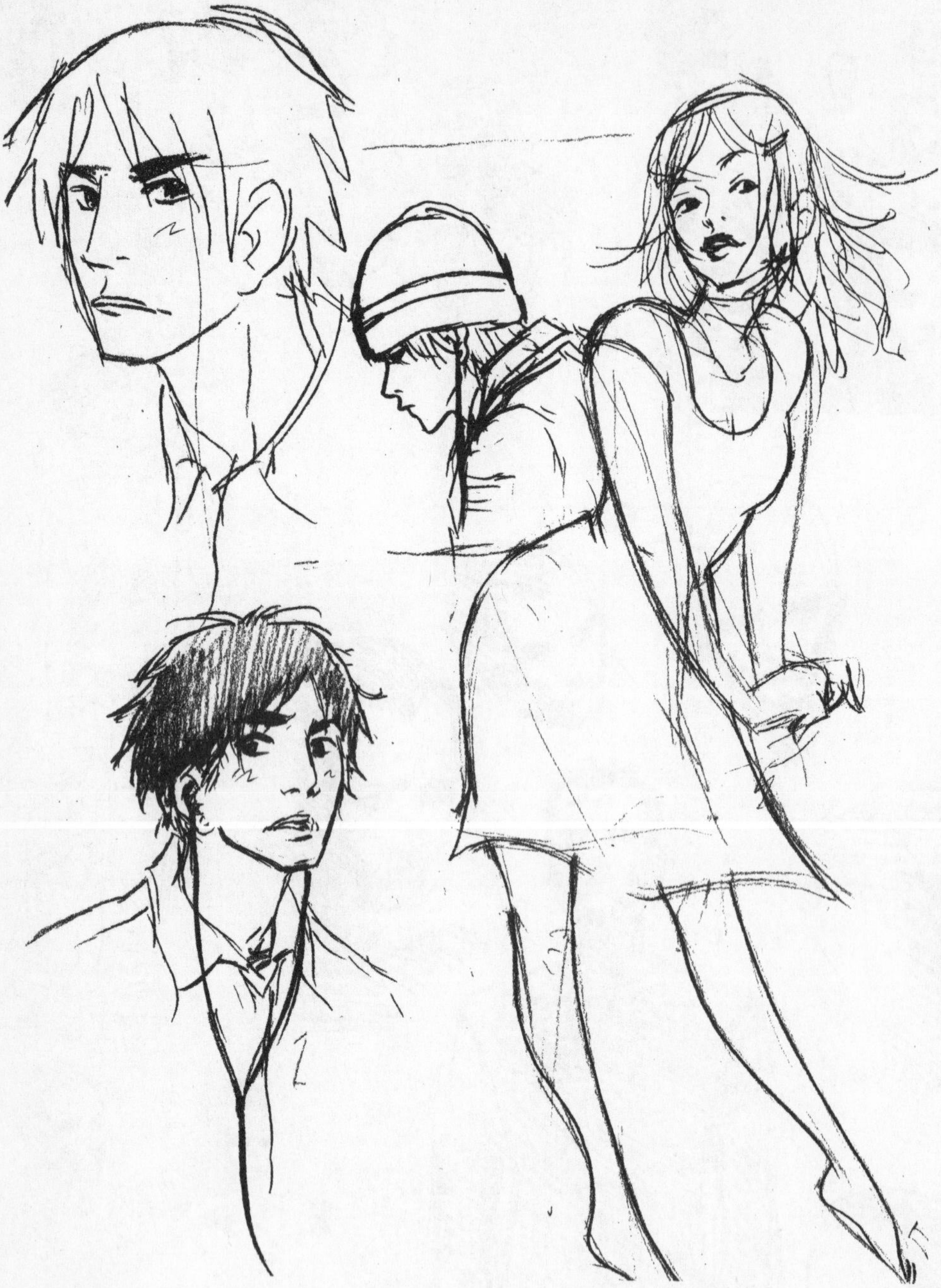

8

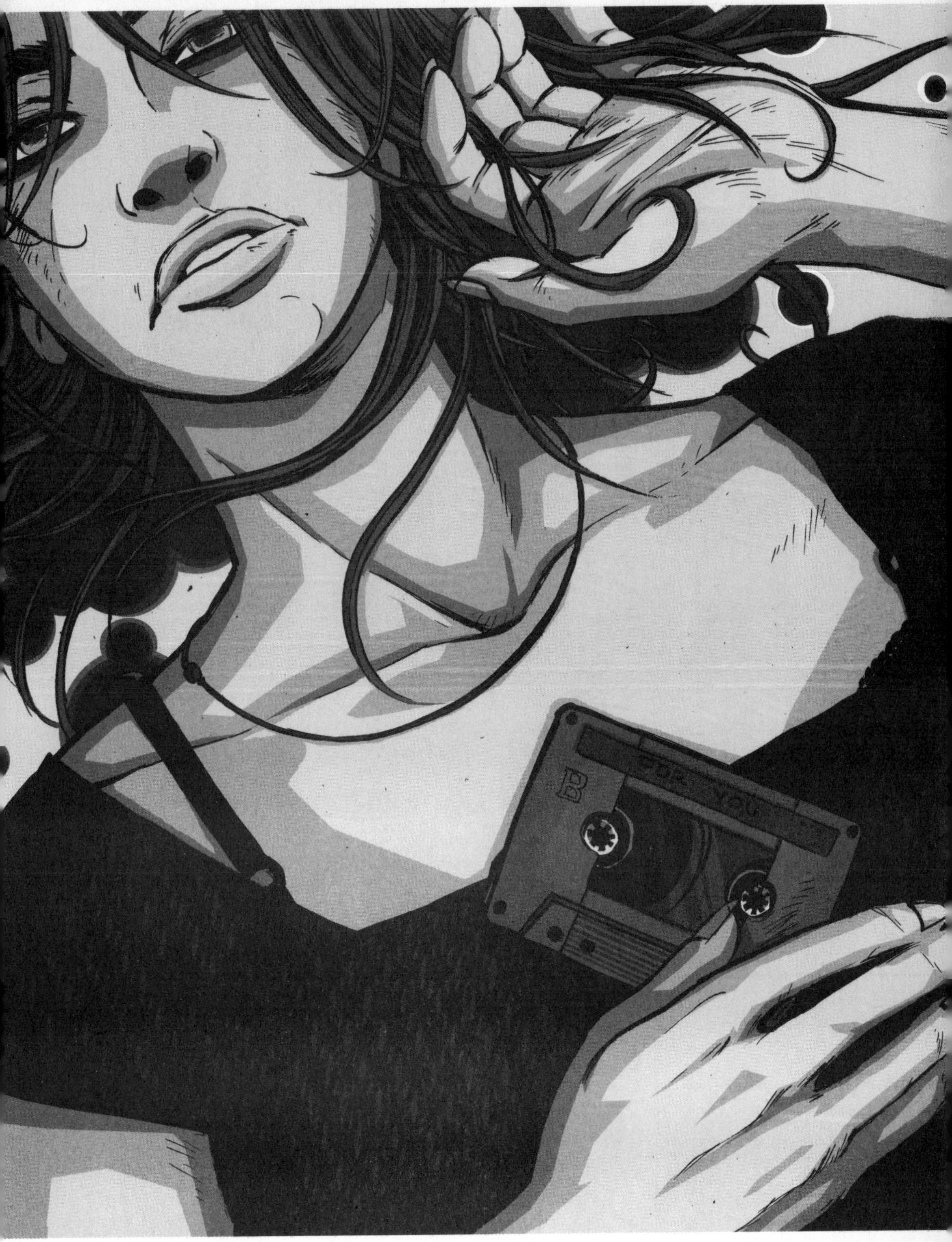
B
FOR YOU

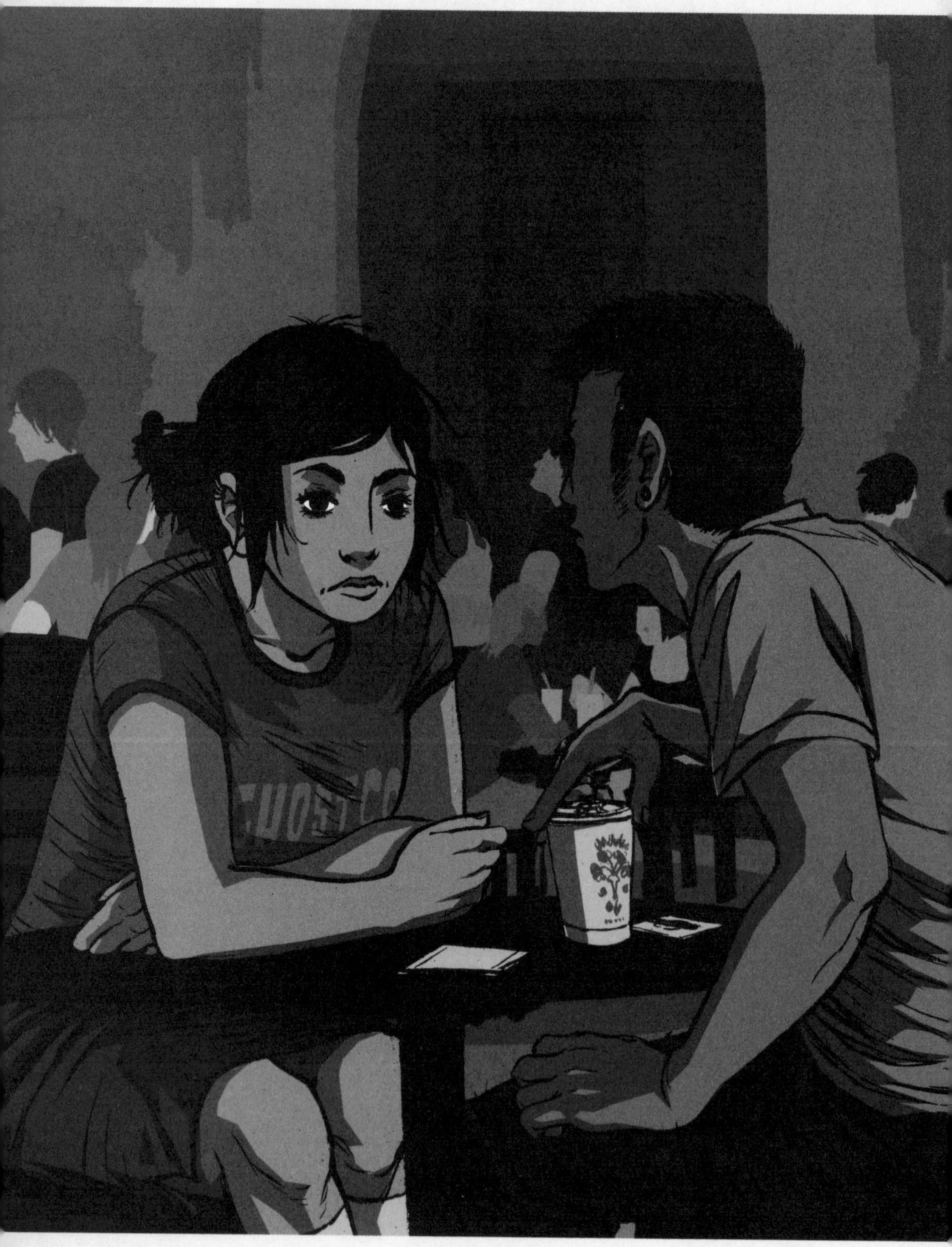

9

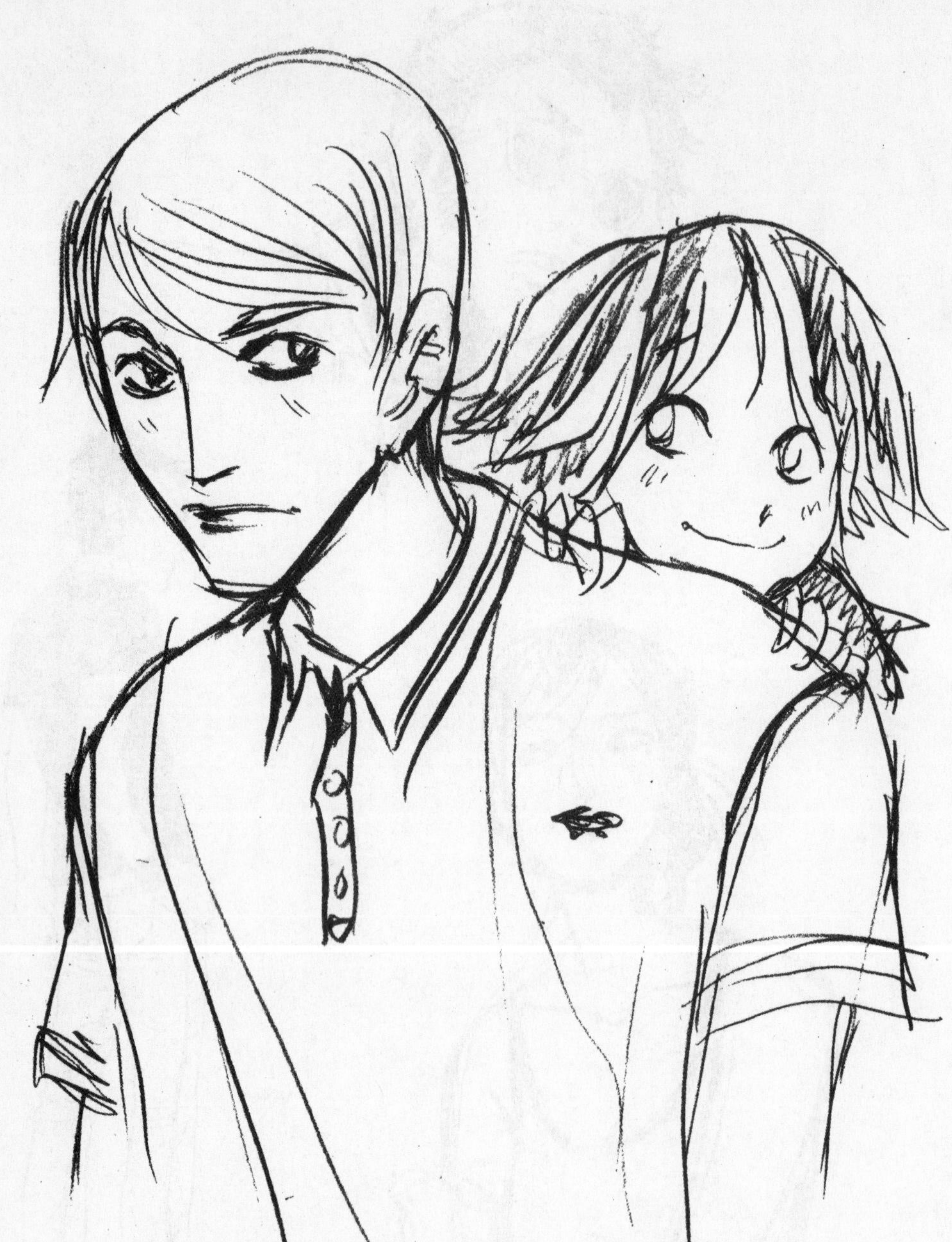

10

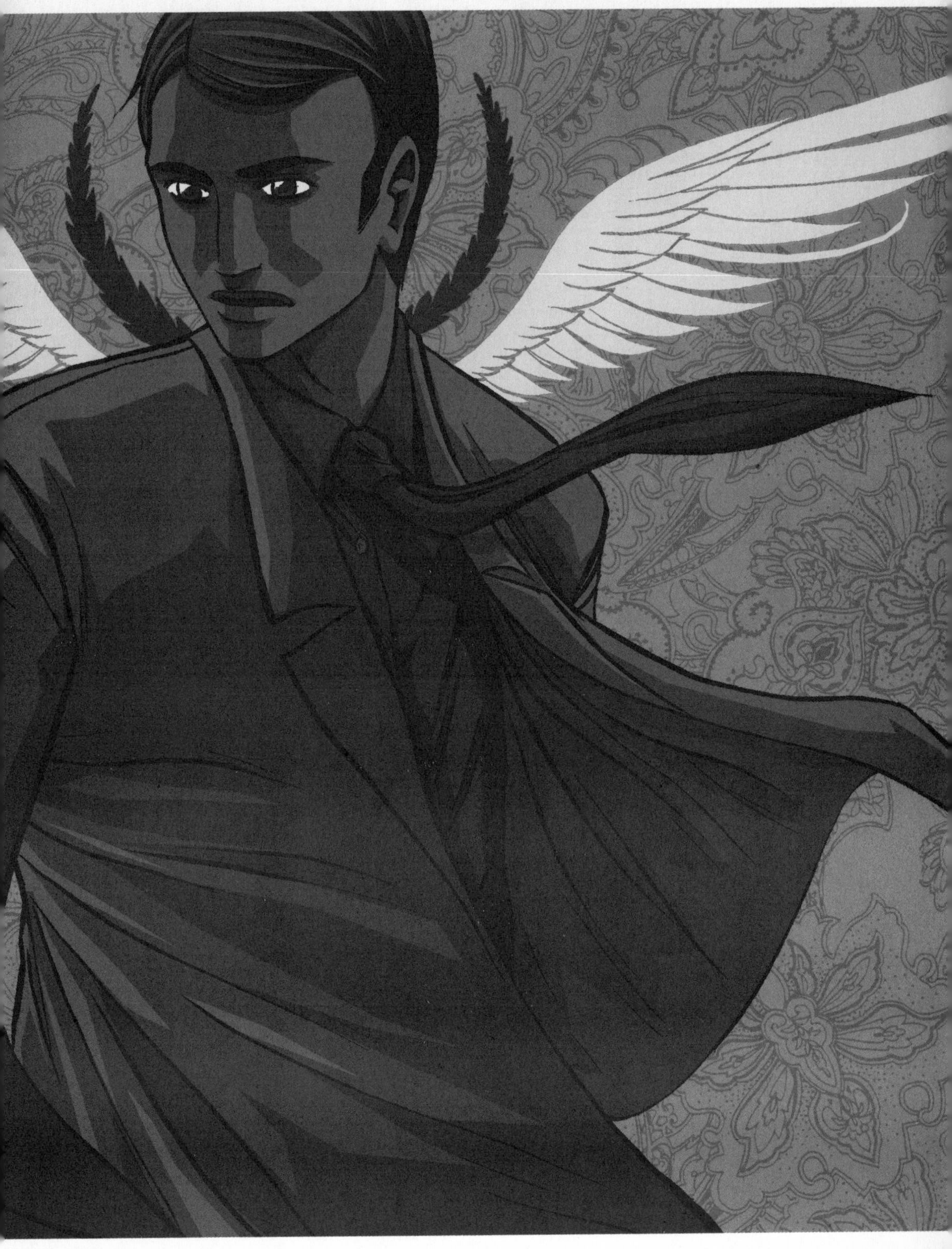

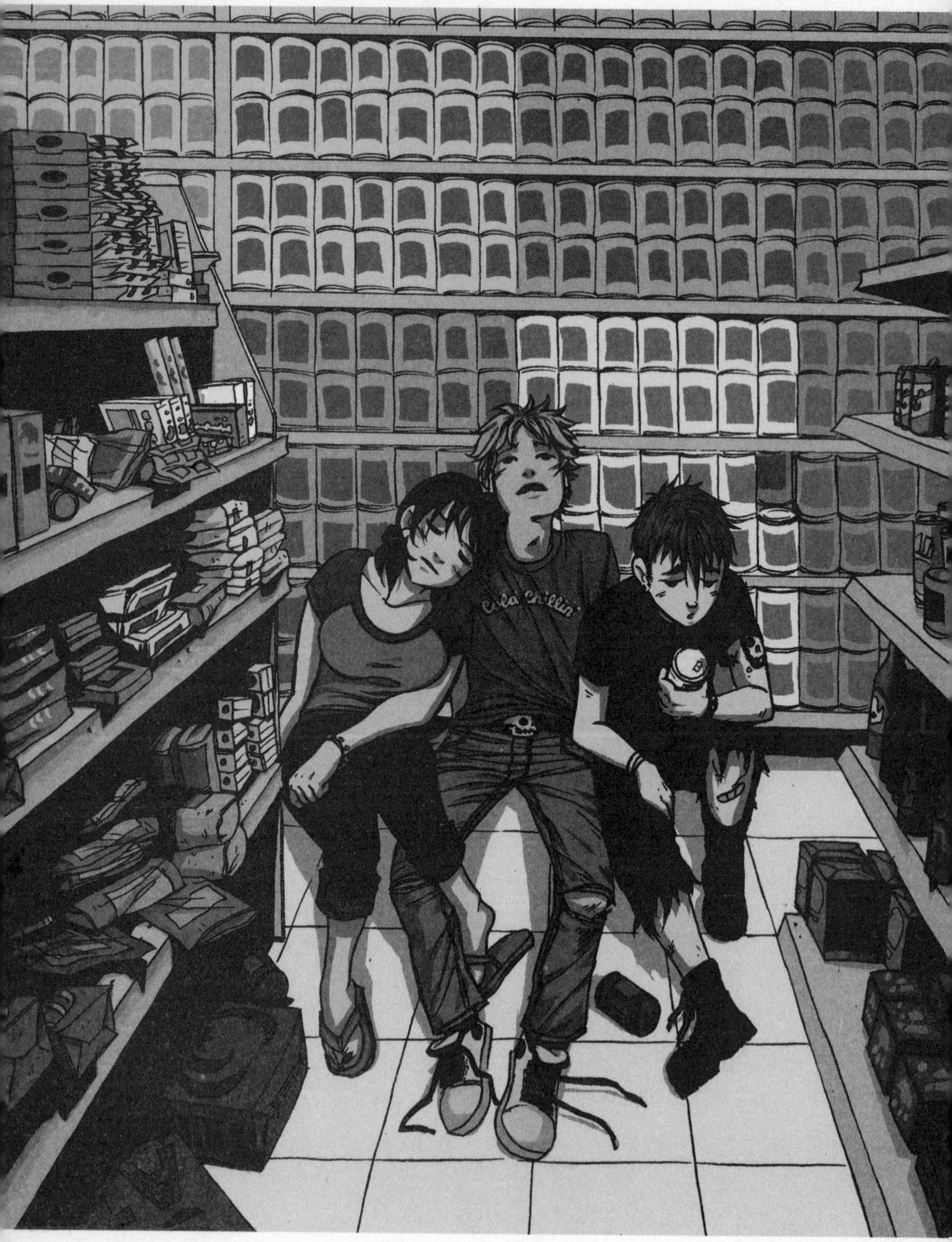

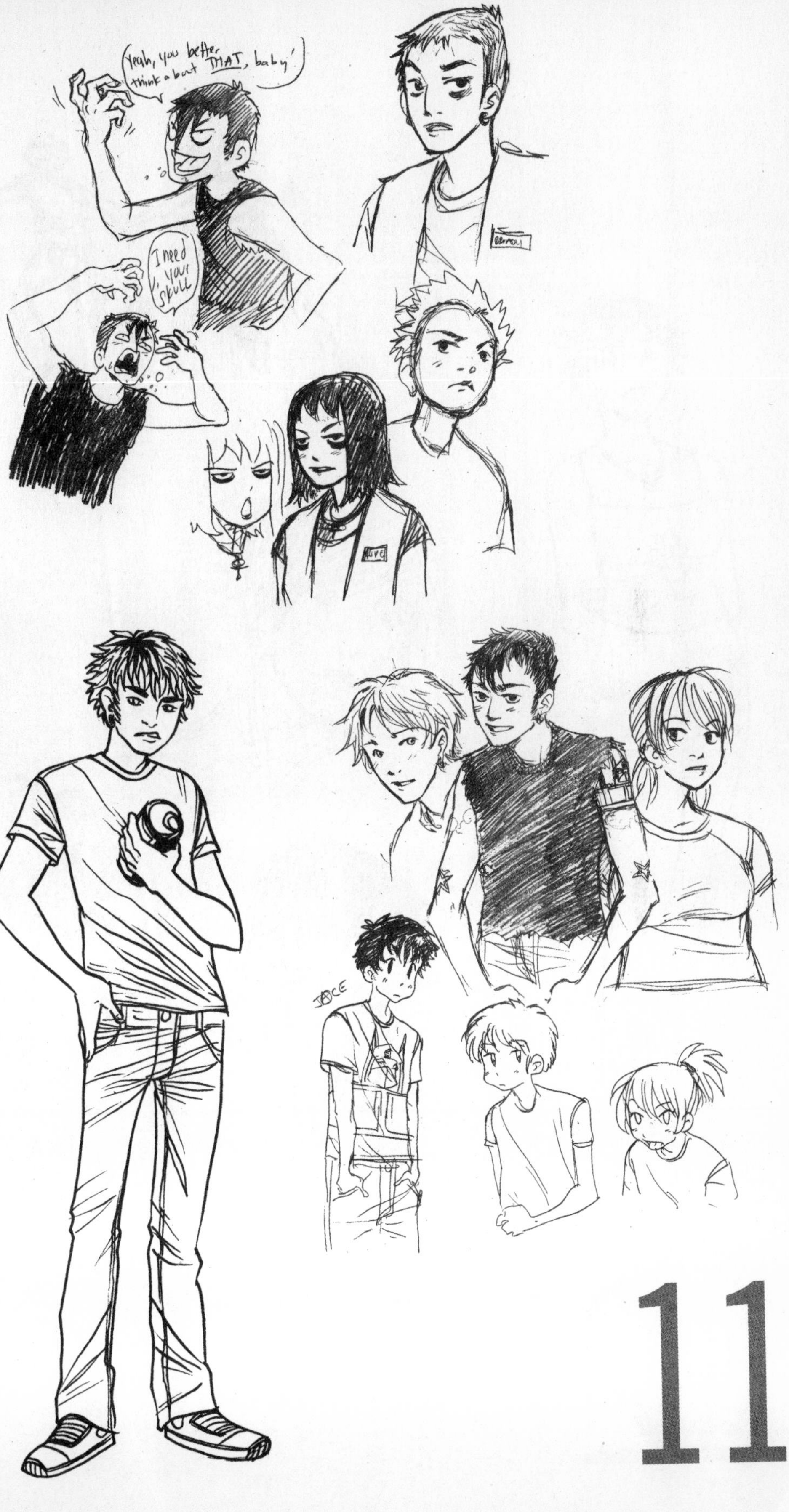
Yeah, you better think about THAT, baby!
I need your skull
JACE

11

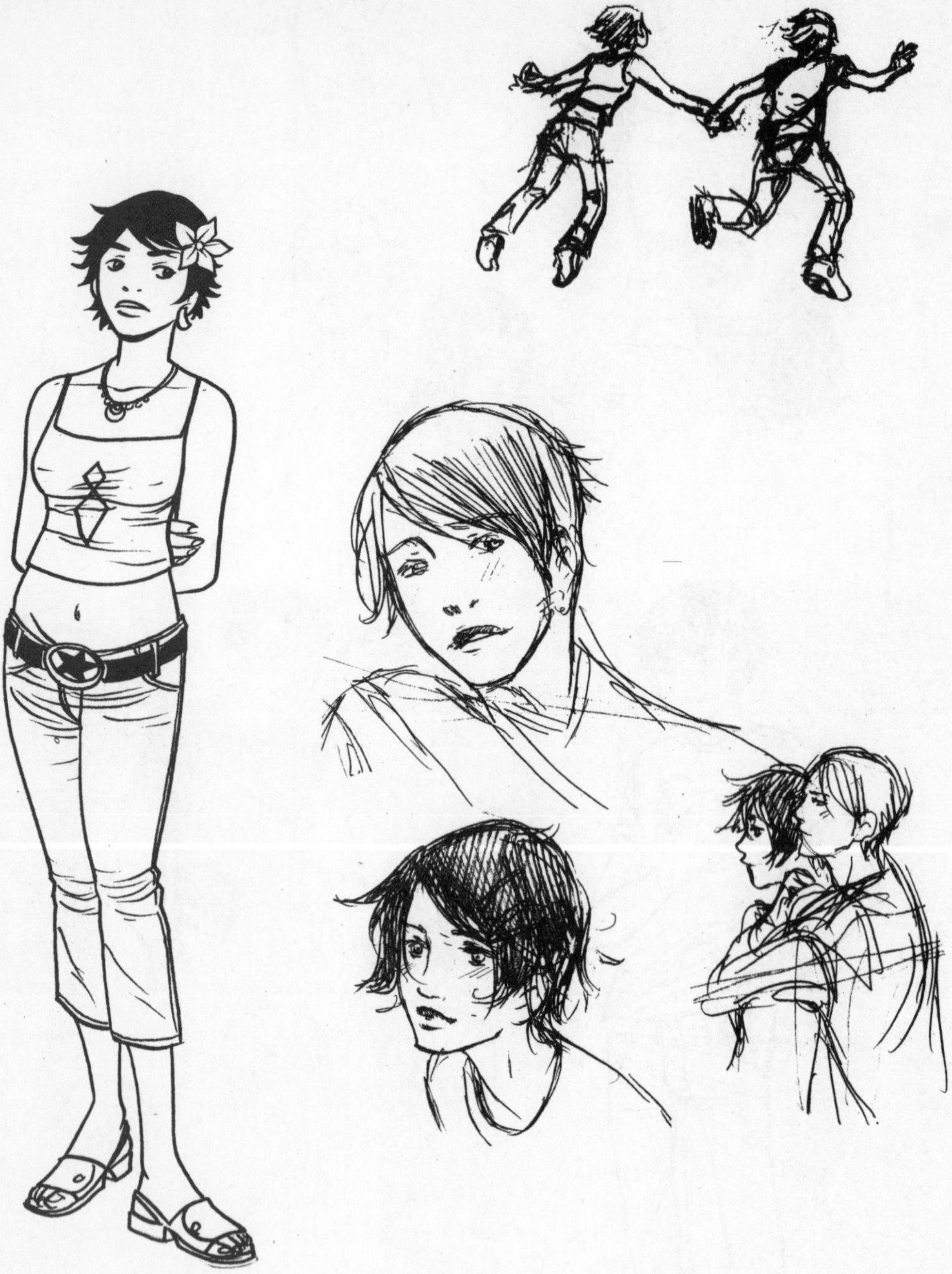

12